S0-APN-911

USA SPORTS

TRAVELER'S AND TV VIEWER'S GOLF TOURNAMENT GUIDE

Preceding page courtesy of Greater Naples IntelliNet Challenge
This page courtesy of Sky Shots

USA SPORTS

TRAVELER'S AND TV VIEWER'S GOLF TOURNAMENT GUIDE

TEXT BY
ROBERT MCCORD
WITH CHUCK STOGEL

EDITED BY
JULIE WARD,
DEPUTY MANAGING EDITOR / USA SPORTS

A BALLIETT & FITZGERALD BOOK
MACMILLAN • USA

A Disclaimer

Readers are advised that prices fluctuate in the course of time and travel information changes under the impact of the varied and volatile factors that affect the travel industry. Neither the author nor the publisher can be held responsible for the experiences of readers while traveling. Readers are invited to write to the publisher with ideas, comments, and suggestions for future editions.

Golf tournaments frequently shift courses from one year to the next. All courses included herein are based on 1995 tour schedules and, when confirmed as of press time, 1996 schedules. A specific year—either 1995 or 1996—for broadcast and purse information is noted. Tournament dates indicated for the PGA Tour and Senior PGA Tour are based on 1996 schedules; LPGA dates, which at press time were pending confirmation, note the month (early, mid- or late) the event occured in 1995.

USA TODAY
Managing Editor, Sports: Gene Policinski
GANNETT NEW MEDIA
Associate Director: Susan Bokern
Manager, Product Development: Silvia Molina Neves
Account Manager: Michelle Mattox
Researcher: Betty Boyd

BALLIETT & FITZGERALD, INC.
Managing Editor: Duncan Bock
Art Editor: Sue Canavan
Consulting Editor: Chris Mitchell
Assistant Editor: Howard Slatkin
Copyeditor: Roger Mooney
Proofreaders: Andrea Mallozzi, Karen Green, Larry Peterson
Page Artists: Peggy Goddard, Barry Koffler
Diagram Artists: Rachel Florman, Tracy Liu, Eric Liftin, Kuen Shon
Editorial Assistant: John Ciba
Special thanks to Brian Phair, Leanne Coupe, and, of course, Mike Spring.

BOOK DESIGN BY MARY TIEGREEN

Macmillan Travel
A Simon & Schuster/Macmillan Company
1633 Broadway
New York, NY 10019

ISBN 0-02-860475-X
Library of Congress Catalog Card No.: 95-080386

Manufactured in the United States

10 9 8 7 6 5 4 3 2 1

First Edition

By David Bean

CONTENTS

THE MAJORS • 10

Courtesy of PGA National Resort and Spa

The PGA Tour • 46

LPGA • 130

By John DeMello

Senior PGA Tour • 174

Tournament Histories• 234

By Dana Edmunds

THE MAJORS

The Masters

AUGUSTA NATIONAL GOLF CLUB

The Masters is a rite of spring; a golfer's heart beats a little faster when the white veranda of the Augusta National clubhouse comes into view. Conceived as the consummate thinking golfer's course, Augusta National is a testament to golf great Bobby Jones's vision. As he wrote of his first visit to the property in 1931, "The long lane of magnolias through which we approached was beautiful...But when I walked out on the grass terrace under the big trees behind the house [built in 1854] and looked down over the property, the experience was unforgettable. It seemed that this land had been lying here for years just waiting for someone to lay a golf course upon it."

The land was then the 365-acre Fruitlands, the South's first commercial nursery, owned by the Berckman family. The rolling pinelands were rich with apple, pear, magnolia, wisteria, camellia and the famous azaleas often seen in full bloom during the Masters. Jones, an amateur golfer who had just won the Grand Slam at age 28 and retired to practice law, joined with Scottish golf architect Alister Mackenzie to turn it into one of the best and most beautiful golf courses in the world. Their layout makes shot and pin placement critical factors, and slight mistakes can lead to big numbers on a scorecard. "There isn't a hole out there that can't be birdied if you just think. But there isn't one that can't be double bogeyed if you stop thinking. A lot of the difference has to do with the weather," said Jones.

A superstar of his era and the only person ever to be accorded two Broadway ticker tape parades, Jones needed a quiet and social club to play golf with his friends. Edward F. Hutton, L. B. Maytag, Eugene G. Grace and other captains of American industry were among Augusta National's early members. Today there are approximately 300 members of Augusta National, mostly from the highest echelons of international business.

TOURNAMENT-AT-A-GLANCE

Course: Augusta National Golf Club
Type: Private
Location: 2604 Washington Rd., Augusta, GA 30903
Phone: (706) 667-6000
When: April 11–14, 1996
How To Get There: From Interstate 20 (150 miles east of Atlanta) take Washington Road Exit south off I-20. The golf course is at Berckman and Washington Road. Augusta is serviced by Bush Field and Daniel Field, local airports.
Broadcast: USA, CBS (1996)
Purse: $2,132,000 (1995)
Tournament Record: 17-under-par 271, Jack Nicklaus, 1965 and Ray Floyd, 1976

In the original plan, the current back nine at Augusta was the front nine, but Jones felt a reversal would bring about dramatic tournament finishes. Augusta opened in 1933 and, after unsuccessful attempts to attract the U.S. Open, the "First Augusta National Invitation Tournament" was inaugurated in 1934. It was won by Horton Smith. Gene Sarazen's "shot heard 'round the world," a dramatic double eagle 2, put the event on the professional golf map in 1935. Sarazen holed a 220-yard, 4-wood on the 500-yard, par-5 15th, then parred the final three holes to tie Craig Wood at 282. In a 36-hole playoff the next day, Sarazen outlasted Wood, 144 to 149, to pick up the $1,500 first prize and a $50 bonus for his playoff efforts. The tournament was rechristened the Masters in 1938.

No golf fan turns off the television set during the final round of the Masters. The 405-yard, par-4 finishing hole has been the scene of many dramatic finishes. A slight dogleg right, it gradually climbs 50 feet to a deep, severely forward-sloping green with a shelf to its rear. In 1942, Ben Hogan caught his fellow Texan, Byron Nelson, with a birdie at the 18th in the final round to tie at 280. Nelson, who started out with a double-bogey 6, won the fiercely fought 18-hole playoff 69 to 70 with the help of an eagle 3 on the eighth and birdies on No. 6 and the three holes at Amen Corner, Nos. 11, 12 and 13. It was on 18 that Art Wall Jr. completed his run of six straight birdies to shoot a final-round 66 for a one-stroke victory in 1959. The next year, Arnold Palmer nailed a 6-iron approach to within 6 feet of the hole, dropped his putt and stole the Masters from Ken Venturi. Sandy Lyle hit his famous 7-iron recovery shot from the left fairway bunker on the final round in 1988 and made birdie to deprive Mark Calcavecchia of the title. And in 1991, Ian Woosnam launched a 280-yard drive over the same fairway bunker to an open spot in the member's practice area, then scrambled for par to win his green

Courtesy of Golfoto

FRONTED BY RAE'S CREEK, AUGUSTA'S FAMOUS 12TH, THE "GOLDEN BELL," HAS BEEN THE SITE OF MANY DISASTERS, INCLUDING TOM WEISKOPF'S 13 IN 1980.

jacket. As Craig Stadler, the 1982 champion, put it, "It's not a difficult hole until you have to par it. Then it becomes a pain in the ass."

Arnold Palmer ushered in the era of big-time televised golf when he hung on to win the 1958 Masters by one stroke over Doug Ford and Fred Hawkins. Palmer won again in 1960, 1962 (in an 18-hole playoff with Gary Player and Dow Finsterwald) and 1964. Jack Nicklaus began his dominance of the event in 1963 at age 23. Over two decades, he won five more—in 1965, 1966 (in an 18-hole playoff with Tommy Jacobs and Gay Brewer, Jr.), 1972, 1975 and 1986. That year, Nicklaus's sixth green jacket and 20th major climaxed one of the most dramatic and emotional finishes in Masters history—he had a final-round 30 on the back nine to edge Tom Kite and Greg Norman by one stroke.

"THERE IS SOMETHING VERY SPECIAL ABOUT THE MASTERS. THE FAMILIARITY OF THE COURSE, THE FACT THAT IT'S PLAYED AT THE SAME PLACE EVERY YEAR GIVES IT A SPECIAL HISTORY YOU DON'T FIND AT ANY OTHER MAJOR CHAMPIONSHIP."

—BEN CRENSHAW,

1984 AND 1995 MASTERS CHAMPION

Bobby Jones played in every Masters until 1947, when he withdrew after the second round because of illness. Diagnosed with a rare spinal disease, he was soon unable to walk. "Playing it as it lies," as Jones would say, he lived gracefully and courageously until 1971.

LODGING

$$$ The Partridge Inn, 2110 Walton Way, Augusta, Ga. (706) 737-8888, (800) 476-6888. 10 minutes from Augusta National GC.
$$ Telfair Inn, 326 Greene St., Augusta, Ga. (706) 724-3315, (800) 241-2407. 5 minutes from Augusta National GC.
$ Comfort Inn, 629 Frontage Rd. NW, Augusta, Ga. (706) 855-6060, (800) 228-5150. 10 minutes from Augusta National GC.
Masters Housing Bureau, 592 Bobby Jones Expwy., No. 8 Anderson Plaza, Martinez, Ga. (706) 855-8898.

DINING

Le Cafe Duteau, 1855 Central Ave., Augusta, Ga. (706) 733-3505.
The King George, 2 Eighth St., Augusta, Ga. (706) 724-4755.
The Boll Weevil— A Cafe and Sweetery, 10 9th St., Augusta, Ga. (706) 722-7772.

PUBLIC COURSES TO PLAY IN THE AREA

Cedar Creek Golf Club, 2475 Club Dr., Aiken, S.C. (803) 648-4206. Public. 18/7,206/72. 30 minutes from Augusta National GC.
Jones Creek Golf Club, 4101 Hammonds Ferry St., Evans, Ga. (706) 860-4228. Public. 18/7,008/72. 20 minutes from Augusta National GC.
Reynolds Plantation, 100 Linger Longer Rd., Greensboro, Ga (706) 467-3159. Resort. Plantation Course: 18/6,656/72. Great Waters: 18/7048/72. 1 hour from Augusta National GC.

TICKETS & ACCESSIBILITY

How to watch: Practice rounds begin three days before tournament. Obtain current information from the Masters Tournament. The waiting list for Masters tickets was closed in 1978 after it reached approximately 5,000. Tickets can be obtained through tour companies such as Best Golf Tours, Box 65, 332 Forrest Ave., Laguna Beach, CA 92652, (800) 458-6888; Fore International, 23200 Chagrin Blvd., Suite 150, Beachwood, OH 44122, (216) 591-0105, (800) 798-FORE; and others. Contact the Masters Tournament for further information: P.O. Box 2086, Augusta, GA 30913, (706) 667-6000.
How to play: The course is closed during the summer months, and you must be a member or play with a member to have access.

●TOUGHEST HOLES

It is usually the par-3s and par-4s that determine the Masters champion. In 1994 the 155-yard, par-3 12th and the 205-yard, par-3 fourth were rated the most difficult holes at the Masters and among the twelve most difficult holes on the PGA Tour.
The fourth hole, called "Flowering Crab Apple," is not etched in the national memory because the front nine is rarely seen on television. It took 56 years of Masters competition for a hole-in-one to be recorded on No. 4. Jeff Sluman aced it with a 4-iron in 1992.

The more famous 12th, "Golden Bell," which Jack Nicklaus calls "the hardest hole in championship golf," is a beautiful and notoriously dangerous hole fronted by Rae's Creek. It was here that Tom Weiskopf recorded a 13 in one round and a 7 in the next in 1980. Jack Nicklaus took his only bogey here when he closed with a 30 in 1986. Fred Couples escaped disaster in 1992 when his final-round tee shot fell short, but somehow did not roll down the bank and into the drink in 1992. Couples got up and down to save par and went on to win the Masters.

●BEST PLACE TO WATCH

Attend the par-3 tournament on Wednesday and walk the course. Visit the practice area any day. Prime spectator spots are behind the 12th tee, where you can also view the 11th; the fourth hole, where you can see the fifth tee; and the left side of the 15th, where you can see the 14th fairway and tee along with the 13th green.

●WHO THE COURSE FAVORS

The course favors a thinking golfer who can plot all the steps needed to reach a particular target on the green in advance and then position the ball accordingly. Because the greens are lightning fast, it is critical to come in high to the target in order to hold the green, preferably below the hole. Accuracy, positioning and putting usually determine the winner of the Masters. When healthy Couples is a threat, and look for two-time U.S. Amateur champion Tiger Woods to do well here in the future.

Toughest Hole

Best Place to Watch

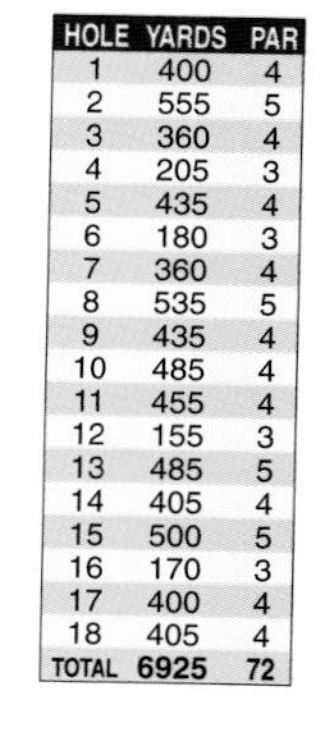

HOLE	YARDS	PAR
1	400	4
2	555	5
3	360	4
4	205	3
5	435	4
6	180	3
7	360	4
8	535	5
9	435	4
10	485	4
11	455	4
12	155	3
13	485	5
14	405	4
15	500	5
16	170	3
17	400	4
18	405	4
TOTAL	6925	72

AUGUSTA NATIONAL GOLF CLUB
ARCHITECT: ALISTER MACKENZIE
WITH ROBERT TYRE JONES JR. (1933),
RENOVATED BY PERRY MAXWELL (1937),
ROBERT TRENT JONES (1946, 1950),
GEORGE FAZIO (1972),
GEORGE W. COBB AND JOHN LAFOY (1977),
JOSEPH S. FINGER AND BYRON NELSON (1979),
JAY MORRISH AND ROBERT CUPP (1982),
JACK NICKLAUS (1985)

United States Open

Oakland Hills Country Club

"The Monster" beckoned. For 54 holes, Oakland Hills had gotten the better of the world's best shotmaker. But as Ben Hogan munched a roast beef sandwich between the final day's two rounds, he steeled himself for one last valiant assault.

TOURNAMENT-AT-A-GLANCE

Course: Oakland Hills Country Club—South Course
Type: Private
Location: 3951 Maple Rd., Birmingham, MI 48012
Telephone: (810) 644-2500
When: June 13–16, 1996
How To Get There: Take I-690 to Telegraph Ave. North. Take Telegraph to Maple Rd. Make a right on Maple to golf course.
Broadcast: NBC (1995)
Purse: $2,000,000 (1995)
Tournament Record: 8-under-par 272, Jack Nicklaus, 1980 and Lee Janzen, 1993 (at par-70 Baltusrol)

The year was 1951, and Hogan's afternoon would transform this U.S. Open into one of the greatest in history on a weekend that had raised the game's popularity to new heights.

Hogan's foe was an 18 conceived by Donald Ross and whipped into a froth by Robert Trent Jones. In Jones's hands, the track had grown to 6,927 yards, its bends and greens had been pocked by 50 new bunkers, its fairways had been narrowed by deep rough, its sharply contoured greens quickened, and its par mercilessly trimmed to 70. Through three rounds, no player had matched par, and Hogan was still two off the lead with a 10-over-par 220.

With record crowds swallowing him each time the ball left his club, Hogan dispatched blow after blow toward what many consider the greatest round of golf ever. His scorecard recorded a modest number, 67, but it came on a round when the average score of the world's best players was more than eight strokes higher. "I'm glad that I brought this course, this monster, to its knees," Hogan said.

The Open, a century-old devotion to golf's highest standards, has become a roving annual pilgrimage among historic but vicious courses that the host United States Golf Association chooses each year to separate the flailers from the game's complete artists. For Oakland Hills, whose rolling Michigan woodlands presented designer Ross with a site "the Lord intended for a golf course," 1996's 96th anniversary of the event marks the Open's sixth visit.

Steel-shafted putters were permitted for the first time when Oakland Hills debuted on the Open's honor roll in 1924. The previous emergence of Bobby Jones and Gene Sarazen had announced the end of Europe's early dominance in the sport, but this time a diminutive Englishman named Cyril Walker bested defending champion Jones by three strokes with steady rounds of 74-74-74-75. A young Sam Snead challenged Ralph Guldahl at Oakland Hills in 1937, but his second-place finish matched the closest he would come to victory in the one major that forever eluded him.

Ten years after Hogan's legendary triumph, the Open returned again to an Oakland Hills whose terrors had been somewhat tamed by a new watering system, kinder bunkers and rough, wider fairways and better equipment. An aging Hogan carded a first-day 71 and said that pace wouldn't win it. Machine-like Gene Littler indeed won by a stroke with a 1-over-par 281, becoming the eighth player ever to capture both the U.S. Open and Amateur titles.

By 1985, the modern player, modern course management and modern equipment had taken much off the edge of Donald Ross's original design and Robert Trent Jones' efforts to humble the pros. The 454-yard, par-4 10th demanded a 2-iron second shot from Hogan in 1951—"my best shot of the tournament"—but Andy North had no problem reaching the green with a 3-wood and a 7-iron in 1985. Fred Couples reached the green of the second hole, a 527-yard par-5, with just a drive and a 6-iron.

A different story line might have saved the event, but its finish, while dramatic, has prompted many observers to rank it among the Open's worst outings. North, an oft-injured player whom no purist seemed to like, had chosen the 1978 Open as the stage of his first Tour victory, and it was a stumbling parade to victory at that. Incredibly, he waited until Oakland Hills to seize his second career win.

The surprise early-round leader in 1985 was T.C. Chen, an ex-sailor in the Chinese Navy who belittled Oakland Hills on only the second hole, a 527-yard par-5, by holing a 240-yard 3-wood for the first dou-

By Mike Klemme

OAKLAND HILLS HOSTED THE CLASSIC 1951 OPEN WHERE BEN HOGAN PLAYED ONE OF CHAMPIONSHIP GOLF'S BEST ROUNDS EVER.

ble-eagle in Open history. Chen birdied the last two holes that day for a 5-under-par 65, then equaled the 36-hole record by tacking on a 69. Chen entered Sunday holding a two-stroke margin over Jay Haas and North.

The second hole yielded a mere birdie to Chen on the final round, but that moved him a comfortable four shots ahead of North. Dufferlike disaster struck three holes later.

On the 457-yard, par-4 fifth, Chen pushed his 4-iron approach into thick rough among a group of trees 30 yards to the right of the green. Chen's wedge, unable to sweep the ball out cleanly, struck the ball again as it popped into the air. The double-hit meant a one-stroke penalty: Chen was suddenly hitting 5 and was not yet on the green.

"THE U.S. OPEN IS OUR NATIONAL CHAMPIONSHIP, THE ONE...EVERYONE WANTS TO WIN. THE WAY THE USGA SETS UP THE COURSES MAKES IT A DIFFICULT CHALLENGE, BUT THAT JUST MAKES THE VICTORY THAT MUCH MORE REWARDING."

—COREY PAVIN,

1995 U.S. OPEN CHMAPION

Three more shots got him down for the most costly 8 in a U.S. Open since Snead triple-bogeyed away the 1939 title on the final hole, at Philadelphia Country Club. By the end of nine, Chen, adding bogeys on six, seven and eight, was two strokes back of North.

It was up to North as he came to the 17th tee. His tee shot caught a bunker fronting the green, but he exploded a sand wedge to within a few feet of the pin and made his par. His 4-iron approach on the long 18th landed in rough between bunkers fronting the green. Informed by a tournament referee that he needed only a bogey to win, North delivered, spending all three strokes to get to the cup. Still, his 74 and 1-under-par total of 287 was enough for victory on a course no other player had conquered.

●TOUGHEST HOLE

The 453-yard, par-4 18th is one of four par-4s in excess of 450 yards at Oakland Hills and one of its most difficult. The tee shot on this dogleg right must negotiate three bunkers to the right and one to the left of the landing area. The approach is to a green severely squeezed in front by bunkers to its left and right. Bunkers farther in front of the green can easily catch errant shots. In the 1951 Open, Ben Hogan cut a drive over the fairway bunker to the right, then hit a 6-iron uphill to within 4 feet of the hole. He sank the putt for his 3, the fourth birdie he recorded on the final nine holes to punctuate his astonishing 67.

●BEST PLACE TO WATCH

The area around the huge Colonial-style clubhouse is convenient to the first tee, ninth green, 10th tee and 18th green. The area around the 11th hole also affords a view of the No. 8 green. But the green area around No. 16, which provides easy access to the 17th tee, is a TV and crowd favorite. A 409-yard dogleg right, the hole's approaches must avoid a pond to the right that runs up to the green, guarded in back by four bunkers. In 1985, Andy North sank a 60-foot putt here for his only birdie of the third round. Gary Player struck one of the most famous 9-irons in history here during the 1972 PGA Championship when he lofted a ball over a weeping willow, miraculously carried the water and presented himself a 4-foot birdie putt as a reward for his courage.

●WHO THE COURSE FAVORS

Because of the high rough and narrower fairways favored for U.S. Open play, accurate tee shots will be required to succeed at Oakland Hills. The large undulating greens, considered by Jack Nicklaus to be among the most difficult on any golf course in the world, could force three or even four putts, especially if they become sun-dried. Well-placed approach shots will be required to set up makeable putts at Oakland Hills. Quality putters like Davis Love III, Brad Faxon and defending champion Corey Pavin should do well here.

HOLE	YARDS	PAR	HOLE	YARDS	PAR
1	436	4	10	454	4
2	527	5	11	411	4
3	199	3	12	560	5
4	433	4	13	172	3
5	457	4	14	465	4
6	359	4	15	399	4
7	405	4	16	409	4
8	139	4	17	201	3
9	217	3	18	453	4
			TOTAL	6996	70

LODGING

$$$ The Townsend Hotel, 100 Townsend St., Birmingham, Mich. (810) 642-7900, (800) 548-4172. 10 minutes from Oakland Hills.
$$ The Village Inn Hotel, 300 N. Hunter Blvd., Birmingham, Mich. (810) 642-6200. 10 minutes from Oakland Hills.
$ Holiday Inn Express, 145 S. Hunter Blvd., Birmingham, Mich. (810) 646-7300. 10 minutes from Oakland Hills.

DINING

The Whitney, 4421 Woodward Ave., Detroit. (313) 832-5700.
Norman's Eton Street Station, 245 S. Eaton Ave., Birmingham, Mich. (810) 647-7774.
Bill Knapp's, 3900 Telegraph Rd., Bloomfield Hills, Mich. (810) 642-2338.

PUBLIC COURSES TO PLAY IN THE AREA

Greystone Golf Club, 6700 Mound Rd., Romeo, Mich. Public. (810) 752-7030. 18/6,860/72. 40 minutes from Oakland Hills.
The Orchards Golf Club, 62900 Campground Rd., Washington, Mich. Public. (810) 786-7200. 18/7,026/72. 1 hour from Oakland Hills.
Stonebridge Golf Club, 5315 Stonebridge Dr. S., Ann Arbor, Mich. Public. (313) 429-8383. 18/6,932/72. 40 minutes from Oakland Hills.

TICKETS & ACCESSIBILITY

How to watch: Mon., practice rounds. Tue., practice rounds. Wed., practice rounds. Thur.-Sun., tournament. Individual, group and sponsor tickets available. The U.S. Open, c/o The United States Golf Association, P.O. Box 708, Far Hills, NJ 07931. (908) 234-9393 (tickets), (908) 234-2300 (USGA).
How to play: Oakland Hills is a private club. You must be a member or the guest of a member to play the course.

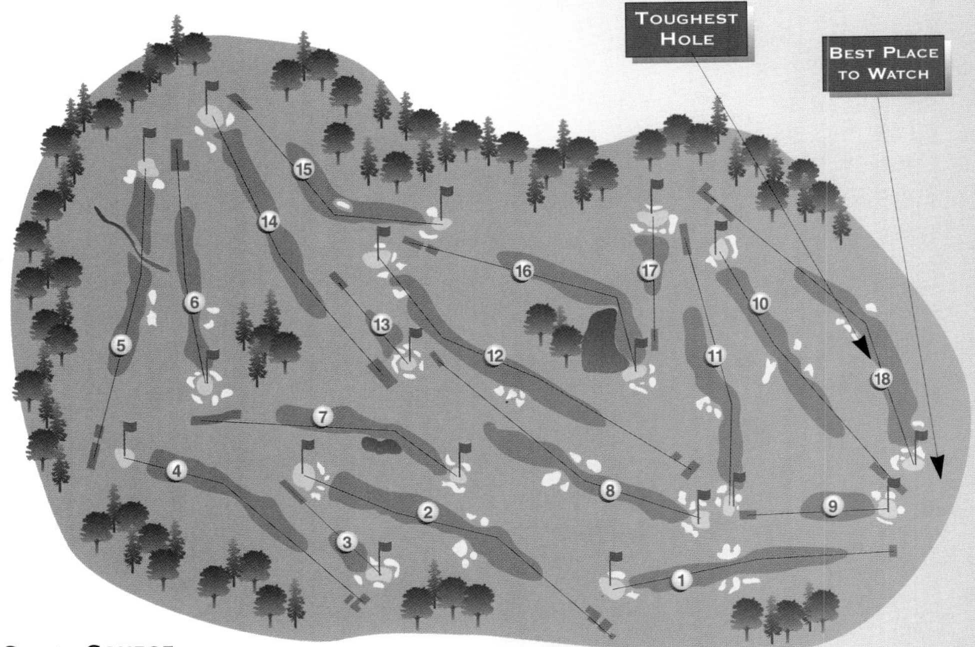

OAKLAND HILLS, SOUTH COURSE
ARCHITECT: DONALD ROSS (1917)
REMODELED BY ROBERT TRENT JONES (1950, 1972, 1984), ARTHUR HILLS (1987, 1994)

British Open

ROYAL LYTHAM AND ST. ANNES GOLF CLUB

The British Open is the granddaddy of all the major tournaments. Its seed was planted in 1857 when eight clubs took part in a three-round foursomes match at a 12-hole layout in Prestwick, Scotland. Though St. Andrews' Old Course would set the standard for a full round of golf at 18 holes, there were still many courses at the time with whatever number of holes accident had bestowed them. Two years later, Allan Robertson, then the acknowledged dominant professional, passed away, and so in 1860 a field of eight professionals from seven Scottish clubs gathered at Prestwick to decide an individual champion in what is now considered the first Open. Willie Park of Musselburgh won that first title contest with a 36-hole total of 174 and would win twice more over the next six years. Runner-up Old Tom Morris of Prestwick would capture the event four times between 1861 and 1867 before Young Tom Morris, the defending champ's aptly named 17-year-old son, overtook the field.

Three consecutive titles later, Young Tom retired Prestwick's Championship belt in 1870. But soon a new trophy was acquired to replace the belt and a rotation was set up among Prestwick, St. Andrews and Musselburgh—a format that has continued, in expanded form, to this day. Playing on his home course, Young Tom won again in 1872 in the first match of the new order.

Americans paid little heed to the venerable Open until the 1920s, when an immensely popular trio—Walter Hagen (winner of the 1922, 1924, 1928 and 1929 titles), Bobby Jones (1926, 1927 and 1930) and Gene Sarazen (1932) made bent-kneed pilgrimages to golf's birthplace and quickly established the Colonies as birthplace of the game's best players. Jones, an idol on both shores, captured his third and final British Open in 1930, the year he became golf's only Grand Slam winner with matching victories in the British Amateur, the U.S. Open and the U.S. Amateur.

TOURNAMENT-AT-A-GLANCE

Tournament: British Open
Course: Royal Lytham and St. Annes Golf Club
Type: Private
Location: Links Gate, St. Annes-On-The-Sea, England FY8 3LQ
Telephone: 011-44-1-253-720094, 011-44-1-253-724206
When: July 18–21, 1996
How To Get There: From London, bus from Euston Station or rail from Victoria Coach Station to St. Annes-on-the-Sea.
Broadcast: ESPN, ABC (1995)
Purse: $1,800,000 (1995)
Tournament Record: 13-under-par 267, Greg Norman, 1993 (at Royal St. George's GC, Sandwich, England)

There is a plaque along the seventeenth hole at Royal Lytham and St. Annes commemorating the shot that won Jones his first British Open in 1926. The course, set on the coast one hour north of Liverpool, was designed in the 1890s by George Lowe Jr., a native of Carnoustie who had moved to England to serve as St. Annes greenskeeper. Inside its clubhouse today is a treasure trove of Jones memorabilia, including a letter in which he professes his love for the course. Tied for the lead when he came to the tournament's 71st hole in 1926, the 24-year-old American hit a heroic mashie recovery from around 170 yards to save par and rattle co-leader Al Watrous into the tournament's decisive bogey.

Royal Lytham did not again host the Open until 1952, well after a five-year break in play caused by World War II. American participation had dwindled during the Great Depression and when Sam Snead, encouraged by Hagen, entered the 1946 Open at St. Andrews and won, he didn't even bother to defend his title. Similarly, Ben Hogan won the Open in 1953 at Carnoustie but never returned.

The event's postwar years were dominated by South African Bobby Locke and Australian Peter Thomson. In 1952, Royal Lytham was the host when Locke won the third of his four Open titles, edging Thomson by a single shot. Thomson's fourth of five titles came at Royal Lytham in 1958, when he defeated D.C. Thomas of England in a 36-hole playoff.

It was not until Arnold Palmer, the game's most popular player, made a concerted effort to play in the tournament that the Open began to regain its international luster. Palmer's arrival reinvigorated the event by importing the rivalries among its new television-era stars, most notably himself, Jack Nicklaus and Gary Player. Player won his first of three British Opens at

Courtesy of Golfoto

OF THE WORLD'S GREAT COURSES, ROYAL LYTHAM AND ST. ANNES IS KNOWN FOR BEING DECEPTIVELY UNDRAMATIC.

Muirfield in 1959, then Palmer, after a second-place finish in his first appearance, won at Royal Birkdale (1961) and Troon (1962).

A young Nicklaus bogeyed the last two holes at Royal Lytham in the 1963 Open to finish a stroke behind Bob Charles and Phil Rodgers, who played the final 36-hole playoff in British Open history to decide a winner. Charles, the lefty, broke open a tight duel over the second 18 to win that showdown by eight strokes.

More recently, Tom Watson established himself as one of golf's all-time greats with five British Open victories, including his 1977 triumph at Turnberry in arguably the greatest Open of all time.

Royal Lytham has played a role in a current trend, as an international field has brought an emphatic end to the era of American domination. Seve Ballesteros captured two of his three Open titles here, in 1979 and 1988. Since Watson's fifth title, in '83, only two Americans—Mark Calcavecchia in 1989 and John Daly in 1995—have won the Open.

"NATURALLY, ROYAL LYTHAM IS ONE OF MY FAVORITE COURSES BECAUSE I WON TWO CHAMPIONSHIPS THERE. THIS YEAR I WOULD LIKE TO MAKE IT THREE."

—SEVE BALLESTEROS,

WINNER OF THE 1979 AND 1988 BRITISH OPENS PLAYED AT ROYAL LYTHAM AND ST. ANNES

Royal Lytham is a course that can lull a player into a false sense of security. The front side is a short 3,302 yards but plays through a minefield of bunkers, sandhills and deep rough that, coupled with unpredictable winds, can quickly add strokes to a scorecard.

The back nine, with only one par-5, is stingy with birdies as the golfers constantly wrestle with club selection and setups for optimum angles to greens protected by tricky rough and deep bunkers. In 1988, Ballesteros fired an 11-under-par 273 to win the Open here, but this venerable layout usually yields only near-par scores to the victor.

LODGING

$$$ Chester Grosvenor, Eastgate St., Chester. Tel: 011-44-1-244-324024, Fax: 011-44-1-244-313246. 50 minutes from Royal Lytham and St. Annes.

$$ Crabwell Manor, Parkgate Rd., Mollington. Tel: 011-44-1-244-851666, Fax: 011-44-1-244-851400. 50 minutes from Royal Lytham and St. Annes.

DINING

Arkle Room in the Chester Grosvenor, Eastgate St., Chester. Tel: 011-44-1-244-324024. Fax: 011-44-1-244-313246.

Brasserie in the Chester Grosvenor, Eastgate St., Chester. Tel: 011-44-1-244-324024. Fax: 011-44-1-244-313246.

PUBLIC COURSES TO PLAY IN AREA

Royal Birkdale, Waterloo Rd., Southport. 011-44-1-704-68857, 011-44-1-704-67920. 18/6,305/71. 30 minutes from Royal Lytham and St. Annes.

Royal Liverpool, Meols Dr., Wirral. 011-44-1-51-632-5868, 011-44-1-51-632-6757. 18/6,810/72. 1 hour from Royal Lytham and St. Annes.

Formby, Golf Rd., Formby. 011-44-1-7048-72164. Formby: 18/6,701/73. Formby Ladies: 18/5,374/71. 45 minutes from Royal Lytham and St. Annes.

TICKETS & ACCESSIBILITY

How to watch: Mon.-Wed., practice rounds. Thurs.-Sun., tournament. Championship Department, Royal and Ancient Golf Club, St. Andrews, Fife, KY169NU. Tel: 011-44-1-334 479463. Fax: 011-44-1-334 478422.

How to play: Royal Lytham and St. Annes is closed to visitors on Tuesday mornings and on weekends. Contact the club through your head pro or directly at 011-44-1-253-720094 or 011-44-1-253-724206 to arrange a tee time.

●TOUGHEST HOLE

The long par-4 15th is usually made longer by an incoming wind. The tee shot must cut off a bit of the dogleg right in order to reach a green bordered by a series of four bunkers that run from its left back out 50 yards into the fairway. The right side of the hole is protected by two bunkers, and dangerous rough awaits errant shots most everywhere else. The 17th, a dogleg left featuring 19 bunkers, is another demanding par-4. In 1963, Jack Nicklaus squandered his final-round lead when he miscalculated and hit a 2-iron through the green into the rough before salvaging a bogey. Nicklaus later recalled: "What I'd forgotten is the effect of adrenaline, which, when you're contending, grows in inverse ratio to the number of holes remaining."

●BEST PLACE TO WATCH

Lytham is a relatively level, compact course with many parallel holes. There are also few trees on the course so it is easy to see great distances, but because of the lack of pronounced elevation changes, other spectators might obstruct your view. The four finishing holes are the ones to watch. The 18th green area, in particular, can provide many adventures. Gary Player, ahead by five shots in the final round of the 1974 Open, ran his approach through the green to the base of the clubhouse wall. He then saved bogey and a four-stroke win by scraping a shot onto the green with his putter.

●WHO THE COURSE FAVORS

Driving accuracy is important at Royal Lytham, especially because of the thick rough and numerous bunkers guarding both the fairways and greens. An ability to hit deft recovery shots from these hazards is also important because the variable winds here can make a ball's destination unpredictable. Player often used a 1-iron off the tee in 1974 to reduce his margin for error. Noted golf journalist Bernard Darwin endorsed the course's greens by writing: "There is no kind of excuse for bad putting at St. Annes."

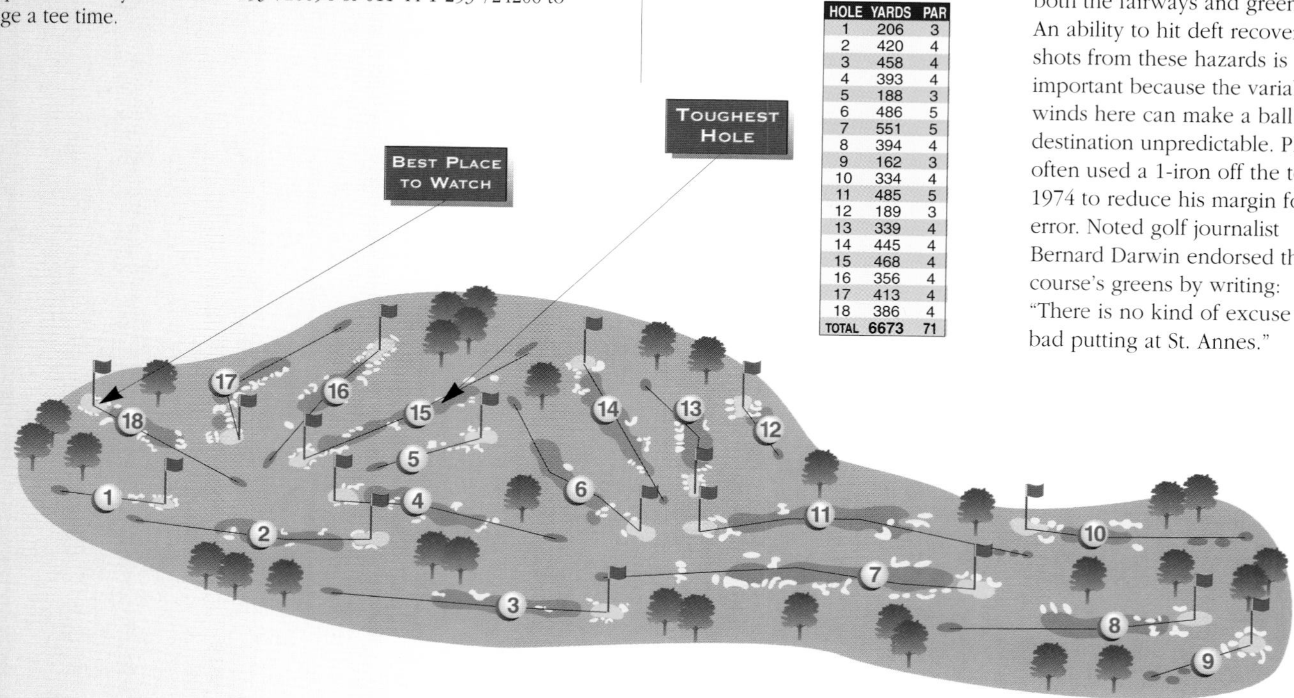

HOLE	YARDS	PAR
1	206	3
2	420	4
3	458	4
4	393	4
5	188	3
6	486	5
7	551	5
8	394	4
9	162	3
10	334	4
11	485	5
12	189	3
13	339	4
14	445	4
15	468	4
16	356	4
17	413	4
18	386	4
TOTAL	6673	71

ROYAL LYTHAM AND ST. ANNE'S
ARCHITECT: GEORGE LOWE, JR. (1897)
REMODELED BY TOM SIMPSON (NA), HERBERT FOWLER (NA), TOM SIMPSON (NA), H.S. COLT AND C.H. ALISON (1923), H.S. COLT AND J.S.F. MORRISON (1932), J.S.F. MORRISON (1936), C.K. COTTON AND J.J.F. PENNINK (1952), D.M.A. STEEL (1987)

PGA Championship

VALHALLA GOLF CLUB

On January 16, 1916, a young U.S. Open champion named Walter Hagen and 34 other New York–area golf professionals gathered at the Taplow Club in New York City to discuss the plight of their profession.

The game's biggest names, like John McDermott and Jock Hutchinson, could make a living from exhibition matches, product endorsements and offering individual lessons to a select clientele. But most top players who weren't born into wealth were, if lucky, locked into jobs as the jack-of-all-trades resident pros at the nation's elite golf clubs.

Department store owner Rodman Wanamaker could see the merchandising possibilities of a professional golfers association, and he offered to put up trophies, medals and $2,580 in prize money to hold the first PGA Championship.

TOURNAMENT-AT-A-GLANCE

Course: Valhalla Golf Club
Type: Private
Location: 15503 Shelbyville Rd., Louisville, KY 40253
Telephone: (502) 245-1238
When: Aug. 8–11, 1996
How To Get There: From Louisville, 20 minutes. Take I-64 east to I-265. Take I-265 Exit north. Proceed 3/4 mile on I-265 north to Hwy. 60/Eastwood-Middletown Exit. Take a right at the bottom of the exit ramp, 2 miles to the golf course.
Broadcast: TBS, CBS (1996)
Purse: $1,700,000 (1995)
Tournament Record: 11-under-par 269, Nick Price, 1994

Thirty-one professionals competed in the first championship, held in October 1916 at the Siwanoy Country Club in Bronxville, N.Y. The final match went the distance, and on the last green, after a measurement to see which ball was away, Englishman "Long Jim" Barnes, a resident of Philadelphia, took advantage of his rival's missed 5-footer by rolling home his own. His victory earned him $500 and a diamond medal.

A world war would intervene before the championship was played again, but when the 1920s arrived, so did America's first great professional champions.

Hagen, the son of a shoemaker, was a flamboyant crowd favorite and a bon vivant. Gene Sarazen, the son of a carpenter from Italy, was only 20 in 1922 when he became the first player to win the U.S. Open and PGA Championship in the same year. They would become the first Americans to make their livings as golfers without being anchored to pro shops, and together they dominated the second decade of the PGA Championship.

Hagen took the title a record five times, and Sarazen claimed it twice. Yet they faced off in the final just once, in 1923, and 36 holes of match play weren't enough to separate them. Hagen forever after contended that a Sarazen fan threw his opponent's drive back into play on the second playoff hole, but the younger player still needed a brilliant recovery from deep rough to send his ball to within an arm's length of the flagstick. Shaken, Hagen dumped his approach into a bunker and missed, just barely, his attempt to prolong the battle.

Hagen did wonders for golf's popularity. He played more than two thousand exhibitions, his bread and butter, between 1914 and the mid-1930s. Though occasionally wild with his loose swing, he was a brilliant recovery player, an excellent putter and a deadly competitor. Yet when the Arnold Palmer of his day quit the game, the pros' tournament circuit was still a loose collection of competitions, and the Great Depression and World War II ensured the pro Tour would not soon become a sure way for a top-flight player to pay his bills.

The popularity of a trio of PGA champions—Byron Nelson (1940, 1945), Sam Snead (1942, 1949, 1951) and Ben Hogan (1946, 1948)—began to change all that, but meanwhile, the PGA tournament itself was becoming a grueling marathon as the field grew. By 1957, the last year of match play, four rounds of 18-hole matches and three rounds of 36-hole matches were played over five days before Lionel Hebert was awarded the Wanamaker Trophy.

The two players who came to define golf's transforming television era, Jack Nicklaus and Arnold Palmer, both spent brief stints as salesmen before daring to make their livings on the pro Tour, but they had widely different career experiences in the PGA's title event. Nicklaus won a record-tying five titles; Palmer never finished better than second.

When Nick Price blew out all comers in the 1994 tournament with a six-stroke victory, his winner's check read: $310,000. His competition included 47 of

By Mike Klemme

A FIRST-TIME PGA CHAMPIONSHIP HOST, VALHALLA HAS A PAR-4 FINISHING HOLE WITH CUNNINGLY PLACED WATER AND TRAPS.

the 50 top-ranked players in the world, making it the strongest field of the year. Rest assured that virtually all the pros among that group at least matched that figure in individual winnings that year.

Among the four majors, the PGA is the most likely to be disparaged by the game's taste-makers. Its crimes? Less brutal or historic courses; perhaps one nobody too many inscribed as champion on the winner's cup.

But the greatest golf stories of the past decade generally belong to the PGA. Thanks to a last-minute cancellation, John Daly found a starting time in the 1991 event and long-balled his way into the public's imagination with a three-stroke victory at Crooked Stick. Greg Norman, desperately seeking to win his first major title on American soil, was robbed once in 1986 when Bob Tway holed a bunker shot on the final hole. In 1993, Paul Azinger caught Norman from behind and then beat him in a playoff, but the new champion couldn't lift the Wanamaker Trophy over his head because of what turned out to be cancerous lymphoma. Just 12 months later, Azinger made it back from chemotherapy in time to attempt to defend his title.

The 1996 PGA Championship will be played on a 10-year-old Jack Nicklaus–designed course, the Valhalla Golf Club in Louisville. The Valhalla features bentgrass greens and landing areas that are well protected by thick rough and strategically placed bunkers. Accuracy off the tee rather than overpowering distance is important on this course, as are the approach shots to greens with a variety of shapes and undulations. If you miss the green on the par-4 12th, for example, you could be in an 8-foot-deep bunker to the right of the green or in heavy rough that requires a delicate but strong touch. The hourglass-shaped green on No. 16, a long par-4, has front and rear shelves with a trough in the center. Pin position and a possible incoming wind will greatly affect the difficulty of arriving at the cup.

When Valhalla hosts its first major, it's unlikely that any contender will skip the tournament to play exhibition matches the way PGA defending champion Walter Hagen did in 1922. The pro's championship will again be one of the ultimate tests of skill under pressure.

"WINNING THE PGA CHAMPIONSHIP AT BELLERIVE WAS THE MOST IMPORTANT TOURNAMENT OF MY CAREER....NONE OF US HAVE PLAYED VALHALLA, BUT FROM EVERYTHING I'VE HEARD IT'S A GREAT TRACK."

—NICK PRICE,

PGA CHAMPION 1992 AND 1994

●TOUGHEST HOLE

The 470-yard, par-4 12th, a slight dogleg right carved through woodlands, plays up to a plateau landing area, then up another level to a tiered green guarded by an extremely deep, right front bunker. Thick rough around the green awaits stray shots, and an incoming wind can often make this hole play like a par-5. The 450-yard, par-4 16th, another slight dogleg right through woodlands, has an hourglass green with a narrow entranceway and a depression in its center that will make this a tough putting hole.

●BEST PLACE TO WATCH

A prime viewing area will be around the 540-yard, par-5 18th, which has mounded viewing areas behind it. There is also an excellent vantage point behind the 12th green, a great place to watch the pros struggle with a long par-4.

●WHO THE COURSE FAVORS

Two distinctly different kinds of golfers, Jack Nicklaus, a power player, and Larry Mize, a finesse player, share the 18-hole course record at Valhalla (66). The golfer must keep tee shots and approach shots out of the thick Kentucky bluegrass rough. And angles of approach to the greens are important because bunkers and pin placements can severely reduce the size of target areas around the holes. A golfer like Davis Love, who is long off the tee and an excellent putter, should do well here as long as he doesn't stray the ball.

HOLE	YARDS	PAR	HOLE	YARDS	PAR
1	425	4	10	565	5
2	525	5	11	165	3
3	205	3	12	470	4
4	355	4	13	350	4
5	460	4	14	210	3
6	415	4	15	410	4
7	605	5	16	450	4
8	155	3	17	420	4
9	415	4	18	540	5
			TOTAL	7130	72

LODGING

$$$ The Seelbach, 500 Fourth Ave., Louisville. (502) 585-3200, (800) 333-3399. 25 minutes from Valhalla.
$$ Residence Inn by Marriott, 120 Hurstbourne Pkwy., Louisville. (502) 425-1821, (800) 331-3131. 5 minutes from Valhalla.
$ Travelodge Louisville-Hurstbourne, 9340 Blairwood Rd., Louisville. (502) 425-8010, (800) 578-7878. 5 minutes from Valhalla.

DINING

Star of Louisville, 151 W. River Rd., Louisville. (502) 589-7827.
The Oakroom, in The Seelbach, 500 Fourth Ave., Louisville. (502) 585-3200.
Blue Boar Cafeteria, 232 Oxmoor Center/Shelbyville Rd., Louisville. (502) 426-3310.

PUBLIC COURSES TO PLAY IN THE AREA

French Lick Springs Country Club, Hwy. 56, French Lick, Ind. Resort. (812) 936-9300. Country Club: 18/6,625/70. Valley: 18/6,056/70. 70 minutes from Valhalla.
Quail Chase Golf Club, 7000 Cooper Chapel Rd., Louisville. Public. (502) 239-2110. South Nine: 9/3,274/36. West: 9/3,241/36. East: 9/3,512/36. 25 minutes from Valhalla.
Sultan's Run Golf Course, 1490 N. Meridian Rd., Jasper, Ind. Public. 18/7000/72. (812) 482-1009. 90 minutes from Valhalla.

TICKETS & ACCESSIBILITY

How to watch: Mon., PGA practice rounds. Tue., PGA practice rounds, champions clinic. Wed., PGA practice rounds. Thur.-Sun., tournament. Individual, group and sponsor tickets available. The PGA Championship, Valhalla Golf Club, 15503 Shelbyville Rd., Louisville, KY 40253, (502) 254-1996, (800) PGA-IN-96.
How to play: Valhalla is a private club. You must be a member or the guest of a member to play the course. Limited reciprocal play is accepted.

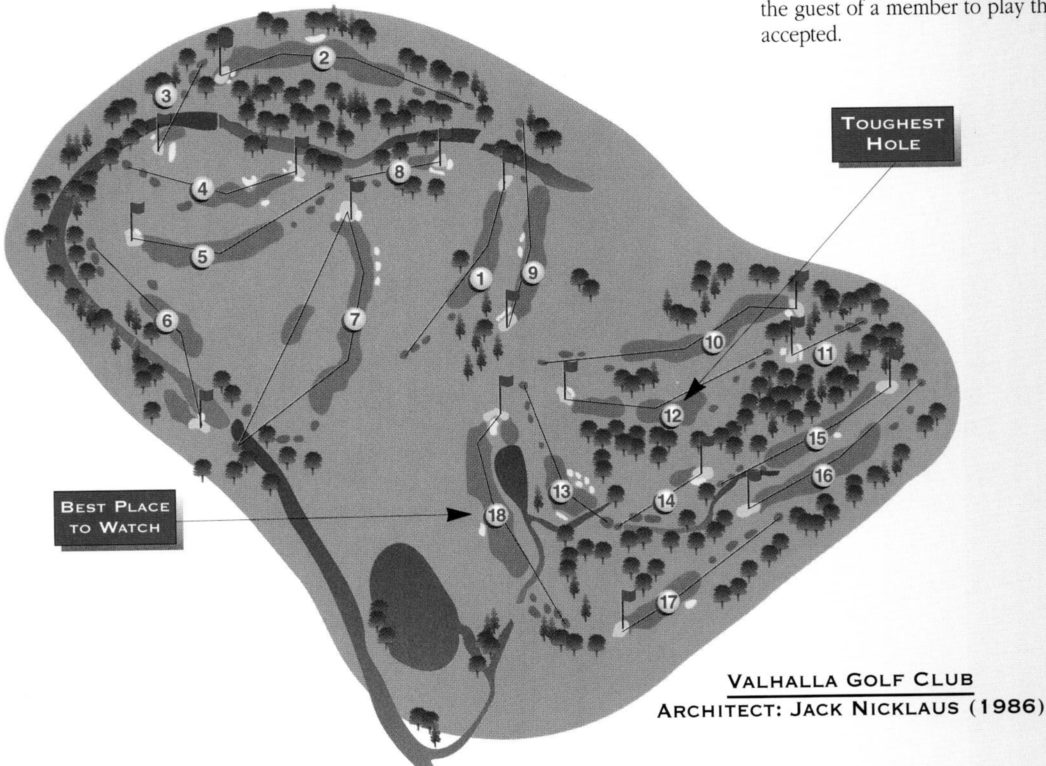

VALHALLA GOLF CLUB
ARCHITECT: JACK NICKLAUS (1986)

Nabisco Dinah Shore

MISSION HILLS COUNTRY CLUB

In 1991, Dinah Shore made Amy Alcott a promise: Win this tournament, and I'll join you in a victory plunge at the pond on the 18th hole.

Three splashes later, Alcott, her caddie and the patron saint of professional women's golf gave fans a memory that will forever define the late TV entertainer's monumental contribution to today's tour.

Shore, the only non-player ever elected to the LPGA Hall of Fame, signed on as celebrity host of the televised Colgate-sponsored event at a time when the U.S. Women's Open was the only LPGA event broadcast consistently, and that because ABC's golf contract required the token coverage. A whole generation of pros grew up knowing nothing else of the ladies' circuit but its one weekend at Mission Hills, where the prize money was four times the purse at any other tour event.

TOURNAMENT-AT-A-GLANCE

Course: Mission Hills Country Club—Old Course
Type: Private
Location: Mission Hills Country Club, 34600 Mission Hills Dr., Rancho Mirage, CA 92270
Telephone: (619) 328-2153
When: Late March
How To Get There: From I-10 take Date Palm Dr. Exit. Proceed south about 4 miles to Gerald Ford Dr. Take left and proceed 1.5 miles to the golf course.
Broadcast: ABC, ESPN (1996)
Purse: $900,000 (1996)
Tournament Record: 15-under-par 273, Amy Alcott, 1991

Shore, who died of cancer in 1994 at the age of 76, used her star power, her talk show and her avid enthusiasm for the game to elevate professional women's sports to a new level of prominence. Her plunge with Alcott, pledged when the 1988 champion was struggling to overcome the death of her mother, merely highlighted all her special gifts as an entertainer, a patron and a friend.

Mission Hills, considered one of the best-conditioned courses on the tour, is a traditional 18 with tree-lined fairways and entranceways that enable the players to roll their approaches onto the large, Bermuda-grass greens. But with its mix of water, sand and desert wind, the Desmond Muirhead–designed Old Course, since renamed the Dinah Shore Tournament Course, has become a formidable mainstay on the women's tour. As Hall of Famer Jo Anne Carner explains, "It has gotten much more difficult over the years, with the trees growing taller and hanging over the fairways. With the second shot, you can't go over the trees now because they are too high. And you can't go under them because most of the greens are elevated."

The course's five finishing holes raise a challenging gauntlet for contenders on the final day.

The 148-yard, par-3 14th requires a tee shot across water to a two-tiered green with a cluster of bunkers to its left, another to the rear and water to the right. The 15th, a 364-yard, par 4, is the most difficult driving hole, with fairway bunkers and out-of-bounds to the left and difficult rough to the right. Trees obstruct the angle from the right side of that fairway to a green that is tiered and bunkered right, left and front.

The 390-yard, par-4 16th is a dogleg right with a huge tree in the middle of the fairway. If the golfer does not again keep her tee shot to the left, the tree can interfere with an approach to a contoured green framed by two large bunkers. Next, the 171-yard, par-3 17th demands a tee shot that carries to an uphill green fronted by sand. Variable winds make club selection critical on this hole.

The 18th is the most difficult par-5 at Mission Hills and, even without the traditional winner's swim, would provide a great tournament finishing hole.

When the prevailing winds are strong, some of the tour's shorter hitters can't even reach this green in three, but the first two shots are always critical in setting up a high-percentage approach to the huge, subtly contoured green. From the tee, water to the left and bunkers to the right are in play. The second shot is usually a layup.

The final green has been the stage for some exciting finishes. Mickey Wright came out of retirement in 1973 and dropped a long putt here to card a 68 on the final round for her 82nd and last LPGA victory. Nancy Lopez completed a course-record 64 on the final round to win the tournament in 1981, and Sally Little equaled that standard a year later to win by three shots.

In 1992, Juli Inkster was looking for her third

Courtesy of Nabisco Dinah Shore

THE MOST CHALLENGING PAR-5 AT MISSION HILLS, THE 18TH IS A CLASSIC TOURNAMENT FINISHING HOLE.

Dinah Shore win when she teed it up on the 18th on the final day, but she left the door open when she missed a 10-foot birdie putt. Her playing partner, Dottie Mochrie, who had nailed a wedge to within 10 feet, promptly dropped her own birdie putt to draw even. The sudden-death playoff took place on the 11th, a 506-yard par-5. Inkster drove into a fairway bunker, caught another bunker with her approach shot and lost by a stroke with her bogey.

In 1995, Nanci Bowen withstood the test of gusting winds and shot a 3-under-par 285 as many contenders, including Nancy Lopez, saw their hopes come to a watery end when they tried to carry the 18th's famous pond.

Perhaps the most heart-stopping finish occurred a year earlier, when Laura Davies and Donna Andrews traded leads twice in the last two holes. Davies led by one stroke at the final tee but pushed her four-iron right and had to chip back into the fairway. Her stunning three-putt then gave Andrews the courage to knock down an 8-footer for a birdie and the victory. Of course, Andrews heeded the crowd's call for the traditional pond plunge.

"I'm sorry Dinah was not there to jump into the water with me," she told reporters later. "But I think she was with me in spirit."

"I WILL ALWAYS BE TIED TO THIS TOURNAMENT...BECAUSE I'VE WON... THREE TIMES AND BECAUSE I WAS FRIENDS WITH DINAH SHORE. THIS WAS THE FIRST WOMEN'S CHAMPIONSHIP TO BE TIED TO CORPORATE SPONSORS. FIRST COLGATE AND NOW NABISCO SHOWCASED WOMEN'S GOLF. DINAH ALWAYS MADE US FEEL SPECIAL."

—AMY ALCOTT,

NABISCO DINAH SHORE CHAMPION, 1983, 1988, AND 1991

NABISCO DINAH SHORE, CONTINUED

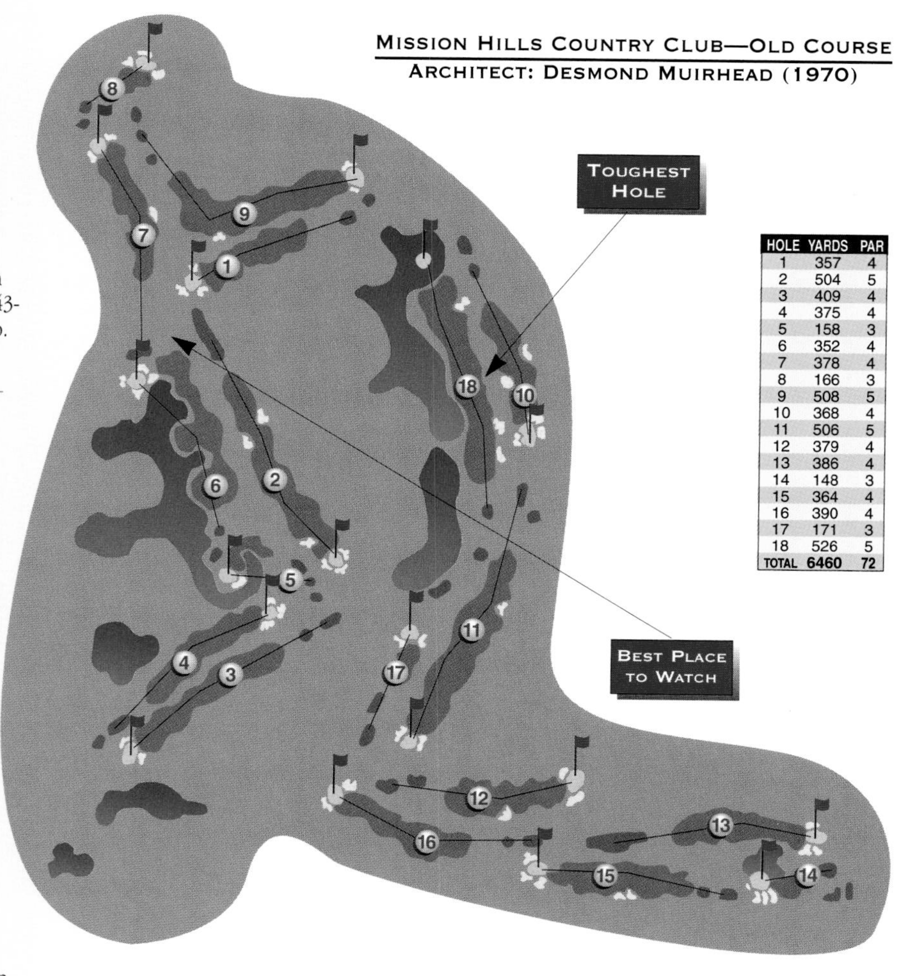

HOLE	YARDS	PAR
1	357	4
2	504	5
3	409	4
4	375	4
5	158	3
6	352	4
7	378	4
8	166	3
9	508	5
10	368	4
11	506	5
12	379	4
13	386	4
14	148	3
15	364	4
16	390	4
17	171	3
18	526	5
TOTAL	6460	72

LODGING

$$$ Westin Mission Hills Resort, 71-333 Dinah Shore Dr., Rancho Mirage, Calif. (619) 328-5955, (800) 999-8284. 2 minutes from Mission Hills Country Club.

$$ Orchard Tree Inn, 261 S. Belardo Rd., Palm Springs, Calif. (619) 325-2791, (800) 733-3435. 20 minutes from Mission Hills Country Club.

$ Courtyard by Marriott, 1300 Tahquitz Canyon Way, Palm Springs, Calif. (619) 322-6100, (800) 443-6000. 20 minutes from Mission Hills Country Club.

DINING

Le Valleuris, 385 W. Tahquitz Canyon Way, Palm Springs, Calif. (619) 325-5059.

LG's Steak House, 74-225 Hwy. 111, Palm Desert, Calif. (619) 779-9799.

Las Casuelas Terraza, 222 S. Palm Canyon Dr., Palm Springs, Calif. (619) 325-2794.

PUBLIC COURSES TO PLAY IN AREA

The Field Golf Club, 19300 Palm Dr., Desert Hot Springs, Calif. Public. (619) 251-5366. 18/6,876/72. 20 minutes from Mission Hills Country Club.

La Quinta, 49-499 Eisenhower Dr., LaQuinta, Calif. Resort. (619) 564-7610 (golf course), (800) 854-1271 (resort). Dunes: 18/6,861/72. Citrus: 18/7,135/72. 10 minutes from Mission Hills Country Club.

PGA West, 56-150 PGA Boulevard, La Quinta, Calif. Resort. (619) 564-7170. Jack Nicklaus Resort Course: 18/7,126/72. TPC Stadium Course: 18/7,261/72. 10 minutes from Mission Hills Country Club.

Westin Mission Hills Resort Golf Course, Westin Mission Hills Resort, 71-333 Dinah Shore Dr., Rancho Mirage, Calif. Resort. (619) 328-5955. 18/6,706/70. 2 minutes from Mission Hills Country Club.

TICKETS & ACCESSIBILITY

How to watch: Mon., LPGA practice rounds with celebrities. Tue., celebrity pro-am event. Wed., celebrity pro-am. Thur.-Sun., tournament. Weekday tickets start at $15, weekends at $20. Group, patron and sponsor packages available. The Dinah Shore, 2 Racquet Club Dr., Rancho Mirage, CA 92270. (619) 324-4546.

How to play: Private club. Play is limited to members and their guests. Reciprocal play is accepted from May 1 to Sept. 30. Starting times can be made in advance. The Arnold Palmer Course (18/6,720/72) and Dinah Shore Course (18/6,899/72) are also on site. (619) 328-2153.

●TOUGHEST HOLE

The course's signature hole is the 526-yard, par-5 18th, one of golf's first island greens with water bordering the entire left side and occasional bunkers to the right of the fairway. It was here Nancy Lopez hit her approach shot into the water on the final round of the 1995 championship to take herself out of contention. The incoming wind made the hole play especially long that day.

●BEST PLACE TO WATCH

From behind hole No. 6, a dangerous par-4 with water to the left and a green surrounded by traps. Here you can see tee shots on No. 7 and No. 2 and incoming shots on No. 1. The 18th is the place to be on the final day of the event. The tournament is often decided there, especially if the wind is blowing in.

●WHO THE COURSE FAVORS

Some holes, especially No. 18, favor big hitters. But shotmaking and positioning are important on this tight and unforgiving course due to wind, water hazards, well-placed trees and heavily bunkered greens.

McDonald's LPGA Championship

DuPont Country Club

Welcome to the land of the big hitters. If anyone doubted the tour's longest drivers have the advantage at DuPont Country Club, the 1995 final-round duel between Laura Davies and Kelly Robbins should have blasted their uncertainties to oblivion. It was the circuit's reigning distance champions, head to head, with the year's second major on the line.

Davies, who seemed to own the back nine in taking consecutive titles at DuPont during the previous two seasons, made the turn on the final day with a three-stroke lead over playing partner Robbins, and the cold, rainy weather looked to favor the defending champion.

But the 25-year-old Robbins, a former All-America at Tulsa who had never won a major tournament, was far from finished. With birdies on the 12th and 14th, she had closed to within a stroke by the time the pair teed up at the 465-yard, par-5 16th.

Robbins pushed her tee shot right, and it settled on a dirt lie slightly stymied by trees. Davies rocketed her ball left, but within 205 yards of the green.

Unnerved by the slow play and her inability to yet score on the back nine, Davies then hit a fat 4-iron to within 50 yards and, without taking a practice swing, lofted a wedge over the green to the rear fringe. Robbins, meanwhile, had recovered with a knock-down runup into a greenside bunker before dropping her sand wedge within 3 feet of a birdie. Davies rolled her fourth shot 5 feet past the hole in response, then missed the comeback. Robbins never looked back after her birdie rattled the leader board.

DuPont could do nothing but play big. With 7,800 members, it's considered the largest private club in the United States. First established in 1920 with a mere 600 members, its early amenities consisted of a two-story frame house, a baseball diamond and a grand-stand. Its first golf course, a nine-hole layout with clay tees and sand greens, was constructed in 1921. Today there are three golf courses, lawn bowling, shuffle-board, tennis—and a much larger clubhouse.

The tournament track is a traditional, mature course featuring small greens, few hazards, rolling hills and fairways lined by tall oaks and maples. It begins with a 384-yard, par-4 slight dogleg left. This seemingly straightforward hole can be difficult to par. Nancy Harvey found that out the hard way in the third round of the 1994 event when she pulled a 3-iron under a tree past the green. She needed four strokes to get back on the putting surface, then two-putted for an eight.

When the players find the rough at DuPont, they often find it difficult to escape. If they miss the small greens, a delicate touch with a wedge is needed to avoid losing strokes.

The long hitters begin to capitalize at the second hole, a 400-yard sharp dogleg right. In 1994, Liselotte Neumann hit a 3-wood 236 yards to the right corner of the turn, just beyond the bunkers protecting the landing area. She then hit a 5-iron to within 15 feet to set up a birdie.

The most difficult hole on the course is the 391-yard, par-4 seventh, which is fringed by trees to the right. The tee shot plays downhill, but the approach is up to a small green guarded by a large bunker to its right front. This hole usually plays into the wind, making it difficult to reach the green safely in two.

TOURNAMENT-AT-A-GLANCE

Course: DuPont Country Club
Type: Private
Location: Rockland and Blackgate Roads, Wilmington, DE 19803
Telephone: (302) 654-4435
When: Mid-May
How To Get There: Take I-95 to Route 202 Exit. Take Rte. 202 north to Rte 141. Turn left on Rte. 141; right on Rockland, 1/4 mile to golf course. Contact tournament office for shuttle bus and parking locations during the tournament.
Broadcast: CBS (1996)
Purse: $1.2 million (1995)
Tournament Record: 17-under-par 267, Betsy King, 1992 (par-71 Du Pont Country Club)

Courtesy of McDonald's LPGA Championship

KNOWN TO FAVOR LONG HITTERS, DUPONT COUNTRY CLUB BECAME HOST OF THE LPGA CHAMPIONSHIP IN 1994 AFTER MAZDA WITHDREW ITS SPONSORSHIP.

The only par-5 on the front side, the 498-yard dogleg ninth, is the easiest of the opening nine holes to par. Kris Monaghan birdied the hole in 1994 by hitting a driver to the middle of the fairway, short of a creek that cuts the hole beyond the turn. She then hit a 3-wood 50 yards short of the green, chipped 8 feet past the cup, and sank the putt.

Two holes on DuPont's front nine were ranked among the six most difficult par-3s on the tour in 1994. The 167-yard fifth usually plays into the wind to a green guarded by traps on both sides. The 192-yard eighth plays uphill, against the wind, to a green flanked by traps to its front.

When Davies and Robbins finished their classic duel on the 399-yard 18th in 1995, they were playing for the top check in an event with total prize money in excess of $1 million. It was a monstrous drive away from the first LPGA Championship, played in 1955 when no purse was at stake. Hall of Famer Louise Suggs captured the first winner's check two years later, when her 285 at Churchill Valley Country Club in Pittsburgh was worth all of $1,316.

"DUPONT COUNTRY CLUB IS A WONDERFUL GOLF COURSE FOR ME BECAUSE IT ALLOWS ME TO HIT MY DRIVER. I'VE WON TWO TOURNAMENTS ON THAT COURSE AND I THINK THAT'S THE REASON. IT REALLY FAVORS A LONG HITTER."

—LAURA DAVIES,

MCDONALD'S LPGA CHAMPIONSHIP WINNER, 1994

●TOUGHEST HOLE

The 391-yard, par-4 seventh, which flows downhill from the tee then sweeps up to a well-bunkered green, was the most difficult hole during the 1995 Championship.

●BEST PLACE TO WATCH

The hill behind the 18th green provides an excellent vantage point to catch the action, especially on the final day. This traditional golf course is an easy course to walk and follow the players.

●WHO THE COURSE FAVORS

The course favors the longer hitter who can hit controlled tee shots and then hit high approaches that will hold the greens. Many of the putting surfaces are crowned, adding to the requirement for accuracy with the shorter irons.

LODGING

$$$ Hotel Du Pont, 11th and Market Sts., Wilmington, Del. (302) 594-3100, (800) 441-9019. 20 minutes from the DuPont CC.
$$ Radisson Hotel Wilmington, 4727 Concord Pike, U.S. Route 202, Wilmington, Del. (302) 478-6000, (800) 333-3333. 10 minutes from the DuPont CC.
$ Courtyard by Marriott, Wilmington Downtown, 1102 West St. (302) 429-7600. 20 minutes from the DuPont CC.

DINING

The Brandywine Room in the Hotel Du Pont, 11th and Market Sts., Wilmington, Del. (302) 594-3156.
The Shipley Grill, 913 Shipley St., Wilmington, Del. (302) 652-7797.
Howard Johnsons, 1811 Concord Pike/Rte. 202, Wilmington, Del. (302) 655-1348.

PUBLIC COURSES TO PLAY IN AREA

DelCastle Golf Club, 801 McKennans Church Rd., Wilmington, Del. Public. (302) 995-1990. 18/6,628/72. 15 minutes from DuPont CC.
Rock Manor Golf Club, 1319 Caruthers Lane, Wilmington, Del. Semi-private. (302) 658-2412. 18/5,779/69. 15 minutes from DuPont CC.
The Three Little Bakers Country Club, 3542 Foxcroft Dr., Wilmington, Del. Semi-private. (302) 737-1877. 18/6,609/71. 5 minutes from the DuPont CC.

TICKETS & ACCESSIBILITY

How to watch: Mon., LPGA practice rounds. Tue., LPGA practice rounds, junior golf clinic. Wed., pro-am tournament. Thur.-Sun., tournament. Daily tickets available from $10. Group and sponsorship packages available. McDonald's LPGA Championship, 601 Rockland Rd., P.O. Box 394, Rockland, DE 19732, (302) 428-1681.
How to play: Private club. You must be the guest of a member to play the course. Nemours (18/6,171/71) and Montchanin (18/4,283/61) courses on site. Reciprocal play can be arranged through the professional. (302) 654-4435.

HOLE	YARDS	PAR	HOLE	YARDS	PAR
1	384	4	10	360	4
2	400	4	11	528	5
3	372	4	12	357	4
4	370	4	13	184	3
5	167	3	14	390	4
6	381	4	15	392	4
7	391	4	16	465	5
8	192	3	17	156	3
9	498	5	18	399	4
			TOTAL	6386	71

DUPONT COUNTRY CLUB
ARCHITECT: ALFRED T. HULL (1950)

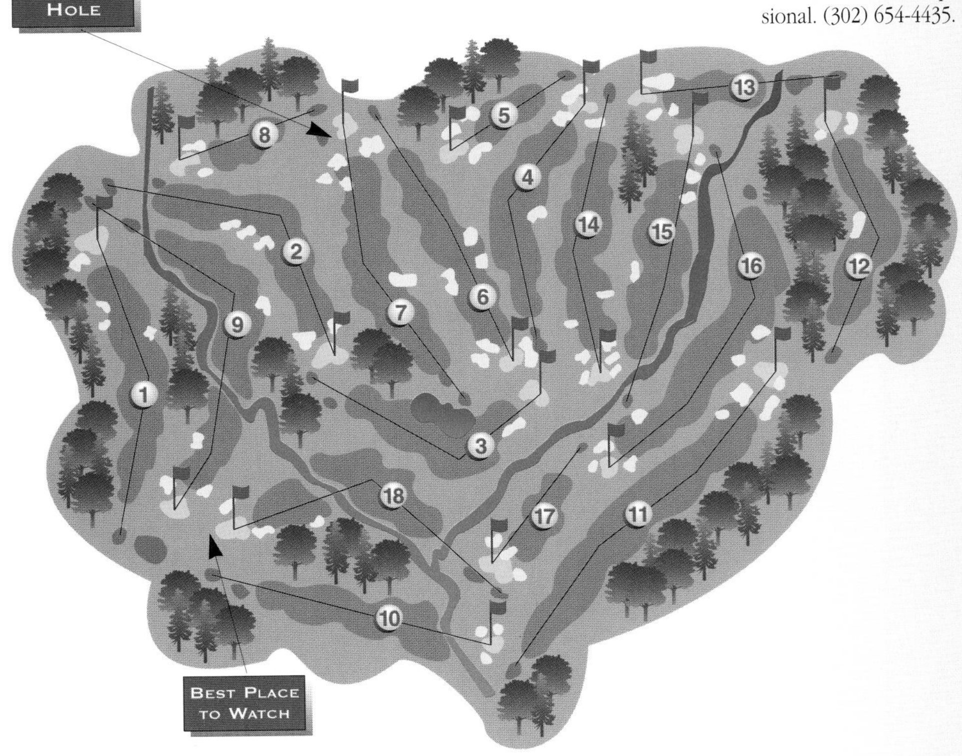

U.S. Women's Open

PINE NEEDLES COUNTRY CLUB

The U.S. Women's Open has never before been played at the picturesque, Donald Ross–designed Pine Needles Resort, but few venues resonate as deeply with the women's tour and America's contribution to the sport's long history.

The resort's owner, Peggy Kirk Bell, was a charter member of the tour in the days when professional women golfers were, at best, an oddity. In 1949, the year she beat Babe Didrickson Zaharias by two strokes to win the Titleholders Championship at Augusta, the newly formed Ladies Pro-fessional Golf Association announced a tournament calendar that boasted 11 events but only $50,000 in total prize money. Little wonder, then, that Kirk maintained her amateur status—playing with America's Curtis Cup team in 1950—until her retirement four years later.

TOURNAMENT-AT-A-GLANCE

Course: Pine Needles Country Club
Type: Resort
Location: Rte. 2, P.O. Box 88, Pinehurst, NC 28374
Telephone: (910) 692-7111
When: Late May, 1996
How To Get There: 15 minutes from Pinehurst. Take U.S. Hwy. 1 to Rte. 2. Take Rte. 2 west 1/4 mile to resort.
Broadcast: ESPN, NBC (1996)
Purse: $1,000,000 (1995)
Tournament Record: 9-under-par 279, Pat Bradley, 1981 (at La Grange Country Club, La Grange, Ill.)

The first Women's Open had been played in 1946 at the Spokane Country Club in Washington, two years after the founding of the pro circuit's progenitor, the Women's Professional Golf Association. That first year, Patty Berg won the qualifying medal with a 73-72–145, then defeated Betty Jameson 5 and 4 in the championship.

Fred Corcoran, a former PGA official who was brought in to manage and promote the women's tour, recalled later that the 1949 reorganization of the WPGA as the LPGA "touched off a national storm of indifference." But the tour was on its way, and with gate attractions like Zaharias and other great players like Berg, Betsy Rawls and Louise Suggs, professional golf would eventually become financially and competitively attractive for women. By 1995, the tour had amassed 38 official events and more than $24 million in prize money.

Such riches and fame were far from the mind of Peggy Kirk, however, when she played in her final Women's Open in 1953. That was the first year the event was hosted by the USGA, which had staged its inaugural Women's Amateur Championship at the Meadow Brook Club in Hempstead, N.Y. in November 1895. (The men's Open had debuted in October at the Newport Golf Club.) Thirty-seven women vied for the 1953 title and a share of the $7,500 purse, including Kirk, who finished tied for 13th with a 72-hole total of 322 on the 6,417-yard layout. She retired that season, married her hometown sweetheart, Warren "Bullet" Bell, and joined PGA professional Julius Boros and another partner in purchasing the Pine Needles Resort.

Pine Needles, constructed in 1928, is the product of a prolific partnership that paired wealthy Boston businessman James Walker Tufts and Donald Ross, the son of a stonemason from Dornoch, Scotland. The two met at the Oakley Country Club in Belmont, Mass., where Ross was the resident pro and greenskeeper. At the time, Tufts was collaborating with Central Park's architect, Frederick Law Olmsted, on the development of a New England–like village resort in North Carolina called Pinehurst, and he persuaded Ross to serve as the resort's winter professional. Ross revamped Pinehurst's original nine-hole course and added another nine to create Pinehurst No. 1 in 1901. Pinehurst No. 2 would become known as his masterpiece, but he later added three more 18s to the popular "golfdom." By the mid-1920s, more than 3,000 men were employed annually in the construction of Donald Ross courses, including the Seminole in Florida (1924), the General Oglethorpe Golf Course in Georgia (1927) and the Aronimink in Pennsylvania (1928).

Pinehurst was such a success that Tufts tried the formula again in nearby Southern Pines, but the stock market crash of 1929 forced the Tufts family to cede Pine Needles and its new Ross creation to his lenders. A series of owners followed before Peggy Kirk Bell and her partners stepped in.

"Bullet" Bell, a former professional basketball player who died in 1984, was largely responsible for the major renovations that steadily improved the 450-acre property over the years. His indomitable widow, the first woman golfer to fly the tour from coast to coast in her own plane, now runs the resort and heads its instructional team. In 1990, she won the USGA's Bobby Jones Award in recognition of her many contributions to the game.

Her course, which is carved out of gently rolling sandhills, wanders through the towering long-leaf pines indigenous to the region. There are only 42 bunkers on the course and just three water hazards, but the small, sloping, bent-grass greens are often elusive, and the ability to hit deft recovery shots around the hole will be important in the Open. The greens' subtle turns will put a premium on aggressive short putting that minimizes the breaks.

"I'VE PLAYED IN 26 OPENS AND IT'S STILL MY FAVORITE EVENT. IT'S THE REASON I'M STILL PLAYING PROFESSIONAL GOLF. IT'S DIFFERENT FROM ANY OTHER TOURNAMENT WE PLAY BECAUSE IT'S ALWAYS ON THE HARDEST COURSE. THE USGA MAKES THE COURSES SO DIFFICULT THEY'RE ALMOST UNFAIR."

—HOLLIS STACY,

U.S. WOMEN'S OPEN CHAMPION, 1977, 1978, AND 1984

The course, which will play at 6,184 yards, or about the distance from the middle tees during normal play, leads off with a 470-yard, par-5 uphill dogleg through the pines but is best known for its postcard-perfect par-3s, particularly the 127-yard third, which plays over a pond to a small green guarded by five shallow bunkers. The 405-yard seventh, a blind dogleg left, may be the most difficult on the front nine. Its tee shot plays over a rise to set up approaches to a deep green with mounds to the left and a bunker to the right.

A tough hole on the back nine is the 412-yard, par-4 17th, a beautiful tree-lined dogleg left that plays to a forward-sloping green flanked by huge bunkers. The finishing hole is a 398-yard par-4 that gradually slopes down to a scenic, deep, two-tiered green with a huge bunker to its right and a small bunker to its left front.

The Women's Open will be the most prestigious event ever held at Pine Needles, but thanks to its designer and its host—two pioneers of the American game—today's great players should be right at home.

LODGING

$$$ Pinehurst Resort and Club, Carolina Vista, P.O. Box 4000, Village of Pinehurst, N.C. (910) 295-6811, (800) ITS-GOLF. 15 minutes from Pine Needles.
$$ Pine Needles Resort, Ridge Road, P.O. Box 88, Southern Pines, N.C. (910) 692-7111, (800) 747-7272. On site.
$ Inn at Bryant House, 214 N. Poplar St., Aberdeen, N.C. (910) 944-3300, (800) 453-4019. 10 minutes from Pine Needles.

DINING

Carolina Room, at the Pinehurst Resort and Club, Carolina Vista, P.O. Box 4000, Village of Pinehurst, N.C. (910) 295-6811.
Jefferson Inn, 150 W. New Hampshire Ave., Southern Pines, N.C. (910) 692-8300.
John's Barbeque & Seafood Restaurant, U.S. Hwy.15-510 North, Southern Pines, N.C. (910) 692-9474.

PUBLIC GOLF COURSES TO PLAY IN THE AREA

Pinehurst Resort & Country Club, Carolina Vista, Village of Pinehurst, Pinehurst, N.C. Resort. (910) 295-6811. Course No.1: 18/5,780/70. No.2: 18/7,020/72. No.3: 18/5,593/70. No.4: 18/6,919/72. No.5: 18/6,827/72. No.6: 18/7,157/72. No.7: 18/7,114/72. 15 minutes from Pine Needles.
Talamore golf course, 1595 Midland Rd., Southern Pines, N.C. Public. (910) 692-5884, (800) 552-6292 (golf packages). 18/7,020/71. 5 minutes from Pine Needles.
Mid Pines Inn & Golf Club, 1010 Midland Rd., Southern Pines, N.C. Public. (910) 692-2114. 18/6,515/72. 5 minutes from Pine Needles.

TICKETS & ACCESSIBILITY

How to watch: Mon.-Wed., LPGA practice rounds. Thur.-Sun., tournament. Individual, group and sponsorship packages available. U.S. Women's Open, P.O. Box 5369, Pinehurst, NC 28374, (800) 295-2094.
How to play: Pine Needles is open to the public. Golf packages are available through the on-site resort, which is open year round. Prime season is mid-March through mid-June and mid-September through November. (910) 692-7111.

●TOUGHEST HOLE

The No.1 handicap hole at Pine Needles is the second, which normally plays 452 yards from the back tees and 369 yards from the forward tees. This demanding par-4 will play 410 yards in the tournament. The tee shot is down a corridor of pine trees to a crowned landing area where the ball can carom to the left or right. The second shot is deceptive, because the green appears to be on the same level as the landing area but is actually downhill. As a result, the golfer can easily select the wrong club and end up in one of three bunkers guarding the small green.

●BEST PLACE TO WATCH

Pine Needles is a fine walking course, with the area around the fifth green providing good sightlines for the No. 6 tee, No. 7 green and No. 8 tee. On the back nine the area around No. 10 offers a clear view of the No. 11 tee, No. 12, the No. 13 green and the No. 14 tee. The U.S. Women's Open has not been won by more than two strokes since 1990, so you'll want to stay around the 18th green on the final day.

●WHO THE COURSE FAVORS

Pine Needles is an open, rolling layout that provides leeway off the tee. The deceptively bunkered greens, with their fast, hard, crowned surfaces will reward the golfer with a good game from 50 yards in.

PINE NEEDLES COUNTRY CLUB
ARCHITECT: DONALD ROSS (1927)

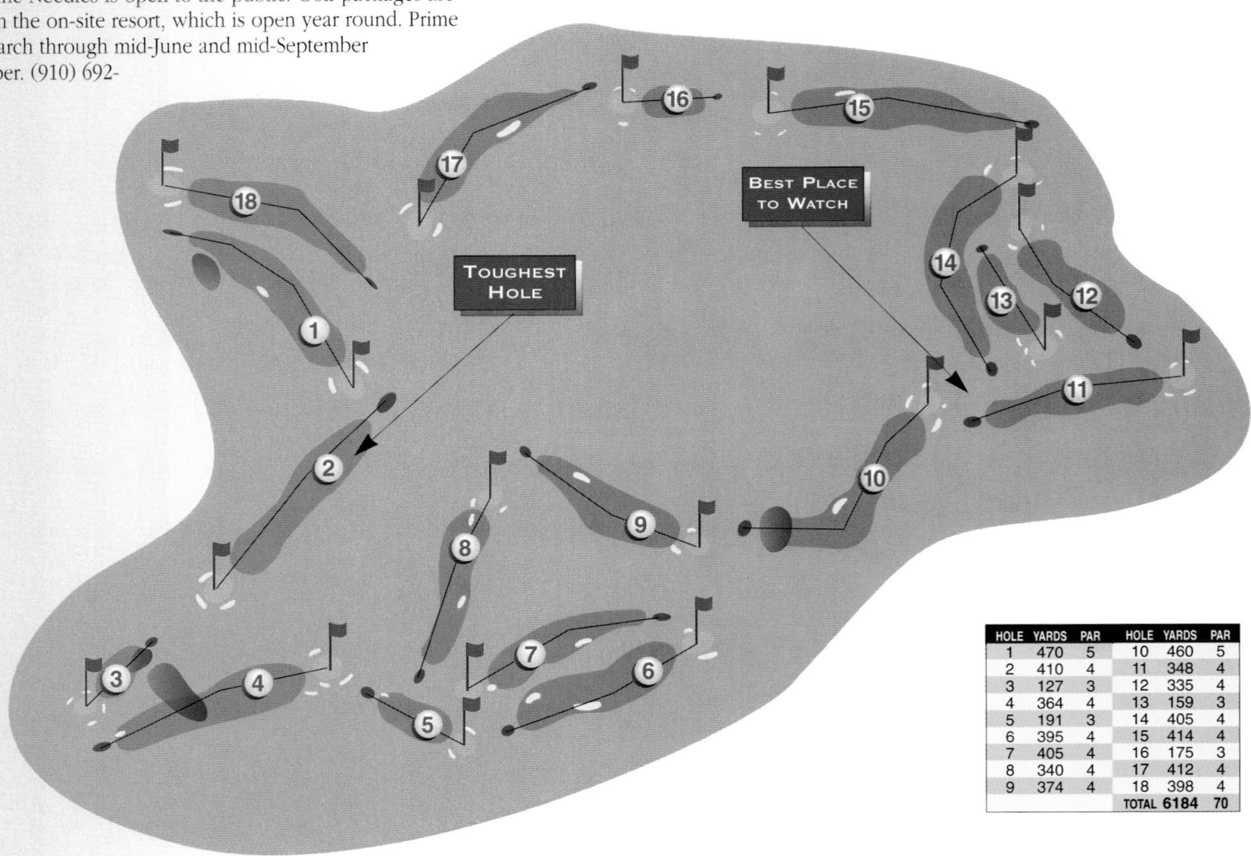

HOLE	YARDS	PAR	HOLE	YARDS	PAR
1	470	5	10	460	5
2	410	4	11	348	4
3	127	3	12	335	4
4	364	4	13	159	3
5	191	3	14	405	4
6	395	4	15	414	4
7	405	4	16	175	3
8	340	4	17	412	4
9	374	4	18	398	4
			TOTAL	6184	70

du Maurier Ltd. Classic

Edmonton Country Club

In the spring of 1896, just a few months before the now legendary Shinnecock Hills of Southampton, N.Y., hosted the second U.S. Open Men's Championship, an elite group of sports enthusiasts established the game in the Northwest Territories by organizing the Edmonton Country Club.

In 1996, the club celebrates its 100th anniversary by hosting the du Maurier Classic, one of the four majors on the women's circuit and the only stop in Canada for most of the world's top players.

"You want to win every tournament," Dawn Coe-Jones, a native of Campbell River, British Columbia, has said of the du Maurier. "But this is the only time I get to showcase my game in Canada, so a win here would be the ultimate."

Canadian soil is home to the continent's oldest continuously operating golf club—the Royal Montreal—but Edmonton Country Club, located along the banks of the North Saskatchewan River near downtown Edmonton, has an engaging history that transcends the sport.

Its first course, a treacherous five-holer that played across railroad tracks and a ferry landing, occupied the present site of the Alberta Legislature building. Its historic clubhouse, commandeered by local health officials as a quarantined hospital for smallpox patients, was burned to the ground in 1906 when the epidemic subsided.

By 1910, a Vancouver entrepreneur had convinced club members that a 426-acre site 8 miles up a rutted dirt road was sufficiently removed from the city's ravenous appetite for land. Its isolation almost killed the venture when the building boom collapsed a few years later, but the beginnings of today's championship course had already been cut into the dramatic terrain.

Cradled within a sharp bend in the North Saskatchewan River, the track traveled for nine holes across a relatively level plateau, then began a punishing hike up and down the steeply sloped hills. The par-3 18th, the course's little-altered signature hole, forced pleasure seekers to lug their bags down an 86-foot-deep ravine before climbing back up to a well-bunkered green. A free-swinging, 100-yard footbridge finally eliminated that challenge in 1920, a year after the future King Edward VIII braved the course's test.

Today's front nine are not much changed from the original 1911 layout, and a slightly less exhausting back nine complete a traditional routing to small greens with subtle breaks. Two or three strategically placed bunkers protect the putting surfaces, and a variety of elm, maple, poplar and other trees guard the fairways.

There are significant elevation changes on the back nine, including holes that run along cliffs with 200-foot drops to the river. Wind can be a factor on some of these holes, most notably the par-3 11th, which experiences swirling winds on the tee, and the par-4 16th and par-5 17th, which generally have tailwinds.

Spectators will find the flatter, more compact front nine an easier venue in which to follow the action, but the three finishing holes provide a scenic and challenging finale. The 16th is a long dogleg right with the river on the right and brush to the left. Approaches on this hole will likely be blind shots up to a plateaued green with two bunkers on its left. The par-5 17th is a long, double dogleg left with two bunkers at the left edge of the first dogleg and another to the right. The treelined fairway turns again 150 yards from a green surrounded by bunkers. A cathedral of oak, birch and pine trees provides a majestic backdrop for the ravine-crossed 18th.

Overall, the course will reward accuracy off the tee and solid approach shots that avoid the deep rough and trees along the fairways, and the bunkers and rough around the greens.

First played as La Canadienne in 1973, the du Maurier Classic took its current moniker in 1984, five years after the nomadic event was designated a major.

TOURNAMENT-AT-A-GLANCE

Course: Edmonton Country Club
Type: Private
Location: 6201 Country Club Rd., Edmonton, Alberta, Canada T6M 2J6
Telephone: (403) 487-1150
When: Late August, 1996
How To Get There: 25 minutes from downtown Edmonton. Drive west to 170th St. then proceed south to 62nd. Ave. Left on 62nd to Wilkin Rd. Right on Wilkin, then bear left to Country Club Rd. and the golf course.
Broadcast: CTV (1995)
Purse: $1,000,000 (1995)
Tournament Record: 16-under-par 276, Cathy Johnson,1990 (at the par-73 Westmount Golf & Country Club, Kitchner, Ontario); 16-under-par 272, Jody Rosenthal, 1987 (Islesmere GC, Laval, Quebec)

LODGING

$$$ Westin Hotel, 10135 100th St., Edmonton, Alberta. (403) 426-3636, (800) 228-3000. 20 minutes from Edmonton CC.

$$ The Inn on 7th St., 10001 107th St., Edmonton, Alberta. (403) 429-2861. 20 minutes from Edmonton CC.

$ Relax Inn, 18320 Stony Plain Rd., Edmonton, Alberta. (403) 483-6031, (800) 578-7878. 15 minutes from Edmonton CC.

DINING

La Boheme, 6427 112th Ave., Edmonton, Alberta. (403) 474-5693.

Pacific Fish Company, Argyll Plaza, 6258 99th St., Edmonton, Alberta. (403) 437-7472.

Chianti, 10501 82nd Ave. South, Edmonton, Alberta. (403) 439-9829.

PUBLIC COURSES TO PLAY IN THE AREA

Goose Hummock Golf Resort, Box 1221/off Hwy. 28, Gibbons, Alberta. Resort. (403) 921-2444. 18/6,560/71. 35 minutes from Edmonton CC.

Kananaskis Country Golf Course, Highway 40, Kananaskis Village, Alberta. Resort. (403) 591-7070, (800) 528-0444. Mt. Kidd: 18/7,050/72. Mt. Lorrette: 18/7,102/72. 2 1/2 hours from Edmonton CC.

Wolf Creek Golf Club, Highway 2, Ponoka, Alberta. Public. (403) 783-6050. No.1/No.2 Courses: 18/6,516/70. No.2/No.3 Course: 18/6,818/70. No.3/No.1: 18/6,730/70. 1 1/2 hours from Edmonton CC.

TICKETS & ACCESSIBILITY

How to watch: Mon., Ladies pro-am practice rounds. Tue., LPGA practice rounds, golf clinic. Wed., pro-am tournament. Thur.-Sun., tournament. Any day single tickets start at $15. Other group and sponsorship packages available. du Maurier Ltd. Classic, 855 rue Irene St., Montreal, Quebec, Canada H4C 2P2, (514) 932-1232

How to play: Private club. You must be the guest of a member in order to play. Limited reciprocal play can be arranged through the club professional. (403) 487-1150.

Hallowed Royal Montreal was the site of the thrilling inaugural event, in which Jocelyne Bourassa, who remains the tournament's sole Canadian champion, defeated Sandra Haynie and Judy Rankin in a playoff. The national dry spell shouldn't last much longer, however, with natives like Coe-Jones, Gail Graham and Lisa Walters all gunning for the top prize and over a dozen Canadians on the LPGA tour. Part of the growth can be credited to a program directed by Bourassa herself. The du Maurier Series, a five-event Canadian season launched in 1990, grooms women golfers for the older pro circuit.

The du Maurier's list of other champions includes Hall of Famers, dark horses and rising stars. Pat Bradley, who won in 1980, 1985 and 1986, is the tournament's only three-time winner. Another Hall member, Betsy King, succumbed to 22-year-old Brandie Burton on the first playoff hole in the 1993 event. "I think I just lost to the next great player on the LPGA tour," King said. "She's going to win more tournaments than anyone in the next 10 years."

No one would have predicted the following year's champion. Martha Nause, a 16-year tour veteran with only two other victories to her name, birdied the final three holes at the Ottawa Hunt Club to edge Michelle McGann by a single stroke.

●TOUGHEST HOLE

Edmonton's 402-yard, par-4 16th is nestled amid treacherous terrain. To the right of the green lies a ravine 100 feet deep; to the left the course slopes away sharply and is heavily treed. The narrow opening to the green demands an accurate second shot from competitors.

●BEST PLACE TO WATCH

A good walking course, Edmonton makes it easy to follow the golfers. On the final day, select a spot behind the No. 9 or No. 18 green. Since 1983 the du Maurier has never been won by more than three strokes, so the tournament will most likely be decided on the last few holes.

●WHO THE COURSE FAVORS

Though the landing areas are wide, errant shots will be penalized by thick rough and strategically placed bunkers around the greens. The golfer who is accurate off the tee, can drop shots onto the small putting surfaces and can read the greens' subtle breaks should do well at Edmonton. Variable winds on back-nine holes like No. 11 and No. 17 also have to be coped with.

EDMONTON COUNTRY CLUB
ARCHITECT: WILLIAM BRINKWORTH (1896)
REMODELED BY
STANLEY THOMPSON (1914, AND IN THE 1920S),
WILLIAM G. ROBINSON AND JOHN F. ROBINSON (1981)

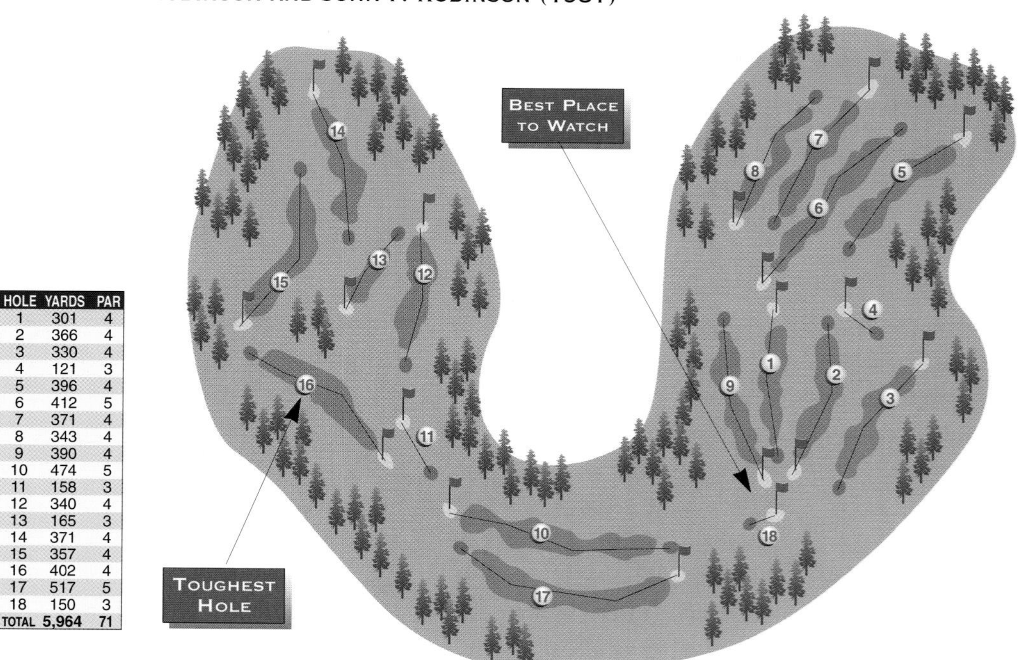

HOLE	YARDS	PAR
1	301	4
2	366	4
3	330	4
4	121	3
5	396	4
6	412	5
7	371	4
8	343	4
9	390	4
10	474	5
11	158	3
12	340	4
13	165	3
14	371	4
15	357	4
16	402	4
17	517	5
18	150	3
TOTAL	5,964	71

The Tradition

Golf Club at Desert Mountain

The pros refer to The Tradition as "The Masters" of the Seniors Tour, which is a pretty precocious label for a tournament born in 1989 on a brand-new desert course. Yet even if only by default, it would be a reasonable parallel to draw: the three other major championships on the Senior Tour have direct counterparts on the PGA circuit, and only The Tradition is moored at one course the way the Masters is rooted at Augusta National. Then there are the parallels between Masters founder Bobby Jones and a later-day legend, Jack Nicklaus, who has teamed with developer Lyle Anderson to design five courses at Desert Mountain in Scottsdale. This includes the gently rolling, impeccably manicured, immensely popular Cochise layout, home of The Tradition.

TOURNAMENT-AT-A-GLANCE

Course: Golf Club at Desert Mountain—Cochise Course
Type: Private
Location: 10333 Rockaway Hills, Scottsdale, AZ 85262
Phone: (602) 443-1597
When: April 4–7, 1996
How To Get There: Go north on Pima Rd. Turn right onto Cave Creek Rd. Turn left onto Desert Mountain Pkwy. Follow signs to the course.
Broadcast: ESPN (1996)
Purse: $1 million (1996)
Tournament Record: 19-under-par 269, Tom Shaw, 1993

But what makes The Tradition special is its annual gathering of so many greats of the game. Since the event's inception, Anderson has invited all champions over the age of 50 who have won at least one major on the PGA or Senior Tours, and the week's events are a celebration of their contributions to the game. Among the extra-curricular activities are a champions' dinner and a two-man scramble on Wednesday for all honorees not competing in The Tradition itself. Such luminaries as Tommy Bolt, Paul Runyan, Billy Casper, Gene Littler, Gary Player, Jack Nicklaus, Lee Trevino, Chi Chi Rodriguez and Arnold Palmer have regaled crowds at the Champions' Clinic with golfing tips and light-hearted heckling. Player and Rodriguez have regularly amused audiences with driving-range impersonations of their famed colleagues.

Desert Mountain comprises 8,000 acres of Sonoran desert and striking mountainsides, tall cactus and lowly sagebrush, open space and foothills, an award-winning clubhouse made of native materials, and four—soon to be five—Nicklaus courses that steer clear of the development's luxury homes.

The first course to open, Renegade, is located at the base of the Tonto Foothills. Cochise opened a year later, in 1988, and was soon followed by Geronimo, which sits on the community's highest stretch of property at 3,500 feet above sea level. "Lyle and I originally planned for the Geronimo to be the Seniors' course because it was the most difficult," Nicklaus has said. "Cochise was going to be the member course. It's softer and prettier. But Geronimo wasn't ready in time, and Cochise was. Funny, but I believe the whole thing worked out for the best."

The Cochise Course features smoother slopes than the edgy, dramatic Geronimo, and places a premium on approach shots and putting. Its rolling fairways wind through desert vegetation and large boulder outcroppings, and the nearby mountains to the north frame the rugged landscape. In the 1993 Tradition, a rattlesnake sunning itself behind the 13th tee almost met its end in Dave Stockton's 2-iron before a spectator persuaded Stockton that the snake wouldn't bother anyone.

One of the traditions at The Tradition has been close, dramatic finishes on Sunday. Four of the first five tournaments were decided on the 72nd hole. Not to be outdone, the 1994 and 1995 Traditions have spilled into playoffs.

In the first Tradition, in 1989, Player rimmed out a 12-foot birdie putt on the final hole that would have netted a playoff with Don Bies. In 1992, another 12-foot would-be birdie putt spun out at No. 18, costing Nicklaus a Tradition three-peat and putting Trevino in the winner's jacket. In 1993, Mike Hill dropped a 10-foot eagle putt on the final hole but little-known Tom Shaw triumphed by a stroke when he sank a 3-footer for birdie. In the process, Shaw shattered the tournament record by five strokes with a 19-under 269.

The 1994 and 1995 editions took the drama a few steps further. In 1994, Dale Douglass' chip shot for eagle—and the victory—at No. 18 hit the pin and bounced away, leaving him with a birdie and a playoff against Raymond Floyd. On the first playoff hole—the par-5 18th again—both players missed the green

THOUGH THE GREEN ON COCHISE'S PAR-5 15TH CAN BE REACHED IN TWO, WATER AND BUNKERS MAY MAKE DISCRETION THE BETTER PART OF VALOR.

trying to get there in two. Floyd got up and down for a birdie, but Douglass had to chip twice to stick on the green.

In 1995, Nicklaus and Isao Aoki staged a desert reenactment of their 1980 U.S. Open battle after they both birdied the 72nd hole of regulation. After both parred No. 18 and No. 17, they returned again to the 18th. This time, Nicklaus reached the green in two shots, using a 3-wood to conquer a wind gusting to 40 miles per hour. Aoki, acknowledged as one of the best golfers in the world from 100 yards in, wasn't quite up to the moment. He under-clubbed his second shot, then, from 96 yards, flew his third into a bunker beyond the green. Just as at Baltusrol in 1980, Nicklaus had outdueled him, and Aoki fell to his knees.

"I thought 12-under would win," Aoki said through an interpreter. "Since Baltusrol, I've played Jack three other times and lost them all. But I'll take him next time."

Nicklaus, who had been talking about retirement, was clearly proud of his newest triumph. "I just made myself play well. I'm very proud of that, because the way I was playing this spring, I didn't know if I would ever win again."

"I HEARD AN AWFUL LOT ABOUT IT FROM OTHER PLAYERS, OF WHAT A GREAT TOURNAMENT IT WAS, THE SURROUNDINGS, WHAT A GREAT VENUE IT WAS. AND AFTER BEING HERE AND HEARING ALL THE RAVES, IT MAY BE EVEN MORE THAN I EXPECTED."

—RAY FLOYD,

1994 WINNER OF THE TRADITION

●TOUGHEST HOLE

The 14th hole on the Cochise Course presents length with a concurrent demand for accuracy. The tee shot must avoid a complex of five bunkers looming on the left side of the fairway's landing zone. To the right, there is a hill rising from the fairway. That is fine when balls bounce back to the fairway, not so good when they come to rest on the hillsides. The approach shot for the pros will be a long iron or fairway wood to a green that slopes away from the golfers, angled slightly front-left to back-right. Being short of the green leaves a difficult pitch. In the 1994 Tradition, this hole exacted 113 bogeys and yielded only 19 birdies.

●BEST PLACE TO WATCH

The par-3 seventh shares the course's signature island double green with the par-5 fifteenth. A swirling wind on the raised tee often complicates club choice. In most cases, the choice will be a long iron and the target will be the center of the green, which slopes from back to front, regardless of the placement of the flagstick. In 1993, this hole was the toughest, averaging 3.331 strokes for the tournament. The par-5 finishing hole has been decisive in a lot of tight finishes, and always has the potential to uncoil a three-stroke swing on the leader board. Long hitters can go for the green in two with their long-irons or fairway woods even though the putting surface is hard to hold. The risk is usually worth it.

●WHO THE COURSE FAVORS

Players named Jack Nicklaus, obviously. Not only did he design the course, he's won The Tradition three of the first seven times it's been held.

LODGING

$$$ Scottsdale Princess, 7575 E. Princess Dr., Scottsdale, Ariz. (602) 585-4848. 20 minutes from Golf Club at Desert Mountain.
$$$ Hyatt Regency Scottsdale, 7500 E. Doubletree Ranch Rd., Scottsdale, Ariz. (602) 991-3388. 35 minutes from Golf Club at Desert Mountain.
$$ Best Western Thunderbird, 7515 E. Butherus Dr., Scottsdale, Ariz. (602) 951-4000. 30 minutes from Golf Club at Desert Mountain.

DINING

Cafe Saguaro, Scottsdale and Pinnacle Peak Rds., Scottsdale, Ariz. (602) 585-6630. 20 minutes from Golf Club at Desert Mountain.
Satisfied Frog & Chili Beer Cantina & Microbrewery, 6245 E. Cave Creek Rd., Cave Creek, Ariz. (602) 488-3317. 15 minutes from Golf Club at Desert Mountain.
Oaxaca, 8711 E. Pinnacle Peak Rd., Scottsdale, Ariz. (602) 998-2222. 20 minutes from Golf Club at Desert Mountain.

PUBLIC COURSES TO PLAY IN AREA

Troon North, 10320 E. Dynamite Blvd., Scottsdale, Ariz. Semi-private. (602) 585-5300. 18/7,008/72. 15 minutes from Golf Club at Desert Mountain.
TPC Scottsdale, 17020 N. Hayden Rd., Scottsdale, Ariz. Public. (602) 585-3800. Stadium: 18/6,992/71. Desert: 18/6,552/71. 25 minutes from Golf Club at Desert Mountain.

TICKETS & ACCESSIBILITY

How to watch: Mon.-Tue., practice rounds. Wed., Honoree Tradition, champions clinic. Thur.-Sun., championship rounds. Tickets: Mon.-Wed., daily grounds-only, $15; Thur.-Sun., daily grounds-only, $25; weekly, grounds-only, $60; Trophy Club, weekly badge, $125; VIP Club, weekly badge, $250. Tickets are limited to 25,000 overall per day. The Tradition, 6263 N. Scottsdale Rd., Suite 215, Scottsdale, AZ 85250. (602) 443-1597.
How to play: The Golf Club at Desert Mountain is a private course. You must play with a member. Cochise: 18/7,045/72. Geronimo: 18/7,437/72. Renegade: 18/7,515/72. Apache: 18/7,300/72.

GOLF CLUB AT DESERT MOUNTAIN—COCHISE COURSE
ARCHITECT: JACK NICKLAUS (1988)

HOLE	YARDS	PAR
1	390	4
2	191	3
3	457	4
4	546	5
5	408	4
6	358	4
7	194	3
8	569	5
9	411	4
10	424	4
11	175	3
12	511	5
13	136	3
14	434	4
15	534	5
16	413	4
17	182	3
18	531	5
TOTAL	6869	72

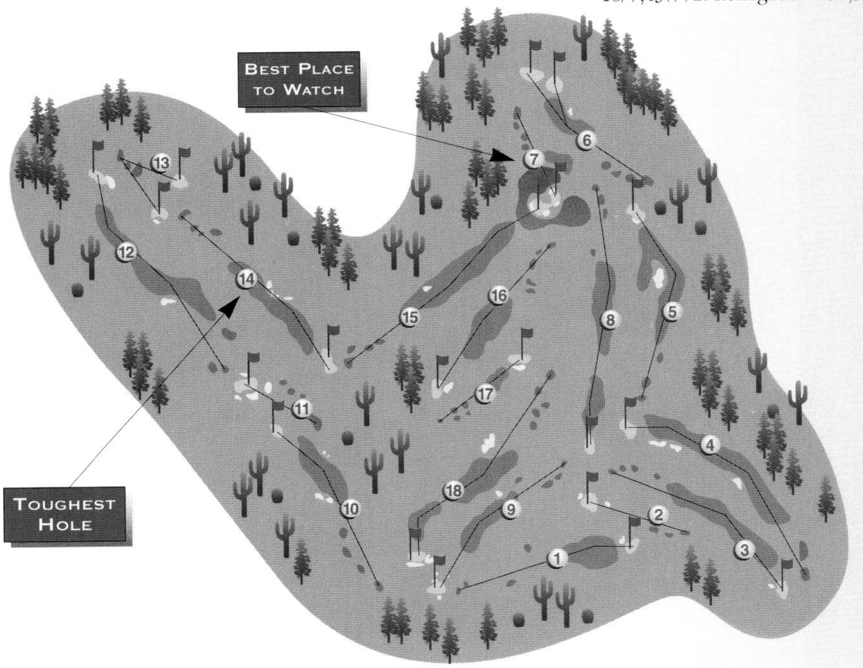

BEST PLACE TO WATCH

TOUGHEST HOLE

PGA Seniors' Championship

PGA National Resort & Spa

Senior statesman of the majors on the Senior PGA Tour, the PGA Seniors' Championship dates back to 1937 when the legendary Jock Hutchinson won the inaugural at Augusta (Ga.) National Golf Club. As the oldest of the Senior events, it boasts a roster of past champions including many of the greats of the game: Gene Sarazen, Paul Runyan, Sam Snead, Julius Boros, Don January and Arnold Palmer, to name just a few. More recent victors include Gary Player, Chi Chi Rodriguez, Jack Nicklaus and Lee Trevino.

Since 1982, the event (not held in 1983 and 1985, though two Seniors championships were held in 1979 and 1984) has been contested on the Champion course at PGA National. Originally a Tom and George Fazio design, the course was closed for major renovations by Jack Nicklaus in 1989 and reopened a year later.

The final seven holes on the back nine are now among the toughest closers in golf. Holes 15, 16 and 17 have been nicknamed "The Bear Trap" to signify the course's challenging conclusion and to honor the Golden Bear, architect Nicklaus. "Forget Amen Corner," said Trevino. "These last four holes, with the wind and water, are the real killers in golf."

Amazingly, the redesign was not meant to toughen the course, but to make the layout more playable and enjoyable at all skill levels. This was accomplished by creating five sets of tees. Also, the fairways and greens were changed from convex repelling areas to concave containing areas. Gallery mounds were constructed to accommodate spectator viewing and media coverage throughout the course.

TOURNAMENT-AT-A-GLANCE

Course: PGA National Resort & Spa—Champion Course
Type: Resort
Location: 100 Ave. of the Champions, Palm Beach Gardens, FL 33418
Phone: (407) 627-2000
When: April 18–21, 1996
How To Get There: From Palm Beach International Airport, take I-95, Florida Tpk. or U.S. 1 north 15 miles to PGA Blvd. Go west to resort entrance.
Broadcast: NBC, USA (1995)
Purse: $1 million (1995)
Tournament Record: 17-under-par 271, Jack Nicklaus, 1991

Still, following the redesign, there was grumbling among the pros. Gary Player's winning score in 1990 was 281, and the average score was 77.71. So Nicklaus was asked to ease the challenge bit. A few changes were made, and the architect responded by winning it himself in 1991 with a 271 as the average score dropped to 75.62, which is still high by tour standards.

The PGA Seniors' event is unique on the Senior circuit because it blends the cream of the touring crop with proficient club pros: The top 55 finishers from the previous year's PGA Senior Club Professional Championship. Yet, come Sunday, it's usually the Tour-tested players who are vying for the title.

The tournament has had its memorable moments, especially since moving north from Turnberry Isle after Miller Barber won in 1981. In 1987, Rodriguez led the Championship at the end of play Friday, but exploded to a 76 on Saturday to fall six strokes behind Dale Douglass. Making a bad day worse, Rodriguez had broken the shaft of his 9-iron during his round and was forced to have a replacement relayed to him from the PGA National's golf shop. "The club felt better than the ones in my bag, and they've won me about $500,000," Rodriguez joked at the time. "So I went to the golf shop and bought the rest of the set."

That did it. Rodriguez fired a 5-under 67 in the final round to beat Douglass by a stroke.

In 1992, Trevino held a two-stroke lead over Mike Hill on Sunday as the pair approached the tee of the par-3 17th. Trevino chose the wrong club, however, and watched his ball drop 45 feet short of the cup. Still

By Mike Klemme

THE FINAL HOLE OF "THE BEAR TRAP," NO. 17 IS THE COURSE'S SHORTEST PAR-3, BUT IT CALLS FOR A FULL CARRY OVER WATER AND OFTEN INTO THE WIND.

seeking a birdie, he blasted his putt 10 feet past the hole before Hill sunk his birdie. Facing a possible two-stroke swing that would knot the score, Trevino shook off the threat by calmly dropping his putt for par. He won when both players parred No. 18, though Trevino needed an 8-foot putt to do it.

When Trevino won again in '94, it was more of a surprise. Trailing by three strokes after 12 holes and by one after 14, Trevino leapfrogged into the lead when Raymond Floyd put two balls into the water on the 15th hole and suffered a quadruple bogey 7. Trevino then finished with par, par and bogey en route to victory.

Undaunted, Floyd came back to win in '95 with an 11-under 277.

"THE CHAMPIONS COURSE AT PGA NATIONAL CAN BE THE TOUGHEST COURSE WE PLAY ALL YEAR...THE GREENS ARE DIFFICULT TO HIT ON A CALM DAY, BUT YOU MIX THE WIND WITH THE WATER AND THE SAND AND IT'S AS TOUGH A COURSE AS WE PLAY. THERE'S JUST NO PLACE THAT YOU CAN RELAX."

—LEE TREVINO,

PGA SENIORS CHAMPION, 1992 AND 1994

LODGING

$$$ PGA National Resort, 400 Ave. of the Champions, Palm Beach Gardens, Fla. (407) 627-2000. Adjacent to course.
$$$ Palm Beach Gardens Marriott, 4000 RCA Blvd., Palm Beach Gardens, Fla. (407) 622-8888. 8 minutes from course.
$$ Radisson Hotel, 4350 PGA Blvd., Palm Beach Gardens, Fla. (407) 622-1000. 10 minutes from course.

DINING

Cafe Chardonnay, 4533 PGA Blvd., Palm Beach Gardens, Fla. (407) 627-2662.
River House, 2373 PGA Blvd., Palm Beach Gardens, Fla. (407) 694-1188.
Prezzo, 2640 PGA Blvd., Palm Beach Gardens, Fla. (407) 775-7444.

PUBLIC COURSES TO PLAY IN AREA

Atlantis CC, 190 Atlantis Blvd., Atlantis, Fla. Semi-private. (407) 968-1300. 18/6,477/72. 25 minutes from the tournament.
PGA National Estate Course, 8581 Marla Moore Lane, Lake Park, Fla. Resort. (407) 627-1614. 18/6,784/72. 14 minutes from tournament.

TICKETS & ACCESSIBILITY

How to watch: Mon.-Wed., practice rounds. Thur.-Sun., championship rounds. Weekly Championship badges are $50, which includes parking and program. Admission to Mon. practice round is free. Daily tickets are $15 Tue.-Wed., for practice rounds. $20 Thur.-Fri., for championship rounds. $25 Sat.-Sun. Juniors (under-17), with ticketed adult, admitted free. PGA Seniors' Championship, 100 Ave. of the Champions, Palm Beach Gardens, FL 33418. (407) 622-4653.
How to play: Champion is part of a four-course complex that also includes General: 18/6,478/72. Haig: 18/6,800/72. Squire: 18/6,768/72. All are open to the public. Three of the courses—Champion, Haig, Squire—were designed by the Fazios, Tom and George. The General was crafted by Arnold Palmer. Preferred times and fees for resort guests. (407) 627-1800.

●TOUGHEST HOLE

At the eleventh, the course begins pouring on the intimidation. This tight-driving, water-daunting par-4 is annually the toughest in this event and one of the three toughest on the entire Senior Tour. Pros will try to hit a driver down the left side of the fairway, avoiding the pond on the right, a body of water that follows the remainder of the hole and goosenecks the land in front of the green. A good drive leaves a mid-iron approach, a not-so-good drive a long iron, over the water to a relatively small green angled from left front to right back. A ridge in the middle of the green leaves no room for error when the flagstick is to the front right, close to the pond.

HOLE	YARDS	PAR	HOLE	YARDS	PAR
1	346	4	10	549	5
2	419	4	11	412	4
3	539	5	12	397	4
4	355	4	13	370	4
5	171	3	14	422	4
6	478	5	15	164	3
7	185	3	16	412	4
8	422	4	17	152	3
9	381	4	18	528	5
			TOTAL	6702	72

●BEST PLACE TO WATCH:

For the gallery, the 17th is an intriguing par-3 and there are plenty of good perches around the green. At 152 yards, it's a couple clubs shorter than the 15th, a similar par-3 over water, but here the wind is more likely to be in the player's faces. Because of its elevated tees, even their knockdown shots can be affected by the gusts, so club choice can mean the difference between a watery grave, a birdie putt or a tough up-and-down from a deep rear bunker.

●WHO THE COURSE FAVORS

Players who have the game, the inner mettle and veteran credentials. Water, sneaky fairway traps and yawning greenside bunkers, target driving areas, humpback swales, long par-4s and, often enough, wind all come into play. Playing well on the tougher back nine is essential. "If the wind blows, and it doesn't have to blow extremely hard, this course becomes very, very difficult," says Lee Trevino.

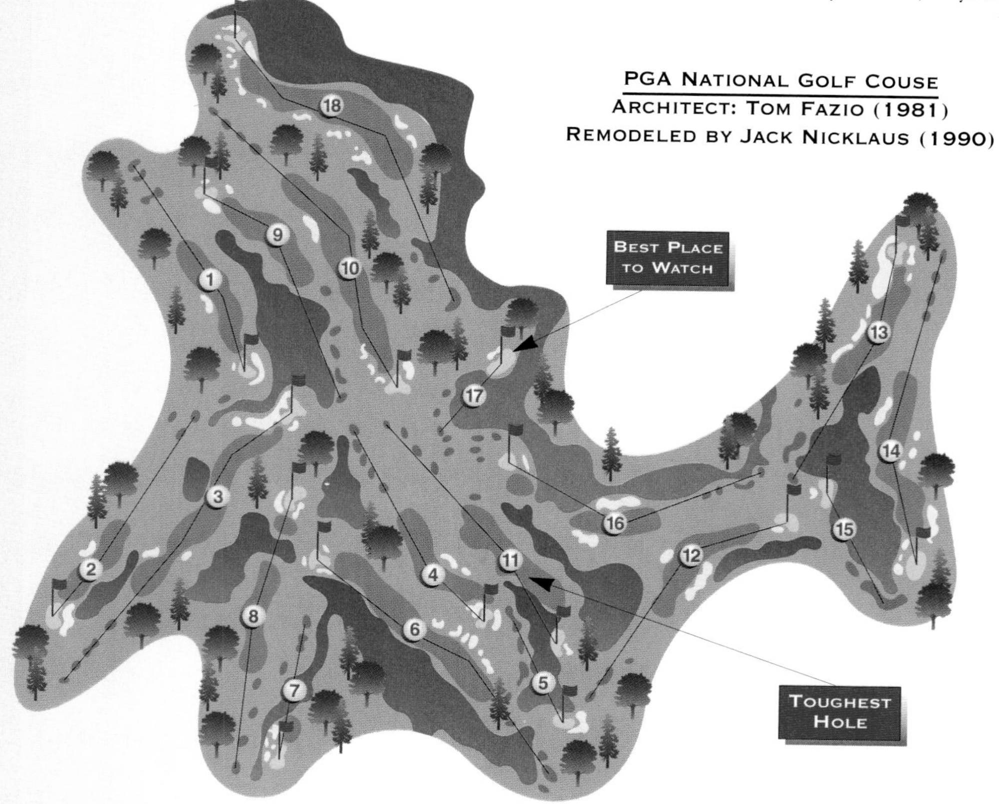

U.S. Senior Open

Canterbury Golf Club

Canterbury Golf Club is no stranger to major golf competition, having hosted two U.S. Opens, two U.S. Amateurs and four Senior Players Championships over its long history. The 1996 U.S. Senior Open coincides with the 75th anniversary of the club, which sits due east of downtown Cleveland.

The architect for Canterbury, Herbert Strong, is the subject of several interesting tales. Strong came to the United States from England at the turn of the century and was a noted club and playing professional. In fact, Strong was right in the thick of things at the historic 1913 U.S. Open that resulted in a playoff between British veterans Harry Vardon and Ted Ray and young American caddie Francis Ouimet, who put golf on the nation's front pages with his surprising victory. Strong was in second place after two rounds but couldn't sustain the momentum. As a course designer, Strong is credited with several well-regarded layouts, including Engineers on Long Island and Metropolis in Westchester County, N.Y.

At Canterbury, Strong crafted an old-time, traditional course, which means the track falls in line with the rolling, but not hilly, topography. Most of the holes have multiple contours, and fairway shots are often off uneven lies. There are numerous doglegs at Canterbury, and the greens are on the small side.

The par-3s are particularly interesting. The seventh stretches 195 yards, the 17th a daunting 215. The 11th seems benign at 143 yards, but the carry from tee to green is across a yawning valley.

History runs deep enough to feel at Canterbury. In a footnote to the 1940 U.S. Open, six players were disqualified for starting the final round here ahead of schedule when, with a storm brewing, they played away. Among the DQs: Ed "Porky" Oliver, who would have had a 287 total and thus joined the playoff between Lawson Little and Gene Sarazen. (Little prevailed in the playoff with a 2-under 70 to Sarazen's 73.)

In 1946, the first official U.S. Open following suspension of the championship during World War II, a three-way playoff developed at 4-under 284 between Lloyd Mangrum, Byron Nelson and Vic Ghezzi. Many feel Nelson should have won outright, but he incurred a penalty stroke in the third round when his caddie kicked his ball. The next day, he fell into a tie by bogeying both the 17th and 18th holes. All three players carded 72s in the first playoff round, and they returned for yet another 18 holes. With Nelson and Ghezzi registering 73s, Mangrum birdied three of the final six holes—interrupted by thunder and finished in the rain—to post a 72 and claim the $1,500 first prize.

In the 1979 U.S. Amateur at Canterbury, Mark O'Meara played 4-under for his first 29 holes and defeated John Cook by a whopping 8 and 7. The medalist in that event was current broadcaster Bobby Clampett, whose qualifying rounds included a Canterbury course record 66 that still stands (it was also 5-under at the time on a course reduced to par 71).

More recently, Canterbury has hosted the first four playings of another of the majors on the Senior Tour—the Senior Players Championship, which was established in 1983. Miller Barber won the inaugural event before Arnold Palmer ran off two in a row. Chi Chi Rodriguez took the 1986 title when rain shortened the

TOURNAMENT-AT-A-GLANCE

Course: Canterbury Golf Club
Type: Private
Location: 22000 S. Woodland Rd., Beachwood, OH 44122
Phone: (216) 561-1996
When: July 4–7, 1996
How To Get There: From downtown Cleveland, take I-77 south to I-480. Go east to I-271. Go north, exit at Chagrin Blvd. Go west to parking lot.
Broadcast: ESPN, NBC (1996)
Purse: $1 million (1996)
Tournament Record: 14-under-par 270, Gary Player, 1987 (at Brooklawn CC, Fairfield, Conn.)

Courtesy of U.S. Senior Open

CANTERBURY'S TRADEMARK DWARF GREENS CAN NEGATE THE ADVANTAGE OF BIG HITTERS.

event to three rounds.

The U.S. Senior Open dates only to 1980, so the lore that enriches each playing here often has more to do with the competitors' younger days or past PGA majors played at the same site. In 1993, Nicklaus held off Tom Weiskopf at Cherry Hills Country Club in Denver, where as a 20-year-old amateur he had finished as runner-up to Arnold Palmer's mythic final-round comeback. In 1995, Weiskopf, a perennial runner-up in the PGA majors, finally finished on top when the Senior Open visited the Congressional Country Club outside Washington, site of Ken Venturi's 1964 sun-baked Open victory.

The 1996 U.S. Senior Open will have a little dramatic twist of its own. Defending champion Weiskopf has close ties with Canterbury: His family used to belong here, and his brother Dan has won four of its club championships.

"CANTERBURY GOLF CLUB IS A MARVELOUS GOLF COURSE. IT HAS THREE OF THE BEST FINISHING HOLES IN GOLF."

—TOM WEISKOPF,

1995 SENIOR OPEN CHAMPION

●TOUGHEST HOLE

The 18th at Canterbury is a long, uphill par-4. One of the course's few straightaways, it presents woods on the left, a fairway bunker and out-of-bounds guarding the right. The tee shot is launched into a hillside elevation. The second shot is uphill to a green where the player can see the flag but hardly see the surface of the green. The approach, from 160 to 200 yards, targets a round green protected by large bunkers left and rear, and small bunkers on the right.

●BEST PLACE TO WATCH

Take your pick between the par-3 third hole, a tee shot over water, or the par-5 13th, which many of the pros will go for—and reach—in two shots.

●WHO THE COURSE FAVORS

Patience is a virtue at Canterbury. Many of the looks are deceiving. Depth perception off the tee and on the approach can be particularly challenging. The best advice is to hit one more club than first instinct would dictate.

HOLE	YARDS	PAR	HOLE	YARDS	PAR
1	430	4	10	344	4
2	365	4	11	143	3
3	167	3	12	373	4
4	436	4	13	485	5
5	412	4	14	381	4
6	522	5	15	365	4
7	195	3	16	608	5
8	358	4	17	215	3
9	543	5	18	430	4
			TOTAL	6772	72

LODGING

$$$ Omni International, 2065 E. 96th St., Cleveland. (216) 791-1900. 25 minutes from Canterbury GC.
$$$ Embassy Suites, 7665 Park East Dr., Beachwood, Ohio. (216) 765-8066. 10 minutes from Canterbury GC.
$$ Holiday Inn Beachwood, 3750 Orange Pl., Beachwood, Ohio. (216) 831-3300. 10 minutes from Canterbury GC.

DINING

Ruby Tuesday's, 24325 Chagrin Blvd., Beachwood, Ohio. (216) 464-2700.
Olive Garden, 2637 Orange Pl., Beachwood, Ohio. (216) 765-1919.
TGI Friday's, Golden Gate Plaza, Mayfield Rd., Mayfield, Ohio. (216) 461-8443.

PUBLIC COURSES TO PLAY IN AREA

Highland Park, 3550 Green Rd., Highland Hills, Ohio. Public. (216) 348-7273. Two courses: Blue, 18/6,562/71. Red, 18/6,090/71. 5 minutes from Canterbury GC.
Fowler's Mill, 13095 Rockhaven Rd., Chesterland, Ohio. Public. (216) 286-9545. Two courses: Blue-White, 18/7,002/72. Red, 9/2,989/35. 20 minutes from Canterbury GC.

TICKETS & ACCESSIBILITY

How to watch: Mon.-Wed., practice rounds. Thur.-Sun., championship rounds. Daily ticket Mon.-Wed., $18; Daily Thur.-Sun., $30; season, with program, $100. All tickets include parking. U.S. Senior Open, Canterbury Golf Club, 22000 S. Woodland Rd., Beachwood, OH 44122. (216) 561-2133.
How to play: Canterbury Golf Club is a private course. Members of other private clubs may be invited but must play with a Canterbury member.

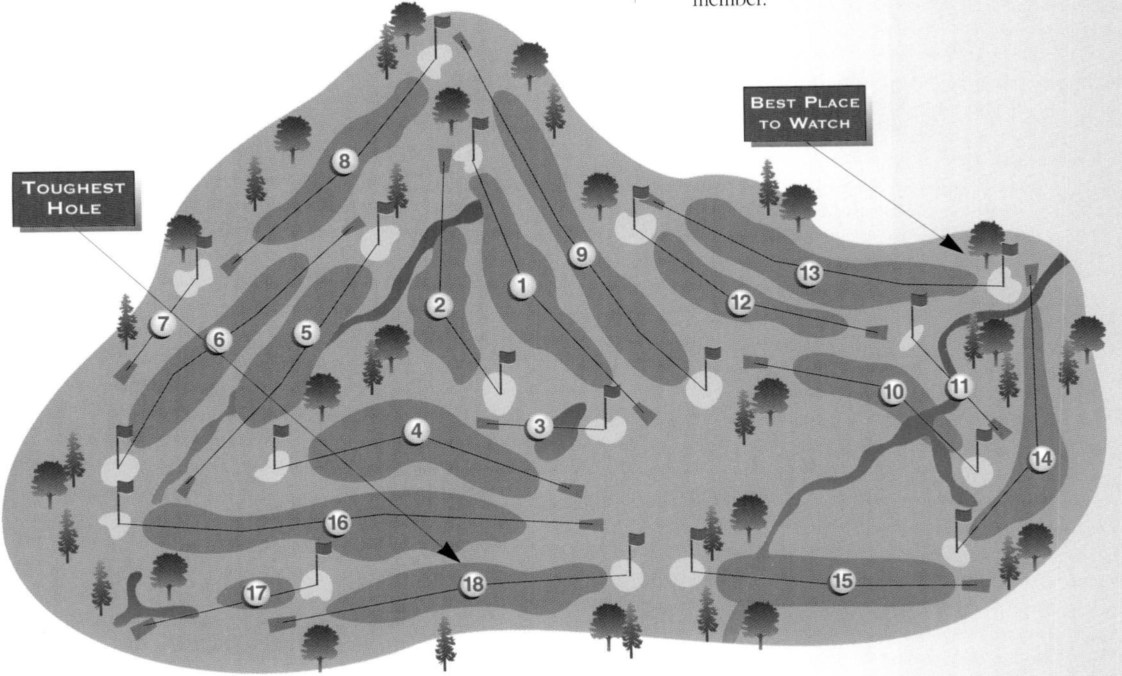

CANTERBURY GOLF CLUB
ARCHITECT: HERBERT STRONG (1921)

Ford Senior Players Championship

TPC OF MICHIGAN

If anyone would seem to have an advantage at this major, it would be Jack Nicklaus, the designer of the host course. But each year since the event moved to Nicklaus' stadium-style course at the TPC of Michigan in 1991, another player has taken the title and stolen the show.

Though he's now one of the leading players on the Senior PGA Tour, Jim Albus was a lowly club professional in 1991 when he stunned the veteran Tour pros by winning the Senior Players, a feat that helped launch his full-time switch from running a golf shop to playing the Tour. Albus opened with a 66 that weekend, but had to survive a second-round 74 before coming from three shots off the lead on the final day to capture his three-stroke victory.

In 1994, Albus matched the course record with a 277 but finished second and six strokes back of Dave Stockton, whose runaway victory helped establish him as the Senior Tour's Player of the Year for the second consecutive season. Stockton, who played all four rounds without a bogey, was in such command during the final round of play that he kept asking the ABC television crew for updates on how his son, Dave Jr., was faring in the PGA Tour's Canon Greater Hartford Open.

Nicklaus, winner of this event in 1990 when it was played at the nearby Dearborn Country Club, nearly triumphed in 1995 when he posted a 67 to catch J.C. Snead on the final day. But Snead, who had led by 4 strokes with only six holes to play, dropped a curling 4-foot birdie putt on the first playoff hole to deny the course architect again.

The Ford Senior Players Championship was first played in 1983 at Canterbury Golf Club in suburban Cleveland, later spent three years near the PGA Tour's headquarters in Ponte Vedra, Fla., and finally settled in Dearborn, Mich., in 1990.

Nicklaus's TPC course provides lots of advantageous spectator mounding overlooking the holes, especially on the back nine. Ponds or wetlands come into play on more than half the holes, and many approaches have to weave their way onto narrow greens amply guarded by bunkers, water and strategically placed cottonwood trees.

In 1993, Jim Colbert overcame problems on the tough finishing hole to win by a stroke over Raymond Floyd. In Saturday's third round, Colbert pulled his drive into wetlands and made double-bogey 6 on the hole. In Sunday's final round, he hit a fine drive but instead of playing relatively safe with a 3-iron, he elected to go with a 5-wood and wound up in a bunker. He blasted out but needed two putts for a bogey, finishing at 69–278. Though Floyd had birdied the 18th with a 1-foot tap-in, he came up a stroke shy.

TOURNAMENT-AT-A-GLANCE

Course: Tournament Players Club of Michigan
Type: Private
Location: 1 Nicklaus Dr., Dearborn, MI 48120
Phone: (313) 441-0300
When: July 11–14, 1996
How To Get There: Take state Rte. 39 (Southfield Fwy.) to Exit 5. Go east on Rotunda Dr. Club is 3/4 mile on left.
Broadcast: ESPN, ABC (1996)
Purse: $1.5 million (1996)
Tournament Record: 27-under-par 261, Jack Nicklaus, 1990 (at Dearborn CC, Dearborn, Mich.)

"MY TWO WINS AT THE TPC OF MICHIGAN WERE COMPLETE REVERSES. I WON THE FIRST IN 1992 WHEN J.C. SNEAD GAVE ME THE TOURNAMENT ON THE LAST HOLE AND I WON THE SECOND IN '94 WHEN I KILLED THE FIELD, WON BY SIX SHOTS."

—DAVE STOCKTON,

FORD SENIOR PLAYERS CHAMPION, 1992 AND 1994

●TOUGHEST HOLE

The 14th hole annually checks in as one of the toughest on Tour. In 1994, it ranked as the fourth-toughest of all Senior PGA Tour holes, averaging 4.487 strokes and yielding only 19 birdies while exacting 88 bogeys from the pros. A slight dogleg left, its entire left side is lined by water that must be respected both on the tee shot and the approach. The prevailing wind on this hole will be into the players' faces. "The thing I think about most on the tee is where to position my drive," says Chi Chi Rodriguez. "You must take a gamble and hit the driver so that you can have a 7- or 8-iron into the green. It doesn't do you any good to lay up, because you'll be hitting a long iron into a green that is narrow and normally very hard. You don't want to be left with a downhill lie and a long iron over the swamp."

●BEST PLACE TO WATCH

The par-3 12th offers both a good view and an interesting challenge. It's "a tough little hole any way you want to play it," says Dale Douglass. "Most players will hit a 5- or 6-iron into this green, but you must guard against everything. If you're short, it's in the pond and a certain double-bogey. The green is difficult to putt, so even if you hit it with your tee shot, you might walk away with a bogey. It will test your patience."

●WHO THE COURSE FAVORS

Like many courses designed by Jack Nicklaus, TPC of Michigan plays somewhat left to right. Greens are narrow but deep. Pinpoint iron play is at a premium.

HOLE	YARDS	PAR	HOLE	YARDS	PAR
1	408	4	10	393	4
2	411	4	11	410	4
3	547	5	12	166	3
4	210	3	13	506	5
5	394	4	14	429	4
6	340	4	15	192	3
7	542	5	16	376	4
8	182	3	17	521	5
9	432	4	18	417	4
			TOTAL	6876	72

TPC OF MICHIGAN
ARCHITECT: JACK NICKLAUS (1990)

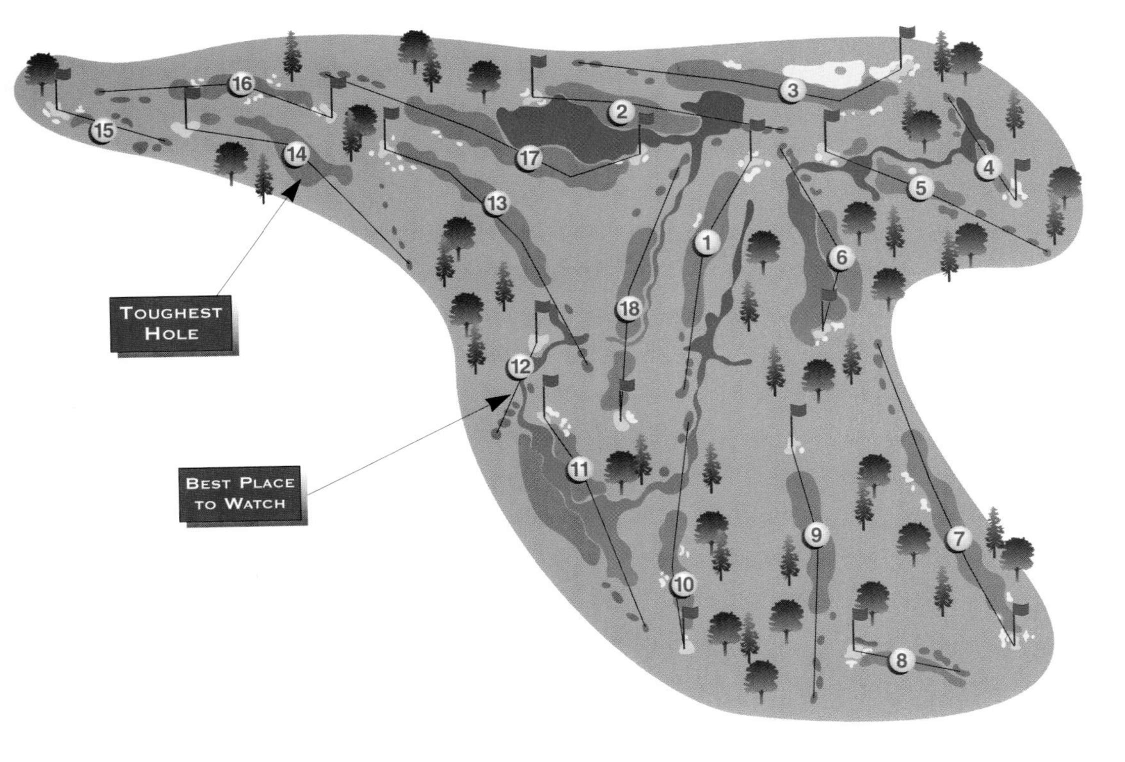

LODGING

$$$ Hyatt Dearborn, Fairlane Town Ctr., Dearborn, Mich. (313) 593-1234. 5 minutes from TPC of Michigan.

$$ Holiday Inn Fairlane, 5801 Southfield Dr., Detroit. (313) 336-3340. 10 minutes from TPC of Michigan.

$ Falcon Inn, 25125 Michigan Ave., Dearborn, Mich. (313) 278-6540. 12 minutes from TPC of Michigan.

DINING

Dearborn Inn, 20301 Oakwood Blvd., Dearborn, Mich. (313) 271-2700.

TGI Friday's, 720 Town Center Dr., Dearborn, Mich. (313) 271-2610.

Chili's, 5707 Southfield Dr., Dearborn, Mich. (313) 271-2339.

PUBLIC COURSES TO PLAY IN AREA

Taylor Meadows, 25360 Ecorse Rd., Taylor, Mich. Public. (313) 295-0506. 18/6,057/71. 15 minutes from TPC of Michigan.

Greystone, 67500 Mound Rd., Romeo, Mich. Public. (810) 752-7030. 18/6,860/72. 60 minutes from TPC of Michigan.

TICKETS & ACCESSIBILITY

How to watch: Mon., practice round. Tue., practice round, Merrill Lynch shoot-out, Coca-Cola golf clinic. Wed., pro-am. Thur.-Sun., championship rounds. Daily grounds, Mon.-Tue., $15 advance/$20 at gate; Wed., $20 advance/$25 at gate; Thur.-Fri., $25 advance/$30 at gate; Sat.-Sun., $30 advance/$35 at gate. Season grounds, $70 advance/$80 at gate. Season clubhouse, $250 advance/$300 at gate. All tickets include parking. Children under 16 admitted free with season badgeholder. Individual, group and sponsor tickets available. A note of interest: All tickets and badges purchased by a predetermined advance date qualify the buyer for a chance to win a spot in the pro-am. Ford Senior Players Championship, 15550 Rotunda St., Dearborn, MI 48120. (313) 441-0300.

How to play: You must be the guest of a member or a member of the TPC network.

Arizona

California

Colorado

Connecticut

Courtesy of Bob Hope Chrysler Classic

PGA Tour

Florida
Bay Hill Club, Orlando • 70
Doral Resort and Country Club, Miami • 68
TPC at Heron Bay, Coral Springs • 65
TPC at Sawgrass, Ponte Vedra Beach • 72
Walt Disney World Resort, Lake Buena Vista • 111

Georgia
Atlanta Country Club, Marietta • 82
Callaway Gardens Resort, Pine Mountain • 110

Hawaii
Kapalua Resort, Lahaina • 120
Waialae Country Club, Honolulu • 50

Illinois
Cog Hill Golf and Country Club, Lemont • 92
Oakwood Country Club, Coal Valley • 109

Louisiana
English Turn Golf and Country Club, New Orleans • 74

Maryland
TPC at Avenel, Potomac • 90

Massachusetts
Pleasant Valley Country Club, Sutton • 98

Michigan
Warwick Hills Golf and Country Club, Grand Blanc • 99

Mississippi
Annandale Golf Club, Madison • 95

Nevada
Las Vegas Country Club, Las Vegas • 114
TPC at Summerlin, Las Vegas • 114

New York
En-Joie Golf Club, Endicott • 108
Westchester Country Club, Rye • 81

North Carolina
Forest Oaks Country Club, Greensboro • 80

Ohio
Firestone Country Club, Akron • 102
Muirfield Village Golf Club, Dublin • 88

Oklahoma
Southern Hills Country Club, Tulsa • 118

South Carolina
Harbour Town Golf Links, Hilton Head Island • 76

Tennessee
TPC at Southwind, Memphis • 94

Texas
Colonial Country Club, Fort Worth • 86
Cottonwood Valley Country Club, Irving • 84
LaCantera Golf Club, San Antonio • 116
TPC at Four Seasons Resort-Las Colinas, Irving • 84
TPC at The Woodlands, The Woodlands • 78

Virginia
Kingsmill Golf Club, Williamsburg • 96

Wisconsin
Brown Deer Park Golf Course, Milwaukee • 104

Canada
Glen Abbey Golf Club, Oakville, Ontario • 106

Mercedes Championships

La Costa Resort and Spa

Only the preceding year's Tour winners are invited to this season-opening tournament, held each year at a world-class resort and spa that makes the invitation a prized windfall for many of the pros' spouses and families.

You might remember this event as the Tournament of Champions, a name it carried from its inception in 1953 until Mercedes took the wheel in 1994—same elite field, and the same great course that has hosted the championship since 1969.

The tournament debuted at the Desert Inn in Las Vegas, awarding winner Al Besselink a then munificent $10,000 first prize, paid—Vegas-style—in silver dollars. Many of golf's greatest players have since won this event, including Gene Littler, who took three consecutive titles in the mid-1950s, triple winners Arnold Palmer and Tom Watson, and Jack Nicklaus, who has won the tournament a record five times.

The 31 players invited to the 1995 event all went home with winnings better than Besselink's. The highest score, Mike Springer's 14-over-par 302, still merited $14,650 for the effort.

La Costa, located in a coastal valley 30 miles north of San Diego, boasts two golf courses, and the tournament selects a 7,022-yard composite of their 18 finest holes.

La Costa is a rolling course, with mature trees, well-bunkered fairway landing areas and greens, and water hazards in the form of a stream and a few small lakes. The wind and hazards make it a thinking man's course

The final four holes, sometimes called "golf's longest mile," measure 1,791 yards into a "two-club" westerly wind. This trek begins with a 378-yard par-4. The 15th is the last hole where players expect birdie opportunities, but it requires a well-placed tee shot over a stream and short of two fairway bunkers. The approach is a short iron to a small green packed inside five bunkers.

The 423-yard par-4 16th plays approximately two clubs longer than it looks because of the wind, and the 569-yard, par-5 17th is usually a three-shot journey to a deep green flanked by two large bunkers to its left and another large bunker to its upper right. A small lake runs along the right of the fairway up to the green. The final hole, a 421-yard par-4, plays straight to a raised, shallow green backed by a bunker and bracketed in front by two more.

During the 1995 championship, Bruce Lietzke had a one-shot lead going into the 17th, but his third shot missed the green and his chip shot left him a 7-foot par putt that he couldn't knock down. In sudden-death, Steve Elkington dropped a 25-foot putt on the second hole, the par-3 11th, for the victory and $180,000 in prize money.

TOURNAMENT-AT-A-GLANCE

Course: La Costa Resort and Spa
Type: Resort
Location: 2100 Costa del Mar Rd., Carlsbad, CA 92009
Telephone: (619) 438-9111, (800) 854-5000
When: Jan. 4–7, 1996
How To Get There: Take I-5 to La Costa Ave. Exit. Take La Costa Ave. east to El Camino Real Rd. Take a left to Costa del Mar Rd. and the resort.
Broadcast: ABC, ESPN (1996)
Purse: $1,000,000 (1995)
Tournament Record: 21-under-par 267, Calvin Peete, 1986

●TOUGHEST HOLE

The 446-yard, par-4 fifth requires a precise tee shot over a stream to a landing area between the stream on the left and a cluster of bunkers on the right. The green, one of the smallest on the course, is protected by a bunker to its left front and another to the rear. The farther and more accurate the tee shot, the easier it is to hold the green with a lofted approach. The 188-yard, par-3 seventh usually plays downwind to a shallow green bordered by water to its left and protected by two bunkers to its front and two more to its rear. The small target and variable wind conditions made this the second-most-difficult hole to par at the 1995 Mercedes Championships.

●BEST PLACE TO WATCH

The final four holes tend to play into the wind and provide for plenty of lead changes. A good place to be at the end is around the 421-yard, par-4 18th, where approach shots are to a raised, shallow green guarded by two bunkers in front and another to the rear.

●WHO THE COURSE FAVORS

A competitor who can hit long, well-positioned tee shots that set up high-percentage approach shots and short putts. The greens are protected by an average of three bunkers each, and many, including the 180-yard, par-3 11th and the 378-yard, par-4 15th, require the golfer to fly the ball into the green. Fairway bunkers and a stream running through the course guard most of the landing areas. The player must also be able to play in the winds that turn the final four holes into "golf's longest mile."

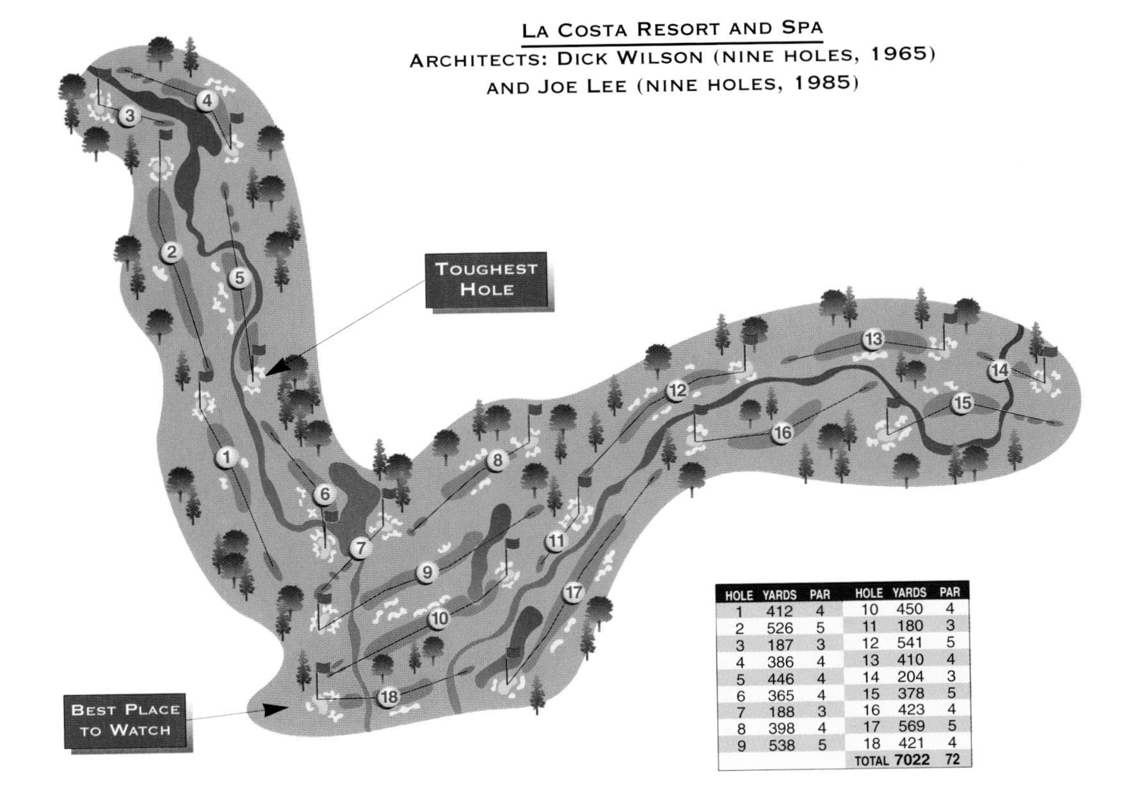

HOLE	YARDS	PAR	HOLE	YARDS	PAR
1	412	4	10	450	4
2	526	5	11	180	3
3	187	3	12	541	5
4	386	4	13	410	4
5	446	4	14	204	3
6	365	4	15	378	5
7	188	3	16	423	4
8	398	4	17	569	5
9	538	5	18	421	4
			TOTAL	7022	72

LODGING

$$$ La Costa Resort and Spa, Costa del Mar Rd., Carlsbad, Calif. (619) 438-9111, (800) 854-5000. On site.

$$ Pelican Cove Inn, 320 Walnut Ave., Carlsbad, Calif. (619) 434-5995. 10 minutes from La Costa.

$ La Jolla Cove Travelodge, 1141 Silverado St., La Jolla, Calif. (619) 454-0791. 30 minutes from La Costa.

DINING

Mille Fleurs, 6009 Paseo Delicias, Rancho Santa Fe, Calif. (619) 756-3085.

Neiman's, 2978 Carlsbad Blvd., Carlsbad, Calif. (619) 729-4131.

Fidel's, 607 Valley Ave., Solana Beach, Calif. (619) 755-5292.

PUBLIC COURSES TO PLAY IN AREA

Four Seasons Resort Aviara, 7447 Batiguitos Dr., Carlsbad, Calif. Public. (619) 929-0077. 18/7,007/72. 5 minutes from La Costa.

Steele Canyon Golf Club, 3199 Stonefield Dr., Jamul, Calif. Semi-private. (619) 441-6900. Canyon/Ranch: 18/6,741/71. Canyon/Meadow: 18/6,672/71. Ranch/Meadow: 18/7,001/72. 20 minutes from La Costa.

Torrey Pines, 11480 N. Torrey Pines Rd., La Jolla, Calif. Public. (619) 452-3226. North: 18/6,659/72. South: 18/7,021/72. 30 minutes from La Costa.

TICKETS & ACCESSIBILITY

How to watch: Mon., PGA practice rounds. Tue., PGA practice rounds. Wed., pro-am event. Thur.-Sun., tournament. Individual and group tickets available. Mercedes Championship, c/o La Costa Resort and Spa, 2100 Costa del Mar Rd., Carlsbad, CA 92009. (619) 438-9111.

How to play: La Costa is a year-round resort with 395 deluxe rooms, 75 one- or two-bedroom suites and executive homes. The resort has five restaurants, two lounges, a full-service spa, tennis, heated swimming pools and other amenities. The North (18/6,987/72) and South (18/6,894/72) courses are both open to resort guests and the public. Golf packages are available through the resort. (619) 438-9111, (800) 854-5000.

United Airlines Hawaiian Open

WAIALAE COUNTRY CLUB

Barbed wire ringed this flat, oceanside course during World War II to fend off landings by the enemy and in 1950 scenes from the classic film *From Here to Eternity* were shot here.

Today this golfer-friendly layout is the site of the Hawaiian Open, an event first won by Gay Brewer in 1965 when he defeated Bob Goalby on the first hole of a sudden-death playoff.

An Eden-like setting, the course is laden with exotic plants like Madagascar olive, cow-itch, Chinese fan-palm, bauhinia, graveyard plameria and monkeypod. Three holes border the Pacific, and prevailing winds blow toward its waves.

The Waialae Country Club, opened in 1927, was designed by Seth Raynor, a protégé of Charles B. Macdonald, "the father of American golf course architecture." Macdonald and Raynor had collaborated on Piping Rock (1913), Sleepy Hollow (1914), the Old White Course at Greenbrier (1915) and the Yale University Golf Club (1926). When Raynor died in 1926, his assistants Charles Banks and Ralph Barton completed his unfinished projects, including Waialae.

Streams cut through the front nine of the tournament course and another comes into play at the par-3 17th. Man-made lakes run along the second and third holes, and palm trees dot the landscape. Deep, sculpted bunkers guard the greens, including six on the 196-yard, par-3 fourth, one of the most difficult holes on the course. A total of sixty-one bunkers protect the greens, while bunkers, trees or water flank the fairway landing areas.

Hawaiian names title the holes at Waialae. "Upiki" (Trapped) is the 182-yard, par-3 seventh, with five traps sur-rounding its green. "Welo" (Float in the Wind), is the 434-yard, par-4 16th. Winds can lengthen holes, such as on the fourth; cut across fairways, as on the tough 460-yard, par-4 fifth; or run downwind with the ball, as on the finishing holes. The 552-yard, par-5 18th, called "Kilou Loa" (Long Hook), is a dogleg left with three bunkers at its left turn and one on its right edge. The approach is downwind to a green guarded by three bunkers.

In a spectacular finish, Isao Aoki holed a 126-yard wedge on the final hole of the 1983 tournament to become the first Japanese player to win a PGA Tour event. The Tour players' assaults on the par-5s at Waialae often provide the weekend's greatest thrills.

Lanny Wadkins, Hubert Green and Corey Pavin are the only two-time winners here.

TOURNAMENT-AT-A-GLANCE

Course: Waialae Country Club
Type: Private
Location: 4997 Kahala Ave., Honolulu, HI 96816
Telephone: (808) 734-2151
When: Feb. 15–18, 1996
How To Get There: Take Kalakaua Ave. east out of Waikiki. Continue onto Diamond Head Rd. (past Diamond Head Lookout) which turns into Kahala Ave. The course is on the left, just before the entrance to the Kahala Hilton.
Broadcast: ABC, cable TBA (1996)
Purse: $1,200,000 (1996)
Tournament Record: 23-under-par, Hale Irwin, 1981; John Cook, 1992

●TOUGHEST HOLE

The two most difficult holes at Waialae come back to back on the front nine. The 196-yard, par-3 fourth plays into the wind to a 55-yard-deep, narrow green with a swale running across its center. Three formidable bunkers guard each side of this hole, which was the most difficult to par in the 1995 championship. Next is the 460-yard, par-4 fifth, named "Auwai" (Two Ditches) in deference to the interruptions in its tree-lined fairway. A solid drive that clears the first ditch leaves a mid-iron to a heavily contoured green with two traps to its right and a large bunker to its left.

●BEST PLACE TO WATCH

Waialae is a flat, easy course to walk. During the early rounds, wander the course and catch the action at the picturesque and difficult par-3s, such as the 196-yard fourth and the 182-yard seventh. During the final round, be sure to catch the action at the 18th, a 552-yard, par-5 dogleg left whose second shot is downwind toward a green fronted by two bunkers that allow a narrow entrance to the putting surface. Another bunker is to the left of the green.

●WHO THE COURSE FAVORS

Because Waialae plays short and the greens putt very true, tournament scores are usually low on this layout. The competitors must be able to accurately read the greens, which break toward the ocean, and cope with the wind. The par-5s on this course are relatively short (three of them are less than 540 yards) providing ample opportunities for birdies and eagles. But virtually all of the greens are well-guarded by three or more bunkers, so solid sand play is an asset.

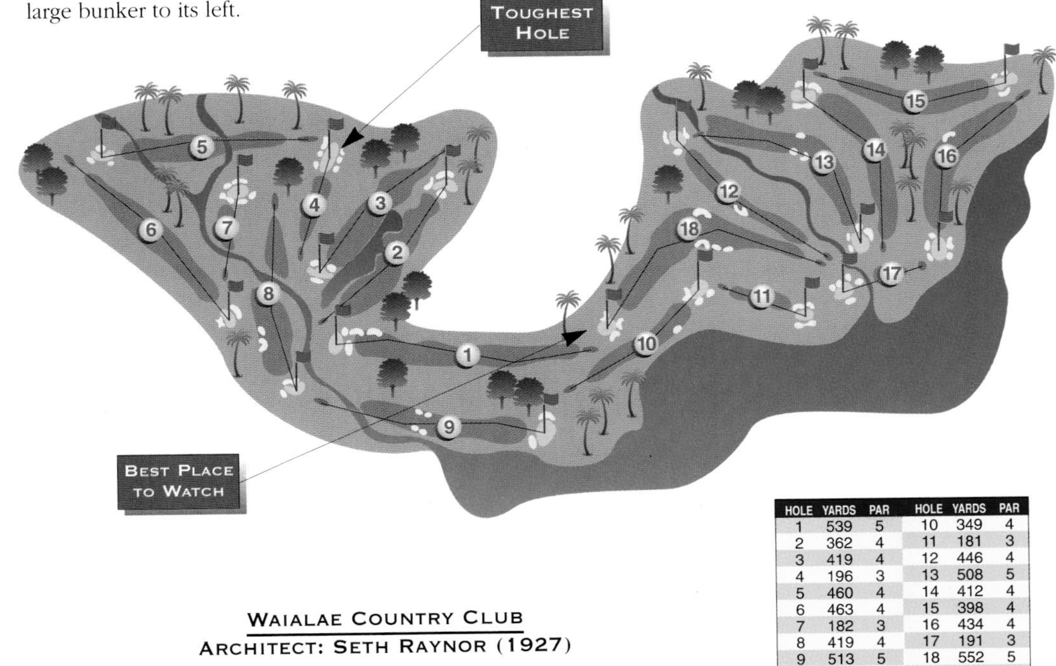

HOLE	YARDS	PAR	HOLE	YARDS	PAR
1	539	5	10	349	4
2	362	4	11	181	3
3	419	4	12	446	4
4	196	3	13	508	5
5	460	4	14	412	4
6	463	4	15	398	4
7	182	3	16	434	4
8	419	4	17	191	3
9	513	5	18	552	5
			TOTAL	7024	72

WAIALAE COUNTRY CLUB
ARCHITECT: SETH RAYNOR (1927)

LODGING

$$$ Kahala Hilton, 5000 Kahala Ave., Honolulu. (808) 734-2211, (800) 367-2525. Within walking distance of Waialae.
$$ Manoa Valley Inn, 2001 Vancouver Dr., Honolulu. (808) 947-6019, (800) 634-5115. 20 minutes from Waialae.
$ Payoda Hotel, 1525 Rycroft St., Honolulu. (808) 941-6611, (800) 367-6060.
Bed and Breakfast Honolulu, 3242 Kaohinani Dr., Honolulu. (808) 595-7533, (800) 288-4666. Provides booking services for the Honolulu area.

DINING

La Mer, in the Halekulani Hotel, 2199 Kalia Rd., Honolulu. (808) 923-2311.
Orchid's in the Halekulani Hotel, 2199 Kalia Rd., Honolulu. (808) 923-2311.
Ono Hawaiian Foods, 726 Kapahulu Ave., Honolulu. (808) 737-2275.

PUBLIC COURSES TO PLAY IN AREA

Ko Olina Golf Club, 3733 Alii Dr., Kapolei, Hawaii. Resort. (808) 676-5300. 18/6,867/72. 50 minutes from Waialae.
Sheraton Makaha Resort & Country Club, 84-626 Makaha Valley Rd., Waianae, Hawaii. Resort. (808) 695-9544. 18/7,091/72. 90 minutes from Waialae.
Waikele Golf Club, 94-200 Paioa Pl., Waipahu, Hawaii. Public. (808) 676-9000. 35 minutes from Waialae.

TICKETS & ACCESSIBILITY

How to watch: Mon., PGA practice rounds. Tue., PGA practice rounds, shoot-out, invitational tournaments, trick shot artist exhibition. Wed., pro-am tournament. Thur.-Sun., tournament. Individual, sponsor and patron packages are available. United Airlines Hawaiian Open, 677 Ala Mouna Blvd., Suite 207, Honolulu, HI 96813. (808) 526-1232.
How to play: The Waialae Country Club is a private club. You must be a member or the guest of a member to play the course.

NorTel Open

TUCSON NATIONAL GOLF RESORT, STARR PASS GOLF CLUB

When the Tucson Open joined the pro circuit's winter tour in 1945, the $5,000 purse was procured through Calcuttas and high-stakes gambling games held in a makeshift casino at the host El Rio Golf and Country Club. The club's short and flat, 6,418-yard, par-70 layout set the stage for some exciting low-scoring shoot-outs.

By David Bean

ONE OF THE MOST PUNISHING FINALES ON THE PGA TOUR, TUCSON NATIONAL'S 18TH YIELDS FEW EASY PARS.

Johnny Miller, with his long, complicated swing, permanently branded the Tucson as a gunner's event in 1975 when he caught fire for a final-round 11-under-par 61 for the second of his three consecutive victories here. That record-setting torching came at the expense of Tucson National, which currently hosts three of the NorTel's four rounds.

Today's Tucson event no longer carries the name of the city, and its combination of an early-season slot and two tameable host course gives it the air of a coming-out party for new talent or resurgent veterans. A 20-year-old Phil Mickelson, then just a junior at Arizona State, became the youngest amateur ever to win a Tour event when he sank an 8-foot birdie putt on the 72nd hole to take the 1991 title.

Tucson National, part of a 167-room conference resort set in the Sonoran Desert, is ranked among the best resort courses in the United States. There are three nine-hole courses on site, and the tournament is played on the Orange/Gold combination, which features large, slightly elevated greens and water hazards on several holes. Tucson National is a old-style layout with no native desert in front of the tee boxes, though it has an abundance of bunkers. Set on a high chaparral desert overlooking the Tucson basin, the course is framed by the dramatic 9,000-foot peaks of the Santa Catalina Mountains.

Two of the toughest holes on the course are the finishing holes on each side. The 440-yard ninth is a slight dogleg right whose tee-shot landing area is guarded by a lake on the right side. The approach is uphill to a large green guarded by a front left side bunker and two more to its rear. The 465-yard, par-4 18th is a dogleg right guarded by a lake on its right side and another farther left. The approach is usually a long iron to a well-guarded green. In the 1995 event Jim Gallagher Jr. three-putted from 60 feet on this hole to finish one stroke behind a 24-year-old Mickelson, who this time kept the winner's check.

Starr Pass Golf Club, host of the tournament players for one round each year, is a more traditional desert-style course where errant shots can end up on lava rock adjacent to the fairways. A rolling layout that often presents tricky, uneven lies, Starr Pass has two of the most difficult holes in the tournament, including the 437-yard, par-4 18th. Its tee shot must carry over desert terrain to a landing area squeezed by bunkers to its right. The approach must avoid a bunker to the right in front of a wide green that is also protected by a large bunker to its left and another to the rear.

Starr Pass provides a tough test in the midst of a playful weekend of golf.

●TOUGHEST HOLE

Played as a par-5 by amateurs, the 456-yard, par-4 10th at Tucson National, a dogleg left with a lake guarding the left side, was rated the most difficult hole to par in the 1995 tournament. A pin placement tucked behind the right front bunker can make this hole especially difficult, and the green is hard to hold with a long-iron approach. Starr Pass' par-4 third has a tight fairway and a table-top green where stopping the ball is a challenge. Along with Nos. 9 and 13, it's the course's hardest.

●BEST PLACE TO WATCH

At Tucson National, walk over to the green area at No. 12, a 182-yard par-3, where you can also see the No. 11 green and tee shots on No. 10. The stands around No. 18 are the place to be on the last day. A short walk away is the ninth green. The clubhouse area at Starr Pass affords views of Nos. 18 and 9 and the tees on Nos. 1 and 10.

●WHO THE COURSE FAVORS

Starr Pass is a desert target course that rewards placement and accurate approach shots to tiered greens. The Tucson National Course is more open, but placement is still important because bunkers and lakes around the landing areas can reduce the competitors' chances to score. The greens at Tucson National do not break in any predictable way so local knowledge and an ability to read these fast, bentgrass surfaces are required.

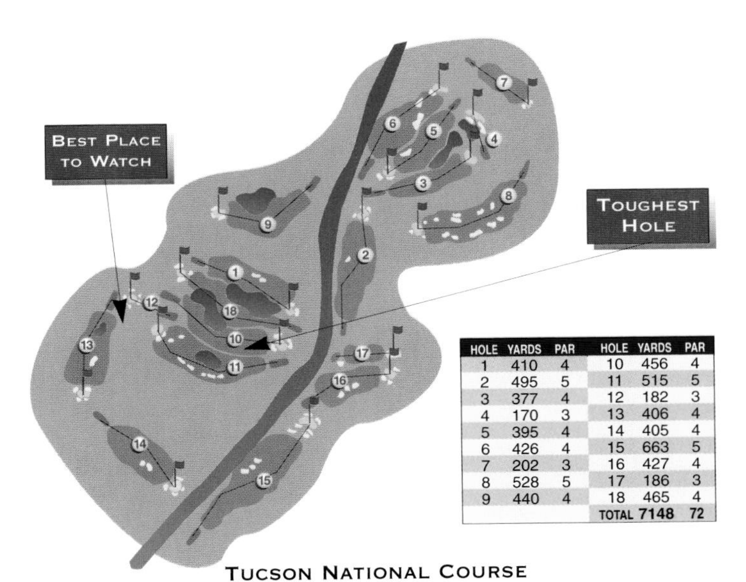

HOLE	YARDS	PAR	HOLE	YARDS	PAR
1	410	4	10	456	4
2	495	5	11	515	5
3	377	4	12	182	3
4	170	3	13	406	4
5	395	4	14	405	4
6	426	4	15	663	5
7	202	3	16	427	4
8	528	5	17	186	3
9	440	4	18	465	4
			TOTAL	7148	72

TUCSON NATIONAL COURSE
ARCHITECT: ROBERT BRUCE HARRIS (18 HOLES, 1961), BRUCE DEVLIN AND ROBERT VON HAGGE (REMODELED 18 HOLES, ADDED 9 HOLES, 1983)

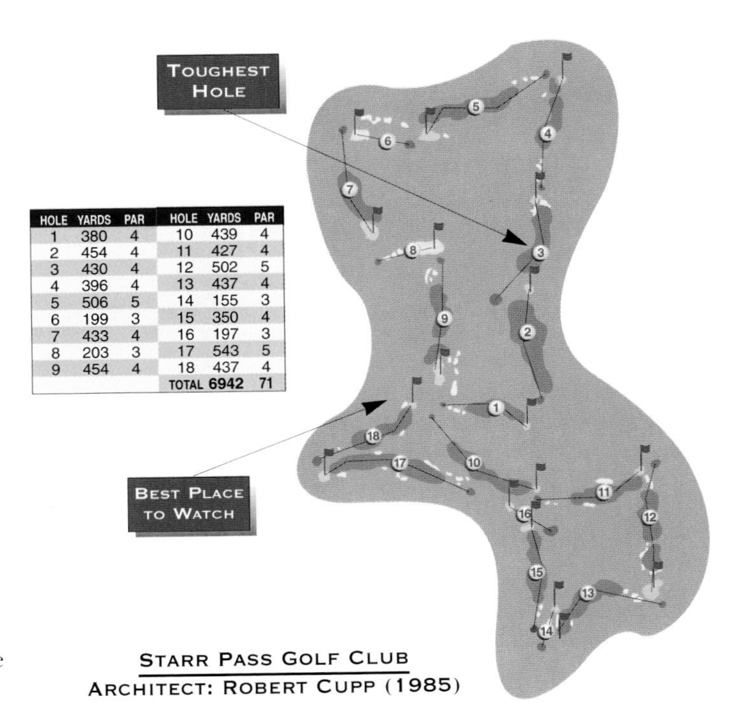

HOLE	YARDS	PAR	HOLE	YARDS	PAR
1	380	4	10	439	4
2	454	4	11	427	4
3	430	4	12	502	5
4	396	4	13	437	4
5	506	5	14	155	3
6	199	3	15	350	4
7	433	4	16	197	3
8	203	3	17	543	5
9	454	4	18	437	4
			TOTAL	6942	71

STARR PASS GOLF CLUB
ARCHITECT: ROBERT CUPP (1985)

TOURNAMENT-AT-A-GLANCE

Courses: Tucson National Golf Resort, Starr Pass Golf Club
Type: Resort
Location: 2727 W. Club Dr., Tucson, AZ 85741
Telephone: (602) 297-2271
When: Jan. 11–14, 1996
How To Get There: Take I-10 to Exit 246/Cortaro Farms. Go east on Cortaro, 3 miles to Shannon. Make a left on Shannon. Proceed north on Shannon to resort on the right.
Broadcast: ESPN (1996)
Purse: $1,250,000 (1996)
Tournament Record: 25-under-par 263, Johnny Miller, 1975 (at Tucson National GC, Tucson, Ariz.)

LODGING

$$$ Loews Ventura Resort, 7000 W. Resort Dr., Tucson, Ariz. (520) 299-2020, (800) 828-5701. 5 minutes from Tucson National.
$$ The Lodge on the Desert, 306 N. Alvernon Way, Tucson, Ariz. (520) 325-3366, (800) 456-5634. 20 minutes from Tucson National.
$ Best Western Inn Suites–Catalina Foothills, 6201 N. Oracle Rd., Tucson, Ariz. (520) 297-8111. 5 minutes from Tucson National.
Arizona Association of Bed & Breakfast Inns, 3661 N. Campbell Ave., Box 237, Tucson, Ariz. (520) 231-6777, 622-7167.

DINING

The Ventura Room, Loews Ventura Resort, 7000 W. Resort Dr., Tucson, Ariz. (520) 299-2020.
Macayo, 7360 N. Oracle Rd., Tucson, Ariz. (520) 742-2141.

PUBLIC COURSES TO PLAY IN AREA

Westin La Paloma Country Club, 3800 E. Sunrise Dr., Tucson, Ariz. Resort. (520) 299-1500 (golf course), (800) 222-1252 (resort). Hill/Ridge: 18/7,017/72. Ridge/Canyon: 18/7,088/72. Canyon/Hill 18/6,996/72. 15 minutes from Tucson National.
Loews Ventura Canyon Golf & Racquet Club, 7000 N. Resort Dr., Tucson, Ariz. Resort. (520) 577-6258 (golf course), (800) 828-5701 (resort). Canyon: 18/6,818/72. Mountain: 18/6,948/72. 5 minutes from Tucson National.
Randolph Park Golf Course, 600 S. Alvernon, Tucson, Ariz. Public. (520) 325-2811. North: 18/6,902/72. South: 18/6,229/70. 25 minutes from Tucson National.

TICKETS & ACCESSIBILITY

How to watch: Mon., PGA practice rounds, golf clinic, Special Olympics clinic. Tue., PGA practice rounds, shoot-out. Wed., Celebrity pro-am. Thur.-Sun., tournament. Daily individual tickets start at $10. Group and sponsorship plans available. NorTel Open, Tucson Conquistadores, 6450 E. Broadway Blvd., Tucson, AZ 85710. (520) 571-0400, (800) 882-7660.
How to play: Both Tucson National and Starr Pass are open to the public year round. Packages available through Tucson National at (520) 277-2271 (golf course), (800) 520-4856 (resort). Starr Pass: (520) 670-0300.

Phoenix Open

TPC of Scottsdale

The Phoenix Open, a venerable tournament and a weeklong community festival in the Arizona desert, owns bragging rights as the world's top spectator golf event. Nearly 400,000 people annually pass through its entrances, drawn by the feats of the game's best players or maybe just by a tent called The Bird's Nest, which for one week of the year is the biggest party in town.

The 1996 edition should be particularly raucous, as sports fans flock to Phoenix that week for Super Bowl XXX. The NFL's showcase will bump the Open schedule back a day, but on Super Sunday itself, CEOs of the world's top businesses will tee up for a charity pro-am with stars of the NFL and PGA, then ride limousines or helicopters to Sun Devil Stadium for a pre–Super Bowl party.

One of the oldest events on the winter Tour, the Phoenix Open has crowned virtually all of the game's legends. Arnold Palmer and Gene Littler, the first inductees into the Open's Hall of Fame, are the event's only three-time winners. Other Hall members include pro-am fixture Bob Hope, longtime celebrity host Glenn Campbell and PING king Karsten Solheim, who started his club-making business in the garage of his Phoenix home. Two-time winner Johnny Miller set a few tournament records in 1975 at the Phoenix Country Club with his astounding 260 total, which resulted in a 14-stroke victory, the largest winning margin in a PGA event during the past four decades.

TOURNAMENT-AT-A-GLANCE

Course: TPC of Scottsdale—Stadium Course
Type: Public
Location: 17020 N. Hayden Rd., Scottsdale, AZ 85255
Telephone: (602) 585-3939 or 585-4334
When: Jan. 24–27, 1996
How To Get There: From airport take 44th St. to Town Blvd. to Bell Rd. Go right on Bell to Pima, then left on Pima, 3/4 miles to golf course.
Broadcast: ESPN (1996)
Purse: $1,300,000 (1995)
Tournament Record: 24-under-par 260, Johnny Miller, 1975

Nestled beneath the McDowell Mountains on a former flood retention plain 15 miles from downtown Phoenix, the TPC of Scottsdale has been the tournament's home since 1987 and was created when designers Tom Weiskopf and Jay Morrish moved more than a million cubic yards of dirt to create a gently rolling links-style course. A rare combination of municipal course and PGA tournament site, it features plenty of grass knolls, several picturesque lakes and amphitheater-type seating. When the pros are in town, dicey flagstick positions on the ample greens heighten the course's challenges. A pin placement to the left at the par-4 11th, for example, throws the approach into the wind and in danger of landing in water to the left.

The front nine has very little water, but prevailing winds demand shot control and proper club selection. The back nine, which has water on six holes, culminates in two good finishing holes. The 332-yard, par-4 17th can be traversed with a strong tee shot, but a lake to the left curls around its deep green. On the par-4 18th, the tee shot must carry 200 yards of water and avoid bunkers that frame the landing area. The approach is to a green guarded by a large, deep bunker to its right. Billy Mayfair landed in this sand in the 1995 tournament but was able to get up and down to finish with a 66 and force a playoff with Vijay Singh. Mayfair hit the bunker again in the playoff but had to settle for a bogey and a second-place finish.

> "IT'S A LITTLE BIT LESS UNNERVING THAN REGULATION PLAY BECAUSE YOU KNOW YOU'VE SECURED SECOND PLACE, SO YOU JUST GO OUT AND PLAY MORE AGGRESSIVE THAN NORMAL."
>
> —VIJAY SINGH,
>
> ON WINNING THE 1995 PHOENIX OPEN AFTER TYING BILLY MAYFAIR AT 269 IN REGULATION

By Rick Bullock

ATTRACTING NEARLY 400,000 FANS ANNUALLY, THE PHOENIX OPEN IS THE PGA TOUR'S FIFTH-OLDEST EVENT.

●TOUGHEST HOLE

The 469-yard, par-4 11th, a slight dogleg right with a lake paralleling its left side. The approach is to a medium-sized green with a large bunker to its front left and another in the rear that's invisible from the fairway. The variable winds on this course can make other holes, like the 453-yard, par-4 fifth, also play tough. Players are forced to quarter into the wind as they try to keep their tee shots at No. 5 out of heavy rough to the left and the out-of-bounds area to the right. The green, protected by two large bunkers and a stream, can be difficult to hit on a windy day.

●BEST PLACE TO WATCH

The hill overlooking the 15th island green and the 16th tee has a party atmosphere and a sweeping view of most of the course. Other great perches: behind the eighth green, where you can also watch the ninth tee and 11th fairway; the 11th green, where you can also see the 12th tee. Of course, the final hole can be an exciting place to be on the last day. In 1988 Sandy Lyle won the event with a bogey on the 18th, the third sudden-death playoff hole. Fred Couples, his opponent, carded a six after hitting his tee shot into the lake.

●WHO THE COURSE FAVORS

The golfer who can overcome mounded fairways, variable winds, thick rough, waste areas and bountiful bunkers. The course penalizes errant shots. Recent champions, including Lee Janzen, Nolan Henke, Mark Calcavecchia and Vijay Singh, have tended to be those who perform well on tight U.S. Open–style courses.

HOLE	YARDS	PAR	HOLE	YARDS	PAR
1	410	4	10	403	4
2	416	4	11	469	4
3	554	5	12	195	3
4	150	3	13	576	5
5	453	4	14	444	4
6	389	4	15	501	5
7	215	3	16	162	3
8	470	4	17	332	4
9	415	4	18	438	4
			TOTAL	6992	71

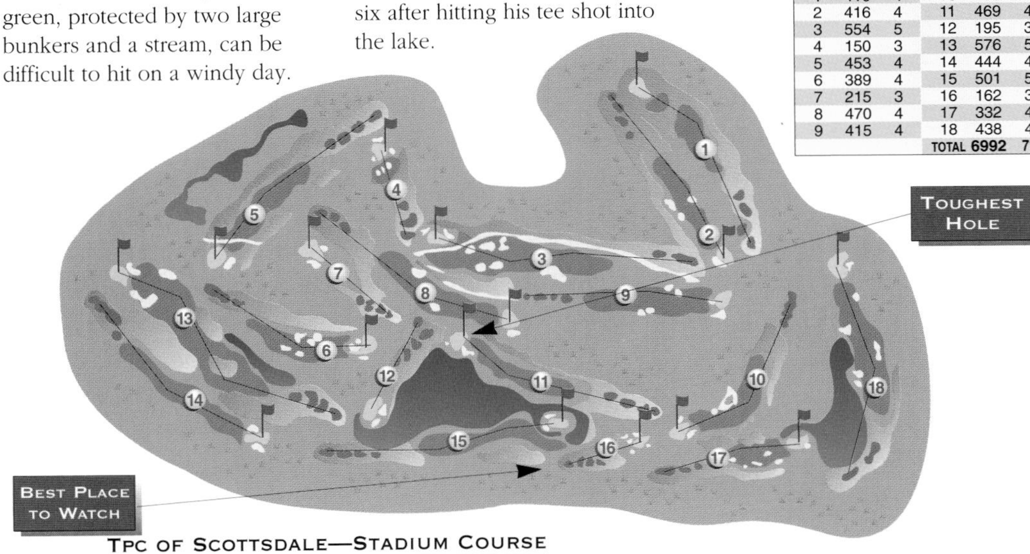

TPC OF SCOTTSDALE—STADIUM COURSE
ARCHITECTS: JAY MORRISH AND TOM WEISKOPF (1986)

LODGING

$$$ Resort Suites of Scottsdale, 7677 E. Princess Blvd., Scottsdale, Ariz. (602) 585-1234, (800) 541-5203. 1 minute from TPC of Scottsdale.

$$$ Scottsdale Princess, 7575 E. Princess Dr., Scottsdale, Ariz. (602) 585-4848, (800) 223-1818. 2 minutes from TPC of Scottsdale.

$ Sunburst Hotel & Conference Center, 4925 N. Scottsdale Rd., Scottsdale, Ariz. (602) 945-7666, (800) 528-7867. 10 minutes from TPC of Scottsdale.

DINING

La Hacienda, at the Scottsdale Princess, 7575 E. Princess Dr., Scottsdale, Ariz. (602) 585-4848.

Piñon Grill, in Regal McCormick Ranch, 7401 N. Scottsdale Rd., Scottsdale, Ariz. (602) 948-5050.

PUBLIC COURSES TO PLAY IN AREA

The Boulders, 34631 N. Tom Darlington Dr., Carefree, Ariz. Resort. (602) 488-9009, (800) 553-1717. North: 18/6,731/72. South: 18/6543/71. 25 minutes from TPC of Scottsdale. Must be a guest of the resort or a member to play.

Stone Creek, 4435 E. Paradise Village Pkwy. S, Paradise Valley, Ariz. Public. (602) 953-9110. 18/6,836/71. 20 minutes from TPC of Scottsdale.

Troon North, 10370 E. Dynamite Blvd., Scottsdale, Ariz. Public. (602) 585-5300. 18/7,000/72. 25 minutes from TPC of Scottsdale.

TICKETS & ACCESSIBILITY

How to watch: Mon., PGA practice rounds, pro-am. Tue., PGA practice rounds, Special Olympics Open, long drive contest, shootout, junior golf clinic. Wed., pro-am, hole-in-one contest. Thur.-Sun., tournament. Daily tickets begin at $12. Children under 17 admitted free. Group and sponsorship packages available. The Thunderbird, 7226 N. 16th St., Suite 100, Phoenix, AZ 85020. (602) 870-0163.

How to play: The Stadium and Desert Courses (18/6,552/71) are public facilities open year-round. Packages are available through the nearby Scottsdale Princess. (602) 585-4848, (800) 223-1818. Seasonal discounts are available at the course. (602) 585-3939.

AT&T Pebble Beach National Pro-Am

PEBBLE BEACH GOLF LINKS, POPPY HILLS GOLF CLUB, SPYGLASS HILL GOLF COURSE

If Hollywood ever needed to cast a golf course, Pebble Beach would get the job. Its white-capped water hazards, cliffside fairways and soft-focus veil of ocean mist long ago created the standard in set design for epic confrontations between the game's legends: Nicklaus versus Watson in the 1982 U.S. Open, Nicklaus versus Palmer in the 1972 Open, Jack Lemmon versus himself in each and every playing of the pro-am.

Bing Crosby's name no longer adorns the most clubby weekend on the pro golfer's calendar, but the mark he made on the game is indelible. The event the late entertainer created in 1937 elevated everything it touched—the game, its stars, and of course, Pebble Beach.

Crosby was already a national treasure when he decided to put up $3,000 in prize money and invite 68 pros and a matching number of amateurs. Zeppo Marx and Fred Astaire also participated in the two days of golf, camaraderie and steak dinners at the host's own Southern California spread, the Rancho Sante Fe Country Club in San Diego. Thus was born "the Clambake," which became a highlight of the Hollywood social season and another nickname for the tournament itself. (A young GI named Clint Eastwood, who's now chairman of the tournament foundation, managed to sneak into his first Clambake in 1951.)

After a World War II sabbatical, the Crosby relocated to the breathtaking Monterey Peninsula in 1947. Just as today, the event was played on three distinguished courses, finishing with a flourish at Pebble Beach. And thanks to Crosby's steadfast refusal to demote the amateur competitors—whose celebrity contingent has lately included Bill Murray, Joe Pesci and George Bush—the format remains almost identical, as both the team and individual titles are decided on the final day of play.

Avid fans of the game know Pebble Beach well. Unmatched in natural beauty, it loops eight holes alongside and across the craggy headlands overlooking Stillwater Cove and Carmel Bay, and weaves 10 challenging inland holes into a track widely regarded as the best in the world. Designer Jack Neville, an amateur champion and career real-estate salesman, had never charted a course before, but on his first effort he got everything just right. He even won the California State Amateur Championship in 1919 when his new course was selected as the event's permanent home. A decade later, a national audience took notice of Pebble Beach when the seemingly invincible Bobby Jones fell to a then unknown Johnny Goodman in the second round of the first U.S. Amateur held more than 10 miles west of the Mississippi.

But it was the Crosby that turned Pebble Beach into an icon. In 1958, a national TV audience tuned in to the pro-am for the first time as Crosby set aside his clubs to offer his unique multisyllabic color commentary. Eventually, the tournament's growing viewership and galleries convinced the USGA that Pebble Beach, though 135 miles south of San Francisco, could draw crowds adequate for a national championship. In 1972, Nicklaus hit a 1-iron straight at the ocean on the par-3 17th and caught the flagstick, clinching the title in the first U.S. Open played on the legend's favorite course.

Ten years later, it was Nicklaus on top again before Tom Watson rolled in a magical chip from the rough just off the same green.

Tom Kite was the last player to enjoy a U.S. Open victory parade past the mansions on his right and the rocky beach to the left on the course's par-5 final hole, and such great moments add to the mystique and luster of the annual pro-am. In 1994, Monterey Peninsula somehow turned the calendar back 15 years to stage a final-round duel between Watson and Johnny Miller. "I don't know what Watson was thinking, but it really was sweet for me," said the eventual winner. "It was a throwback, a Miller-Watson duel in the rain at Pebble Beach."

"IF I COULD PLAY, LIFT, CLEAN AND PLACE ALL THE TIME, I'D BE IN THE HALL OF FAME."

—PETER JACOBSEN,

1995 AT&T PEBBLE BEACH NATIONAL PRO-AM WINNER, AFTER WET CONDITIONS ALLOWED PLAYERS TO CLEAN AND PLACE THE BALL

TOURNAMENT-AT-A-GLANCE
Courses: Pebble Beach Golf Links, Poppy Hills Golf Club, Spyglass Hill Golf Course **Type:** Resort **Location:** Pebble Beach Golf Links, 17-Mile Drive, Pebble Beach, CA 93953 **Telephone:** (408) 624-3811 **When:** Feb. 1–4, 1996 **How To Get There:** Take Hwy. 101 to Monterey Peninsula turnoff. Take Rte. 156 west to Hwy. 1 and go south to 17-Mile Drive/Pebble Beach Exit. A guard at the entrance provides directions to the golf courses. **Broadcast:** USA, CBS (1996) **Purse:** $1,400,000 (1996) **Tournament Record:** 17-under-par 271, Peter Jacobsen, 1995

By Steve Burton

THE FAMOUS PAR-3 SEVENTH AT PEBBLE BEACH PLAYS ALONG THE "CLIFFS OF DOOM" TO AN OCEANSIDE GREEN.

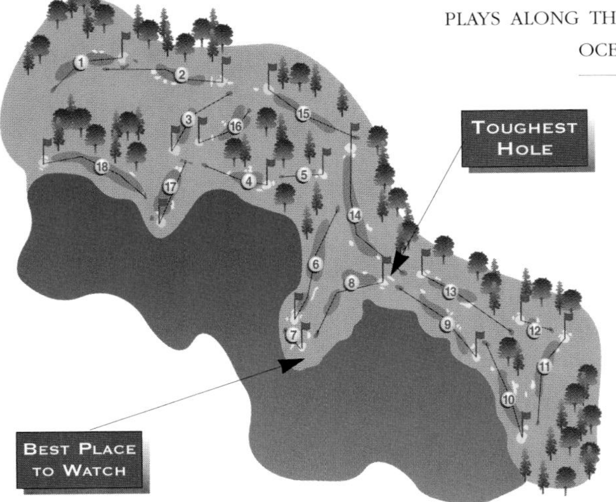

PEBBLE BEACH GOLF LINKS
ARCHITECT: JACK NEVILLE (1919)

HOLE	YARDS	PAR	HOLE	YARDS	PAR
1	373	4	10	426	4
2	502	5	11	384	4
3	388	4	12	202	3
4	327	4	13	392	4
5	166	3	14	565	5
6	516	5	15	397	4
7	107	3	16	402	4
8	431	4	17	209	3
9	464	4	18	548	5
			TOTAL	6799	72

●TOUGHEST HOLE

The toughest Pebble Beach hole during the 1995 AT&T was the 431-yard, par-4 eighth, which plays along the ocean to its right, and squeezes to a very narrow fairway into a small green, guarded by a large bunker to its right and two more bunkers to its rear. The approach shot must carry the ocean chasm that cuts into the right fairway and reach the severely forward-sloping target. A right-to-left wind off the ocean is another major factor on this hole.

●BEST PLACE TO WATCH

The three-course spread of this event on its first three days gives spectators a lot of marvelous golf terrain to cover, but you will no doubt want to spend most of your time at dramatic Pebble Beach. It's an easy course to walk. Two prime viewing areas are the green area around No. 7, the famous 107-yard par-3, and the 548-yard, par-5 18th, which runs along the ocean.

●WHO THE COURSE FAVORS

The variable winds coming off the ocean, the small greens and the subtly sloping fairways make Pebble Beach a shotmaker's course. The golfer has to come into the green with precision, especially on the ocean holes, or the ball will be in a bunker, thick rough or somewhere in the ocean.

LODGING

$$$ The Lodge at Pebble Beach, 17-Mile Dr., Pebble Beach, Calif. (408) 624-3811, (800) 654-9300. On site.

$$ Pine Inn, Ocean Ave. and Lincoln St., Box 250, Carmel, Calif. (408) 624-3851, (800) 228-3851. 5 minutes from Pebble Beach.

$ Arbor Inn, 1058 Muras Ave., Monterey, Calif. (408) 372-3381. 15 minutes from Pebble Beach.

DINING

Club XIX at The Lodge at Pebble Beach, 17-Mile Dr., Pebble Beach, Calif. (408) 624-3811.

Flaherty's Seafood Grill & Oyster House, 6th Ave. and San Carlos St., Carmel, Calif. (408) 625-1500 (Seafood Grill), (408) 624-0311 (Oyster House).

The Tinnery, 631 Ocean View Blvd., Pacific Grove, Calif. (408) 646-1040.

PUBLIC COURSES TO PLAY IN AREA

The Links at Spanish Bay, 2700 17-Mile Dr., Pebble Beach, Calif. Resort. (408) 624-3811, (800) 654-9300. 18/6,820/72. 5 minutes from Pebble Beach Golf Links.

Carmel Valley Ranch Golf Club, 1 Old Ranch Rd., Carmel Valley, Calif. Resort. (408) 625-9500, (800) 4 CARMEL. 18/6,515/70. 15 minutes from Pebble Beach Golf Links. You must stay at resort to play course.

Golf Club at Quail Lodge, 8205 Valley Greens Dr., Carmel, Calif. Resort. (408) 624-1581, (800) 538-9516. 18/6,515/71. 15 minutes from Pebble Beach Golf Links. You must stay at resort to play course.

TICKETS & ACCESSIBILITY

How to watch: Mon., PGA practice rounds. Tue., PGA practice rounds, shoot-out. Wed., PGA practice rounds, Celebrity Challenge, youth golf clinic. Thur.-Sun., tournament. Individual daily tickets start at $10. Group and sponsorship packages available. Spectators 12 years of age and under admitted free if accompanied by an adult. AT&T Pebble Beach National Pro-Am, P.O. Box 869, Monterey, CA 93942. (408) 649-1533, (800) 541-9091.

How to play: Pebble Beach is open year-round and tee times can be reserved by resort guests up to 18 months in advance, the public up to 24 hrs. in advance. (408) 624-3811, (800) 654-9300. Packages available through the resort. Poppy Hills is open year-round and takes tee time reservations a month in advance. (408) 625-2035. Spyglass is open year-round and tee times can be made 18 months in advance by guests of The Lodge at Pebble Beach or the Inn at Spanish Bay. Packages are available through the resort. Groups of two or more players may make reservations 60 days in advance. (408) 625-8563 (golf course), (800) 654-9300 (resort).

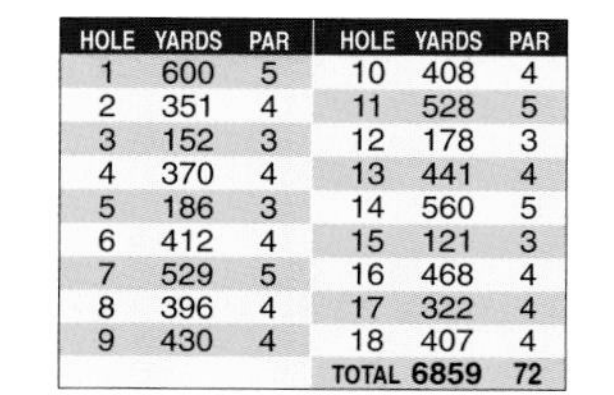

HOLE	YARDS	PAR	HOLE	YARDS	PAR
1	600	5	10	408	4
2	351	4	11	528	5
3	152	3	12	178	3
4	370	4	13	441	4
5	186	3	14	560	5
6	412	4	15	121	3
7	529	5	16	468	4
8	396	4	17	322	4
9	430	4	18	407	4
			TOTAL	6859	72

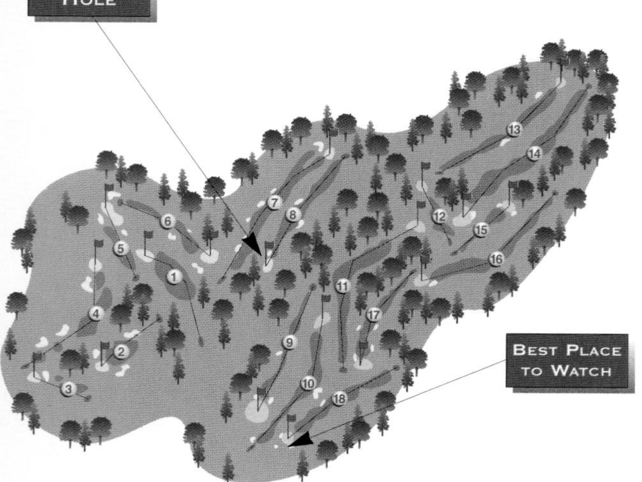

SPYGLASS HILL GOLF COURSE
ARCHITECT: ROBERT TRENT JONES SR. (1966)

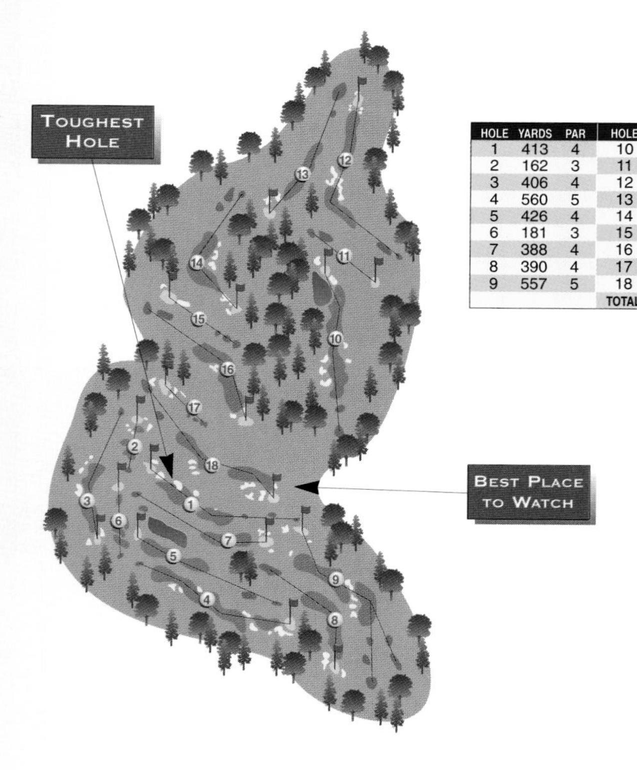

HOLE	YARDS	PAR	HOLE	YARDS	PAR
1	413	4	10	511	5
2	162	3	11	214	3
3	406	4	12	531	5
4	560	5	13	393	4
5	426	4	14	417	4
6	181	3	15	210	3
7	388	4	16	439	4
8	390	4	17	163	3
9	557	5	18	500	5
			TOTAL	6861	72

POPPY HILLS GOLF CLUB
ARCHITECT: ROBERT TRENT JONES JR. (1986)

●TOUGHEST HOLE

The eighth at Robert Trent Jones's Spyglass is a 396-yard par-4 that plays to a left-to-right sloping fairway bordered by trees. The approach shot is severely uphill and must avoid the large bunker to its right front. Robert Trent Jones Jr.'s Poppy Hills leads off with its toughest tournament hole, a 413-yard par-4 that takes a sharp right turn to a well-bunkered green.

●BEST PLACE TO WATCH

At Spyglass, check out the No. 18 green, No. 9 green, No. 1 tee and No. 10 tee, all in the golf shop area. The first five holes, reminiscent of Pine Valley, should be walked. At Poppy Hills, catch the action from near the 18th green or the ninth, both close to the spacious clubhouse.

●WHO THE COURSE FAVORS

Spyglass is considered by some to be a better golf course than Pebble Beach. More penal than Pebble Beach, Spyglass requires precision shotmaking from the tee to the demanding greens, which range in size from 18 to 50 yards in depth. Poppy Hills requires distance and accuracy off the tees because of trees and bunkers guarding the landing areas. The large greens can be forgiving on approach shots but three-putts are possible once you get there.

Buick Invitational of California

Torrey Pines Golf Courses

Torrey Pines Golf Courses, two municipal layouts set beside the 1,100-acre Torrey Pines State Preserve above the Pacific Ocean, are a justifiable focus of civic pride in the San Diego area. They are consistently ranked among the nation's top public courses.

The Spaniards who colonized this area called it La Jolla, "The Jewel," and the rolling terrain along its oceanside bluffs is dotted with cypress, eucalyptus and torrey pines, and populated with deer, bobcat and a variety of birds.

Both courses, the North and the South, opened in 1957 and were designed by William P. Bell and his son, William F. Bell, who saw the project through after his father's death. The Torrey Pines courses are characterized by strong winds off the Pacific, a variety of elevation changes and mildly undulating, quick, bentgrass greens that can be difficult to read. The shorter North Course offers a variety of doglegs, including a 421-yard par-4 13th that turns sharply left around a canyon, with trees and bunkers guarding the bend.

The longer South Course, the sole course used for the final two rounds of the tournament, starts off with one of the tougher tournament holes, a 447-yard par-4 that plays to a deep, forward sloping green. But the finishing hole, a 498-yard par-5, is often the scene of critical lead changes in this event.

Bruce Devlin was three shots off the lead coming into the 18th in 1975, but he caught the elongated pond in front of the green and took a 10 on the hole to drop into 30th place. A plaque commemorating this event now marks the spot.

Tom Weiskopf dropped an eagle putt from just off the 18th green to win the 1968 tournament by one stroke. In 1982, Jack Nicklaus hit a 3-wood to within 8 feet of the cup, then eagled the hole for a course record-tying 64. But Johnny Miller, who had a seven-shot lead at the beginning of the round, cautiously parred the same hole to win by a stroke. La Jolla High School graduate Craig Stadler withstood a final-hole birdie by runner-up Steve Lowery to take the 1994 event, and 1995 champion Peter Jacobsen birdied the 18th to punctuate a decisive four-stroke victory in his second consecutive Tour win.

Inaugurated in 1952 as the San Diego Open, this tournament bore the name of celebrity host Andy Williams for 21 years beginning in 1968.

TOURNAMENT-AT-A-GLANCE

Course: Torrey Pines—North and South Courses
Type: Public
Location: 11480 Torrey Pines Rd., La Jolla, CA 92037
Telephone: (619) 452-3226
When: Feb 8–11, 1996
How To Get There: Take I-5 to Gennessee Exit, take Gennessee Ave. west to North Torrey Pines Rd., turn north to golf course.
Broadcast: NBC, cable TBA (1996)
Purse: $1,200,000 (1996)
Tournament Record: 22-under-par 266, George Burns, 1987

●TOUGHEST HOLE

The toughest hole to par on the North Course during the 1995 event was the 400-yard, par-4 seventh, an uphill dogleg right with a canyon to the left and trees to the right. The ball tends to bounce left on the tee shot; the approach is to a small green guarded by three traps. Another difficult par-4 is the 453-yard seventh on the South Course, home of the two final rounds. This dogleg right plays into the wind to an angled green that's set into the hill.

●BEST PLACE TO WATCH

There are many excellent vantage points on these beautiful oceanside courses. The green at the 173-yard, par-3 third on the South Course offers a good view of the ocean, the fourth tee and the fifth green. The third hole on the North Course, a 121-yard par-3, is another good spectator spot, as are the finishing holes on both courses. The South Course's eighth hole, a 171-yard par-3, has sightlines to the 17th green and to the ninth and 18th tees.

●WHO THE COURSE FAVORS

The golfer who can successfully negotiate the ocean winds with distance and accuracy yet has touch and patience on the fast greens. Stormy and wet weather can greatly affect play at tournament time. For example, in 1986, heavy rains canceled third-round action. In 1992, the third round was canceled due to fog.

A birdie hole, the North Course's No. 3 is the tournament's shortest, at 121 yards.

HOLE	YARDS	PAR	HOLE	YARDS	PAR
1	447	4	10	373	4
2	365	4	11	207	3
3	173	3	12	468	4
4	453	4	13	535	5
5	404	4	14	398	4
6	535	5	15	356	4
7	453	4	16	203	3
8	171	3	17	425	4
9	536	5	18	498	5
			TOTAL	7000	72

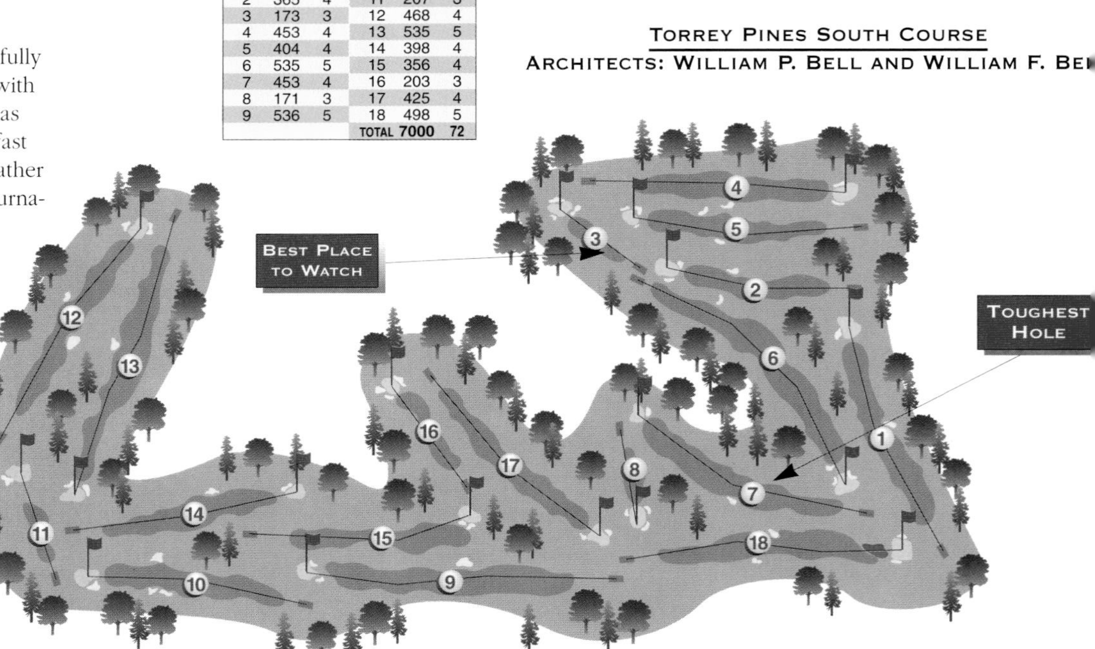

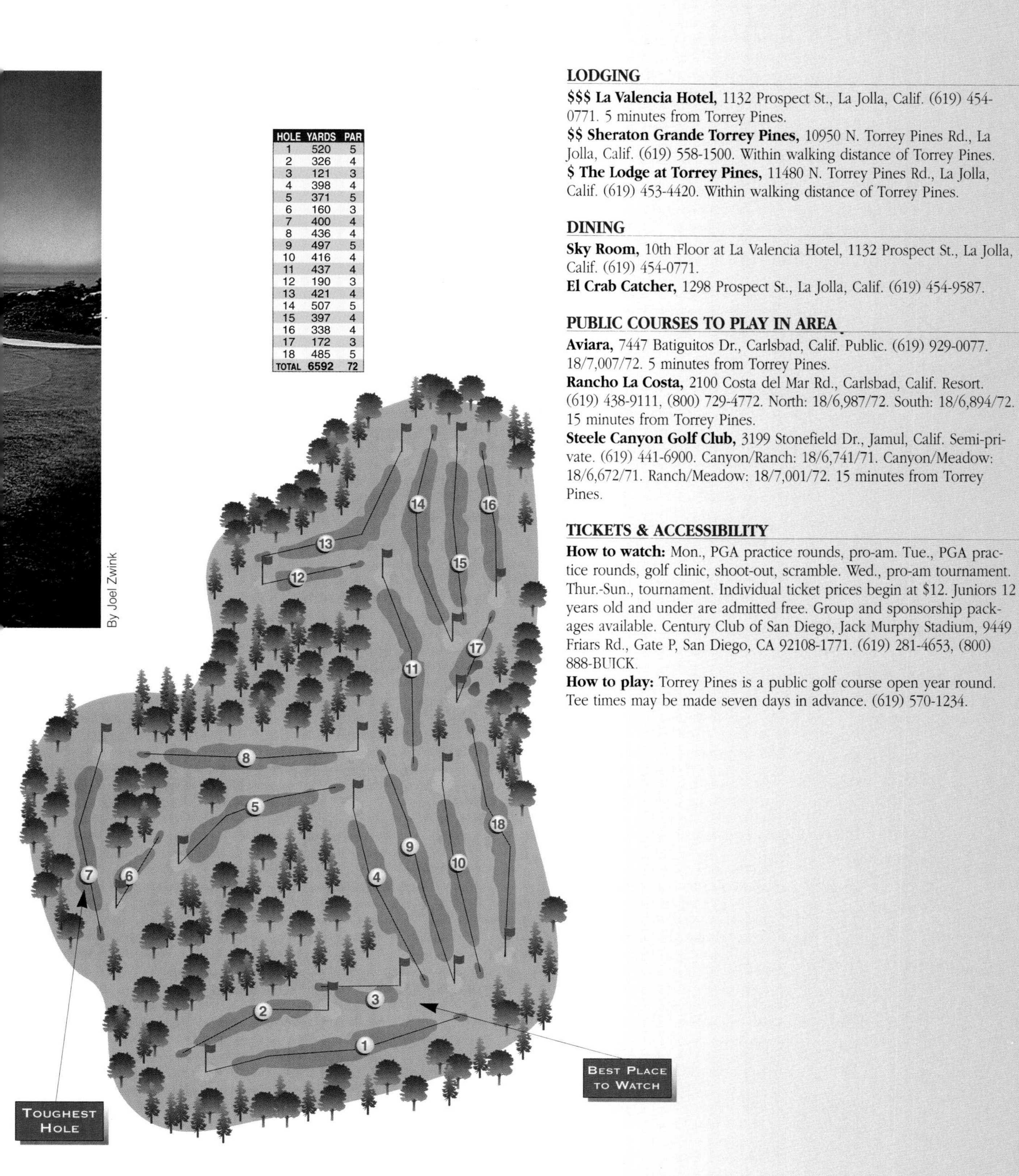

HOLE	YARDS	PAR
1	520	5
2	326	4
3	121	3
4	398	4
5	371	5
6	160	3
7	400	4
8	436	4
9	497	5
10	416	4
11	437	4
12	190	3
13	421	4
14	507	5
15	397	4
16	338	4
17	172	3
18	485	5
TOTAL	6592	72

Torrey Pines North Course
Architects: William P. Bell and William F. Bell

LODGING

$$$ La Valencia Hotel, 1132 Prospect St., La Jolla, Calif. (619) 454-0771. 5 minutes from Torrey Pines.

$$ Sheraton Grande Torrey Pines, 10950 N. Torrey Pines Rd., La Jolla, Calif. (619) 558-1500. Within walking distance of Torrey Pines.

$ The Lodge at Torrey Pines, 11480 N. Torrey Pines Rd., La Jolla, Calif. (619) 453-4420. Within walking distance of Torrey Pines.

DINING

Sky Room, 10th Floor at La Valencia Hotel, 1132 Prospect St., La Jolla, Calif. (619) 454-0771.

El Crab Catcher, 1298 Prospect St., La Jolla, Calif. (619) 454-9587.

PUBLIC COURSES TO PLAY IN AREA

Aviara, 7447 Batiguitos Dr., Carlsbad, Calif. Public. (619) 929-0077. 18/7,007/72. 5 minutes from Torrey Pines.

Rancho La Costa, 2100 Costa del Mar Rd., Carlsbad, Calif. Resort. (619) 438-9111, (800) 729-4772. North: 18/6,987/72. South: 18/6,894/72. 15 minutes from Torrey Pines.

Steele Canyon Golf Club, 3199 Stonefield Dr., Jamul, Calif. Semi-private. (619) 441-6900. Canyon/Ranch: 18/6,741/71. Canyon/Meadow: 18/6,672/71. Ranch/Meadow: 18/7,001/72. 15 minutes from Torrey Pines.

TICKETS & ACCESSIBILITY

How to watch: Mon., PGA practice rounds, pro-am. Tue., PGA practice rounds, golf clinic, shoot-out, scramble. Wed., pro-am tournament. Thur.-Sun., tournament. Individual ticket prices begin at $12. Juniors 12 years old and under are admitted free. Group and sponsorship packages available. Century Club of San Diego, Jack Murphy Stadium, 9449 Friars Rd., Gate P, San Diego, CA 92108-1771. (619) 281-4653, (800) 888-BUICK.

How to play: Torrey Pines is a public golf course open year round. Tee times may be made seven days in advance. (619) 570-1234.

Bob Hope Chrysler Classic

INDIAN RIDGE COUNTRY CLUB, BERMUDA DUNES COUNTRY CLUB, INDIAN WELLS COUNTRY CLUB, TAMARISK COUNTRY CLUB

When the motion picture industry set roots in the arid terrain outside Los Angeles, it doomed many of its early stars—like W.C. Fields, Harold Lloyd, Douglas Fairbanks, Bob Hope and Bing Crosby—to become golf addicts.

Crosby, a one-time British Amateur competitor, developed his own celebrity golf tournament in 1937, and his *Road* movie sidekick followed suit almost three decades later when the five-year-old Palm Springs Golf Classic was redubbed the Bob Hope Desert Classic in 1965. These celebrity pro-am events have played a significant role in golf's modern history, adding a glitzy entertainment element to the game, popularizing its players through expanded television coverage, and raising millions of dollars for charity.

The Bob Hope Chrysler Classic is a bit unusual in that it's a 90-hole event played on four Palm Springs–area golf courses. Pros circulate among three-player amateur teams for the first four days, then the professionals play alone on the final day. Amateurs who have participated include Clint Eastwood, Mike Ditka, John Denver, Jim Palmer, Joe Pesci, Willie Mays and many others. The 1995 event featured a pro-am foursome that grouped President Clinton with former Presidents Ford and Bush. Bob Hope, now in his 90s, played an 18-hole round to celebrate the occasion.

The courses in the Bob Hope rotation are open, well-manicured and rolling, with an abundance of bunkers, especially around the greens.

Bermuda Dunes, opened in 1959 and one of the desert's oldest golf courses, has been in the rotation since the tournament began. Surrounded by the Santa Rosa, San Jacinto and Shadow mountain ranges, its tree-lined fairways require precise drives and second shots. There are more than 60 bunkers on the course, but water comes into play on only four holes. The course concludes with the signature 513-yard, par-5 18th, a beautiful dogleg right whose second shot must at times cross a sculpted pond to the right front of a deep green guarded by three bunkers.

The Indian Wells Country Club, another old desert course, opened in 1956 but was remodeled by Ted Robinson in the 1980s. The greens on this layout are large and well-bunkered. Water can come into play on five holes, including the 501-yard, par-5 finishing hole, whose approach is uphill to a green guarded by a bunker to its right and a pond to its left.

The Tamarisk Country Club opened in 1952 and is the third-oldest club in the desert, but the first to add water hazards. Recently, lakes have been moved and new bunkers added, while the greens, most of which are fairly large, have been redesigned and the course recontoured. One of the best holes on this course is the 225-yard, par-3 14th, which plays to a large green guarded by four traps.

The Indian Ridge Country Club, an Arnold Palmer design, is the host club for the 1996 tournament. Citrus and palm trees dot this rolling layout, which has large, sculpted bunkers and water hazards on 11 holes. The professionals will play from tees set at 7,037 yards in the tournament and the amateurs will tee it up at 6,530 yards. If past is prologue, there is likely to be an exciting finish at the 423-yard, par-4 18th. The approach on this hole is to a deep green bordered to the right by bunkers and to the left by a lake fed by multilevel pools. There have been 13 sudden-death playoffs in this tournament, so this is the place to be on the final day.

Kenny Perry squeaked by to win the 1995 event with rounds of 63-71-64-67-70–335 to edge David Dural by one stroke. Arnold Palmer won a record five Desert Classics, including his 60th and last PGA Tour win, which he seized by outdueling Jack Nicklaus in 1973.

TOURNAMENT-AT-A-GLANCE

Courses: Indian Ridge Country Club, Bermuda Dunes Country Club, Indian Wells Country Club, Tamarisk Country Club
Type: Private
Location: Indian Ridge Country Club, 76-375 Country Club Dr., Palm Desert, CA 92211
Telephone: (619) 772-7272
When: Jan. 17–21, 1996
How To Get There: Take I-10 to Washington Exit. Proceed south on Washington to Country Club Dr., right on Country Club Dr. to Indian Ridge Dr. and the golf course.
Broadcast: NBC (1996)
Purse: $1,300,000 (1996)
Tournament Record: 35-under-par 325, Tom Kite, 1993

Courtesy of Bob Hope Chrysler Classic

ONE OF THE CLASSIC'S FOUNDING CLUBS, TAMARISK WAS THE FIRST PALM DESERT SPREAD TO USE WATER HAZARDS.

●TOUGHEST HOLE

Indian Ridge has two strong holes coming down the stretch. The 452-yard, par-4 16th has a generous tee-shot landing area, but large traps around the green provide trouble. The 423-yard, par-4 18th plays straight to a deep green bordered to the right by large bunkers and to the left by multilevel pools and a lake. The toughest hole on the course, however, is the 459-yard, par-4 12th. One of Tamarisk's toughest is its 13th, a 417-yard dogleg left that plays to a deep green guarded by a bunker to its front left and another to the right. The three-tiered green adds to its difficulty.

●BEST PLACE TO WATCH

These desert courses are relatively flat and easy to walk as you follow your favorite celebrities and players. You will want to catch the action on some of the excellent par-3s on these courses, most notably the 13th at Indian Wells, the fourth and 17th at Bermuda Dunes, and the ninth and 14th at Tamarisk. The finishing holes are good places to be as the rounds and tournament draw to a close, especially the scenic final hole at Indian Ridge, which is an easy walk from the clubhouse, practice range, first tee, ninth green, 15th green and 16th tee.

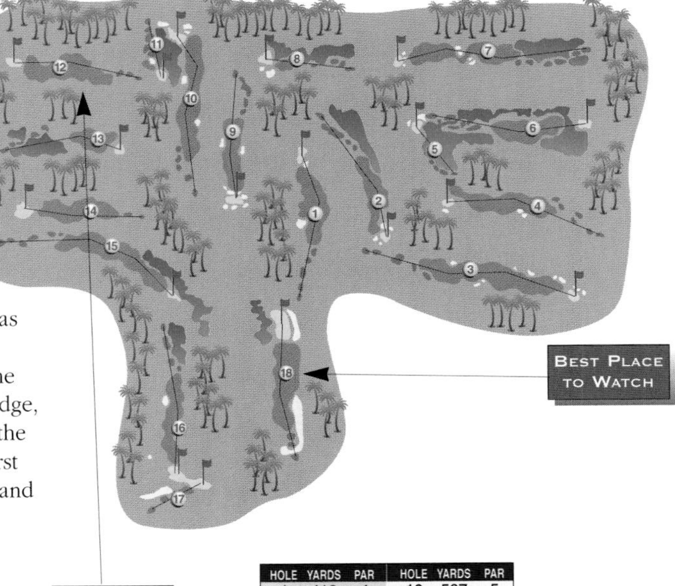

HOLE	YARDS	PAR	HOLE	YARDS	PAR
1	482	5	10	407	4
2	171	3	11	191	3
3	443	4	12	550	5
4	509	5	13	417	4
5	199	3	14	225	3
6	375	4	15	423	4
7	331	4	16	404	4
8	393	4	17	395	4
9	439	4	18	527	5
			TOTAL	6881	72

TAMARISK COUNTRY CLUB (NOT PICTURED)
ARCHITECT: WILLIAM P. BELL (1952)

HOLE	YARDS	PAR	HOLE	YARDS	PAR
1	418	4	10	507	5
2	408	4	11	152	3
3	609	5	12	459	4
4	427	4	13	335	4
5	209	3	14	424	4
6	430	4	15	530	5
7	524	5	16	452	4
8	203	3	17	159	3
9	368	4	18	423	4
			TOTAL	7037	72

INDIAN RIDGE
ARCHITECT: ARNOLD PALMER (1993)

LODGING

$$$ The Ritz-Carlton Rancho Mirage, 68-900 Frank Sinatra Dr., Rancho Mirage, Calif. (619) 321-8282, (800) 241-3333. 10 minutes from tournament courses.

$$ Hyatt Regency Suites Palm Springs, 285 N. Palm Canyon Dr., Palm Springs, Calif. (619) 322-9000, (800) 233-1234. 10 minutes from tournament courses.

$ Courtyard by Marriott, 1300 Tahquitz Way, Palm Springs, Calif. (619) 322-6100. 10 minutes from tournament courses.

DINING

The Dining Room at the Ritz-Carlton Rancho Mirage, 68-900 Frank Sinatra Dr., Rancho Mirage, Calif. (619) 321-8282.

Las Casuelas Original, 368 N. Palm Canyon Dr., Palm Springs, Calif. (619) 325-3213.

Marie Callendors, 69-830 Hwy. 111, Rancho Mirage, Calif. (619) 328-0844.

PUBLIC COURSES TO PLAY IN AREA

The Field Golf Club, 19300 Palm Dr., Desert Hot Springs, Calif. Public. (619) 251-5366. 18/6,876/72. 20 minutes from tournament courses.

PGA West, 56-150 PGA Blvd., La Quinta, Calif. Resort. (619) 564-7170. Jack Nicklaus Resort Course: 18/7,126/72. The Stadium Course: 18/7,261/72. 10 minutes from tournament courses.

La Quinta, 49-499 Eisenhower Dr., La Quinta, Calif. Resort. (619) 564-7610 (golf course), (800) 854-1271 (resort). 10 minutes from tournament courses.

TICKETS & ACCESSIBILITY

How to watch: Mon., PGA and amateur practice rounds. Tue., PGA and amateur practice rounds, shoot-out. Wed.-Sun., tournament. Individual tickets begin at $10. Group and sponsorship plans available. Bob Hope Chrysler Classic, P.O. Box 865, 3900 Bob Hope Dr., Rancho Mirage, CA 92270, (619) 346-8184.

How to play: Bermuda Dunes, Indian Wells, Indian Ridge and Tamarisk are private clubs reserved for members and their guests only. Reciprocal play can be arranged at Indian Wells. Bermuda Dunes, (619) 345-2232; Indian Ridge, (619) 772-7272; Indian Wells, (619) 345-2561; Tamarisk, (619) 328-2141.

●TOUGHEST HOLE

The toughest hole at Indian Wells is the 446-yard, par-4 10th, where the tee shot plays uphill and the green is squeezed by traps in front. Another challenge on this course is the 197-yard, par-3 13th, which plays to a green framed by two large bunkers. A cluster of trees to the right of the green could cause trouble if the ball is strayed. Among the most difficult holes to par on the Bermuda Dunes course are two par-3s. The 209-yard fourth requires extreme accuracy with a long iron in order to avoid the four traps surrounding the small green. The 212-yard 17th also has four traps guarding its putting surface. Out-of-bounds is to the left.

●WHO THE COURSE FAVORS

These short courses were built for club players and tourists. The weather here is usually perfect, the conditions immaculate and the scores low. The courses tend to favor players who can manage their overall games while playing with amateurs for the first four rounds of this five-round marathon. Players with good all-around games like Tom Kite, Billy Casper, Jack Nicklaus, Corey Pavin, Johnny Miller and Peter Jacobsen have all won here. Also, it helps to have played here before, because competitors will play four different courses in five days and the hybrid Bermuda-grass greens can be tricky. The local lore is that all greens break toward Indio, a town southeast of the tournament venues.

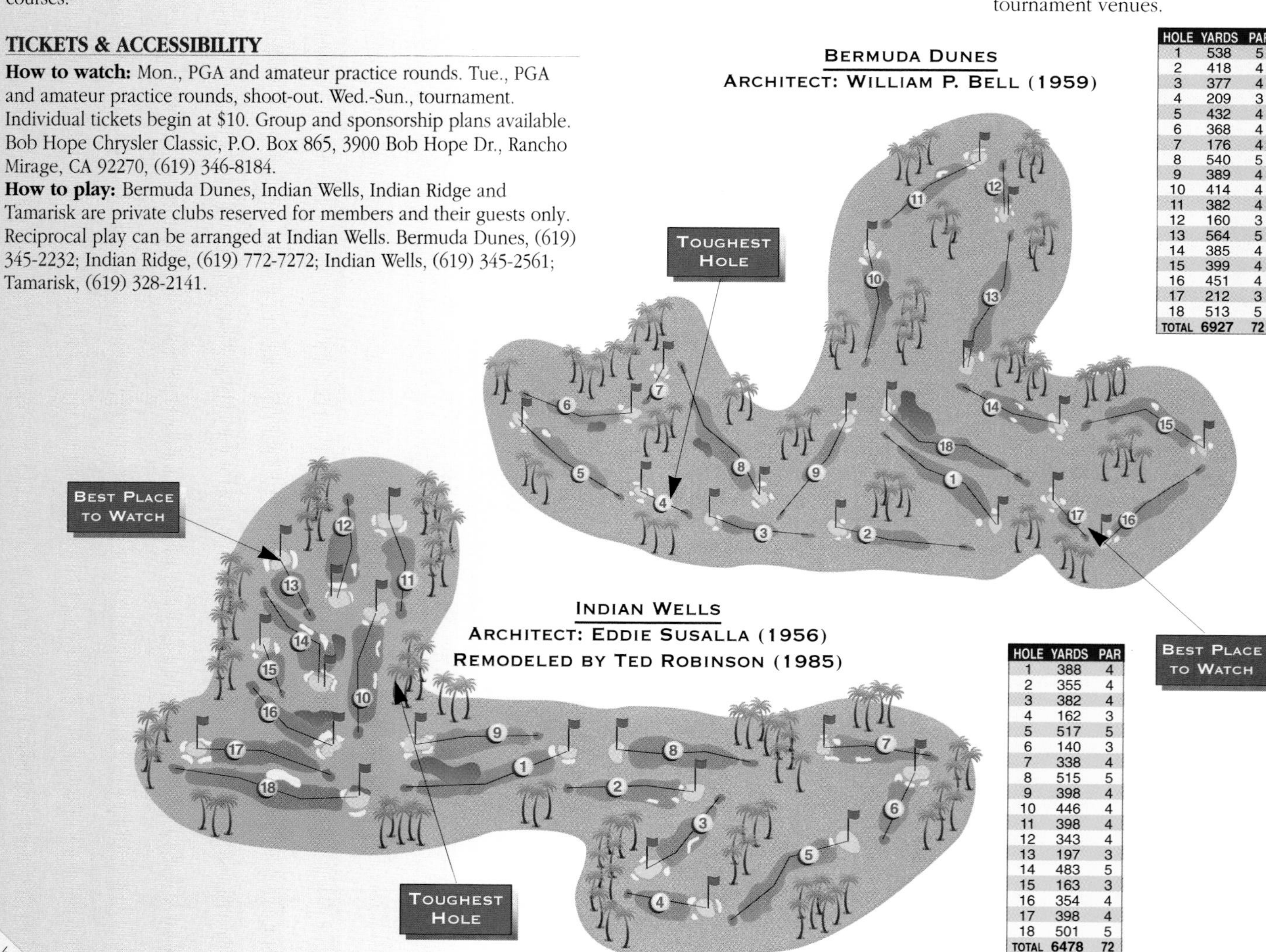

HOLE	YARDS	PAR
1	538	5
2	418	4
3	377	4
4	209	3
5	432	4
6	368	4
7	176	4
8	540	5
9	389	4
10	414	4
11	382	4
12	160	3
13	564	5
14	385	4
15	399	4
16	451	4
17	212	3
18	513	5
TOTAL	6927	72

HOLE	YARDS	PAR
1	388	4
2	355	4
3	382	4
4	162	3
5	517	5
6	140	3
7	338	4
8	515	5
9	398	4
10	446	4
11	398	4
12	343	4
13	197	3
14	483	5
15	163	3
16	354	4
17	398	4
18	501	5
TOTAL	6478	72

Honda Classic

TPC at Heron Bay

LODGING

$$$ Marriott's Harbor Beach Resort, 3030 Holiday Dr., Fort Lauderdale, Fla. (305) 525-4000, (800) 222-6543. 30 minutes from TPC at Heron Bay.
$$ Carriage House Resort Motel, 250 S. Ocean Blvd., Deerfield Beach, Fla. (305) 427-7670. 15 minutes from TPC at Heron Bay.
$ Riverside Hotel, 620 E. Las Olas Blvd., Fort Lauderdale, Fla. (305) 467-0671, (800) 325-3280. 25 minutes from TPC at Heron Bay.

DINING

Sheffield's, in Marriott's Harbor Beach Resort, 3030 Holiday Dr., Fort Lauderdale, Fla. (305) 525-4000.
Cap's Place, Cap's Dock, 2765 N.E. 28th Ct., Lighthouse Point, Fla. (305) 941-0418.
Grainary Cafe, 847 S. Federal Hwy., Deerfield Beach, Fla. (305) 360-0883.

PUBLIC COURSES TO PLAY IN AREA

Arrowhead Country Club, 8201 S.W. 24th St., Fort Lauderdale, Fla. Semi-private. (305) 475-8200. 18/6,506/71. 10 minutes from TPC at Heron Bay.
PGA National Golf Club, 400 Avenue of Champions, Palm Beach Gardens, Fla. Resort. (407) 627-2000, (800) 633-9150. Champion: 18/7,022/72. Haig: 18/6,806/72. Squire: 18/6,498/72. General: 18/6,768/72. Estate: 18/6,784/72. 30 minutes from TPC at Heron Bay.
West Palm Beach Country Club, 7001 Parker Ave., West Palm Beach, Fla. Public. (407) 582-2019. 18/6,789/72. 45 minutes from TPC at Heron Bay.

TICKETS & ACCESSIBILITY

How to watch: Mon.-Wed., PGA practice rounds. Thur.-Sun., tournament. Individual tickets begin at $25 for the week. Group and sponsorship plans available. Honda Classic, 2608 Country Club Way, Fort Lauderdale, FL 33332. (305) 346-4000.
How to play: TPC Heron Bay is a privately owned public course open year-round. (305) 340-3852.

TOURNAMENT-AT-A-GLANCE

Course: TPC at Heron Bay
Type: Public
Location: 66100 Coral Ridge Dr., Coral Springs, FL 33076
Telephone: (305) 340-3852
When: March 7–10, 1996
How To Get There: From Miami, 50 minutes. Take I-95 to Rte. 595. Take Rte. 595 West to Sawgrass Hwy. Take Sawgrass north to Coral Ridge Drive Exit. Follow signs to golf course.
Broadcast: NBC (1996)
Purse: $1,200,000 (1995)
Tournament Record: 22-under-par 266, Blaine McCallister, 1989

The Honda Classic originated in 1972 as Jackie Gleason's Inverrary Classic, named after the portly comedian who loved golf and had a fully equipped bar in his air-conditioned, customized golf cart. Many of golf's great players, including Jack Nicklaus, Lee Trevino and Johnny Miller, have won this event, which in 1996 takes up residence at a new home on the edge of the Everglades.

The recently completed TPC at Heron Bay, designed by Mark McCumber, is an open, windswept golf course with young oaks and sable palms that in the short term will have little impact on shotmaking. There are more than 100 sizeable bunkers at Heron Bay, and they heavily guard most of the medium-size, Bermuda-grass greens. The shifting winds are a key factor, especially in March.

●TOUGHEST HOLE

The most difficult hole on the new TPC at Heron Bay could be the 445-yard, par-4 finishing hole, which is bordered on the right by water from tee to green. Variable March winds will make the approach shot to the medium-sized green a test of nerves. The putting surface is guarded by a bunker to its front left and another to the back right. The green slopes toward the water, which borders it to the right.

●BEST PLACE TO WATCH

The final four holes are likely to decide the outcome of the tournament the final day. A spectator hub with telephone, food service and other amenities is conveniently located near the 18th hole and enables you to see the 16th tee, 17th green, the 11th green and tee, and the 18th tee. Similar spectator hubs are near Nos. 4 and 7, behind No. 15, and in an area near Nos. 12, 13 and 14.

●WHO THE COURSE FAVORS

The TPC at Heron Bay favors a big hitter who can keep the ball out of the more than 100 bunkers on the course and adjust to the variable wind conditions that can suddenly cause a downwind hole to play into the wind. An ability to recover from bunkers is essential on this open course.

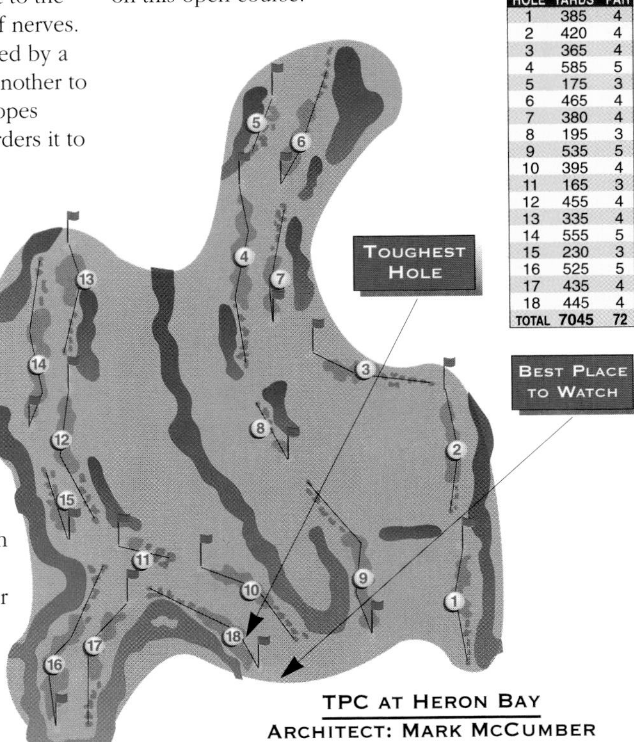

HOLE	YARDS	PAR
1	385	4
2	420	4
3	365	4
4	585	5
5	175	3
6	465	4
7	380	4
8	195	3
9	535	5
10	395	4
11	165	3
12	455	4
13	335	4
14	555	5
15	230	3
16	525	5
17	435	4
18	445	4
TOTAL	7045	72

TPC at Heron Bay
Architect: Mark McCumber and Associates (1995)

Nissan Open

RIVIERA COUNTRY CLUB

One of the most elite golf clubs in the Los Angeles area began with a dare and a plot of land that looked hopeless.

Built in the 1920s as a refuge from the anti-Semitic policies of the city's other tony clubs, the Riviera Country Club was carved out of 240 acres of tangled brush, cactus, eucalyptus, pin oaks and sycamore in the Santa Monica Canyon. Gauging the land's prospects, course architect George Thomas at first refused the task, then accepted the challenge for no fee when property owners at the Los Angeles Country Club suggested he might not be man enough for the job.

TOURNAMENT-AT-A-GLANCE

Course: Riviera Country Club
Type: Private
Location: 1250 Capri Dr., Pacific Palisades, CA 90272
Telephone: (310) 454-6591
When: Feb. 22–25, 1996
How To Get There: Take Sunset Blvd. to Capri Dr., turn south onto Capri to clubhouse.
Broadcast: USA, CBS (1996)
Purse: $1,200,000 (1996)
Tournament Record: 20-under-par 264, Lanny Wadkins, 1985

That dare would cost the club $650,000, making Riviera the most expensive golf course in the world at the time, but when a work crew of more than 200 had cut down many trees, planted others, and transported tons of sand and topsoil under the direction of Thomas and his assistant William P. Bell, one of the nation's finest courses was ready to test early members like Clark Gable, W.C. Fields, Spencer Tracy and Will Rogers. By 1929, it was suitable to the honor of co-hosting the fourth annual Los Angeles Open, the richest tournament in golf.

An arduous test of strategic shotmaking, Riviera is loaded with distinctive holes, including a doughnut-shaped green with a pot bunker at its center on No. 6. The pros practically gush over some other classics: Ben Hogan called the 238-yard fourth "the greatest par-3 hole in America." Tom Watson named both the par-4 10th and the par-4 finishing hole to his "Dream 18."

Mature trees today add to the challenge and complexity of Riviera, which has many deep, sculpted traps and fast, bentgrass greens that range in size from 20 yards deep to just 38 yards on the par-5 17th. The fairways, carpeted by tightly clipped kikuyu grass, an African weed that tends to hold the ball up, are soft, minimizing roll. Though dormant and less troublesome during the Nissan Open's mid-winter visit, the kikuyu can be deadly when it grows into rough, especially around the greens.

Among the most difficult holes is the 447-yard, par-4 15th, a dogleg right that leads to a deep green protected by a huge trap to its right. But the toughest is probably the 447-yard, par-4 18th, which plays to a small green overlooked by a grand Spanish-style clubhouse and framed by a natural amphitheater hillside. More than 53,000 fans watched as Corey Pavin, a graduate of UCLA, parred this hole to win the first of two straight Los Angeles Opens in 1994. Another noteworthy L.A. Open repeat winner was Hogan, who won in 1942, 1947 and 1948, then returned to Riviera that summer to add the 1948 U.S. Open title. Dubbed "Hogan's Alley" by pundits—a nickname also claimed by Colonial Country Club in Fort Worth, Texas—Riviera was the scene of Hogan's comeback in 1950, less than a year after he nearly died in an automobile accident. Hogan, not expected to contend, lost to Sam Snead that weekend in an 18-hole playoff.

The 1948 Open and the 1983 and 1995 PGA Championships add luster to Riviera's history, but the annual event hosted by the high-tone club can also boast of a tradition of breaking barriers. In 1952, the tournament defied a PGA ban on black players by allowing Joe Louis to compete. Fourteen years earlier, Babe Didrickson Zaharias had become the first woman to play in a PGA men's event when she entered the 1938 L.A. Open, staged that year at nearby Griffith Park.

"[THE 10TH IS] ONE OF THE GREATEST PAR-4 HOLES IN THE WORLD. IT'S ONLY [311] YARDS, DOESN'T HAVE ANY OUT OF BOUNDS OR A WATER HAZARD, BUT IT'S A VERY DEMANDING HOLE."

—JERRY PATE,
1976 U.S. OPEN CHAMPION

RIVIERA'S PAR-4 NINTH HAS A TRICKY, UPHILL APPROACH TO A SLOPING GREEN.

●TOUGHEST HOLE

Riviera starts off with a benign 501-yard, par-5 birdie opportunity but then hits you with a 460-yard par-4, the most difficult hole to par in the 1995 Nissan event. The tee shot must be positioned to the right side of the narrow fairway in order to have an angle of approach past two bunkers guarding the left front and right front of the green. This hole, a par-5 for Riviera members, plays into a cutting wind. A difficult par-3 on this side is the 238-yard fourth hole whose tee shot is to a shallow green framed by a large bunker to its left. The green slopes severely from right to left, making it difficult to land a long iron or a wood.

●BEST PLACE TO WATCH

The natural amphitheater around the 18th green provides an excellent view of the final hole. The grove refreshment area is the central site for seeing the action on the No. 9 tee, No. 13 green and No. 18 green. The area between greens No. 3 and 17 is another good place to monitor a number of holes. At the far end of the course, fans can see the action next to the 16th green and can also watch tee shots on No. 6, a 170-yard par-3 with a trap in the middle of the green.

HOLE	YARDS	PAR	HOLE	YARDS	PAR
1	501	5	10	311	4
2	460	4	11	561	5
3	434	4	12	413	4
4	238	3	13	420	4
5	426	4	14	180	3
6	170	3	15	447	4
7	406	4	16	168	3
8	468	4	17	578	5
9	418	4	18	447	4
			TOTAL	6946	71

●WHO THE COURSE FAVORS

You have to have all the shots at Riviera and an ability to manage your game. Though short-hitting Corey Pavin is a two-time champion here, distance is a major benefit on the course's 460-yard, par-4 second; the 238-yard, par-3 fourth; the 468-yard, par-4 eighth; and the long par-5s on the back nine, the 561-yard, 11th and the 578-yard 17th. Holes like the 311-yard, par-4 10th, a tempting hole well guarded by bunkers, requires distance if you want to go for the green, but finesse if you miss. The tough kikuyu rough requires a deft touch around the greens to avert skidding balls across the hard, slick putting surfaces.

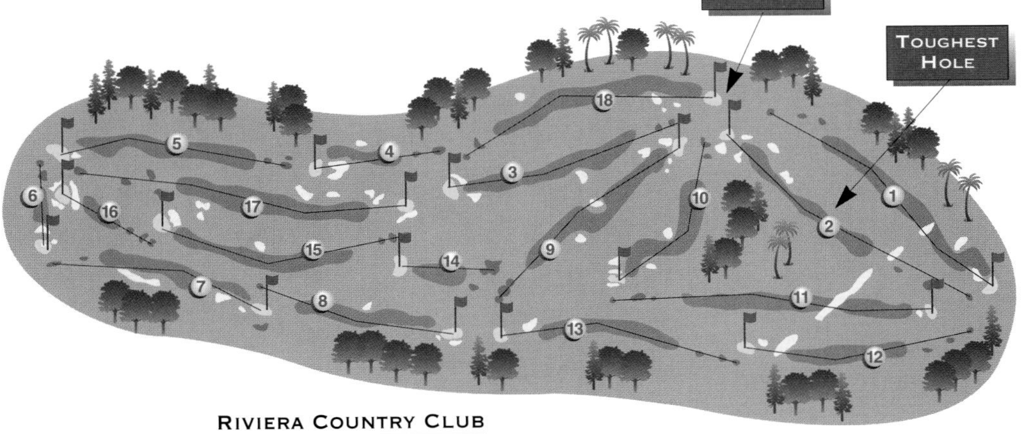

RIVIERA COUNTRY CLUB
ARCHITECTS: GEORGE THOMAS AND WILLIAM F. BELL (1926)

LODGING

$$$ Loews Santa Monica Beach Hotel, 1700 Ocean Ave., Santa Monica, Calif. (310) 458-6700, (800) 223-0888. 10 minutes from Riviera CC.

$$ Pacific Shore, 1819 Ocean Ave., Santa Monica, Calif. (310) 451-8711, (800) 622-8711. 10 minutes from Riviera CC.

$ Channel Road Inn Bed & Breakfast, 219 W. Channel Rd., Santa Monica, Calif. (310) 459-1920. 10 minutes from Riviera CC.

DINING

Beau Rivage, 26025 Pacific Coast Hwy., Malibu, Calif. (310) 456-5733.

Gladstone's 4 Fish, 17300 Pacific Coast Hwy., Pacific Palisades, Calif. (310) 454-3474.

Judy Maroni's Sausage Kingdom, 2011 Ocean Front Walk, Venice, Calif. (310) 306-1995.

PUBLIC COURSES TO PLAY IN AREA

Industry Hills, One Industry Hills Pkwy., City of Industry, Calif. Public. (818) 810-GOLF (golf course). Eisenhower: 18/7,181/72. The Babe: 18/6,778/71. 50 minutes from Riviera CC.

Pelican Hill Golf Club, 22653 Pelican Hill Rd. Newport Coast, Calif. Public. (714) 760-0707. Ocean: 18/6,647/70. Links: 18/6,856/71. 2 hours from Riviera CC.

Ojai Valley Inn and Country Club, Country Club Rd., Ojai, Calif. Resort. (805) 646-5511, (800) 422-OJAI. 18/6,252/70. 1 hour and 15 minutes from Riviera CC.

TICKETS & ACCESSIBILITY

How to watch: Sun., celebrity-am golf tournament, senior golf clinic. Mon., PGA practice rounds. Tue., PGA practice rounds, long drive competition, shoot-out. Wed., pro-am. Thur.-Sun., tournament. Ticket prices begin at $5. Groups and sponsorship packages available. Nissan Open, c/o Los Angeles Junior Chamber of Commerce, 350 Bitel St., Suite 100, Los Angeles, CA 90017. (213) 482-1311, (800) 752-OPEN.

How to play: Riviera Country Club is a private club. You must be a member or the guest of a member to play the course.

Doral-Ryder Open

DORAL RESORT & COUNTRY CLUB

The 667-room Doral Resort and Country Club is situated on 2,400 acres of former swampland within minutes of Miami International Airport. The resort features 99 holes of golf, but the centerpiece at Doral is "the Blue Monster," or Blue Course, a flat, 6,939-yard layout rich with tropical landscaping, eight man-made lakes, a network of streams and canals and more than 108 sand bunkers. The fairways are tightly guarded by water, bunkers and mature palms, and swirling winds off the nearby Atlantic can greatly complicate its challenges. The Bermuda-grass greens come in a variety of shapes and sizes ranging from the shallow but wide and well-bunkered dance floor on the par-4 second to the 61-yard-deep three-tiered stage on the par-4 17th.

TOURNAMENT-AT-A-GLANCE

Course: Doral Resort & Country Club—Blue Course
Type: Resort
Location: 4400 N.W. 87th Ave., Miami, FL 33178
Telephone: (305) 592-2000, (800) 327-6334
When: Feb. 29–March 3, 1996
How To Get There: From Miami International Airport, 15 minutes. Take Hwy. 836 west 2 miles to N.W. 87th Ave. Proceed north on N.W. 87th Ave. to resort.
Broadcast: USA, CBS (1996)
Purse: $1,500,000 (1996)
Tournament Record: 23-under-par 265, Greg Norman, 1993

The Blue Monster is noted for its difficult and long par-3 holes, including the 237-yard fourth, where a lake borders the right side from the fairway to a deep but narrow green guarded by three bunkers. The 174-yard par-3 15th provides a wide, shallow target backed by a bunker and fronted by two more. Incoming winds or crosswinds can make this green very elusive. It was here that John Huston hit an 8-iron tee shot to within 6 feet of the cup to ensure a win in the 1994 Doral.

The 1995 tournament illustrated why Raymond Floyd calls the 425-yard, par-4 18th "the toughest par-4 in the world" and how the entire course earned its nickname. Nick Faldo, playing ahead of third-round leaders Greg Norman and Peter Jacobsen, pulled his tee shot into the water and then, after dropping near the point of entry, hit a 3-wood to the green, bogeyed the hole and finished with 69 on the last day. Norman, who needed a par to win, pulled his drive into the heavy left rough, then yanked a 6-iron approach way left into the water and took a double-bogey six. Jacobsen was on the lower part of the deep green in two but could not sink his birdie attempt for a tie. Faldo took advantage of final round 73s by Norman and Jacobsen to win his first PGA event of the 1995 season and the $270,000 top prize.

"This hole is a monster," tournament director Frank Strafaci had said during the event's 1962 debut. "A blue monster."

Doral's developer, Alfred Kaskel, brought the PGA to Southern Florida with a splash in 1962 by putting up the richest purse on the Tour that year—$50,000. So pleased was Kaskel with Doral's monstrous reputation that in 1963, when Jack Nicklaus and Arnold Palmer exposed a shortcut on the dogleg 16th, Kaskel ordered groundskeeping crews to venture out under the dark of night to plant a row of palm trees at the bend.

Raymond Floyd is the only player to claim three victories at the Doral Open, including a gutsy win in 1992 just after the 49-year-old's nearby home was destroyed in a fire. Two-time winner Jack Nicklaus, who has finished second a record five times in the Doral, was victimized by Floyd in a playoff in 1980 when Floyd recovered from the trees to make par on the 18th. Nicklaus noted, "That hole can do it to you. I've seen it happen there plenty of times. You can hit two great shots and still not make par." Still Greg Norman shot his record 62 (twice!) on this course.

"SINCE 1987, WHEN I STOPPED COMING TO THE PGA TOUR REGULARLY, I FELT YOU HAD TO COME IN AND ACCLIMATIZE [TO CONDITIONS] IF YOU WANTED TO WIN."

—NICK FALDO,

WHO TOOK UP RESIDENCE IN FLORIDA IN 1995 IN ORDER TO PLAY MORE PGA TOUR EVENTS

Courtesy of Doral Resort & Country Club

CALLED "THE TOUGHEST PAR-4 IN THE WORLD" BY RAYMOND FLOYD, THE 18TH IS RESPONSIBLE FOR DORAL'S "BLUE MONSTER" NICKNAME.

●TOUGHEST HOLE

The 18th, birthplace of Doral's "Blue Monster" nickname, has provided a number of memorable finishes. This 425-yard, par-4 dogleg left is bordered by water on its left from tee to green. If the tee shot is to the left, it is either in the water or the golfer has to come into the right-to-left angled green over water. A pair of traps lurk on the other side of the putting surface. If the tee shot is too far right, the approach could be stymied by trees guarding the fairway. The wind often blows into the golfer on this hole, making it even more difficult. The most difficult par-3 on the course is the 246-yard 13th, which plays to a small, elevated green with two traps to its right and another to the left. Competitors have a difficult time holding this green with a long iron or wood.

●BEST PLACE TO WATCH

The Doral Blue Course is an easy layout to walk. Examine all the holes during the early rounds of the event, especially the long par-3s. The 237-yard fourth is a place to start. A limited number of bleacher seats overlook the ninth, 10th, 15th and 18th greens. The final hole often decides the tournament.

●WHO THE COURSE FAVORS

Winners at Doral are those who can hit the ball far but with enough control to negotiate the wind, water and sand. Approach shots are demanding because the smaller putting surfaces are well guarded by traps and mediocre shots onto the larger greens, like those on the seventh or the 18th, can easily lead to three putts. Champions here have included big hitters like Nicklaus, Norman and Tom Weiskopf, as well as solid shotmakers like Floyd, Billy Casper and Ben Crenshaw.

DORAL RESORT & COUNTRY CLUB—BLUE COURSE
ARCHITECTS: DICK WILSON WITH ROBERT VON HAGGE (1961)

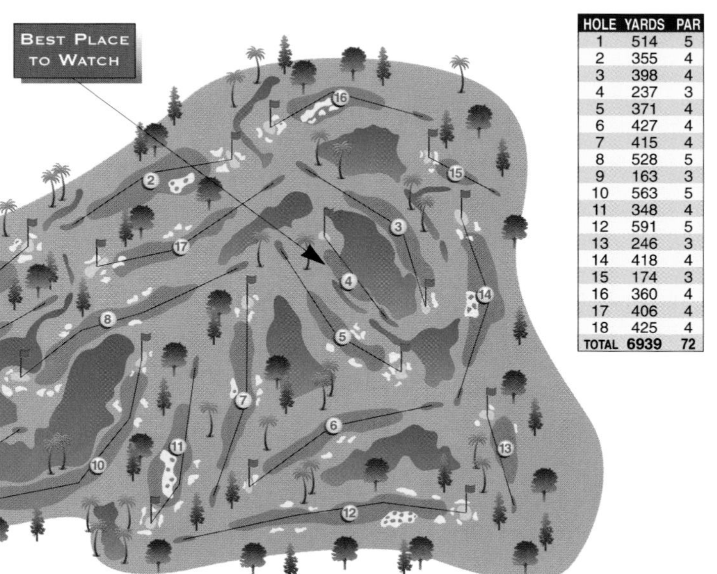

HOLE	YARDS	PAR
1	514	5
2	355	4
3	398	4
4	237	3
5	371	4
6	427	4
7	415	4
8	528	5
9	163	3
10	563	5
11	348	4
12	591	5
13	246	3
14	418	4
15	174	3
16	360	4
17	406	4
18	425	4
TOTAL	6939	72

LODGING

$$$ The Doral Golf Resort and Spa, 4400 N.W. 87th Ave., Miami. (305) 592-2000, (800) 327-6334. On site.

$$ Biscayne Bay Marriott Hotel & Marina, 1633 N. Bayshore Dr., Key Biscayne, Fla. (305) 374-3900, (800) 228-9290. 30 minutes from The Doral.

DINING

Biscayne Wine Merchants and Bistro, 12953 Biscayne Blvd., North Miami, Fla. (305) 899-1997.

PUBLIC COURSES TO PLAY IN AREA

The Links at Key Biscayne, Crandon Blvd., Key Biscayne, Fla. Public. (305) 361-9139. 18/7,070/72. 25 minutes from The Doral.

PGA National Golf Club, 400 Avenue of Champions, Palm Beach Gardens, Fla. Resort. (407) 627-1800, (800) 633-9150. Champion: 18/7,022/72. Haig: 18/6,806/72. Squire: 18/6,498/72. General: 18/6,768/72. Estate: 18/6,784/72. 30 minutes from The Doral.

Turnberry Isle Yacht and Country Club, 19999 West Country Club Dr., North Miami Beach, Fla. Resort. (305) 932-6200, (800) 327-7028. North: 18/6,323/70. South: 18/7,003/72. 35 minutes from The Doral.

TICKETS & ACCESSIBILITY

How to watch: Sun., pro-am tournament, PGA practice rounds. Mon., pro-am tournament, PGA practice rounds. Tue., Skins game, PGA practice rounds. Wed., pro-am. Thur.-Sun., tournament. Individual tickets start at $25. Group and sponsorship packages available. Doral-Ryder Open, P.O. Box 522927, Miami, FL 33152. (305) 477-4653.

How to play: The Doral is a year-round complete destination resort with five other courses besides the "Blue Monster." Red: 18/6,120/71. Gold: 18/6,384/70. White: 18/6,208/72. Silver: 18/6,801/72. Green: 9/1,085/27 (par-3). Tee times can be made at the time a resort reservation is made. Golf packages and seasonal discounts are available through the resort. The public can make tee times 24 hours in advance. The busiest season is late December through March. (305) 592-2000, (800) 327-6334.

Bay Hill Invitational

BAY HILL CLUB

By the time Arnold Palmer purchased Orlando's Bay Hill Golf Club in 1976, he had played most of the great golf courses of the world and had won 60 PGA Tour events, including four Masters (1958, 1960, 1962, 1964), two British Opens (1961, 1962) and the U.S. Open (1960).

This tournament has become a tribute to his legacy.

As a designer, Palmer has had a hand in creating more than 200 courses worldwide, but Bay Hill, designed in 1961 by Dick Wilson along with Joe Lee and Robert von Hagge, is Palmer's home track. The host has toughened it up for tournament play, and the course now merits a 74.6 USGA rating from the championship tees. Known for its length and its many lakes and ponds, Bay Hill stretches across relatively flat and open earth, but it has strategically placed bunkers, water or mature trees squeezing almost every landing area. A relentless strategic challenge, it offers a variety of doglegs, a range of green sizes and contours and a wide assortment of challenging approach angles. What's more, the difficult par-4s tend to play directly into the north wind, rewarding golfers like Palmer who can hit low tee shots for distance.

The course's tenacity can be felt from the first tee to the final green. The 441-yard par-4 first, rated the third most difficult hole in the 1995 Invitational, is a slight dogleg left with a string of three bunkers that forces big hitters to hold back. The approach must drop a dart between four large bunkers encircling a small, subtly contoured green.

Originally called the Bay Hill Citrus Classic, this Tour stop has been won by some of the biggest names in golf, including Palmer (1971), Lee Trevino (1975), Tom Kite (1982 and 1989), Payne Stewart (1987), Paul Azinger (1988), Fred Couples (1992), and Ben Crenshaw (1993). But the most dramatic finish to this competition occurred when Robert Gamez, then a 21-year-old Tour rookie, holed a 176-yard 7-iron on the classic finishing hole for an eagle to win the 1990 Invitational.

After a three-putt bogey on the 17th, Vijay Singh came to the final hole in 1994 tied for the lead. He hit his tee shot into the rough and couldn't reach the green in two. His second consecutive bogey dropped him into a second-place finish with Nick Price and Fuzzy Zoeller, and handed a long-awaited first Tour victory to veteran Loren Roberts.

Title-tempered now, Roberts returned in 1995 to become the first repeat winner in the tournament's history when he compensated for his short distance off the tee by consistently sinking key putts. Despite matching Singh's 1994 collapse with two finishing bogeys, Roberts topped a strong-finishing Brad Faxon by two strokes.

TOURNAMENT-AT-A-GLANCE

Course: Bay Hill Club—Challenger and Champion Nines
Type: Resort
Location: 9000 Bay Hill Blvd., Orlando, FL 32819
Telephone: (407) 876-2429, (800) 523-5999
When: March 14–17, 1996
How To Get There: From Orlando International Airport, 20 minutes. Take Bee Line Expressway (Hwy. 582) west to I-4. Take I-4 east to Exit 29 (State Rd. 482/Sand Lake Rd.), go west on Sand Lake to Apopka-Vineland Rd., then right on Apopka-Vineland, 1/2 mile to Bay Hill entrance (Bay Hill Blvd.) on left. Follow Bay Hill Blvd. to club on the right.
Broadcast: NBC (1996)
Purse: $1,200,000 (1995)
Tournament Record: 23-under-par 265, Brian Allin, 1973, (at par-72 Rio Pinar CC)

"THIS TOURNAMENT LAST YEAR GAVE ME CONFIDENCE TO PLAY AS WELL AS I DID. I'VE BEEN WORKING HARD, AND I FELT LIKE I WAS COMING AROUND. BUT HERE [AT BAY HILL] MY ATTITUDE CHANGES."

—LOREN ROBERTS,

WHO WON HIS SECOND STRAIGHT INVITATIONAL AT BAY HILL IN 1995

By Steve Hosid

THE INVITATIONAL HAS BECOME A TRIBUTE TO ARNOLD PALMER, BAY HILL'S OWNER AND HOST SINCE 1976.

●TOUGHEST HOLE

The 441-yard, par-4 18th is bordered by water to the right on the approach shot; the deep green is also guarded to its rear by a bunker and by two more to its left. The green used to be elevated, but when Arnold Palmer remodeled the course, he lowered its right side so that it is very easy to find the water. Bunker shots hit from the left or rear of the green can easily skid across the slick putting surface into the water. In 1983, 27 consecutive Tour players missed this green.

●BEST PLACE TO WATCH

The 18th hole is the place to be during the final day. The area around the ninth green, a 467-yard par-4, is another good spot. A series of mounds and bunkers surrounds this large putting surface, which is near the clubhouse. The bleachers around the green on the 481-yard, par-5 16th are another good vantage point as players decide whether to try to clear the pond in front of the green in two. This hole is in the middle of a sequence of five difficult finishing holes where much of the tournament drama takes place.

●WHO THE COURSE FAVORS

Bay Hill is long and tough. Because of the numerous sand bunkers and water hazards, a player must be long but in control; it is easy to roll up penalty strokes if you forget to think your way through this layout. Poorly placed approaches on the ample putting surfaces can easily lead to three putts.

BEST PLACE TO WATCH

TOUGHEST HOLE

HOLE	YARDS	PAR
1	401	4
2	218	3
3	395	4
4	530	5
5	365	4
6	543	5
7	197	3
8	424	4
9	467	4
10	400	4
11	428	4
12	570	5
13	364	4
14	206	3
15	425	4
16	481	5
17	219	3
18	441	4
TOTAL	7114	72

BAY HILL CLUB—CHALLENGER AND CHAMPION NINES
ARCHITECTS: DICK WILSON, JOE LEE AND ROBERT VON HAGGE (1961)
REMODELED BY ARNOLD PALMER (1981)

LODGING

$$$ Villas of Grand Cypress, One North Jacaranda, Orlando, Fla. (407) 239-4700, (800) 835-7377. 15 minutes from Bay Hill.
$$ Residence Inn by Marriott, 8800 Meadow Creek Dr., Lake Buena Vista, Fla. (407) 239-7700, (800) 331-3131. 20 minutes from Bay Hill.

DINING

Chatham's Place, 7575 Dr. Phillips Place, Orlando, Fla. (407) 345-2992.
Wekiwa Marina Restaurant, 1000 Miami Springs Rd., Longwood, Fla. (407) 862-9640.

PUBLIC COURSES TO PLAY IN AREA

Bay Hill Club, 9000 Bay Hill Blvd., Orlando, Fla. Resort. (407) 876-2429, (800) 523-5999. Challenger/Champion: 18/7,114/72. Charger: 9/3,060/36. 5 minutes from Bay Hill.
Hunters Creek Golf Course, 14401 Sports Club Way, Orlando, Fla. Public. (407) 240-4653. 18/7,432/72. 15 minutes from Bay Hill.
Walt Disney World, Lake Buena Vista, Fla. Resort. (407) 824-4321. Palm: 18/6,957/72. Magnolia: 18/7,190/72. Lake Buena Vista: 18/6,829/72. Osprey Ridge: 18/7,101/72. Eagle Pines: 18/6,772/72. Oak Trail: 9/2,913/36. 5 minutes from Bay Hill.

TICKETS & ACCESSIBILITY

How to watch: Mon., PGA practice rounds. Tue., pro-am tournament. Wed., PGA practice rounds, junior clinic. Thur.-Sun., tournament. Individual tickets start at $28. Group and sponsorship plans are available. PGA Tournament Office, Bay Hill Club and Lodge, Bay Hill Blvd., Orlando, FL 9000 Bay Hill Blvd., Orlando, FL 32819. (407) 876-2429, ext. 615.
How to play: Bay Hill is a resort course open to the public year round. The Challenger and Champion nines are used for the PGA tournament and another nine, the Charger, is available for play. Tee times can be made at the time of reservations at the resort, up to 1 year in advance. There are 70 rooms and two restaurants on site. Golf and seasonal discounts are available through the resort. This is also the headquarters for the Arnold Palmer Golf Academy. (407) 876-2429.

THE PLAYERS CHAMPIONSHIP

TPC AT SAWGRASS—STADIUM COURSE

A perpetual bridesmaid to golf's Grand Slam events, The Players Championship may finally be getting the respect it deserves. In recent years it has drawn a strong field including top international players like José María Olazábal and Bernhard Langer, who see the TPC at Sawgrass—an extremely challenging layout for golfers of all abilities—as a valuable tune-up for the Masters two weeks later. In 1994, Greg Norman wowed spectators and fellow Tour pros alike by opening with a 63 that tied Fred Couple's course record … and then firing three straight 67s for a 24-under total.

TOURNAMENT-AT-A-GLANCE

Course: TPC at Sawgrass—Stadium Course
Type: Resort
Location: Marriott at Sawgrass Resort, 1000 TPC Boulevard, Ponte Vedra Beach, FL 32082
Telephone: (904) 285-2261 (golf course), (800) 457-GOLF (resort)
When: March 28–31, 1996
How To Get There: Take I-95 to J. Turner Butler Blvd. (State Rd. 202), continue east 14 miles across Intracoastal Waterway to the beach. Proceed south on A1A 3 miles to resort.
Broadcast: NBC
Purse: $3,000,000 (1995)
Tournament Record: 24-under-par 264, Greg Norman, 1994

As the prototype for former Tour commissioner Deane Beman's vision of "stadium golf," the Players Course was built to showcase golf as a modern spectator sport and has spawned imitations nationwide. Famously innovative architect Pete Dye hacked his way through wild jungle, reclaimed land from swamps and marshes and formed, from the remaining muck, stadium mounds for spectators. He even imported a small herd of goats to eat the undergrowth without damaging the Bermuda fairway grass.

Dye's notorious par-3 island 17th came about by accident. Having already excavated the sand from around the green, Dye decided to flow water around this apple-shaped target that measured 28 yards long and 35 yards wide. At the bottom of the forward-sloping green was a bunker, and around it was trouble everywhere. Dye recalls realizing that "I had created a hole that was planted in the player's mind from the very first tee…. Competitors subconsciously realize that no lead is secure until their ball is safely on the green."

Many golfers expressed dismay and shock after first confronting the course in practice rounds. Craig Stadler said of the 17th, "There's just too much luck involved here." Jack Nicklaus's reaction to the greens was, "I've never been very good at stopping a 5-iron on the hood of a car." Fuzzy Zoeller mused, "Where are the windmills and animals?" These were some of the more polite remarks. Even though Jerry Pate shot an 8-under-par 280 to win the first Players Tournament played here in 1982, Beman and Dye regrouped, making the greens less severe and performing other modifications. Ben Crenshaw, an early critic of the course, now says that "through evolution it has become very playable."

Sawgrass is difficult because it has variable winds that can reach over 40 miles per hour, water hazards on every hole, an abundance of bunkers guarding fairways and greens, and putting surfaces that often yield three putts.

Lee Janzen closed with a 71 and an overall 5-under-par 283 to win the 1995 Players Championship by a single stroke over Bernhard Langer. Players agreed that the course conditions, including the rough and pin placements, approximated U.S. Open conditions. Perhaps this is what Pete Dye and Deane Beman had originally intended.

"THE PLAYERS CHAMPIONSHIP HAS BECOME ONE OF THE BEST TOURNAMENTS IN THE WORLD. IT GETS A GREAT FIELD BECAUSE THE TOP PLAYERS FROM THE EUROPEAN TOUR COME AND NOW THAT THE COURSE HAS BEEN TOUGHENED UP, IT PRODUCES GREAT WINNERS."

—GREG NORMAN,
WINNER OF THE 1994 PLAYERS CHAMPIONSHIP

●TOUGHEST HOLE

The 440-yard par-4 18th was the most difficult hole early in the 1995 Tour. Following the notorious par-3, island-green 17th, this great finishing hole provides no respite for the stressed competitor. Water borders the left side from tee to green, making it difficult to hit a driver off the tee without a bit of anxiety. A cluster of thickly grassed mounds guards the right side of the green, and grass bunkers protect the back. A huge spectator mound that accommodates more than 40,000 people lies to the right of the green. In the 1995 Players Championship, the most difficult par-3 was not the 17th but the 172-yard 13th. Water borders the left side of the hole. Phil Mickelson aced this hole in 1995.

●BEST PLACE TO WATCH

Over 850,000 feet of earth was excavated and elevated to build Dye's spectator mounds, some of these mounds as high as three-story buildings and positioned to block out prevailing winds from the northwest. The spectator areas at the par-3 island 17th and the finishing hole are the places to be during the tournament, but the course is designed for the spectator to easily walk to several holes. Play returns to or near the clubhouse several times, making it convenient to see Nos. 1, 2, 3, 5, 9, 10, 16, 17 and 18.

●WHO THE COURSE FAVORS

Sawgrass is a windswept, target golf course that favors the player who can strategically plan and execute a sequence of shots without being rattled by the penal aspects of this layout. Jerry Pate, winner of that first tournament, threw architect Pete Dye into the lake after firing an 8-under-par 280 to win. The course has been modified over the years to be less punishing, and by 1994 Tom Kite was complaining that the course was too easy.

Courtesy of Golfoto

THOUGH NOT AS FAMOUS AS PETE DYE'S ISLAND 17TH, THE FINISHING PAR-4 AT SAWGRASS LEAVES LITTLE LEEWAY FOR ERRANT DRIVES OR APPROACHES.

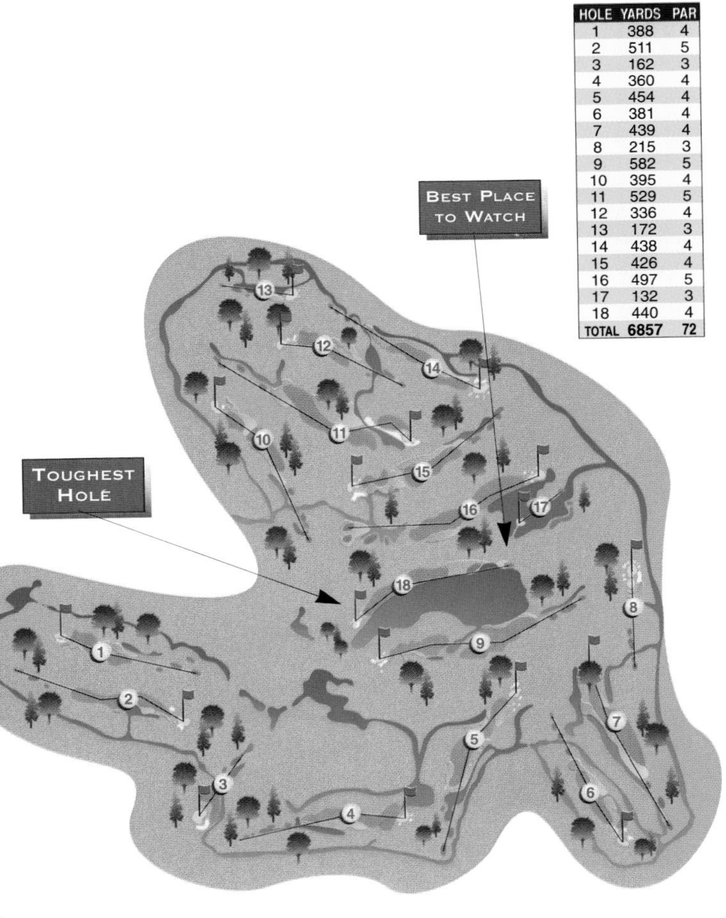

HOLE	YARDS	PAR
1	388	4
2	511	5
3	162	3
4	360	4
5	454	4
6	381	4
7	439	4
8	215	3
9	582	5
10	395	4
11	529	5
12	336	4
13	172	3
14	438	4
15	426	4
16	497	5
17	132	3
18	440	4
TOTAL	6857	72

TPC STADIUM COURSE AT SAWGRASS
ARCHITECT: PETE DYE (1982)

LODGING

$$$ The Marriott at Sawgrass Resort, 1000 TPC Blvd., Ponte Vedra Beach, Fla. (800) 457-GOLF. On site.

$$ Lodge & Bath Club at Ponte Vedra Beach, 607 Ponte Vedra Blvd., Ponte Vedra Beach, Fla. (904) 273-9500. On site.

DINING

Homestead, 1712 Beach Blvd., Jacksonville Beach, Fla. (904) 249-5240.

PUBLIC COURSES TO PLAY IN AREA

Amelia Island Plantation, Highway A1A S., Amelia Island, Fla. Resort. (904) 261-6161 (golf course), (800) 874-6878 (resort). Amelia Links: Oakmarsh/Oceanside (18/6,140/71); Oyster Bay/Oceanside (18/6,026/71); Oakmarsh/Oyster Bay (18/6,502/72). Long Point: 18/6,775/72. 1 hour from TPC at Sawgrass.

Windsor Park Golf Club, 4747 Hodges Blvd., Jacksonville, Fla. Public. (904) 223-4653. 18/6,742/72. 10 minutes from TPC at Sawgrass.

TICKETS & ACCESSIBILITY

How to watch: Mon.-Tue., PGA practice rounds. Wed., PGA practice rounds, shoot-out, junior golf clinic. Thur.-Sun., tournament. Daily tickets, group and sponsorship plans available. The Players Championship, P.O. Box 829, 103 TPC Blvd., Ponte Vedra Beach, FL 32082. (904) 273-3392, (800) 741-3161.

How to play: The TPC Stadium is a resort course open to the public year-round. Note that by staying at the 538-room Marriott you have unlimited access and more advantageous tee time reservation options to area golf courses. High season is January through the first week of June. Packages are available through the Marriott at Sawgrass as well as The Lodge and Bath Club at Ponte Vedra Beach and the Ponte Vedra Inn (904-285-1111). Other golf courses on site include: TPC Valley: 18/6,838/71, (904) 273-3235; Sawgrass Country Club, East: 9/3,476/36, West: 9/3,424/36, and South: 9/3,440/36, (904) 285-2261; Marsh Landing: 18/6,841/72, (904) 285-6514; and Oak Bridge: 18/6,383/70, (904) 285-5552.

Freeport-McDermott Golf Classic

English Turn Golf and Country Club

Legend has it that in 1699, a handful of French explorers in two canoes escaped harm by bluffing an armed British ship into changing its course at a bend in the Mississippi River now known as English Turn. Less than 30 minutes from Bourbon Street in the Big Easy, the site is now home to the English Turn golf course, a Jack Nicklaus–designed challenge punctuated by mounding, pocked with ample bunkering, and lined with water on every hole. Miscalculated or poorly executed shots on this layout will find sand, water or deep rough.

Nicklaus nicely varied the length and configuration of the holes on this course. For example, the par-4s range from the 370-yard ninth to the 471-yard finishing hole. The tee shot on the ninth requires positioning, ideally on the left, in order to have a clear angle of approach to a green guarded by bunkers on both sides and a pond to its front right. But if the tee shot is too far left, it will land in a waste bunker or water farther left. If it is long and right, it could find the water that begins 278 yards from the tee.

The course toughens up considerably on the back nine, culminating in the long 18th, the most difficult hole at English Turn. The tee shot must avoid a cluster of five bunkers to the right and a waste bunker burdened by water all the way down the left side. The hole's deep green curls to the left in an amphitheater setting and is almost entirely framed by sand, save for a narrow entrance. This hole was rated the most difficult on the PGA Tour in 1991.

Mike Standly played the front nine at a cumulative 13-under-par and the back at six over to win the 1993 Freeport-McDermott Classic by a stroke over Russ Cochran and Payne Stewart. Stewart left his birdie putt inches short on the final hole to narrowly miss forcing sudden-death. The following year, Ben Crenshaw posted the 18th victory of his 22-year career when he held on to win this tournament as José María Olazábal's heroic birdie-birdie finish fell short.

Davis Love III desperately needed a win the next year to qualify for the 1995 Masters, which follows the Freeport-McDermott on the PGA Tour calendar. Love, a native of Georgia who has won over $5 million in his career, arrived at the 17th tee on the final day and looked as if he had the tournament won after his nearest rival, Mike Heinen, hit his approach into the water on No. 18 for a double bogey. But Love bogeyed 17th and 18th after hitting into greenside bunkers on both holes. Fortunately, Love regrouped to win a sudden-death playoff against Heinen with a birdie on the second playoff hole.

Originated in 1938 as the Greater New Orleans Open, this event's past champions include golf immortals like Picard, Demaret, Nelson, Casper, Player, Nicklaus, Trevino, Watson and Crenshaw.

English Turn has made this tournament a fitting prelude to the Masters: Ian Woosnam took both titles in 1991, Olazábal captured the 1994 Masters a week after his runner-up finish at English Turn, and the 1995 Masters saw Davis Love finish second to 1994 Freeport-McDermott Classic champion Crenshaw.

TOURNAMENT-AT-A-GLANCE

Course: English Turn Golf and Country Club
Type: Private
Location: 1 Clubhouse Dr., New Orleans, LA 70131
Telephone: (504) 392-2200
When: March 21–24, 1996
How To Get There: From New Orleans, 15 minutes. Take Mississippi River Bridge to General DeGaulle East Exit. Take General DeGaulle to Intracoastal Bridge. Take right on Hwy. 406 just off bridge. Proceed 3/4 mile to English Turn sign. Take right, 1 mile to club.
Broadcast: NBC (1996)
Purse: $1,200,000 (1996)
Tournament Record: 26-under-par 262, Chip Beck, 1988

Courtesy of Freeport McMoRan Golf Classic

WATER, WATER EVERYWHERE, AND NOT A PUTT TO SINK: PATIENCE AND THE COURSE'S LARGEST GREEN HELP THE PLAYERS MAKE A FAIR FIGHT OF THE 542-YARD ISLAND 15TH AT ENGLISH TURN.

●TOUGHEST HOLE

The 471-yard, par-4 18th at English Turn is a monster bordered by water on the left from tee to green. A waste bunker guards the entire left fairway, and a collection of five bunkers protects the right landing area. The approach is to a shallow green guarded by sand everywhere except at its entranceway. The farther left the tee shot, the narrower the target becomes. José María Olazábal, who had a first-round 63, holed a bunker shot on this hole to birdie and finish second to Ben Crenshaw in 1994. Payne Stewart left a 25-foot putt inches short here in 1993 to finish one stroke behind the winner, Mike Standly.

●BEST PLACE TO WATCH

The front and back nines flow from the clubhouse in opposite directions, then loop back. The first tee, ninth green, 10th tee and 18th green are all easily reached from the clubhouse. The 207-yard 17th, the most difficult par-3 on the course, is a good place to watch the golfers, as is the green area around the 463-yard fifth and the 469-yard 14th, two of the most difficult par-4s on the course.

HOLE	YARDS	PAR	HOLE	YARDS	PAR
1	398	4	10	420	4
2	519	5	11	550	5
3	200	3	12	158	3
4	349	4	13	380	4
5	463	4	14	469	4
6	557	5	15	542	5
7	445	4	16	442	4
8	176	3	17	207	3
9	370	4	18	471	4
			TOTAL	7116	72

●WHO THE COURSE FAVORS

English Turn is long, has water hazards on every hole, and the greens, many of them less than 30 yards in depth, are well-protected by sand and water. Architect Nicklaus has allowed a reasonable amount of room on tee shots, but the golfer must be able to come into the greens with a high degree of accuracy. As on many of Nicklaus' earlier courses, the ability to hit the ball long and high is rewarded

ENGLISH TURN GOLF AND COUNTRY CLUB
ARCHITECT: JACK NICKLAUS (1988)

LODGING

$$$ Windsor Court Hotel, 300 Gravier St., New Orleans. (504) 523-6000, (800) 262-2662. 20 minutes from English Turn.
$$ Le Meridien New Orleans, 614 Canal St., New Orleans. (504) 525-6500, (800) 543-4300. 20 minutes from English Turn.
$ Le Richelieu in the French Quarter, 1234 Chartres St., New Orleans. (504) 529-2492, (800) 535-9653. 25 minutes from English Turn.

DINING

The Grill Room, in the Windsor Court Hotel, 300 Gravier St., New Orleans. (504) 522-1992.
Antoine's, 713-717 Rue St. Louis, New Orleans. (504) 581-4422.
Acme Oyster House, 724 Iberville, New Orleans. (504) 522-5973.

PUBLIC COURSES TO PLAY IN AREA

The Bluffs on Thompson Creek, Freeland Rd. at Hwy. 965, St. Francisville, La. Resort. (504) 634-5551 (golf course), (504) 634-5222 (lodge). 18/7,126/72. 2 hours from English Turn.
Bayou Oaks, 1040 Fillmore Ave., New Orleans. Public. (504) 483-9396. 18/7,061/72. Four other golf courses on site. 20 minutes from English Turn.
Oak Harbor Golf Club, 201 Oak Harbor Blvd., Slidell, La. Public. (504) 646-0110. 18/6896/72. 45 minutes from English Turn.

TICKETS & ACCESSIBILITY

How to watch: Mon., PGA practice rounds, pro-am. Tue., PGA practice rounds, shoot-out. Wed., classic pro-am. Thur.-Sun., tournament. Individual tickets start at $15. Group and sponsorship plans available. Freeport-McDermott Classic, 110 Veterans Blvd., Suite 170, Metairie, LA 70005, (504) 831-4653.
How to play: English Turn is a private club. You must be a member or the guest of a member to play the course.

MCI Classic

HARBOUR TOWN GOLF LINKS

Located on the inland coastline of Hilton Head Island, Harbour Town set a new trend in golf course design when it opened in 1969.

This Pete Dye–layout, which winds among 300 acres of trees and marshland, measured only 6,657 yards when Arnold Palmer won the first Heritage Classic that year. The course has fewer than 50 bunkers, and the greens tend to be very small. At the time, the dominant practice in American golf course architecture was to build large runway tees, long holes, huge and abundant bunkers and large greens. Dye, working with Jack Nicklaus and Alice Dye, his wife and long-time business partner, instead developed a shotmaker's course woven through mature forests of oak, pine and magnolia. Where these trees stand in groves near the fairways, they tend to make the landing areas seem much smaller than they actually are. There are no significant elevation changes on this lowland course and the bunkers around the greens provide sight lines that enable a golfer to judge perspective and distance. Pot bunkers, bulkheaded banks and a variety of grasses were used to highlight the contour of the land at Harbour Town. The area in back of the greens, for example, was sodded with centipede, a thick-leaf grass, while bahia grass was used in the rough. It is likely that a golfer will spend some strokes in these areas, the bunkers or nearby water as he tries to reach the small targets.

The Harbour Town Golf Links offers a variety of distances, angles and hazards. Its shorter par-5s, such as the 505-yard second and the 535-yard fifth, provide birdie opportunities, but the par-3s and longer par-4s, including the 466-yard eighth and the final hole—one of the best in golf—are likely to reclaim strokes. Tour players have made some pointed comments about the course. Lee Trevino noted that the 15th hole, a 575-yard par-5 is "... so long that it doesn't favor the long hitters. Even King Kong couldn't get on the green in two."

The final two holes at Harbour Town are among the most difficult on the course and provide for exciting finishes. The 192-yard, par-3 17th plays over a lagoon to a deep, narrow green bracketed by a long waste bunker to its left and another bunker to its right front. Signature Dye railroad ties bulkhead the green. An incoming wind often complicates the tee shot, as does the late-afternoon sun, which is directly in front of the golfer at the end of the tournament. In a sudden-death playoff in 1995, Bob Tway hit a tee shot to within a few feet of the hole here to defeat Nolan Henke, who had birdied three of the final four regulation holes. Earlier in the tournament, Tway had pushed his tee shot to the right but holed a 30-yard chip for a birdie.

The 18th hole is similar in design to the par-5 final hole at Pebble Beach. However, this lengthy challenge is a par-4 whose first two shots must be played over the marshlands of Calibogue Sound, which borders the left side. The approach is to a small green fronted by an 80-yard-long waste bunker that runs out along the left edge of the fairway. Another bunker is to the rear of the green. Out-of-bounds borders the right side of the fairway. Arnold Palmer birdied the hole on the final day in his 1969 win. David Frost hit his drive into the marsh to end his chances of catching David Edwards in 1993. Hale Irwin parred this hole during the final round in 1994 to preserve his two-shot lead over Greg Norman and set a course-record 18-under-par 266. Irwin had claimed his first Tour victory when he won the Classic in 1971.

TOURNAMENT-AT-A-GLANCE

Course: Harbour Town Golf Links
Type: Resort
Location: 11 Lighthouse Ave., Hilton Head, SC 29928
Telephone: (803) 842-8484, (800) 845-6131
When: April 18–21, 1996
How To Get There: Take U.S. 278 (William Hilton Pkwy.) to Hilton Head Island. Proceed 12 miles to first traffic circle, take second right off circle to Greenwood Dr., Sea Pines Resort and the golf course.
Broadcast: CBS (1996)
Purse: $1,300,000 (1995)
Tournament Record: 18-under-par 266, Hale Irwin, 1994

●TOUGHEST HOLE

Harbour Town's 466-yard, par-4 eighth has been the most difficult hole to par in tournament play. A dogleg left, its tee shot landing area is guarded by trees and a pond on each side of the fairway. The approach is to a narrow green with a pond and a long bunker to its left from 100 yards out. The par-3s at Harbour Town are difficult to make, especially the 198-yard fourth and the 192-yard 17th. No. 4 is bordered by water from tee to a green backed by a huge bunker. The 17th has a deeper green, but a huge waste bunker guards its left side from 100 yards into the green. Farther left and to the rear is water. Another trap squeezes the right front of the green.

●BEST PLACE TO WATCH

The 18th, a 478-yard par-4, has been the scene of some great finishes. Position yourself behind the small green and watch water-defying approach shots come in over the marshlands of Calibogue Sound. The green areas around the par-3s, especially the difficult 192-yard 17th and the 198-yard fourth, are good places to view the action. Other tough holes where the golfers are severely challenged are the 466-yard, par-4 eighth and the 436-yard, par-4 10th.

●WHO THE COURSE FAVORS

Harbour Town is characterized by tight landing areas and small greens guarded by strategically placed water and bunkers. The 180-yard, par-3 seventh is almost completely surrounded by bunkers, the 535-yard, par-5 fifth offers a 27-yard-deep green protected by a bunker to its left front, and the 378-yard, par-4 13th has a huge trap surrounding its front, forcing the golfer to fly the approach in. Variable winds off the nearby Atlantic Ocean and some well-placed mature trees necessitate excellent course-management skills.

By David S. Soliday

SMALL GREENS AND A VERITABLE SALAD OF GRASSES WHICH VARY THE TERRAIN MAKE HARBOUR TOWN SHOTMAKERS' TURF.

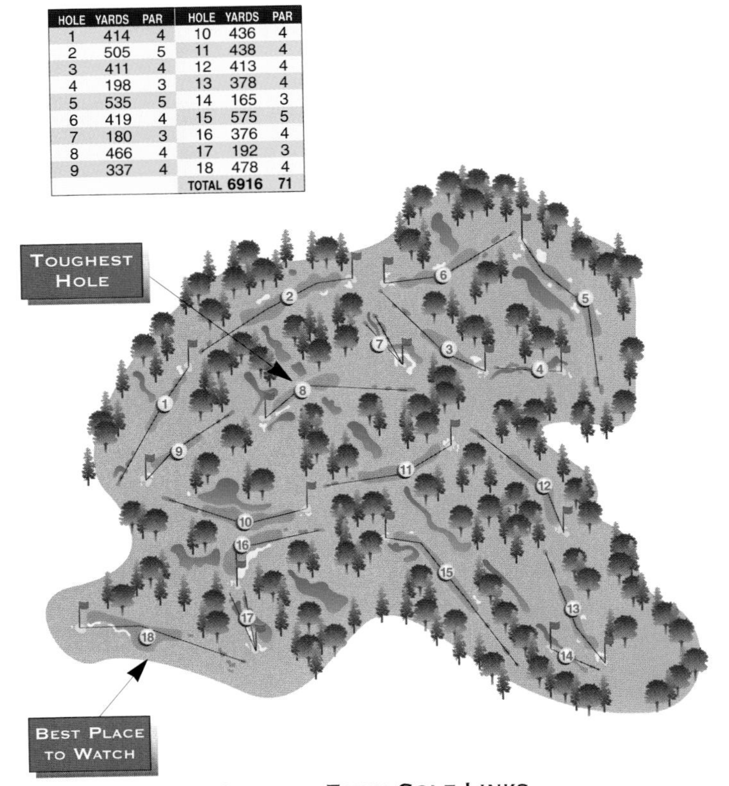

HOLE	YARDS	PAR	HOLE	YARDS	PAR
1	414	4	10	436	4
2	505	5	11	438	4
3	411	4	12	413	4
4	198	3	13	378	4
5	535	5	14	165	3
6	419	4	15	575	5
7	180	3	16	376	4
8	466	4	17	192	3
9	337	4	18	478	4
			TOTAL	6916	71

HARBOUR TOWN GOLF LINKS
ARCHITECT: PETE DYE AND JACK NICKLAUS (1969)

LODGING

$$$ Hilton Head Island Resort, 23 Ocean Lane, Hilton Head Island, S.C. (803) 842-8000, (800) 845-8001. 15 minutes from Harbour Town Golf Links.

$ Fairfield Inn by Marriott, 9 Marina Side Dr., Hilton Head Island, S.C. (803) 842-4800. 15 minutes from Harbour Town Golf Links.

DINING

King Fisher, 8 Harbour Lane, Hilton Head Island, S.C. (803) 785-4442.

Aunt Chilada's Easy Street Cafe, 69 Pope Ave., Hilton Head Island, S.C. (803) 785-7700.

PUBLIC COURSES TO PLAY IN AREA

Palmetto Dunes Resort, 2 Leanington Lane, Hilton Head Island, S.C. Resort. (803) 785-1138, (800) 826-1649 (resort). Fazio: 18/6,873/70. Jones: 18/6,710/72. Hills: 18/6,651/72. 10 minutes from Harbour Town Golf Links.

Palmetto Hall Plantation, 108 Fort Howell Dr., Hilton Head Island, S.C. Resort. (803) 689-4100. Hills: 18/6,918/72. Cupp: 18/7,079/72. 10 minutes from Harbour Town Golf Links.

Oyster Reef Golf Club, 155 High Bluff Rd., Hilton Head Island, S.C. Public. (803) 681-7717. 18/7,027/72. 15 minutes from Harbour Town Golf Links.

TICKETS & ACCESSIBILITY

How to watch: Mon., pro-am event, PGA practice rounds. Tue., shoot-out, youth golf clinic, PGA practice rounds. Wed., pro-am. Thur.-Sun., tournament. Individual tickets start at $75 for weekly admission to tournament. Daily tickets prior to the tournament are available beginning from $10. Group and sponsorship packages available. MCI Classic, 71 Lighthouse Rd., Suite 414, Hilton Head Island, S.C. 29928. (803) 671-2448.

How to play: Sea Pines Resort is a year-round resort with Harbour Town Golf Links and two other courses, Ocean: 18/6,614/72, and Sea Marsh: 18/6,515/72, open to the public. Resort guests can make tee times 90 days in advance, the public 14 days in advance. Peak season is March to May and Sept. to Nov. Packages are available through resort. (803) 785-3333, (800) 845-6131.

Shell Houston Open

TPC at The Woodlands

The Shell Houston Open has been around for five decades, but it sure has the look and feel of a new tournament.

Maybe it's the recent winners. Before Payne Stewart broke through in 1995, five consecutive champions had never won a Tour event before.

Or maybe it's the course. Opened in 1978, the stadium-style TPC at Woodlands East is as well-treed as its name might suggest. Its tabletop terrain, however, inspired designers Robert von Hagge and Bruce Devlin to load it with the most routine enemies of the modern pro: lots of water, a couple of island greens and contoured bunkers everywhere the golfer hopes to land. The very first hole, a 515-yard, par-5 dogleg right, culminates in a small, oval green that sits behind a virtual moat of necklaced bunkers. Another par-5, the 530-yard 13th, sets its island green in water. These holes are the weekender's nightmares, but they offer few subtleties for the pros.

The Woodlands itself is a planned community, including a resort and an executive conference center, tucked discreetly into a forested area near Lake Harrison, less than 20 miles north of Houston. The TPC course is swept by winds that can alter strategic decisions, and its fast Bermuda-grass greens help put a premium on precision approaches.

Like many other Tour events, this Houston event began with the efforts of a group of civic boosters who believed their city deserved a visit by the game's finest players. The first showdown was all the Houston Golf Association could hope for, as Byron Nelson edged Ben Hogan by two strokes and Sam Snead finished five strokes back in third.

Hogan and Snead would stretch their cameos here through four and five decades, respectively, but Nelson never returned. Big names have since topped the leader board, but few ever made Houston an annual pilgrimage. Curtis Strange is one of the exceptions, and the three wins he collected in Houston during the 1980s are the most in the event's history.

A 25-year-old Corey Pavin earned his first Tour win in the 1984 Houston Open, and the event crowned an unlikely string of first-time winners for five straight years to start this decade—Tony Sills (1990), Fulton Allem (1991), Fred Funk (1992), Jim McGovern (1993) and Mike Heinen (1994), a 27-year-old rookie who finished three strokes ahead of Jeff Maggert, Tom Kite and his boyhood idol, Hal Sutton.

The 1995 tournament broke that string, but it proved how unsettling the back nine's hazards can be. Scott Hoch, who missed an 18-inch putt that would have won the 1989 Masters in a playoff with Nick Faldo, made the turn on the final day at 16-under-par for the tournament. But he bogeyed 12 and 14, then double-bogeyed 17, before sinking a courageous 35-foot birdie putt on No. 18 to tie Stewart at 12-under.

The 18th was also the first playoff hole, and Hoch landed his second shot in a left bunker. He fell down on his way into the bunker, then just missed the pin on a sand shot that rolled all the way to the opposite fringe. When that bogey ended his hopes, Hoch could only say, "It was pitiful. I couldn't have had an easier tournament to win."

TOURNAMENT-AT-A-GLANCE

Course: TPC at The Woodlands
Type: Resort
Location: The Woodlands Executive Conference Center and Resort, 2301 North Millbend Dr., The Woodlands, TX 77380.
Telephone: (713) 367-1100, (800) 533-3052
When: May 2–5, 1996
How To Get There: From Houston, 45 minutes. Take I-45 north to Rayford-Sawdust Exit, turn left at light under highway on Sawdust Rd., bear right onto Grogan's Mill Rd., take right onto South Mill Bend. Follow signs to course.
Broadcast: ABC (1996)
Purse: $1,400,000 (1995)
Tournament Record: 18-under-par 266, Curtis Strange, 1980

Courtesy of Houston Golf Association

DESPITE ITS IMPOSING MOATED GREEN, THE WOODLANDS' 13TH HOLE IS HANDLED FAIRLY EASILY BY TOURNAMENT COMPETITORS.

●TOUGHEST HOLE

Two of the most difficult holes at the TPC Woodlands are the finishing holes. The 383-yard, par-4 17th requires a well-placed tee shot that avoids water on the left and trees to the right. The approach is likely to be over a pond. The next hole is a 445-yard par-4 with water bordering the right side of the fairway from 175 yards to the front of the green. Behind the large putting surface is a cluster of bunkers and a large stadium bank.

●BEST PLACE TO WATCH

The Woodlands is a TPC stadium-style course redesigned in the 1980s to accommodate spectators on viewing mounds. The 18th is the prime place to watch on the final day; the area around the 17th is also a good spot. Errant shots coming into these greens can find water in front or a bunker behind, requiring some interesting recovery shots. Other difficult holes on the course worth visiting are the 195-yard, par-3 14th, which plays over water to a very shallow green fronted by two bunkers and backed by two more; the 413-yard, par-4 fourth, which also requires an approach over water; and the 413-yard, par-4 seventh, bordered by water on the left from 130 yards into the green.

●WHO THE COURSE FAVORS

The TPC at The Woodlands has large, fast undulating Bermudagrass greens with water hazards on half its holes. Tee-shot landing areas are usually protected by bunkers. Because of these hazards and the demanding pin placements of tournament play, the course favors a strategic shotmaker who can come into the greens with accurate approach shots.

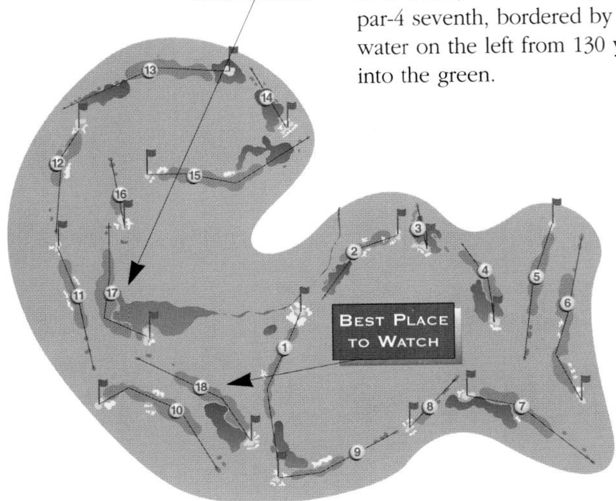

HOLE	YARDS	PAR	HOLE	YARDS	PAR
1	515	5	10	428	4
2	365	4	11	421	4
3	165	3	12	388	4
4	413	4	13	525	5
5	457	4	14	195	3
6	577	5	15	530	5
7	413	4	16	177	3
8	218	3	17	383	4
9	427	4	18	445	4
			TOTAL	7042	72

TPC AT THE WOODLANDS
ARCHITECTS:
ROBERT VON HAGGE AND BRUCE DEVLIN (1978)
REMODELED BY CARLTON GIPSON (1984)

LODGING

$$$ The Ritz-Carlton Houston, 1919 Briar Oaks Lane, Houston. (713) 840-7600, (800) 241-3333. 45 minutes from TPC at The Woodlands.
$$ The Woodlands Executive Conference Center Resort and Country Club, 2301 N. Millbend Dr., The Woodlands, Texas. (713) 367-1100, (800) 433-2624. On site.
$ Sam Houston Inn, 3296 I-45 south, Huntsville, Texas. (409) 295-9151, (800) 395-9151. 45 minutes from the TPC at The Woodlands.

DINING

Ruggles Grill, 903 Westheimer, Houston. (713) 524-3839.
Green's Barbecue, 5404 Almeda, Houston. (713) 528-5501.

PUBLIC COURSES TO PLAY IN AREA

Waterwood National Country Club, 1 Waterwood Pkwy, Huntsville, Texas. Resort. (409) 891-5211, (800) 441-5211. 18/6,872/71. 2 hours from the TPC at The Woodlands.
South Wyck Golf Club, 2901 Clubhouse Dr., Pearland, Texas. Public. 18/7,015/72. (713) 436-9999. 45 minutes from the TPC at The Woodlands.
Cypresswood Golf Club, 21602 Cypresswood Dr., Spring, Texas. Public. (713) 821-6300. Creek: 18/6,930/72. Cypress: 18/6,906/72. 45 minutes from the TPC at The Woodlands.

TICKETS & ACCESSIBILITY

How to watch: Mon., pro-am event. Tue., PGA practice rounds, pro-celebrity pitch/putt contest, shoot-out, junior golf clinic. Wed., pro-am. Thur.-Sun., tournament. Individual, group and sponsor ticket plans available. Shell Houston Open, Houston Golf Association, 1830 South Millbend Dr., The Woodlands, TX 77380. (713) 367-7999.
How to play: The TPC at The Woodlands is part of the Woodlands Executive Conference Center and Resort and is open to the public. Tee times can be made at the time of reservations or outside play can be booked up to two weeks in advance. The North Course: 18/6,881/72 is also available for play. Packages can be obtained through the resort. (409) 891-5211, (800) 441-5211.

Kmart Greater Greensboro Open

Forest Oaks Country Club

One of the oldest tournaments on the PGA Tour, the Greensboro Open came to life at a moment of golfing glory for the North Carolina city that hosts the event.

In 1936, Tony Manero, a member of Greensboro's Sedgefield Country Club, surprised the world when he carded a U.S. Open record 282 at Baltusrol for a two-stroke victory over Harry Cooper. In 1937, Sedgefield's Estelle Lawson Page and Bobby Dunkelberger added victories in the U.S. Women's Amateur and the men's French Amateur. Two thousand fans showed up on a Sunday in March that year to see Dunkelberger and Manero in an exhibition. That cinched it. The Greensboro Jaycees were determined to squeeze their own tournament in a week before the Masters.

Sam Snead ruled this tournament from the beginning. On his way to a PGA record 81 career Tour wins, Snead racked up an unequaled eight victories in Greensboro, including a five-stroke romp in the 1938 debut event. He became such an integral part of the event that when he was banned from Starmount Country Club after his 1960 Greensboro victory there (he had joked that the club owner ought to "dig up a couple of cans of money and fix up the course"), tournament officials quickly settled down for 16 years at Sedgefield.

TOURNAMENT-AT-A-GLANCE

Course: Forest Oaks Country Club
Type: Private
Location: 4600 Forest Oaks Dr., Greensboro, NC 27406
Telephone: (910) 674-0126
When: April 25–28, 1996
How To Get There: Take Hwy. 421 7 miles south from Greensboro to Hagon Stone Brook Exit. Exit to stop sign, follow signs to the country club.
Broadcast: CBS (1996)
Purse: $1,500,000 (1996)
Tournament Record: 17-under-par 267, Chi Chi Rodriguez, 1973 (at the par-71 Sedgefield CC); and 17-under-par 271, Sandy Lyle, 1988 (at par-72 Forest Oaks CC).

●TOUGHEST HOLE

One of the most difficult holes on the Tour, the 409-yard, par-4 third requires an accurate tee shot that avoids trees to the left and a water hazard on the right. The approach is to a large, two-level green with a bunker to its left front and two bunkers to its right. Another large bunker protects the rear.

●BEST PLACE TO WATCH

The area around the 18th, a 435-yard par-4 and one of the toughest holes on the course, has been the scene of many close finishes.

●WHO THE COURSE FAVORS

Forest Oaks is long, with large greens, large bunkers and out-of-bounds on 17 holes. The large, undulating greens at Forest Oaks are inviting, but once you get there, it's easy to spend three putts or even more. Long, accurate tee shots are required to set up approaches that stay close to the flagstick.

HOLE	YARDS	PAR
1	411	4
2	523	5
3	409	4
4	179	3
5	420	4
6	393	4
7	379	4
8	221	3
9	584	5
10	400	4
11	392	4
12	185	3
13	521	5
14	439	4
15	559	5
16	414	4
17	198	3
18	435	4
TOTAL	7062	72

FOREST OAKS COUNTRY CLUB
ARCHITECT: ELLIS MAPLES (1962)

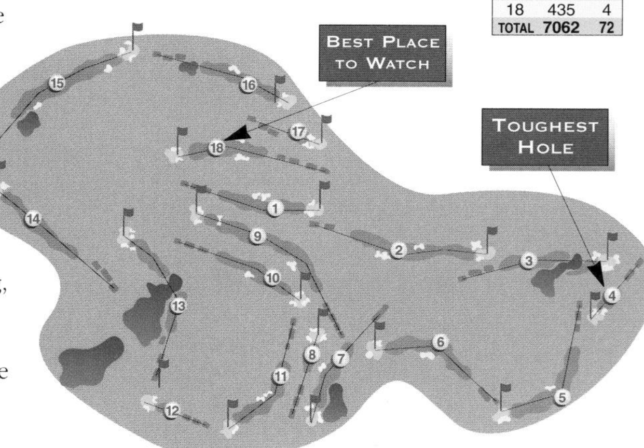

LODGING

$$$ Sheraton Greensboro Hotel and Conference Center, 303 N. Elm St., Greensboro, N.C. (910) 379-8000. 5 minutes from Forest Oaks CC.
$$ Residence Inn by Marriott, 2000 Veasley St., Greensboro, N.C. (910) 294-8600. 10 minutes from Forest Oaks CC.
$ Ramada Inn–Airport, 7067 Albert Pick Rd., Greensboro, N.C. (910) 668-3900. 25 minutes from Forest Oaks CC.

DINING

The Madison Park Restaurant, 616 Dolly Madison Rd., Greensboro, N.C. (910) 294-6505.
Kyoto Japanese Steakhouse, 1200 S. Holden Rd., Greensboro, N.C. (910) 299-1003.
Cracker Barrel Old Country Store, 4402 Landview Dr., Greensboro, N.C. (910) 294-0911.

PUBLIC COURSES TO PLAY IN AREA

Bryan Park and Golf Club, 6275 Bryan Park Rd., Brown Summit, N.C. Public. (910) 375-2200. Champions: 18/7,135/72. Players: 18/7,076/72. 35 minutes from Forest Oaks CC.
Oak Hollow Golf Course, 1400 Oakview Rd., High Point, N.C. Public. (919) 883-3260. 18/6,483/72. 30 minutes from Forest Oaks CC.
Tanglewood Park, Route 40, Clemmons, NC Public. (919) 766-5082. Championship: 18/7,048/72. Reynolds: 18/6,469/72. 50 minutes from Forest Oaks CC.

TICKETS & ACCESSIBILITY

How to watch: Mon., pro-am tournament, PGA practice rounds. Tue., long drive competition, shoot-out, youth golf clinic, PGA practice rounds. Wed., celebrity pro-am, PGA practice rounds. Thur.-Sun., tournament. Daily tickets start at $18. Group and sponsor packages available. Kmart Greater Greensboro Open, c/o Greensboro Jaycees, 401 N. Greene St., Greensboro, NC 27401. (910) 379-1570.
How to play: Forest Oaks is a private club. You may play the course as a member or as a guest of a member. The course is open year round.

Buick Classic

Westchester Country Club

LODGING

$$$ Doral Arrowwood, Anderson Hill Rd., Rye Brook, N.Y. (914) 939-5500. 10 minutes from Westchester CC.
$$ The Stouffer Westchester Hotel, 80 W. Red Oak Ln., White Plains, N.Y. (914) 694-5400. 20 minutes from Westchester CC.
$ Courtyard by Marriott, 631 Midland Ave., Rye, N.Y. (914) 921-1110. 10 minutes from Westchester CC.

DINING

The Atrium in the Doral Arrowwood, Anderson Hill Rd., Rye Brook, N.Y. (914) 939-5500.
Cobble Creek Cafe, 578 Anderson Hill Rd., Purchase, N.Y. (914) 761-0050.

PUBLIC COURSES TO PLAY IN AREA

Bethpage Black Course, Round Swamp Rd., Farmingdale, Long Island, N.Y. Public. (516) 249-0701. 18/7,065/71. 1 hour from Westchester CC.
Doral Arrowwood, Anderson Hill Rd., Rye Brook, N.Y. Resort. (914) 939-5500, (800) 22-DORAL. 18/6,300/70. 10 minutes from Westchester CC.
Spook Rock Golf Course, 199 Spook Rock Rd., Ramapo, N.Y. Public. (914) 357-6466. 18/6,894/72. 1 hour from Westchester CC.

TICKETS & ACCESSIBILITY

How to watch: Mon., pro-am. Tue., PGA practice rounds, golf clinic. Wed., pro-am. Thur.-Sun., tournament. Individual, group and sponsor tickets available. The Buick Classic, P.O. Box 200, Rye, NY 10580. (800) 765-4742.
How to play: Westchester Country Club is a private club. You must be a member or the guest of a member to play. In addition to the West Course, there is also the South Course (18/6,039/70).

TOURNAMENT-AT-A-GLANCE

Course: Westchester Country Club—West Course
Type: Private
Location: 99 Biltmore Ave., Rye, NY 10580
Telephone: (914) 967-6000
When: June 6–9, 1996
How To Get There: From New England Thruway, take Rte. 287 West. Take Hutchinson River Pkwy to Exit 25. Make right at end of ramp onto North St. At first light, left onto Polly Park Rd. Golf club 1 1/2 miles up on the right. Via Hutchinson River Pkwy. from New York City, 30 minutes. Take North Street Exit 25E/Harrison to golf club on the left.
Broadcast: USA, CBS (1996)
Purse: $1,200,000 (1996)
Tournament Record: 19-under-par 261, Bob Gilder, 1982

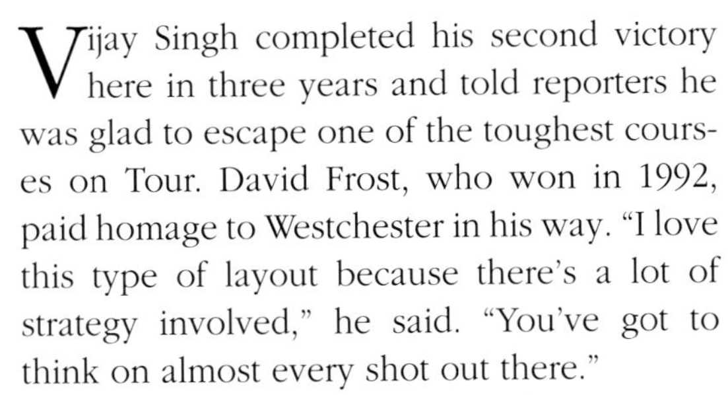

Vijay Singh completed his second victory here in three years and told reporters he was glad to escape one of the toughest courses on Tour. David Frost, who won in 1992, paid homage to Westchester in his way. "I love this type of layout because there's a lot of strategy involved," he said. "You've got to think on almost every shot out there."

Back in its normal slot as the last warm-up before the U.S. Open, the Buick Classic draws a strong field for the challenges of its compact, rolling, tree-lined course and its small, tricky, traditional greens. To use a cliché, this course, designed in the 1920s by three-time U.S. Amateur champion Walter Travis, requires the use of every club in the bag, and it is usually the adaptable, smarter players who win this event.

Westchester Country Club
—West Course
Architect: Walter J. Travis (1922)
Remodeled by William S. Flynn,
Alfred H. Tull (1969),
Joseph Finger (1971),
Rees Jones (1982)

Best Place to Watch

Toughest Hole

HOLE	YARDS	PAR
1	192	3
2	386	4
3	419	4
4	422	4
5	573	5
6	133	3
7	333	4
8	455	4
9	505	5
10	314	4
11	444	4
12	476	4
13	381	4
14	154	3
15	477	4
16	204	3
17	376	4
18	535	5
TOTAL	6779	71

●TOUGHEST HOLE

The tee shot on the 12th plays down to a valley and a likely downhill-sidehill lie, then up to a small green. This hole was rated the third most difficult on the Tour in 1994. Almost as tough is the 15th, a dogleg right protected at the turn by a huge white oak tree. The approach is downhill to a green guarded by a trap on each side.

●BEST PLACE TO WATCH

There are many parallel holes here, making it easy to catch a lot of action. Toward the end of your day at this event, you'll want to be at the tree-lined 18th, a par-5 dogleg left. Bob Gilder double-eagled this hole from 251 yards in 1982 on his way to a record 72-hole score.

●WHO THE COURSE FAVORS

The tight fairways, elevation changes and relatively small greens demand excellent course-management skills and shotmaking talent. A poorly positioned shot can easily find heavy rough or an uneven lie that can lead to bogeys or worse. Only Jack Nicklaus, Seve Ballesteros and Vijay Singh have won this event more than once.

BellSouth Classic

ATLANTA COUNTRY CLUB

Sportsman Jim Clay couldn't find a local course willing to bring a PGA tournament to Atlanta, so he built his own.

Pooling his resources with a half dozen friends in the mid-1960s, Clay purchased hundreds of acres of rolling, wooded farmland near the Chattahoochee River in Cobb County. The terrain had been the site of brutal skirmishes during the Civil War, partly because of a paper mill on the site that had printed Confederate money. Along Sope Creek, which meanders through today's championship golf course, the ruins of the mill can be seen through the trees from the 13th tee.

Designed by William Byrd, the Atlanta Country Club course opened in 1967, the same year that Bob Charles captured a two-stroke victory in the first Atlanta Golf Classic. The course hosted the first Players Championship in 1974, and Jack Nicklaus has since refashioned the course by moving some greens and tees, and adding breaks to the putting surfaces. The pros have ranked it among the top five best-maintained courses on the Tour.

The 499-yard, par-5 finishing hole at Atlanta leaves few leads safe on the final day, because a big tee shot opens eagle opportunities. John Daly hit a driver and an 8-iron into a green-side bunker during the 1994 BellSouth Classic and finished with a birdie to win the tournament by a stroke. Calvin Peete birdied this hole in 1983 to finish with a back-nine score of 31 and a final-round total of 63 to win the 54-hole rain-shortened tournament.

In 1995, Mark Calcavecchia birdied four of the final six holes for his first win in three years. A major turning point in his back-nine score of 31 was an eagle on the 548-yard, par-5 11th. Calcavecchia hit a 3-wood to within 18 feet of the cup, then sank his putt. He also landed a 3-wood on the 18th green in two, then two-putted for a birdie. On the way to his 17-under-par two-shot win, Calcavecchia birdied No. 18 three times and eagled the hole during the second round.

Steve Keppler of Snellville, Ga., played almost well enough in 1995 to become the first club professional to win a Tour event since Richie Karl won the B.C. Open in 1974. Entering the final day as a co-leader, Keppler shot a credible 71, and finished third, three strokes behind Calcavecchia. John Daly, 1994 champion, finished six shots back, but he stunned Sunday's crowd when he almost holed his drive on No. 14, a 335-yard par-4.

TOURNAMENT-AT-A-GLANCE

Course: Atlanta Country Club
Type: Private
Location: 500 Atlanta Country Club Dr., Marietta, GA 30067
Telephone: (404) 953-2100
When: April 4–7, 1996
How To Get There: From Atlanta, 20 minutes. Take I-75 north to Exit 111 (Delk Rd.). Take left on Delk to Paper Mill Rd. Go right on Paper Mill approximately 3 miles to Atlanta Country Club Dr. Take a right to the club.
Broadcast: CBS, cable TBA (1996)
Purse: $1,300,000 (1995)
Tournament Record: 23-under-par, Andy Bean, 1979; Dave Barr, 1987

"I LOOKED UP AT THE LEADER BOARD ON 17 AND SAW MY NAME UP THERE. I SAID 'WOW! THIS MUST BE A MISTAKE.'"

—STEVE KEPPLER,

A GEORGIA CLUB PRO WHO RECEIVED HIS BIGGEST PAYCHECK ($88,400) WHEN HE FINISHED THIRD IN THE 1995 BELLSOUTH CLASSIC.

By Clate Sanders

WITH A LONG TEE SHOT, A COMPETITOR CAN FINISH WITH A BIRDIE OR AN EAGLE ON ATLANTA'S 499-YARD 18TH HOLE.

●TOUGHEST HOLE

The 452-yard 15th has historically been the stiffest challenge on the course, though the 421-yard, par-4 ninth won that honor in 1994 and '95. The 15th is a sharp dogleg right with Sope Creek running up the right side and cutting across the fairway approximately 50 yards from a deep green framed by two large bunkers. Most professionals will play a draw to the center of the fairway, then play for the green with a long iron. The more daring, or foolish, will try to draw the ball over the stately oaks and pines in order to have an easier approach. The ninth, a dogleg left, travels uphill to a two-level green guarded by a bunker to its left front and another to its right front.

The toughest par-3 on the course is the 190-yard sixth, which plays over a creek that guards the right side of the green; four bunkers sit to its left. Trees behind and to the left of this hole make it difficult to gauge wind conditions.

●BEST PLACE TO WATCH

The 499-yard, par-5 18th, whose approach shot plays over water to a green protected by three bunkers, is a good place to catch the final round. John Daly hit his approach into a greenside bunker on the final round in 1994 but got up and down to win the tournament by one stroke over Nolan Henke and Brian Henninger. Bleachers are set up during the tournament on holes No. 15, 16 and 18. Sky boxes were recently built on No. 16, a 206-yard, uphill par-3. Other good vantage points are behind the third tee, where you can view that 188-yard par-3 and the green of the 563-yard, par-5 second hole. This hilly course is not easy to walk, so it's best to pick a few good vantage points from which to catch the action.

●WHO THE COURSE FAVORS

The course favors a long hitter like Daly who can keep the ball in play during the tournament. Shorter hitters who can keep the ball in play and manage the course intelligently may also succeed.

HOLE	YARDS	PAR
1	407	4
2	563	5
3	188	3
4	427	4
5	432	4
6	190	3
7	340	4
8	550	5
9	421	4
10	457	4
11	548	5
12	426	4
13	156	3
14	335	4
15	452	4
16	206	3
17	421	4
18	499	5
TOTAL	7018	72

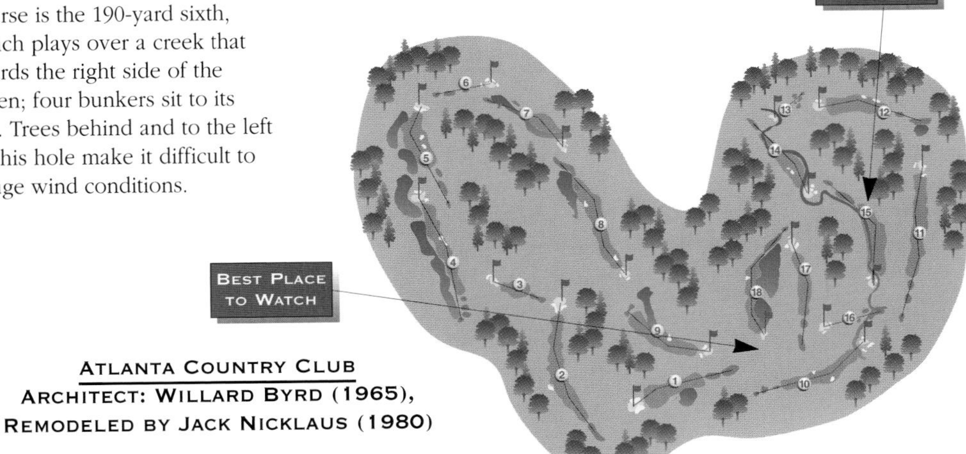

ATLANTA COUNTRY CLUB
ARCHITECT: WILLARD BYRD (1965),
REMODELED BY JACK NICKLAUS (1980)

LODGING

$$$ The Ritz-Carlton Buckhead, 3434 Peachtree Rd. NE, Atlanta. (404) 237-2700. 25 minutes from Atlanta CC.

$$ Hyatt Regency Suites Hotel, 2999 Windy Hill Rd., Marietta, Ga. (404) 956-1234. 10 minutes from Atlanta CC.

$ Best Western–Bon Air Motel, 859 Cobb Pkwy. SE, Marietta, Ga. (404) 427-4676. 5 minutes from Atlanta CC.

DINING

The Dining Room in the Ritz-Carlton Buckhead, 3434 Peachtree Rd. NE, Atlanta. (404) 237-2700.

Buckhead Diner, 3073 Piedmont Rd., Atlanta. (404) 262-3336.

Houck's Steakhouse, 805 Village Pkwy., Marietta, Ga. (404) 859-0041.

PUBLIC COURSES TO PLAY IN AREA

Château Elan Golf Club, 6060 Golf Club Dr., Braselton, Ga. Resort. (404) 932-0900, (800) 233-9463. 18/7,030/71. Also has private 18-hole course and 9-hole walking course. 1 hour 10 minutes from Atlanta CC.

Southerness Golf Course, 4871 Flat Bridge Rd., Stockbridge, Ga. Semi-private. (404) 808-6000. 18/6,766/72. 30 minutes from Atlanta Country Club.

White Columns Golf Club, 300 White Columns Dr., Alpharetta, Ga. Public. (404) 343-9025. 18/7,053/72. 30 minutes from Atlanta CC.

TICKETS & ACCESSIBILITY

How to watch: Mon., PGA practice rounds, pro-am event. Tue., PGA practice rounds, shoot-out. Wed., pro-am events. Thur.-Sun., tournament. Individual, group and sponsorship plans available. The BellSouth Classic, 380 Interstate North, Suite 160, Atlanta, GA 30339. (770) 951-8777.

How to play: The Atlanta Country Club is a private club. You must be a member or the guest of a member to play the course, which is open year-round.

GTE Byron Nelson Classic

TPC AT FOUR SEASONS RESORT—LAS COLINAS

Byron Nelson was born in 1912 on a cotton farm outside of Waxahachie, Texas, and he retired to a 630-acre ranch in Roanoke less than 35 years later. In between, he established himself as one of the greatest golfers of all time, with a swing so fluid that the mechanical device used by the USGA to test equipment is still called "Iron Byron."

Nelson was 16 when he entered and won his first significant tournament, defeating another bag mule named Ben Hogan in a nine-hole playoff at a Fort Worth country club's 1928 caddie championship. He won the first of his 52 PGA events in the middle of the Depression, in 1936, and he claimed his first Masters title a year later.

In 1944, Nelson won the inaugural Dallas Open and seven other events on his way to being named the Associated Press Sportsman of the Year. But his best was yet to come. While crowding his calendar with appearances and exhibitions at military camps or USO and Red Cross shows, he demolished a war-depleted pro circuit with a record 18 Tour victories—including an astonishing 11 in a row—and a record-low 68.33 year-long scoring average. A season later, he retired to the ranch 22 miles north of Fort Worth that he had purchased with his 1945 winnings.

The Dallas Open took on Byron Nelson's name in 1968 when Nelson was convinced that the cause—raising money for children's camps for the less fortunate—was worth dedicating himself to. It is still the sole PGA Tour event named for a player.

TOURNAMENT-AT-A-GLANCE

Course: Four Seasons Resort and Club at Las Colinas—Tournament Players Course and Cottonwood Valley Course
Type: Resort
Location: 4200 N. MacArthur Blvd., Irving, TX 75038
Telephone: (214) 717-2500
When: May 9–12, 1996
How To Get There: Take Rte. 635 LBJ Freeway to MacArthur Blvd. Proceed south 4 miles to resort. From Rte. 114 to MacArthur, proceed south 2 miles to resort. Or take Rte. 183 to MacArthur, north 2 miles to resort.
Broadcast: ABC (1996)
Purse: $1,300,000 (1996)
Tournament Record: 17-under-par 263, Ernie Els, 1995

In 1986 the event settled just outside of Dallas at a brand-new TPC designed by Jay Morrish, with Nelson and Ben Crenshaw as consultants. Just across the road is the Cottonwood Valley Golf Course, a hybrid of Morrish and Robert Trent Jones Jr. layouts that now hosts half the tournament field on each of the first two days.

In Texas, the wind has to be taken into consideration on any golf course. At Las Colinas the wind comes from the south, and the holes have been routed to be into the wind, against the wind and to have crosswinds in an equitable fashion. A stream cuts through much of the course, paralleling six holes and cutting across the fifth and 14th. After a jaunt into the woods during the middle holes, the course opens up from the par-4 15th to the par-4 finishing hole, where stadium mounding and spectator areas provide ample viewing areas.

Prior to the 1995 Byron Nelson, Ernie Els, the young star many pick to become the game's next dominant player, took a three-week away-from-golf vacation in his native South Africa, then opened here with a 69, set the Cottonwood course record with a second-round 61 and shot a third-round 65 at the TPC to enter the final day with a three-shot lead. After bogeying the eighth and 11th, Els regrouped to birdie the 13th, 14th and 16th, and went on to win by three strokes, setting a new tournament record with a 17-under-par 263.

"MY GAME HAD GOTTEN SO GOOD, THERE WERE TIMES [DURING THE STREAK] WHEN I ACTUALLY WOULD GET BORED PLAYING."

—BYRON NELSON,

IN 1995, REMEMBERING THE 11-TOURNAMENT VICTORY STREAK HE HAD IN 1945, STILL A PGA RECORD

HOLE	YARDS	PAR
1	385	4
2	176	3
3	490	4
4	425	4
5	176	3
6	396	4
7	533	5
8	457	4
9	439	4
10	447	4
11	347	4
12	426	4
13	183	3
14	409	4
15	445	4
16	554	5
17	196	3
18	415	4
TOTAL	6899	70

TPC AT LAS COLINAS
ARCHITECTS: JAY MORRISH, BYRON NELSON AND BEN CRENSHAW (1986)

•TOUGHEST HOLE

The toughest hole at the TPC at Las Colinas in 1995 was the 409-yard, par-4 14th, a dogleg right into the wind where tee shots can easily kick off a mounded fairway into the rough. The approach is to a small green surrounded by water. As Tom Kite describes it, "The 14th hole at TPC Las Colinas is one of the trickiest holes we play on Tour all year. It requires a long iron off the tee to a fairway that is very difficult to hit because it is hogbacked ... If the drive finds the rough, then a layup to the water short of the green is a strong possibility." Cottonwood's toughest, the 15th hole, is a picturesque par-4 dogleg left ending on a two-level green.

•BEST PLACE TO WATCH

In the early stages of the tournament, some of the tough holes at Cottonwood Valley are worth watching, including the 15th, the par-3 ninth and the par-4 finishing hole. The 18th, a dogleg right, plays up to a green well protected by four traps. This hole is convenient to the first tee and the practice area just behind the 18th green. The TPC Stadium Course, just across MacArthur Blvd., is the sole tournament venue after the 36-hole cut. The first tee, practice range and 18th green are a short walk from the Four Seasons Resort and Club Hotel. You'll want to view the difficult holes, especially the 196-yard, par-3 17th, and the finishing hole, a 415-yard par-4.

•WHO THE COURSE FAVORS

The designers of the TPC at Las Colinas tried to balance the impact of Texas winds by positioning some holes into the wind, some against and others that would be swayed by crosswinds. As a result, the successful competitor will have to calibrate his shots accordingly. Accuracy off the tee is important at Las Colinas because water, sand and trees can affect errant shots on most holes, as can the thick rough. Cottonwood is not a target course; it has room to spray drives and large, relatively tame greens. Big hitters like Els have the advantage.

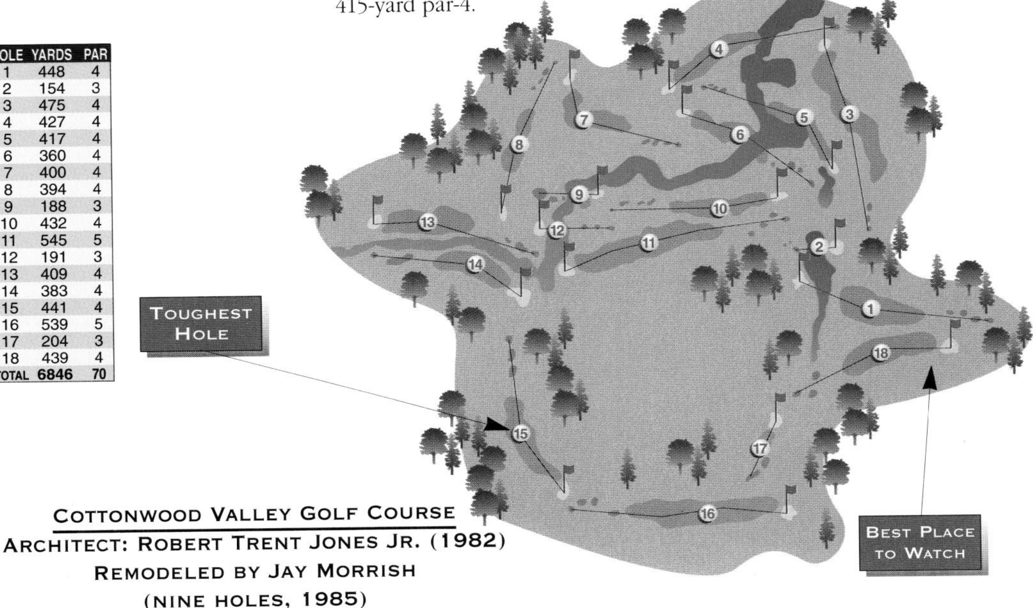

HOLE	YARDS	PAR
1	448	4
2	154	3
3	475	4
4	427	4
5	417	4
6	360	4
7	400	4
8	394	4
9	188	3
10	432	4
11	545	5
12	191	3
13	409	4
14	383	4
15	441	4
16	539	5
17	204	3
18	439	4
TOTAL	6846	70

COTTONWOOD VALLEY GOLF COURSE
ARCHITECT: ROBERT TRENT JONES JR. (1982)
REMODELED BY JAY MORRISH
(NINE HOLES, 1985)

LODGING

$$$ The Four Seasons Resort and Club, 4150 N. MacArthur Blvd., Irving, Texas. (214) 717-0700, (800) 332-3442. On site.
$$ Wyndham Garden Hotel, 110 W. John Carpenter Frwy., Irving, Texas. (214) 650-1600, (800) WYNDHAM. 5 minutes from Las Colinas.
$ Red Roof Inn, 8150 Esters Blvd., Irving, Texas. (214) 929-0020. 5 minutes from Las Colinas.

DINING

The Riviera, 7709 Inwood Rd., Dallas. (214) 351-0094.
Lawry's The Prime Rib, 3008 Maple Ave., Dallas. (214) 521-7777.
La Calle Doce, 415 W. 12th St., Oak Cliff, Texas. (214) 941-4304.

PUBLIC COURSES TO PLAY IN AREA

Hyatt Bear Creek Golf and Racquet Club, 3000 Bear Creek Court (off West Air Field Drive), Dallas–Fort Worth Airport, Euless, Texas. Resort. (214) 615-6800 (golf course), (800) 233-1234 (resort). East: 18/6,670/72. West: 18/6,677/72. 25 minutes from Las Colinas.
Firewheel Golf Park, 600 W. Blackburn Rd., Garland, Texas. Public. (214) 205-2795. Lakes: 18/6,625/71. Old: 18/7,054/72. 30 minutes from Las Colinas.
Marriott's Golf Club at Fossil Creek, 3401 Clubgate Dr., Fort Worth. Public. (817) 847-1900. 18/6,865/72. 25 minutes from Las Colinas.

TICKETS & ACCESSIBILITY

How to watch: Sun., pro-am event. Mon., pro-am, PGA practice rounds. Tue., PGA practice rounds, shoot-out, junior golf clinic. Wed., pro-am. Thur.-Fri., tournament at Cottonwood Valley and TPC courses. Sat.-Sun., tournament at TPC course. Individual, group and sponsorship plans available. GTE Byron Nelson Classic, c/o Salesmanship Club of Dallas, 350 Union Station, 400 South Houston St., Dallas, TX 75202-4811. (214) 742-3896.
How to play: The Four Seasons Resort and TPC at Las Colinas is open to the public. Resort guests may make tee times 45 days in advance. Golf packages are available. (214) 717-2530 (golf course), (800) 332-3442 (resort).

MasterCard Colonial

COLONIAL COUNTRY CLUB

Ben Hogan's home course, often ranked the best in Texas, was the inspiration of a scratch golfer named Marvin Leonard. Leonard believed Fort Worth deserved a championship course with bentgrass greens, a luxury virtually unheard of in the Lone Star State at the time.

Purchasing some brush-covered land near the Trinity River, Leonard hired John Bredemus in 1935 to lay out the course. Bredemus, a graduate of Princeton in civil engineering, held a dubious distinction in the history of sports due to his second-place finish to Jim Thorpe in the 1912 AAU National All-Around Competition in track and field. When Thorpe was stripped of his Olympic and AAU titles for having been paid to play semi-pro baseball a few years earlier, his AAU medals were sent to Bredemus. Bredemus would later became a professional golfer and establish Texas's first bentgrass greens at the San Angelo Country Club. However, Colonial, which opened in 1936, is no doubt the best golf course he ever designed.

The first National Invitational, held in 1946, was won by the local favorite, a Fort Worth native who had already earned his place in golf history. Ben Hogan would also pocket the second NIT title, and his record five victories here would brand the course "Hogan's Alley." His final victory here came in 1959, when the 59-year-old legend seized his 63rd and final Tour event in the tournament's first play-off. Modern players seeking inspiration need only stop in the clubhouse, where the Hogan trophy room displays an impressive collection.Holes three, four and five at Colonial are called "the Horrible Horseshoe." The 476-yard, par-4 third, a dogleg left, has a large tree and a cluster of bunkers to the left of the landing area and two huge bunkers protecting its green. The 246-yard, par-3 fourth plays to a green only 27 yards in depth and guarded to its left by deep bunkers. The 459-yard, par-4 fifth has trees and a stream to its right from tee to green.

Virtually all the fast, hard, bent-grass greens, which range in depth from 23 to 41 yards, are guarded by large bunkers and, in the case of the 13th, 15th and 18th, by water. Wind can play a role at Colonial, as Jim Colbert will attest. On the final hole of the 1983 Colonial, an unexpected tail-wind carried his 5-iron approach into the water to the left of the green. But Colbert was able to salvage a tie with Fuzzy Zoeller at 278, then win on the sixth hole of a sudden-death playoff.

Payne Stewart bogeyed the final hole in 1984 to fall into another sudden-death playoff, which Peter Jacobsen won on the first extra hole. In 1992, Corey Pavin, who had won this event in 1985 with a 14-under-par 266, birdied the 17th to tie Bruce Lietzke in regulation, but Lietzke birdied the same hole to take the sudden-death playoff.

Tom Lehman, who had minor cancer surgery four weeks prior to the 1995 Colonial, ran in a 30-foot birdie putt on the 18th to win by one stroke. Lehman had carded four sub-par rounds on a course many professionals consider the toughest par-70 in golf.

TOURNAMENT-AT-A-GLANCE

Course: Colonial Country Club
Type: Private
Location: 3735 Country Club Circle, Fort Worth, TX 76109
Telephone: (817) 927-4200
When: May 16–19, 1996
How To Get There: From downtown Fort Worth, 15 minutes. Take I-30 to University Exit (TCU). Take University south to Colonial Dr. (across from zoo). Take right on Colonial, follow the hedges approximately 1 mile to the golf course.
Broadcast: CBS, USA (1996)
Purse: $1,400,000 (1995)
Tournament Record: 16-under-par 264, Fulton Allem, 1993

"I LOVE THIS COURSE. THIS IS A STANDARD BY WHICH ALL GOLF COURSES SHOULD BE BUILT."

—PAYNE STEWART

●TOUGHEST HOLE

The 476-yard, par-4 third is a dogleg left with three bunkers guarding the turn on the left side. The drive should be hit to the left-center for a good angle to a hard, fast, medium-sized green flanked by a large bunker on each side. Another challenging hole is the 427-yard, par-4 18th, a slight dogleg left. The tee shot has to be hit near the center of the fairway to keep out of play the water to the left and behind the green and the large bunkers that straddle the deep putting surface. Greg Norman birdied this hole on the final round of the 1993 Colonial, forcing Fulton Allem to make a 4-foot par putt to win. In 1994 Nick Price fired a final-round 64, including five consecutive birdies, to make up seven strokes and tie Scott Simpson. Simpson hit his approach to within 20 feet on the 18th, the first extra hole, but missed his putt. Price, who had approached to within 9 feet, sank yet another birdie for the win.

●BEST PLACE TO WATCH

Colonial is a flat course with many parallel holes. Eight of the par-4s at Colonial had better-than-par stroke averages in the 1994 tournament, including Nos. 3, 18, 5, 14, 9, 15, 12 and 7 in descending order of difficulty. While standing behind No. 9, you have a vantage point to the 10th tee, first tee and 18th green. The area behind the 15th green affords a view of the scenic 188-yard 16th. On the final day, the final five holes can easily be monitored without walking too far from the clubhouse.

●WHO THE COURSE FAVORS

The trees, bunkers and water hazards at Colonial, an extremely long par-70 course, require restraint and accuracy from the tee. Colonial also requires an ability to hit accurate mid- and long irons into the greens, especially on long par-4s such as the 476-yard third and the 459-yard fifth.

HOLE	YARDS	PAR
1	565	5
2	400	4
3	476	4
4	246	3
5	459	4
6	393	4
7	420	4
8	192	3
9	391	4
10	404	4
11	599	5
12	433	4
13	178	3
14	426	4
15	430	4
16	188	3
17	383	4
18	427	4
TOTAL	7010	70

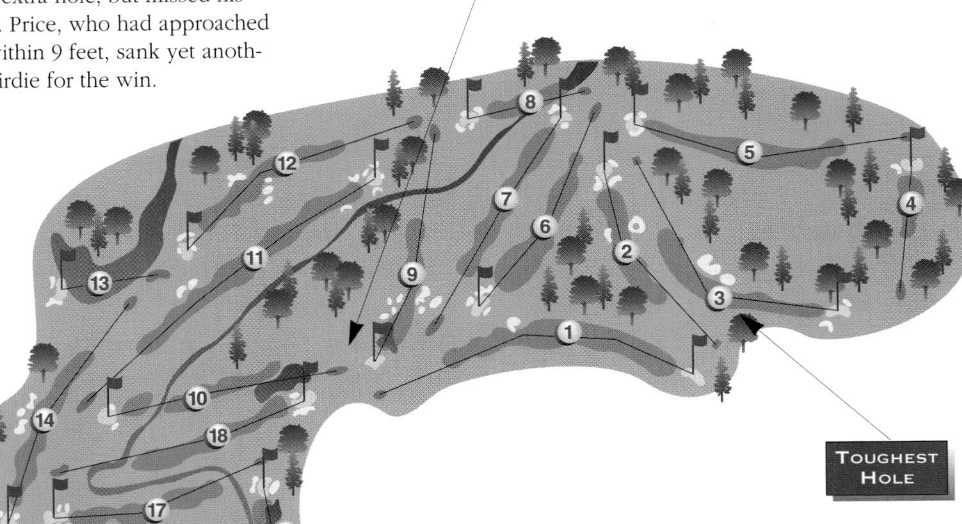

Colonial Country Club
Architect: John Bredemus (1936)
Additional three, Perry Maxwell (1940)
Remodeled by Dick Wilson (1956),
Robert Trent Jones (1960),
Jay Morrish and Robert Cupp (1982)

LODGING

$$$ The Worthington Hotel, 200 Main St., Fort Worth. (800) 433-5677 (outside Texas), (800) 477-8274 (Texas). 10 minutes from Colonial CC.

$$ Residence Inn by Marriott Fort Worth–River Plaza, 1701 S. University Dr., Fort Worth. (817) 870-1011. 5 minutes from Colonial CC.

$ La Quinta Motor Inn–Northeast, 7920 Bedford–Euless Rd., Fort Worth. (817) 485-2750. 20 minutes from Colonial CC.

DINING

Reflections, Worthington Hotel, 200 Main St., Fort Worth. (817) 870-1000.

Joe T. Garcia's, 2201 N. Commerce St., Fort Worth. (817) 626-4356.

J&J Oyster Bar, 929 University Dr., Fort Worth. (817) 335-2756.

PUBLIC COURSES TO PLAY IN AREA

Buffalo Creek Golf Club, 624 Country Club Dr., Rockwell, Texas. Public. (214) 771-4003. 18/7,018/71. 1 hour from Colonial CC.

Four Seasons Resort and Club, 4150 North MacArthur Blvd., Irving, Texas. Resort. (214) 717-0700, (800) 332-3442. TPC Course: 18/6,826/70. 45 minutes from Colonial CC.

Hyatt Bear Creek Golf and Racquet Club, 3000 Bear Creek Court (off West Air Field Drive), Dallas–Fort Worth Airport, Texas. Resort. (214) 615-6800, (800) 233-1234. East: 18/6,670/72. West: 18/6,677/72. 45 minutes from Colonial CC.

TICKETS & ACCESSIBILITY

How to watch: Mon., PGA practice rounds, pro-am. Tue., PGA practice rounds, shoot-out, junior clinic. Wed., pro-am. Thur.-Sun., tournament. Admission is free on Mon. and Tue. Individual tickets begin at $25. Group and sponsorship plans available. The MasterCard Colonial, 3735 Country Club Circle, Fort Worth, TX 76109. (817) 927-4277, (817) 927-4278.

How to play: Colonial is a private club. You must be a member or the guest of a member to play the course.

Memorial Tournament

MUIRFIELD VILLAGE GOLF CLUB

The Memorial is sometimes called "The Masters of the Midwest." Jack Nicklaus, its founder, could dream of no greater tribute.

Nicklaus, considered by most to be the greatest golfer of all time, grew up in nearby Columbus, Ohio, as a golf prodigy not unlike like his boyhood idol, Bobby Jones. Jones, a golden boy of the Roaring Twenties whose engineering degree, Harvard English degree and Emory law studies accredited him as golf's premier Renaissance Man, co-designed Augusta National and established the Masters shortly after retiring from the game in 1930 at the ripe age of 28. Nicklaus collaborated in the layout of Muirfield while in his competitive prime, and he began a tradition of honoring golf's legends by dedicating the first Memorial to Jones himself. When he won the event's second running, in 1977, Nicklaus called the victory "my biggest thrill in golf."

TOURNAMENT-AT-A-GLANCE

Course: Muirfield Village Golf Club
Type: Private
Location: 5750 Memorial Dr., Dublin, OH 43017
Telephone: (614) 889-6700
When: May 30–June 2, 1996
How To Get There: From Columbus, I-270 west to Exit 17. Take Rte. 33 to Avery Rd./Muirfield. Turn right; Avery Rd. becomes Muirfield Dr. north of Rte. 33. Follow signs to the golf course.
Broadcast: ABC, ESPN (1995)
Purse: $1,700,000 (1995)
Tournament Record: 20-under-par 268, Tom Lehman, 1994

Situated on rolling, wooded land west of Columbus, Muirfield is named for the site of Nicklaus's first British Open victory and would delight Jones with its blend of majestically treed fairways, Scottish-inspired bunkering and fast, undulating greens. Ponds and streams play into "18 shots," according to Tom Weiskopf, a fellow Ohioan and architect who christened the layout in an exhibition with Nicklaus on Memorial Day, 1974. Designed to accommodate TV cameras and large crowds, Muirfield is one of the toughest up-and-down courses on the Tour.

The opening hole is a slight dogleg right and an early indicator that the par-4s will be long and well-protected by hazards, and that once you get to the green, it will be like putting on glass. One of the best holes on the front side is the par-4 ninth, which flows up from the tee over a rise, then down to a deep green fronted by a bunker and a stream that wends its way along the right side.

The four finishing holes usually provide the turning point for this tournament, and the last three are rated among the four most difficult in the tournament. Nicklaus parked his drive under a picnic table on the 17th during the final round of the 1984 Memorial. He took a bogey on the hole but parred the 18th to tie Andy Bean at 280. The sudden-death playoff was then decided on the 17th when Bean missed a 3-foot par putt to hand his host a second Memorial title.

One of the most electric finishes in recent Tour history occurred at the 1993 Memorial, when close friends Paul Azinger and Payne Stewart, deadlocked atop the leader board, hit their approach shots into the left greenside bunker on the final hole. Stewart looked like the winner when he hit a bunker shot to within 8 feet of the cup, but Azinger holed his wedge and broke into tears. Stunned, Stewart missed his 8-footer to fall into third place. In a few short minutes, Stewart's apparent winnings had fallen by $155,000.

Tom Lehman didn't need any last-hole heroics when he scorched the course with four straight 67s and a course-record 268 in 1994. That same year, Bob Tway equaled a Tour record by carding two aces in one tournament—one on the eighth in the first round and the other on his third crack at the 12th.

In 1995, Greg Norman fired a 269 to win the Memorial, but it was an older great's turn to be honored when the groundbreaking took place for a Jack Nicklaus Museum.

●TOUGHEST HOLE

The 437-yard, par-4 18th, a dog-leg right, has a landing area bordered by sand on the right and a stream on the left. The approach shot is to a medium-sized left-to-right-angled green with a pair of bunkers to its left, another to its right and a fourth to its rear. The entranceway is squeezed by rough and bunkers. Jack Nicklaus just avoided the tree guarding the left side of the green on his 3-iron approach during the final round of the 1977 event, which he won by two strokes.

●BEST PLACE TO WATCH

The three final holes, among the most difficult on the course, usually provide the most memorable shots on the final day. But Muirfield was one of the first golf courses in the United States built for spectators and the requirements of television coverage, so many other holes will provide good vantage points, including the green areas around two tough par-3s—the 204-yard fourth and the 156-yard 12th, which is similar to the 12th at Augusta.

●WHO THE COURSE FAVORS

The course favors a long, accurate hitter off the tee who can stay out of the bunkers, trees, water and heavy rough guarding landing areas. It helps to be able to come high into the greens in order to hold and properly position the ball on these fast, well-guarded surfaces.

Courtesy of Muirfield Village Golf Club

WITH LIMITED APPROACH ANGLES, WELL-PLACED DRIVES ARE MUSTS AT MUIRFIELD'S NINTH.

HOLE	YARDS	PAR	HOLE	YARDS	PAR
1	446	4	10	441	4
2	452	4	11	538	5
3	392	4	12	156	3
4	204	3	13	442	4
5	531	5	14	363	4
6	430	4	15	490	5
7	549	5	16	204	3
8	189	3	17	430	4
9	410	4	18	437	4
			TOTAL	7104	

TOUGHEST HOLE

BEST PLACE TO WATCH

MUIRFIELD VILLAGE GOLF CLUB
ARCHITECTS:
JACK NICKLAUS WITH DESMOND MUIRHEAD (1974)

LODGING

$$$ Stouffer Renaissance Dublin Hotel, 600 Metro Place North, Dublin, Ohio. (614) 764-2200. 5 minutes from Muirfield Village.

$$ Courtyard by Marriott–Dublin, 5175 Post Rd., Dublin, Ohio. (614) 764-9393, (800) 321-2211. 10 minutes from Muirfield Village.

$ Red Roof Inn–Dublin, 5125 Post Rd., Dublin, Ohio. (614) 764-3993, (800) 843-7663. 5 minutes from Muirfield Village.

DINING

Lindey's, 169 East Beck St., Columbus, Ohio. (614) 228-4343.

Nickleby's Bookstore Cafe, 1425 Grandview Ave., Columbus, Ohio. (614) 488-2665.

Bob Evans Farms Restaurant, 5067 Post Rd., Dublin, Ohio. (614) 889-8883.

PUBLIC COURSES TO PLAY IN AREA

Bent Tree Golf Club, 350 Bent Tree Rd., Sunbury, Ohio. Public. (614) 965-5140. 18/6,850/72. 25 minutes from Muirfield Village.

Eagle Sticks Golf Club, 1300 Country Club Dr., Zanesville, Ohio. Public. (614) 454-4900. (800) 782-4493. 18/6,857/72. 1 hour from Muirfield Village.

Indian Springs Golf Club, 11111 State Rte. 161, Mechanicsburg, Ohio. Public. (513) 834-2111. 18/7,123/72. 45 minutes from Muirfield Village.

TICKETS & ACCESSIBILITY

How to watch: Mon., PGA practice rounds. Tue., PGA practice rounds, Skins game, junior golf clinic. Wed., PGA practice rounds, golf clinic. Thur.-Sun., tournament. Individual, group and sponsorship tickets available. The Memorial Tournament, P.O. Box 396, Dublin, OH 43017. (614) 889-6700.

How to play: Muirfield Village is a private club. You must be a member or the guest of a member to play the course.

Kemper Open

TPC at Avenel

The Kemper, which has had the same title sponsor longer than any other American sporting event, arrived with the thunder of cavalry when Arnold Palmer staged one of his patented final-round charges to take its inaugural title in 1968. The win at Pleasant Valley Country Club in Massachusetts earned the 14-year veteran a $30,000 check that made him the Tour's first player to reach $1 million in career earnings.

The Kemper has moved three times since then, passing the 1970s at Quail Hollow in North Carolina, most of the 1980s at Congressional in Bethesda, Md., and finally crossing the street in 1987 to take up residence at the TPC at Avenel.

The 1995 Kemper boasted its best field in years, arriving as it did just a week before the U.S. Open. Lee Janzen birdied the tough final hole for the fifth time in four days to win a playoff with Corey Pavin, then consoled his friend by telling him the U.S. Open is usually won by the previous weekend's second-place finisher. A week later, Pavin proved him right.

TOURNAMENT-AT-A-GLANCE

Course: The Tournament Players Club at Avenel
Type: Private
Location: 10000 Oaklyn Dr., Potomac, MD 20854
Telephone: (301) 469-3700
When: May 23–26, 1996
How To Get There: From Washington, D.C., 40 minutes. Take River Rd. across Beltway to third stoplight. Go left on Bradley to intersection, 0.6 mile to Club Dr.
Broadcast: CBS (1996)
Purse: $1,500,000 (1996)
Tournament Record: 21-under-par 263, Billy Andrade, 1991

●TOUGHEST HOLE

A long slight dogleg to the right, the 18th requires a tee shot to the right center in order to take the bunker to the left out of play. Two more bunkers, one to the right and another toward the rear of the green, can also catch approach shots. In '95, Davis Love completed a back-nine collapse here by hitting his tee shot into the left fairway bunker, pulling his next shot way left and finishing with a double bogey that dropped him from final-round leader all the way to fourth place.

●BEST PLACE TO WATCH

During the early rounds you'll want to catch the action around tough holes like the 239-yard, par-3 third and the 472-yard, par-4 12th. During the final round watch the finish at four of the best finishing holes in golf. The stadium-style TPC course at Avenel will accommodate 50,000 spectators at the 18th hole alone.

●WHO THE COURSE FAVORS

The TPC at Avenel favors a long, accurate hitter who can come into the greens from the proper angles to take the water, bunkers and deep rough out of play. The tee shot on the 453-yard, par-4 eighth must be hit long and to the right-center, for example, in order to come into a small green surrounded by bunkers. A tee shot to the left will catch a fairway bunker or deep rough.

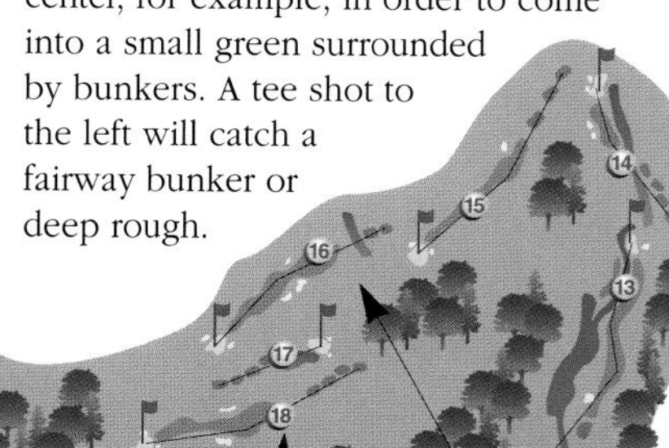

HOLE	YARDS	PAR	HOLE	YARDS	PAR
1	393	4	10	374	4
2	622	5	11	165	3
3	239	3	12	472	4
4	435	4	13	524	5
5	359	4	14	301	4
6	520	5	15	467	4
7	461	4	16	415	4
8	453	4	17	195	3
9	166	3	18	444	4
			TOTAL	7005	71

TPC at Avenel
Architects: Edmund Ault, Brian Ault, Tom Clark, Bill Love, Ed Sneed (1986)

LODGING

$$$ Hyatt Regency Bethesda, One Bethesda Metro Center, Bethesda, Md. (301) 657-1234. 15 minutes from TPC at Avenel.
$$ Residence Inn by Marriott Bethesda, 7335 Wisconsin Ave., Bethesda, Md. (301) 897-9400, (800) 331-3131. 15 minutes from TPC at Avenel.
$ Clarion Hotel and Suites, 1251 W. Montgomery Ave., Rockville, Md. (800) 366-1251. 15 minutes from TPC at Avenel.

DINING

Old Anglers Inn, 10801 MacArthur Blvd., Potomac, Md. (301) 365-2425.
O'Donnell's, 8301 Wisconsin Ave., Bethesda, Md. (301) 656-6200.
The Original Pancake House, 7703 Woodmont Ave., Bethesda, Md. (301) 986-0285.

PUBLIC COURSES TO PLAY IN AREA

Lansdowne Golf Club, 44050 Woodridge Pkwy., Leesburg, Va. Resort. (703) 729-8400, (800) 541-4801. 18/7,040/72. 35 minutes from TPC at Avenel.
Penderbrook Golf Club, 3700 Golf Trail Lane, Fairfax, Va. Public. (703) 385-3700. 18/6,151/71. 30 minutes from TPC at Avenel.
Queenstown Harbor Golf Links, 310 Link Lane, Queenstown, Md. Public. (410) 827-6611, (800) 827-5257. Harbor Nine: 9/3,070/35. River: 9/3,612/36. Woods: 9/3,498/36. 1 hour from TPC at Avenel.

TICKETS & ACCESSIBILITY

How to watch: Mon., PGA practice rounds, pro-am. Tue., PGA practice rounds, shoot-out, junior golf clinic. Wed., pro-am. Thur.–Sun., tournament. Individual tickets start at $10 for practice rounds. Group and sponsorship plans available. Kemper Open, 10,000 Oaklyn Dr., Potomac, MD 20854. (301) 469-3737.
How to play: The TPC at Avenel is a private club. You must be a member or the guest of a member to play the course.

Canon Greater Hartford Open

TPC at River Highlands

LODGING

$$$ Griswold Inn, 36 Main St., Essex, Conn. (203) 767-1776. 40 minutes from River Highlands.

$$ Radisson Inn and Conference Center, 100 Berlin Rd., Cromwell, Conn. (203) 635-2000, (800) 333-3333. 5 minutes from River Highlands.

$ Comfort Inn, 111 Berlin Rd., Cromwell, Conn. (203) 635-4100, (800) 221-2222. 10 minutes from River Highlands.

DINING

Griswold Inn, 36 Main St., Essex, Conn. (203) 767-1776.

Chart House, W. Main St. at Rte. 9, Chester, Conn. (203) 526-9898.

PUBLIC COURSES TO PLAY IN AREA

Blackledge Country Club, 180 West St., Hebron, Conn. Public. (203) 228-0250. Links: 9/3,086/36. Anderson: 9/3,201/36. Gilead: 9/3,193/36. 25 minutes from River Highlands.

Lyman Meadow Golf Club, Rte. 157, Middlefield, Conn. Public. (203) 349-8055. 18/7,011/72. 15 minutes from River Highlands.

Portland Golf Course, 169 Bartlett St., Portland, Conn. Public. (203) 342-2833. 18/6,213/71. 10 minutes from River Highlands.

TICKETS & ACCESSIBILITY

How to watch: Mon., PGA practice rounds. Tue., Celebrity long drive competition, golf clinic, shoot-out, PGA practice round. Wed., Celebrity pro-am. Thur.-Sun., tournament. Individual tickets start at $8. Group and sponsorship plans available. Canon Greater Hartford Open, One Financial Plaza, 2nd Floor, Hartford, CT 06103-2601. (203) 522-4171.

How to play: The TPC at River Highlands is a private club. You must be a member or a guest of a member to play the course.

TOURNAMENT-AT-A-GLANCE

Course: TPC at River Highlands
Type: Private
Location: Golf Club Rd., Cromwell, CT 06416
Telephone: (203) 635-5000
When: June 27–30, 1996
How To Get There: From Hartford, 20 minutes. Take I-91 south to Exit 23. Take left off exit ramp to Rte. 99. Take right onto Rte. 99, go 2 miles to TPC sign on left. Follow signs to golf course.
Broadcast: CBS, ESPN (1996)
Purse: $1,200,000 (1995)
Tournament Record: 25-under-par 259, Tim Norris, 1982 (at par-72 Wethersfield CC, Hartford)

In the days when giants named Jack Nicklaus, Lee Trevino and Arnold Palmer shook the fairways, there was the Crosby, there was the Bob Hope Desert Classic, and then there was Sammy.

In fact, the Greater Hartford event that bore Sammy Davis Jr.'s name for 16 years has a history that predates his involvement by almost two decades, twice crowning Palmer the champion of the Insurance City Open.

As the 1990s approached, the event took on a new identity when Davis stepped out of the spotlight and the competition departed the Wethersfield Country Club in quest of a stiffer challenge. Today, the Canon Greater Hartford Open is played at the River Highlands Course, a TPC Stadium reconfiguration of a traditional course, just southeast of downtown Hartford. Stronger fields have produced a star-studded roster of champions, including Greg Norman (1995), Nick Price (1993) and Lanny Wadkins (1992).

TPC at River Highlands
Architects:
Robert J. Ross and Maurice Kearny (1928)
Remodeled by Orrin Smith (1951),
Pete Dye and David Postlethwait (1984)
Bobby Weed (1991)

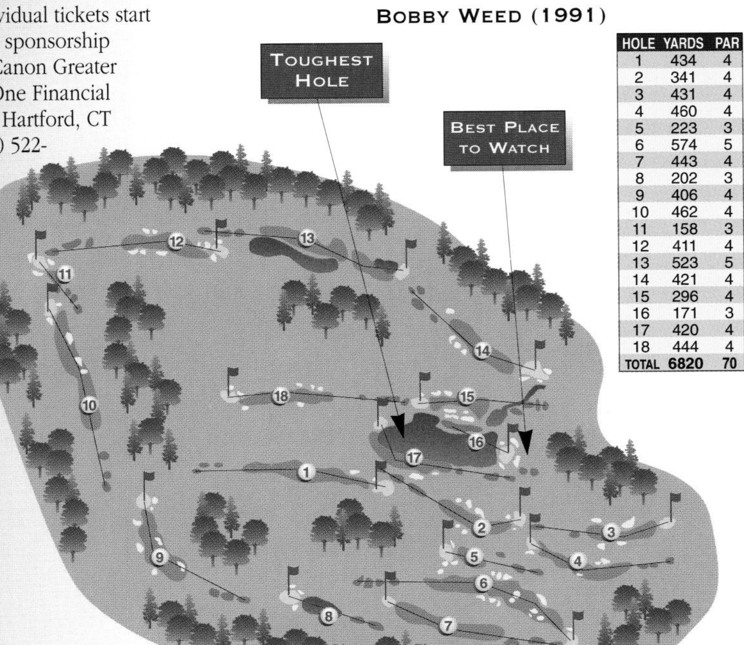

HOLE	YARDS	PAR
1	434	4
2	341	4
3	431	4
4	460	4
5	223	3
6	574	5
7	443	4
8	202	3
9	406	4
10	462	4
11	158	3
12	411	4
13	523	5
14	421	4
15	296	4
16	171	3
17	420	4
18	444	4
TOTAL	6820	70

●TOUGHEST HOLE

Part of a nail-biting, three-hole spin around a lake, the 420-yard, par-4 17th has a dogleg right that wraps around water below the green. In 1993, winner Nick Price hit his second shot just over the green, then hit a bump-and-run recovery to within 4 feet and saved his par on the final round.

●BEST PLACE TO WATCH

The tournament has not been won by more than two strokes since 1982, when it was still played in Wethersfield, so position yourself somewhere around the final holes. A hillside seat at "The Blue Triangle"—Nos. 15, 16 and 17—affords views of all three lakeside holes. Also try the 10th green, a 462-yard par-4, which is easily accessible to the 158-yard, par-3 11th.

●WHO THE COURSE FAVORS

The TPC at River Highlands demands that the golfer weave through an obstacle course of bunkers off the tee and coming into the greens. The 574 yard, par-5 sixth, for example, has more than a dozen bunkers, and the 411 yard, par-4 12th has eight.

Motorola Western Open

COG HILL GOLF AND COUNTRY CLUB

The USA's second-oldest golf tournament after the U.S. Open has been played at Cog Hill's Dubsdread since 1991.

The Masters? The PGA? You call that tradition? The Western Open predates them both and ranks second only to the U.S. Open among the longest-running American events on the PGA Tour. Of course, its creators—representatives from 14 Chicago-area clubs—probably wouldn't want to hear that. They founded the Western Golf Association in 1899 to challenge the East Coast–centered USGA for control of the booming sport.

Scotsman Willie Smith, who ran away with an 11-stroke victory in the U.S. Open that year, captured the first Western title in an 18-hole playoff at the Glen/View Club in Golf, Ill. Since then, the tournament has roamed as far west as the Presidio Club in San Francisco (1956), as far south as the River Oaks Country Club in Houston (1940) and as far east as the Brookfield Country Club in New York state (1948). The event ended its nomadic tradition in 1962 when it moved back to Illinois. Since 1991 it has been played at Cog Hill, 32 miles southwest of downtown Chicago.

Virtually every great golfer has played in the Western Open, and many have held its sterling cup (though the 1923 original disappeared only three years later). Walter Hagen won this championship a record five times (1916, 1921, 1926, 1927, 1932), Willie Anderson four times (1902, 1904, 1908, 1909), and the other multiple winners include names like Hogan, Snead, Palmer, Casper, Nicklaus, Watson and Price.

Yet the first amateur to win this event put his stamp on its history like none of its other champions. Chick Evans, who in 1916 would become the first player ever to capture the U.S. Amateur and the U.S. Open in the same year, won the 1910 Western Open 6 and 5 in a match-play final. His most enduring contribution, however, was his establishment in 1928 of a trust fund to help caddies pay for college. Since 1930, Evans scholars have been the sole charity beneficiaries of the Western Open, and the program currently awards grants to more than 800 men and women who are attending some 20 universities, mostly in the Midwest.

Cog Hill, a privately owned public facility, includes four golf courses, a formidable clubhouse, and an excellent practice and teaching facility. The complex was purchased in 1951 by the legendary Joe Jemsek, once a caddie at 65 cents a round and a young golf professional during the Great Depression. Jemsek now owns eight golf courses in the Chicago area and is considered a patron saint of American public golf.

Dubsdread, opened in 1964, is a beautifully designed, mature course that rolls gently toward greens that are distinctively guarded by clusters of sculptured, amoeba-like traps. Players who spray the ball might be stymied by a large tree or ambushed by an occasional water hazard.

TOURNAMENT-AT-A-GLANCE

Course: Cog Hill Golf and Country Club—Cog Hill No. 4 (Dubsdread)
Type: Public
Location: 12294 Archer Ave. at 119th St., Lemont, IL 60439
Telephone: (708) 257-5872
When: July 4–7, 1996
How To Get There: From Chicago, 32 miles. Take Hwy. 55 south to Hwy. 83 south to Hwy. 171 south. The course is on the right (199th St./Parker Rd.), 6 miles from intersection of I-55 and Hwy. 83.
Broadcast: CBS (1996)
Purse: $2,000,000 (1995)
Tournament Record: 20-under-par 268, Sam Snead, 1949 (at Keller Golf Club, St. Paul, Minn.)

●TOUGHEST HOLE

Twelve of Cog Hill's holes had over-par scoring averages during the 1994 event. The 452-yard, par-4 18th topped the list with a stroke average of 4.286. The tee shot on this hole must avoid three bunkers to the right of the landing area and one to the left in order to set up an approach to a green protected by a pond on its left and two bunkers to its right. Nick Price missed a 5-foot putt on this hole in the final round of the 1994 Western Open but was given a reprieve when Greg Kraft hit a bunker on his tee shot, another bunker on his approach, and then bogeyed the hole. Kraft finished with a final-round 73 and a 72-hole total of 278, one stroke and $86,400 behind Price.

●BEST PLACE TO WATCH

The area around the 16th green, a tough 409-yard par-4, provides easy access to the 14th green, 15th tee and 17th tee. The area around the 12th green, the most difficult par-3 on the course, has easy access to the 13th tee. Be sure to be around the 18th hole on the final day. This green is convenient to the clubhouse, the first tee, the 10th tee and the ninth green. The ninth, a 568-yard par-5, is guarded by two large traps towards its front but provides birdie and eagle opportunities for those who can reach the flat, uncomplicated putting surface in two.

●WHO THE COURSE FAVORS

Dubsdread is a scenic, tree-lined course that rewards the long hitter who can accurately set up high, well-placed approaches to the well-bunkered greens. The 410-yard, par-4 seventh, for example, is guarded by four large traps. Pin placements near these bunkers can easily create bogeys. The same is true of the 192-yard, par-3 14th, which is surrounded by six bunkers.

COG HILL GOLF CLUB—COG HILL NO. 4 (DUBSDREAD)
ARCHITECTS: DICK WILSON AND JOE LEE (1964)
REMODELED BY
JOE LEE (1977), ROCKY ROGUEMORE (1990)

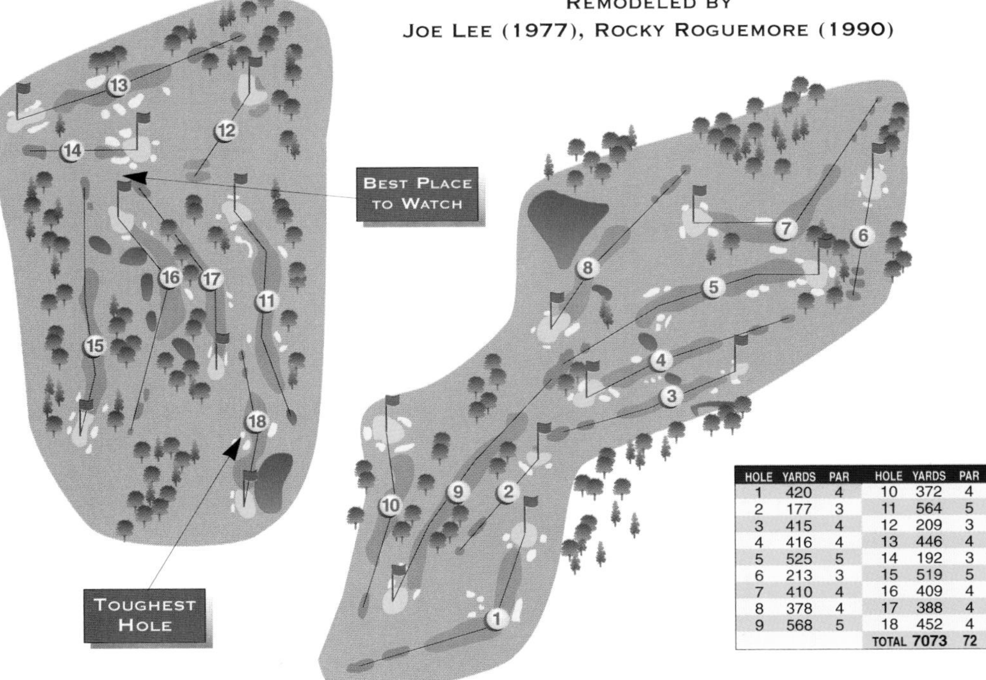

HOLE	YARDS	PAR	HOLE	YARDS	PAR
1	420	4	10	372	4
2	177	3	11	564	5
3	415	4	12	209	3
4	416	4	13	446	4
5	525	5	14	192	3
6	213	3	15	519	5
7	410	4	16	409	4
8	378	4	17	388	4
9	568	5	18	452	4
			TOTAL	**7073**	72

LODGING

$$$ Ritz-Carlton Chicago, 160 E. Pearson St., Chicago. (312) 266-1000, (800) 241-3333. 50 minutes from Cog Hill.
$$ The Whitehall Hotel, 105 E. Delaware Pl., Chicago. (312) 944-6300, (800) 948-4255. 50 minutes from Cog Hill.
$ Courtyard by Marriott, 1155 E. Diehl Rd., Naperville, Ill. (708) 505-0550, (800) 321-2211. 30 minutes from Cog Hill.

DINING

Ambria, 2300 N. Lincoln Park West, Chicago. (312) 472-5959.
Meson Sabika, 1025 Aurora Ave., Naperville, Ill. (708) 983-3000.
Cog Hill Clubhouse, 12294 Archer Ave., Lemont, Ill. (708) 257-5872.

PUBLIC COURSES TO PLAY IN AREA

Cantigny Golf Course, 27 W. Mack Rd., Wheaton, Ill. Public. (708) 668-8463. Woodside/Lakeside: 18/6,709/72. Hillside: 9/3,253/36. 50 minutes from Cog Hill.
Kemper Lakes, Old McHenry Rd., Long Grove, Ill. Public. (708) 320-3950. 18/7,217/72. 1 hour from Cog Hill.
Pine Meadow Golf Club, 1 Pine Meadow Lane, Mundelein, Ill. Public. (708) 566-4653. 18/7,129/72. 45 minutes from Cog Hill.

TICKETS & ACCESSIBILITY

How to watch: Mon., PGA practice rounds, two pro-ams. Tue., PGA practice rounds, junior golf clinic, celebrity Skins game. Wed., PGA practice rounds, two pro-ams. Thur.-Sun., tournament. Individual tickets available from $20. Group and sponsor plans available. Motorola Western Open, Western Golf Association, One Briar Rd., Golf, IL 60029. (708) 724-4600.
How to play: Cog Hill is a privately owned public golf course open year round. There are four courses, including No. 1 (18/6,294/72), No. 2 (18/6,295/72), No. 3 (18/6,437/72) and No. 4 (Dubsdread), which are open from April through October. There is also an excellent golf learning and practice facility on site. (708) 257-5872.

FedEx St. Jude Classic

TPC at Southwind

Lightning struck twice at this Memphis classic in 1977. Former President Gerald Ford thrilled viewers at the Wednesday pro-am that year with "the shot heard 'round the world"—a hole-in-one on Colonial Country Club's 177-yard fifth. But when the next issue of *Sports Illustrated* acclaimed "one of the most significant athletic achievements of the century," Al Geiberger was the golfer they had in mind.

Playing the longest course on the Tour that year, the 39-year-old Californian fired a second-round 59 to break a barrier that had seemed impenetrable.

There have been plenty of other great moments, and name changes, in the history of this event, which began in 1958 as the Memphis Open. The late Danny Thomas became its celebrity host in 1970, and the St. Jude Children's Research Hospital has been its sole charity ever since.

The TPC at Southwind, a rolling, tree-lined course on the outskirts of Memphis, has been the tournament's home since 1989. Many of its fairways have few or no bunkers in the landing areas, but the thick rough will slow up any golfer who strays the ball.

TOURNAMENT-AT-A-GLANCE

Course: TPC at Southwind
Type: Private
Location: 3325 Club at Southwind, Memphis, TN 38125
Telephone: (901) 748-0330
When: June 20–23, 1996
How To Get There: From Memphis, 45 minutes. Proceed to Rte. 240 to Poplar Ave. Exit. Go east to Germantown Rd., then take a right on Germantown to stop sign. Take a left onto Poplar Pike to the next stop sign, then take a left onto Hacks Cross Rd. Proceed to Southwind entrance on the left.
Broadcast: CBS (1996)
Purse: $1,250,000 (1995)
Tournament Record: 21-under-par 263, Jay Haas, 1992

•TOUGHEST HOLE

The tee shot on the par-4 17th should finish 25 to 40 yards in front of a creek cutting the fairway at the bottom of a long drop. The approach is to a deep green with three bunkers to its right and another two left. Tom Kite hit his "best shot ever in competition—a 30-foot banana" from behind a tree on this hole for a final-round birdie that set up his playoff victory in 1990.

•WHO THE COURSE FAVORS

This long 7,006-yard, par-71 layout favors a big hitter who won't stray too far from the ample landing areas into the deep rough. Approaches are critical because the greens are either small, like the 17-yard-deep putting surface on the fourth, or overly generous, like the par-4 ninth's 51-yard-deep green, a fertile field for three-putts.

HOLE	YARDS	PAR
1	426	4
2	387	4
3	525	5
4	194	3
5	527	5
6	427	4
7	458	4
8	169	3
9	450	4
10	447	4
11	146	3
12	375	4
13	430	4
14	231	3
15	385	4
16	528	5
17	464	4
18	437	4
TOTAL	7006	71

•BEST PLACE TO WATCH

From the clubhouse, it's easy to move among the 18th, first, and ninth greens and the 10th tee. If the summer Tennessee heat doesn't bother you, the green area around No. 17, one of the most difficult holes on the course, is a good place to watch, or you might want to set up behind the scenic 231-yard, par-3 14th, the toughest par in 1994.

TPC at Southwind
Architect: Ron Pritchard with Fuzzy Zoeller and Hubert Green (1988)

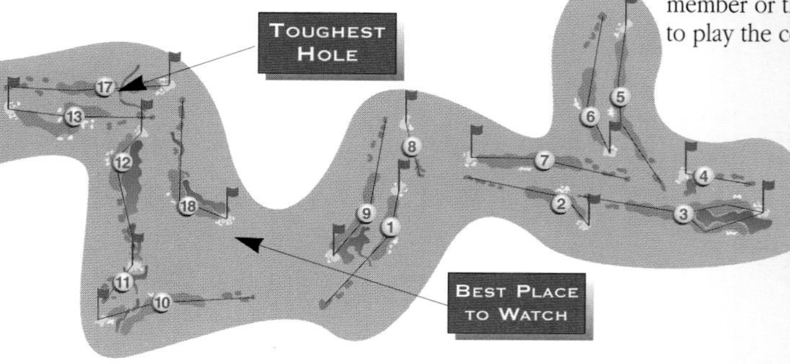

LODGING

$$$ The Peabody Memphis Hotel, 149 Union Ave., Memphis. (901) 529-4000, (800) PEABODY. 45 minutes from Southwind.

$$ Marriott Residence Inn, 6141 Poplar Pike, Germantown, Tenn. (901) 685-9595, (800) 228-9290. 10 minutes from Southwind.

$ Econo Lodge, 3280 Elvis Presley Blvd., Memphis. (901) 345-1425, (800) 446-6900. 45 minutes from Southwind.

Bed and Breakfast in Memphis Reservation Service, Box 41621, Memphis. (901) 726-5920.

DINING

Chez Philippe at The Peabody Memphis Hotel, 149 Union Ave., Memphis. (901) 529-4188.

Paulette's, 2110 Madison Ave., Memphis. (901) 726-5128.

John Wills' Barbecue Pit, 5101 Sanderlin St., Memphis. (901) 761-5101.

PUBLIC COURSES TO PLAY IN AREA

Big Creek Golf Club, 6195 Woodstock Cuba Rd, Memphis, Tenn. Public. (901) 353-1654. 18/7,056/72. 45 minutes from Southwind.

Orgill Park Golf Course, 9080 Bethuel Rd., Millington, Tenn. Public. (901) 872-3610. 18/6,284/70. 45 minutes from Southwind.

Stonebridge Golf Course, 3049 Davies Plantation Rd. South, Memphis. Public. (901) 382-1886. 18/6,788/71. 15 minutes from Southwind.

TICKETS & ACCESSIBILITY

How to watch: Mon., PGA practice rounds, pro-am. Tue., PGA practice rounds, youth golf clinic, trick-shot show, shoot-out. Wed., PGA practice rounds, celebrity pro-am. Thur.-Sun., tournament. Individual, group and sponsor ticket plans available. FedEx St. Jude Classic, 3325 Club at Southwind, Memphis, TN 38125. (901) 748-0534.

How to play: TPC at Southwind is a private club. You must be a member or the guest of a member to play the course.

Deposit Guaranty Golf Classic

Annandale Golf Club

LODGING

$$$ Millsaps Blue Horse Bed & Breakfast, 628 N. State St., Jackson, Miss. (601) 352-0221. 20 minutes from Annandale.

$$ Residence Inn by Marriott, 881 E. River Place, Jackson, Miss. (601) 355-3599. 20 minutes from Annandale.

$ Cabot Lodge of Jackson North, 120 Dyess Rd., Jackson, Miss. (601) 957-0757. 10 minutes from Annandale.

DINING

The Restaurant at the Edison Walthal Hotel, 225 E. Capitol St., Jackson, Miss. (601) 948-6161.

Iron Horse Grill, 320 W. Pearl St., Jackson, Miss. (601) 355-8419.

Morrison's Cafeteria, 1200 E. Country Line Rd., Jackson, Miss. (601) 956-0016.

PUBLIC COURSES TO PLAY IN AREA

Bay Pointe Country Club, 800 Bay Pointe Dr., Brandon, Miss. Semi-private. (601) 829-1862. 18/6,320/72. 30 minutes from Annandale.

Timberton Golf Club, 22 Club House Rd., Hattiesburg, Miss. Public. (601) 584-4653. 18/7,003/72. 95 minutes from Annandale.

Windance Country Club, 19385 Champion Circle, Gulfport, Miss. Public. (601) 832-5374. 18/6,705/72. 2 1/2 hours from Annandale.

TICKETS & ACCESSIBILITY

How to watch: Mon., PGA practice rounds. Tue., PGA practice rounds. Wed., pro-am. Thur.-Sun., tournament. Individual, group and sponsor tickets available. Deposit Guaranty Golf Classic, P.O. Box 1939, Madison, MS 39130, (601) 856-9290, (800) 856-9290.

How to play: Annandale is a private club. You must be a member or the guest of a member to play the course.

TOURNAMENT-AT-A-GLANCE

Course: Annandale Golf Club
Type: Private
Location: 837 Mannsdale Rd., Madison, MS 39110
Telephone: (601) 856-3882
When: July 18–21, 1996
How To Get There: From Jackson, 25 minutes. Take I-55 north to Madison Exit 108. Take a left on Hwy. 463 (5 miles), Annandale is on the left side.
Broadcast: Golf Channel (1995)
Purse: $700,000 (1995)
Tournament Record: 25-under-par 263, Dan Halldorson, 1986 (at par-72 Hattiesburg Country Club)

The world's best golfers are playing the British Open on the weekend this PGA Tour event is played, so newcomers get a chance here to boost their earnings and put their names on the winners' lists.

Elevated to full PGA tournament status in 1994—its first year at the Jack Nicklaus-designed Annandale Golf Club, the Classic traces its roots as a PGA Tour satellite event to 1968.

Rain spoiled the event's 1994 coming-out party as officials were forced to cancel two rounds, including all but a sudden-death playoff on the final day. Playing the soggy 532 yard, par-5 18th, which runs along the right edge of a scenic lake, Brian Henninger sank an 18-foot birdie putt that day to defeat Mike Sullivan.

Located 20 minutes north of Jackson, Miss., Annandale is a collection of consistently strong golf holes featuring ample landing areas, wiry rough, strategically placed bunkers and waste areas, and several water hazards. Trees frame many holes, but are set back from the fairways. The pencross bentgrass greens—rare this far south—are large, with tricky undulations and terraces.

●TOUGHEST HOLE

The 465-yard, par-4 fourth requires a 230-yard carry over a fairway bunker on the tee shot, then usually requires a 3- or 4-iron approach to a large green that slopes a bit left toward two bunkers on that side.

●BEST PLACE TO WATCH

This gently rolling course has no severe elevation changes, making it easy to follow the action. There's plenty of intrigue on the three finishing holes, including the scenic 17th, which plays to an island landing area whose center is about 230 yards from the tee. The farther left the tee shot, the longer and more difficult the approach to a green that's difficult to hold with a mid-iron.

●WHO THE COURSE FAVORS

The landing areas are generous at Annandale, as are the rolling greens. But winds can kick up, water comes into play on half the holes, and the rough will be high and tough. If the golfer doesn't pay attention to position, there is a good chance he will be penalized by low-percentage shots to well-guarded flags.

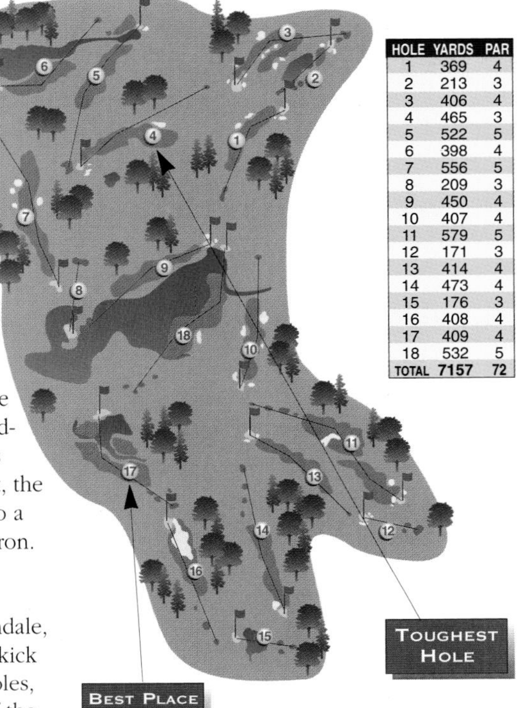

HOLE	YARDS	PAR
1	369	4
2	213	3
3	406	4
4	465	3
5	522	5
6	398	4
7	556	5
8	209	3
9	450	4
10	407	4
11	579	5
12	171	3
13	414	4
14	473	4
15	176	3
16	408	4
17	409	4
18	532	5
TOTAL	7157	72

Annandale Golf Club
Architect: Jack Nicklaus (1981)

ANHEUSER-BUSCH GOLF CLASSIC

KINGSMILL GOLF CLUB

This event, established in 1968 amid the vineyards of Napa Valley, Calif., was moved across the continent in 1981 to the Pete Dye–designed centerpiece of Anheuser-Busch's own Kingsmill development, a 2,900-acre resort and residential community in historic Williamsburg, Va.

The River Course cuts through rolling woodland terrain, around four ponds and finishes with spectacular views of the James River, but its three-rail fences and snaking railroad-tie embankments give its open holes the feel of an ancient horse-breeding farm. A shotmaker's course, it requires accurate tee shots to avoid uneven lies, trees, 90 bunkers and unfavorable angles to its fast, multi-tiered greens.

TOURNAMENT-AT-A-GLANCE

Course: Kingsmill Golf Club—River Course
Type: Resort
Location: 100 Golf Club Rd., Williamsburg, VA 23185
Telephone: (804) 253-3906
When: July 11–14, 1996
How To Get There: From east or west, take I-64 to Williamsburg. Take Exit 57A (Busch Gardens) and follow Rte. 199W to the first traffic light. The Kingsmill entrance is on the left.
Broadcast: ESPN (1995)
Purse: $1,100,000 (1995)
Tournament Record: 18-under-par 266, Lanny Wadkins, 1990 and Mike Hulbert, 1991

The three finishing holes on the River Course are among the finest on the Tour. Remnants of Civil War fortifications run along the left of the scenic 17th, a wind-crossed 177-yard, par-3 with a cathedral of trees behind it and the river downslope to its right.

It's here that Kingsmill resident and two-time U.S. Open champion Curtis Strange can count on hearing cheers from the rowdy flotilla that commentators have christened "Curtis's Strange Navy."

Mark McCumber chipped in for birdies on the 15th and 16th holes during the final round of the 1994 tournament and went on to win the event by three shots.

Courtesy of Anheuser-Busch Golf Classic

WITH THE 17TH HOLE PLAYING DIRECTLY BESIDE THE JAMES RIVER, IT HAS BECOME A FAVORITE GATHERING SPOT FOR BOATERS KNOWN AS "CURTIS'S STRANGE NAVY."

●TOUGHEST HOLE

The 413-yard, par-4 eighth hole requires a tee shot dropped just right-of-center of the severely banked fairway in order to set up a clear approach to a two-level hillside green that is guarded by three bunkers to its left and another to the top right. The most difficult par-3 in 1994 was the 204-yard second.

●BEST PLACE TO WATCH

The rolling, well-treed River Course is an easy course to walk, but the humid heat of a Williamsburg July might deter you from following the golfers around the course. Close to the clubhouse are the 18th green, 11th tee, 10th tee, first tee and ninth green. Toward the end of the tournament you will want to be around the final three holes. All three of these beautiful holes had an over-par stroke average in 1994. An incoming wind on No. 16 and variable winds on No. 17 can make these holes difficult and interesting to watch.

●WHO THE COURSE FAVORS

Pete Dye courses tend to favor a thinking golfer. Kingsmill, because of its trees, sloped fairways, variable winds, multi-tiered greens and strategically placed bunkers, requires proper club selection and shotmaking rather than distance. The par-4 first hole, for example, has a double fairway that enables the golfer to choose an angle to the flagstick. As Dye once said, "When you get those dudes thinking, they're in trouble."

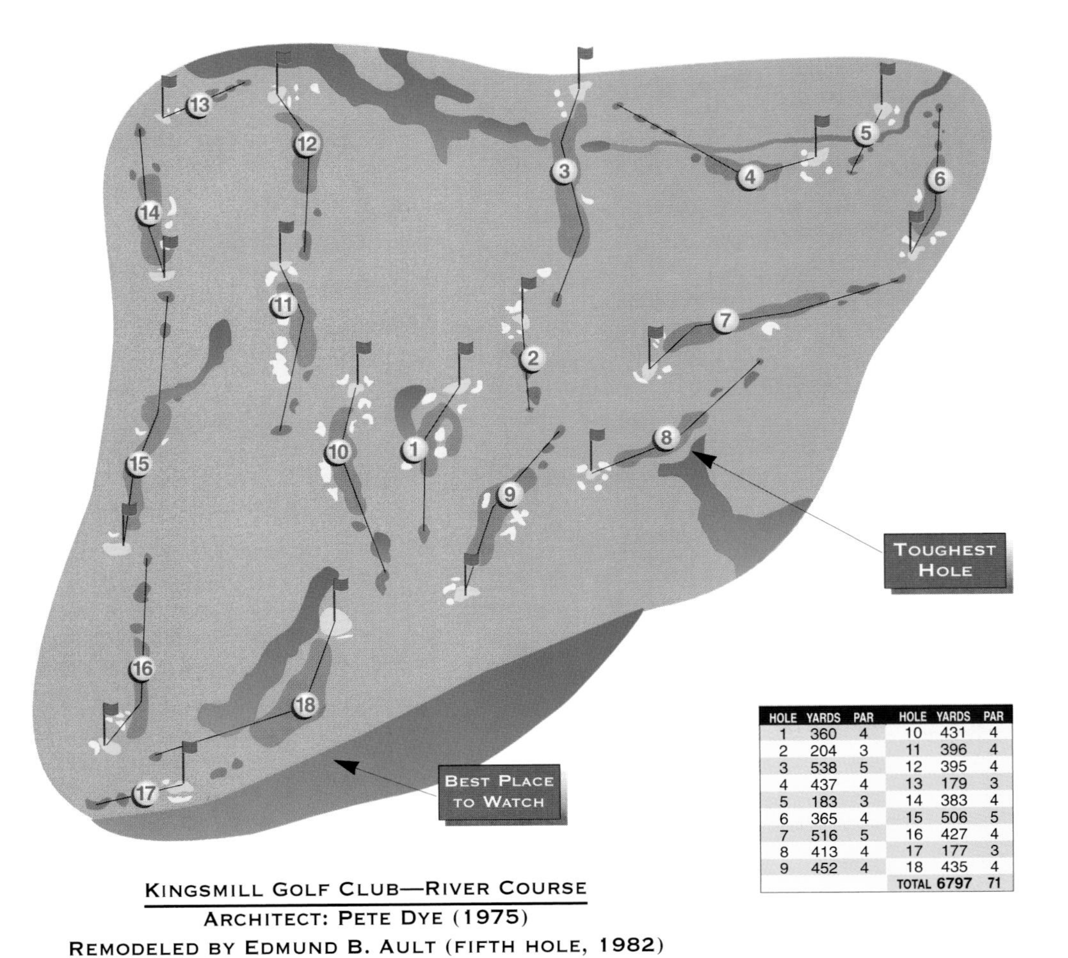

HOLE	YARDS	PAR	HOLE	YARDS	PAR
1	360	4	10	431	4
2	204	3	11	396	4
3	538	5	12	395	4
4	437	4	13	179	3
5	183	3	14	383	4
6	365	4	15	506	5
7	516	5	16	427	4
8	413	4	17	177	3
9	452	4	18	435	4
			TOTAL	6797	71

KINGSMILL GOLF CLUB—RIVER COURSE

ARCHITECT: PETE DYE (1975)

REMODELED BY EDMUND B. AULT (FIFTH HOLE, 1982)

LODGING

$$$ Williamsburg Inn, 137 Francis St., Williamsburg, Va. (804) 221-8840. 10 minutes from Kingsmill.

$$ The Kingsmill Resort and Conference Center, 1010 Kingsmill Rd., Williamsburg, Va. (804) 253-1703, (800) 832-5665. On site.

$ Econo Lodge Parkway, 442 Parkway Dr., Williamsburg, Va. (804) 229-7564, (800) 424-4777. 5 minutes from Kingsmill.

DINING

The Regency Room, in the Williamsburg Inn, 137 Francis St., Williamsburg, Va. (804) 229-1000.

The Dining Room at Ford's Colony, 240 Ford's Colony Dr., Williamsburg, Va. (804) 258-4100.

Thomas Pettus Grille, at Kingsmill, 1010 Kingsmill Rd., Williamsburg, Va. (804) 253-1703.

PUBLIC COURSES TO PLAY IN AREA

Ford's Colony Country Club, 240 Ford's Colony Dr., Williamsburg, Va. Semi-private. (804) 254-4100, (800) 548-2978. Red/White: 18/6,755/72. Blue/Gold: 18/6,787/71. 10 minutes from Kingsmill.

Golden Horseshoe Golf Course, 401 S. England St., Williamsburg, Va. Resort. (804) 220-7696. Gold: 18/6,700/71. Green: 18/7120/72. Spotswood: 18/3,745/62 (executive course). 10 minutes from Kingsmill.

The Tides Inn, King Carter Dr., Irvington, Va. Resort. (804) 438-5000, (800) 843-3746. 18/6,963/72. 35 minutes from Kingsmill.

TICKETS & ACCESSIBILITY

How to watch: Mon., PGA practice rounds, pro-am. Tue., PGA practice rounds, shoot-out. Wed., PGA practice rounds. Thur.-Sun., tournament. Individual, group and sponsorship plans available. Anheuser-Busch Golf Classic, 328 McLaws Circle, Williamsburg, VA 23185. (804) 253-3985.

How to play: Kingsmill is a resort with golf packages available year round. There are a variety of one- to three-bedroom accommodations on site. In addition to the River Course, golf courses include Plantation (18/6,590/72), Woods (18/6,784/72) and Bray Links (9/740/27). (804) 253-1703, (800) 832-5665.

New England Classic

Pleasant Valley Country Club

The Pleasant Valley Country Club in Massachusetts has been the regular host of a PGA Tour tournament since 1965, but the event's identity has changed about as often as the New England weather.

In the first and only Carling World Open, Tony Lema outdueled Arnold Palmer down the stretch after Lema's wild approach shot on the tough 17th hit a spectator. But Palmer's approach was even more damaging: It flew the green and landed in a brook. As fate would have it, this was the last tournament "Champagne" Tony would win. Lema, who had captured the British Open at St. Andrews in 1964, died at 32 in a small-plane crash outside of Chicago in 1966.

Pleasant Valley is a rolling, tree-lined course approximately 1 hour west of Boston. Set on the site of a former apple orchard, it's a long course with a variety of doglegs, numerous elevation changes, many parallel holes, few fairway bunkers and large, fast bentgrass greens. The landing areas at Pleasant Valley are generous and usually level, so the course has tended to favor longer hitters like Palmer.

TOURNAMENT-AT-A-GLANCE

Course: Pleasant Valley Country Club
Type: Private
Location: Armsby Rd., Sutton, MA 01590
Telephone: (508) 865-4441
When: July 25–28, 1996
How To Get There: Take Rte. 146 south from Worcester (7 miles), turn right at Armsby Rd., proceed 1/2 mile to the golf course.
Broadcast: Golf Channel (1996)
Purse: $1,000,000 (1995)
Tournament Record: 17-under-par 267, George Burns, 1985

•TOUGHEST HOLE

During the 1994 Classic, the 455-yard, par-4 eighth and the 480-yard, par-4 11th were the toughest holes. The eighth is a long dogleg right that plays to a narrow, two-tiered green with a bunker to its right. The 11th plays straight up a fairway cut by bunkers 165 yards from the green. The putting surface is a huge 60 yards deep and is guarded by four bunkers to its left and two more to the right.

•WHO THE COURSE FAVORS

Pleasant Valley has some of the largest greens on the tour. Approach shots and putting are extremely important. The tree-lined fairways demand driving accuracy in order to avoid being stymied. But because the event follows the British Open by a week, it favors any elite player who hustles back in time to compete here.

HOLE	YARDS	PAR
1	183	3
2	426	4
3	386	4
4	547	5
5	606	5
6	430	4
7	180	3
8	455	4
9	383	4
10	467	4
11	480	4
12	377	4
13	394	4
14	230	3
15	371	4
16	200	3
17	412	4
18	583	5
TOTAL	7110	71

•BEST PLACE TO WATCH

There are many parallel holes at Pleasant Valley making it easy to move from hole to hole. Just outside the clubhouse is the course's toughest par-3, the 183-yard first hole, which plays to a green that sharply drops off to a cluster of bunkers to its right. Be certain to watch the action on the three finishing holes, including the 18th, a 583-yard, par-5 birdie opportunity.

Best Place to Watch

Toughest Hole

PLEASANT VALLEY COUNTRY CLUB
ARCHITECT: DONALD HOENIG (1959–1960)
REMODELED BY GEOFFREY CORNISH AND WILLIAM ROBINSON (1976); AND BY BRIAN AULT, TOM CLARK, EDMUND B. AULT (1984)

LODGING

$$$ Servico Crowne Plaza, 10 Lincoln Sq., Worcester, Mass. (508) 791-1600. (800) HOLIDAY. 20 minutes from Pleasant Valley.
$$ Clarion Suites Hotel, 70 Southbridge St., Worcester, Mass. (508) 753-3512, (800) 252-7466. 20 minutes from Pleasant Valley.
$ Days Inn–Lodge of Worcester, 50 Oriol Dr., Worcester, Mass. (508) 852-2800, (800) 329-7466. 20 minutes from Pleasant Valley.

DINING

Beechwood Restaurant, in the Beechwood Inn, 363 Plantation St., Worcester, Mass. (508) 754-5789.
Legal Seafoods, 1 Exchange Place, Worcester, Mass. (508) 792-1600.
Tony's Sutton Pizza Restaurant, Boston Rd. & Rte. 146, Sutton, Mass. (508) 865-9544.

PUBLIC COURSES TO PLAY IN AREA

Shaker Hills Golf Club, Shaker Rd., Harvard, Mass. Public. (508) 772-2227. 18/6,850/72. 40 minutes from Pleasant Valley.
Sterling Country Club, 33 Albright Rd., Sterling, Mass. Public. (508) 422-3335. 18/6,640/71. 25 minutes from Pleasant Valley.
Stow Acres Country Club, 58 Randall Rd., Stow, Mass. Public. (508) 568-8690. North: 18/6,909/72. South: 18/6,520/72. 30 minutes from Pleasant Valley.

TICKETS & ACCESSIBILITY

How to watch: Mon., PGA practice rounds, pro-am. Tue., PGA practice rounds. Wed., pro-am. Thur.-Sun., tournament. Admission free Monday. Individual tickets begin at $10. Group and sponsorship plans available. New England Classic, P.O. Box 420, Sutton, MA 01590. (508) 865-1491.
How to play: Pleasant Valley is a private club. You must be a member or the guest of a member to play the course.

Buick Open

Warwick Hills Golf and Country Club

Tournament-at-a-Glance

Course: Warwick Hills Golf and Country Club
Type: Private
Location: G-9057 S. Saginaw St., Grand Blanc, MI 48439
Telephone: (810) 694-4103
When: Aug. 1–4, 1996
How To Get There: From Detroit, 60 minutes. Take I-75 north to Grand Blanc Exit. Make right onto Grand Blanc Rd. to Saginaw Rd. Take right on Saginaw 4 miles to golf course.
Broadcast: CBS (1996)
Purse: $1,200,000 (1995)
Tournament Record: 26-under-par, Robert Wrenn, 1987

The first Buick Open, held in 1958, celebrated General Motors' 50th anniversary with $1 admission prices, free parking and a hefty winner's check for Billy Casper. The years since have been a bumpy ride, but in the 1980s the automaker spurned the PGA's recommendation that the event be moved from Flint, Mich., and rededicated itself to staging a first-class event.

Part of the tournament's initial decline was due to Warwick Hills' overly long layout, which was shortened in 1967. The course is still fairly long and flat, with bunkers positioned mostly around the large, well-groomed putting surfaces.

Now scheduled just before the PGA Championship, the Buick is regularly drawing a first-class field. In 1993, Fuzzy Zoeller sank a 35-foot putt from the edge of the 17th green to draw within a stroke of playing partner Larry Mize, but Mize parred the final hole to win.

•Toughest Hole

The 15th hole at Warwick Hills is a slight dogleg left with trees and out-of-bounds on the left side. This 457-yard par-4 plays into the wind, usually leaving a long-iron approach to a green flanked by bunkers to its left and right. Recently added trees on the right side of the fairway can stymie approach shots. The most difficult par-3 at Warwick Hills is the 199-yard eighth, which plays to a two-level, raised green flanked by three bunkers. George Bayer scored a hole-in-one here during the 1963 Buick Open, but Julius Boros won the tournament.

•Best Place to Watch

Relatively level, Warwick Hills is an easy course to walk. Many of the holes are parallel, including Nos. 1, 9, 10 and 18, which are a short distance from the clubhouse. Position yourself under a tree on No. 17, and you can easily catch the action on the 199-yard, par-3 eighth.

•Who the Course Favors

The course favors a long hitter who can keep the ball in-bounds. Warwick Hills also rewards a shotmaker who can come into the large greens with accuracy. A long hitter, Fred Couples, and a tenacious shotmaker, Corey Pavin, finished first and second in 1994.

HOLE	YARDS	PAR	HOLE	YARDS	PAR
1	567	5	10	401	4
2	431	4	11	190	3
3	187	3	12	335	4
4	401	4	13	548	5
5	437	4	14	322	4
6	421	4	15	457	4
7	584	5	16	580	5
8	199	3	17	197	3
9	413	4	18	435	4
			TOTAL	7105	72

Best Place to Watch

Warwick Hills Golf and Country Club
Architects: James Gilmore Harrison and Ferdinand Garbin (1957)
Remodeled by Joe Lee (1967)

Lodging

$$$ Radisson, One Riverfront Center West, Flint, Mich. (810) 239-1234. 15 minutes from Warwick Hills.
$$ Holiday Inn Gateway Centre, 5353 Gateway Centre, Flint, Mich. (810) 232-5300. 10 minutes from Warwick Hills.
$ Hampton Inn, 1150 Robert T. Longway Blvd., Flint, Mich. (810) 238-7744. 10 minutes from Warwick Hills.

Dining

Makuch's Red Rooster, 3302 Davison Rd., Flint, Mich. (810) 742-9310.
The Olive Garden, G-3699 Miller Rd., Flint, Mich. (810) 732-4260.
Old Country Buffet, G-3583 Miller Rd., Flint, Mich. (810) 733-5511.

Public Courses to Play in Area

Greystone Golf Club, 7500 Mound Rd., Romeo, Mich. Public. (810) 752-7030. 18/6,860/72. 30 minutes from Warwick Hills.
Pine Trace Golf Club, 3600 Pine Trace Rd., Rochester Hills, Mich. Public. (810) 852-7100. 18/6,610/72. 40 minutes from Warwick Hills.
Timber Ridge Golf Course, 16339 Park Lake Rd., East Lansing, Mich. Public. (517) 339-8000. 18/6,497/72. 60 minutes from Warwick Hills.

Tickets & Accessibility

How to watch: Mon., PGA practice rounds, pro-am. Tue., PGA practice rounds, youth golf clinic, pro-celebrity Skins game. Wed., pro-am. Thur.-Sun., tournament. Individual, group and sponsor tickets available. Buick Open, Marketing Office, 902 E. Hamilton Ave., Flint, MI 48550-0135. (800) 878-OPEN.
How to play: Warwick Hills is a private club. You must be a member or the guest of a member to play the course.

The Sprint International

CASTLE PINES GOLF CLUB

The Sprint International is PGA golf on a high wire. Nowhere else does the ball fly so far; perhaps nowhere else do the players take so many risks.

Drives soar a little farther at this 7,559-yard Jack Nicklaus–designed course. It's perched in Rocky Mountain woodlands more than 6,000 feet above sea level. The golfers get a little reckless because it's the only tournament on the calendar that uses the unusual Stableford point system, which means pars do a player no good.

In this format, a double eagle is worth 8 points, an eagle 5 points, a birdie 2 points and par is null. On the wrong side of the number line, a bogey is a -1 and a double bogey or worse is a -3. A field of 144 is cut in half after two rounds and then to an elite two dozen for the final day. In the past, every player who made the final cut started Sunday back at even, but under a new format initiated in 1993, the points are cumulative over the four rounds.

Steve Lowery, a seven-year Tour veteran who had never won a tournament, was seven points back of leader Ernie Els and looked to be out of the hunt after nine holes on the final round of 1994. It didn't help matters when he bogeyed holes 11, 12 and 13. But Lowery rapped a curling 3-iron within 25 feet on the par-5 14th and a 5-iron to 15 inches on the par-5 17th. His two eagles sent his total soaring 10 points, and he beat Rick Fehr on the first sudden-death playoff hole.

A year before, Phil Mickelson racked up 29 points on the final day in an exhibition that again had the media comparing him to the young Nicklaus.

Nicklaus's course, one of his early solo projects, has been ranked among the nation's Top 40 by *Golf Digest.* Its track through pine and oak forests is one of the longest on the Tour, but it plays 10% to 15% shorter due to the thinner air. This fact might provide solace when the golfer tees up on the 644-yard, par-5 opening hole, which drops more than 120 feet to a deep green guarded by a series of three bunkers. Most of the bunkers at Castle Pines are near the greens, but ponds, gulches and streams can come into play on more than half the holes.

Nicklaus prefers elevated tees that offer the golfer an opportunity to see what's in store for him. The 197-yard, par-3 11th, for example, plays 75 feet down to a two-tiered green protected by a gulch and a series of bunkers. The 623-yard, par-5 14th plays downhill and, like the monster first hole, can be reached in two shots.

TOURNAMENT-AT-A-GLANCE

Course: Castle Pines Golf Club
Type: Private
Location: 1000 Hummingbird Dr., Castle Rock, CO 80104
Telephone: (303) 688-6000
When: Aug. 15–18, 1996
How To Get There: From Denver, 40 minutes. Take I-25 south to Exit 187 (Happy Canyon Rd.), go west (right) 1 mile to golf club.
Broadcast: CBS
Purse: $1,600,000
Tournament Record: Plus 45, Phil Mickelson, 1993 (total points for four rounds); Plus 17, Joey Sindlear, 1988 (total points for final round)

"IF I COULD DESIGN MY IDEAL GOLF COURSE, ALL THE HOLES WOULD PLAY DOWNHILL SO THAT ON EACH TEE THE GOLFER COULD SEE EVERYTHING THAT HE WAS ABOUT TO PLAY."

—JACK NICKLAUS,
CASTLE PINES ARCHITECT

Courtesy of Castle Pines Golf Club

DRIVERS ARE THANKFUL FOR THE THIN MOUNTAIN AIR WHEN THEY CONTEND AGAINST CASTLE PINES, ONE OF THE TOUR'S LONGEST SPREADS.

●TOUGHEST HOLE

Castle Pines plays 7,559 yards from the championship tees, and even with the 10% to 15% additional length in the thin Rocky Mountain air, this is still a long day's journey through the rolling woods. The downhill 485-yard, par-4 10th is a case in point. The tee shot is down a tree-lined fairway to a landing area that will most likely require a long iron or mid-iron from an uneven lie to a green guarded by bunkers to its left and rear and a pond to its right. Another tough par-4 is the 477-yard fifth, which plays uphill over an battalian of bunkers guarding the front of an elevated green.

●BEST PLACE TO WATCH

Because of the severe elevation changes, this is a difficult course to walk. You might want to hang around the No. 1 and No. 10 tees or the greens around No. 9 and No. 18., all of which are near the clubhouse. The Stableford scoring system used in this tournament is likely to produce final-round back-nine excitement as it did in 1994 when Steve Lowery had eagles on No. 14 and No. 17, and Rick Fehr had birdies on Nos. 13, 14, 15 and 17 to force a playoff.

●WHO THE COURSE FAVORS

Because this is a point system rather than a stroke-play event, the course favors an aggressive, attacking player who can take high-percentage chances and succeed. Lowery's two final-round eagles provided him with 10 of his 35 points for the four-day competition. Club selection and positioning are essential because of the effect of the altitude on distance, the numerous elevation changes on the course and the trees, bunkers and water hazards that can punish errant shots.

HOLE	YARDS	PAR
1	644	5
2	408	4
3	462	4
4	205	3
5	477	4
6	417	4
7	185	3
8	535	5
9	458	4
10	485	4
11	197	3
12	440	4
13	439	4
14	623	5
15	403	4
16	209	3
17	492	5
18	480	4
TOTAL	7559	72

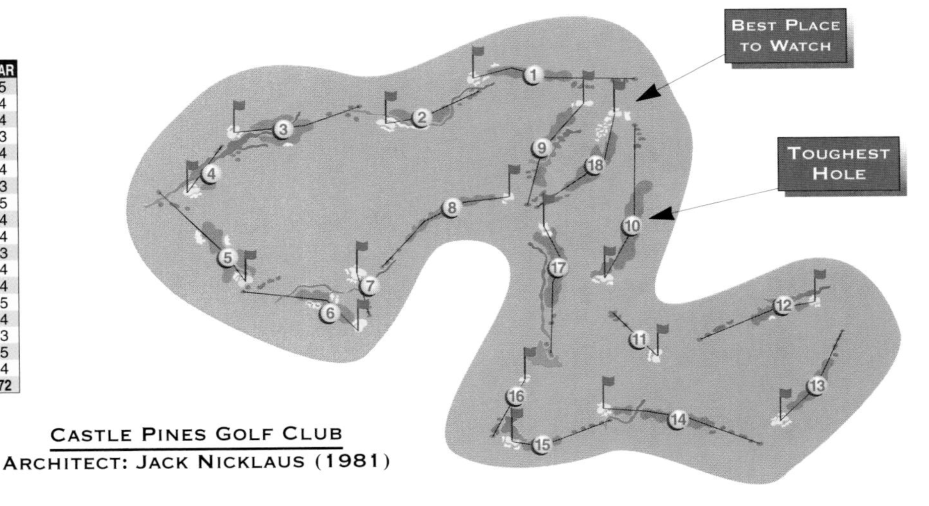

CASTLE PINES GOLF CLUB
ARCHITECT: JACK NICKLAUS (1981)

LODGING

$$$ The Broadmoor, Lake Ave. and Lake Circle, Colorado Springs. (719) 577-5775, (800) 634-7711. 45 minutes from Castle Pines.

$$ Embassy Suites Tech Center, 10250 E. Costilla Ave., Englewood, Colo. (303) 792-0433, (800) 362-2779. 25 minutes from Castle Pines.

$ Courtyard by Marriott Denver-Tech Center, 6565 S. Boston St., Englewood, Colo. (303) 721-0300, (800) 321-2211. 25 minutes from Castle Pines.

DINING

The Swan, 200 Inverness Dr., Englewood, Colo. (303) 799-5800.

Palace Arms at the Brown Palace Hotel, 321 17th St., Denver. (303) 297-3111.

The Harvest Restaurant and Bakery, 7730 E. Belleview Ave., Englewood, Colo. (303) 779-4111.

PUBLIC COURSES TO PLAY IN AREA

The Arrowhead Golf Club, 10850 W. Sundown Trail, Littleton, Colo. Public. (303) 973-9614. 18/6,682/70. 35 minutes from Castle Pines.

The Broadmoor Golf Club, Lake Ave. and Lake Circle, Colorado Springs. Resort. (719) 577-5790, (800) 634-7711. East: 18/7,218/72. West: 18/6,937/72. South: 18/6,781/72. 1 hour from Castle Pines.

Plum Creek Golf & Country Club, 331 Player's Club Dr., Castle Rock, Colo. Public. (303) 688-2611, (800) 488-2612. 18/6,633/72. 10 minutes from Castle Pines.

TICKETS & ACCESSIBILITY

How to watch: Mon.-Tue., practice rounds. Wed., pro-am. Thur.-Sun., championship rounds. Tickets: Week-long pass, $150. Individual, group and sponsor tickets available. The Sprint International, 1000 Hummingbird Dr., Castle Rock, CO 80104. (303) 660-8000, (303) 220-4771.

How to play: Castle Pines is a private course. You must be a member to play.

NEC World Series of Golf

FIRESTONE COUNTRY CLUB

The Firestone Country Club was founded in the 1920s when Harvey Firestone, the millionaire tire industrialist, decided to provide his employees with a quality venue for golfing. Today there are three golf courses on this site just outside of downtown Akron, but the South Course, remodeled by Robert Trent Jones in the late 1950s and again by Ohioan Jack Nicklaus in the mid-1980s, has been lengthened and toughened up for PGA Tour play. Firestone was chosen to host the 1960, 1966 and 1975 PGA Championships.

Before that major's first visit, Robert Trent Jones added 50 bunkers and two ponds, and Jack Nicklaus has since enlarged and recontoured the small greens. A good long-iron player, like Nicklaus, who won this event in 1962, 1963, 1967, 1970 and 1976, has an edge on this old-style, par-70 course because of its abundance of long par-4s

Firestone has hosted a PGA event annually since 1954, when Tommy Bolt won the title in the Rubber City Open. The World Series event debuted here in 1962, as a 36-hole contest among the most recent winners of the Masters, the U.S. Open, the British Open and the PGA Championship. That format immediately yielded a legendary three-man field of Arnold Palmer, Gary Player and Nicklaus. In 1976, the tournament's elite field was expanded, and the event now draws the most recent winners of 52 events worldwide.

The long par-4s at Firestone include four on the front side that stretch at least 450 yards. The 458-yard fourth, which plays down a right-to-left sloping fairway to a green squeezed by two bunkers in front, is one of the most difficult on the course.

The back nine concludes with four great finishing holes. Bunkers, green size and water make approach shots to these last holes difficult in their own distinctive ways. The 15th plays into the prevailing wind and has two bunkers to the right and another to the left of the deep, thin green. Monstrous No. 16 has one of the smallest greens on the course, which is well-guarded by a pond to its right front and bunkers to its left. The 17th is fronted by a bunker, forcing the approach to be flown to the green. And the long final hole plays to a fast, deep green guarded by bunkers to its left front and deep bunkers to its rear.

In 1993, Fulton Allem birdied the 18th to complete a final-round 62 that earned him a five-stroke victory over the world's best players. José María Olazábal won his second World Series Championship in 1994 when he fired a 269 on Firestone's par-70 North Course. Olazábal shot a tournament-record 262 to win his first NEC in 1990.

TOURNAMENT-AT-A-GLANCE

Course: Firestone Country Club—South Course
Type: Private
Location: 452 E. Warner Rd., Akron, OH 44319
Telephone: (216) 644-8441
When: Aug. 22–25, 1996
How To Get There: From downtown Akron, 15 minutes. Take I-77 south to Waterloo Rd. Exit. Turn left off exit, go 3/4 mile to Arlington Rd. Turn right on Arlington to Warner Rd. Turn right on Warner to golf course.
Broadcast: USA, CBS (1995)
Purse: $2,000,000 (1995)
Tournament Record: 18-under-par 262, José María Olazábal, 1990

"GOOD FOR THE RECORDS."

—JOSÉ MARÍA OLAZÁBAL,

AFTER WINNING THE 1994 NEC WORLD SERIES OF GOLF AND BECOMING THE FIRST TO WIN ON BOTH THE FIRESTONE NORTH AND SOUTH COURSE

Courtesy of NEC World Series of Golf

DEEP BUNKERS AROUND THE GREEN MAKE THE PAR-4 18TH A TOUGH FINALE.

●TOUGHEST HOLE

The par-4 fourth, with its sloping fairway and green, is the course's toughest, but there are plenty of stern tests on the back nine. The 625-yard, par-5 16th plays downhill, tempting the big hitters to reach the green in two, as Palmer, Nicklaus and others have done. But the drive has to avoid bunkers to the right, and the second shot is likely to be from a downhill lie. To the right front of the green is a pond that has caught many an errant approach. The par-4 18th is a dogleg left with a fairway that tilts left at its bend. Its deep, narrow green is surrounded by bunkers to the left, front right and rear. The thick rough just off the fairway and the bunker to the right of the landing area increase its difficulty.

●BEST PLACE TO WATCH

Like many old-style golf courses, Firestone has several parallel holes, making it easy for the spectator to follow the action. Three difficult par-4s on the front side—Nos. 4, 6 and 9—are good places to catch the action. From the teeing area on No. 4, it is easy to move to the No. 3 green. From the No. 9 green, it is an easy walk to the No. 1 tee, No. 10 tee, No. 18 green, No. 17 tee and No. 16 green. Another difficult par-4 is the 13th, where an oak tree protects the dogleg turn. From the green area around No. 13 it is an easy walk to the No. 14 tee, No. 17 green, No. 18 tee and No. 10 green.

●WHO THE COURSE FAVORS

Firestone South plays over 7,100 yards yet is only a par-70. The long par-3s and par-4s often require precision long irons into the contoured greens. The thick rough and intermittent mature trees throughout the course can quickly penalize errant tee shots.

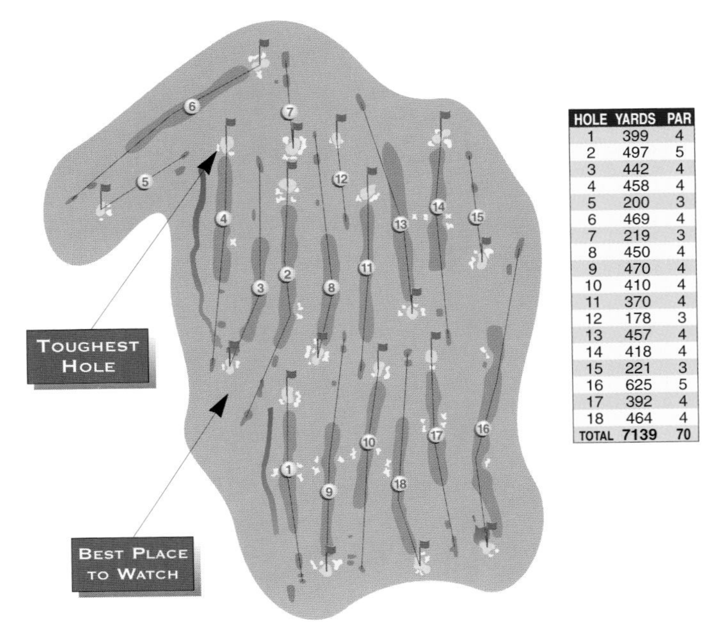

HOLE	YARDS	PAR
1	399	4
2	497	5
3	442	4
4	458	4
5	200	3
6	469	4
7	219	3
8	450	4
9	470	4
10	410	4
11	370	4
12	178	3
13	457	4
14	418	4
15	221	3
16	625	5
17	392	4
18	464	4
TOTAL	7139	70

FIRESTONE COUNTRY CLUB SOUTH COURSE
ARCHITECT: BERT WAY (1929)
REMODELED BY ROBERT TRENT JONES (1959),
JACK NICKLAUS (1986)

LODGING

$$$ Akron Hilton Inn at Quaker Square, 135 S. Broadway, Akron, Ohio. (216) 253-5970, (800) HILTONS. 15 minutes from Firestone.

$$ Sheraton Suites Cuyahoga Falls, 1989 Front St., Cuyahoga Falls, Ohio. (216) 929-3000. 25 minutes from Firestone.

$ Holiday Inn–Akron South, I-77 and Arlington Rd., Akron, Ohio. (216) 644-7126, (800) HOLIDAY. 5 minutes from Firestone.

DINING

Tangier Restaurant and Cabaret, 532 W. Market St., Akron, Ohio. (216) 376-7171.

Diamond Grill, 77 W. Market St., Akron, Ohio. (216) 253-0041.

Country Manor Family Restaurant, 1886 State Rd., Cuyahoga Falls, Ohio. (216) 644-0525.

PUBLIC COURSES TO PLAY IN AREA

Sleepy Hollow Golf Course, 9445 Brecksville Rd., Brecksville, Ohio. Public. (216) 526-4285. 18/6,500/70. 30 minutes from Firestone.

Tam O'Shanter Golf Course, 5055 Hills and Dales Rd., Canton, Ohio. (216) 477-5111, (800) 462-9964. Dales: 18/6,569/70. Hills: 18/6,385/70. 30 minutes from Firestone.

Turkeyfoot Lake Golf Links, 294 W. Turkeyfoot Lake Rd., Akron, Ohio. Public. (216) 644-5971. First Nine: 9/3,249/36. Second: 9/3,067/36. Third: 9/2,203/35. 15 minutes from Firestone.

TICKETS & ACCESSIBILITY

How to watch: Mon., PGA practice rounds. Tue., shoot-out, junior golf clinic. Wed., pro-am. Thur.-Sun., tournament. Individual, group and sponsor tickets available. NEC World Series of Golf, 445 E. Warner Rd., Akron, OH 44319, (216) 644-2299.

How to play: Firestone is a private club. You must be a member or the guest of a member to play. In addition to the South Course, the North Course (18/7,139/70) and the West Course (18/6,581/72) are on site.

Greater Milwaukee Open

Brown Deer Park Golf Course

The Greater Milwaukee Open is now a rarity: a full-fledged PGA event played on a true public course.

The underdog in that unusual pairing is Brown Deer Park, the finest in a fine collection of the county's public courses. Designed in 1929 by longtime park superintendent George Hansen, the richly treed layout already boasted a credible pedigree as host of the 1951, 1966 and 1977 national Public Links Championships but it's benefited from $3 million in renovations it received in time for the pros' first visit in 1994.

Former Public Links titlist Billy Mayfair was the defending Greater Milwaukee champion when the event moved from Tuckaway Country Club, where it had resided for 21 of its 26 years. But on the final day, Mike Springer and Mark Calcavecchia were the co-leaders, fighting it out at the 557-yard, par-5 finishing hole.

Springer, who had come from two shots back to establish a one-stroke lead as he arrived at the 72nd tee, hit a good drive, but then pushed a 3-wood to the right and had to settle for par on one of the easiest holes on the course.

Calcavecchia, playing in the group behind Springer, needed a birdie to tie. But he drove into heavy rough on the left, hit a recovery into the fairway, launched his approach into a greenside bunker and needed three shots to get down for a bogey. The 34-year-old, who had lost a playoff in Milwaukee a year earlier, fell into a tie for third.

TOURNAMENT-AT-A-GLANCE

Course: Brown Deer Park Golf Course
Type: Public
Location: 7835 N. Green Bay Ave., Milwaukee, WI 53209
Telephone: (414) 352-8080
When: Aug. 29–Sept. 1, 1996
How To Get There: Take I-43 north to Good Hope Rd. exit. Proceed west on Good Hope (3 miles) to Rangeline Rd. Take a right (north) on Rangeline 1/3 mile to course.
Broadcast: ABC (1996)
Purse: $1,000,000 (1995)
Tournament Record: 22-under-par 266, Bill Kratzert, 1980 (at the par-72 Tuckaway Country Club, Franklin, Wis.)

"It was tough out there," Springer said later. "The wind was blowing. I hit some good shots out there, and I didn't get rewarded. Fortunately enough for me, the guys didn't really play all that well."

He sounded like a champion who had just been humbled by a public course.

Brown Deer can do that. It immediately challenges the players with two tough par-4s, the 447-yard straightaway first and the uphill 417-yard second. Both averaged above par in 1994, as did three par-3s, the 215-yard seventh, the 198-yard 11th and the 188-yard 14th. The fairways and greens aren't heavily bunkered, but the putting surfaces are large, and the 12 remaining original greens are particularly conducive to three putts.

The 10th hole, a 461-yard dogleg right, was the toughest hole to par, but a more intriguing par-4 is the 381-yard 17th, where the drive must thread a pair of willows to set up the approach. The second shot must be flown over bunkers to one of the smallest greens on the course. As Springer noted, wind can come into play on some of the holes, with headwinds sometimes making the finishing holes play extremely long.

But it's the rough that is the great equalizer at Brown Deer. Maintained at 6 to 8 inches, it can make the pros pay dearly, as Calcavecchia did in 1994, if they stray the ball from the fairways.

●TOUGHEST HOLE

The 417-yard, par-4 second plays up a corridor of trees to a heavily contoured green guarded by bunkers on the front left and the front right. A slight dogleg left, it demands a well-placed tee shot to create a clear shot to the green. The first hole, a 447-yard par-4, is another tree-lined challenge. The green of this straightaway hole is framed by two bunkers. Together, the first two holes are a rigorous beginning to a fine, parkland golf course.

●BEST PLACE TO WATCH

Brown Deer Park is a rolling golf course with many scenic, tree-lined, parallel holes. Tees No. 1, 7, 10 and 15 are easily accessible from the stone clubhouse, as are greens No. 6, 9, 14 and 18. The most difficult par-4s are the No. 1, No. 8 and No. 2 holes, and the most difficult par-3s are No. 11 and No. 14. It is convenient to stand behind the 14th, then move over to tee No. 15, green No. 16, tee No. 17 and the green at the par-5 finishing hole. This hole usually plays into the wind, providing for some dramatic moments. Mark Calcavecchia sank a 40-foot eagle putt on No. 18 during the third round of the 1994 tournament.

●WHO THE COURSE FAVORS

A player who can hit with accuracy off the tee. It's easy to lose strokes if you hit the ball into thick rough or too close to the trees. There are few fairway bunkers and a minimal number of bunkers around most greens, but you have to be able to hit out of that rough at times to score here.

HOLE	YARDS	PAR	HOLE	YARDS	PAR
1	447	4	10	461	4
2	417	4	11	196	3
3	171	3	12	367	4
4	485	5	13	414	4
5	170	3	14	188	3
6	550	5	15	531	5
7	215	3	16	371	4
8	426	4	17	381	4
9	359	4	18	557	5
			TOTAL	6706	71

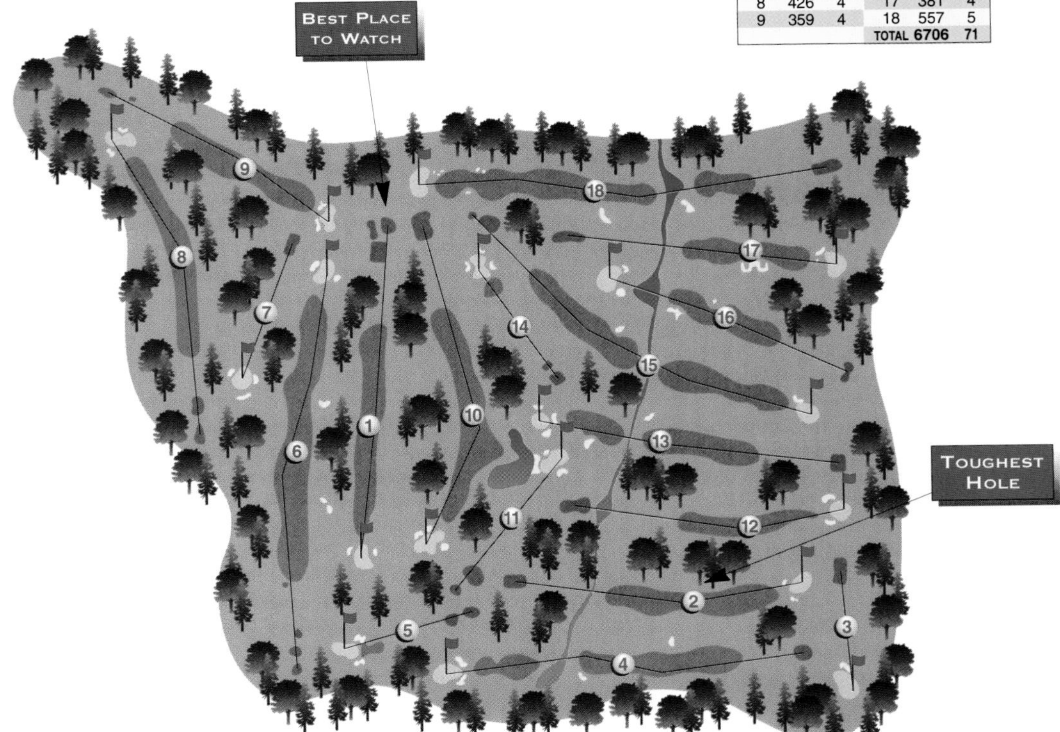

BROWN DEER PARK GOLF COURSE
ARCHITECT: GEORGE HANSEN (1929)
REMODELED BY ROGER PACKARD AND ANDY NORTH (1994)

LODGING

$$$ Pfister Hotel, 424 E. Wisconsin Ave., Milwaukee. (414) 273-8222. 25 minutes from Brown Deer.

$$ Wyndham Milwaukee Center, 139 E. Kilbourn Ave., Milwaukee. (414) 276-8686, (800) WYNDHAM. 20 minutes from Brown Deer.

$ Residence Inn by Marriott, 7275 N. Port Washington Rd., Glendale, Wis. (414) 352-0070. (800) 331-3131. 5 minutes from Brown Deer.

Bed and Breakfast of Milwaukee, Inc., 823 2nd St., Milwaukee. (414) 277-8066. Reservations booking service.

DINING

English Room, in Pfister Hotel, 424 E. Wisconsin Ave., Milwaukee. (414) 273-8222.

Mador's German Restaurant, 1037 N. Old World 3rd St., Milwaukee. (414) 271-3377.

PUBLIC COURSES TO PLAY IN AREA

Grand Geneva Resort, Hwy. 50 East, Lake Geneva, Wis. Resort. (414) 248-8811, (414) 652-3668. Briar Patch: 18/6,742/71. Brute: 18/7,258/72. 50 minutes from Brown Deer.

Blackwolf Run, 1111 W. Riverside Ave., Kohler, Wis. Resort. (414) 457-4446 (golf course), (800) 344-2838 (American Club). Meadow/Valleys: 18/7,142/72. River: 18/6,991/72. 70 minutes from Brown Deer.

Geneva National Golf Course, 1331 Geneva Ave. S, Lake Geneva, Wis. Public. (414) 245-7010. Trevino Course: 18/7,120/72. Palmer Course: 18/7,171/72. 50 minutes from Brown Deer.

TICKETS & ACCESSIBILITY

How to watch: Mon., PGA practice rounds, pro-am. Tue., PGA practice rounds, shoot-out. Wed., pro-am. Thur.-Sun., tournament. Individual tickets begin at $12. Group and sponsorship plans available. Greater Milwaukee Open, 4000 W. Brown Deer Rd., Milwaukee, WI 53209. (414) 365-4466.

How to play: Brown Deer is a public golf course open April-November. (414) 352-8080 (pro shop), (414) 643-4653 (tee time reservations).

Bell Canadian Open

GLEN ABBEY GOLF CLUB

The Canadian Open, one of the game's oldest national championships, premiered in 1904 at the Royal Montreal, North America's first golf club. American players have long since dominated the event, the only PGA stop north of the United States, but its list of great Yankee champions—Leo Diegel, Tommy Armour, Walter Hagen, Lawson Little, Sam Snead, Byron Nelson, Arnold Palmer, Lee Trevino, Tom Weiskopf—has one glaring omission: Jack Nicklaus who has been the runner-up in the Canadian Open seven times but never been crowned Canada's champion. Perhaps that's what made him the perfect candidate to design the tournament's home course.

TOURNAMENT-AT-A-GLANCE

Course: Glen Abbey Golf Club
Type: Public
Location: 1333 Dorval Dr., R.R. 2, Oakville, Ontario, Canada, L6J 423
Telephone: (905) 844-1800
When: Sept. 5–8, 1996
How To Get There: Take Queen Elizabeth Hwy. (QEW) to Oakville/Dorval Dr. Exit. Proceed north 1 mile to golf course. Glen Abbey is 20 miles west of Toronto.
Broadcast: ESPN, CTV (1995)
Purse: $1,300,000 (1995)
Tournament Record: 17-under-par 271, Steve Jones, 1989

Glen Abbey, located 30 minutes northwest of Toronto on 200 wooded acres that once belonged to a Jesuit seminary, was Nicklaus's first solo project as a designer. When he laid the plans for the course in the mid-1970s, he explained the philosophy behind all of his early creations. "I regard the emphasis on length and huge greens as the two worst faults of modern golf course design," he said. "Many people assume my golf courses will be long monsters, but I consider golf to be a game of precision, not strength."

Glen Abbey, a public course and home of the Royal Canadian Golf Association, does have four tee distances, and even from the championship tees its par-3s run only 141 to 197 yards, its par-4s from 414 to 458 yards and its par-5s from 508 to 529 yards.

Sixteen Mile Creek, which can be more like a roaring river when swollen by rain, snakes through the fairways on Nos. 11, 12, 13 and 14, where rolling terrain and tree-lined bluffs make for some of the most scenic and difficult holes on the course. More than a million cubic feet of earth were moved to contour the level land where 12 of the holes were sited. The result is an almost relentless challenge: In the 1980s, holes nine through 12 were all rated among the 70 most difficult holes on the PGA Tour.

Three of the course's par-5s are among its six finishing holes, opening the way for a flourish of tournament-turning birdies. The 516-yard, par-5 16th, a dogleg left, plays to a contoured fairway with no bunkers but dangerous rough. The green, shaped like a pistol pointed left, is 30 yards deep at the "handle" and only 14 yards deep near the tip of the "muzzle." A pin position to the left can make this hole extremely difficult. The finishing hole, a 508-yard par-5, requires a tee shot to the left-center of a fairway bordered by nine bunkers. If the golfer decides to go for it in two, he normally must carry a pond that begins on the right, 107 yards from the green, and runs up to the angled putting surface bordered by traps to its left.

In 1994, Mark Calcavecchia eagled this final hole by sinking a 40-foot putt on the last day. But Nick Price matched him shortly thereafter when he eagled the 16th by hitting a 2-iron 217 yards to within 2 feet of the flag. Price's total of 275 edged Calcavecchia by a single stroke.

In 1993, David Frost needed a birdie on the final hole to beat Fred Couples, so he ripped a 5-wood over the water and two-putted for the victory.

Walt Disney World/Oldsmobile Classic

Walt Disney World Resort

One of America's best golf destinations is the Walt Disney World Resort, just southwest of Orlando, Fla., in Lake Buena Vista. The "Magic Linkdom," as it is aptly called, encompasses five 18-hole golf courses, four of which have been PGA Tour or LPGA tournament sites. The Joe Lee–designed Lake Buena Vista, Palm and Magnolia courses host the Disney World/Oldsmobile Classic which began in 1971. Jack Nicklaus won the first three titles before team play became the chosen format for the next eight years.

Recent champions have found there are advantages—and disadvantages—to playing in an event hosted by Disney. In the rain-soaked 1993 event, the sky was dark by the time winner Jeff Maggert hit his approach to the 36th and final green of his marathon Sunday, but Disney's floodlights assured that every player finished. In 1994, winner Rick Fehr almost didn't make his final-round starting time because his wife and kids had taken the car to Disney World.

Course designer Lee, a Florida native, teamed with Dick Wilson to create many fine courses, including Bay Hill in Orlando and Cog Hill No. 4 near Chicago, but his trio at Disney are among his best.

Purists may argue whether a Mickey Mouse–shaped bunker belongs on the sixth hole of any championship course, but the rolling, relatively open Magnolia course is the longest and most difficult of the three, and thus the obvious choice to host the final round.

The layout's two finishing holes are a difficult combination. The tee shot on the 427-yard, par-4 17th must carry water guarding the dogleg left. The approach is to a deep, narrow, forward-sloping green framed by bunkers, with a pond farther right. Fehr hit his approach to within 3 feet on the final round in 1994 and won the tournament by two strokes. The 455-yard, par-4 18th plays straight to a deep, forward-sloping green with three bunkers arrayed on its left.

Lake Buena Vista, despite an island green at its par-3 16th and lagoons on a handful of other holes, is the easiest of the three courses. The Palm, a tighter layout, is ranked among *Golf Digest*'s top 25 resort courses in the nation.

TOURNAMENT-AT-A-GLANCE

Course: Walt Disney World Resort—Magnolia, Palm and Lake Buena Vista Golf Courses
Type: Resort
Location: Lake Buena Vista, FL 32830
Telephone: (407) 824-2270
When: Oct. 17–20, 1996
How To Get There: Disney World is southwest of Orlando, off I-4. Take I-4 west from I-95 or Hwy. 1 to resort exit. Take I-4 east from I-75 to resort exit. Traveling on Florida Turnpike, use Kissimmee–St. Cloud interchange and Hwy. 192 to resort and tournament golf courses.
Broadcast: Golf Channel (1995)
Purse: $1,200,000 (1995)
Tournament Record: 26-under-par 262, John Houston, 1992

"IT WAS A LOUSY WAY TO END IT. MY SHORT GAME IS SO SCREWED UP AT THE MOMENT. SOMEWHERE I'M OFF BY ABOUT 10 TO 15 YARDS."

—CRAIG STADLER,

WHO HAD SOME TROUBLE WITH HIS SHORT GAME DOWN THE STRETCH. FINISHED WITH A 70 ON THE FINAL ROUND AND TIED FOR SECOND IN THE 1994 DISNEY

CAREFUL APPROACHES ARE NEEDED TO REACH THE NARROW 16TH GREEN AT THE PALM COURSE IN ORDER TO AVOID THE WATER.

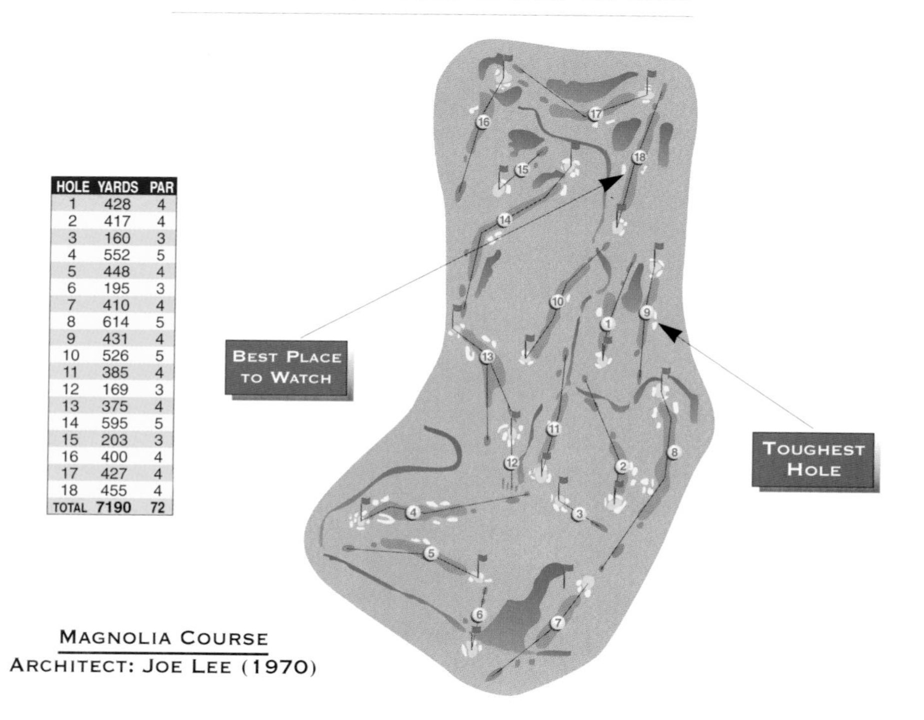

HOLE	YARDS	PAR
1	428	4
2	417	4
3	160	3
4	552	5
5	448	4
6	195	3
7	410	4
8	614	5
9	431	4
10	526	5
11	385	4
12	169	3
13	375	4
14	595	5
15	203	3
16	400	4
17	427	4
18	455	4
TOTAL	7190	72

●TOUGHEST HOLE

The finishing holes on both sides of the Magnolia Course are among the most difficult. The ninth, a 431-yard, par-4 dogleg right, plays to a landing area guarded by bunkers to the right and a pond to the left that begins 278 yards from the championship tees. The right side is well-treed from tee to green, and the approach must avoid water to the left, two bunkers straddling the front entranceway to the green and two more bunkers to the rear. The 455-yard, par-4 18th plays to a landing area squeezed by bunkers 200 yards from a deep, forward-sloping green. The left front of the putting surface is guarded by two bunkers, and another waits to the left rear. Payne Stewart birdied this hole in 1990 to complete his course-record 61.

●BEST PLACE TO WATCH

The three finishing holes on the Magnolia are good to watch. The approach on the 400-yard, par-4 16th crosses a pond to a green fronted by three bunkers and guarded by another trap to its left. The 17th, a 427-yard, par-4 dogleg left, has been called "the most dangerous hole on the course" by Lanny Wadkins. The tee shot must carry a large pond yet avoid two bunkers to the right. The approach is usually a mid-iron to a narrow green with two bunkers to its left and another to the right. A large pond is farther to the right. The 18th hole, a 455-yard par-4, is usually among the most difficult to par on this course.

●WHO THE COURSE FAVORS

Accuracy off the tee is important on these courses, whose landing areas are guarded by sand, water, deep rough and trees. The greens are heavily bunkered and must be approached with accuracy in order to score. The par-4 second on the Magnolia Course is surrounded by five bunkers, forcing the golfer to fly the ball in with accuracy to a small green. The same is true on the 552-yard, par-5 fourth, which has seven bunkers around its putting surface.

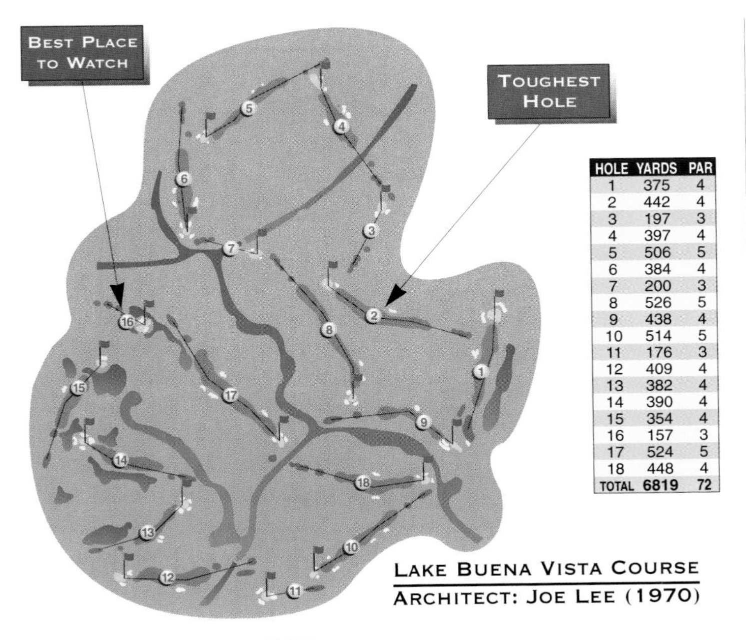

HOLE	YARDS	PAR
1	375	4
2	442	4
3	197	3
4	397	4
5	506	5
6	384	4
7	200	3
8	526	5
9	438	4
10	514	5
11	176	3
12	409	4
13	382	4
14	390	4
15	354	4
16	157	3
17	524	5
18	448	4
TOTAL	6819	72

LAKE BUENA VISTA COURSE
ARCHITECT: JOE LEE (1970)

•BEST PLACE TO WATCH

Lake Buena Vista's island 157-yard, par-3 sixteenth is not as severe as No. 17 at Sawgrass, but it provides an exciting target which seems to get smaller as the tournament progresses. On the Palm Course, the green area around No. 18 is easily accessible to the No. 10 and No. 1 tees and the No. 9 green as well as the clubhouse and practice area.

•TOUGHEST HOLE

Two par-4s on Lake Buena Vista's front nine are among the most difficult holes on the course. The 442-yard second, a dogleg right, demands a long and accurate tee shot to avoid out-of-bounds to the left and a large bunker to the right. The approach is to a crowned green with a trap to its front right. The 438-yard ninth, another dogleg right, has woods to the right and out-of-bounds to the left. The approach is to an elevated green guarded by two bunkers to its front right and another to its rear left. The Palm Course's 454-yard par-4 finishing hole has been ranked as high as No. 4 on the PGA's toughest hole list. The tee shot is down a treelined alleyway and the approach is to a small, forward-sloping peninsula green, a bunker to its front, left and rear.

•WHO THE COURSE FAVORS

The variety of doglegs, abundant bunkers, omnipresent trees and strategically placed water hazards require a golfer to hit a variety of shots and manage the courses in order to succeed. The Palm Course demands that a golfer hit the fairways in order to avoid rough, trees and water. Approaches into the well-guarded greens are critical and, if you miss, good sand play or a new ball is required.

Best Place to Watch
Toughest Hole

HOLE	YARDS	PAR	HOLE	YARDS	PAR
1	495	5	10	450	4
2	389	4	11	552	5
3	165	3	12	199	3
4	422	4	13	364	4
5	403	4	14	547	5
6	412	4	15	426	4
7	532	5	16	172	3
8	205	3	17	397	4
9	373	4	18	454	4
			TOTAL	6957	72

PALM COURSE
ARCHITECT: JOE LEE (1970)

LODGING

Walt Disney World has accommodations in every price range from camping and travel sites to fully equipped vacation homes that can accommodate 12 guests. Contact: Walt Disney World, P.O. Box 10000, Lake Buena Vista, FL 32830-0040. (407) W-DISNEY (reservations). Suggested are:

$$$ Disney's Grand Floridian Beach Resort, 4401 Grand Floridian Way, Lake Buena Vista, Fla. (407) W-DISNEY. 10 minutes from golf courses.

$$ Hilton at Walt Disney World Village, 1751 Hotel Plaza Blvd., Lake Buena Vista, Fla. (407) 827-4000, (800) 782-4414, (800) 445-8667. 10 minutes from golf courses.

$ Disney's Fort Wilderness Reserve and Campground (trailer homes and campsites), 4510 N. Fort Wilderness Trail, Lake Buena Vista, Fla. (407) W-DISNEY. 10 minutes from golf courses.

DINING

Dux, in the Peabody Hotel, 9811 International Dr., Orlando, Fla. (407) 345-4550.

Café de France, 526 S. Park Ave., Winter Park, Fla. (407) 647-1869.

Bubbalou's Bodacious Bar-B-Q, 1471 Lee Rd., Winter Park, Fla. (407) 628-1212.

PUBLIC COURSES TO PLAY IN AREA

Bay Hill Club, 9000 Bay Hill Blvd., Orlando, Fla. Resort. (407) 876-2429, (800) 523-5999. Challenger/Champion: 18/7,114/72. Charger: 9/3,090/36. 20 minutes from Walt Disney World.

Grand Cypress, 1 N. Jacaranda, Orlando, Fla. Resort. (407) 239-4700, (800) 835-7377 (Villas of Grand Cypress), (407) 239-1234, (800) 233-1234 (Hyatt Regency). North/South: 18/7,024/72. South/East: 18/6,955/72. East/North: 18/6,937/72. New Course: 18/6,773/72. Grand Cypress Golf Academy (3 holes): 3/1,104/12. 5 minutes from Walt Disney World.

Greenlefe Resort and Conference Center, 3200 State Road 546, Haines City, Fla. Resort. (813) 422-7511, (800) 237-9549 (outside Fla.). West: 18/7,325/72. East: 18/6,802/72. South: 18/6,869/71. 30 minutes from Walt Disney World.

TICKETS & ACCESSIBILITY

How to watch: Mon., PGA and amateur practice rounds. Tue., PGA and amateur practice rounds, shoot-out, ladies tournament. Wed., PGA and amateur practice rounds, PGA father-child tournament. Thur.-Sun., tournament. Thur.-Sat., competition held on Lake Buena Vista, Palm and Magnolia Courses. Final round is played on Magnolia. Individual, group and sponsorship tickest available. Walt Disney World/Oldsmobile Golf Classic, 4510 N. Fort Wilderness Trail, Lake Buena Vista, FL 32830. (407) 824-2250.

How to play: Golf packages are available year-round with lowest rates from May to December. Tee times can be made 30 days in advance if you have a reservation at a Disney resort hotel. The public can make reservations seven days in advance May-Dec. and four days in advance Jan.-April. Ninety-nine holes of golf on site include: Eagle Pines: (18/6,772/72). Lake Buena Vista: (18/6,829/72). Magnolia: (18/7,190/72). Oak Trail: (9/2,913/36). Osprey Ridge: (18/7,101/72). Palm: (18/6,772/72). (407) 824-2270 for tee time reservation information.

Las Vegas Invitational

TPC AT SUMMERLIN, LAS VEGAS COUNTRY CLUB

Like the Bob Hope Chrysler Classic, the Las Vegas Invitational is a marathon, five-round, 90-hole pro-am event that's played on a handful of courses and finishes with a pro-only final 18 at the event's host course.

Fuzzy Zoeller won the 1983 inaugural and later joined with architect Bobby Weed to design the TPC at Summerlin course, which now hosts both this event and the Las Vegas Seniors Classic.

Situated not far from downtown Vegas in an enormous luxury community developed by the Howard Hughes Corporation, TPC at Summerlin is an open, stadium-style course that has always been prone to low scores, as have the event's secondary layouts. In 1991, third-place finisher Chip Beck tied Al Geiberger's all-time PGA Tour tournament record by firing a 13-under-par 59 at the Sunrise Golf Club during the third round.

In 1993, Davis Love III finished with rounds of 65 and 66 here to win by eight shots. In 1994, Bruce Lietzke holed an eagle on the 16th and finished with a 66 and 65 to edge Robert Gamez by a stroke.

TOURNAMENT-AT-A-GLANCE

Course: TPC at Summerlin, Las Vegas Country Club
Type: Private
Location: 1700 Village Center Circle, Las Vegas, NV 89134
Telephone: (702) 256-0111
When: Oct. 2–6, 1996
How To Get There: From Las Vegas airport, 20 minutes. Take Tropican to I-15. Turn right on I-15 toward downtown. Proceed to I-95, then take I-95 north to Summerlin Pkwy. Exit. Bear right off exit onto Summerlin. Proceed 2 miles to traffic circle, bear right at traffic circle to the club.
Broadcast: ESPN (1996)
Purse: $1,500,000 (1995)
Tournament Record: 29-under-par 331 (5 rounds), Davis Love III, 1993

"IT'S HARD TO CONCENTRATE ON EVERY SHOT WHEN YOU KNOW WHAT'S GOING TO HAPPEN. I MEAN, WHEN I GOT AN 11-SHOT LEAD, THERE WAS NO WAY I COULD FIGURE OUT HOW TO LOSE IT. I KEPT TELLING MYSELF TO GET 32 OR 33 UNDER, AND I WAS TRYING, BUT WHAT I REALLY WANTED TO DO WAS GET MY SECOND WIN OF THE YEAR."

—DAVIS LOVE III,

AFTER SETTING A TOURNAMENT RECORD WITH A SCORE OF 331 TO WIN THE LAS VEGAS INVITATIONAL IN 1993

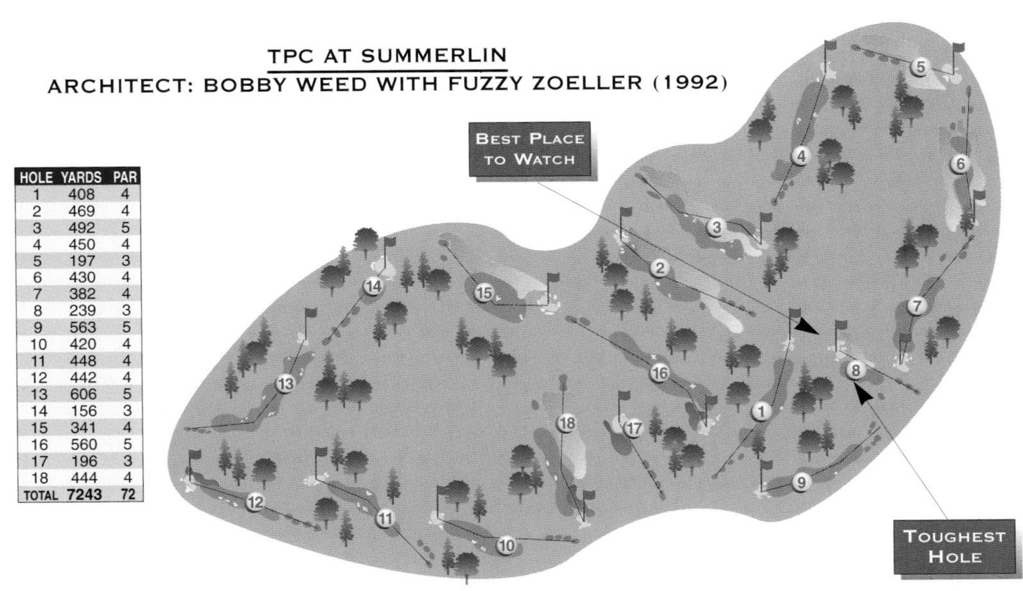

HOLE	YARDS	PAR
1	408	4
2	469	4
3	492	5
4	450	4
5	197	3
6	430	4
7	382	4
8	239	3
9	563	5
10	420	4
11	448	4
12	442	4
13	606	5
14	156	3
15	341	4
16	560	5
17	196	3
18	444	4
TOTAL	7243	72

●TOUGHEST HOLE

Summerlin's 239-yard, par-3 eighth was rated the most difficult hole to par on the course in 1994. Desert waste guards the right side and the 47-yard-deep green is protected by four bunkers to its right, one to its front left and another to its rear. The Las Vegas Country Club's greens are well protected by palm, pine and olive trees. A difficult hole here is the 442-yard, par-4 sixth, a dogleg left with out-of-bounds to the right and a small green well protected by three bunkers.

●BEST PLACE TO WATCH

The TPC course is relatively flat and easy to walk. The par-3s that tend to average above par—all but the 14th—are good places to watch. The mounds around the par-3 eighth hole provide views of No. 3, No. 2 and No. 9. The two finishing holes are also good spectator holes. A good place to watch at the Las Vegas Country Club is to the right of the green on the 346-yard, par-4 13th. This affords easy access to holes No. 10, 14, and 15.

●WHO THE COURSE FAVORS

The TPC course is toughened up for the tournament by moving the tees back to 7,243 yards, but finishing round scores indicate that the pros can easily handle this open desert layout. The ability to hit accurate approach shots to set up birdie opportunities on this course is critical. The Las Vegas Country Club rewards the golfer who can play a controlled, strategic game and avoid its hazards, but its short layout makes it easy to rack up birdies.

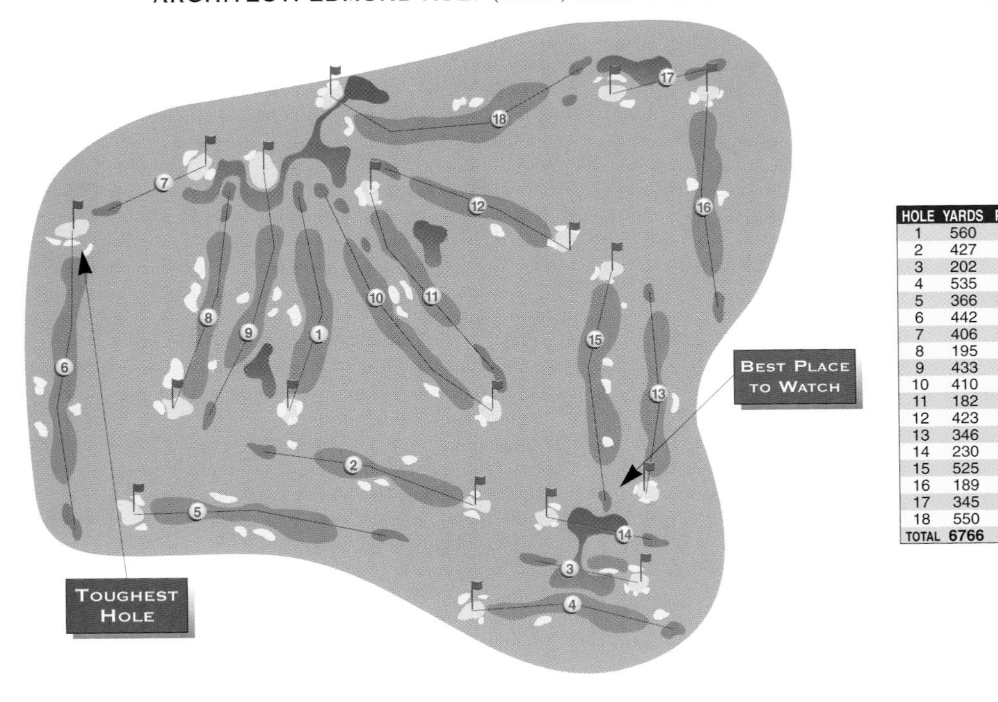

HOLE	YARDS	PAR
1	560	5
2	427	4
3	202	3
4	535	5
5	366	4
6	442	4
7	406	4
8	195	3
9	433	4
10	410	4
11	182	3
12	423	4
13	346	4
14	230	3
15	525	5
16	189	3
17	345	4
18	550	5
TOTAL	6766	71

LODGING

$$$ Residence Inn by Marriott, 3225 Paradise Rd., Las Vegas. (702) 796-9300, (800) 331-3131. 5 minutes from TPC Summerlin.

$$ Alexis Park Resort, 375 E. Harmon Ave., Las Vegas. (702) 796-3300. (800) 582-2228. 5 minutes from TPC Summerlin.

$ Rio Suite Hotel & Casino, 3700 W. Flamingo Rd., Las Vegas. (702) 252-7777, (800) PLAY-RIO. 10 minutes from TPC Summerlin.

DINING

Fisherman's Port at the Alexis Park Resort, 375 E. Harmon Ave., Las Vegas. (702) 796-3300.

Fiore's Restaurant at the Rio Suite Hotel and Casino, 3700 W. Flamingo Rd., Las Vegas. (702) 252-7777.

Hard Rock Cafe, adjacent the Hard Rock Hotel and Casino, 4455 Paradise Rd., Las Vegas. (702) 693-5000, (800) HRD-ROCK.

PUBLIC COURSES TO PLAY IN AREA

Desert Inn Country Club, Desert Inn Hotel and Casino, 3145 Las Vegas Blvd., South Las Vegas. Resort. (702) 733-4444, (800) 634-6906. 18/7,111/72. 5 minutes from TPC Summerlin.

The Legacy Golf Club, 130 Par Excellence Dr., Henderson, Nev. Resort. (702) 897-2187. 18/7,233/72. 15 minutes from TPC Summerlin.

Painted Desert Golf Club, 5555 Painted Mirage Way, Las Vegas. Public. (702) 645-2568. 18/6,840/72. 10 minutes from TPC Summerlin.

TICKETS & ACCESSIBILITY

How to watch: Mon., PGA practice rounds. Tue., PGA practice rounds, shoot-out. Wed.-Sun., tournament. Individual, group and sponsor ticket information is available from Las Vegas Invitational, 801 S. Rancho Dr., Suite C-3, Las Vegas, NV 89106. (702) 382-6616.

How to play: The TPC Summerlin is a private club. You must be a member or the guest of a member to play the course.

LaCantera Texas Open

LACANTERA GOLF CLUB

One of the oldest events on the pro Tour, the Texas Open debuted in 1922 with a purse of $5,000, then the largest in professional golf history and almost twice the total winnings paid out at the PGA Championship. This early foray into high-stakes golf was the brainchild of Jack O'Brien, the editor of the *San Antonio Evening News,* who sold the San Antonio Chamber of Commerce on the idea that a February golf tournament would publicize the mild winters of the nation's 37th largest city. Four years later, the Los Angeles Jaycees would follow San Antonio's lead, and the PGA Tour was finally on the path to today's year-round calendar of million-dollar events and national television audiences.

The Texas Open's champions over seven-plus decades are a proud line of great PGA golfers, among them Walter Hagen, Bill Mehlhorn, Byron Nelson, Ben Hogan, Sam Snead, Jack Burke Jr., Arnold Palmer, Ben Crenshaw, Lee Trevino and Nick Price. Over the years, the Texas Open has witnessed many of the Tour's lowest scores ever. In 1955, big Mike Souchak charged from the gates with an 8-under-par front nine at San Antonio's Brackenridge Park Golf Course, on his way to a 27-under-par 72-hole total of 257, still a PGA Tour record.

The event was one of very few PGA Tour tournaments to enter 1995 without a national television deal, but its image was sure to be burnished by its move to a sparkling new Jay Morrish and Tom Weiskopf–designed course called La Cantera. Located about 20 minutes northwest of the Alamo in a 1,600-acre development that includes the Fiesta theme park, LaCantera was rated one of the best new golf courses to open in the United States in 1994. Cut into Texas Hill Country, it features views of the San Antonio skyline, a fascinating variety of tee distances and hole configurations, and large, well-bunkered greens. A plethora of natural elements—ponds, streams, elevation changes, limestone outcroppings, variable winds and such foliage as oak and mesquite—add challenge and beauty to the course. Holes have been routed in various ways to make the most of 15 mph prevailing winds. And the huge greens allow for many interesting pin placements.

LaCantera wastes no time in getting your attention. The first hole is a par-5 that stretches a daunting 665 yards, but it usually plays downwind and it drops 125 feet from the hilltop tee. Bunkers guard the front and both sides of its large green, and a pond lurks in back to catch overclubbed and windblown shots. By the fourth tee, the golfer has played the longest par-5, the longest par-4 and the longest par-3 on the course, but some of the most difficult holes are yet to come.

One of these is the 415-yard 12th, whose tee shot must avoid bunkers to the left and a sharp drop to a ravine on the right. The green is large but angled slightly, and it is guarded by a waterfall and two creeks which meet to run in front of the green.

Variety, and the well-integrated natural features of the land, make LaCantera a scenic challenge. A privately owned daily-fee course, it has five tee-distance options and can graciously accommodate any golfer, including the best in the world.

TOURNAMENT-AT-A-GLANCE

Course: LaCantera Golf Club
Type: Public
Location: 16401 LaCantera Pkwy, San Antonio, TX 78256
Telephone: (210) 558-4653
When: Oct. 10–13, 1996
How To Get There: From San Antonio, 15 minutes. Take I-10/McDermott Freeway to LaCantera Pkwy Exit. Exit onto LaCantera Pkwy. LaCantera Golf Club entrance is 1 miles up on the right.
Broadcast: Golf Channel (1995)
Purse: $1,100,000 (1995)
Tournament Record: 27-under-par 257, Mike Souchak, 1957 (at Brackenridge Park Golf Course, San Antonio)

"I THOUGHT I WAS GOING TO HAVE TO BIRDIE UNTIL DARK TO WIN."

—JAY HAAS,

WINNER OF THE 1993 TEXAS OPEN, WHO BIRDIED FOUR OF THE LAST FIVE HOLES, INCLUDING THE SUDDEN-DEATH PLAYOFF HOLE, TO WIN THE EVENT.

By Oscar Williams

FROM ITS HIGH PERCH, THE 10TH HOLE AT LACANTERA HAS PANORAMIC VIEWS OF SAN ANTONIO AND THE SURROUNDING TEXAS HILL COUNTRY.

•TOUGHEST HOLE

Co-designer Tom Weiskopf is betting that the 415-yard, par-4 12th hole "will someday be considered one of the foremost par-4s in Texas, not only due to the challenge it provides the golfer but also because of its beauty." The tee shot plays to a tight landing area guarded by a ravine and by a series of four bunkers 240 yards from the tournament tee. A lateral hazard lurks on the right. Two creeks and a waterfall guard the green, and the approach must be lofted over the water to a large, side-angled green protected by a bunker to its left and another at its rear. Another challenging par-4 at LaCantera is the 466-yard 15th, which plays uphill to a deep, lightbulb-shaped green with a huge bunker to its left. The tee shot should be hit to the right-center of the fairway to avoid trees on the left. Approaches can be run onto the putting surfaces, but a deep bunker waits on the left, a rock outcropping rises to the back right, and a lateral hazard is hidden behind the green.

•BEST PLACE TO WATCH

The two finishing holes provide prime viewing spots. Position yourself near the green at the 190-yard, par-3 17th, where contenders will probably try to squeeze more out of the hole than they can possibly get. Two large bunkers guard the right and left side of the deep, doglegged putting surface. The 442-yard, par-4 finishing hole, a dogleg left, should provide dramatic conclusions to this venerable tournament. The first shot must avoid a bunker that encroaches into the right fairway, and the approach is uphill to a deep green framed by a horseshoe of bunkers. Within an easy walk of the No. 18 green are the No. 4 green, No. 1 tee, No. 9 green, No. 5 tee, the practice area and the clubhouse.

•WHO THE COURSE FAVORS

LaCantera demands shotmaking skills because of the variable winds, elevation changes, hole distance variations and obstacles such as water, sand and trees. The par-5s, for example, range from the dogleg right, 665-yard opening hole, which plays downwind and downhill, to the dogleg-left, 537-yard 14th, a bunker-free hole where a creek crossing in front of the green protects the flagstick.

HOLE	YARDS	PAR
1	665	5
2	470	4
3	215	3
4	438	4
5	535	5
6	183	3
7	315	4
8	348	4
9	405	4
10	558	5
11	467	4
12	415	4
13	144	3
14	537	5
15	466	4
16	353	4
17	190	3
18	442	4
TOTAL	7146	72

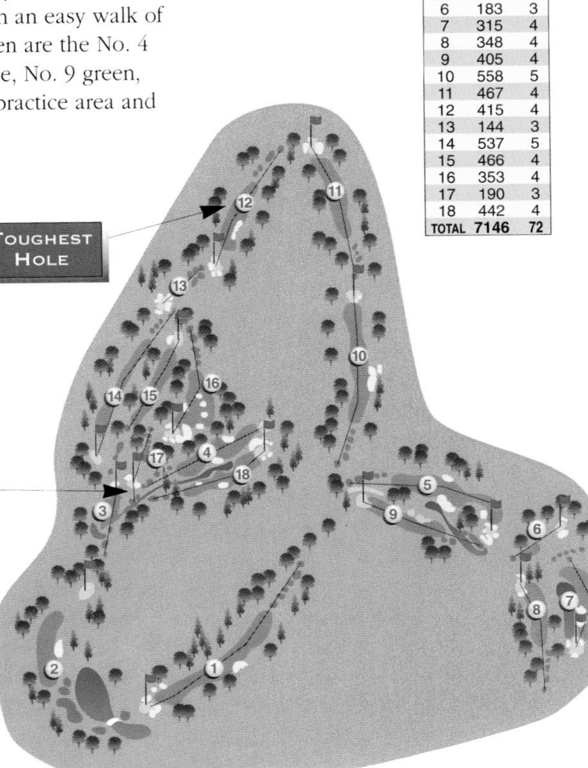

LACANTERA GOLF CLUB
ARCHITECTS: JAY MORRISH AND TOM WEISKOPF (1994)

LODGING

$$$ Hyatt Regency Hill Country Resort, 9800 Hyatt Resort Dr., San Antonio. (210) 647-1234, (800) 233-1234. 20 minutes from La Cantera.
$$ Marriott Rivercenter, 101 Bowie St., San Antonio. (210) 223-1000, (800) 228-9290. 20 minutes from La Cantera.
$ Hampton Inn–Fiesta Park, 11010 Interstate 10 at Huebner Rd., San Antonio. (210) 561-9058, (800) 426-7866. 5 minutes from La Cantera.

DINING

Chez Ardid, 1919 San Pedro Ave., San Antonio. (210) 732-3203.
Ports O' Call, 4522 Fredericksburg Rd., San Antonio. (210) 732-3663.
La Margarita, 120 Produce Row, San Antonio. (210) 227-7140.

PUBLIC COURSES TO PLAY IN AREA

Barton Creek Resort and Country Club, Austin, Texas. Resort. (512) 329-4000, (800) 336-6158. Crenshaw: 18/6,678/71. Fazio: 18/6,956/72. 1 hour from La Cantera.
Hill Country Golf Club, 9800 Hyatt Resort Dr., San Antonio. Resort. 18/6,913/72. (210) 520-4040. 20 minutes from La Cantera.
Pecan Valley, 4700 Pecan Valley, San Antonio. Public. (210) 333-9018, (800) 336-3418. 18/7,116/72. 20 minutes from La Cantera.

TICKETS & ACCESSIBILITY

How to watch: Sun., celebrity pro-am. Mon., classic pro-am, PGA practice rounds. Tue., PGA practice rounds, shoot-out. Wed., celebrity pro-am. Thur.-Sun., tournament. Admission is free Mon. Individual tickets begin at $10. Group and sponsorship plans available. LaCantera Texas Open, San Antonio Golf Association, 70 N.E. Loop 410, Suite 370, San Antonio, TX 78216, (210) 341-0823.
How to play: LaCantera is a daily fee course open to the public year-round. Contact the pro shop for tee times at (210) 558-4653.

The Tour Championship

SOUTHERN HILLS COUNTRY CLUB

In 1810 the land on which Southern Hills now stands was given to the Creek tribe by the U.S. Government "for as long as the grass grows and the water runs." After Oklahoma achieved statehood in 1907, the land was sold off at $10 per acre.

Waite Phillips, a co-founder of Phillips Petroleum and a major beneficiary of that land sale, offered to provide 300 acres for a family-style country club in south Tulsa during the middle of the Depression if club organizers could come up with $150,000 in three weeks. The group collected enough pledges, 140 at $1,000 each, to satisfy Phillips, and Perry Maxwell, a former banker, was retained to build Southern Hills.

TOURNAMENT-AT-A-GLANCE

Course: Southern Hills Country Club
Type: Private
Location: 2636 East 61st Street, Tulsa, OK 74136
Telephone: (918) 492-3351
When: Oct. 24–27, 1996
How To Get There: From downtown Tulsa, take I-75 south to 71st St. bridge. Take 71st St. east to Lewis. Go left on Lewis to 61st St. and the golf course.
Broadcast: ABC, ESPN (1996)
Purse: $3,000,000 (1995)
Tournament Record: 12-under-par 268, Tom Watson, 1987 (at par-72 Oak Hills CC, San Antonio)

Maxwell—a good friend of Bobby Jones and who later remodeled Augusta National and Pine Valley—had begun designing courses in 1913 and in the early 1930s had worked in partnership with the great Alister Mackenzie. Southern Hills was built with mules and panscrapers, making it, along with Augusta National, one of the few golf courses of note to be built in the United States during the Depression. Maxwell lived on-site during construction and earned his fee from cost control of the $100,000 budget.

Southern Hills is noted for its variable, strong winds, its steel wool-tough Bermuda and rye rough, its heavily contoured greens and the 85 powdery bunkers that penalize errant drives and approaches. The course is flat, despite its name, except for the ninth and the 18th, which play uphill to the stately clubhouse. Three of its holes—the second, 14th and 18th—were ranked among the 50 toughest on the Tour in 1994.

Often ranked among the nation's 10 best courses, Southern Hills has been the scene of many great marches up its legendary 430-yard, par-4 finishing hole to the elevated green backed by a steep hillside and overlooked by the clubhouse. Nick Price set the course record at 269 with his runaway victory here in the 1994 PGA Championship. Two other PGA Championships (1970, 1982), a U.S. Senior Amateur (1961), a U.S. Amateur (1965) and two U.S. Opens (1958, 1977) have also been decided here. In 1946, the great Babe Didrikson Zaharias won the 1946 U.S. Women's Amateur here, 11 and 9 in match play.

The Tour Championship, first won by Tom Watson at Oak Hills in San Antonio in 1987, arrived at Southern Hills in 1995. The year's top-30 money-winners tee it up for the final official event of the season, and half the time a sudden-death playoff has determined the outcome. In 1994, Mark McCumber and Fuzzy Zoeller tied at 274 at San Francisco's Olympic Club, but McCumber drained a right-to-left, uphill 40-foot putt for birdie on the first extra hole to stun the runner-up and claim the year's biggest winner's check: $540,000.

> "HEY, I'M TRYING TO GET MY NAME ON TROPHIES. BY THE TIME I'M DEAD, ALL THE MONEY WILL BE GONE, BUT THE TROPHIES WILL STILL BE THERE."
>
> —FUZZY ZOELLER,
>
> WHO ESTABLISHED A TOUR RECORD BY EARNING $1,016,804 IN 1994 WITHOUT WINNING A TOURNAMENT

●TOUGHEST HOLE

The most difficult hole on the front side of Southern Hills is the 458-yard second, where tee shots must fly 225 yards in the air to clear three bunkers and a creek that turns and runs up the left side of the fairway. From there, the bunker-wrapped green is still a long-iron away. The back nine reserves its most demanding hole until last. This 430-yard, par-4 dogleg again punctuates the need to drive well at Southern Hills, because if you don't, the wiry rough or one of three fairway bunkers in a region 250 to 275 yards off the tee will create major problems. The next shot is to a sloping green that can be a nightmare if you land above the hole. The ideal approach to this target is from a plateau on the left side of the fairway. A safe tee shot usually finds a downhill slope, thus leaving a difficult uphill shot to the green.

●BEST PLACE TO WATCH

The ideal place to watch is from the steep hill behind the tough and famous finishing hole. Approaches to the green are often with long irons from difficult downhill lies, and the steep slope and contours of the green make for interesting putts. The green area of the par-4 ninth, also on a slope up to the clubhouse, provides another good vantage point. The rest of the golf course is flat and easy to walk.

●WHO THE COURSE FAVORS

Southern Hills is a driver's course. The tee shot must be well executed to avoid the thick Bermuda rough that has been compared to steel wool. Ben Hogan had to withdraw from the 1958 U.S. Open here when he hurt his wrist trying to extract a ball from ankle-deep grass. Talcum powder–like sand bunkers can often produce buried lies, and water hazards come into play on six holes. Solid shotmakers like Nick Price, Raymond Floyd and Dave Stockton have won the PGA Championship here.

HOLE	YARDS	PAR	HOLE	YARDS	PAR
1	456	4	10	376	4
2	458	4	11	164	3
3	405	4	12	448	4
4	368	4	13	537	5
5	614	5	14	207	3
6	175	3	15	405	4
7	382	4	16	468	4
8	215	3	17	352	4
9	374	4	18	430	4
			TOTAL	6834	70

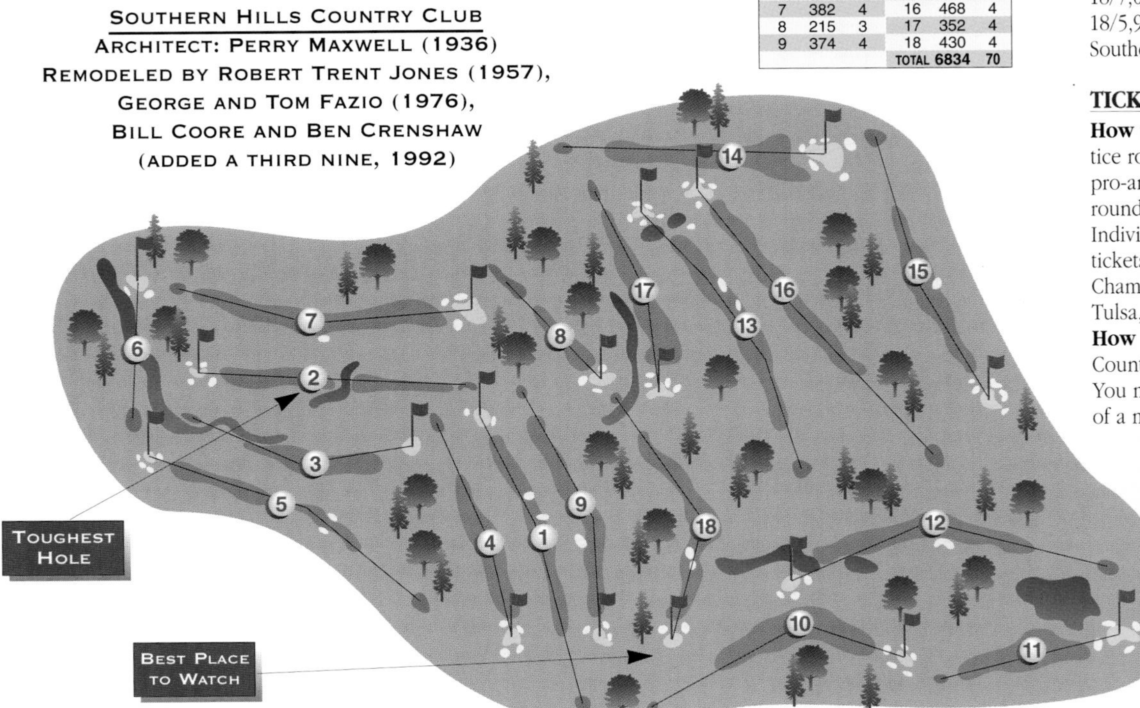

LODGING

$$$ Doubletree Hotel Downtown, 616 W. 7th St., Tulsa. (918) 587-8000, (800) 528-0444, (800) 222-8733. 15 minutes from Southern Hills.
$$ Tulsa Marriott, 10918 E. 41st St., Tulsa. (918) 627-5000, (800) 228-9290. 15 minutes from Southern Hills.
$ Residence Inn by Marriott, 8181 E. 41st St., Tulsa. (918) 664-7241, (800) 331-3131. 15 minutes from Southern Hills.

DINING

Warren Duck Club, in the Doubletree Hotel at Warren Place, 6110 South Yale St., Tulsa. (918) 495-1000, (800) 528-0444.
7 West Café & Grille, in the Doubletree Hotel Downtown, 616 W. 7th St., Tulsa. (918) 587-8000.
Chimi's Mexican Foods, 6109 E. 31st St., Tulsa. (918) 587-4411.

PUBLIC COURSES TO PLAY IN AREA

Forest Ridge Golf Club, 7501 E. Kenosha, Broken Arrow, Okla. Public. (918) 357-2282. 18/7,069/72. 25 minutes from Southern Hills.
Page Belchor Golf Course, 6666 S. Union, Tulsa. Public. (918) 446-1529. Olde Page: 18/6,826/71. Stone Creek: 18/6,539/71. 10 minutes from Southern Hills.
Shangri La, Rte. 3 and Hwy. 125, Afton, Okla. Resort. (918) 257-4204, (800) 331-4060. Blue Course: 18/7,012/72. Gold Course: 18/5,932/70. 90 minutes from Southern Hills.

TICKETS & ACCESSIBILITY

How to watch: Mon., PGA practice rounds, junior clinic. Tue., pro-am. Wed., PGA practice rounds. Thur.-Sun., tournament. Individual, group and sponsorship tickets available. The Tour Championship, P.O. Box 702620, Tulsa, OK 74170, (918) 497-4653.
How to play: Southern Hills Country Club is a private club. You must be a member or a guest of a member to play the course.

Lincoln-Mercury Kapalua International

KAPALUA RESORT

Kapalua, set beside the Pacific on the island of Maui, is one of those places you'll not want to leave once you cast your eyes upon its three golf courses that run through hillside pineapple plantations, across ravines, and through coconut palms, ironwoods and cool pines.

This post-season pro-am uses two of the resort's courses: the Arnold Palmer–designed Bay Course, built in the mid-1970s, and the Plantation Course, a 1991 addition designed by Ben Crenshaw and Bill Coore and used for the event's final two, pro-only rounds. The select professionals invited to this event are paid no matter what their score. Mark Rolfing shot a hefty 338 in 1994 and still received $7,700 for his effort.

The Plantation Course, a robust par-73, features large bunkers, rolling terrain and dramatic views of the ocean and the west Maui mountains. Winds and elevation changes require smart club selection and precise shotmaking.

Fred Couples enjoys Kapalua's hospitality, taking consecutive victories in the 1993 and 1994 events.

This tournament, which started in obscurity in 1982, put itself on the map a year later when a national TV audience watched Greg Norman, framed by Kapalua's memorable backdrop, storm to a six-stroke victory.

TOURNAMENT-AT-A-GLANCE

Course: Kapalua Resort—Plantation and Bay Courses
Type: Resort
Location: 2000 Plantation Club Dr., Lahaina, HI 96761
Telephone: (808) 669-8800 (golf course), (800) 367-8000 (resort)
When: Nov. 7–10, 1996
How To Get There: From Lahaina, 25 minutes. Take Hwy. 30 to Office Rd. Turn left onto Office Rd. at Kapalua exit. Follow signs to resort and golf courses.
Broadcast: ABC, ESPN (1996)
Purse: $1,050,000 (1996)
Tournament Record: 20-under-par 264, David Peoples, 1990 (at the Bay Course)

"HERE WE HAVE THE RAREST COMBINATION YOU CAN FIND IN GOLF, A STRIKINGLY BEAUTIFUL LOCATION THAT IS ALSO A NATURAL FOR PLAY. OUR DESIGN DIDN'T REALLY HAVE TO CREATE NEW HOLES AS MUCH AS TAKE THE EXISTING LAND AND NATURAL CHARACTERISTICS AND ADAPT THEM TO CREATE THE MOST EXCITING, CHALLENGING PLAY POSSIBLE."

—BEN CRENSHAW,
OF THE PLANTATION COURSE AT KAPALUA

Plantation Course

Architects: Bill Coore and Ben Crenshaw (1991)

HOLE	YARDS	PAR	HOLE	YARDS	PAR
1	473	4	10	354	4
2	218	3	11	164	3
3	380	4	12	373	4
4	382	4	13	407	4
5	532	5	14	305	4
6	398	4	15	555	5
7	484	4	16	365	4
8	203	3	17	486	4
9	521	5	18	663	5
			TOTAL	7263	73

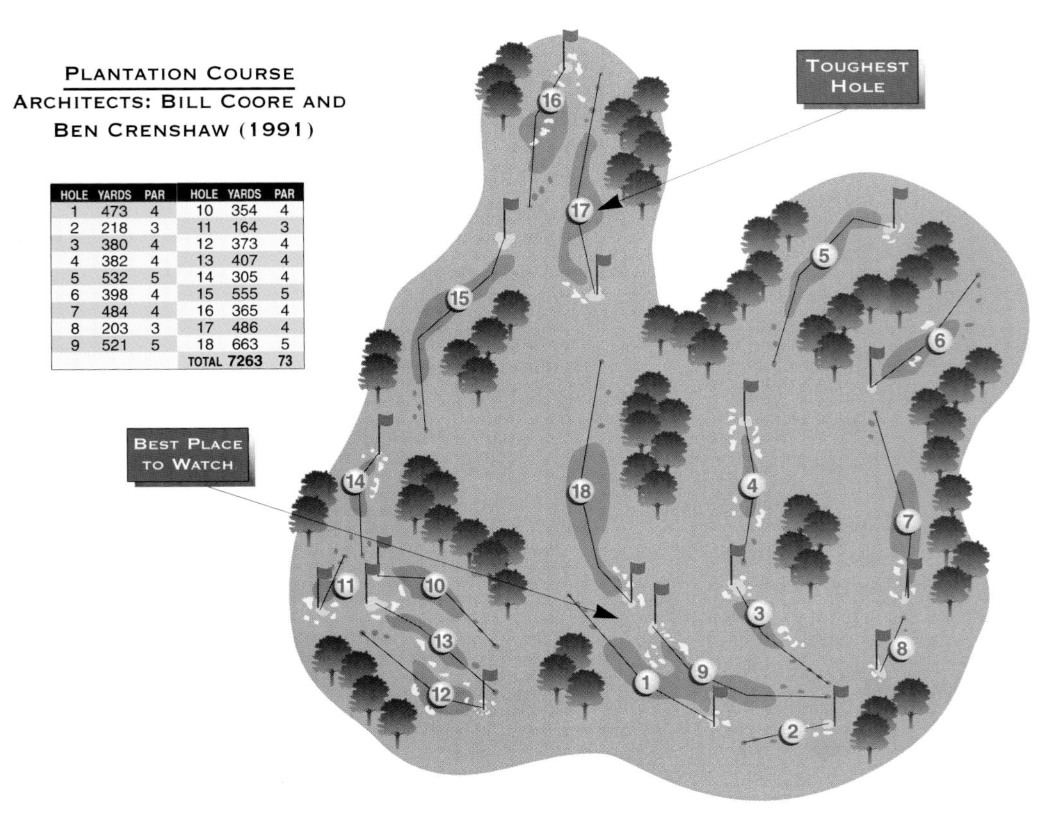

•TOUGHEST HOLE

At 486 yards, the Plantation course's dogleg left par-4 17th demands plenty of length and good club selection to account for its 150-foot downhill drop. The approach crosses a broad ravine to a deep green defended by three bunkers to its right rear. One of the toughest holes on the Bay Course is the 372-yard, par-4 second, an uphill challenge whose second shot is to a green well protected by bunkers to its left, rear and front.

•BEST PLACE TO WATCH

The No. 1 tee, No. 9 green, No. 10 tee and No. 18 green are all close to the Plantation course clubhouse. The 663-yard, par-5 18th, which is somewhat shortened by its downhill, downwind routing, is especially fun to watch as the pros try to make up strokes by going for the deep green in two. At the Bay Course, unless you want to walk up hills, the clubhouse has easy access to the No. 1 and 10 tees and No. 9 and 18 greens.

•WHO THE COURSE FAVORS

The Plantation Course would seem to favor a shotmaker who can adjust to wind conditions and elevation changes, but Fred Couples and Davis Love, two players known more for length than craft, notched three straight titles from 1992 to 1994. A solid putting game is also required. Most of the holes on the Bay Course play up, down or across hills. Club selection, an ability to hit off uneven lies, and green reading skills are important assets on this course.

Bay Course

Architect: Arnold Palmer (1975)

HOLE	YARDS	PAR
1	504	5
2	372	4
3	189	3
4	357	4
5	205	3
6	500	5
7	355	4
8	162	3
9	453	4
10	527	5
11	408	4
12	220	3
13	345	4
14	349	4
15	470	4
16	371	4
17	192	3
18	552	5
TOTAL	6531	71

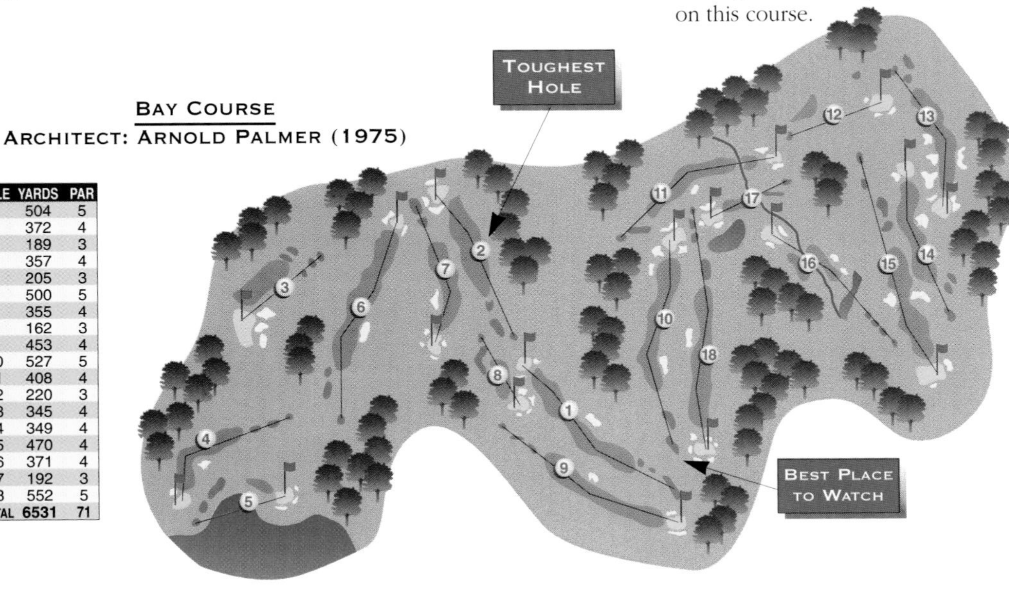

LODGING

$$$ Kapalua Bay Hotel, 1 Bay Dr., Kapalua, Hawaii. (808) 669-5656, (800) 367-8000. On site.

$ Pioneer Inn, 658 Wharf St., Lahaina, Hawaii. (808) 661-3636, 20 minutes from Kapalua resort.

DINING

The Plantation Veranda, in the Kapalua Bay Hotel, 1 Bay Dr., Kapalua, Hawaii. (808) 669-5656.

Avalon Restaurant and Bar, 844 Front St., Lahaina, Hawaii. (808) 667-5559.

PUBLIC COURSES TO PLAY IN AREA

Royal Kaanapali Golf Course, Kaanapali Beach Resort, Lahaina, Hawaii. Resort. (808) 661-3691. North: 18/6,994/71. South: 18/6,555/71. 25 minutes from Kapalua.

Waikapu Sandalwood Golf Course, 2500 Honoapiilani Hwy., Wailuki, Hawaii. Public. (808) 242-4653. 18/6,469/72. 50 minutes from Kapalua.

TICKETS & ACCESSIBILITY

How to watch: Mon.-Tue., all-amateur tournament, PGA professional practice rounds. Wed., PGA professional practice rounds. Thur.-Sun., tournament. Thur.-Fri., half the field on the Bay, half on the Plantation Course. Sat.-Sun., Plantation Course. Individual, group and sponsor tickets available. The Lincoln-Mercury Kapalua International, c/o Kapalua Marketing Company, 500 Bay Dr., Lahaina, Maui, HI 96761, (808) 669-5433.

How to play: The Kapalua Golf Club is part of the Kapalua Bay Hotel and Villa Resort, which includes 154 guest rooms and 124 one- and two-bedroom villas. The resort is open year round, and golf packages are available mid-April to mid-December. In addition to the Bay and Plantation courses, there is also the Village course on site: 18/6,632/71. (808) 669-8044 (golf course), (800) 367-8000 (resort).

Andersen Consulting World Championship of Golf

GRAYHAWK GOLF CLUB

Native plants and views of the McDowell Mountains are the backdrop at Grayhawk's 18th hole, "Five Falls," noted for its unique five-tiered waterfall.

This world championship is a new postseason match-play event that begins with head-to-head regional matches between outstanding professionals from four regions: the United States, Europe, Japan and "the rest of the world." Seven golfers who led the previous year's Sony rankings plus one sponsorship exempt player play elimination rounds on courses throughout the world, and the four finalists come to Scottsdale, Ariz., to decide the championship.

The Talon Course at Grayhawk, set above the Phoenix Valley and magnificently landscaped with native desert plants and trees, is a sequence of adventures. A 40-foot-deep canyon cuts through the back nine of the course, where the eleventh tee is served by a swinging bridge, an island green adds flair to the seventeenth, and cascading waterfalls wrap the 18th green. Arizona natives Phil Mickelson and Howard Twitty called the David Graham/Gary Panks layout their home course even before it opened in 1994.

"FROM THE START, GRAYHAWK GOLF CLUB HAS BEEN DESIGNED TO BE A HOME FOR THOSE WHO LOVE THE GAME OF GOLF."

—PHIL MICKELSON,

GRAYHAWK PGA TOUR REPRESENTATIVE

TOURNAMENT-AT-A-GLANCE

Course: Grayhawk Golf Club—Talon Course
Type: Public
Location: 19600 N. Pima Rd., Scottsdale, AZ 85255
Telephone: (602) 502-1800
When: Jan. 3–5, 1997
How To Get There: From Phoenix/Sky Harbor Airport, 45 minutes. Take 44th St. north to Camelback Rd. Make a right on Camelback to Scottsdale Rd. Go left on Scottsdale approximately 20 minutes to light. Take a right onto Frank Lloyd Wright Rd., proceed to second light, then take a left north on Pima about 3 1/2 miles to golf course on the left.
Broadcast: ABC (1996)
Purse: $3,650,000 (1996)
Tournament Record: New event in 1995

●TOUGHEST HOLE

For the professionals, the toughest hole on the front side is likely to be "Death Valley," No. 6, a 465-yard, par-4 dogleg left whose tee shot must carry 200 yards of desert terrain to reach a rolling fairway. The approach is to a medium-sized green with a shelf to its rear left. Another tough par-4 is "Double Cross," the 12th, a dogleg left that measures 445 yards to a green with slight shelves on its left and right. Both of these holes are likely to play into headwinds. A noteworthy par-3 is the 130-yard 17th, which plays to an island green with two bunkers to its left. There is a bit of rough, but not much, around this memorable target, called "Devil's Drink." A tailwind is likely to force the golfer to aim for the center of the green and hope for the best. Green speeds of up to 12 on the Stimpmeter will add to the difficulty of Grayhawk.

●BEST PLACE TO WATCH

The intersection of holes Nos. 12, 13, 14 and 15 provides good viewing opportunities, but because only four of the world's best players will compete in the finals of this event, you'll want to stay just ahead of them on this easy-to-walk layout.

●WHO THE COURSE FAVORS

Grayhawk demands accuracy and distance off the tee in order to overcome variable wind conditions and to set up high-percentage approach shots and putts. Errant approach shots will leave difficult lies on tricky mounds or tough bunker shots from deep traps. If the approach is ill-placed, the fast, undulating greens—the first in Arizona to use a hybrid called Crenshaw bent grass—will cause major problems.

HOLE	YARDS	PAR	HOLE	YARDS	PAR
1	435	4	10	450	4
2	348	4	11	168	3
3	500	5	12	445	4
4	405	4	13	305	4
5	150	3	14	525	5
6	465	4	15	451	4
7	408	4	16	420	4
8	230	3	17	130	3
9	550	5	18	575	5
			TOTAL	6960	72

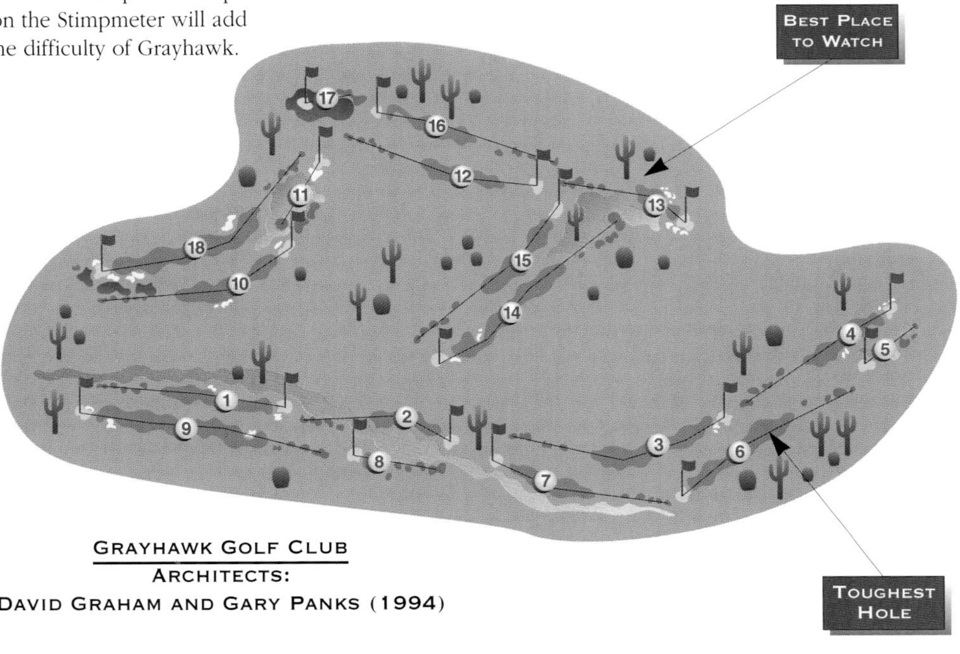

BEST PLACE TO WATCH

TOUGHEST HOLE

GRAYHAWK GOLF CLUB
ARCHITECTS:
DAVID GRAHAM AND GARY PANKS (1994)

LODGING

$$$ The Phoenician, 6000 E. Camelback Rd., Scottsdale, Ariz. (602) 941-8200, (800) 888-8234. 25 minutes from Grayhawk.
$$ Marriott Suites Scottsdale, 7325 E. Third Ave., Scottsdale, Ariz. (602) 945-1550, (800) 228-9290. 25 minutes from Grayhawk.
$ Residence Inns by Marriott, 6040 N. Scottsdale Rd., Scottsdale, Ariz. (602) 948-8666, (800) 331-3131. 20 minutes from Grayhawk.

DINING

Mary Elaine's Restaurant, at The Phoenician, 6000 E. Camelback Rd., Scottsdale, Ariz. (602) 941-8200.
The Grill Room, at the Ritz-Carlton Phoenix, 1401 E. Camelback Rd., Phoenix. (602) 468-0700, (800) 241-3333.
Z' Tejas Grill, Scottsdale Fashion Sq. Mall, 7014 E. Camelback Rd., Scottsdale, Ariz. (602) 946-4171.

PUBLIC COURSES TO PLAY IN AREA

Tournament Players Club of Scottsdale, 17020 N. Hayden Rd., Scottsdale, Ariz. Resort. (602) 585-3800, (800) 223-1818 (Scottsdale Princess Resort). Stadium: 18/6,992/71. Desert: 18/6,552/71. 13 minutes from Grayhawk.
Troon North Golf Club, 10370 E. Dynamite Blvd., Scottsdale, Ariz. Public. (602) 585-5300. 18/7,008/72. 10 minutes from Grayhawk.
Wigwam Resort, 451 Litchfield Rd., Litchfield Park, Ariz. Resort. (602) 272-4653, (800) 327-0396. Resort. Blue: 18/6,030/70. Gold: 18/7,021/72. West: 18/6,867/72. 55 minutes from Grayhawk.

TICKETS & ACCESSIBILITY

How to watch: Fri., pro-am. Sat., semifinal rounds. Sun., final rounds. Individual, group and sponsorship tickets available. International Sports and Entertainment Strategies, 1100 Spring St., Suite 600, Atlanta, GA 30309. (404) 873-5669.
How to play: Grayhawk is a high-end daily fee golf course open year round. The new 18-hole Tom Fazio–designed course, also available to the public, will be open late December 1995. On site is the Kostis/McCord Learning Center for golf instruction. Contact the pro shop for tee time reservation, rates, seasonal discounts and other information. (602) 502-1800.

THE SKINS GAME

BIGHORN GOLF CLUB

An anchor of the postseason's "greed tour"—where popular players compete for enormous purses in largely unofficial, made-for-TV events—the Skins Game is also one of the most-watched televised golf events after the Masters. And well it should be. Each year it pits four stars against each other in a favorite format of weekend golfers everywhere. Add a postcard backdrop and multiply the duffers' stakes by about a thousand, and you have 36 holes of entertaining golf drama. The formula worked so well for the PGA players that both the Senior and the women's tours have since added their own Skins showdowns.

TOURNAMENT-AT-A-GLANCE

Course: Bighorn Golf Club
Type: Private
Location: 255 Palowet Dr., Palm Desert, CA 92260
Telephone: (619) 341-4653
When: Nov. 30–Dec. 1, 1996
How To Get There: From Hwy. 111, 3 minutes. Take Hwy. 74 south toward mountains, golf course on the left.
Broadcast: ABC (1996)
Purse: $540,000 (1995)
Tournament Record: $370,000 in skins, Fuzzy Zoeller, 1985 (TPC at PGA West, La Quinta, Calif.)

The first Skins Game, played in 1983 at Desert Highlands Country Club in Scottsdale, Ariz., featured four all-time greats: Gary Player, Arnold Palmer, Tom Watson and Jack Nicklaus. Player dropped a critical 4-foot putt on the second-to-last hole to win with seven skins and $170,000. A parade of terrific players have followed, including Lee Trevino, Payne Stewart, Fred Couples, Tom Kite, Greg Norman, John Daly, Curtis Strange, Nick Faldo, Raymond Floyd, Paul Azinger and Fuzzy Zoeller. Stewart is the all-time money winner with $840,000 in earnings through 1994.

Bighorn, home of the Skins since 1992, is a scenic, Arthur Hills–designed desert course that meanders up, down and through the foothills of the majestic Santa Rosa Mountains in Palm Desert. With seven holes that cut manicured grass into barren cliffs, elevation varies from 810 to 1,150 feet, and each target area, including the small greens on the long par-3s, is enveloped by natural desert.

Bighorn requires strategic shotmaking and a good short game rather than distance. The 280-yard, par-4 fifth, for instance, dares the pros to go for the green in one, but an errant shot is likely to find the desert or a bunker adjacent to the two-tiered green. The 205-yard, par-3 eighth, called "Geronimo," drops severely to a narrow green surrounded by natural desert. The 166-yard, par-3 17th is all carry over a pond to a three-tiered green, making club selection and accuracy essential.

The first six holes of the Skins Game are played for $20,000 each, the next six for $30,000 and the last six for $40,000. Tied holes are carried over.

Stewart won the most money on one hole, with $260,000 in 1991.

Watson, breaking a long winless streak, captured the 1994 event by sinking a 15-foot playoff birdie putt for $160,000 and a total of $210,000.

And lest you think the game's heroes are too greedy, each Skins winner donates 20% of his earnings to a charity of his choice.

"I HAD CHANCES TO WIN FOUR TO FIVE TOURNAMENTS, BUT IT WAS NOT TO BE. SO THIS IS NOT THE ICING ON THE CAKE. IT'S JUST THE ICING. THE CAKE ISN'T THERE. BUT IT'S STILL VERY SWEET."

—TOM WATSON,

AFTER WINNING $210,000 AND THE SKINS GAME AT BIGHORN IN 1994.

●TOUGHEST HOLE

One of the tougher holes on the front side is the 459-yard, par-4 ninth, which plays down a desert-engulfed fairway to a small green protected by a lake and a waterfall to its left. Another tough hole on this side is the deceptive 205-yard, par-3 eighth, which drops severely and can be affected by swirling winds. A tough hole on the back side is the 426-yard, par-4 18th, whose tee-shot landing area is guarded by bunkers on the right. The approach must avoid a sea of sand to the rear, left and right of the green. A large pond on the left will catch errant shots from 150 yards into the green in that direction.

●BEST PLACE TO WATCH

Both nines loop out from the clubhouse through native desert and back to the starting point. It's an easy walk from the clubhouse to the practice area, the tees on Nos. 1, 10, 14 and 16, as well as the greens on Nos. nine, 13, 15 and 18. For the more adventuresome, it's easy to follow the select field around the course, which has refreshment outposts and rest rooms in several locations.

●WHO THE COURSE FAVORS

Bighorn is a short course by PGA standards. The par-5s range from 501 to 524 yards, the par-4s from 280 to 459 yards and the par-3s from 166 to 205 yards. Elevation changes and the omnipresent native desert areas can affect play, but short-iron play and putting is going to make the difference in this event, especially when multiple skins are on the line.

HOLE	YARDS	PAR
1	503	5
2	367	4
3	501	5
4	185	3
5	280	4
6	505	4
7	392	4
8	205	3
9	459	4
10	421	4
11	197	3
12	524	5
13	391	4
14	425	4
15	505	5
16	436	4
17	166	3
18	426	4
TOTAL	6888	72

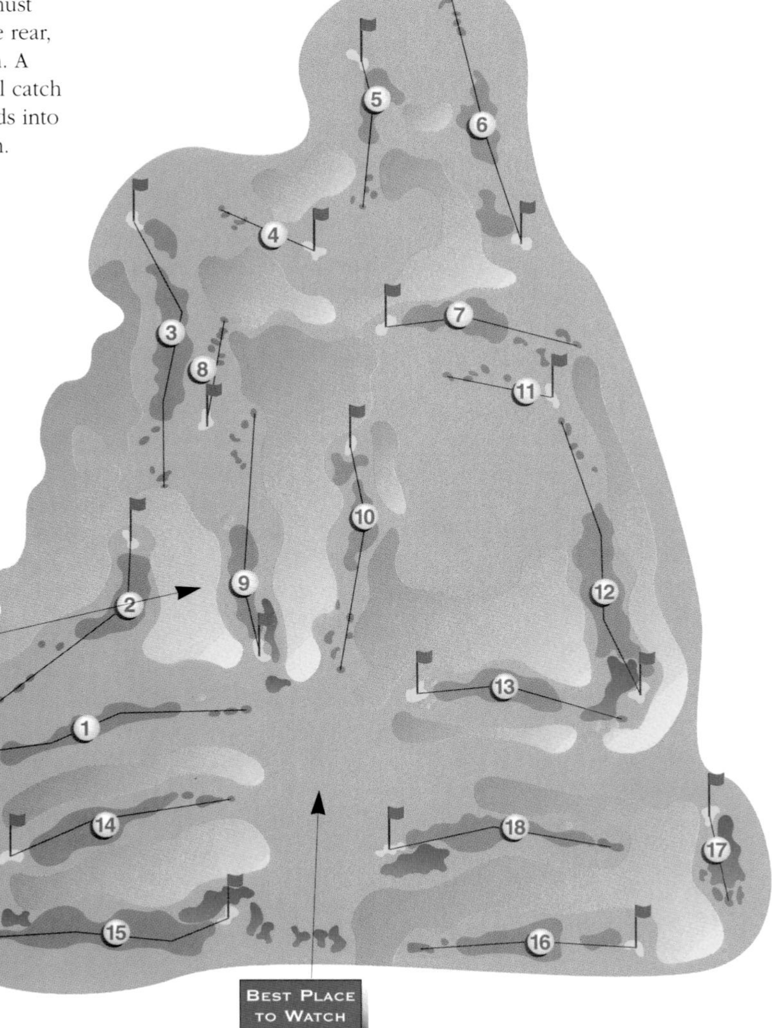

BIGHORN GOLF CLUB
ARCHITECT: ARTHUR HILLS (1991)

LODGING

$$$ The Ritz-Carlton Rancho Mirage, 68-900 Frank Sinatra Dr., Rancho Mirage, Calif. (619) 321-8282, (800) 241-3333. 15 minutes from Bighorn.

$$ Marriott's Rancho Las Palmas, 41000 Bob Hope Dr., Rancho Mirage, Calif. (619) 568-2727, (800) 458-8786. 15 minutes from Bighorn.

$ Courtyard by Marriott, 1300 Tahquitz Canyon Way, Palm Springs, Calif. (619) 322-6100, (800) 321-2211. 20 minutes from Bighorn.

DINING

The Club Grill at the Ritz-Carlton Rancho Mirage, 68-900 Frank Sinatra Dr., Rancho Mirage, Calif. (619) 321-8282.

Casuelas Cafe, 73-703 Hwy. 111, Palm Desert, Calif. (619) 568-0011.

PUBLIC COURSES TO PLAY IN AREA

The Field Golf Club, 19300 Palm Dr., Desert Hot Springs, Calif. Public. (619) 251-5366. 18/6,876/72. 5 minutes from Bighorn.

PGA West, 56-150 PGA Blvd., La Quinta, Calif. Resort. (619) 564-7170. Jack Nicklaus Resort Course: 18/7,126/72. TPC Stadium Course: 18/7,261/72. 15 minutes from Bighorn.

Westin Mission Hills Resort Golf Course, Westin Mission Hills Resort, 71-333 Dinah Shore Dr., Rancho Mirage, Calif. Resort. (619) 328-5955, (800) 358-2211. Player: 18/7,062/72. Dye: 18/6,706/70. 20 minutes from Bighorn.

TICKETS & ACCESSIBILITY

How to watch: Fri., pro-am. Sat.-Sun., tournament. Individual, group or sponsor tickets available. The Skins Game, OCC Sports, 962 N. La Cienega, Los Angeles, CA 90069. (310) 358-5300.

How to play: Bighorn is a private club open year round. You must be a member or the guest of a member to play the course.

Franklin Templeton Shark Shootout

Sherwood Country Club

The Shark Shootout—hosted by the Shark himself, Greg Norman—is a 54-hole, three-day event that pairs 20 top players in two-man teams. The field is open to the two defending champions, the year's top-three money-makers on the PGA Tour, the 10 top all-time money-winners and enough exemptions to complete the field.

The format of the first round is best ball, the second round is alternate shot, and the final round is a scramble.

The Sherwood Country Club is a Jack Nicklaus creation within a luxury development north of Los Angeles. Though the course is young, its builders cultivated its mature look by relocating dozens of sycamore and oak trees. Pools, waterfalls, streams and volcanic rock also adorn its rugged setting. Nicklaus's touch is evident in the layout's generous, bowl-like landing areas and the challenging approaches to amply bunkered, undulating greens.

Fred Couples, who does extraordinarily well in post-season special events like this, teamed with Brad Faxon to win the $300,000 team prize with scores of 68-64-58–190 in 1994. Raymond Floyd is the event's all-time leading money winner with $440,750.

TOURNAMENT-AT-A-GLANCE

Course: Sherwood Country Club
Type: Private
Location: 320 W. Strafford Rd., Thousand Oaks, CA 91361
Telephone: (805) 496-3036
When: Nov. 21–24, 1996
How To Get There: From downtown Los Angeles, 45 minutes. Take 101 North (Ventura Freeway) to Westlake Blvd. Turn left after 2 miles onto Potrero Rd. Turn right after 2 miles onto Trentwood and Sherwood Country Club.
Broadcast: ESPN, CBS (1995)
Purse: $1,100,000 (1995)
Tournament Record: 34-under-par 182, Fred Couples/Raymond Floyd, 1990

●TOUGHEST HOLE

One of the most difficult holes at Sherwood is the 435-yard, par-4 fourth, a dogleg right that often plays into a headwind. Water lines the right side from tee to green, and a large bunker runs to the right side of the green from 50 yards out.

●BEST PLACE TO WATCH

The adventuresome can follow the golfers around the course, but near the clubhouse there's easy access to the practice range and putting green as well as tees Nos. 1 and 10, and greens Nos. 9 and 18. The greens of the picturesque and difficult par-3s are also excellent places to watch.

●WHO THE COURSE FAVORS

Confronted with only three par-4s under 400 yards, a player would do well to be long and accurate off the tee at Sherwood, where landing areas are protected by water or bunkers. In this tournament format, if you can't consistently birdie, your team won't be competitive.

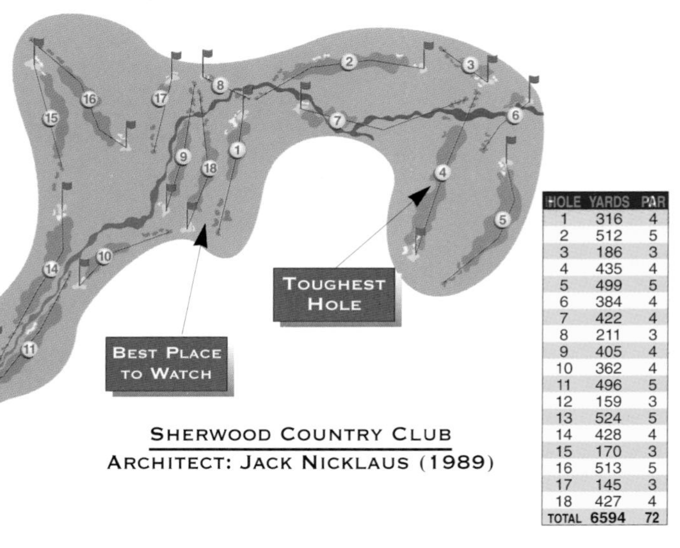

HOLE	YARDS	PAR
1	316	4
2	512	5
3	186	3
4	435	4
5	499	5
6	384	4
7	422	4
8	211	3
9	405	4
10	362	4
11	496	5
12	159	3
13	524	5
14	428	4
15	170	3
16	513	5
17	145	3
18	427	4
TOTAL	6594	72

Sherwood Country Club
Architect: Jack Nicklaus (1989)

LODGING

$$$ Hyatt Westlake Plaza Hotel, 880 S. Westlake Blvd., Westlake Village, Calif. (805) 497-9991, (800) 223-1234. 10 minutes from Sherwood CC.
$$ Warner Center Marriott Hotel, 21850 Oxnard St., Woodland Hills, Calif. (818) 887-4800, (800) 228-9290. 20 minutes from Sherwood CC.
$ Thousand Oaks Inn, 75 W. Thousand Oaks Blvd., Thousand Oaks, Calif. (805) 497-3701, (800) 600-6878. 5 minutes from Sherwood CC.

DINING

Pearl's, A California Restaurant, in the Warner Center Marriott Hotel, 21850 Oxnard St., Woodland Hills, Calif. (818) 887-4800.
Black Angus, 139 W. Thousand Oaks Blvd., Thousand Oaks, Calif. (805) 497-0757.

PUBLIC COURSES TO PLAY IN AREA

Elkins Ranch Golf Club, 1386 Chambersburg Rd., Fillmore, Calif. Public. (805) 524-1440. 18/6,302/71. 35 minutes from Sherwood CC.
Malibu Country Club, 901 Encinal Canyon Rd., Malibu, Calif. Public. (818) 889-6680. 18/6,740/72. 50 minutes from Sherwood CC.
Ojai Valley Inn and Country Club, Country Club Rd., Ojai, Calif. Resort. (805) 646-5511, (800) 422-6524. 18/6,252/70. 45 minutes from Sherwood CC.

TICKETS & ACCESSIBILITY

How to watch: Mon., PGA practice rounds. Tue., PGA practice rounds. Wed., pro-am, first round. Thur., pro-am, second round. Fri.-Sun., tournament. Attendance is limited to 5,000 per day. Individual tickets begin at $30. Season tickets, weekend passes, daily tickets, business, entertainment and sponsorship packages available. Franklin Templeton Shark Shootout, P.O. Box 7657, Thousand Oaks, CA 91359, (805) 379-2664.
How to play: Sherwood Country Club is a private club. You must be a member or the guest of a member to play the course.

Diners Club Matches

PGA WEST

The 1994 debut of this event couldn't have been scripted better. Jack Nicklaus and Arnold Palmer, those legendary money players, were teamed again in a reunion recalling their domination of World Cup matches in the 1960s. They had advanced to the finals, and after being down four with 10 holes gone, they had rallied with a barrage of birdies that put them up by one at the final tee.

The Diners Club Matches, four flights of better-ball, match-play team competition, are an end-of-season innovation that brings together on one course the best players from all three pro tours—the PGA, the LPGA and the Senior PGA.

The three tours plus an over-70 men's field play in four separate brackets, but the format for each bracket is the same: two-player teams go head to head in match play over 18 holes; the players each play one ball, and the better score among the partners counts as the team's score.

One player on each team wins an invitation based on the year's money standings and performance in significant tournaments, then chooses a partner from the pool of pros who don't qualify on their own.

In the 1994 Seniors final, neither Nicklaus, the course's designer, nor Palmer came out the hero. Nor were they beaten by a third legend of the game, rival Raymond Floyd, who had led the Seniors Tour that year in scoring average. The deciding moments instead belonged to Floyd's uncelebrated partner, Dave Eichelberger, who forced a playoff by hitting a 5-iron out of the rough and dropping a birdie putt on a hole dubbed "Jack's Revenge." Eichelberger then birdied the first playoff hole to give his team the $250,000 first prize.

TOURNAMENT-AT-A-GLANCE

Course: PGA West—Jack Nicklaus Resort Course
Type: Resort
Location: 55-955 PGA Blvd., La Quinta, CA 92253-4604
Telephone: (619) 564-7170
When: Dec. 12–15, 1996
How To Get There: Take I-10 to Washington St. Exit. Take Washington St. south to Rte. 111. Make a left on Rte. 111 to Jefferson St., then take a right on Jefferson to the end and the golf course.
Broadcast: ABC, ESPN (1996)
Purse: $2,110,000 (1995)
Tournament Records: PGA Tour—19 holes, Jeff Maggert and Jim McGovern; LPGA—2-and-1, Kelly Robbins and Tammie Green; Senior Tour—2-and-1, Dave Eichelberger and Raymond Floyd

Kelly Robbins and Tammie Green captured the first LPGA final with a tough 2-and-1 victory over Dottie Mochrie and Juli Inkster. Green made an 8-foot birdie putt on the 164-yard, par-4 17th to close out the competition.

In the 1994 PGA final, Jim McGovern and Jeff Maggert were down four holes with five to play against Rocco Mediate and Lee Janzen, but they rode a string of birdies to a playoff, and Maggert sank an 8-foot birdie putt on the first sudden-death hole for the win.

The four-day event is played on reversed nines at the Jack Nicklaus–designed Resort Course at PGA WEST in La Quinta, California—just a short walk from the Pete Dye–designed TPC Stadium Course, which now hosts the Seniors' Legends of Golf competition.

The Nicklaus course is a demanding target layout set against the Santa Rosa Mountains within this 2,010-acre resort and residential development near Palm Springs. Foreboding names like "Fatal Attraction," "Bear Trap" and "Jagged Edge" characterize each hole, and few overstate the dangers: Dramatic mounding, massive fringed waste bunkers and several gaping water hazards heighten the stakes on each gamble, and punish partners who can't muster one great shot out of every two.

"I THINK THAT'S THE FIRST TIME I'VE EVER BEATEN NICKLAUS AND PALMER."

—DAVE EICHELBERGER,

AFTER TEAMING WITH RAYMOND FLOYD TO BEAT PALMER AND NICKLAUS IN A SUDDEN-DEATH PLAYOFF TO WIN THE SENIORS SECTION OF THE 1994 DINERS CLUB MATCHES.

"IMAGES," THE PAR-4 FOURTH AT PGA WEST'S JACK NICKLAUS RESORT COURSE, HAS A HUGE DESERT-WASTE BUNKER OFF THE FAIRWAY LANDING AREA AS ITS HALLMARK.

●TOUGHEST HOLE

"Jack's Revenge," the par-4 finishing hole for tournament play (No. 9 regularly), is the most difficult hole from all three tees. A precise tee shot allows the player to choose between crossing a lake to the left or finding the narrow entranceway on the right to the large double green. Fly the green, and a huge bunker waits behind on the left side.

●BEST PLACE TO WATCH

The practice area within walking distance of the clubhouse is a good place to catch the players in this elite field. Also within an easy walk of the clubhouse is the first tee, the ninth green, 10th tee and 18th green. It makes sense that you'll want to follow your favorite pairings around the course, and the flat terrain makes that easy to do. But the final hole is the place to be when matches are on the line.

●WHO THE COURSE FAVORS

This course is a target golf course just like its counterpart, the more diabolical Pete Dye–designed Stadium Course nearby: If you miss the landing areas, the sand, water and rough won't forgive you.

Courtesy of KSL Recreation Corporation

PGA TOUR					
HOLE	YARDS	PAR	HOLE	YARDS	PAR
1	364	4	10	401	4
2	525	5	11	440	4
3	182	3	12	187	3
4	417	4	13	542	5
5	435	4	14	357	4
6	561	4	15	457	4
7	436	4	16	520	5
8	210	3	17	164	4
9	458	4	18	470	4
			TOTAL	7126	72

LPGA					
HOLE	YARDS	PAR	HOLE	YARDS	PAR
1	364	4	10	351	4
2	482	5	11	388	4
3	151	3	12	156	3
4	371	4	13	482	5
5	377	4	14	324	4
6	446	4	15	379	4
7	366	4	16	451	5
8	171	3	17	146	4
9	383	4	18	390	4
			TOTAL	6178	72

SENIOR PGA TOUR					
HOLE	YARDS	PAR	HOLE	YARDS	PAR
1	364	4	10	401	4
2	525	5	11	440	4
3	165	3	12	187	3
4	381	4	13	542	5
5	435	4	14	357	4
6	504	4	15	412	4
7	433	4	16	520	5
8	184	3	17	164	4
9	432	4	18	438	4
			TOTAL	6884	72

PGA WEST JACK NICKLAUS RESORT COURSE

ARCHITECT: JACK NICKLAUS (1987)

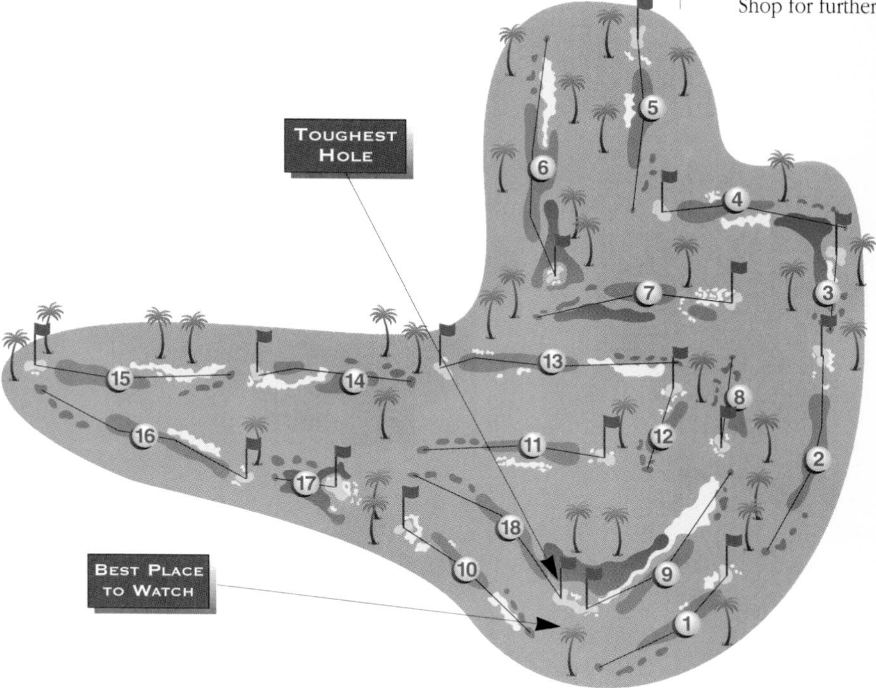

LODGING

$$$ La Quinta Hotel, Golf and Tennis Resort, 49-499 Eisenhower Dr., P.O. Box 69, La Quinta, Calif. (619) 564-4111, (800) 472-4316 (in Calif.), (800) 854-1271. 5 minutes from Jack Nicklaus Resort Course at PGA West.

$$ Embassy Suites Hotel, 74-700 Hwy. 111, Palm Desert, Calif. (619) 340-6600, (800) 362-2779. 15 minutes from Jack Nicklaus Resort Course at PGA West.

$ Vacation Inn, 74-715 Hwy. 111, Palm Desert, Calif. (619) 340-4441, (800) 231-8675. 15 minutes from Jack Nicklaus Resort Course at PGA West.

DINING

La Mirage in the La Quinta Hotel, 49-499 Eisenhower Dr., La Quinta, Calif. (619) 564-4111.

PUBLIC COURSES TO PLAY IN AREA

The Field Golf Club, 19300 Palm Dr., Desert Hot Springs, Calif. Public. (619) 251-5366. 18/6,876/72. 20 minutes from Jack Nicklaus Resort Course at PGA West.

Golf Course at Indian Wells, 44-600 Indian Wells Lane, Indian Wells, Calif. Resort. (619) 346-4653. East: 18/6,665/72. West: 18/6,480/72. 20 minutes from Jack Nicklaus Resort Course at PGA West.

Westin Mission Hills Resort, 71-333 Dinah Shore Dr., Rancho Mirage, Calif. Resort. (619) 770-9496, (800) 358-2211. Player: 18/7,062/72, Dye: 18/6,706/70. 30 minutes from Jack Nicklaus Resort Course at PGA West.

TICKETS & ACCESSIBILITY

How to watch: Mon., practice rounds. Tue., pro-am, practice rounds. Wed., pro-am, practice rounds. Thur.-Sun., tournament. Individual, group and sponsor tickets available. Diners Club Matches, 56-150 PGA Blvd., La Quinta, CA 92253. (619) 777-0150, (800) 307-6444.

How to play: The PGA West Jack Nicklaus Resort Course is open to the public as is the PGA West Course served by the same clubhouse. Golf packages are offered through nearby resort hotels. Contact the Pro Shop for further information: (619) 564-7170.

Courtesy of Nabisco Dinah Shore

LPGA

Chrysler-Plymouth Tournament of Champions

Grand Cypress Resort

The lush, lunar-like terrain of this acclaimed Jack Nicklaus–designed course sets a dramatic backdrop for one of the most selective tournaments on the women's tour. The Chrysler-Plymouth Tournament of Champions, launched in 1994, extends invitations only to LPGA winners from the previous two years and to members of the exclusive LPGA Hall of Fame.

Inaugural winner Dottie Mochrie said Grand Cypress' tough January gusts helped separate her from the field's non-Floridians, but the players had plenty of other troubles to contend with, too. A pockmarked landscape crowds the fairways with treacherous mounds, hollows and sandy dunes, while lakes or ponds come into play on more than half the holes on this tournament course combining holes from the North and South courses.

The mid-1980s are sometimes called Nicklaus' "hateful years," and the fast, elevated greens he placed in this 1984 layout are a reason why: If you miss them, you can easily find yourself attempting to chip while standing 8 to 10 feet below the cup.

In 1995's rain and windswept showdown, Beth Daniel matched Mochrie's standard-setting score, but her 1-under-par 287 left her six strokes back of Dawn Coe-Jones, who simply avoided Nicklaus' nasty streak by hitting more greens than anybody ese.

Hotel guests at the 1,500-acre resort may also want to play the friendlier New Course, Nicklaus' tribute to the pot bunkers and open links of St. Andrews' legendary Old Course.

A short walk from the opulent Mediterranean-style clubhouse at Grand Cypress is the Grand Cypress Academy of Golf, an excellent learning facility that includes a Nicklaus-designed par-3, par-4 and par-5 simulating many of the conditions found on the courses nearby.

Courtesy of Chrysler-Plymouth Tournament of Champions

January winds can make the 16th tournament hole (normally No. 6 on the South Course) a major shotmaking challenge.

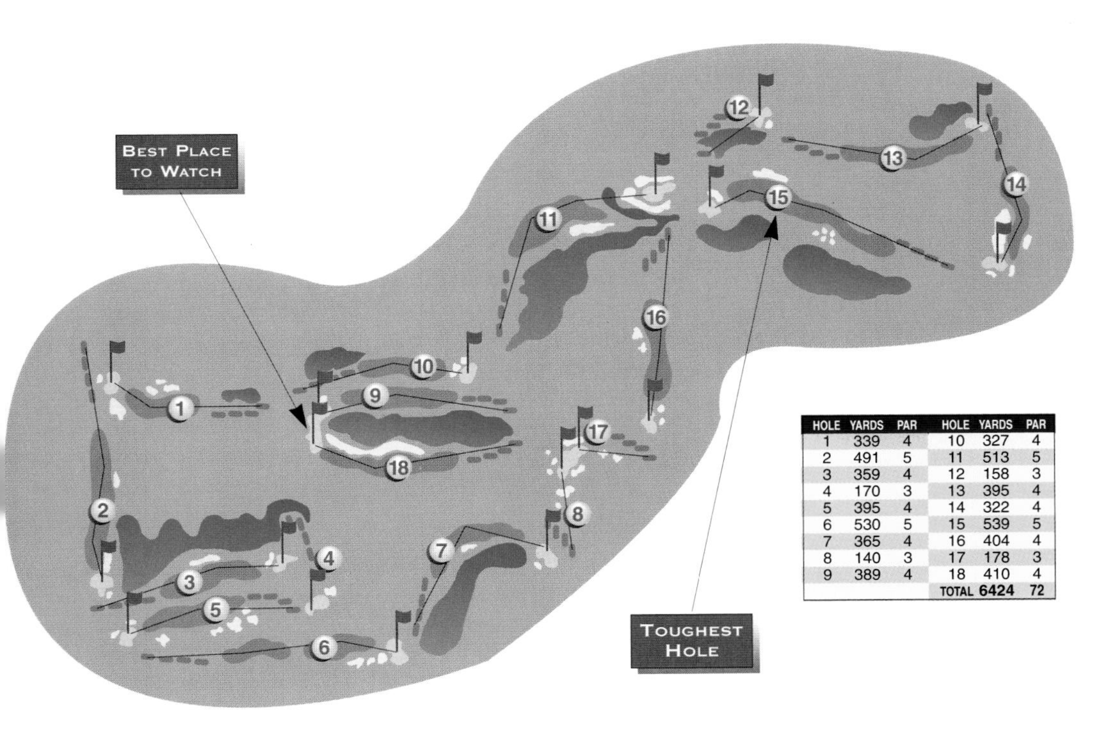

HOLE	YARDS	PAR	HOLE	YARDS	PAR
1	339	4	10	327	4
2	491	5	11	513	5
3	359	4	12	158	3
4	170	3	13	395	4
5	395	4	14	322	4
6	530	5	15	539	5
7	365	4	16	404	4
8	140	3	17	178	3
9	389	4	18	410	4
			TOTAL	6424	72

GRAND CYPRESS RESORT—NORTH/SOUTH TOURNAMENT COURSE
ARCHITECT: JACK NICKLAUS WITH ROBERT CUPP (1984)

●TOUGHEST HOLE

The tournament's 539-yard, par-5 15th, the sixth hole on the South Course, is bordered by water on the left and punctuated by mounds and pot bunkers. The plateaued green is framed by water on the left and a huge bunker on the right. January winds can make this hole a major shotmaking challenge, especially down the tournament stretch.

●BEST PLACE TO WATCH

The bleachers at the 410-yard, par-4 finishing hole let you view the action on both the front and back nines because the large double green is shared by the North Course's 389-yard, par-4 ninth.

●WHO THE COURSE FAVORS

Virtually every hole on this course is flanked by mounds, swales, water, sand or all of these elements. The elevated greens are extremely fast, requiring accurate approach shots, strong wedge play and a steady putting stroke.

TOURNAMENT-AT-A-GLANCE

Course: Grand Cypress Resort—North and South Courses
Type: Resort
Location: 1 N. Jacaranda, Orlando, FL 32819
Telephone: (407) 239-4700, (800) 835-7377 (Villas of Grand Cypress), (800) 233-1234 (Hyatt Regency)
When: Early March
How To Get There: Via I-4 E, take Exit 27 and make left at light onto State Rd. 535 north of I-4 two lights. Take left at second light, follow signs two miles to golf course on the right.
Broadcast: Prime Network/Family Channel, NBC (1996)
Purse: $700,000 (1996)
Tournament Record: 7-under-par 281, Dawn Coe-Jones, 1995

LODGING

$$$ Villas at Grand Cypress, 1 N. Jacaranda, Orlando Fla. (407) 239-4700, (800) 835-7377.
$$ Disney's Village Resort, 10100 Lake Buena Vista, Lake Buena Vista, Fla. Central Reservations, (407) 827-1100. 10 minutes from Grand Cypress.
$ Casa Rosa Inn, 4600 W. Orlo Bronson Memorial Hwy., Kissimmee, Fla. (407) 396-2020, (800) 432-0665. 20 minutes from Grand Cypress.

DINING

Chalet Suzanne, U.S. 27, north of Lake Wales, 3800 Chalet Suzanne Dr., Lake Wales, Fla. (813) 676-6011.
Hemingway's, in the Hyatt Regency Grand Cypress, 1 Grand Cypress Blvd., Orlando, Fla. (407) 239-3854.
Fairways Lounge, in the clubhouse at Grand Cypress, 1 N. Jacaranda, Orlando, Fla. (407) 239-4700.

PUBLIC COURSES TO PLAY IN AREA

Bay Hill Club, 9000 Bay Hill Blvd., Orlando, Fla. Resort. (407) 876-2429, (800) 523-5999. Challenger/Champion: 18/7,114/72. Charger: 9/3,060/36. 5 minutes from Grand Cypress.
Hunters Creek Golf Course, 14401 Sports Club Way, Orlando, Fla. Public. (407) 240-4653. 18/7,432/72. 15 minutes from Grand Cypress.
Walt Disney World, Lake Buena Vista, Fla. Resort. (407) 824-4321. Palm: 18/6,957/72. Magnolia: 18/7,190/72. Lake Buena Vista: 18/6,829/72. Osprey Ridge: 18/7,101/72. Eagle Pines: 18/6,772/72. Oak Trail: 9/2,913/36. 5 minutes from Grand Cypress.

TICKETS & ACCESSIBILITY

How to watch: Mon., skills challenge. Tue., LPGA practice rounds, Skins game. Wed., pro-am event. Thur.-Sun., tournament. Tickets are $10 per day for individuals. Group and sponsorship packages available. Chrysler-Plymouth Tournament of Champions, c/o Grand Cypress Resort, 60 Grand Cypress Blvd., Orlando, FL 32826. (407) 774-LPGA, (800) 655-LPGA.
How to play: Resort guests may reserve tee times 60 days in advance, the public one week in advance. Golf packages available year round. (407) 239-4700.

HealthSouth Classic

Walt Disney World Resort

Golf is billed as "more fun and exciting" at Walt Disney World's 99-hole "Magic Linkdom" than anywhere else in the world, but someone must have forgotten to tell Pete Dye about the fun part. There are few easy putts on the undulating greens of Eagle Pines, Dye's 1992 addition to Disney's 28,000-acre resort.

Served by a futuristic, pastel-colored clubhouse and decorated at the entrances by a collection of Dumbo-size golf-tee sculptures, this relatively flat course doesn't lack for visual interest. Its pine-straw rough, extensive waste bunkers, adjacent wetlands and unusual native grasses add color to a layout marked by a wide variety of hole designs.

Dye designed the course to minimize penalties and delays for resort golfers, but it also provides a fine test of championship golf. Water enters play on 16 holes, though there are no forced carries from the course's concave, dishlike fairways.

Hall of Famer Pat Bradley closed with a strong 68 to seize a one-shot victory in 1995, the HealthSouth tournament's first year in Mickey's backyard.

TOURNAMENT-AT-A-GLANCE

Course: Walt Disney World Resort—Eagle Pines Golf Course
Type: Resort
Location: Lake Buena Vista, FL 32830-1000
Telephone: (407) 824-2270 (tee times, tournaments), (407) 934-7639 (resort)
When: Early February
How To Get There: Westbound take I-4 W from I-95 or Hwy. 1 to resort exit. Eastbound take I-4 E from I-75 to resort exits. Northbound on Florida Turnpike, take Kissimmee–St. Cloud interchange and Hwy. 192 to resort.
Broadcast: The Golf Channel (1996)
Purse: $450,000 (1996)
Tournament Record: 5-under-par 211, Pat Bradley, 1995

•TOUGHEST HOLE

The 405-yard, par-4 fifth, a dogleg right, requires length off the tee to reach the corner, leaving the golfer a mid-iron to a sloping, deep green with a large trap on the left and water to the far left and rear.

•BEST PLACE TO WATCH

The 18th green, near the clubhouse, where the tournament is likely to be decided. Another good spot is behind the 12th green, which is adjacent to the eighth and 13th tees.

•WHO THE COURSE FAVORS

The competitor who can cope with the wind conditions and play position golf to set up solid approach shots to greens with a variety of entrance angles.

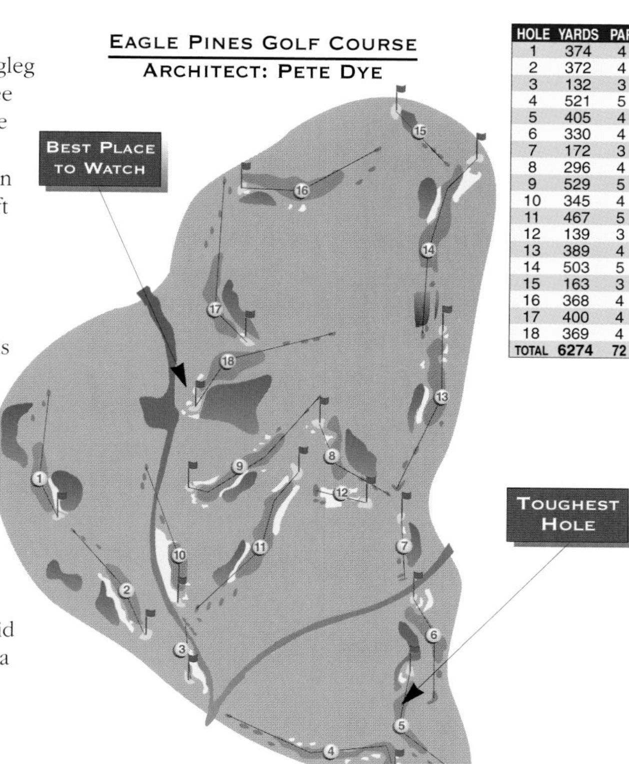

HOLE	YARDS	PAR
1	374	4
2	372	4
3	132	3
4	521	5
5	405	4
6	330	4
7	172	3
8	296	4
9	529	5
10	345	4
11	467	5
12	139	3
13	389	4
14	503	5
15	163	3
16	368	4
17	400	4
18	369	4
TOTAL	6274	72

LODGING

Walt Disney World has accommodations in every price range from camping and trailer sites to fully equipped vacation homes for up to 12 guests. Walt Disney World, P.O. Box 10,000, Lake Buena Vista, Fla. (407) W-DISNEY (reservations).

DINING

At Walt Disney World:
Yachtsman Steakhouse, Disney Yacht Club and Resort. (407) 934-3356.
Beaches and Cream Soda Shop, Disney's Yacht and Beach Club. (407) 934-7000, ext. 6109.

PUBLIC COURSES TO PLAY IN AREA

Grenelefe Golf & Tennis Center, 3200 State Road 546, Haines City, Fla. Resort. (813) 422-7511, (800) 237-9549 (outside Florida). West: 18/7,325/72. East: 18/6,802/72. South 18/6,869/71. 30 minutes from Eagle Pines.
Mission Inn Resort, 3200 State Road 546, Howey-in-the-Hills, Fla. Resort. (904) 324-3101, (800) 874-9053. El Campeon: 18/6,842/72. Las Colinas: 18/6,867/72. 45 minutes from Eagle Pines.
Palisades Country Club, 16510 Palisades Blvd., Clermont, Fla. Public. (904) 394-0085. 18/7,002/72. 35 minutes from Eagle Pines.

TICKETS & ACCESSIBILITY

How to watch: Daily tickets available from $10. Various group and sponsorship packages. Tue., LPGA qualifier. Wed., pro-am event. Thur., LPGA practice rounds. Fri.-Sun., tournament. HealthSouth, 3200 South Hiawassee Rd., Suite 206, Orlando, FL 32835-6331, (407) 292-9992.
How to play: Golf packages available year round with lowest rates from May to December. Tee times can be made 30 days in advance if you have a reservation at a Disney resort hotel. The public can make reservations 7 days in advance May to December and 4 days in advance January to April. 99 holes of golf on site. Eagle Pines: 18/6,772/72. Lake Buena Vista: 18/6,829/72. Magnolia: 18/7,190/72. Oak Trail: 9/2,913/36. Osprey Ridge: 18/7,101/72. Palm: 18/6,772/72. (407) 824-2270.

Cup Noodles Hawaiian Ladies Open

Ko Olina Golf Club

LODGING

$$$ Ihilani Resort and Spa, 92-1001 Olani St., Kapolei, Hawaii. (808) 679-0079, (800) 626-4446. 5 minutes from Ko Olina.

$$ Waikikian on the Beach, 1811 Ala Moana Blvd., Honolulu, Hawaii. (808) 949-5331, (800) 922-7866. 30 minutes from Ko Olina.

$ Less expensive accommodations can be located through **Bed and Breakfast Hawaii,** Box 449, Kapaa, Hawaii. (808) 822-7771, (800) 733-1632. Or **Bed and Breakfast Honolulu,** 3242 Kaohinani Dr., Honolulu, Hawaii. (808) 262-6026, (800) 999-6026.

DINING

Azul, in the Ihilani Resort and Spa, 92-1001 Olani St., Kapolei, Hawaii. (808) 679-0079.

Orchids, in the Halekulani Hotel, 2199 Kalia Rd., Waikiki, Honolulu, Hawaii. (808) 923-2311.

Monterrey Bay Canners, 981005 Moanalua Rd., Pearl Ridge, Hawaii. (808) 487-0048.

PUBLIC COURSES TO PLAY IN AREA

The Links at Kulima, Kahuku, Hawaii. Resort. (808) 293-8574. 18/7,199/72. 45 minutes from Honolulu.

Poli Municipal Golf Course, 45-050 Kamehameha Hwy., Kaneohe, Hawaii. Public. (808) 261-9784. 18/6,494/72. 15 minutes from Honolulu.

Sheraton Makaha Resort and Country Club, 84-626 Makaha Valley Rd., Wainae, Hawaii. Resort. (808) 695-9544 (pro shop), (808) 695-9511 (resort). 18/7,091/72. 1 hour from Honolulu.

TICKETS & ACCESSIBILITY

How to watch: Mon., LPGA qualifying rounds, practice rounds. Tue., LPGA practice rounds. Wed., pro-am tournament. Thur.-Sat., tournament. Daily tickets start at $10. A variety of group and sponsorship packages are available. Hawaiian Ladies Open, Ko Olina Resort, 91-100 Kamoana Place, Kapolei, HI 96707. (808) 671-5050.

How to play: Open to the public year round. Golf packages available through the resort. Tee time reservations can be made up to one week in advance. (808) 676-5300.

TOURNAMENT-AT-A-GLANCE

Course: Ko Olina Golf Club
Type: Resort
Location: 92-1220 Alinui Dr., Kapolei, HI 96707
Telephone: (808) 676-5300 (golf course), Ihilani Resort (808) 679-0079
When: Late February
How To Get There: From Honolulu (30 min.), take Hwy. 1 West to Ko Olina exit, follow signs to resort.
Broadcast: Mainichi Broadcasting System (1995)
Purse: $600,000 (1996)
Tournament Record: 12-under-par 204, Barb Thomas, 1995

Architect Ted Robinson moved more than 2 million cubic feet of dirt to create this beautifully landscaped course along the Pacific Ocean. Abundant with palm and coconut trees and adorned with brilliant tropical flowers, Ko Olina has lush, rolling fairways, undulating greens protected by a variety of bunkers, and waterfalls, lakes or streams on six holes.

The trade winds and Kona winds greatly affect shotmaking on this layout, as do flag positions on the tricky, tiered, Bermuda-grass greens. The variable winds, lurking bunkers, occasional rock gardens and even the cascading water near the par-3 12th make a precise short game essential here.

From the championship tees, the par-3s tend to be the most difficult holes, but par-4s are also counted among Ko Olina's more challenging tests.

An international cast has won this event since its inception at the Turtle Bay Resort in 1987. Cindy Rarick won the inaugural. Ayako Okamoto of Japan (1988), Lisa Walters of Canada (1992, 1993) and Marta Figueras-Dotti of Spain (1994) have also won the event, which always features a large contingent of competitors from the Japanese Ladies Professional Golf Association tour.

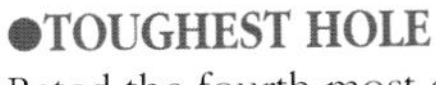

●TOUGHEST HOLE

Rated the fourth most difficult on the tour in 1994, the 385-yard, par-4 finishing hole plays to a landing area guarded by water in front, seven pools to the right and bunkers to the left. The approach shot is over a broad lake to a tiered green with a bunker in the rear and waterfalls on the left. With prevailing tail winds and trouble everywhere, club selection is critical.

●BEST PLACE TO WATCH

The 18th green on the final day. If you arrive early, you can get a seat in the clubhouse restaurant/bar overlooking the finishing hole.

●WHO THE COURSE FAVORS

Big hitters like playing Ko Olina because it has wide fairways and few landing-area hazards. But the tournament is usually decided by approach shots and putting on the tricky greens.

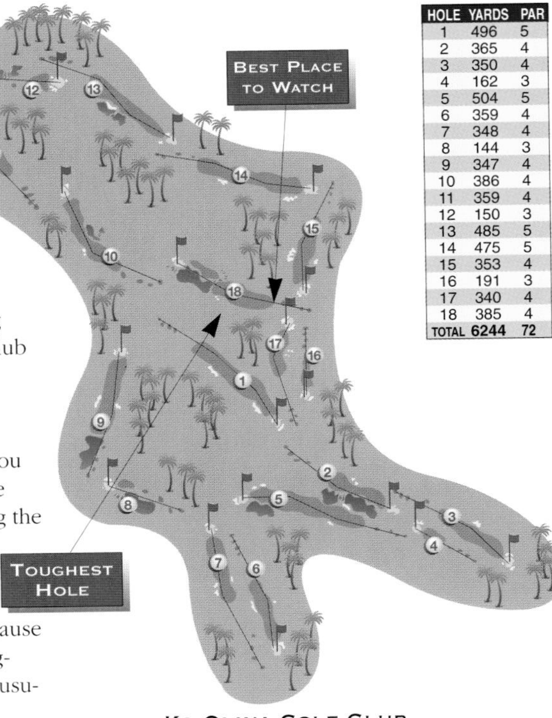

HOLE	YARDS	PAR
1	496	5
2	365	4
3	350	4
4	162	3
5	504	5
6	359	4
7	348	4
8	144	3
9	347	4
10	386	4
11	359	4
12	150	3
13	485	5
14	475	5
15	353	4
16	191	3
17	340	4
18	385	4
TOTAL	6244	72

Ko Olina Golf Club
Architect: Ted Robinson (1990)

PING/Welch's Championship (Arizona)

RANDOLPH PARK

With its wide, flat greens and generous landing areas, this park-like course in the middle of the Arizona desert is tailored for public play, so the top prize in the PING/Welch's Championship is usually seized by the player who subdues the slightly updated 1930 layout with the soundest all-around game.

After eight years of undistinguished finishes, Dottie Mochrie did just that in 1995, firing a 10-under-par 278 for a five-stroke victory over Cindy Rarick and Annika Sorenstam.

As its name suggests, Randolph Park looks more like a park than a golf course. Mature sycamores and Aleppo pines line its adjacent fairways, an ideal configuration for tournament spectators soaking in distant views of the Catalina Mountains surrounding nearby Tucson.

Stray drives can be costly at tournament time, when normally close-cropped rough is grown long. Approach shots from the rough often skid across the firm greens, and winds can sometimes severely test the players' knock-down touch.

With so much riding on the setup for high approach shots, the right-to-left hitter gains an edge from the course's abundance of doglegs left.

The course begins with some of its easiest holes, has a cluster of more difficult holes in the middle, then finishes on a more benign note with a 458-yard straight par-5 whose approach to a well-bunkered green must carry a stream.

TOURNAMENT-AT-A-GLANCE

Course: Randolph Park—North Golf Course
Type: Public
Location: 600 South Alvernon, Tucson, AZ 85711
Telephone: (520) 325-2811
When: Mid-March
How To Get There: Take I-10 to Exit 259 and W. 22nd St. Follow 22nd St. east to South Alvernon, go left on South Alvernon. Follow 1 block to the golf course between 22nd and Broadway.
Broadcast: Golf Channel (1995)
Purse: $450,000 (1996)
Tournament Record: 16-under-par 272, Chris Johnson, 1984, and Meg Mallon, 1993

Some of the more difficult tournament holes at Randolph Park have been the fourth, a lengthy 402-yard par-4 and the fifth, a 408-yard par-4. The fourth is a slight dogleg left whose tee shot is to a landing area pinched by trees to the left of the fairway. The approach is to a medium-sized green squeezed in the front by traps on either side. The fifth comes back, parallel to the fourth, with trees on the left and a slightly smaller green, also with a narrow opening between two front bunkers. Many of the greens have tiers, and there are usually a few traps framing each green, but all of the doglegs are right-to-left. The fairways are intermittently bordered with a handsome array of mature palm, orange, tamarisk, mesquite, pine and eucalyptus.

The first PING/Welch's Championship, held in 1981, was won by Nancy Lopez, who closed with a pair of 68s to win by four strokes over Pat Bradley. The following year Ayako Okamoto and Sally Little went to extra holes after Little finished with a 66. Okamoto won on the second sudden-death hole.

There has only been one two-time winner (Chris Johnson) in the 15-year history of this event. Dottie Mochrie, who had played the PING/Welch's in each of her eight seasons on the tour, never finished higher than a tie for fifteenth until she posted a five-stroke victory over Cindy Rarick and Annika Sorenstam in 1995.

"IT'S NOT THAT LONG. THE PAR-5s ARE FAIRLY ACCESSIBLE AND THE GREENS ARE PRETTY BIG. AND I COME IN HERE AND SHOOT A MILLION EVERY YEAR."

DOTTIE MOCHRIE,

BEFORE WINNING THE 1995 PING/WELCH'S WITH A 70-68-72-68–278

Courtesy of Tuscon Parks & Recreation

A lake wraps along the right side of the 15th at Randolph North, awaiting both errant drives and approaches.

●TOUGHEST HOLE

The 402-yard, par-4 fourth was rated among the fifty most difficult holes on the LPGA tour in 1994. Another tough hole is the 152-yard, par-3 15th, which plays over the right edge of a lake to a green protected by water to its left and rear. Any tee shot to the left or long means bogey or more on this great spectator's hole.

●BEST PLACE TO WATCH

The mounded areas behind the ninth and 18th greens are great vantage points, as is the mounded area behind No. 6. A mound between Nos. 6 and 7 offers several places to catch action on both holes.

●WHO THE COURSE FAVORS

With its abundant supply of dogleg left holes, Randolph Park favors the right-to-left player who can hit for distance to set up high approach shots that will hold the firm greens.

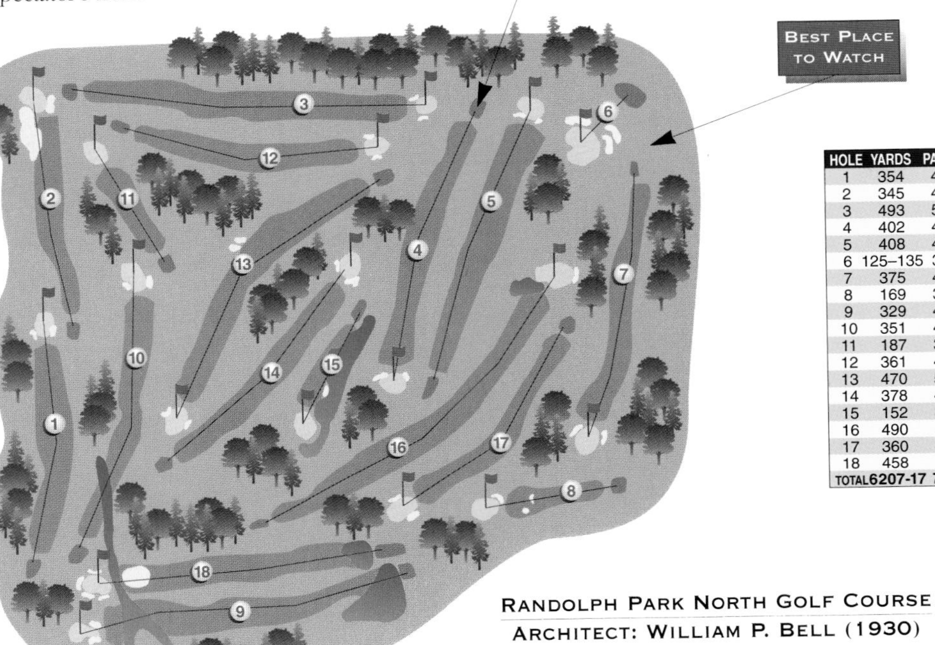

HOLE	YARDS	PAR
1	354	4
2	345	4
3	493	5
4	402	4
5	408	4
6	125–135	3
7	375	4
8	169	3
9	329	4
10	351	4
11	187	3
12	361	4
13	470	5
14	378	4
15	152	3
16	490	5
17	360	4
18	458	5
TOTAL	6207-17	72

Randolph Park North Golf Course
Architect: William P. Bell (1930)
Remodeled by Pete Dye (4 holes, 1980)

LODGING

$$$ Loews Ventana Canyon Resort, 7000 N. Resort Dr., Tucson, Ariz. (520) 299-2020. 25 minutes from Randolph Park.

$$ Doubletree Hotel, 445 South Alvernon Way, Tucson, Ariz. (520) 881-4200. Within a few minutes walk to Randolph Park.

$ Comfort Inn, 715 W. 22nd St., Tucson, Ariz. (520) 791-9282. 5 minutes from Randolph Park.

DINING

The Ventana Room, Loews Ventana Canyon Resort, 7000 N. Resort Dr., Tucson, Ariz. (520) 299-2020.

Scordatos in the Foothills, 4405 W. Speedway Blvd., Tucson, Ariz. (520) 624-8946.

Pinnacle Peak Restaurant, 6541 E. Tanque Verde Rd., Tucson, Ariz. (520) 296-0911.

PUBLIC COURSES TO PLAY IN AREA

Loews Ventana Canyon Golf & Racquet Club, 7000 N. Resort Dr., Tucson, Ariz. Resort. (520) 577-1400, (800) 828-5701. Canyon: 18/6,909/72. Mountain: 18/6,984/72. 25 minutes from Randolph Park.

Tournament Players Club at Starr Pass, 3645 W. 22nd St., Tucson, Ariz. Public. (520) 670-0300. 18/7,010/72. 20 minutes from Randolph Park.

The Westin La Paloma, 3800 E. Sunrise Dr., Tucson, Ariz. Resort. (520) 299-1500, (800) 222-1249. Hill/Ridge: 18/7,017/72. Ridge/Canyon: 18/7,088/72. Canyon/Hill: 18/6,996/72. 25 minutes from Randolph Park.

TICKETS & ACCESSIBILITY

How to watch: Mon., pro-am tournament, LPGA qualifying rounds. Tue., LPGA practice rounds, shootout. Wed., celebrity pro-am. Thur.-Sun., tournament. Daily individual tickets start from $10. Group packages and sponsorships are available. Tucson Parks Foundation, 900 S. Randolph Way, Tucson, AZ 85716. (520) 791-5742.

How to play: Randolph Park is open to the public year round. South Course is par 70 and plays 6,000 yards; North Course plays 7,000 yards from the back tees. Contact within 6 days of desired tee time. (520) 791-4336.

Standard Register PING

MOON VALLEY COUNTRY CLUB

Just off the practice green at the Moon Valley Country Club, tucked behind the trees, is the modest, concrete-block home of one of golf's wealthiest industrialists and one of the LPGA's most prominent sponsors. From time to time, white-bearded octogenarian Karsten Solheim will still give a call to the pro shop for a lift to the first tee of this Dick Wilson-designed course that he purchased in the late 1960s. And when the LPGA come to town each year, he's out there every day, playing the perfect host.

Solheim, who crafted the world's first PING putters in his Phoenix garage, has supported this event as a title sponsor since 1991, four years after it moved to his back yard and 11 years after its founding. As sponsor of a Portland area "PING" tournament since 1977, Solheim had established himself as an important patron of women's golf when he founded the Solheim Cup matches in 1990, pitting the best pros in the United States against the best in Europe. PING has since lent its name to two other LPGA events, the PING/Welch's championships, which are played in both the Tucson and Boston areas.

At 6,483 yards and par 73, Solheim's Moon Valley plays longer than most courses on the women's tour, but its traditional, tree-lined layout is relatively flat, with few water hazards. Well-placed trees and long tournament rough are the most persistent hazards, but wind is often a critical enemy as the track weaves through this subdivision's homes. "Any time I don't hit the ball in someone's back yard, I've played well," Laura Davies said in 1994 after capturing the first of her two consecutive titles. On some holes, like the 149-yard, par-3 second and 160-yard, par-3 fifth, the wind direction can change between tee and green, making club selection critical. Distance and accuracy off the tee are also important, especially on the par-5 10th, a dogleg left whose corner can be cut, and the finishing hole, a dogleg left whose landing area is squeezed by a lake on the left and a large bunker on the right. Many holes finish in multi-tiered greens.

Patty Sheehan set the tournament record here in 1993 when she fired rounds of 70-70-65-70 to post a 17-under-par total of 275. Sheehan birdied the 384-yard ninth on the final round and holed a bunker shot on the 480-yard, par-5 13th to leave her closest challengers five shots back. Still, she admitted she was nervous until the 18th green because the victory, her 30th on tour, qualified her for the LPGA Hall of Fame.

Long-ball champion Davies became the third two-time winner of the tournament (Pat Bradley won in 1987 and 1990 and the short-hitting Danielle Ammaccapane won back-to-back titles in 1991 and 1992) when she stumbled home with a 69-68-70-73–280 to defeat Beth Daniel by a single stroke in 1995. Davies two-putted each of the last two holes from within 5 feet to narrowly avert a playoff.

TOURNAMENT-AT-A-GLANCE

Course: Moon Valley Country Club
Type: Private
Location: 151 W. Moon Valley Dr., Phoenix, AZ 85023
Telephone: (602) 942-1278
When: Mid-March 1996
How To Get There: Take I-10 to Exit 210 at Thunderbird. Proceed east on Thunderbird, past 19th St. to second light (Coral Gables). Take a left at Coral Gables, then the first right to Moon Valley Country Club.
Broadcast: ESPN (1995)
Purse: $500,000 (1995)
Tournament Record: 17-under-par 275, Patty Sheehan, 1993

WITH WATER ON THE LEFT AND TREES ON THE RIGHT, MOON VALLEY'S NINTH EMPHASIZES DRIVING ACCURACY.

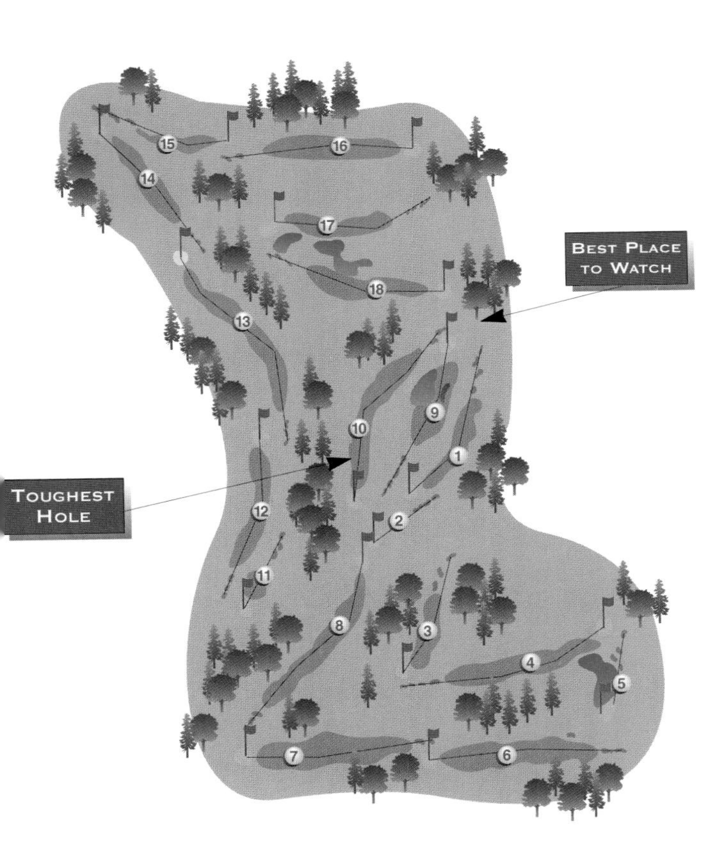

MOON VALLEY COUNTRY CLUB
ARCHITECT: DICK WILSON (1958)

●TOUGHEST HOLE

The 530-yard, par-5 10th is a dogleg left bordered by a gully on the left, trees on the right and a series of bunkers on both sides. If a player lets her ball stray into the thick rough, this hole can be particularly costly.

●BEST PLACE TO WATCH

From the bleachers on the par-4 finishing hole the final day of the event. Also check out the viewing mounds behind the ninth green, where you can see players make the turn and tee off on No. 10.

●WHO THE COURSE FAVORS

Tournament winners have included big hitters like Laura Davies as well as strategic shorter-hitting players like Danielle Ammaccapane. At almost 6,500 yards, Moon Valley ideally suits the longer hitter who can keep the ball on the fairway and position approach shots to the greens.

HOLE	YARDS	PAR	HOLE	YARDS	PAR
1	350	4	10	530	5
2	149	3	11	165	3
3	324	4	12	385	4
4	485	5	13	480	5
5	160	3	14	345	4
6	398	4	15	340	4
7	345	4	16	402	4
8	490	5	17	360	4
9	384	4	18	390	4
			TOTAL	6483	73

LODGING

$$$ Ritz Carlton–Phoenix, 2401 E. Camelback Rd. at 24th St., Phoenix. (602) 468-0700. 15 minutes from Moon Valley CC.

$$ The Pointe Hilton at Tapatio Cliffs, 1111 N. 7th St., Phoenix. (602) 866-7500. 5 minutes from Moon Valley CC.

$ Best Western Inn Suites Phoenix Squaw Peak, 1615 E. Northern Ave. at 16th St., Phoenix. (602) 997-6285. 10 minutes from Moon Valley CC.

DINING

Different Pointe of View, at The Pointe Hilton Restaurant at Tapatio Cliffs, 1111 N. 7th St., Phoenix. (602) 866-7500.

Ammaccapane Sports Bar, 13470 N. 7th St. at Thunderbird, Phoenix. (602) 863-1199.

Chili's, 2057 E. Camelback Rd., Phoenix. (602) 955-1195.

PUBLIC COURSES TO PLAY IN AREA

The Boulders, 34631 N. Tom Darlington, Carefree, Ariz. Resort. (602) 488-9028 (golf course), (800) 553-1717 (resort). North: 18/6,731/72. South: 18/6,543/71. 30 minutes from Moon Valley CC.

Tournament Players Club of Scottsdale, Scottsdale Princess, 17020 N. Hayden Rd., Scottsdale, Ariz. Public. (602) 585-3939, (800) 344-4758. Stadium: 18/6,992/71. Desert: 18/6,552/71. 20 minutes from Moon Valley CC.

Troon North, 10370 E. Dynamite Blvd., Scottsdale, Ariz. Public. (602) 585-5300. 18/7,008/72. 30 minutes from Moon Valley CC.

TICKETS & ACCESSIBILITY

How to watch: Mon., two pro-am tournaments, LPGA practice rounds. Tue., LPGA practice rounds, junior clinic, shoot-out. Wed., pro-am. Thur.-Sun., tournament. Daily tickets start at $10. Group and individual sponsorship packages available from Standard Register PING, 1441 N. 12th St., Phoenix, AZ 85006. (602) 495-4483.

How to play: Moon Valley is a private course. You must be a member or the guest of a member to play, or arrange reciprocal play through the club professional.

Sprint Championship

LPGA International

Courtesy of Sky Shots

THE 18TH AT LPGA INTERNATIONAL ENTICES BIRDIE ATTEMPTS, BUT DURING THE 1995 SPRINT CHAMPIONSHIP THREE OF THE LAST NINE GOLFERS PUT THEIR TEE SHOTS IN THE LAKE.

Moved from the nearby Indigo Lakes Golf Club in Daytona Beach, the 1995 Sprint Championship showcased the new Rees Jones–designed LPGA International course at the LPGA headquarters. This beautiful links-style layout features large, contoured greens, elaborate mounding in and around the fairways, 83 strategically placed white-sand bunkers, and long views of placid lakes and surrounding wetlands. To make this public course playable for all skill levels, Jones gave many holes a generous selection of tee angles, shot options and yardage variations. His contoured greens aim, he says, "to reward accurate approach shots." The wind coming off the nearby Atlantic Ocean adds to the challenge of this scenic venue.

During the 1995 championship, golfers had trouble reading the fast, tricky greens. Errant tee shots tended to run through the windswept fairways into sand, water or rough. Fluffy bunker sand made recovery shots especially difficult. As Alice Ritzman exclaimed after ineffectually slashing a 3-iron out of one: "This bunker has too much sand!"

As predicted, the 452-yard, par-5 finishing hole played a major part in determining the winner. An enticing birdie or eagle opportunity, this dogleg left wraps a mounded fairway around a lake and flows into a deep green bordered by the lake. Three of the final nine golfers put their tee shots in the water, including Val Skinner, who had a three-shot lead over playing partner Kris Tschetter when she stepped onto the 72nd tee. Aided by a heroic recovery from the right rough, Skinner saved par to close out a two-stroke victory.

"THIS BUNKER HAS TOO MUCH SAND!"

ALICE RITZMAN,

DURING THE BAPTISMAL PRO TOURNAMENT AT LPGA INTERNATIONAL

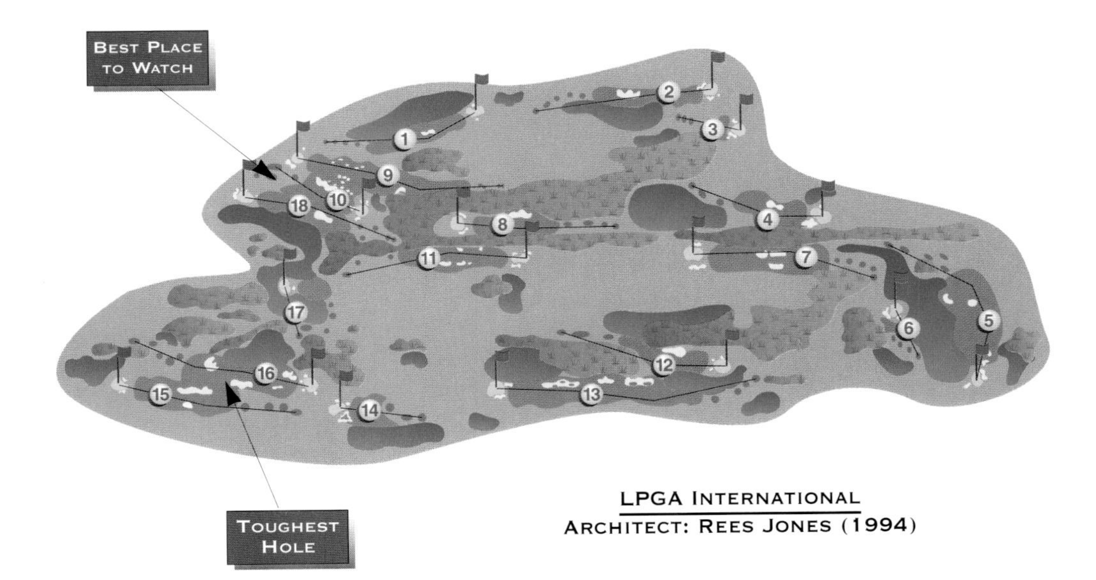

LPGA International
Architect: Rees Jones (1994)

●TOUGHEST HOLE

The 383-yard, par-4 16th usually plays 40 yards longer because approaches are hit uphill to the green and usually into the wind. Many players hit long irons and woods onto the undulating green, which is squeezed by a pair of bunkers in front and another to its right.

●BEST PLACE TO WATCH

Bleachers provide seating at the first tee, ninth green, 10th tee and 18th green. The 18th, which plays as a short par-5, provides eagle opportunities and possible dramatic finishes. The course is difficult to walk because of the length between the greens and the next tee.

●WHO THE COURSE FAVORS

Longer hitters like Beth Daniel, Laura Davies, Michelle McGann and Val Skinner are able to cope with the wind, which lengthens the course. Shotmakers like Patty Sheehan and Kris Tschetter can turn delicate wedge shots into stroke savers around the greens.

HOLE	YARDS	PAR	HOLE	YARDS	PAR
1	388	4	10	338	4
2	408	4	11	378	4
3	179	3	12	363	4
4	355	4	13	533	5
5	473	5	14	162	3
6	145	3	15	369	4
7	377	4	16	383	4
8	369	4	17	172	3
9	522	5	18	452	5
			TOTAL	6393	72

TOURNAMENT-AT-A-GLANCE

Course: LPGA International
Type: Public
Location: 300 Champions Dr., Daytona Beach, FL 32114
Telephone: (904) 274-3880
When: Late April to Early May
How To Get There: From the north, take I-95 to Daytona Beach West Exit. Go 2 miles to the light, then take a left onto LPGA Blvd., follow signs 7 miles to the golf course. From the south, take I-95 to Exit 87, take left at traffic light, proceed 3 miles to LPGA Blvd., take right on LPGA Blvd. to golf course.
Broadcast: CBS (1995)
Purse: $1.2 million (1996)
Tournament Record: 17-under-par 271, Beth Daniel, 1990

LODGING

$$$ Adams Mark, 100 N. Atlantic Ave., Daytona Beach, Fla. (904) 254-8200, (800) 872-9269. 5 minutes from LPGA International.
$$ Indigo Lakes Holiday Inn, 2620 W. International Speedway Blvd., Daytona Beach, Fla. (904) 258-6333, (800) HOLIDAY. 5 minutes from LPGA International.
$ Howard Johnson Hotel, 600 N. Atlantic Ave., Daytona Beach, Fla. (904) 255-4471, (800) 767-4471. 15 minutes from LPGA International.

DINING

Live Oak Inn Dining Room, 448 S. Beach St., Daytona Beach, Fla. (904) 252-4667.
Major Moultries Restaurant at Indigo Lakes Holiday Inn, 2620 International Speedway Blvd., Daytona Beach, Fla. (904) 254-3600.

PUBLIC COURSES TO PLAY IN AREA

Indigo Lakes Golf Club, 312 Indigo Dr., Daytona Beach, Fla. Public. (904) 254-3607. 18/7,168/72. 7 minutes from LPGA International.
Palm Coast Resort, 300 Clubhouse Dr., Palm Coast, Fla. Resort. Matanzas Woods: 18/6,985/72. Cypress Knoll: 18/6,591/72. Palm Harbor: 18/6,514/72. Pine Lakes: 18/7,074/72. (904) 445-3000, (800) 654-6538. 40 minutes from LPGA International.
Pelican Bay Country Club—South Course, 550 Sea Duck Dr., Daytona Beach, Fla. Public. (904) 788-6496. 18/6,630/72. 15 minutes from LPGA International.

TICKETS & ACCESSIBILITY

How to watch: Mon., LPGA qualifier, shootout, junior golf clinic, LPGA practice rounds. Tue., Skins game, LPGA practice rounds. Wed., pro-am tournament. Thur.-Sat., tournament. Various individual, group and sponsorship ticket purchase options available. Sprint Championship Tournament Headquarters, 101 Corsair Dr., Suite 202, Daytona Beach, FL 32114. (904) 255-3606.
How to play: The course is open to the public year round. Tee times are taken seven days in advance at (904) 274-3880. Golf packages and accommodations are available through Golf Daytona Beach at (800) 881-7065.

Chick-fil-A Charity Championship

Eagle's Landing Country Club

A mammoth, white-columned plantation-style clubhouse overlooks the rolling fairways of this Tom Fazio–designed course, which is nestled in an Old South–inspired commercial and residential development 20 minutes south of Atlanta.

The terrain at Eagle's Landing is intermittently treed, with wetlands, ponds and streams on many holes. The well-bunkered putting surfaces are firm, fast, large and undulating. It is easy to hit through the greens, or to three-putt once you get there.

The Chick-fil-A Charity Championship, then called the SEGA Women's Championship, was first played in 1992 when Dottie Mochrie shot an 11-under-par 72-hole total of 277 to edge Danielle Ammaccapane. The tournament was shortened to a three-day event in 1994, and Val Skinner fired a closing-round 68 to capture a one-stroke victory over Liselotte Neumann, who had opened the final round with a triple-bogey seven on the 380-yard par-4 first hole.

Because of wet weather at the 1995 event, big hitters like Laura Davies had a decided advantage. By recording three consecutive rounds of 67, Davies broke the tournament record by four strokes.

TOURNAMENT-AT-A-GLANCE

Course: Eagle's Landing Country Club
Type: Private
Location: 100 Eagle's Landing Way, Stockbridge, GA 30281
Telephone: (404) 389-2000
When: Mid-April
How To Get There: Take I-75 South from Atlanta to Exit 73. Turn left off exit; golf course is 1 mile ahead, on the right.
Broadcast: Golf Channel (1996)
Purse: $550,000 (1996)
Tournament Record: 15-under-par 201, Laura Davies, 1995

●TOUGHEST HOLE

The tee shot on the 404-yard, par-4 15th must negotiate water to the left and transitional bunkers to the right. The approach is to a deep green with a huge bunker to its right and wetlands to the left. The incoming wind makes this hole especially challenging.

●BEST PLACE TO WATCH

The 18th tee, where you can also catch the action on the No. 17 green and incoming shots to No. 10.

●WHO THE COURSE FAVORS

The course favored long hitters in 1995 because of wet weather. Ordinarily the course favors players with a good short game who can approach the firm, undulating, bentgrass greens and hit finesse shots out of greenside bunkers and Bermuda and zoysia rough.

HOLE	YARDS	PAR	HOLE	YARDS	PAR
1	380	4	10	380	4
2	382	4	11	171	3
3	440	5	12	340	4
4	146	3	13	515	5
5	355	4	14	346	4
6	476	5	15	404	4
7	306	4	16	152	3
8	163	3	17	378	4
9	388	4	18	465	5
			TOTAL	6187	72

Toughest Hole

Best Place to Watch

Eagle's Landing Country Club
Architect: Tom Fazio (1989)

LODGING

$$$ Ritz-Carlton Buckhead, 3434 Peachtree Rd. NE, Atlanta. (404) 237-2700, (800) 241-3333. 25 minutes from Eagle's Landing.
$$ Residence Inn by Marriott Buckhead, 2960 Piedmont Rd. NE, Atlanta. (404) 239-0677. 25 minutes from Eagle's Landing.
$ Best Western Atlanta South, 3509 Highway 138, Stockbridge, Ga. (404) 474-8771, (800) 528-1234. 5 minutes from Eagle's Landing.

DINING

The Dining Room, in the Ritz-Carlton, 3434 Peachtree Rd. NE, Atlanta. (404) 237-2700, (800) 241-3333
The Bistro at St. Andrews Square, 56 E. Andrews Dr. NW, Atlanta. (404) 231-5733.
St. Charles Deli, 752 N. Highland Ave., Atlanta. (404) 876-3354.

PUBLIC COURSES TO PLAY IN AREA

Callaway Gardens, Hwy. 27, Pine Mountain, Ga. Resort. (706) 663-2281. Mountain View: 18/7,040/72. Garden View: 18/6,392/72. Lake View: 18/6,006/70. Sky View: 9/2,096/31. 1 hour from Eagle's Landing.
Southerness Golf Course, 4871 Flat Bridge Rd., Stockbridge, Ga. Semi-private. (404) 808-6000. 18/6,766/72. 5 minutes from Eagle's Landing.
White Columns Golf Club, 300 White Columns Dr., Alpharetta, Ga. Public. (404) 343-9025. 18/7,053/72. 50 minutes from Eagle's Landing.

TICKETS & ACCESSIBILITY

How to watch: Mon., pro-am event, LPGA qualifier. Tue., LPGA practice rounds, junior golf clinic. Wed.-Thur., pro-am. Fri.-Sun., tournament. Ticket prices range from $20 for a weekly badge to $800 for "Golf Patron" packages. Sponsorships available. Chick-fil-A Charity Championship, 100 Eagle's Landing Way, Stockbridge, GA 30281. (404) 474-4653.
How to play: Private club. You must be the guest of a member or arrange reciprocal privileges through the club pro.

Sara Lee Classic

Hermitage Golf Course

LODGING

$$$ Union Station Hotel, 1001 Broadway, Nashville. (615) 726-1001. 30 minutes from Hermitage GC.

$$ Courtyard by Marriott, 103 Eastpark Dr., Brentwood, Tenn. (615) 371-9200. 10 minutes from Hermitage GC.

$ Travelers Rest Inn, 107 Franklin Rd., Brentwood, Tenn. (615) 373-3033. 10 minutes from Hermitage GC.

DINING

Mario's, 2005 Broadway, Nashville. (615) 327-3232.

Outback Steakhouse, 8005 Moores Lane, Brentwood, Tenn. (615) 661-9150.

Luby's Cafeteria, 4050 Nolensville Rd., Nashville. (615) 333-7490.

PUBLIC COURSES TO PLAY IN AREA

Forrest Crossing Golf Course, 750 Riverview Dr., Franklin, Tenn. Public. (615) 794-9400. 18/6,968/72. 30 minutes from Hermitage GC.

Legends Club of Tennessee, 1500 Legends Club Lane, Franklin, Tenn. Public. (615) 790-1300. North: 18/7,190/72. South: 18/7,113/71. 30 minutes from Hermitage GC.

Springhouse Golf Club and Opryland Hotel, 18 Springhouse Lane, Nashville. Resort. (615) 871-7759. 18/7,007/72. 15 minutes from Hermitage GC.

TICKETS & ACCESSIBILITY

How to watch: Mon., LPGA qualifying rounds, LPGA practice rounds, celebrity Skins game. Tue., LPGA practice rounds, junior golf clinic. Wed., pro-am event. Thur., pro-am. Fri.-Sun., tournament. Admission free Mon. and Tue. Individual tickets begin at $5. Group and sponsorship packages available. Tournament Office, Sara Lee Classic, 3939 Old Hickory Blvd., P.O. Box 390, Old Hickory, TN 37138. (615) 847-5018.

How to play: Hermitage is a public golf course open year round. High season is March through October. (615) 847-4001.

TOURNAMENT-AT-A-GLANCE

Course: Hermitage Golf Course
Type: Public
Location: 3939 Old Hickory Blvd., Old Hickory, TN 37138
Telephone: (615) 847-4001
When: Early May
How To Get There: From Nashville, 20 minutes. Take I-40 E. to Exit 221A. Go left onto Old Hickory Blvd. Follow 5 miles to the golf course.
Broadcast: Golf Channel (1995)
Purse: $525,000 (1995)
Tournament Record: 14-under-par 202, Michelle McGann, 1995

The Sara Lee Classic, inaugurated in 1988, is played in the rolling, tree-lined hills just outside Nashville and only a short drive from the original Hermitage, home of Andrew Jackson. With its tight fairways, strategically placed bunkers, and a medley of water and trees protecting landing areas and greens, this Gary Roger Baird layout affords a fine test of championship golf.

The front nine opens with a friendly 350-yard, par-4. But as you work your way around the course you notice the shelves and undulations that make the bentgrass greens tricky. The subtle mounds, dropoffs and sprawling traps demand good recovery skills.

The 344-yard par-4 finishing hole appears at first to be harmless. The tee shot should be played to the left, but there is a risk of pulling it into the trees or hitting one of three fairway bunkers. The approach is blind up to a forward-sloping, fast putting surface. It was here Meg Mallon missed a short birdie putt that would have forced a play-off with Laura Davies in the 1994 Classic.

Michelle McGann, the lady who wears many hats, shot a tournament record 202 to win the 1995 Classic, her first victory since turning professional in 1988.

●TOUGHEST HOLE

The landing area off the tee of the 480-yard, par-5 11th is framed tightly by trees to the right and a lake to the left. Water bordering the left and cutting in front of the green creates a tough second shot to the green for eagle opportunities. If the golfer lays up in front of the water hazard, a shallow green with water in front and a bunker to its rear makes the approach potentially dangerous.

●BEST PLACE TO WATCH

The bleachers on No. 17 provide an excellent view of that par-3 as well as a look at the approach to No. 11 and tee shots on No. 18.

●WHO THE COURSE FAVORS

A right-to-left player and a good shotmaker from 150 yards.

HERMITAGE GOLF COURSE
ARCHITECT: GARY ROGER BAIRD (1987)

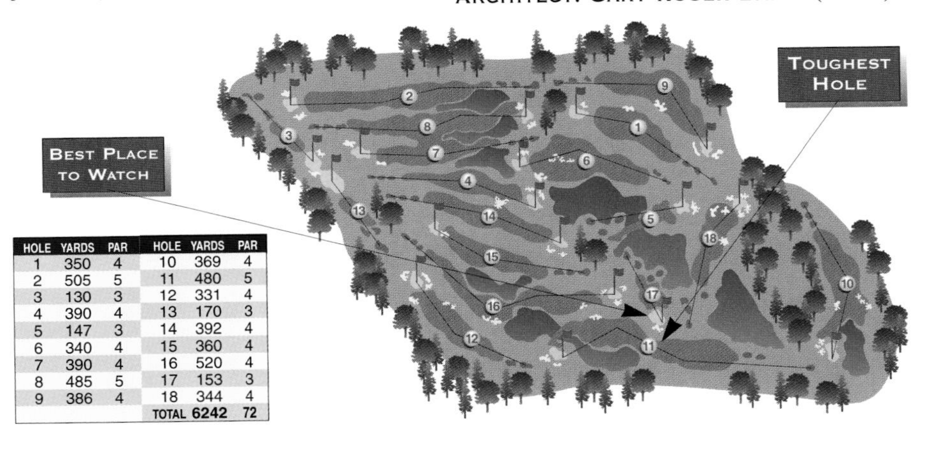

HOLE	YARDS	PAR	HOLE	YARDS	PAR
1	350	4	10	369	4
2	505	5	11	480	5
3	130	3	12	331	4
4	390	4	13	170	3
5	147	3	14	392	4
6	340	4	15	360	4
7	390	4	16	520	4
8	485	5	17	153	3
9	386	4	18	344	4
			TOTAL	6242	72

Star Bank LPGA Classic

Country Club of the North

The Country Club of the North, 10 miles southeast of downtown Dayton, Ohio, is situated on valley terrain in a 450-acre residential development bordered by the Little Miami River. Creeks, lakes, forests and open meadows fringe the home sites, which come into view on half the holes.

The signature hole on this Jack Nicklaus–designed, fully bentgrass layout is the 489-yard, par-5 eighth, which starts with a tee shot to a landing area framed by a lake to the right and bunkers to the left. The second shot must avoid a stream cutting the fairway and bordering a deep, narrow green framed by two bunkers.

The Country Club of the North is a shotmaker's course, with relatively short par-3s and par-5s, a variety of doglegs, water hazards on five holes and a series of strategically placed bunkers. Long hitters have a decided advantage in birdie opportunities on the par-5s and some of the shorter par-4s.

LPGA representatives accompanied Nicklaus during the design stages of this layout to ensure a suitable LPGA site. As with many Nicklaus courses, the golfer is given some leeway off the tee but must hit solid approach shots to score.

TOURNAMENT-AT-A-GLANCE

Course: Country Club of the North
Type: Private
Location: 1 Club North Dr., Beavercreek, OH 45385
Telephone: (513) 374-5000
When: Mid to Late May
How To Get There: From Cincinnati, 55 miles. I-75 N. to I-675 N. to Indian Ripple Road Exit. Go right (east) onto Indian Ripple Rd.; 4 miles to course. From Columbus, 75 miles. I-70 W to I-675 S, to U.S. 35 E. Take U.S. 35 to Factory Rd., turn right and follow signs to the course. From Indianapolis, 150 miles. I-70 E to I-75 S to U.S. 35 E. Follow directions above.
Broadcast: Golf Channel (1995)
Purse: $500,000 (1995)
Tournament Record: 6-under-par 210, Maggie Will, 1994

●TOUGHEST HOLE

The 397-yard, par-4 18th, a dogleg right, hugs marshlands and has crosswinds from right to left. A deep and tight green tilts to the rear and has an ominous bunker flanking its right and back sides.

●BEST PLACE TO WATCH

The hillside near the 18th provides a great view of the finishing hole. Bleacher seating at the 403-yard, par-4 ninth is another good vantage point.

●WHO THE COURSE FAVORS

Big hitters have the advantage on this relatively open layout; large greens are protected by a maximum of three bunkers.

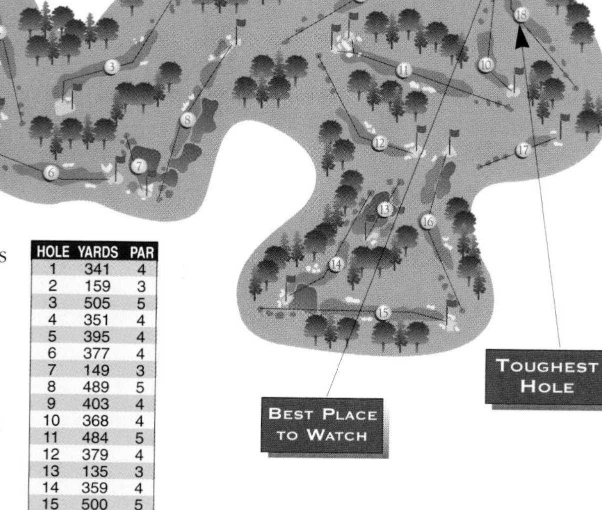

HOLE	YARDS	PAR
1	341	4
2	159	3
3	505	5
4	351	4
5	395	4
6	377	4
7	149	3
8	489	5
9	403	4
10	368	4
11	484	5
12	379	4
13	135	3
14	359	4
15	500	5
16	358	4
17	170	3
18	397	4
TOTAL	6318	72

The Country Club of the North
Architect: Jack Nicklaus (1992)

LODGING

$$$ Homewood Suites, 2750 Presidential Dr., Fairborne, Ohio. (513) 429-0600. 15 minutes from Country Club of the North.
$$ Holiday Inn Conference Center, 2800 Presidential Dr., Fairborne, Ohio. (513) 426-7800, (800) HOLIDAY. 15 minutes from Country Club of the North.
$ Red Roof Inn, 2850 Colonel Glenn Hwy., Fairborne, Ohio. (513) 426-6116, (800) THE-ROOF. 15 minutes from Country Club of the North.

DINING

The Pine Club, 1926 Brown St., Dayton, Ohio. (513) 228-7463.
The Diner on St. Clair, 101 S. St. Clair St., Dayton, Ohio. (513) 228-2201.

PUBLIC COURSES TO PLAY IN AREA

The Golf Club of Yankee Trace, 10,000 Yankee Dr., Centerville, Ohio. Public. (513) 438-4653. 18/7,139/72. 20 minutes from Country Club of the North.
Heatherwoode Golf Club, 88 Heatherwoode Blvd., Springboro, Ohio. Public. (513) 748-3222. 18/6,730/72. 25 minutes from Country Club of the North.
Weatherwax Golf Course, 5401 Middletown Rd., Middletown, Ohio. Public. (513) 425-7886. Valley/Highlands: 18/6,756/72. Woodside/Meadows: 18/7,174/72. 40 minutes from Country Club of the North.

TICKETS & ACCESSIBILITY

How to watch: Mon., LPGA practice rounds, junior golf clinic, pro-am event. Tue., LPGA practice rounds, shootout. Wed., pro-am. Thur., pro-am. Fri.-Sun., tournament. No charge for Mon. and Tue. Daily tickets from $13. Group and sponsorship packages available. Star Bank LPGA Classic, 1 Club North Dr., Beavercreek, OH 45385, (513) 291-4230, (800) 551-LPGA.
How to play: Private club. You must be the guest of a member to play the course. No reciprocals.

Corning Classic

Corning Country Club

LODGING

$$$ Radisson Hotel Corning, 125 Denison Pkwy. East, Corning, N.Y. (607) 962-5000. 10 minutes from the Corning CC.

$$ Rosewood Inn, 134 E. 1st St., Corning, N.Y. (607) 962-3253. 10 minutes from the Corning CC.

$ Red Jacket Motor Inn, Rte 17, Elmira, N.Y. (607) 734-1616. 20 minutes from the Corning CC.

DINING

Pierce's 1894 Restaurant, 228 Oakwood Ave., Elmira Heights, N.Y. (607) 734-2022.

London Underground Cafe and Club, 69 East Market St., Corning, N.Y. (607) 962-2345.

Sorge's, 66-68 W. Market St., Corning, N.Y. (607) 937-5422.

PUBLIC COURSES TO PLAY IN AREA

En-Joie Golf Club, 722 West Main St., Endicott, N.Y. Public. (607) 785-1661. 18/7,016/72. 1 hour and 15 minutes from Corning CC.

Soaring Eagles Golf Club, 4229 Middle Rd., Horseheads, N.Y. Public. (607) 739-0551. 18/6,625/72. 10 minutes from Corning CC.

Willow Creek Golf Course, Route 352, Big Flats, N.Y. Semi-private. (607) 562-8898. Pines/Bittercreek: 18/6,820/72. Willowcreek: 9/3,300/36. 10 minutes from Corning CC.

TICKETS & ACCESSIBILITY

How to watch: Mon., LPGA practice rounds, pro-am tournament, junior golf clinic. Tue., LPGA practice rounds, shootout. Wed., pro-am. Thur.-Sun., tournament. Daily tickets start at $8. Group and sponsorship packages available. LPGA Corning Classic, P.O. Box 1048, Corning, NY 14830-1048. (607) 962-4441.

How to play: Private club. You must be the guest of a member or arrange reciprocals through the club professional.

TOURNAMENT-AT-A-GLANCE

Course: Corning Country Club
Type: Private
Location: E. Corning Road, P.O. Box 17, Corning, NY 14830
Telephone: (607) 936-3711 (club), (607) 962-5985 (pro shop)
When: Late May
How To Get There: From the east, Rte. 17, Exit 47. Right at the light; first left to the golf course. From the west, Rte. 17, East Corning Road Exit; follow left 3 miles to the club.
Broadcast: ABC, ESPN (1996)
Purse: $550,000 (1996)
Tournament Record: 16-under-par 272, Patty Sheehan, 1993; Patti Rizzo, 1985; Ayako Akamoto, 1989

A popular small-town stop where, according to Amy Alcott, players "feel at home," the Corning Country Club is a well-treed, tight, rolling, traditional golf course. Significant elevation changes on several holes, small strategically bunkered greens, few water hazards and occasional doglegs such as the 364-yard, par-4 ninth make Corning a shotmaker's challenge. The course starts out with one of its toughest holes, a 402-yard, par-4 slight dogleg right that plays to a narrow landing area with an approach to a small two-tiered green. This hole, with a tournament stroke average of 4.57, was rated the most difficult on the LPGA circuit in 1994.

The finishing hole, a 377-yard, par-4 dogleg left, plays to a green protected by three bunkers. In 1993 Kelly Robbins and Alison Nicholas, tied going into the 18th on the final round, both bogeyed the hole, forcing a sudden-death playoff. Robbins then parred the same hole to win her first LPGA tournament at the age of 23.

●TOUGHEST HOLE

The 402-yard par-4 first hole and the 412-yard, par-4 13th, which plays from an elevated tee then uphill to a two-tiered green with two traps to its left. A good tee shot is required.

●BEST PLACE TO WATCH

The 18th hole near the clubhouse has bleachers and skyboxes from which to view the par-4 finishing hole. Because there are many adjacent fairways on this traditional course, it is easy to move to various vantage points.

●WHO THE COURSE FAVORS

Corning Country Club requires controlled, well-positioned drives down the tightly treed fairways and excellent approach shots to small greens that usually measure no more than 31 yards deep. This is a true shotmaker's course.

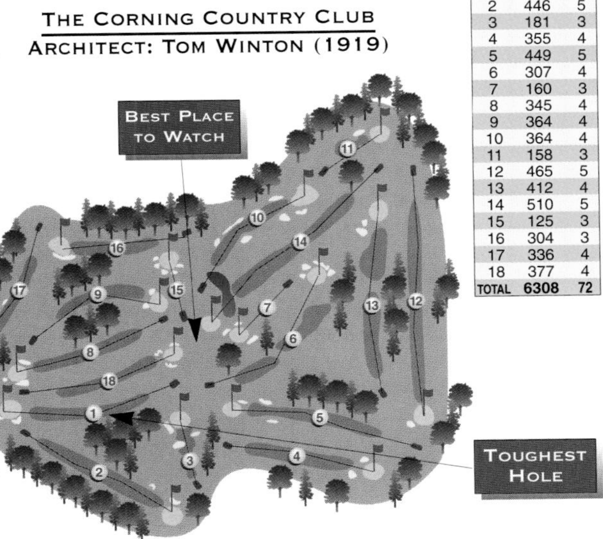

The Corning Country Club
Architect: Tom Winton (1919)

HOLE	YARDS	PAR
1	402	4
2	446	5
3	181	3
4	355	4
5	449	5
6	307	4
7	160	3
8	345	4
9	364	4
10	364	4
11	158	3
12	465	5
13	412	4
14	510	5
15	125	3
16	304	3
17	336	4
18	377	4
TOTAL	6308	72

"PEOPLE HERE ARE WONDERFUL... THE SMALL TOWN IS REALLY THE LIFEBLOOD OF GOLF."

—AMY ALCOTT

JCPenney/LPGA Skins Game

STONEBRIAR COUNTRY CLUB

The women's tour joined one of the most popular and lucrative traditions in modern golf in 1990 when Jan Stephenson, JoAnne "Big Mama" Carner, Nancy Lopez and Betsy King teed it up at the Stonebriar Country Club for the first LPGA Skins Game.

On the 17th hole, Stephenson tapped in an 18-inch putt and raised her arms to the heavens in thanks.

Her par was worth six skins and $200,000.

After a one-year hiatus, the unique drama of the Skins Game was back, and this time it was Hall of Famer Pat Bradley's turn, as she birdied the par-4 13th to earn $200,000.

Betsy King won the 1993 event with seven skins and $185,000, but Nancy Lopez earned $110,000 on a single hole by three-putting the 492-yard eighth for a par-5.

Patty Sheehan set the LPGA Skins record in 1994 when she collected 13 skins and $285,000, defeating Betsy King and shutting out both Lopez and Brandie Burton.

The Stonebriar Country Club is set in a gated, luxury residential community and features a 52,000-square-foot clubhouse with fine dining facilities, a grand ballroom and other amenities. The rolling, open golf course has large, bentgrass greens, water hazards that can come into play on eight holes, and several large bunkers guarding landing areas and greens. The wind, which can reach gusts of more than 40 miles per hour, is a major factor.

Stonebriar gradually builds in difficulty, culminating in the 490-yard, par-5 18th, which plays well over 500 yards because of the incoming wind. The tee shot is to a landing area narrowed by water, bunkers and trees. The second shot must negotiate three bunkers to the right on the way to a three-tiered green guarded by a large pond and a collection of bunkers.

The Skins Game began on the PGA Tour in 1983 and has since become one of golf's most popular television events. In the LPGA Skins Game, $20,000 is at stake on each of the first six holes, $30,000 each on the middle six and $40,000 each on the final holes. If a hole is halved, the prize carries over to the next tee. Patty Sheehan, Laura Davies, Dottie Mochrie and Nancy Lopez competed for $540,000 in the 1995 contest. This was the first time the Ladies' event had a purse equal to the men's.

TOURNAMENT-AT-A-GLANCE

Course: Stonebriar Country Club
Type: Private
Location: 5050 Country Club Dr., Frisco, TX 75034
Telephone: (214) 625-5050
When: Late May
How To Get There: Dallas Tollway N to Legacy Exit. Go left off exit ramp, follow 1 1/2 miles to golf course.
Broadcast: ABC (1996)
Purse: $540,000 (1996)
Tournament Record: 13 skins, $285,000, Patty Sheehan, 1994

"I HAD NEVER EXPERIENCED COMPETING IN A SKINS GAME. I ROLLED IN A 30-FOOTER FOR MY FIRST SKIN AND $90,000. WHAT A GREAT FEELING! YOU TALK ABOUT PRESSURE—THIS IS IT!"

PATTY SHEEHAN,

WINNER OF A RECORD $285,000 IN THE 1994 LPGA SKINS GAME.

●TOUGHEST HOLE

The 405-yard, par-4 ninth plays around a large pond to the right. A bunker to the rear and two to the left of the green make approach shots challenging, especially if the competitor has been cautious off the tee. An incoming wind from the south can make this hole play very long.

●BEST PLACE TO WATCH

Because the four golfers play only nine holes each day, it is easy to follow the weekend drama.

●WHO THE COURSE FAVORS

Stonebriar favors a player who can approach the green from 150 yards in, especially under incoming windy conditions that generally prevail on holes No. 7, 8, 9, 15 and 18.

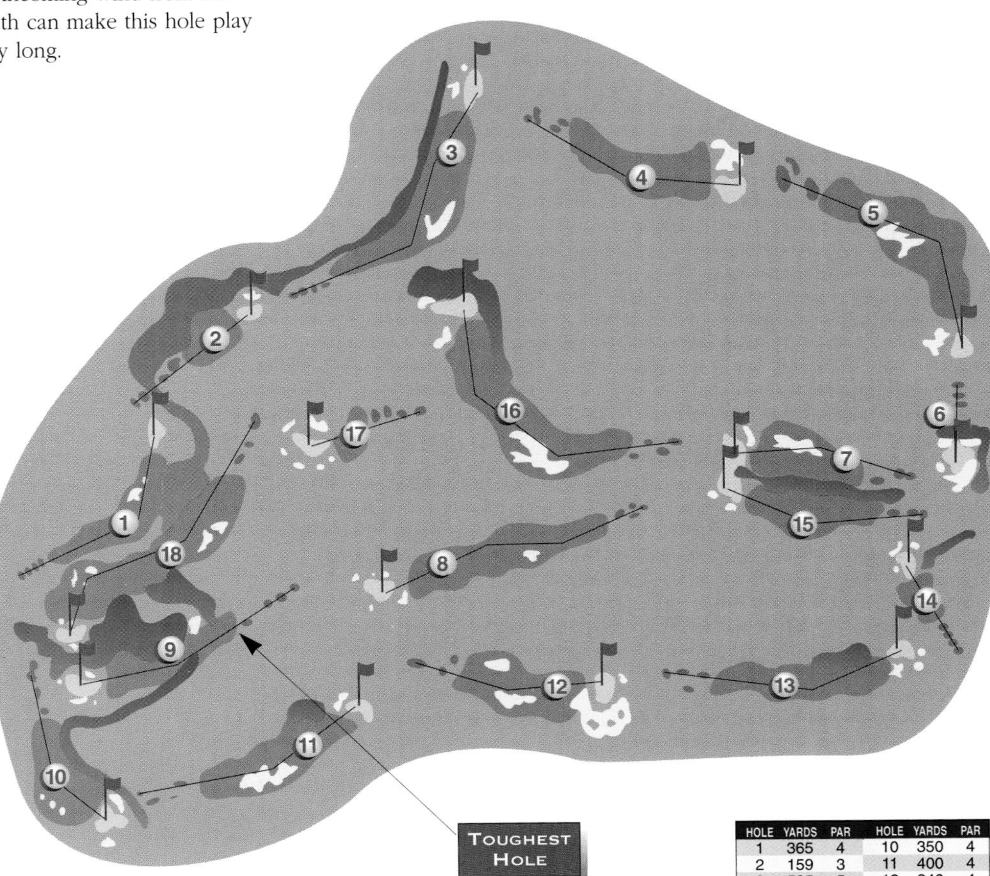

HOLE	YARDS	PAR	HOLE	YARDS	PAR
1	365	4	10	350	4
2	159	3	11	400	4
3	525	5	12	340	4
4	425	4	13	400	4
5	395	4	14	170	3
6	123	3	15	352	4
7	290	4	16	475	5
8	492	5	17	140	3
9	405	4	18	490	5
			TOTAL	6296	72

STONEBRIAR COUNTRY CLUB
ARCHITECTS: KEN DYE AND BAXTER SPANN (1988)

LODGING

$$$ The Grand Kempinski Dallas, 15201 Dallas Pkwy., Dallas. (214) 386-6000, (800) 426-3135. 20 minutes from Stonebriar CC.

$$ Doubletree at Campbell Centre, 8250 N. Central Expwy., Dallas. (214) 691-8700. 20 minutes from Stonebriar CC.

$ La Quinta Inn, 1820 N. Central Pkwy., Plano, TX 75093. (214) 423-1300. 10 minutes from Stonebriar CC.

DINING

The French Room, Adolphus Hotel, 1321 Commerce St., Dallas. (214) 742-8200.

Javier's Ristorante, 4912 Cole Ave., Dallas. (214) 521-4211.

Luby's Cafeteria–Collin Creek Mall, 811 N. Central Expwy., Plano, Texas. (214) 423-9120.

PUBLIC COURSES TO PLAY IN AREA

Chase Oaks Golf Club, 7201 Chase Oaks Blvd., Plano, Texas. Public. (214) 517-7777. Blackjack: 18/6,811/72. Sawtooth: 18/6,496/72. 15 minutes from Stonebriar CC.

Four Seasons Resort and Club, 4150 North MacArthur Blvd., Irving, Texas. Resort. (214) 717-2530 (golf course), (800) 332-3442 (resort). 18/6,826/70. 25 minutes from Stonebriar CC.

Hyatt Bear Creek Golf and Racquet Club, 3000 Bear Creek Court. (off W. Air Field Dr.), Dallas–Fort Worth Airport. Resort. (214) 615-6800 (golf course), (800) 233-1234 (resort). East: 18/6,670/70. West: 18/6,677/72. 25 minutes from Stonebriar CC.

TICKETS & ACCESSIBILITY

How to watch: Sat.-Sun., tournament. Individual, group and sponsorship packages are available. JC Penney Skins Game, c/o JC Penney Company, P.O. Box 10001, 6501 Legacy Dr., Plano, TX 75024-3698. (214) 431-4159.

How to play: Private Club. You must be the guest of a member to play the course. Limited reciprocals can be arranged through the club professional.

Oldsmobile Classic

Walnut Hills Country Club

Beth Daniel set up one of the best 72-hole totals in LPGA history in 1994 when she played the back nine at Walnut Hills in 31 strokes to record a 70 on the third round. Daniel, the 1994 LPGA Player of the Year, had shot a course-record 63 the previous day, and her 268 total tied her with Nancy Lopez for the all-time record in a 72-hole tournament.

Walnut Hills is a shotmaker's layout, with well-treed, narrow fairways and small greens. The course rewards accuracy off the tee and on approach shots.

Daniel and other long hitters like Laura Davies and Val Skinner have an advantage on this traditional course because its soft, lush fairways and uphill slopes often supply minimum roll. The golfer must be able to play strategically and hit off uneven lies to be able to score.

"I think this course plays much, much tougher when it's wet," Daniel said after her record-book weekend. "The conditions this weekend were wonderful. I can't remember the greens being like this. They were true and smooth, with great speed."

TOURNAMENT-AT-A-GLANCE

Course: Walnut Hills Country Club
Type: Private
Location: 2874 Lake Lansing Rd., East Lansing, MI 48823
Telephone: (517) 332-8647
When: Early June
How To Get There: Take I-96 to Okomos Road Exit. Follow Okomos Road to Lake Lansing Road and the golf course.
Broadcast: ESPN (1995)
Purse: $600,000 (1996)
Tournament Record: 20-under-par 268, Beth Daniel, 1994

HOLE	YARDS	PAR	HOLE	YARDS	PAR
1	373	4	10	375	4
2	152	3	11	506	5
3	402	4	12	329	4
4	159	3	13	171	3
5	511	5	14	440	5
6	460	4	15	397	4
7	344	4	16	175	3
8	362	4	17	286	4
9	385	4	18	364	4
			TOTAL	6191	72

Walnut Hills Country Club
Architect: John A. Roseman (circa 1920s)
Remodeled by Bruce and Jerry Mathews (1962), Jerry Mathews (1984), Jeff Gorney (1990)

●TOUGHEST HOLE

The 385-yard, par-4 ninth plays straight down an intermittently treed fairway to an elevated green that slopes severely forward and is protected by three bunkers. It was rated the 14th most difficult hole on the LPGA Tour in 1994.

●BEST PLACE TO WATCH

Between Nos. 9 and 18, where you can watch the golfers come up to the clubhouse.

●WHO THE COURSE FAVORS

The long-ball hitter with control will do well at Walnut Hills, whose uphill slopes require extra carry. Short par-5s, especially the 440-yard 14th, the 506-yard 11th and the 460-yard sixth, offer eagle opportunities.

LODGING

$$$ East Lansing Marriott, 300 M.A.C., East Lansing, Mich. (517) 337-4440, (800) 228-9290. 10 Minutes from Walnut Hills CC.
$$ Park Inn International Quality Suites, 901 Delta Commerce Dr., Lansing, Mich. (517) 886-0600. 20 minutes from Walnut Hills CC.
$ Red Roof Inn–East, 3615 Dunckel Rd., Lansing, Mich. (517) 332-2575, (800) THE-ROOF. 20 minutes from Walnut Hills CC.

DINING

Chesapeake Crab House at the East Lansing Marriott, 300 M.A.C., East Lansing, Mich. (517) 337-4440.
Mountain Jack's–Lansing, 5800 W. Saginaw Hwy., Lansing, Mich. (517) 321-2770.
Clara's, 637 E. Michigan Ave., Lansing, Mich. (517) 372-7120.

PUBLIC COURSES TO PLAY IN AREA

Cascades Golf Course, 1992 Warren Ave., Jackson, Mich. Public. (517) 788-4323. 18/6,614/72. 50 minutes from Walnut Hills CC.
Forest Akers Golf Course, Harrison Rd. at Mt. Hope, at Michigan State University, East Lansing, Mich. Public. (517) 355-1635. East: 18/6,510/72. West: 18/6,750/71. 20 minutes from Walnut Hills CC.
Timber Ridge Golf Course, 16339 Park Lake Rd., East Lansing, Mich. Public. (517) 339-8000. 18/6,497/72. 5 minutes from Walnut Hills CC.

TICKETS & ACCESSIBILITY

How to watch: Mon., LPGA practice rounds, pro-am event. Tue., LPGA practice rounds. Wed., pro-am. Thur.-Sun., tournament. Admission free on Mon. Daily tickets start at $5. Group and sponsorship packages available. Oldsmobile Classic, P.O. Box 12240, Lansing, MI 48901, (517) 372-4653.
How to play: Private club. You must be the guest of a member or arrange reciprocals through the club professional.

ROCHESTER INTERNATIONAL

LOCUST HILL COUNTRY CLUB

LODGING

$$$ Oliver Loud's Inn, 1474 Marsh Rd., Pittsford, N.Y. (716) 248-5200. 5 minutes from Locust Hill.

$$ Residence Inn by Marriott, 1300 Jefferson Rd., Rochester, N.Y. (716) 272-8850, (800) 331-3131. 5 minutes from Locust Hill.

$ Super 8 Motel, 100 Lehigh Station Rd., Henrietta, N.Y. (716) 359-1630. 5 minutes from Locust Hill.

DINING

Richardson's Canal House, 1474 Marsh Rd., Pittsford, N.Y. (716) 248-5000.

The Depot Restaurant, 41 N. Main St., Pittsford, N.Y. (716) 381-9991.

Applebees, 3050 Winton Rd. S., Rochester, N.Y. (716) 272-7753.

PUBLIC COURSES TO PLAY IN THE AREA

Bristol Harbor Golf Club, 5500 Seneca Point Rd., Canandaigua, N.Y. Semi-private. (716) 396-2460. 18/6,692/72. 40 minutes from Locust Hill.

Shadow Pines Golf Club, 600 Whalen Rd., Penfield, N.Y. (716) 385-8550. 18/6,763/72. 20 minutes from Locust Hill.

Wildwood Golf Club, 1201 West Rush Rd., Rush, N.Y. Semi-private. (716) 334-9210. 18/6,431/71. 15 minutes from Locust Hill.

TICKETS & ACCESSIBILITY

How to watch: Mon., LPGA practice rounds. Tue., LPGA practice rounds, pro-am event. Wed., pro-am. Thur.-Sun., tournament. Ticket sales start at $10. Group and sponsorship packages available. The Rochester International, Locust Hill Country Club, 2000 Jefferson Rd., Pittsford, NY 14534. (716) 427-7100.

How to play: Private club. The course is open from April through October. You must be the guest of a member. Reciprocal play can be arranged through the club professional.

TOURNAMENT-AT-A-GLANCE

Course: Locust Hill Country Club
Type: Private
Location: 2000 Jefferson Blvd., Pittsford, NY 14534
Telephone: (716) 427-7040
When: Mid-June
How To Get There: South on Rte. 390 to Rte. 252 (Jefferson Rd.). Go right 3 1/2 miles to golf course. Or go north on Rte. 390 to Exit 15A (Rte. 252/Jefferson Rd.); left on Jefferson Rd. Follow 3 1/2 miles to golf course.
Broadcast: The Golf Channel (1995)
Purse: $500,000 (1995)
Tournament Record: 19-under-par 269, Patty Sheehan, 1992

Tightly treed and dotted with small, slippery greens, this rolling, traditional layout makes an apt home for a tournament with a rich history.

Opened in 1928 as a nine-hole course, Locust Hill was remodeled and completed three years later by the masterful Robert Trent Jones. Strategic shot placement, careful club selection and deft approaches from uneven lies are critical here, but the winner usually earns her crown around the tiered putting surfaces, which are easy to miss.

Some of the tour's great names have added luster to this event with their accomplishments here: Hall of Famer Pat Bradley took the debut event in 1977, then repeated her win in 1983. Nancy Lopez, a three-time Rochester champion, won her record fifth-straight tournament here in 1978 during her astonishing rookie year. In 1984, Kathy Whitworth broke a Sam Snead standard when she graced Locust Hill with her 85th sanctioned tournament victory. And in 1989, Patty Sheehan launched a barrage of victories and top-5 finishes here when she sank a rare double eagle on the go-for-broke, 443-yard, par-5 17th.

●TOUGHEST HOLE

The 158-yard, par-3 fifth hole, an uphill test of mid-iron accuracy to a three-level green framed by two large bunkers. Three putts are not uncommon on the slick putting surface.

●BEST PLACE TO WATCH

The stands around No. 18, a 362-yard par-4; the mounds in back of No. 17, a 443-yard par-5 where Patty Sheehan scored a double eagle in 1989; and the bleachers around No. 9, a scenic 150-yard par-3.

●WHO THE COURSE FAVORS

Length is not the issue at Locust Hill. But tee-shot positioning down tree-lined fairways and accurate approaches to the well-bunkered, tiered greens are extremely important. Some holes, such as the 391-yard, par-4 dogleg left first, are difficult for short hitters.

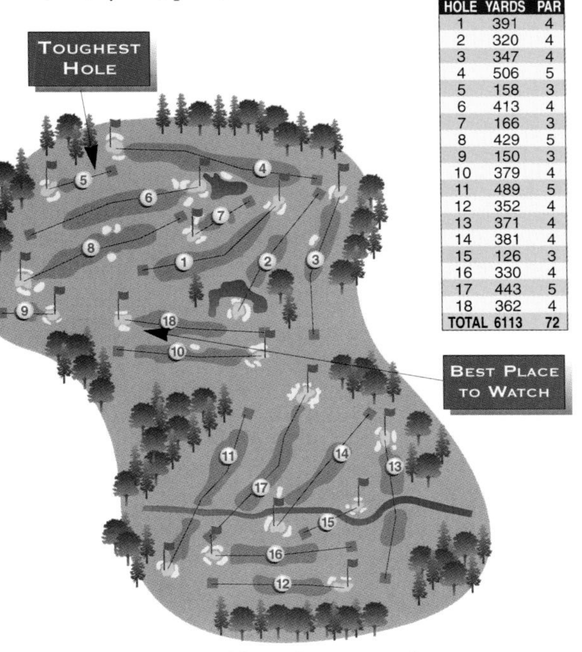

HOLE	YARDS	PAR
1	391	4
2	320	4
3	347	4
4	506	5
5	158	3
6	413	4
7	166	3
8	429	5
9	150	3
10	379	4
11	489	5
12	352	4
13	371	4
14	381	4
15	126	3
16	330	4
17	443	5
18	362	4
TOTAL	6113	72

LOCUST HILL COUNTRY CLUB
ARCHITECT: SEYMOUR DUNN (NINE HOLES, 1928)
COURSE REMODELED AND SECOND NINE ADDED BY ROBERT TRENT JONES SR. (1931)

Edina Realty LPGA Classic

EDINBURGH USA GOLF COURSE

Carved into Minnesota farmland that can easily yield bland golfing terrain, this Robert Trent Jones Jr. layout creates its own drama with rolling fairways, ample wooded areas, deep bunkers and water hazards worthy of the "Land of 10,000 Lakes."

Recognized as one of the best public courses in America, Edinburgh USA begins with an open Scottish-style front nine before turning to a less spacious back nine highlighted by two memorable holes. The 15th, a 490-yard par-5, is sometimes called "The Brooklyn Tunnel" because of a corridor of trees that leads to a small green guarded by two large bunkers. Consistently one of the toughest holes faced by the LPGA, the signature 17th has a narrow, island fairway and plays over the surrounding lake to an angled peninsula green.

The 18th finishes with an uphill approach to a vast, one-acre green shared by the ninth hole and by practice putters.

In one of the most unlikely finishes in the Classic's brief history, Hiromi Kobayashi made up eight strokes in the final 11 holes to force a playoff with Cindy Rarick in 1993. Rarick then three-putted from 12 feet on the first playoff hole to let the tournament slip away.

Edinburgh's signature 17th requires shooting from an island fairway to a peninsula green.

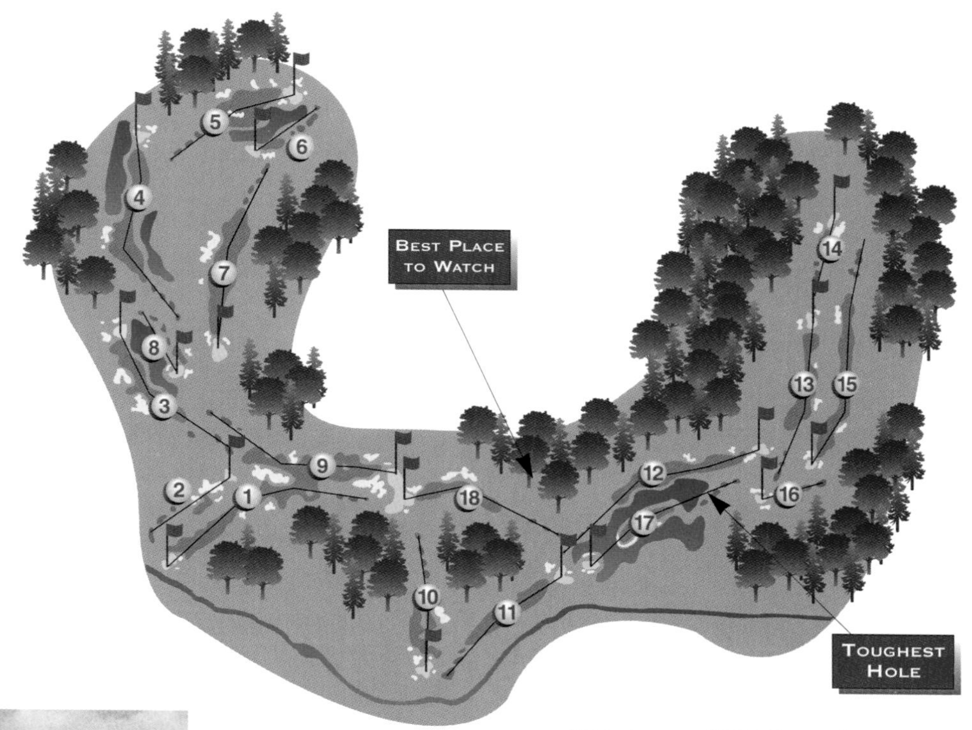

EDINBURGH USA GOLF COURSE
ARCHITECT: ROBERT TRENT JONES JR.

HOLE	YARDS	PAR	HOLE	YARDS	PAR
1	492	4	10	335	4
2	176	3	11	404	5
3	373	5	12	467	4
4	490	4	13	390	3
5	325	4	14	180	4
6	166	4	15	490	5
7	349	3	16	124	4
8	150	5	17	365	3
9	495	4	18	370	4
			TOTAL	6141	72

Courtesy of Edina Realty LPGA Classic

TOURNAMENT-AT-A-GLANCE

Course: Edinburgh USA Golf Course
Type: Public
Location: 8700 Edinbrook Crossing, Brooklyn Park, MN 55443
Telephone: (612) 424-7060
When: Early to Mid-June
How To Get There: From downtown Minneapolis, 15 miles. I-94 west to Hwy. 252, Hwy. 252 north to 85th Ave., left on 85th to golf course, 1 mile on the right.
Broadcast: Golf Channel (1996)
Purse: $500,000 (1995)
Tournament Record: 13-under-par 203, Beth Daniel, 1990

●TOUGHEST HOLE

The picturesque 365-yard, par-4 17th plays over water to an island fairway that narrows to 35 yards at its far end. The approach is over water to a green protected by bunkers and framed by water on three sides. This hole was rated the third most difficult hole on the LPGA tour in 1994.

●BEST PLACE TO WATCH

The bleachers to the right of the clubhouse at the 18th or behind the signature No. 17.

●WHO THE COURSE FAVORS

Accuracy off the tee is required to negotiate the wind, bunkers, water hazards and mature trees. Approach shots from uneven lies must be mastered in order to avoid sand and water.

LODGING

$$$ The Northland Inn, 7025 Northland Dr., Brooklyn Park, Minn. (612) 536-8300, (800) 441-6422. 5 minutes from Edinburgh USA GC.
$$ Holiday Inn North, 2200 Freeway Blvd., Brooklyn Center, Minn. (612) 566-8000, (800) HOLI-DAY. 10 minutes from Edinburgh USA GC.
$ Best Western Northwest Inn, 6900 Lakeland Blvd., Brooklyn Park, Minn. (612) 566-8855. 5 minutes from Edinburgh USA GC.

DINING

Wadsworth's Restaurant, in The Northland Inn, 7025 Northland Dr., Brooklyn Park, Minn. (612) 536-8300.
W.A. Frost & Company Restaurant, 374 Selby Ave., Minneapolis. (612) 224-5715.
McDivots, at Edinburgh USA, 8700 Edinbrook Crossing, Brooklyn Park, Minn. (612) 424-7060.

PUBLIC COURSES TO PLAY IN AREA

Braemar Golf Course, 6364 Dewey Hill Rd., Edina, Minn. Public. (612) 941-2072. 18/6,695/71. 30 minutes from Edinburgh USA GC.
Bunker Hills Golf Course, Hwy. 242 and Foley Blvd., Coon Rapids, Minn. Public. (612) 755-4141. North: 9/3,373/36. East: 9/3,426/36. West: 9/3,520/36. 15 minutes from Edinburgh USA GC.
Fox Hollow Golf Club, 4780 Palmgren, Rogers, Minn. Public. (612) 428-4468. 18/6,701/72. 1 hour from Edinburgh USA GC.

TICKETS & ACCESSIBILITY

How to watch: Mon., charity event with LPGA players. Tue., LPGA practice rounds. Wed., pro-am event. Thur., pro-am. Fri.-Sun., tournament. Tickets start at $10. Group and sponsorship packages available. The Edina Realty LPGA Classic, 8600 Edinbrook Crossing, Brooklyn Park, MN 55443, (612) 493-7000.
How to play: Edinburgh USA is open to the public mid-April through October. Group package rates and other discounts available. Reserve tee times up to 4 days in advance. (612) 424-7060.

ShopRite LPGA Classic

GREATE BAY RESORT AND COUNTRY CLUB

Built when Atlantic City was the playground of Philadelphia's elite, this rolling seashore course has been rejuvenated over the past decade to become a challenging arena for championship golf.

Willie Park Jr., a two-time British Open winner in the 1880s, laid out the original 18 in 1921 for the private enjoyment of Ocean City real estate developer Harvey Lake. Decades of public play followed before George and Tom Fazio were called in by a new team of private developers for a major upgrade in the early 1970s. Today's owner, Eugene Gatti, has pampered the course with hundreds of new plantings and a rigorous maintenance program that has revived once unpredictable greens.

Though mature trees define many of its holes, Greate Bay is relatively open to both imperfect drives and the swirling northerly winds coming off nearby Egg Harbor Bay. The gusts usually start blowing on summer afternoons, giving tournament leaders fits as they try to hold the small, firm putting surfaces. Water or wetlands come into play on only two holes, but the course's abundant bunkers guard the straightest paths to many of the contoured greens.

TOURNAMENT-AT-A-GLANCE

Course: Greate Bay Resort and Country Club
Type: Resort
Location: 901 Mays Landing Rd., Somers Point, NJ 08244
Telephone: (609) 927-0066
When: Late June
How To Get There: From the north and Garden State Pkwy., take Exit 30. Go east to the first stop sign and make a right. Take a left at the first traffic light to the golf course. From the south and Garden State Pkwy., take Exit 29 (Somers Point/Ocean City). Go right at first light and proceed north on Rte. 9 to light (Mays Landing Rd.). Turn right; 1/2 mile to the golf course.
Broadcast: WNYW-TV (New York), WTXF-TV (Philadelphia), WMGM-TV (South Jersey) (1995)
Purse: $650,000 (1995)
Tournament Record: 9-under-par 204, Shelley Hamlin, 1993 (54-hole record); 5-under-par 275, Chris Johnson, 1990 (72-hole record)

The winds blow most fiercely on the course's eastern holes, which include a relatively easy opening set of four. The longer holes begin when the players cross under Route 9 to the fifth. The 390-yard, par-4 18th, whipped by the winds east of the highway, is rated among the most difficult on the LPGA tour. The second shot on this dogleg right must carry a bunker guarding the front of the green and avoid another to the left.

First played in 1986 as the Atlantic City Classic, the area's LPGA showdown was held the first two years just up the road on a shorter, links-style course at Marriott's Seaview Country Club. Juli Inkster, the only two-time winner of the event, won the debut tournament, then captured the title again two years later during its first spin through Greate Bay.

One of the most popular former champions here is Shelley Hamlin, who at age 44 fired a tournament-record 9-under-par 204 in 1993. Hamlin, who had a modified radical mastectomy in the summer of 1991, returned to post her best tour years ever during the following two seasons. Breast cancer awareness became a theme of the 1994 event, when Hamlin returned as defending champion and a featured speaker at a women's health forum.

That year's champion, Donna Andrews, proved how tough an afternoon at Greate Bay can be when—after posting a 67 and a 66 in the opening rounds—she bogeyed the 15th, double-bogeyed the 16th and bogeyed the 17th before righting herself for a finishing par and a two-stroke victory.

"JUMPING IN THE LAKE IS MY NATURE. BUT MENTALLY I'M EXHAUSTED."

—DONNA ANDREWS,

WINNER OF THE 1994 SHOPRITE CLASSIC, WHO HAD JUMPED INTO THE LAKE AFTER WINNING THE NABISCO DINAH SHORE IN 1994 BUT ELECTED NOT TO TAKE THE PLUNGE AT GREATE BAY

By John R. Johnson

New plantings and top-notch greenskeeping have revived once unpredictable greens at Greate Bay.

•TOUGHEST HOLE

The 390-yard, par-4 18th can play especially long with an incoming wind. Another difficult hole is the 380-yard, par-4 13th, whose tee shot crosses wetlands to a landing area bordered by trees to the right and more wetlands to the left. The approach is over water to a three-tiered green fronted by a bunker.

•WHO THE COURSE FAVORS

The golfer who can play in the wind, which is usually incoming on Nos. 2 through 7, and on 10 and 11. Club selection, positioning and an ability to adjust to the swirling winds, especially on approach shots, is critical.

•BEST PLACE TO WATCH

The skyboxes, grandstand and other vantage points around 18. The central area among holes Nos. 5 through 9 is a good place to wander.

HOLE	YARDS	PAR	HOLE	YARDS	PAR
1	365	4	10	395	4
2	165	3	11	330	4
3	360	4	12	185	3
4	125	3	13	380	4
5	370	4	14	170	3
6	385	4	15	360	4
7	390	4	16	535	5
8	435	5	17	360	4
9	535	5	18	390	4
			TOTAL	6235	71

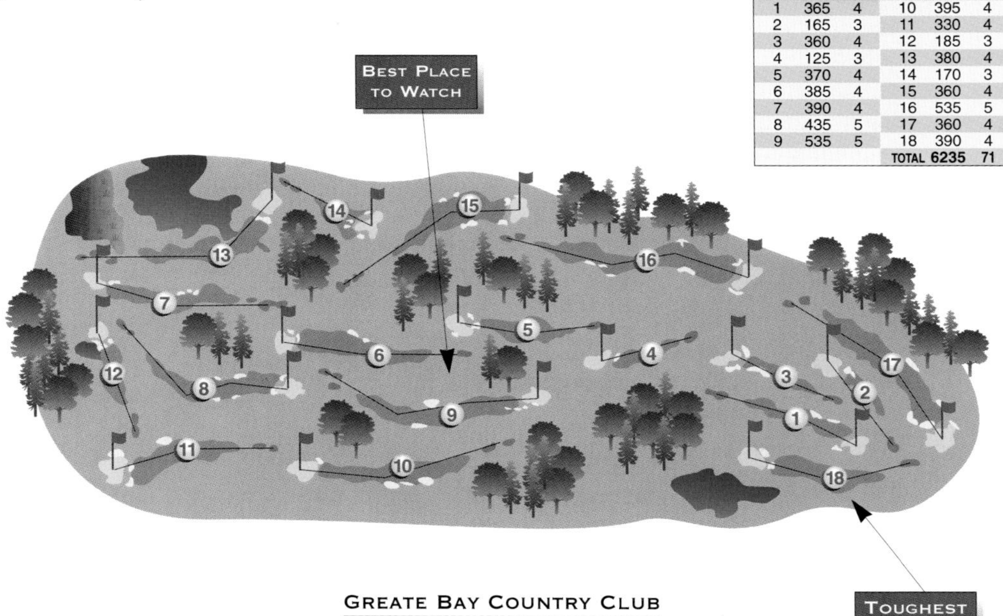

Greate Bay Country Club
Architect: William Park Jr. (1921)
Remodeled by Tom Fazio (1972),
additional three holes by Ron Garl (1989)

LODGING

$$$ Marriott's Seaview Golf Resort, U.S. Rte. 9/Shore Rd., Absecon, N.J. (609) 652-1800, (800) 228-9290. 40 minutes from Greate Bay.

$$ Marriott's Residence Inn, 900 Mays Landing Rd., Somers Point, N.J. (609) 927-6400, (800) 331-3131. Within walking distance of Greate Bay.

$ Biscayne Suites, 820 Ocean Ave., Ocean City, N.J. (609) 391-8800. 5 minutes from Greate Bay.

For other accommodations contact: Accommodations Express, 1095 Blackhorse Pike, West Atlantic City, N.J. (800) 444-7666.

DINING

Ram's Head Inn, 9 W. White Horse Pike, Absecon, N.J. (609) 652-1700.

19th Hole Bar and Grill, at the Greate Bay clubhouse, 901 Mays Landing Rd., Somers Point, N.J. (609) 927-0066.

PUBLIC COURSES TO PLAY IN AREA

Blue Heron Pines Golf Club, 550 W. Country Club Dr., Galloway, N.J. Public. (609) 965-4653. 18/6,777/72. 30 minutes from Greate Bay.

Marriott's Seaview Golf Resort, U.S. Route 9/Shore Rd., Absecon, N.J. Resort. (609) 652-1800, (800) 228-9290. Pines: 18/6,885/71. Bay: 18/6,263/71. 40 minutes from Greate Bay.

Ocean County Golf Course at Atlantis, Country Club Blvd., South Tuckerton, N.J. Public. (609) 296-2444. 18/6,848/72. 30 minutes from Greate Bay.

TICKETS & ACCESSIBILITY

How to watch: Mon., LPGA practice rounds. Tue., pro-am event. Wed., pro-am. Thur., LPGA practice rounds, shootout, junior golf clinic. Fri.-Sun., tournament. Daily individual tickets start at $8. Group and sponsorship packages available. ShopRite LPGA Classic, 599 Shore Rd., Suite 202, Somers Point, NJ 08244, (609) 927-7888.

How to play: Greate Bay is open to the public year round. High season is May through September. Reservations can be made up to three days in advance. (609) 927-0066. Packages available through on-site Marriott's Residence Inn. Tee times can be reserved when you book your hotel room. (609) 927-6400, (800) 331-3131.

Youngstown-Warren LPGA Classic

AVALON LAKES GOLF COURSE

A 1968 creation of Pete Dye, Avalon Lakes is a long, flat shotmaker's course like his 1964 masterpiece, Crooked Stick, but its fairways are narrowed slightly by majestic oaks, pines, maples and several lakes and ponds. Its well-bunkered, undulating greens make difficult target practice for mid-iron approaches.

Dye's wife and business partner, Alice—an outstanding amateur golfer and the first woman named to the American Society of Golf Course Architects—assisted him in the course's design and most notably influenced the positioning and distance of the red tees.

But the LPGA players step back to the blue or white tees to play Avalon Lakes at slightly over 6,300 yards, just 150 yards shy of the distance from the regular tees. While the par-3s are considered very difficult for men (at 184, 235, 209 and 183 yards from the back tees), the par-4s have been the tough holes at the Youngstown-Warren Classic. The 365-yard first hole, for example, plays to a landing area framed by large trees to the left and a pond to the right. Incoming winds can make No. 15, a 392-yard par-4; No. 17, a 380-yard par-4; and No. 18, a 451-yard par-5, play much longer. With hazards pinching its landing areas and bunkers or trees narrowing the approach angles, Avalon Lakes requires you to position your tee shots well before taking aim at the windswept targets.

The LPGA professionals have more success with the par-5s, which have all played under par in stroke average for the field. It was at the 18th that Nancy Lopez, down by two, fired an eagle to force a playoff with Deb Richard in 1993. Lopez then birdied the same hole to seize a victory in sudden-death. With crowds shouting, "Go Ohio, Go Ohio," Tammie Green—the pride of nearby Somerset—led almost wire-to-wire in 1994, when she had to play 32 holes the final day because of rain. Green finished with 67-69-70–206 to edge Colleen Walker by two strokes, marking the first time that this tournament, which debuted as the Phar-Mor in 1990, was not decided by a playoff.

TOURNAMENT-AT-A-GLANCE

Course: Avalon Lakes Golf Course
Type: Public
Location: One American Way, Warren, OH 44484
Telephone: (216) 856-8898
When: Late June to Early July
How To Get There: From Pittsburgh, 70 miles via Rte. 76 to Rte. 680 to I-80. East on I-80 to Rte. 11. North on Rte. 11 to second exit, Rte. 82. Take Rte. 82 west to Howland-Wilson Rd.; make right on Howland-Wilson to stop sign. Take right (E. Market St.) to Avalon Inn and golf course.
70 miles from Cleveland via I-80 east to Rte. 5 bypass to Howland-Wilson exit. Take left on Howland-Wilson Rd. to stop sign (E. Market St.). Make right on East Market to Avalon Inn and golf course.
Broadcast: None (1995)
Purse: $600,000 (1996)
Tournament Record: 13-under-par 203, Nancy Lopez, 1993

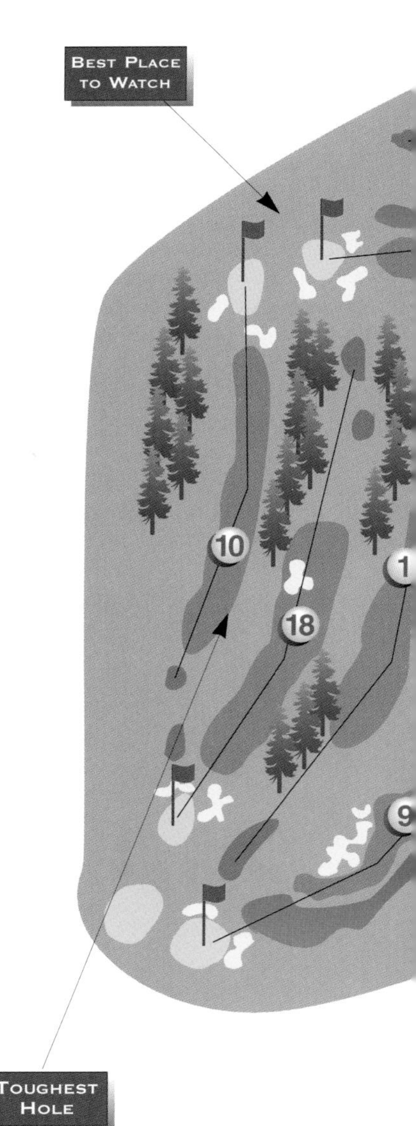

FEATURING A STEEP ASCENT FROM TEE TO FAIRWAY, WYKAGYL'S 18TH HAS STAGED MANY MEMORABLE FINISHES.

●TOUGHEST HOLE

The 377-yard, par-4 14th, whose tee shot must lay up just short of a brook that crosses a left-side landing area. From there, it's a long approach to a green flanked by two large bunkers. Another difficult hole is the 233-yard, par-3 seventh, which plays down a steep drop to a deep green with a horseshoe-shaped cluster of six bunkers to its sides and rear.

●BEST PLACE TO WATCH

The corner of the course near No. 12 enables you to follow the action on a variety of holes within a short walking distance. Other prime vantage points are behind the greens of Nos. 9 and 18, and the gallery areas behind the tees of Nos. 1 and 2.

●WHO THE COURSE FAVORS

Long hitters like Davies and Daniel, who can cut the corners on doglegs and hit lofted irons on approach shots. Control off the tee is also required, as is a solid short game around the heavily bunkered greens.

HOLE	YARDS	PAR	HOLE	YARDS	PAR
1	493	5	10	401	4
2	155	3	11	365	4
3	472	5	12	398	4
4	197	3	13	138	3
5	387	4	14	377	4
6	347	4	15	430	5
7	223	3	16	157	3
8	353	4	17	384	4
9	343	4	18	475	5
			TOTAL	6095	71

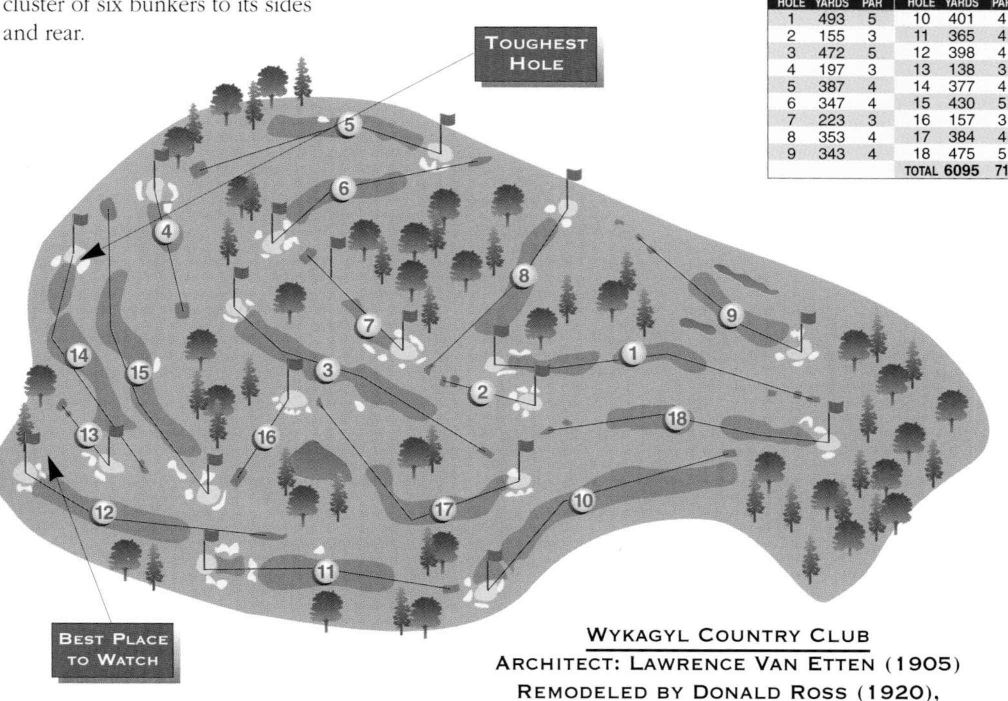

WYKAGYL COUNTRY CLUB
ARCHITECT: LAWRENCE VAN ETTEN (1905)
REMODELED BY DONALD ROSS (1920),
ROBERT WHITE (1923), A.W. TILLINGHAST (1931),
HAL PURDY (1966), STEPHEN KAY (1990)

LODGING

$$$ Doral Arrowwood, Anderson Hill Rd., Rye Brook, N.Y. (914) 939-5500. 20 minutes from Wykagyl.
$$ Stouffer Westchester Hotel, 80 W. Red Oak Lane, White Plains, N.Y. (914) 694-5400. 15 minutes from Wykagyl.
$ Courtyard by Marriott, 631 Midland Ave., Rye, N.Y. (914) 921-1110. 20 minutes from Wykagyl.

DINING

Mama Francesca, 414 Pelham Rd., New Rochelle, N.Y. (914) 636-1229
Cobble Creek Cafe, 578 Anderson Hill Rd., Purchase, N.Y. (914) 761-0050.
The Rye Grill & Bar, 1 Station Plaza, Rye, N.Y. (914) 967-0332.

PUBLIC COURSES TO PLAY IN AREA

Bethpage Black Course, Round Swamp Rd., Farmingdale, Long Island, N.Y. Public. (516) 249-0701. 18/7,065/71. 1 hour from Wykagyl.
Doral Arrowwood Golf Club, Anderson Hill Rd., Rye Brook, N.Y. Resort (must be a guest to play). (914) 939-5500, (800) 22-DORAL. 18/6,300/70. 15 minutes from Wykagyl.
Spook Rock Golf Course, 199 Spook Rock Rd., Ramapo, N.Y. Public. (914) 357-6466. 18/6,894/72. 45 minutes from Wykagyl.

TICKETS & ACCESSIBILITY

How to watch: Mon., celebrity pro-am, LPGA qualifier. Tue., LPGA practice rounds, shootout, junior golf clinic. Wed., pro-am. Thur.-Sun., tournament. Any day single ticket prices begin at $5 with group and sponsorship packages available. JAL Big Apple Classic, 1266 East Main St., 7th Floor, Stamford, CT 06902. (203) 363-1095, (800) 444-LPGA.
How to play: Private club. You must be the guest of a member to play. Limited reciprocal play is permitted. The course is open from mid-April through October. (914) 636-8700.

McCall's LPGA Classic at Stratton Mountain

Stratton Mountain Country Club

The grass-covered ski runs of southern Vermont's majestic Green Mountains loom just above this challenging 18-hole hike. Crossed by picturesque brooks and rippled by rolling hills, its tree-lined Geoffrey Cornish layout is a natural preserve for three of the LPGA tour's toughest 20 holes.

Besides its mountain scenery, the course is distinguished by uneven lies, abundant water hazards, and mounds, swales and dropoffs around its amicably large greens.

One of the most difficult holes is the 390-yard, par-4 second, a sharp dogleg left on the Lake nine. Mature trees and a bunker guard the left turn of the fairway, forcing players to drive wide. The approach is slightly uphill to a sizable green with a ridge in its center and a deep bunker to its left front. A mounded amphitheater frames the back of the green and a stream cuts in front. Hitting the target can be even more challenging when wind kicks up off the nearby lake.

The Mountain Course, played as the back nine in this tournament, can unsettle the players with its 270-yard, par-4 12th and its 525-yard, par-5 14th. The 12th demands a precise drive to the right, while the two streams that cross the 14th limit the field of players who can gun for birdies.

There is a fine finishing hole, a 465-yard, par-5 dogleg left with a fairway bunker in the left landing area. The tee shot is blind, but when the players come over a rise midway to the green, their eyes take in the clubhouse and a forward-sloping putting surface that is sandwiched by large traps and guarded by a pond farther to the right.

In the inaugural Classic, Cathy Gering won a sudden-death playoff by cutting the dogleg and then knocking a 4-iron approach to within 5 feet of the hole. 1994 champion Carolyn Hill, who had not won an event in 14 years on the LPGA tour, made the ninth another memorable hole when she dared a three-wood approach to its pond-protected green. Her shot landed just off the green, and her bold birdie restored a one-stroke lead that she never relinquished.

TOURNAMENT-AT-A-GLANCE

Course: Stratton Mountain Country Club—Mountain and Lake Courses
Type: Resort
Location: Stratton Mountain, VT 05155
Telephone: (802) 297-2200, (800) 843-6867
When: Early August
How To Get There: Take Rte. 30 to Bondville. Turn onto Stratton Mountain Access Rd. to resort, which is 81 miles northeast of Albany, N.Y.
Broadcast: ESPN (1996)
Purse: $500,000 (1995)
Tournament Record: 13-under-par 275, Dana Lofland-Dormann, 1993 and Carolyn Hill, 1994

Courtesy of McCall's

THE SKI SLOPES OF THE GREEN MOUNTAINS OVERLOOK THE EQUALLY TREACHEROUS TERRAIN OF STRATTON MOUNTAIN'S LAKE AND MOUNTAIN COURSES.

Stratton Mountain Country Club–Mountain and Lake Courses

Architect: Geoffrey Cornish (1965)

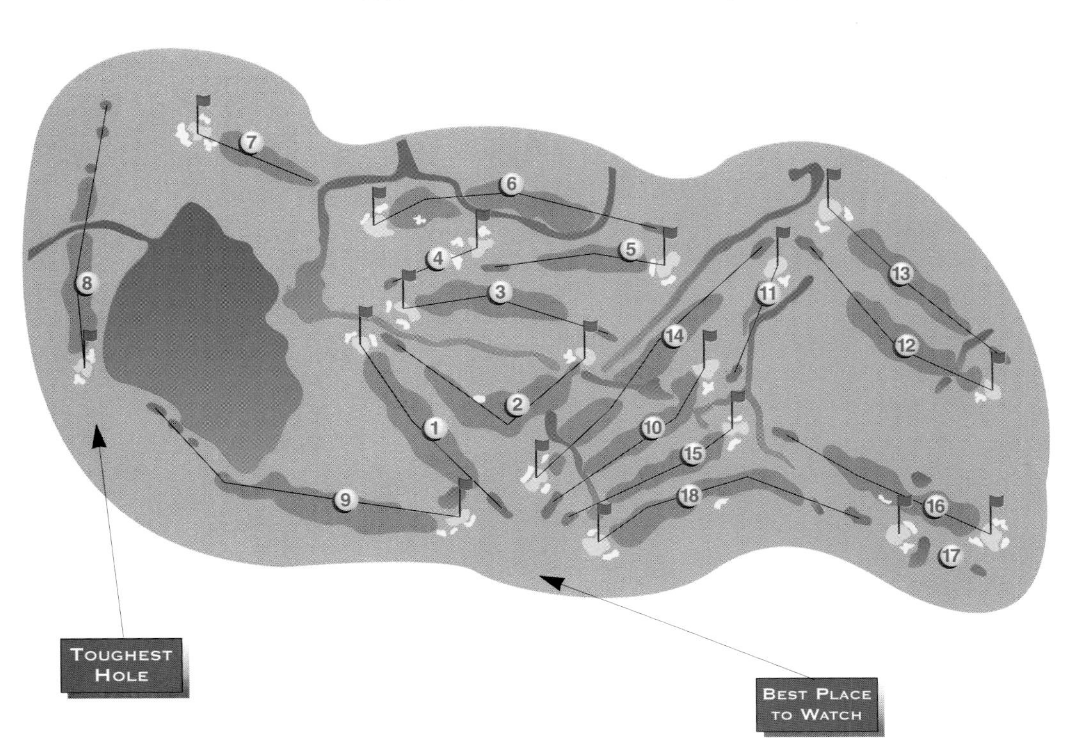

HOLE	YARDS	PAR
1	385	4
2	390	4
3	355	4
4	164	3
5	305	4
6	492	5
7	150	3
8	390	4
9	430	5
10	354	4
11	160	3
12	270	4
13	382	4
14	525	5
15	327	4
16	385	4
17	158	3
18	465	5
TOTAL	6087	72

●TOUGHEST HOLE

The 390-yard, par-4 eighth was rated the 12th most difficult on the tour in 1994. It plays from an elevated tee over a stream to a landing area framed by trees to the left and a stream to the right. The approach is to a slightly raised, deep green guarded by two bunkers to its right and another to the left front. A left-to-right crosswind from Stratton Lake can make the hole play longer.

●BEST PLACE TO WATCH

Both tournament nines finish near a hilltop clubhouse where you can take in the action from an outdoor restaurant. If you wander out to the lake side of the 18th you'll also have a good view of tee shots on the 10th.

●WHO THE COURSE FAVORS

Stratton Mountain plays a long 6,087 yards because of its elevation changes, uneven lies and wind conditions. Distance off the tee and shot placement are critical because of some blind shots and a variety of hazards that can alter approach-shot strategies. Good shotmaking is required when coming into greens protected by water and sand.

LODGING

$$$ The Equinox, Historic Rte. 7A, Manchester Village, Vt. (802) 362-4700, (800) 362-4747. 25 minutes from Stratton Mountain Country Club.

$$ Stratton Mountain Inn, Stratton Mountain, Vt. (802) 297-2200, (800) 843-6867. 5 minutes from Stratton Mountain Country Club.

$ Red Fox Inn, Windhall Hollow Rd., Bondville, Vt. (802) 297-2488. 10 minutes from Stratton Mountain Country Club.

DINING

The Arlington Inn, Historic Rte. 7A, Arlington, Vt. (802) 375-6532.

The Red Fox Inn, Windhill Hollow Rd., Bondville, Vt. (802) 297-2488.

Mulligan's, Village Square, Stratton Mountain, Stratton, Vt. (802) 297-9293.

PUBLIC COURSES TO PLAY IN AREA

Gleneagles Golf Course, Historic Route 7A, Manchester Village, Vt. Resort. (802) 362-3223. 18/6,423/71. 25 minutes from Stratton Mountain Country Club.

Manchester Country Club, Beech St., Manchester, Vt. Private (tee times available if you stay at selected hotels such as The Equinox). (802) 362-2233. 18/6,742/72. 25 minutes from Stratton Mountain Country Club.

Rutland Country Club, North Grove St., Rutland, Vt. Semi-private. (802) 773-3254. 18/6,062/70. 1 hour from Stratton Mountain Country Club.

TICKETS & ACCESSIBILITY

How to watch: Mon., LPGA practice rounds. Tue., LPGA practice rounds, junior golf clinic. Wed., pro-am tournament. Thur.-Sun., tournament. Individual tickets from $6. Group and sponsorship plans available. McCall's LPGA Classic, P.O. Box 638, Stratton Mountain, Vermont 05155, (802) 297-3616.

How to play: All three nine-hole resort courses (Lake, Mountain, Forest) are open to guests and the public. Packages are available through the resort. Courses open mid-May through October. Stratton Mountain Golf School on site at its Geoffrey Cornish/Arnold Palmer–designed, 22-acre facility. (802) 297-2200.

Friendly's Classic
CRESTVIEW COUNTRY CLUB

Home of the only LPGA tournament played in two states, Crestview Country Club is an open farmland course with 15 holes in Massachusetts and three in Connecticut. Course designer Geoffrey Cornish, whose Stratton Mountain Country Club hosts the McCall's LPGA Classic, spiced this late 1950s layout with water hazards on eight holes and tiered greens well protected by medium-sized bunkers. The bentgrass greens hold incoming shots well, but once you get there the slick surfaces make it easy to miss putts. Variable winds can also affect play at Crestwood, putting a premium on accuracy and distance off the tee, club selection and well-positioned approaches. Incoming winds on No. 10, a 355-yard par-4; No. 15, a 390-yard par-4; and No. 16, a 365-yard par-4, should add drama to concluding rounds at Friendly's fledgling Classic.

TOURNAMENT-AT-A-GLANCE

Course: Crestview Country Club
Type: Private
Location: Shoemaker Lane, Agawam, MA 01001
Telephone: (413) 786-2593
When: Late July
How To Get There: I-91 south to Exit 3. Bear right over bridge, take first exit and go around rotary to Rte. 57. Take third exit off Rte. 57. Turn left onto Rte. 75. At third set of lights, turn right onto Shoemaker Lane; follow 3/4 mile to golf course.
Broadcast: None (1995)
Purse: $500,000 (1995)
Tournament record: 12-under-par 276, Becky Iverson, 1995

●TOUGHEST HOLE
The 372-yard, par-4 4th, which the LPGA plays from the back tees, is rated the most difficult hole on the course. A slight dogleg right, the tee shot landing area is guarded by a bunker to the right. If the tee shot is not properly positioned to the left-center of the fairway, a trap guarding the right front of the green can come into play. A large trap guards the back of the small green.

●WHO THE COURSE FAVORS
Crestview favors a big hitter who can fly the ball into greens well-protected by bunkers and rough. The variable winds on this layout can also curtail distance and accuracy. The soft fairways give little roll.

HOLE	YARDS	PAR
1	401	4
2	536	5
3	155	3
4	372	4
5	390	4
6	185	3
7	445	5
8	359	4
9	408	4
10	355	4
11	150	3
12	462	5
13	380	4
14	154	3
15	390	4
16	365	4
17	495	5
18	379	4
TOTAL	6381	72

●BEST PLACE TO WATCH
Crestview is an easy course for the spectator to walk. A dramatic amphitheater-like setting behind the 18th provides an excellent view of the 379-yard, par-4 finishing hole, which plays uphill to a well-bunkered, steep, sloped green. You should also try the areas around the first green, which provide views of the No. 17 and No. 7 tees, and of the No. 6 and No. 16 greens.

CRESTVIEW COUNTRY CLUB
ARCHITECT: GEOFFREY S. CORNISH (1957)

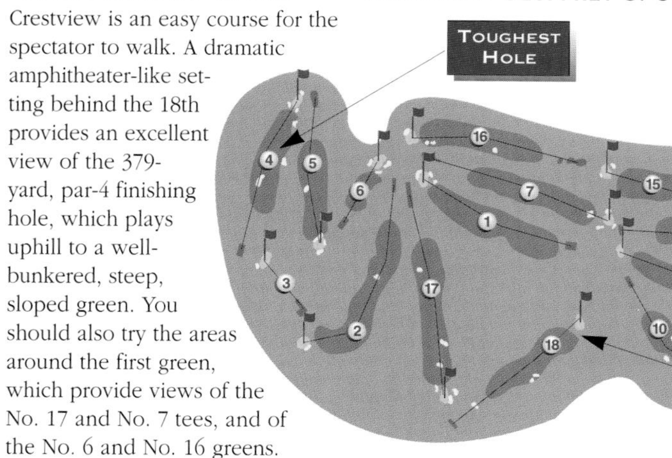

LODGING
$$$ Springfield Marriott Hotel, Boland Way and Columbus Ave., Springfield, Mass. (413) 781-7111. 20 minutes from Crestview.
$$ Ramada Hotel, 1080 Riverdale St. (U.S. 5), West Springfield, Mass. (413) 781-8750. 10 minutes from Crestview.
$ Howard Johnson Bed & Breakfast, 1150 Riverdale St., West Springfield, Mass. (413) 739-7261. 10 minutes from Crestview.

DINING
The Delaney House, Rte. 5 at Smith's Ferry, Holyoke, Mass. (413) 532-1800.
Barclay's at the Ramada Hotel, 1080 Riverdale St. (U.S. 5), West Springfield, Mass. (413) 781-8750.
Sorrowtown Tavern, 1305 Memorial Ave., West Springfield, Mass. (413) 732-4188.

PUBLIC COURSES TO PLAY IN AREA
Crumpin-Fox Club, Parmeater Rd., Bernardston, Mass. Public. (413) 648-9101. 18/7,007/72. 1 hour from Crestview.
Hampden Country Club, 128 Wilbraham Rd., Hampden, Mass. Semi-private. (413) 566-8010. 18/6,833/72. 45 minutes from Crestview.
Oak Ridge Golf Club, 850 South Westfield, Feeding Hills, Mass. Semi-private. (413) 789-7307. 18/6,819/70. 10 minutes from Crestview.

TICKETS & ACCESSIBILITY
How to watch: Mon., LPGA qualifier, LPGA practice rounds, junior golf clinic. Tues., pro-am event, shootout. Wed., pro-am. Thurs.-Sun., tournament. Admission free Mon. Individual tickets start at $5 thereafter. Group and sponsorship plans available. Friendly's Classic, c/o Friendly's Ice Cream Corp., 1855 Boston Rd., Wilbraham, MA 01095. (413) 543-2400.
How to play: Private club. You must be the guest of a member to play the course. Limited reciprocal play. Open year round. Prime season April to October. (413) 786-0917.

STATE FARM RAIL CLASSIC

RAIL GOLF CLUB

LODGING

$$$ Springfield Hilton, 700 E. Adams St., Springfield, Ill. (217) 789-1530. 15 minutes from the Rail GC.
$$ Holiday Inn East, 3100 S. Dirkson Pkwy., Springfield, Ill. (217) 529-7171, (800) HOLIDAY. 30 minutes from the Rail GC.
$ Red Roof Inn, 3200 Singer Ave., Springfield, Ill. (217) 753-4302, (800) THE ROOF. 10 minutes from the Rail GC.

DINING

City Lights on 30, at the Springfield Hilton, 700 E. Adams St. at 7th, Springfield, Ill. (217) 789-1530.
Saputo's, 801 E. Monroe St., Springfield, Ill. (217) 544-2523.
Feed Store, 516 E. Adams St., Springfield, Ill. (217) 528-3355.

PUBLIC COURSES TO PLAY IN AREA

Eagle Creek Resort Golf Course, Eagle Creek State Rd., Findlay, Ill. Resort. (217) 756-3456, (800) 876-3245. 18/6908/72. 1 1/2 hours from the Rail GC.
Lincoln Greens Golf Club, 700 E. Lake Dr., Springfield, Ill. Public. (217) 786-4000. 18/6,500/72. 15 minutes from the Rail GC.
Spencer T. Olin Community Golf Course, 4701 College Ave., Alton, Ill. Public. (618) 465-3111. 18/6,941/72. 1 hour from the Rail GC.

TICKETS & ACCESSIBILITY

How to watch: Tue., LPGA practice rounds. Wed., LPGA practice rounds, pro-am event. Thur., LPGA practice rounds, supershot contest, pro-am. Fri., pro-am. Sat.-Mon., tournament. Admission to practice rounds free through Wed. Individual, group and sponsorship packages available. State Farm Rail Classic, 427 E. Monroe St., Suite 301, Springfield, IL 62701, (217) 528-5742, (800) 545-7300 (lodging information).
How to play: The Rail is a public golf course open March through December. Call five days in advance for tee times. (217) 525-0365.

TOURNAMENT-AT-A-GLANCE

Course: Rail Golf Club
Type: Public
Location: Rural Rte. 5 and Rural Rte. 124 N., Springfield, IL 62707
Telephone: (217) 525-0365
When: Early September
How To Get There: From Springfield, 20 minutes. Take I-55 north to Sherman Exit. South on Sherman; follow signs to golf course.
Broadcast: Prime Network (1995)
Purse: $575,000 (1996)
Tournament Record: 17-under-par 271, Hollis Stacy, 1977 (72-hole record); 19-under-par 197, Pat Bradley, 1991 (54-hole record)

Open fairways and true-rolling greens set the stage for an annual Labor Day shootout at this public, farmland course just north of Springfield, Ill., burial place of that old rail-splitter, Abraham Lincoln.

Some of the tour's lowest scores have been recorded on this Robert Trent Jones Jr. layout, including Pat Bradley's standard-setting 19-under-par 197 in 1991. The course, opened just two years before this long-running event's 1976 debut, is now dotted with maturing oaks, maples, and white and Australian pines. Birdie opportunities still abound, but its rough is now grown longer for tournament play, and softer sand has toughened up some of its bunkers. Shifting winds can sometimes make club selection an adventure.

Before calling the course easy, consider Laura Davies' 1994 collapse. Leading by four strokes entering the final round, she ballooned to a 77 after dumping two shots into one of The Rail's troubling water hazards.

●TOUGHEST HOLE

The 531-yard, par-5 17th has water running up its right side and fronting an elevated green protected by three traps. An incoming wind forces most players to lay up in two and settle for par. Accuracy on both the tee shot and second shot is essential to score here.

HOLE	YARDS	PAR	HOLE	YARDS	PAR
1	367	4	10	366	4
2	183	3	11	391	4
3	506	5	12	378	4
4	370	4	13	491	5
5	399	4	14	135	3
6	505	5	15	372	4
7	167	3	16	168	3
8	335	4	17	531	5
9	363	4	18	376	4
			TOTAL	6403	72

●BEST PLACE TO WATCH

The skyboxes above the 18th and the bleachers around nine and 18 are prime viewing spots. The course is easy to walk; a vantage point behind green No. 8 offers views of No. 18, and the area behind green No. 14 has views of green No. 16 and tee No. 17.

●WHO THE COURSE FAVORS

Although the maturing trees have filled in The Rail, it is still easy to reach the greens. The golfer who can putt well and avoid the water hazards, especially on No. 17, has a solid chance in this tournament.

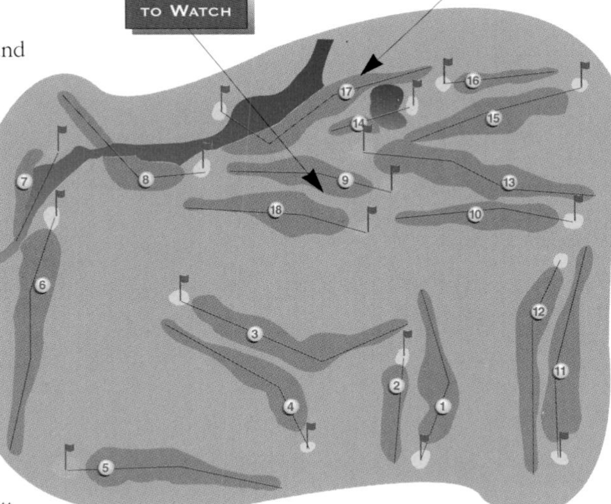

RAIL GOLF CLUB
ARCHITECT: ROBERT TRENT JONES JR. (1974)

PING/Welch's Championship (Mass.)

BLUE HILL COUNTRY CLUB

Blue Hill was designed by an apprentice to Donald Ross, but it has all the earmarks of the master.

Woven gracefully into rolling, tree-lined hills 30 minutes southwest of Boston, the course is somewhat forgiving from the tees but requires ingenuity to fly from its uneven lies to its well-guarded greens.

Skip Wogan, who apprenticed under Ross at the Essex Country Club in Manchester, Mass., often had his mentor by his side when he laid out the first nine at Blue Hill in 1950. Five years later, Wogan and his son Philip completed the course just in time to host the 1956 PGA Championship, which Jack Burke Jr. won in the event's next-to-last year of match play.

The undulating greens at Blue Hill are well-protected by sculpted sand traps nestled close to the putting surfaces. There are relatively few fairway bunkers, but mature oaks, pines and maples punish shots that go astray. The soft fairways provide little roll, and uneven lies are routine.

The front nine plays tougher than the back, with the 417-yard, par-4 first, the 386-yard, par-4 third and the 176-yard, par-3 fourth all averaging higher than par in tournament play. The toughest holes on the back nine are the 405-yard, par-4 11th and the 389-yard, par-4 14th.

Strokes tend to be made up on the par-5s, including the 469-yard finishing hole, which big hitters can tame in two. This hole, along with the 451-yard, par-5 ninth and the 325-yard, par-4 second, tend to be the easiest holes for the LPGA pros.

The 1993 PING/Welch's Championship featured one of the event's most exciting finishes, when defending champion Dottie Mochrie and then-winless tour veteran Missie Berteotti went five extra holes in sudden death. After watching Mochrie two-putt from 18 feet on the deciding hole, Berteotti knocked her own 18-footer in for a birdie. The 1994 event brought sweet redemption for winner Helen Alfredsson. A week earlier, the 29-year-old Swede had plummeted from an early eight-stroke lead to finish tied for ninth in the U.S. Women's Open. At Blue Hill, she fought off Juli Inkster and hometown favorite Pat Bradley by sinking birdies on holes 10, 12, 14, 15 and 18 to close with a 66 and a four-stroke victory.

TOURNAMENT-AT-A-GLANCE

Course: Blue Hill Country Club
Type: Private
Location: 23 Pecunit St., Canton, MA 02021
Telephone: (617) 828-2000
When: Mid-August
How To Get There: Take Rte. 128 to Exit 2A. Exit to first lights, take right onto Washington St. and proceed 3/4 mile to Blue Hill sign. Take right to the club.
Broadcast: WCVB-TV (Needham, Mass.) (1995)
Purse: $450,000 (1995)
Tournament Record: 16-under-par 272, Amy Alcott, 1989 (at par-72 Sheraton Tara Hotel Resort, Danvers, Mass.)

By Leonard M. Burg

The obstacles and uneven lies at Blue Hill can turn a stray shot into a wild goose chase.

●TOUGHEST HOLE

Blue Hill's two most difficult holes are past by the time a player leaves the third green. The 417-yard first hole, one of the longest par-4s on the tour, was rated the fifth-most-difficult hole on the tour in 1994. It has a wide fairway, but many players will be hitting fairway woods from a downhill lie to a green trapped on its front left. The 386-yard, par-4 third has a narrow landing area with out-of-bounds to the left. A large bunker sits in front and to the left of the green.

●BEST PLACE TO WATCH

Blue Hill is an easy course on which to follow the players. From behind the 11th green you can see the No. 16 tee, No. 15 green, and No. 12 tee. The natural amphitheater setting behind No. 18 is another good vantage point.

●WHO THE COURSE FAVORS

Blue Hill plays a long 6,137 yards because its soft fairways yield little roll, its elevation changes create uneven lies and its well-bunkered greens demand high approaches from lofted clubs. Pat Bradley, born in nearby Westford, Mass., is always a crowd favorite here but has never won the event.

BLUE HILL COUNTRY CLUB

ARCHITECTS: SKIP WOGAN (NINE HOLES, (1950)
ADDITIONAL NINE BY SKIP AND PHIL WOGAN (1955)
REMODELED BY MANNY FRANCIS (1956),
BRIAN SILVA AND GEOFFREY CORNISH (1985)

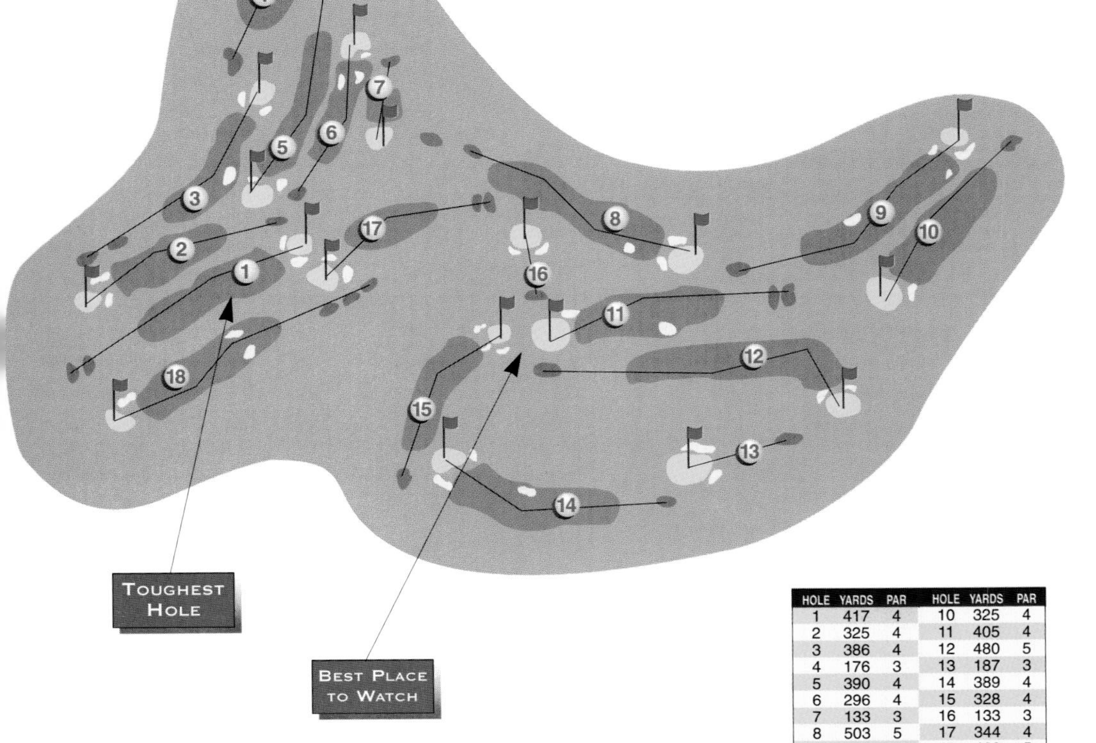

HOLE	YARDS	PAR	HOLE	YARDS	PAR
1	417	4	10	325	4
2	325	4	11	405	4
3	386	4	12	480	5
4	176	3	13	187	3
5	390	4	14	389	4
6	296	4	15	328	4
7	133	3	16	133	3
8	503	5	17	344	4
9	451	5	18	469	5
			TOTAL	6137	72

LODGING

$$$ Sheraton Tara Hotel–Braintree, 37 Forbes Rd., Braintree, Mass. (617) 848-0600. 20 minutes from Blue Hill.

$$ Courtyard by Marriott–Stoughton, 200 Technology Center Dr., Stoughton, Mass. (617) 297-7000. 15 minutes from Blue Hill.

$ Super 8 Motel, 395 Old Post Rd., Sharon, Mass. (617) 784-1000. 15 minutes from Blue Hill.

Bed and breakfast reservation service in the region: Bed & Breakfast Associates Bay Colony Ltd., P.O. Box 57166, Babson Park Branch, Boston, MA 02157, (617) 449-5302.

DINING

Gables, at the Hilton at Dedham Place, 95 Dedham Pl., Dedham, Mass. (617) 329-7900.

Aesop's Tables, Wellesley, Mass. (508) 349-6450.

Union Oyster House, 41 Union St., Boston, Mass. (617) 227-2750.

PUBLIC COURSES TO PLAY IN AREA

New England Country Club, 180 Paine St., Bellingham, Mass. Public. (508) 883-2300. 18/6,815/72. 20 minutes from Blue Hill.

New Seabury Resort and Conference Center, Great Neck Rd., New Seabury, Mass. Resort. (508) 477-9110. Blue: 18/7,200/72. Green: 18/5,939/72. 1 hour from Blue Hill.

Shaker Hills Golf Club, Shaker Rd., Harvard, Mass. Public. (508) 772-2227. 18/6,850/71. 45 minutes from Blue Hill.

TICKETS & ACCESSIBILITY

How to watch: Mon., LPGA practice rounds, pro-am tournament. Tue., LPGA practice rounds, junior golf clinic. Wed., pro-am. Thur.-Sun., tournament. Individual tickets start at $6. Group and sponsorship plans available. Ping/Welch's Championship, 1320 Centre St., Suite 206, Newton Center, MA 02159, (617) 965-4114.

How to play: Private club. You must be the guest of a member to play.

PING AT&T Wireless Services LPGA Golf Championship

COLUMBIA EDGEWATER COUNTRY CLUB

Set in the forested northeastern corner of Portland—home of abundant rainfall, beautiful parks and ardent golfers—Columbia Edgewater is gentle to the eye but a stern test of strategy and concentration.

This softly rolling traditional course was designed by A. Vernon Macan, an amateur from Victoria, British Columbia, who turned to golf architecture after losing a leg in World War I. Hemmed by towering cedar forests and mature oaks, birches and pines, the layout has water on five holes and small to mid-size greens protected by large, shallow bunkers. Smart shotmaking, proper club selection and a deft touch around the greens are required at this site, which has hosted an LPGA tournament 14 times since 1974.

The subtle challenges of Columbia Edgewater—the sentinel trees, the tricky lies created by its little hills and swales—become evident as the player works through the front nine. The variety of optimum distances and angles of approach forces the golfer to plan well or risk penalties. The 355-yard, par-4 opener requires a well-placed tee shot to the left to allow a clear approach that must carry two bunkers to a back-to-front-sloping green. The most difficult hole on the front side is the 401-yard, par-4 ninth, which plays straight to a green squeezed by large traps in front.

The tournament could well be decided on the last two holes, ranked among the most difficult on the women's tour. The 372-yard, par-4 17th, a dogleg right, demands a well-placed tee shot between heavy trees and a hidden pond. The well-bunkered, three-tiered green requires precision mid-irons to avoid as many putts. The finishing hole, a 382-yard, par-4 dogleg left, again presents a narrow angle of attack from the tree-lined fairway landing area. A pond to the front left and massive willows to the right protect the front-sloping green, probably the fastest on the course. Nancy Lopez holed an 8-foot putt here to win the 1987 event by one stroke.

Founded as the Portland Classic in 1972, this event was played as a team championship from 1977 to 1982 before returning to its original format as a 54-hole title event in 1983. Lopez, who won in 1985, 1987 and 1992, teamed with Jo Ann Washam for a victory in the 1979 team event. From 1987 through 1993 the tournament was decided by a single stroke in regulation or a sudden-death playoff. In 1993, Donna Andrews parred the final hole while Tina Barrett and Missie McGeorge both finished with bogeys to tie for second. McGeorge came back a year later to fire a final-round 66 that secured her first LPGA victory with a tournament record–tying, nine-under-par total of 207. She holed a 15-foot birdie putt from the fringe on the final hole to seal her three-shot victory.

Columbia Edgewater holes come in all shapes and sizes, from the 138-yard, par-3 eighth to the 497-yard, par-5 12th. It's unlikely that a golfer would ever tire of matching wits with its challenges.

TOURNAMENT-AT-A-GLANCE

Course: Columbia Edgewater Country Club
Type: Private
Location: 2220 N.E. Marine Dr., Portland, OR 97211
Telephone: (503) 285-8354
When: Early September
How To Get There: From downtown Portland, 15 minutes. Take I-5 north to Marine Dr. East (Exit 307). Follow the signs to Marine Dr., take Marine Dr. 2.8 miles east to the golf course. From Portland Airport, 10 minutes. Follow signs to Columbia Blvd. Take Columbia Blvd. west 2 miles to 33rd. Travel north 1 1/2 miles to the end of 33rd to Marine Dr. and golf course.
Broadcast: KGW-TV (Portland) (1995)
Purse: $500,000 (1995)
Tournament Record: 9-under-par, Ayako Okamoto, 1986 and Missie McGeorge, 1994

●TOUGHEST HOLE

The 401-yard, par-4 ninth, normally the finishing hole at Columbia Edgewater, was ranked the seventh most difficult on the tour in 1994. The tee shot must be long enough to afford an approach that avoids a large right-front bunker—and accurate enough to avoid sliding down the humpbacked fairway into the rough. The 382-yard, par-4 18th punishes stray tee shots by leaving a tree-stymied approach to a fast green sloped from back to front. A cluster of willows guards the putting surface to the front right and a pond guards it to the left.

●BEST PLACES TO WATCH

The 18th green is usually the site of dramatic finishes. An easy walking course for a spectator, Columbia Edgewater has several other primary viewing points, including behind the 13th, a par-3 that plays 155 yards to a two-tiered green; the areas around the green of No. 8, a scenic 138-yard par-3; and No. 17, a 372-yard, par-4 with a severely sloping tri-level putting surface.

●WHO THE COURSE FAVORS

This tight, traditional course demands accurate tee shots to avoid being blocked by trees. But distance is required to create birdie opportunities on longer holes like the 400-yard, par-4 third, the fourth most difficult hole on the course. Big hitters like Michelle McGann and Kelly Robbins could play this course with irons only and do quite well if their short games stand the test around the small to medium-sized greens.

COLUMBIA EDGEWATER COUNTRY CLUB
ARCHITECT: A. VERNON MACAN (1925)
REMODELED BY ROBERT MUIR GRAVES (1966),
WILLIAM F. BELL (1970),
ROBERT CUPP (1993)

HOLE	YARDS	PAR	HOLE	YARDS	PAR
1	355	4	10	451	5
2	151	3	11	308	4
3	400	4	12	497	5
4	382	4	13	155	3
5	466	5	14	346	4
6	350	4	15	357	4
7	450	5	16	170	3
8	138	3	17	372	4
9	401	4	18	382	4
			TOTAL	6131	72

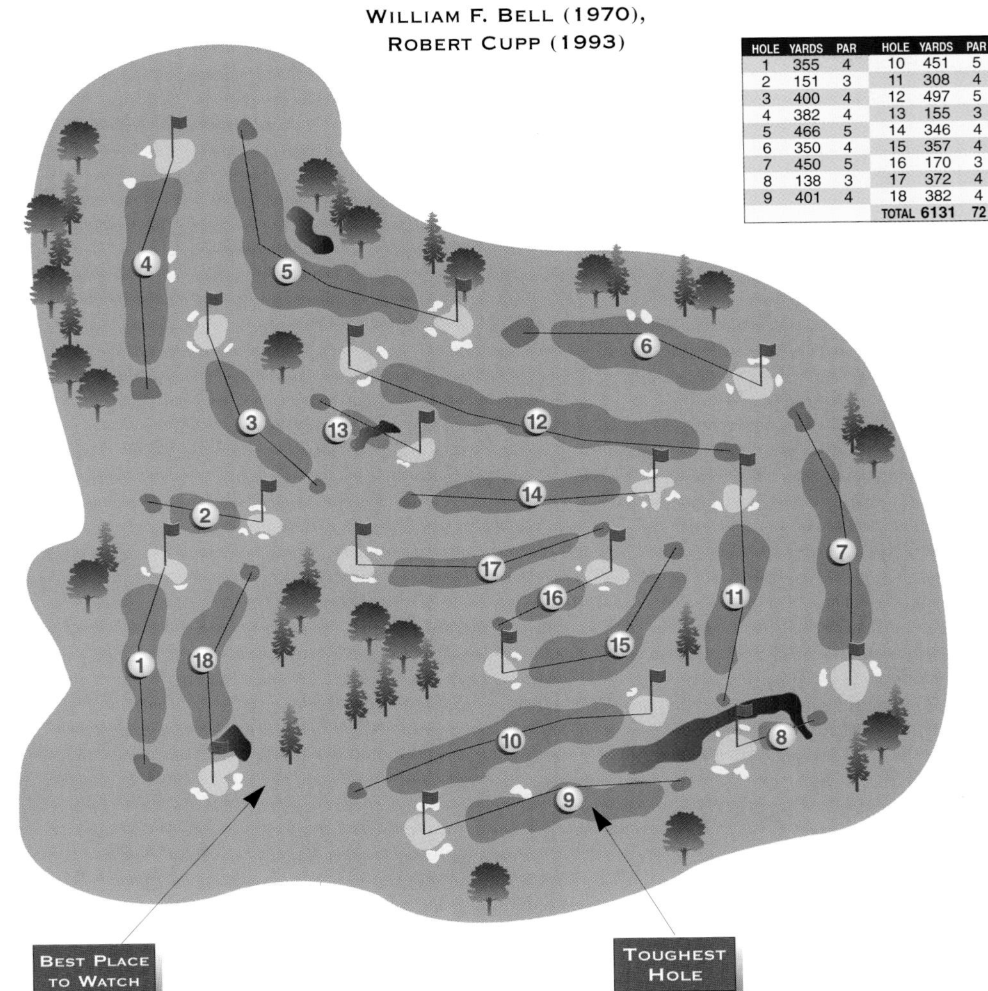

LODGING

$$$ Heathman Hotel, 1001 S.W. Broadway, Portland, Ore. (503) 241-4100, (800) 551-0011. 20 minutes from Columbia Edgewater.
$$ Red Lion Hotel–Jantzen Beach, 909 N. Hayden Island Dr., Portland, Ore. (503) 283-4466. 10 minutes from Columbia Edgewater.
$ The Red Lion And The Rose Victorian Bed & Breakfast, 1810 N.E. 15th Street, Portland, Ore. (503) 287-9245. 15 minutes from Columbia Edgewater.

DINING

L'Auberge, 2601 N.W. Vaughn, Portland, Ore. (503) 223-3302.
Jake's Famous Crawfish Restaurant, 401 S.W. 12th Ave., Portland, Ore. (503) 226-1419.
Dan & Louis Oyster Bar, 208 S.W. Ankeny St., Portland, Ore. (503) 227-5906.

PUBLIC COURSES TO PLAY IN AREA

Eastmoreland Golf Course, 2415 S.E. Bybee Blvd., Portland, Ore. Public. (503) 775-2900. 18/6,508/72. 10 minutes from Columbia Edgewater.
Heron Lakes Golf Course, 3500 North Victory Blvd., Portland, Ore. Public. (503) 289-1818. Greenback: 18/6,579/72. Great Blue: 18/6,916/72. 20 minutes from Columbia Edgewater.
Pumpkin Ridge Golf Club, 12930 Old Pumpkin Ridge Rd., Cornelius, Ore. Public. (503) 647-9977. Ghost Creek: 18/6,839/71. 15 minutes from Columbia Edgewater.

TICKETS & ACCESSIBILITY

How to watch: Tue., LPGA practice rounds. Wed., pro-am tournament, shootout, celebrity/LPGA putt-off. Thur., pro-am. Fri.-Sun., tournament. Daily tickets start at $15 with group and sponsorship packages available. AT&T Wireless Services, LPGA Golf Championship, 6775 SW 111th Street, Suite 100, Beaverton, OR 97005-5378, (503) 626-2711.
How to play: Private club. You must be the guest of a member to play. Limited reciprocals accepted. Open year round.

SAFECO Classic

MERIDIAN VALLEY COUNTRY CLUB

Meridian Valley has a knack for staging dramatic finishes. Just ask Rosie Jones, who found herself one notch short of victory in four consecutive SAFECO Classics.

"I've stood at No. 18 looking at putts that could either win the title or put me in a playoff," she said in 1993 after her third-straight runner-up finish, on this traditional, tree-lined layout. "To my dismay, three years in a row I've looked into the crowd with a half-smile and a wrench in my heart, knowing the check and the trophy is handed to another player. My memories always end at No. 18, but I'll be back. I promise."

Since two-time champion Patty Sheehan set the tournament record here in 1990 with an 18-under-par 270, the title in this event has been regularly decided on the three crucial finishing holes of this well-treed course that snakes amid streams, ponds and rolling hills about 30 minutes southeast of Seattle.

In 1993, Brandie Burton powered her way to a birdie on the track's toughest hole, the 371-yard, par-4 16th, on her way to a blistering final-round 65 that erased Jones' five-stroke edge. Most players hit a mid-iron at this dogleg right's well-bunkered, elevated green, but Burton lofted an 8-iron to within 8 feet of the cup.

The relatively easy 365-yard 17th, a dogleg left, was Chris Johnson's undoing in 1994. She eluded the pond at the left side of the fairway turn but missed both a 15-foot birdie putt and an 18-inch tap-in. "That's where I lost the tournament," she said. "Who knows where my mind was?" Another failed birdie putt on 18 gave Deb Richard the lead and dropped Johnson into a tie with three others, including, of course, Rosie Jones.

Jones used the 470-yard par-5 finishing hole to set up one of the event's most dramatic curtain-closers. Bordered by a stream on the right and playing to a green framed by a stadium-like hill, the 18th often offers birdies to SAFECO's leaders, and that's just what Jones delivered in the 1991 edition. Alas, Pat Bradley answered with a par to withstand the challenge and then knocked Jones out with a birdie on the second hole of sudden death. While Jones' near-misses now seem perennial, the SAFECO Classic's leaderboard has been topped by a variety of great champions, including Juli Inkster and Sheehan, the event's two-time winners, as well as fellow Hall of Famers Kathy Whitworth and Pat Bradley and local favorite JoAnne Carner, who hails from nearby Kirkland, Wash.

By John R. Johnson

Since 1990, the final three holes at Meridian Valley have supplied a series of finishes as dramatic as the local scenery.

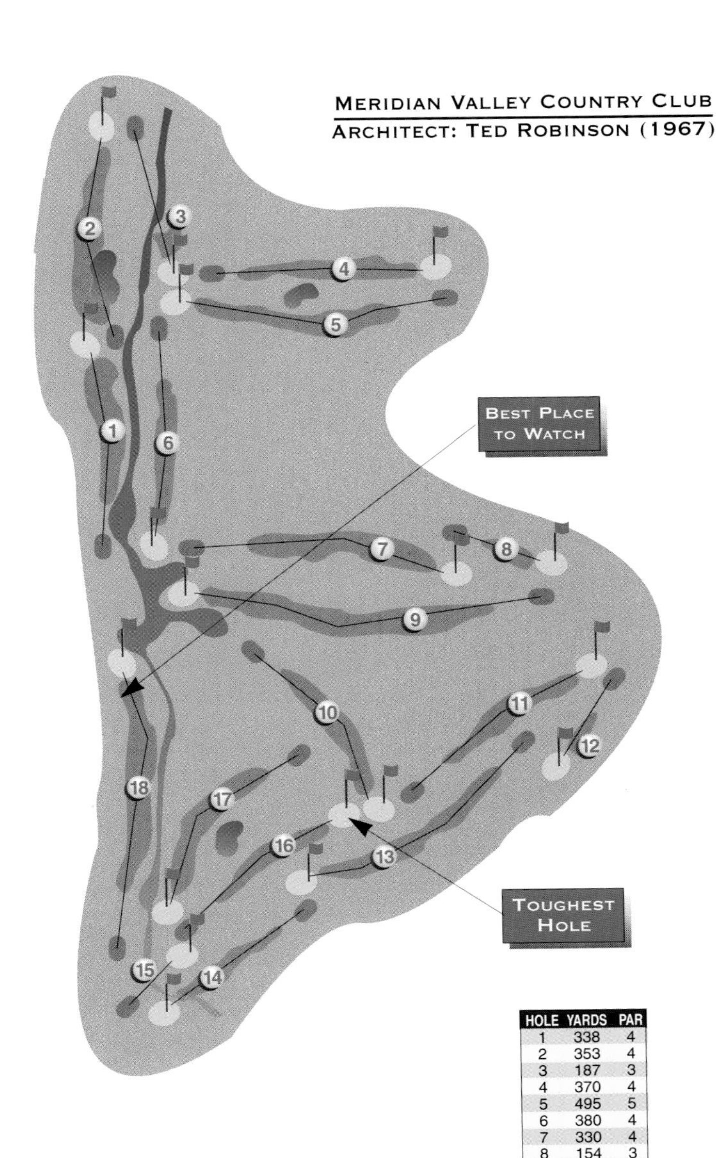

●TOUGHEST HOLE

The 371-yard 16th is set up to accommodate a slight fade to the right then a mid-iron approach to an elevated green with two bunkers to its left and one to its right. Brandie Burton hit an 8-iron to within 8 feet for a final-round birdie on this hole during her 1993 victory march.

●BEST PLACE TO WATCH

The amphitheater-like hill or the grandstands behind No. 18 are ideal for watching the final round. Try following play from behind No. 16, a 371-yard par-4, or behind No. 17, a 365-yard par-4 dogleg left whose green is protected by four bunkers.

●WHO THE COURSE FAVORS

Iron play and putting decide the tournament on this straightforward golf course. Many of the greens are elevated and well-bunkered, requiring accurate approach shots and proper club selection.

HOLE	YARDS	PAR
1	338	4
2	353	4
3	187	3
4	370	4
5	495	5
6	380	4
7	330	4
8	154	3
9	522	5
10	347	4
11	334	4
12	170	3
13	521	5
14	363	4
15	164	3
16	371	4
17	365	4
18	470	5
TOTAL	6234	72

TOURNAMENT-AT-A-GLANCE

Course: Meridian Valley Country Club
Type: Private
Location: 24830 136th Ave. SE, Kent, WA 98042
Telephone: (206) 631-3133
When: Mid-September
How To Get There: From Seattle, 30 minutes. Take I-5 south to 405 north. Take second exit to Valley Fwy. 167 south. Exit at N. Central Ave. Drive south to James then turn right onto 132nd Ave. SE; golf club on the left.
Broadcast: KIRO-TV (Seattle) (1995)
Purse: $500,000 (1995)
Tournament Record: 18-under-par 270, Patty Sheehan, 1990

LODGING

$$$ Westin Hotel Seattle, 1900 5th Ave., Seattle. (206) 728-1000. 30 minutes from Meridian Valley.
$$ Doubletree Suites, 16500 South Center Pkwy., Seattle. (206) 575-8220, (800) 222-8733. 25 minutes from Meridian Valley.
$ Best Western Choice Lodge, 24415 Russell Rd., Kent, Wash. (206) 854-8767. 5 minutes from Meridian Valley.

DINING

Metropolitan Grill, 820 2nd Ave., Seattle. (206) 624-3287.
Brooklyn Seafood, Steak and Oyster House, 1212 2nd. Ave., Seattle. (206) 224-7000.
Rose's Highway Inn, 26915 Pacific Highway South, Kent, Wash. (206) 839-7277.

PUBLIC COURSES TO PLAY IN AREA

Harbour Pointe Golf Course, 11817 Harbour Pointe Blvd., Mukliteo, Wash. Public. (206) 355-6060, (800) 233-3128 (WA). 18/6,880/72. 1 hour from Meridian Valley.
McCormick Woods, 5155 McCormick Woods Dr. Southwest, Port Orchard, Wash. Public. (360) 895-0130, (800) 323-0130 (WA). 18/7,012/72. 1 hour from Meridian Valley.
Riverbend Golf Complex, 2019 West Meeker, Kent, Wash. Public. (206) 854-3673. 18/6,603/72. 10 minutes from Meridian Valley.

TICKETS & ACCESSIBILITY

How to watch: Mon., LPGA qualifying rounds, pro-am. Tue., LPGA practice rounds, shootout, junior golf clinic. Wed., pro-am. Thur.-Sun., tournament. Individual, group and sponsorship plans available. SAFECO Classic, P.O. Box 6488, Kent, WA 98064, (206) 624-6818.
How to play: Meridian Valley is a private club. You must be the guest of a member to play. The course is open year round. Reciprocals can be arranged through the professional.

GHP Heartland Classic

Forest Hills Country Club

Laid out on rolling pastures in 1964, this course in the suburbs west of St. Louis has matured into a true test of championship golf with its tightly treed fairways, sculpted white-sand bunkers and fast, sloping greens. Designer Dick Nugent refined Chick Adam's original layout just in time for the 1994 debut of the GHP Heartland Classic.

Pearl Sinn, a 27-year-old Korean-American and former U.S. Amateur champion, captured the gallery's heart at the inaugural event when she raced out to a five-under 67 on the first round. But Liselotte Neumann, the 1988 U.S. Women's Open winner, seized the lead on the third round with her own 67, then held on for victory with birdies at two, five, nine, 11, and 12 on the final day. Sinn, who joined the tour in 1991, finished tied for second with Elaine Crosby, three shots off the pace at 281.

TOURNAMENT-AT-A-GLANCE

Course: Forest Hills Country Club
Type: Private
Location: 36 Forest Club Dr., Clarkson Valley, MO 63005
Telephone: (314) 227-1528
When: Late September
How To Get There: 20 minutes from St. Louis. Take Hwy. 40 west to the Clarkson Rd. Exit. Proceed south approximately 2 1/2 miles to the golf course.
Broadcast: None (1995)
Purse: $525,000 (1995)
Tournament Record: 10-under-par 278, Liselotte Neumann, 1994

●TOUGHEST HOLE

The 349-yard, par-4 sixth plays straight to a severely sloping green guarded by a pair of large bunkers to its front right and more bunkers to its left. This hole was ranked among the fifty most difficult holes on the Tour in 1994. Another tough hole is the 365-yard, par-4 17th, whose large, deep green wraps around a huge bunker guarding its right side.

●BEST PLACE TO WATCH

Behind No. 18, a 515-yard par-5 with a slight rise up to a green pinched by bunkers. Also, the area behind green No. 9, which plays up to a shallow green with dropoffs to one bunker on its left and two to its right.

HOLE	YARDS	PAR
1	338	4
2	402	4
3	175	3
4	392	4
5	460	5
6	349	4
7	153	3
8	507	5
9	385	4
10	365	4
11	339	4
12	375	4
13	163	3
14	334	4
15	186	3
16	560	5
17	365	4
18	515	5
TOTAL	6363	72

●WHO THE COURSE FAVORS

Forest Hills favors a complete player who can keep the ball in fairways tightly guarded by trees, bunkers and streams. Shots onto the large, fast greens must be accurate to avoid sliding down slopes into the deep bunkers.

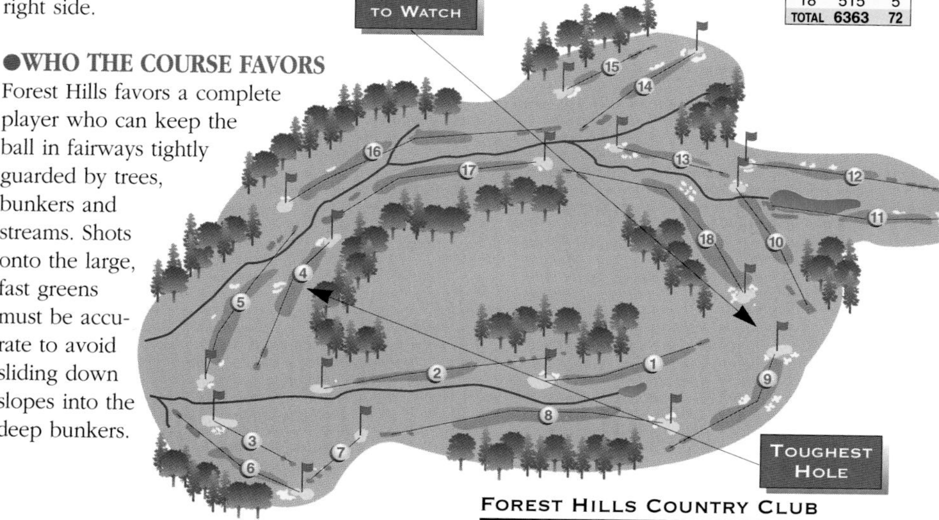

Forest Hills Country Club
Architect: Chick Adams (1965)
Remodeled by Dennis Griffiths (1987), Richard Nugent (1994)

LODGING

$$$ Ritz-Carlton St. Louis, 100 Corondelet Plaza, Clayton, Mo. (314) 863-6300. 10 minutes from Forest Hills.
$$ Residence Inn by Marriott–St. Louis Galleria, 1100 McMurrow Ave., Richmond Heights, Mo. (314) 862-1900. 15 minutes from Forest Hills.
$ Holiday Inn–Clayton Plaza, 7730 Bonhomme Ave., Clayton, Mo. (314) 863-0400. 10 minutes from Forest Hills.
For bed & breakfast accommodation information contact: Bed & Breakfast Inns of Missouri, P.O. Box 775294, St. Louis, MO 63177. (800) 83-BOOKS.

DINING

The Grill, in the Ritz-Carlton St. Louis, One Ritz-Carlton Dr., Clayton, Mo. (314) 863-6300.
Bernard's Bistro, in the Seven Gables Inn, 26 North Maramec, Clayton, Mo. (314) 863-8400.
St. Louis Bread Company, 10 South Central Ave., Clayton, Mo. (314) 725-9666.

PUBLIC COURSES TO PLAY IN THE AREA

Annbriar Golf Course, 1524 Birdie Lane, Waterloo, Ill. Public. (618) 939-4653. 18/6,841/72. 45 minutes from Forest Hills.
Crystal Highlands Golf Club, 3030 U.S. 61, Festus, Mo. Public. (314) 931-3880. 18/6,542/72. 25 minutes from Forest Hills.
Spencer T. Olin Community Golf Course, 4701 College Ave., Alton, Ill. Public. (618) 465-3111. 18/6,941/72. 1 hour from Forest Hills.

TICKETS & ACCESSIBILITY

How to watch: Mon., LPGA qualifier, celebrity pro-am event. Tue., LPGA practice rounds, shootout. Wed., pro-am. Thur.-Sun., tournament. Individual, group and sponsorship ticket plans are available. MetroTix, P.O. Box 63411, St. Louis, MO 63163. (314) 534-1111.
How to play: Private Club. You must be the guest of a member to play. Limited reciprocals with other private clubs. Open year round.

Fieldcrest Cannon Classic

Peninsula Country Club

LODGING

$$$ Hilton at University Place, 8629 Jim Keynes Dr., Charlotte, N.C. (704) 547-7444. 30 minutes from Peninsula CC.

$$ Holiday Inn–Lake Norman, 19901 Holiday Lane, Cornelius, N.C. (704) 892-9120, (800) HOLI-DAY. 5 minutes from Peninsula CC.

$ Best Western–Lake Norman, 19608 Liverpool Pkwy., Cornelius, N.C. (704) 896-0660. 5 minutes from Peninsula CC.

DINING

La Biblioteque, 1901 Roxborough Rd., Charlotte, N.C. (704) 365-5000.

Dilworth Brewing Company, 1301 East Blvd., Charlotte, N.C. (704) 377-2739.

The Olive Garden, 4336 E. Independence Blvd., Charlotte, N.C. (704) 532-9631.

PUBLIC COURSES TO PLAY IN THE AREA

Highland Creek Golf Club, 7001 Highland Creek Ave., Charlotte, N.C. Public. (704) 875-9000. 18/7,008/72. 30 minutes from Peninsula CC.

River Bend Golf Club, 3005 Longwood Dr., Shelby, N.C. Public. (704) 482-4286. 18/6,800/72. 1 hour from Peninsula CC.

Woodbridge Golf Links, 1007 New Camp Creek Church Rd., Kings Mountain, N.C. Public. (704) 482-0353. 18/6,743/72. 50 minutes from Peninsula CC.

TICKETS & ACCESSIBILITY

How to watch: Mon., LPGA practice rounds, pro-am event. Tue., LPGA practice rounds. Wed., pro-am. Thur.-Sun., tournament. Tickets start at $40 for a week-long package. Other individual, group and sponsorship plans are available. Carolina LPGA Challenge, P.O. Box 33367, Charlotte, NC 28233-3367. (704) 378-4410.

How to play: Private club. You must be the guest of a member to play the course. Limited reciprocal play can be arranged through the club professional.

TOURNAMENT-AT-A-GLANCE

Course: Peninsula Country Club
Type: Private
Location: 1800 Jetton Rd., Huntersville, NC 28078
Telephone: (704) 896-7060
When: Late September
How To Get There: From Charlotte, 20 minutes north. Take I-77 to Exit 28/Lake Norman. Drive west 1 mile to Jetton Rd., follow signs to golf course.
Broadcast: The Golf Channel (1995)
Purse: $500,000 (1995)
Tournament Record: New tournament in 1995

Jutting into Lake Norman just north of Charlotte is Peninsula Country Club, which wends its way through a 611-acre country-club community. This rolling, Rees Jones layout, carved through tall pine and oak woodland, features mounded fairways and large, ridged greens protected by sculpted bunkers and water hazards. Lake Norman sits beside or cuts into seven holes.

Variable winds can greatly affect play, especially on the par-3 seventh, which plays downhill to a small green framed by the lake to its rear, and on the approach to the well-bunkered 17th green.

The finishing hole, a 499-yard, par-5 dogleg left, will be the scene of many exciting finales. The tee shot must negotiate a series of bunkers to the left. Then the issue is whether to carry the lake in two. Errant shots are likely to find the water or one of the three traps protecting the green.

●TOUGHEST HOLE

The 400-yard, par-4 17th, a dogleg left that can play even longer with variable incoming winds. The tee shot must be left-center but avoid bunkers in order to create a good angle to a green with a large bunker in front of it and another to its right.

●WHO THE COURSE FAVORS

Every player will enjoy the lies on the zoysia fairways, but the golfer with a solid short game and superior putting stroke should win here.

●BEST PLACE TO WATCH

There are few adjacent holes, but the green area around No. 2 will provide easy access to the par-3 third hole and the fourth tee. If you position yourself behind the par-3 seventh green, you can look across the water to view shots being played on the eighth, a short par-4. The clubhouse area has easy access to the No. 18 green, No. 14 green, No. 1 tee, No. 10 tee, No. 15 tee and No. 9 green.

HOLE	YARDS	PAR
1	510	5
2	375	4
3	178	3
4	363	4
5	380	4
6	381	4
7	185	3
8	322	4
9	441	5
10	511	5
11	393	4
12	379	4
13	160	3
14	340	4
15	379	4
16	132	3
17	400	4
18	499	5
TOTAL	6328	72

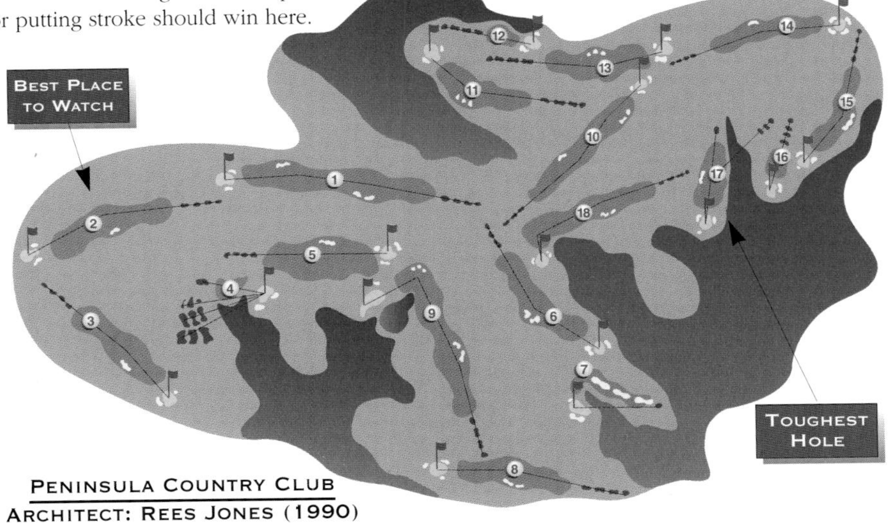

Peninsula Country Club
Architect: Rees Jones (1990)

JCPenney Classic

INNISBROOK HILTON RESORT

The JCPenney Classic is a postseason tournament that matches top LPGA and PGA Tour players in 52 two-person teams. Played on Florida's top-rated course, the 72-hole event is a fun, birdie-rich test of shotmaking and strategy.

First the rules: The qualifying players pick their own partners, with the women choosing one year and the men the next. On days one and three, the teams tally their better-ball score on each hole. On days two and four, the players must alternate shots on each hole. Both tee off—normally from separate tees—then decide which ball to play.

Golfweek's year-in, year-out top-ranked Florida course, the Copperhead at Innisbrook wends its way through 172 acres of wooded, rolling, sandy soil about 20 minutes northwest of Tampa. Water hazards can come into play on 10 holes, and more than 70 sculpted bunkers protect the landing areas and undulating Bermuda-grass greens. Copperhead's dips and turns are a bit snakelike, and its few pine-hugged fairways feel more like North Carolina than the Sunshine State.

The course is the centerpiece of a 63-hole collection laid out by Larry Packard at Innisbrook, an award-winning 1,000-acre resort developed by Stan and Brent Wadsworth, builders of more than 300 top courses throughout the nation.

The par-4s are difficult at Copperhead, and the 456-yard, par-4 sixth is the toughest hole on the front side. A dogleg right, it plays down a tree-lined fairway to a large green fronted by a bunker to its left. The front nine make it clear that par has some fierce defenders in the slithering bunkers, the encroaching forests and the sheer length of some of its holes. The greens vary in depth from 21 yards to a gigantic 47 yards, and are easy to three-putt.

The course concludes with an uphill par-4 that flows 432 yards (369 yards for the women) to a deep green protected to the right by a series of bunkers that run from 125 yards to the front of the putting surface. To the left front is another bunker.

In 1994, Marta Figueras-Dotti of Spain and Brad Bryant, who had never won a PGA Tour event, were deadlocked at 22-under-par after 72 holes with former Tour Rookies of the Year Robert Gamez and Helen Alfredsson. A sudden-death showdown ended four holes later when Alfredsson missed a 3-foot putt and the opposition walked away with $150,000 each.

TOURNAMENT-AT-A-GLANCE

Course: Innisbrook Hilton Resort—Copperhead Course
Type: Resort
Location: 36750 U.S. Highway 19 N, Palm Harbor, FL 34684
Telephone: (813) 942-2000, (800) 456-2000
When: Early December
How To Get There: From Tampa International Airport, 35 miles. Take Hwy. 275 south to Hwy. 60 west to Clearwater to Hwy. 19 north. Take Hwy. 19 approximately 10 miles north to the main gate of the Innisbrook Hilton Resort (between Alderman and Klosterman Rds.)
Broadcast: ABC, ESPN (1995)
Purse: $1,300,000 (1995)
Tournament Record: 22-under-par 262, Marta Figueras-Dotti/Brad Bryant and Helen Alfredsson/Robert Gamez, 1994 (Figueras-Dotti/Bryant won the play-off).

Courtesy of Innisbrook Hilton Resort

WITH ITS PINE TREE-LINED FAIRWAY AND METICULOUSLY KEPT TEE AREA, COPPERHEAD'S NO. 5 IS JUST ONE REASON INNISBROOK IS OFTEN CALLED FLORIDA'S TOP COURSE.

●TOUGHEST HOLE

One of the most difficult of Innisbrook's tough par-4s is the 458-yard 16th (402 yards for LPGA), a dogleg right with bunkers to the right of the tee shot landing area. Trees border the left side up to and behind a deep green, with two huge bunkers bracketing its front. The entrance to this forward-sloping putting surface is quite narrow. The two finishing holes add an element of drama and danger to Copperhead. The 211-yard, par-3 17th (153 yards for LPGA) may be affected by variable winds that can blow a tee shot into one of four bunkers surrounding the green. The 432-yard, par-4 18th (369 yards for LPGA) has a narrow fairway protected by two large bunkers to its left. The approach is to a deep green guarded by huge bunkers.

●BEST PLACE TO WATCH

The last three holes are the ones to watch, especially as the tournament draws to a close. Two scenic and tough par-3s, the 175-yard 13th and the 212-yard 15th, are also good holes to watch, as is the 572-yard, par-5 14th, a double dogleg to a deep green with water to its front and bunkers to its left and right.

●WHO THE COURSE FAVORS

Copperhead favors long hitters who can position the ball to come into the large, well-bunkered greens with high-percentage approach shots, especially in this team competition, where birdies are the rule rather than the exception.

LPGA			PGA TOUR		
HOLE	YARDS	PAR	HOLE	YARDS	PAR
1	501	5	1	561	5
2	354	4	2	406	4
3	391	4	3	452	4
4	132	3	4	176	3
5	517	5	5	576	5
6	404	4	6	456	4
7	337	4	7	378	4
8	170	3	8	235	3
9	377	4	9	418	4
10	372	4	10	444	4
11	496	5	11	546	5
12	340	4	12	379	4
13	145	3	13	175	3
14	527	5	14	572	5
15	162	3	15	212	3
16	402	4	16	458	4
17	153	3	17	211	3
18	369	4	18	432	4
TOTAL	6149	71	TOTAL	7087	71

TOUGHEST HOLE

BEST PLACE TO WATCH

INNISBROOK HILTON RESORT—COPPERHEAD COURSE
ARCHITECT: LARRY PACKARD (1972)

LODGING

$$$ The Innisbrook Hilton Resort, U.S. Hwy. 19, Tarpon Springs, Fla. (813) 942-2000, (800) 456-2000. On site.

$$ Wyndham Harbour Island Hotel, 725 S. Harbour Island Blvd., Tampa. (813) 229-5000, (800) WYNDHAM. 50 minutes from Innisbrook.

$ Inn on the Bay, 1420 Bayshore Blvd., Dunedin, Fla. (813) 734-7689. 35 minutes from Innisbrook.

DINING

Louis L. Pappas Riverside Restaurant, 10 W. Dodecanese Blvd., Tarpon Springs, Fla. (813) 937-5101.

PUBLIC COURSES TO PLAY IN AREA

Bloomingdale Golfers Club, 1802 Nature's Way Blvd., Valrico, Fla. Public. (813) 685-4105. 18/7,165/72. 65 minutes from Innisbrook.

Saddlebrook Resort, 5700 Saddlebrook Way, Wesley Chapel, Fla. Resort. (813) 973-1111, (800) 729-8383. Palmer: 18/6,469/71. Saddlebrook: 18/6,603/70. 30 minutes from Innisbrook.

World Woods Golf Club, 17590 Ponce De Leon, Brooksville, Fla. Public. (904) 796-5500. Pine Barrens: 18/6,902/71. Rolling Oaks: 18/6,985/72. 50 minutes from Innisbrook.

TICKETS & ACCESSIBILITY

How to watch: Mon., professional practice rounds. Tue., pro-am. Wed., pro-am. Thur.-Sun., tournament. For individual, group and sponsor ticket information, contact: JCPenney Classic, Innisbrook Hilton Resort, P.O. Box 1088, Tarpon Springs, FL 34688-1088, (813) 942-5566.

How to play: Golf packages are available year round. In addition to the Copperhead, Innisbrook golf courses include Island (18/6,999/72), Sandpiper One/Two (18/5,969/70), Sandpiper Two/Three (18/6,210/70), and Sandpiper Three/One (18/6,245/70). An excellent golf school, The Golf Institute, headed by PGA professional Jay Overton, offers a variety of golf learning options. (813)942-2000, (800) 456-2000.

By Douglas Avery

Senior PGA Tour

Hyatt Senior Tournament of Champions

HYATT DORADO BEACH

The Senior Tournament of Champions, for 11 years played in tandem with the PGA's sister event, split off on its own in 1995. While the PGA's Tour's Mercedes Championship remained at La Costa in California, the Senior Tour's inaugural event of the season moved to the exotic Hyatt Dorado Beach in Puerto Rico.

The site was not new to the tour. Dorado hosted a season-ending Senior event for four years, from 1990 to 1993, before that event moved to Myrtle Beach, S.C.

The Senior TOC's history boasts a roster of true champions who have claimed its title, including Jim Colbert, Jack Nicklaus, Al Geiberger, Bruce Crampton, George Archer, Miller Barber and Don January.

Any of the four courses at the two-hotel Hyatt resort complex in Dorado would be worthy of hosting a tour event. But the East not only has the variety of challenges required for a professional test of golf, it probably has the most scenic routing. The resort is set on a former plantation that was developed into a vacation retreat in the 1950s by Laurance Rockefeller. Dorado Beach is the older of two hotels at the site, and the more intimate of the pair. Cerromar Beach, opened in 1972, is a high-rise known for its free-flowing river pool.

TOURNAMENT-AT-A-GLANCE

Course: Hyatt Dorado Beach—East Course
Type: Resort
Location: Dorado, Puerto Rico 00646
Phone: (809) 796-1234
When: Jan. 19–21, 1996
How To Get There: From San Juan International Airport via regular shuttle. 40 minutes.
Broadcast: ABC, ESPN (1995)
Purse: $750,000 (1995)
Tournament Record: 9-under-par 279, Bruce Crampton, 1991

When it was staged in California, the Tournament of Champions was contested over 72 holes, but since moving to Puerto Rico, it's been adjusted to a 54-hole championship. Ray Floyd set the 54-hole standard with a whopping 19-under-par 197 in the season-ending event formerly hosted by Hyatt Dorado Beach. In 1993, Simon Hobday won with 199, edging Floyd by two shots. "I ducked out on my mates before they could get me into a bar," the free-spirited South African said later about his Saturday-night restraint. Though he referred only to a bar, we'll assume Hobday also skipped the Hyatt hotels' cozy casinos.

Jim Colbert, a.k.a. The Hat, shot a 7-under-par 209 to win in 1995. He captured the $148,000 first prize with a birdie on the third playoff hole to defeat Jim Albus.

What makes this tournament a challenge is not the course so much as its being the first tour outing in quite a while for the players. Still, conditions do play a part, and golf at Dorado can definitely be affected by winds. For instance, at 1995's event, a weakened Lee Trevino—recuperating from back surgery—was unable to go for the par-5s in two because of the prevailing gusts. "Other guys are two-putting for birdie on a couple of these par-5s, and I've had to knock it close with a wedge," said Trevino, who finished tied for sixth.

"EVERYONE'S TRYING TO GET OUT OF THE BOX STRONG, BUT IT'S BEEN A LONG TIME BETWEEN TOURNAMENTS."

—RAY FLOYD,

WHO TIED FOR SIXTH IN 'THE 1995 SEASON OPENER

Courtesy of Hyatt Dorado Beach

The third hole on Dorado's East Course is a straight par-3 that demands good club selection.

●TOUGHEST HOLE

An unforgiving par-5, the fifth demands caution, as foliage encroaches on either side of the sloping fairway. Making par is no small achievement.

HOLE	YARDS	PAR	HOLE	YARDS	PAR
1	360	4	10	520	5
2	530	5	11	215	3
3	175	3	12	360	4
4	375	4	13	540	5
5	570	5	14	205	3
6	370	4	15	430	4
7	410	4	16	455	4
8	185	3	17	415	4
9	440	4	18	415	4
			TOTAL	6970	72

●BEST PLACE TO WATCH

Around the green at the 13th hole, a notorious par-5 double dogleg hole beyond which sits the Atlantic Ocean. Long hitters can reach the green in two, but the drive will have to cut across pond No. 1 on the left and the first dogleg, and the approach will have to carry pond No. 2 on the right and negate the second dogleg. Spectators perched here can hear the waves, smell the salty air, try to guess whether a pro will try for the green in two and then watch what happens.

●WHO THE COURSE FAVORS

Robert Trent Jones sculpted a well-rounded layout, with doglegs right, doglegs left, even a double dogleg; holes toward the ocean, away from the ocean and alongside the ocean; short, strategic par-4s, and a few long par-4s. The course is a mixture of length and shotmaking, but it can be influenced when the wind kicks up. With wind a factor, the sand wedge becomes important for getting up and down because when it's windy, there'll definitely be some bunker play involved.

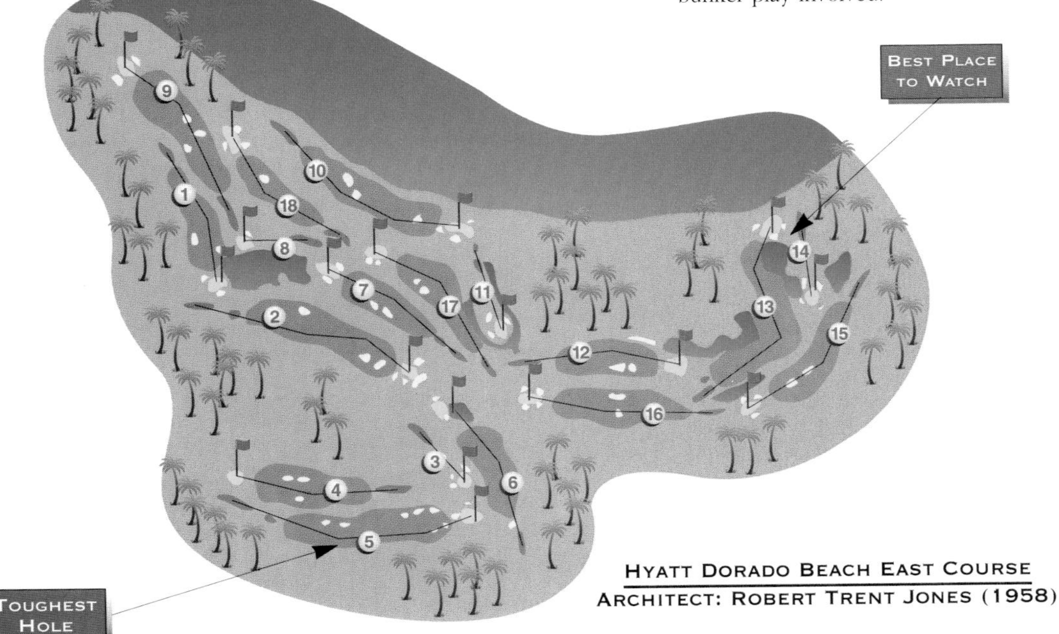

Hyatt Dorado Beach East Course
Architect: Robert Trent Jones (1958)

LODGING

$$$ Hyatt Dorado Beach, Dorado, Puerto Rico. (809) 796-1234.

$$$ Hyatt Regency Cerromar Beach, Dorado, Puerto Rico. (809) 796-1234. 5 minutes from Dorado Beach.

$$$ Best Western Pierre, 105 De Diego Ave., San Juan, Puerto Rico. (809) 721-1200. 40 minutes from Dorado Beach.

DINING

Su Casa, on the grounds of Hyatt Dorado Beach. (809) 796-1234.

Medici's, Hyatt Regency Cerromar Beach, Puerto Rico. (809) 796-1234.

Metropol, Avenida Roosevelt #724, Hato Rey, Puerto Rico. (809) 751-4022.

PUBLIC COURSES TO PLAY IN AREA

Hyatt Regency Cerromar Beach, Road 693, Dorado, Puerto Rico. Resort. (809) 796-1234. North: 18/6,841/72; South: 18/7,047/72.

Hyatt Dorado Beach, Road 693, Call Box BB, Dorado, Puerto Rico. Resort. (809) 796-1234. West: 18/6,913/72.

TICKETS AND ACCESSIBILITY

How to watch: Mon.-Tue., practice rounds. Wed.-Thur., pro-am rounds. Season tickets are $15; daily tickets for the three championship rounds are $8. Individual, group and sponsor tickets available. Hyatt Dorado Beach, attention: Golf Department, Road 693, Dorado, PR 00646. (809) 796-1234.

How to play: All four of the courses at the two adjacent Hyatt complexes in Puerto Rico were designed by noted architect Robert Trent Jones and are open to the public. Resort guests receive preferred reservations, fees.

SENIOR SKINS GAME
MAUNA LANI RESORT

By Bob Fewell

THE SOUTH COURSE'S SIGNATURE PAR-3 15TH FEATURES A TEE SHOT OVER FIERCE SURF.

The largest number of resorts on the Big Island of Hawaii are concentrated on the Kohala Coast along the island's leeward side, where there is scant rainfall—about nine inches a year, compared to more than 40 inches on the Hilo side of the island—and plenty of sunshine. The volcanic island is young, at barely a million years, and most of the Big Island courses have been carved out of 5,000-year-old lava flows. The emerald fairways and greens resemble jewels in a rough setting of black and brown lava. The Big Island also features two of the largest mountains in the Pacific, Mauna Kea at 13,796 feet and Mauna Loa at 13,679 feet. It's the mountain range that separates the island into two distinct coastal regions and climates.

The Mauna Lani Resort was developed in the 1970s. The South Course snakes through the stark, rugged landscape formed by the prehistoric Kaniku lava flow. Spectators and golfers alike are treated to a panorama of mountain and ocean views. The fairways are framed by traps, mounding and lava rock. The Senior Skins Game, annually held the weekend of the NFL's Super Bowl, began in 1988 and has been played at Mauna Lani since 1990.

Arnold Palmer has won three of the Senior Skins at Mauna Lani and Jack Nicklaus one. Ray Floyd won 1994 and 1995, including a record-setting $420,000 out of a $540,000 total purse in 1995. En route to that victory, Floyd earned a whopping $290,000 on a single hole, another record. To do it, he holed an 8-foot birdie putt at No. 17 after the ante had been inflated by seven skins.

"IT'S TOUGH TO MAKE A PUTT FOR THAT MUCH MONEY. IF ARNOLD [PALMER] HAD MADE HIS [PUTT], THE HOLE WOULD HAVE LOOKED ABOUT THE SIZE OF A THIMBLE."

—RAY FLOYD,

WHO WON $290,000 WITH A BIRDIE AT THE 17TH HOLE IN 1995

TOURNAMENT-AT-A-GLANCE

Course: Mauna Lani Resort—South Course
Type: Resort
Location: 68-150 Ho'Ohana St., Kohala Coast, HI 96743
Phone: (808) 885-6655
When: Jan. 27–28, 1996
How To Get There: From Keahole-Kona Airport, go north on Rte. 19 for 20 miles.
Broadcast: ABC (1996)
Purse: $540,000 (1996)
Tournament Record: Raymond Floyd, $420,000, 1995

•TOUGHEST HOLE

They call the third hole on the South Course the "Mother of Long Holes." It's a par-5 with a slight dogleg to the right. The landing area for the tee shot is guarded by water to the left of the fairway and by a series of five traps to the right. The second-shot landing area is guarded by another body of water left and a narrow fairway neck about 100 yards in front of the green. Most troubling of all, however, is the long, narrow, sloping green.

•BEST PLACE TO WATCH

The 15th is Mauna Lani's signature hole. Crosswinds affect shots over the water to a large, two-tiered green surrounded by deep bunkers. Frolicking whales offshore in the Pacific Ocean can be a distraction not found at too many courses on the U.S. mainland. This is one of the most photographed golf holes in the world. Bring a camera.

•WHO THE COURSE FAVORS

Patience is a virtue, not only in dealing with the format of a Skins game but also in negotiating this course. Golfers must keep the ball in play and make the safe approach; then good things can happen.

MAUNI LANI RESORT—SOUTH COURSE
ARCHITECTS: RAY CAIN (NINE HOLES 1980)
NELSON WRIGHT HAWORTH (NINE HOLES 1991)

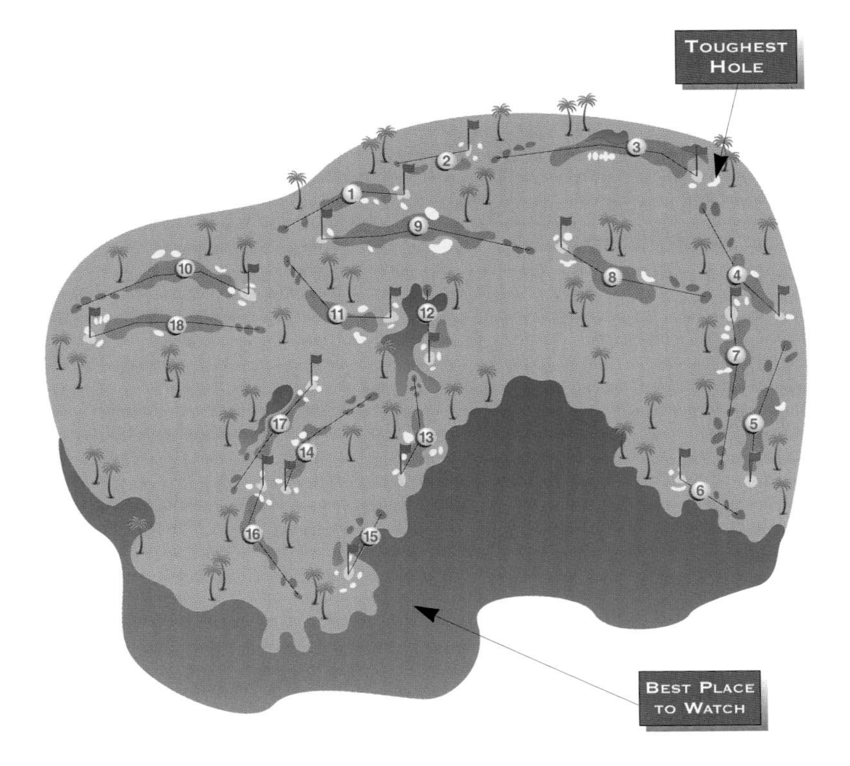

HOLE	YARDS	PAR
1	390	4
2	218	3
3	601	5
4	395	4
5	403	4
6	221	3
7	398	4
8	390	4
9	572	5
10	535	5
11	408	4
12	202	3
13	387	4
14	413	4
15	202	3
16	368	4
17	411	4
18	515	5
TOTAL	7029	72

LODGING

$$$ Mauna Lani Bay, 68-1400 Mauna Lani Dr., Kohala Coast, Hawaii. (808) 885-6622. At Mauna Lani Resort.
$$$ Ritz-Carlton, 1 No. Kaniku Dr., Kohala Coast, Hawaii. (808) 885-2000. At Mauna Lani Resort.
$$ Hilton Waikoloa, Village 425 Waikoloa Beach Dr., Kamuela, Hawaii. (808) 885-1234. 15 minutes from Mauna Lani Resort.

DINING

Donatoni's, at Hilton Waikoloa Village, Kamuela, Hawaii. (808) 885-1234.
Bay Terrace, at Mauna Lani Bay, Kohala Coast, Hawaii. (808) 885-6622.
Canoe House, at Mauna Lani Bay, Kohala Coast, Hawaii. (808) 885-6622.

PUBLIC COURSES TO PLAY IN AREA

Mauna Kea, 62-100 Mauna Kea Beach Dr., Kamuela, Hawaii. Public. (808) 880-3480. 18/7,114/72. 20 minutes from Mauna Lani Resort.
Waikoloa Village, 68-1792 Melia St., Waikoloa, Hawaii. Public. (808) 883-9621. 18/6,687/72. 15 minutes from Mauna Lani Resort.

TICKETS & ACCESSIBILITY

How to watch: Fri., pro-am. Sat.-Sun., championship rounds. Tickets: Fri., $30 daily; Sat.-Sun., $60 daily; three-day pass, $80 until Jan. 15, then $100. Each ticket includes parking, shuttle, program and poster. Individual, group and sponsor tickets available. Senior Skins Game, Mauna Lani Resort, 68-150 Ho'Ohana St., Kohala Coast, HI 96743. (808) 885-4277.
How to play: Preference given to resort guests. Two courses: North (18/6,913/72) and South (18/6,938/72). (808) 885-6655.

Royal Caribbean Classic

THE LINKS AT KEY BISCAYNE

Each winter there's a unique feeling of renewal when the sun's first rays greet the early pairings in the Royal Caribbean Classic. The tournament, traversing The Links at Key Biscayne, represents the first full-field tournament of the Senior season, following several restricted outings in January. Players who have been away for two months are coming back. New qualifiers are joining the Tour. The money list starts anew.

All this is dropped into a vast public complex, Crandon Park, which is also home to a world-class tennis center, a 2-mile span of beach, botanical gardens, a full-service marina, a regulation running track, biking and hiking trails, and two sports meadows.

Prior to the '94 Royal Caribbean Classic the course underwent a $1.8 million renovation. New TifDwarf putting surfaces were installed, adding additional contours to the greens. Mounding was built around the greens to improve the depth field on approach shots and to enhance spectator viewing. Greenside bunkers were added or redone.

"Key Biscayne, before the work was done, was one of the finer courses down here. We are definitely the best now," said Bob Scarbert, assistant director of Dade County's parks department.

TOURNAMENT-AT-A-GLANCE

Course: The Links at Key Biscayne
Type: Public
Location: 6700 Crandon Blvd., Key Biscayne, FL 33149
Phone: (305) 365-0365
When: Feb. 2–4, 1996
How To Get There: Take I-95 to Exit 1. Follow signs to Key Biscayne. After crossing two bridges, go 1/3 mile to course on right.
Broadcast: ESPN (1996)
Purse: $850,000 (1996)
Tournament Record: 14-under-par 199, Jim Colbert, 1993

To many folks, Key Biscayne represents the best municipal course in South Florida. The bay, the vistas and the elements all play a role in the sport here. When the Royal Caribbean is in town, the weather can be windy, cold, or both—or it can be calm and sunny—and sometimes all of that in the same day. In the second round of the '95 event, with the wind at 40 miles per hour, Tom Wargo snagged a greenside bunker at No. 11 and then, while waiting for his playing partners to hit their approaches, watched his ball disappear beneath drifting sands.

The finishing hole, surrounded by grandstands and skyboxes at the green, can stage a dramatic conclusion. With Biscayne to their right and more water to their left, tournament contenders can't afford to stray their tee shots. Most players then face a mid-iron approach to a tightly guarded green.

In 1994, the 18th was the decision-maker in a playoff between Trevino and Kermit Zarley. It was the fourth extra hole after the two had tied in regulation at 8-under 205. In the end, Zarley found water with a hooked drive, and Trevino's par was good enough for another title.

"KEY BISCAYNE IS PROBABLY THE BEST PUBLIC GOLF COURSE AROUND AS FAR AS ITS BEAUTY, TOUGHNESS AND CONDITION. IT IS JUST BEAUTIFUL."

—LEE TREVINO,
TWO-TIME WINNER OF THE ROYAL CARIBBEAN CLASSIC

By Michael O'Bryon

PLAYERS MUST CLEAR MANGROVES EN ROUTE TO THE GREEN ON THE PAR-3 SIXTH AT KEY BISCAYNE.

●TOUGHEST HOLE

Water to the right and two traps to the left demand precise tee shots past the bend of No. 7's dogleg right. After that, depending on position in the fairway, it's a 150- to 200-yard approach shot across a salt water lagoon to an angled green protected front and rear by bunkers. Bold players will try to set up a shorter approach shot off the tee, but they risk water to the right of the fairway. Playing the tee shot more conservatively down the left side of the fairway leaves a much longer approach because of the dogleg heading to the right.

●BEST PLACE TO WATCH

The viewing is best from behind the 12th green, a medium-sized par-3 with water running along the left side. When the wind kicks up, club selection is crucial; the danger increases when the flagstick is placed.to the back left.

●WHO THE COURSE FAVORS

It used to be a player could beat the wind by playing bump and run-up shots to the greens, but since the redesign installed numerous greenside bunkers, that option has almost disappeared. In a sense, though, wind management—or, more precisely, club selection—becomes even more crucial because of the need for higher-lofted approaches and the vagaries of the prevailing breezes.

HOLE	YARDS	PAR	HOLE	YARDS	PAR
1	538	5	10	533	5
2	451	4	11	384	4
3	187	3	12	168	3
4	593	5	13	390	4
5	423	4	14	521	5
6	182	3	15	424	4
7	434	4	16	389	4
8	151	3	17	187	3
9	380	4	18	419	4
			TOTAL	6754	71

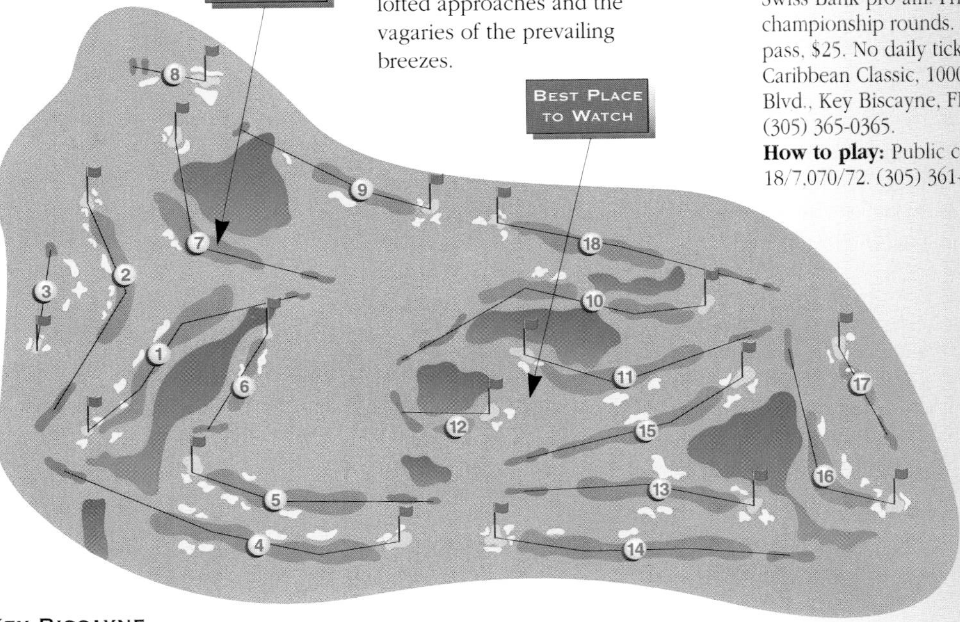

THE LINKS AT KEY BISCAYNE
ARCHITECTS: R. VON HAGGE AND BRUCE DEVLIN (1972)
REMODELED BY R. VON HAGGE (GREENS, 1993)

LODGING

$$$ Sonesta Beach, 350 Ocean Dr., Key Biscayne, Fla. (305) 361-2021. 10 minutes from The Links at Key Biscayne.
$$$ Intercontinental, 100 Chopin Plaza, Key Biscayne, Fla. (305) 577-1000. 15 minutes from The Links at Key Biscayne.
$$$ Sheraton Biscayne Bay, 495 Brickell Ave., Miami, Fla. (305) 373-6000. 10 minutes from The Links at Key Biscayne.

DINING

Rusty Pelican, 3201 Rickenbacker Causeway, Key Biscayne, Fla. (305) 361-3818.
Sunday's By The Bay, 5420 Crandon Blvd., Key Biscayne, Fla. (305) 361-6777.
Monty Trainer's, 2550 S. Bayshore Dr., Coconut Grove, Fla. (305) 858-1431.

PUBLIC COURSES TO PLAY IN AREA

Biltmore, 1210 Anastasia Ave., Coral Gables, Fla. Public. (305) 460-5364. 18/6,800/71. 20 minutes from The Links at Key Biscayne.
Golf Club Of Miami, 6801 Miami Gardens Dr., Miami. Public. (305) 829-8456. 18/7,500/72. 45 minutes from The Links at Key Biscayne.

TICKETS & ACCESSIBILITY

How to watch: Mon., Crown & Anchor pro-am. Tue., Merrill Lynch Shoot-Out. Wed., Swiss Bank pro-am, junior clinic. Thur., Swiss Bank pro-am. Fri.-Sun., championship rounds. Season pass, $25. No daily tickets. Royal Caribbean Classic, 1000 Crandon Blvd., Key Biscayne, FL 33149. (305) 365-0365.
How to play: Public course. 18/7,070/72. (305) 361-9129.

Greater Naples IntelliNet Challenge

LELY PLANTATION

For the third time since it began in 1988, the newly renamed Greater Naples IntelliNet Challenge moves to a new venue. The first three playings of the event, won by Gary Player, Gene Littler and Lee Trevino, the Club at Pelican Bay hosted the southwest Florida event. Then for five years, the IntelliNet was played on the South Course at The Vineyards. Now it's on to Lely Resort for 1996.

The Lely complex, being constructed in stages, contains two courses, and plans call for a lodging and dining facility, and a third course. The public-access Flamingo Island Club Course adjacent to the tournament site is well-regarded itself, having been designed by Robert Trent Jones.

The Classics Course, which the Senior pros will play, was designed by Gary Player and opened in 1991. The layout is considered a "membership" track, which means some bunkers and water enter play but not an overabundance of either. Most greens allow a front alleyway for golfers to run an approach or pitch onto the putting surface. The greens have been slow coming around, and some have been redone since opening, but they are reportedly improving in consistency.

As a young facility, Lely has yet to host an event of major magnitude. The course record is a 5-under 67 co-held by former Tour pro Paul Trittler and by assistant club pro Richie Stanford, who won the biggest tournament held to date on the Classics Course, the Trittler Invitational, in 1994.

TOURNAMENT-AT-A-GLANCE

Course: Lely Plantation—The Classics Course
Type: Private
Location: 8004 Lely Resort Blvd, Naples, FL 33962
Phone: (813) 435-1600
When: Feb. 9–11, 1996
How To Get There: Take I-75 to Exit 15. Go south on State Rte. 951 approximately 4 miles to course on right.
Broadcast: ESPN (1996)
Purse: $600,000 (1995)
Tournament Record: 19-under-par 197, Jimmy Powell, 1992 (at The Vineyards, Naples, Fla.)

●TOUGHEST HOLE

The ninth hole presents a long par-4 with a sharp dogleg to the right. Players cannot see the green from the tee. The fairway landing area varies in elevation and is sprinkled with uncut rough patches within the fairway bounds, putting a premium on a long, pinpoint tee shot. Approaches from these rough patches can be troublesome.

HOLE	YARDS	PAR	HOLE	YARDS	PAR
1	387	4	10	427	4
2	381	4	11	523	5
3	581	5	12	162	3
4	185	3	13	352	4
5	375	4	14	417	4
6	181	3	15	365	4
7	512	5	16	190	3
8	407	4	17	507	5
9	426	4	18	427	4
			TOTAL	6805	72

LELY PLANTATION
ARCHITECT: GARY PLAYER (1991)

●BEST PLACE TO WATCH

The terrain surrounding the green at No. 18 provides a stadium setting for spectators at the end of a challenging finishing hole. This par-4 demands a tee shot over water to reach the fairway, which is protected on its right-side landing zone by a 60-yard-long waste area. The approach is over water again to a small, elevated green.

●WHO THE COURSE FAVORS

Players with a fine-tuned short game or those shorter hitters who can proficiently play the bump-and-run can score.

BEST PLACE TO WATCH

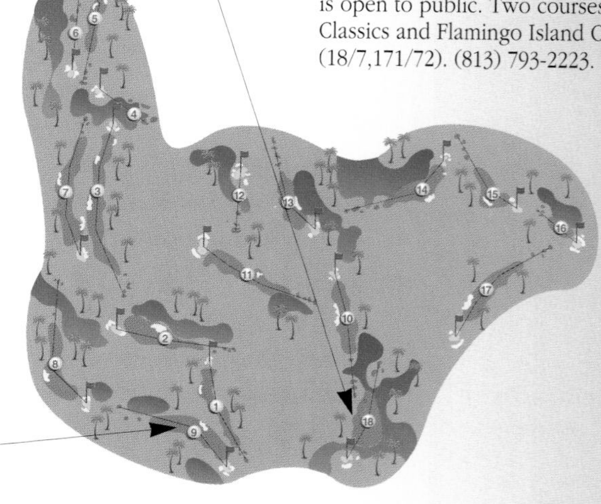

TOUGHEST HOLE

LODGING

$$$ Registry Resort, 475 Seagate Dr., Naples, Fla. (813) 597-3232. 20 minutes from Lely Resort.
$$ Inn Of Naples, 4055 N. Tamiami Trail (Rte. 41), Naples, Fla. (813) 649-5500. 15 minutes from Lely Resort.
$ Hampton Inn, 3210 N. Tamiami Trail (Rte. 41), Naples, Fla. (813) 261-8000. 15 minutes from Lely Resort.

DINING

Villa Pescatore, 8920 N. Tamiami Trail (Rte. 41), Naples, Fla. (813) 597-8119.
Truffles, 1200 Third St. S, Naples, Fla. (813) 262-5500.
Chef's Garden, 1200 Third St. S, Naples, Fla. (813) 262-5500.

PUBLIC COURSES TO PLAY IN AREA

Flamingo Island Club, 8004 Lely Resort Blvd., Naples, Fla. Public. (813) 793-2223. 18/7,171/72. On site.
Pelican's Nest, 4450 Pelican's Nest Dr., Bonita Springs, Fla. Public. (813) 947-4600. Hurricane: 9/3,458/36. Gator: 9/3,558/36. Seminole: 9/3,514/36. Panther: 9/3,461/36. 30 minutes from Lely Resort.

TICKETS & ACCESSIBILITY

How to watch: Mon.-Tue, practice rounds. Wed.-Thur., pro-am. Fri.-Sun., championship rounds. Daily tickets, Mon.-Tue., $5; Wed.-Thur., $10; Fri.-Sun., $15. Weeklong Challenge Club pass, $40, includes complimentary greens fees during off-season at choice of 30 private courses in region. Greater Naples IntelliNet Challenge, 2150 Goodlette Rd., Suite 308, Naples, FL 33940. (813) 435-1600.
How to play: Classics Course is private. Pro may extend invitation. Lely's Flamingo Island Club Course is open to public. Two courses: Classics and Flamingo Island Club (18/7,171/72). (813) 793-2223.

Senior Golf Classic

TPC at Prestancia

LODGING

$$$ Hyatt Sarasota, 1000 Blvd. of the Arts, Sarasota, Fla. (813) 953-1234. 25 minutes from TPC at Prestancia.
$$ Days Inn, 6600 S. Tamiami Trail, Sarasota, Fla. (813) 924-4900. 8 minutes from TPC at Prestancia.
$$ Ramada Inn South, 1660 S. Tamiami Trail, Osprey, Fla. (941) 966-2121. 15 minutes from TPC at Prestancia.

DINING

Outback Steakhouse, 7202 S. Tamiami Trail, Sarasota, Fla. (813) 924-4329.
Lone Star, 7275 S. Tamiami Trail, Sarasota, Fla. (813) 927-2233.
Woody's Bar-B-Q, 7500 S. Tamiami Trail, Sarasota, Fla. (941) 925-7049.

PUBLIC COURSES TO PLAY IN AREA

University Park, 7671 Park Blvd., Sarasota, Fla. Public. (813) 359-2995. 18/6,950/72. 15 minutes from TPC at Prestancia.
Tatum Ridge, 421 N. Tatum Rd., Sarasota, Fla. Semi-private. (813) 378-4211. 18/6,757/72. 10 minutes from TPC at Prestancia.

TICKETS & ACCESSIBILITY

How to watch: Mon., pro-am and practice rounds. Tue., Baseball Legends long-drive contest, Dial 8 driving contest, Hot Box shoot-out, practice rounds. Wed.-Thur., Baseball Legends pro-am. Fri.-Sun., Senior Tour championship rounds. (703) 905-3300.
How to play: TPC at Prestancia is a private course. You must be the guest of a member or a member of the TPC network. Stadium and Club (18/6,536/72).

TOURNAMENT-AT-A-GLANCE

Course: TPC at Prestancia—Stadium Course
Type: Private
Location: 4409 TPC Dr., Sarasota, FL 34238
Phone: (941) 922-2800
When: Feb. 23–25, 1996
How To Get There: Take I-75 to Exit 37. Go west on State Rte. 72 approximately 2 miles. Turn left on McIntosh, go south 1 mile. Turn right on Palmer Ranch Pkwy, entrance 1/4 mile on left.
Broadcast: TBA (1996)
Purse: $800,000 (1996)
Tournament Record: New event

The TPC Prestancia layout on the West Coast of Florida is no stranger to the Senior PGA Tour. The Ron Garl–designed Stadium Course was host to the Chrysler Cup team match for seven years before that event moved to Acapulco in 1995.

The Senior Golf Classic will conclude with a standard three-day stroke-play competition among the pros, but earlier in the week 54 former baseball stars, including several Hall of Famers, will also tee it up for a two-day pro-am and a variety of special events.

Prestancia's Stadium Course presents a contrast in nines. The front is more wide-open; it looks like a links course but, with its open greens, doesn't really play like one. The back nine has a more traditional placement of trees, bunkers and water, and it plays tougher. Still, the course is not overly long, and it favors the shotmaker.

●TOUGHEST HOLE

The 11th hole, which can play as long as 442 yards, requires a drive down the left-center of the fairway to set up the best approach to the green. Oak trees border the fairway while small pines guard the right side of the green. Also, a 25-foot-wide drainage ditch crosses the fairway 120 yards from the green, which is more of a mental factor for golfers than a real hazard.

HOLE	YARDS	PAR
1	396	4
2	512	5
3	416	4
4	167	3
5	390	4
6	511	5
7	192	3
8	409	4
9	370	4
10	363	4
11	412	4
12	519	5
13	198	3
14	435	4
15	525	5
16	169	3
17	418	4
18	381	4
TOTAL	6783	72

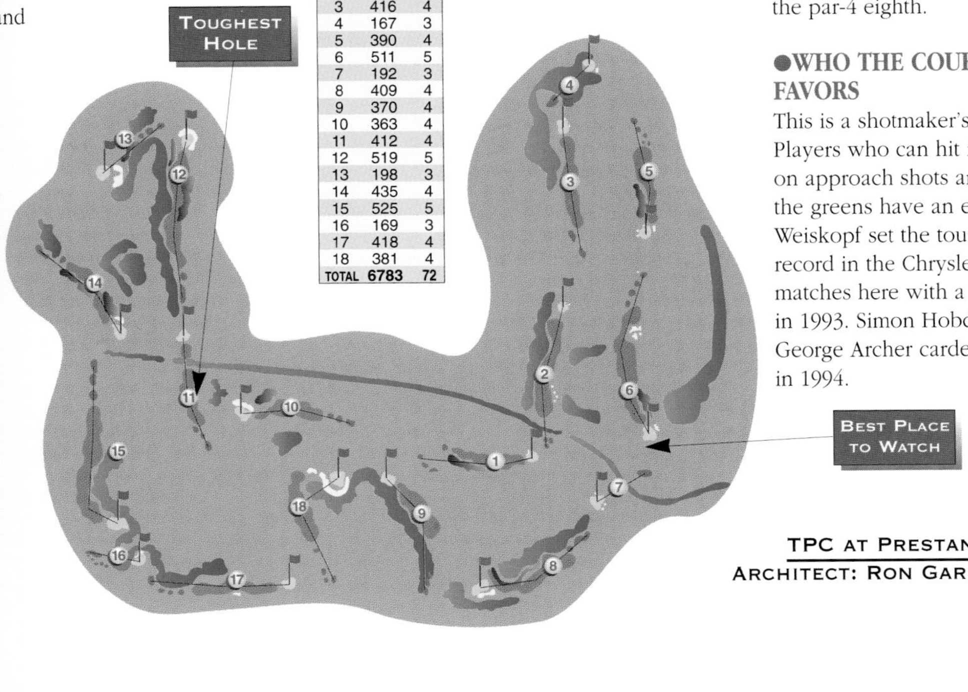

Toughest Hole

Best Place to Watch

TPC at Prestancia
Architect: Ron Garl (1985)

●BEST PLACE TO WATCH

A station on higher ground around the sixth green affords multi-viewing opportunities. The drives and approach shots should all be visible on the par-5 sixth, as should much of the action on the par-3 seventh and tee shots at the par-4 eighth.

●WHO THE COURSE FAVORS

This is a shotmaker's course. Players who can hit it close on approach shots and master the greens have an edge. Tom Weiskopf set the tournament record in the Chrysler Cup matches here with a 202 total in 1993. Simon Hobday and George Archer carded 203s in 1994.

GTE Suncoast Classic

TPC OF TAMPA BAY AT CHEVAL

On a non-tournament day, wildlife may appear at any turn at this distinctive course, which weaves its track among lagoons, wetlands and majestic stands of mature cypress. A member of both the Audubon Society and the PGA Tour's network of TPC courses, the club is an annual host to golf legends but a daily host to sunbathing alligators, back-stroking otters, preening egrets and grazing deer.

The wiser critters take cover, however, when the GTE Suncoast Classic rolls in every February. Each year the tournament draws among the largest galleries on the tour, and in 1995 it logged attendance of better than 187,000 over the course of the week.

Crafted by architect Bobby Weed with Senior Tour star Chi Chi Rodriguez serving as design consultant, the TPC layout has yielded some low scores and dramatic finishes.

Two of the most exciting conclusions in tournament history were produced in 1993 and '94.

In '93, Jim Albus registered a two-shot winning margin, but his triumph wasn't assured until the final hole. Albus went to the par-4 18th with a one-shot lead and then, despite a narrow landing area and water stretching along the entire right side, decided to hit a driver. His errant tee shot rolled into the rough, just 5 feet from the hazard. Later, he said he should have laid up. Nonetheless, he hit his approach from that precarious perch to within three feet of the pin, and dropped the putt for a birdie.

In 1994, Rocky Thompson's all-or-nothing philosophy yielded a record-tying 61 in the final round for a miraculous come-from-behind victory. Previously, only Johnny Miller had shot a final-round score as low as 61 to come from behind and win—at the PGA Tour's 1975 Tucson Open. Thompson ripped off 10 birdies in his final round to nip Raymond Floyd by a stroke.

But in 1995, Thompson's free-swinging style dropped him into a tie for 29th and Dave Stockton highlighted the week's fireworks by sinking an 80-yard sand wedge for eagle on the par-4 fifth. Stockton's final-round 68 was good for a 204 total and a two-stroke victory over Jim Colbert, Bob Charles and J.C. Snead.

TOURNAMENT-AT-A-GLANCE

Course: TPC of Tampa Bay at Cheval
Type: Semi-private
Location: 5100 Terrain de Golf Dr., Lutz, FL 33549
Phone: (813) 949-0090
When: Feb. 16–18, 1996
How To Get There: From Tampa, take I-275 to Veterans Expwy., north past Tampa International Airport. Take last exit onto Dale Mabry Hwy., then left on Lutz-Lake Fern Rd. Course will be on the left.
Broadcast: ESPN (1996)
Purse: $750,000 (1996)
Tournament Record: 13-under-par 202, Jim Colbert and George Archer, 1992 (Colbert won the playoff)

"THIS [TOURNAMENT] HAS OUTSTANDING CROWDS. IT'S ALWAYS AN EXCITING TOURNAMENT BECAUSE OF THE STADIUM CONCEPT WITH ALL OF THE PEOPLE RIGHT THERE."

—JIM COLBERT,
1992 GTE SUNCOAST CLASSIC WINNER

ARNOLD PALMER LINED UP A PUTT ON THE 17TH DURING THE 1994 CLASSIC.

●TOUGHEST HOLE

Lagoon and wetlands flank the entire left side of the dogleg left 15th hole. The green sits on the lagoon, with cypress looming in the distance, water on the left and bunkers on both sides. It demands sharp, long-iron second shots.

●BEST PLACE TO WATCH

Greenside at the par-3 17th hole affords views of action on the 10th green, 11th tee and 18th tee, making it a highly enjoyable vantage point. The 17th hole requires a longish tee shot over water to a green measuring 11,000 square feet. Birdies are scarce on the subtly breaking green.

●WHO THE COURSE FAVORS

Second-shot maestros should have the advantage on a course that's not long by pro standards. Hitting the greens and making a few putts along the way will provide the keys to victory.

HOLE	YARDS	PAR	HOLE	YARDS	PAR
1	395	4	10	395	4
2	191	3	11	179	3
3	425	4	12	495	5
4	415	4	13	345	4
5	332	4	14	528	5
6	144	3	15	425	4
7	533	5	16	413	4
8	391	4	17	197	3
9	420	4	18	415	4
			TOTAL	6638	71

LODGING

$$$ Marriott Westshore, 1001 No. Westshore Blvd., Tampa. (813) 287-2555.
$$ Holiday Inn Busch Gardens, 2701 E. Fowler Ave., Tampa. (813) 971-4710.
$ Days Inn State Fairgrounds, 9942 Adamo Dr., Tampa. (813) 623-5121.

DINING

Ristorante Francesco, 1441 E. Fletcher Ave., Tampa (in La Place Village). (813) 971-3649.
Columbia, 7th Ave. from 21st to 22nd Sts., Tampa. (813) 248-4961.

PUBLIC COURSES TO PLAY IN AREA

Westchase Golf Course, 10307 Radcliffe Dr., Tampa. Public. (813) 854-2331. 18/6,710/72. About 20 minutes from TPC of Tampa Bay.
Saddlebrook Resort, 5700 Saddlebrook Way, Wesley Chapel, Fla. Resort. (813) 973-1111. Palmer: 18/6,469/71. Saddlebrook: 18/6,603/70. About 25 minutes from TPC of Tampa Bay.

TICKETS & ACCESSIBILITY

How to watch: Mon., one-day pro-am. Tue., Merrill Lynch Shoot-Out. Wed-Thur., pro-am. Season badge is two-for-$75 before Dec. 31, $75 per person thereafter. Daily tickets are $12 purchased before Dec. 31, $15 thereafter. Seniors 50-and-over admitted free on Wed. Individual, group and sponsorship tickets available. GTE Suncoast Classic, 16002 N. Dale Mabry 2nd. Fl., Tampa, FL 33618. (813) 265-4653.
How to play: Reservations are taken seven days in advance. Daily greens fee varies by season. TPC offers $125 Associate and $275 Eagle memberships that provide a round of golf, discounts on further greens fees, range use, shop merchandise and tournament tickets.

FHP HEALTH CARE CLASSIC

OJAI VALLEY COUNTRY CLUB

Only 90 minutes from Hollywood, director Frank Capra found his Shangri-La.

Ojai Valley had come to the world's attention several decades earlier, in the 1870s, when Washington Post travel writer Charles Nordhoff had raved about its sunny climate and sweeping vistas. Soon, wealthy Easterners dotted the lush valley and rugged mountain range with their winter residences.

One of them, Edward Drummond Libbey, a millionaire glass manufacturer from Toledo, Ohio, dreamed of importing the spirit of southern Spain to his favorite getaway, and in the early 1920s he commissioned the construction of several charming adobe landmarks, including the gracious hacienda clubhouse that overlooks one of southern California's premiere golf courses.

By the time Capra came along, scouting locations for a silver-screen incarnation of the mythic paradise in *Lost Horizon*, many of filmdom's biggest names had already discovered Ojai's pleasures. Among those who made cameos on the resort's early guest lists were Clark Gable, Irene Dunne, Walt Disney and Lana Turner.

Ojai's rolling, scenic golf course, designed in 1924 by George Thomas Jr. and updated in 1988 by Jay Moorish, has long been one of the resort's primary attractions. The Senior Tour, which played four early versions of this championship in the Los Angeles area, has been coming to Ojai since 1989.

TOURNAMENT-AT-A-GLANCE

Course: Ojai Valley Country Club
Type: Resort
Location: 702 Country Club Rd., Ojai, CA 93023
Phone: (800) 422-6524
When: March 1–3, 1996
How To Get There: From Los Angeles, take I-405 north, exit onto U.S. Rte. 101 north. Follow to last exit, Hwy. 33 (Ojai). Take Hwy. 33 for 14 miles to Hwy. 150. Bear right and follow to town. Turn right at light onto Country Club Dr.
Broadcast: ESPN (1996)
Purse: $800,000 (1996)
Tournament Record: 15-under-par 195, Bruce Crampton, 1992

The 1994 event is memorable because Senior Tour rookie Jay Sigel, who had turned 50 four months earlier, rallied from a 10-stroke deficit to shoot a final-round 62 and then defeated veteran Jim Colbert on the fourth hole of a sudden-death playoff.

The 1993 winner was local favorite Al Geiberger, who scored a two-shot victory over Isao Aoki and George Archer. The tournament record for 54 holes belongs to Bruce Crampton, who won in 1992 with a 15-under 195.

Despite its reputation for sunshine, Ojai and its tournament course can suffer from rain, as witnessed by the 1995 event. Rain dampened play during the first two rounds, and Sunday's final round had to be cancelled, except for a playoff, due to an additional 2-inch downpour. Only 10 miles away, a major landslide caused by the persistent precipitation hit La Conchita. Tour officials called for a televised Sunday playoff between Bruce Devlin and Dave Eichelberger, who were tied for the lead after 36 holes. Because of TV demands, the pair were relegated to competing for a $112,500 first prize over a pair of par-3s perched above the flood level. Devlin won on the second par-3 playoff hole.

> "THERE WERE RIVERS ON EVERY FAIRWAY. I WOULD HAVE HAD A LITTLE ADVANTAGE IF WE WOULD HAVE PLAYED A PAR-4."
>
> —DAVE EICHELBERGER,
>
> AFTER LOSING TO BRUCE DEVLIN IN THE 1995 PLAYOFF

●TOUGHEST HOLE

No. 13 ranks with the best par-4s around. To get a good angle at a green fronted by two fierce bunkers, players must thread their tee shots down a tight chute of trees. Even then, the uphill second shot must carry a ravine to a green with a narrow neck, where club choice can vary by two or three clubs depending on flagstick position.

●BEST PLACE TO WATCH

The par-5 18th never lacks in drama, demanding finesse and nerves after two long shots. For players who take a risk and reach the green in two, it can yield eagles. Missed approaches on the right, however, mean a tough pitch to an excruciatingly tricky putting surface.

●WHO THE COURSE FAVORS

Long hitters can do well on this course, with its plenitude of driving holes, but there's also a mix of short par-4s that, tempting as they may be, require some decision-making off the tee to provide the most advantageous approach shot.

Courtesy of Ojai Valley Country Club

NESTLED IN THE SUN-BAKED HILLS OF CENTRAL CALIFORNIA'S COASTAL RANGE, OJAI HAS BEEN A RURAL RETREAT SINCE THE 1870S.

LODGING

$$ Best Western Casa Ojai, 1302 E. Ojai Ave., Ojai, Calif. (805) 646-8175. 10 minutes from course.
$$ Doubletree, 2055 Harbor Blvd., Ventura, Calif. (805) 643-6000. 30 minutes from course.
$ Oakridge Inn, 780 Ventura Ave., Oak Ridge, Calif. (805) 649-4018. 20 minutes from course.

DINING

L'Auberge, 314 El Paseo, Ojai, Calif. (805) 646-2288.
Suzanne's, 502 W. Ojai Ave., Ojai, Calif. (805) 640-1961.
Ranch House, S. Lomita Ave., Ojai, Calif. (805) 646-2360.

PUBLIC COURSES TO PLAY IN AREA

Soule Park Golf Course, 1033 E. Ojai Ave., Ojai, Calif. Public. (805) 646-5633. 18/6,398/72. Used as tournament qualifying site.
Saticoy Regional Golf Course, 1025 So. Wells Rd., Ventura, Calif. Public. (805) 647-6678. 9/2,712/34.

TICKETS & ACCESSIBILITY

How to watch: Mon., one-day pro-am. Tue., Wells Fargo Bank Shoot-Out. Wed.-Thur., pro-am rounds. Season clubhouse badge is $60. Mon.-Wed. tickets are $5, Thur. is $8, Fri.-Sat. $10 and Sun. $12. Parking is $3. Individual, group and sponsorship tickets available. FHP Health Care Classic, Tournament Office, 702 Country Club Rd., Ojai, CA 93023. (805) 640-2800.
How to play: A resort course with daily greens fees and reduced fees for resort guests. (805) 646-5511.

BEST PLACE TO WATCH

HOLE	YARDS	PAR
1	412	4
2	358	4
3	115	3
4	297	4
5	440	4
6	312	4
7	392	4
8	128	3
9	517	5
10	405	4
11	203	3
12	562	5
13	442	4
14	177	3
15	359	4
16	402	4
17	181	3
18	487	5
TOTAL	6189	70

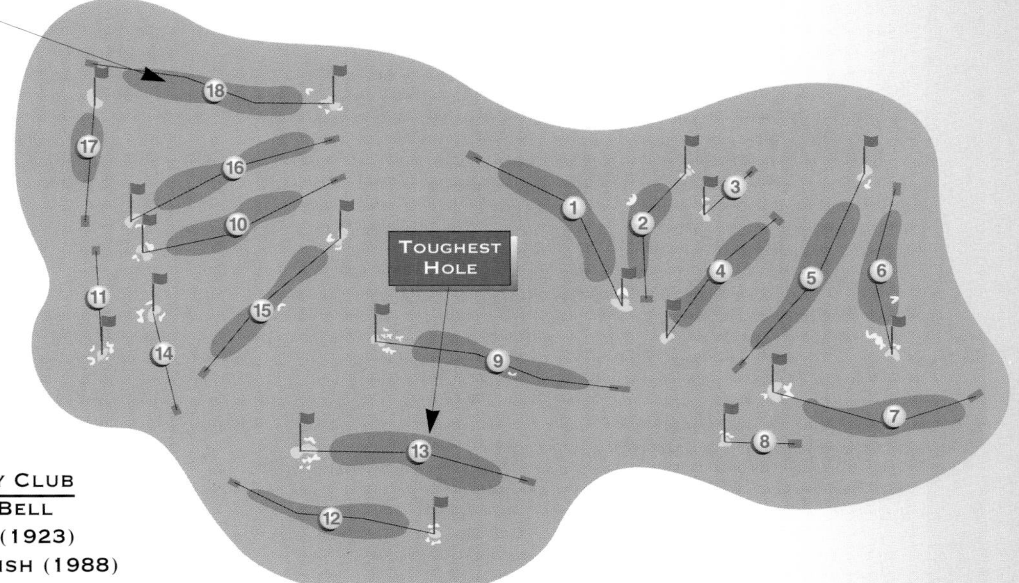

OJAI VALLEY COUNTRY CLUB
ARCHITECTS: BILLY BELL
AND GEORGE THOMAS (1923)
REMODELED BY JAY MORRISH (1988)

Toshiba Senior Classic

MESA VERDE COUNTRY CLUB

Tour golf and Mesa Verde Country Club go way back—in fact, right back to the year the Billy Bell–designed course opened (1959).

The PGA Tour's Orange County Open was played here the next four years, with Jay Hebert, Charles Sifford, Bob McCallister and Tony Lema crowned the winners. In 1968, Bob Dickson won the Tour's Haig Open at Mesa Verde. The LPGA has also visited Mesa Verde six times. The Women's Kemper was held on the course from 1979 to '81; the Uniden from 1984 to '86. Women's winners have included JoAnne Carner, Nancy Lopez and Pat Bradley.

The course is relatively flat, with water on six holes. For the Senior Tour, the nines are reversed. Though the course is not long overall, only one of its par-5s, the tournament 10th hole, is considered easily reachable by the pros in two shots.

The course can yield low scores. Marion Heck set the course record with a 7-under 63 in the final round of the 1995 Toshiba, while winner George Archer and runner-up Dave Stockton both posted 64s. Archer converted six birdie putts in the final round from 10 feet or more, including a 25-footer at the 17th hole.

TOURNAMENT-AT-A-GLANCE

Course: Mesa Verde Country Club
Type: Private
Location: 3000 Clubhouse Rd., Costa Mesa, CA 92626
Phone: (714) 549-0377
When: March 15–17, 1996
How To Get There: Take I-405 to Harbor Blvd. Exit in Costa Mesa. Go south, turn right on Baker St. Go 3/4 mile to Mesa Verde West, turn right, go to Clubhouse Rd.
Broadcast: ESPN (1996)
Purse: $1 million (1996)
Tournament Record: 11-under-par 199, George Archer, 1995

●TOUGHEST HOLE

The tournament 18th proved most difficult in the 1995 inaugural Senior event at Mesa Verde. It's not the longest par-4 on the course by any means, but when played into the kona wind, the second-shot approach over water, which seeps in and narrows the head of the fairway, can call for a stern choice of clubs. This is not a birdie hole.

●BEST PLACE TO WATCH

Anywhere around the clubhouse, where a spectator can easily catch action from the tees for holes No. 1 and 10, and the greens for Nos. 9 and 18.

●WHO THE COURSE FAVORS

The player who keeps the ball in play off the tee on the tight driving zones of this tree-lined layout should be able to set up for mid- to short-iron approaches and scoring opportunities.

MESA VERDE COUNTRY CLUB
ARCHITECT: BILLY BELL (1959)

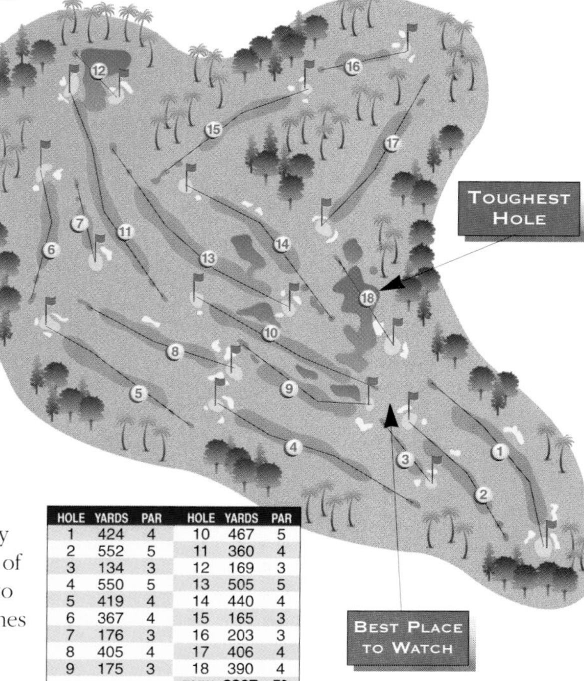

HOLE	YARDS	PAR	HOLE	YARDS	PAR
1	424	4	10	467	5
2	552	5	11	360	4
3	134	3	12	169	3
4	550	5	13	505	5
5	419	4	14	440	4
6	367	4	15	165	3
7	176	3	16	203	3
8	405	4	17	406	4
9	175	3	18	390	4
			TOTAL	6307	70

LODGING

$$$ Westin South Coast Plaza, 666 Anton Blvd., Costa Mesa, Calif. (714) 540-2500. 10 minutes from Mesa Verde CC.

$$ Holiday Inn Express, 1600 E. First St., Santa Ana, Calif. (714) 835-3051. 15 minutes from Mesa Verde CC.

$ Costa Mesa Motor Inn, 2277 Harbor Blvd., Costa Mesa, Calif. (714) 645-4840. 10 minutes from Mesa Verde CC.

DINING

Legends, 580 Anton Blvd., Costa Mesa, Calif. (714) 966-5338.

Planet Hollywood, 1641 W. Sunflower, Santa Ana, Calif. (714) 434-7827.

TGI Friday's, 601 Anton Blvd., Costa Mesa, Calif. (714) 540-2227.

PUBLIC COURSES TO PLAY IN AREA

Costa Mesa Golf & Country Club, 1701 Golf Course Dr., Costa Mesa, Calif. Public. (714) 540-7500. Los Lagos: 18/6,542/72. Mesa Linda: 18/5,486/70. 5 minutes from Mesa Verde CC.

Mile Square, 10401 Warner Ave., Fountain Valley, Calif. Public. (714) 968-4556. 18/6,200/72. 20 minutes from Mesa Verde CC.

TICKETS & ACCESSIBILITY

How to watch: Mon., Kraft Foods pro-am. Tue., senior shoot-out, junior clinic. Wed.-Thur., pro-am. Fri.-Sun., championship rounds. Tickets: Mon.-Thur., $10 daily; Fri.-Sun., $15 daily; season clubhouse badge, $50. Toshiba Senior Classic, 1730 W. Coast Hwy., Newport Beach, CA 92663. (714) 646-9007.

How to play: Mesa Verde is a private course. You must be a member or accompanied by one.

SBC Presents the Dominion Seniors

Dominion Country Club

TOURNAMENT-AT-A-GLANCE

Course: Dominion Country Club
Type: Private
Location: 1 Dominion Dr., San Antonio, TX 78257
Phone: (210) 698-3582
When: March 29–31, 1996
How To Get There: Take I-10 westbound. Exit at Camp Bullis Rd. Stay on service road 1 mile to club.
Broadcast: None (1995)
Purse: $650,000 (1996)
Tournament Record: 15-under-par 201, Larry Mowry (1989), Lee Trevino (1992)

It may be warm or cool when the Senior PGA Tour visits Dominion Country Club each March, but it always seems to be windy.

In 1995, Lee Trevino, after a birdie on the 10th hole, trailed leader Jim Albus by a shot on the final day. Both golfers had to contend with a stiff headwind gusting up to 25 mph for holes No. 10 through 14, and defending champion Albus handled the wind and the course better. Trevino, who bogeyed 12 and 14 as Albus birdied 11, was suddenly out of it.

"It was tough out there with that wind," said Trevino. "Tough, tough, tough. A couple bad iron shots, a couple of bogeys and it was over."

In 1993, J.C. Snead, who usually likes playing in the wind, got plenty of it for the final round. As the only pro to turn in a bogey-free card that day, Snead's 2-under final-round 70 paved his way to victory. "This weather came and really threw everything out of kilter," said a relieved Snead.

The Dominion course, designed by Bill Johnston as part of a real-estate development, has hosted the Dominion Seniors every year since the tournament began in 1985. The course features some of the toughest holes on the Tour. Besides the 16th, the par-4 12th is exacting. In '93, when it averaged 4.502 strokes and ranked seventh-hardest on Tour for the season, the 12th yielded just 15 birdies while chalking up 92 bogeys and 17 double-bogeys or worse. The course record is 64, held by four players.

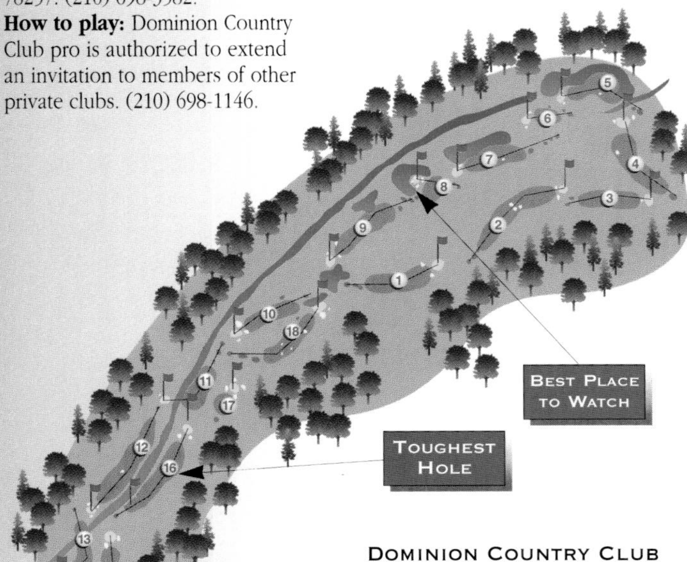

Dominion Country Club
Architect: Bill Johnston (1984)

●TOUGHEST HOLE

The 16th is a long, straightaway par-5 with trees to the left and water on the right all the way to the green. The hole is annually among the top-30 toughest on Tour, averaging 4.3 strokes plus. The approach shot is stern because it means hitting a long iron or fairway wood to an elevated green that is wide but not deep and protected by a grass bunker in front, sand in the rear and a slope toward the water on the right.

HOLE	YARDS	PAR	HOLE	YARDS	PAR
1	423	4	10	413	4
2	522	5	11	363	4
3	406	4	12	385	4
4	381	4	13	405	4
5	438	4	14	202	3
6	167	3	15	360	4
7	436	4	16	538	5
8	153	3	17	189	3
9	545	5	18	508	5
			TOTAL	6834	72

●BEST PLACE TO WATCH

A spot at the 8th green affords a view of a fun par-3 and the 9th tee. The 8th green slopes back to front, is protected by five bunkers and surrounded by water, and can present a perplexing club selection when there's wind.

●WHO THE COURSE FAVORS

The patient player who can handle variable wind and putt well on the fast, bentgrass greens. The par-5s are mostly three-shot holes, so long hitters don't have an advantage there. In general the course does not demand length off the tee. Position for approach is more important.

LODGING

$$$ Wyndham, 9821 Colonnade, San Antonio. (210) 691-8888. 10 minutes from Dominion CC.
$$ Siena Royale, 6300 Rue Marielyne, San Antonio. (210) 647-0041. 15 minutes from Dominion CC.
$$ Hawthorn Suites, 4041 Bleumel, San Antonio. (210) 561-9660. 10 minutes from Dominion CC.

DINING

Alamo Cafe, 10060 I-10 West, San Antonio. (210) 691-8827.
Chester's, 9980 I-10 West, San Antonio. (210) 699-1222.
Mi Tierra, 218 Produce Row, San Antonio. (210) 225-1262.

PUBLIC COURSES TO PLAY IN AREA

Cedar Creek, 8250 Vista Colina, San Antonio. Public. (210) 695-5050. 18/7,150/72. 20 minutes from Dominion CC.
Pecan Valley, 4700 Pecan Valley Dr., San Antonio. Semi-private. (210) 333-9018. 18/7,116/71. 45 minutes from Dominion CC.

TICKETS & ACCESSIBILITY

How to watch: Mon., practice round (free admission). Tue., Merrill Lynch shoot-out, practice round. Wed.-Thur., pro-am. Fri.-Sun., championship rounds. Tickets: Daily grounds, Tues.-Fri., $10; daily Sat.-Sun., $15; season grounds, $50; season clubhouse, $75. Dominion Seniors, 1 Dominion Dr., San Antonio, TX 78257. (210) 698-3582.
How to play: Dominion Country Club pro is authorized to extend an invitation to members of other private clubs. (210) 698-1146.

Liberty Mutual Legends of Golf

PGA West

Some pros call this layout the "golf course from hell." For sure, it's a legendary course, and in 1995 the unique event that launched the Senior Tour moved to it.

The Legends is a two-man better-ball competition, which softens the rigors of a Pete Dye links-style desert course built for developers who wanted La Quinta equipped with "the hardest damn golf course in the world."

"I think you'd get the Senior players boycotting the tournament if you had to play it as an individual-ball event," says Tour pro Bruce Devlin.

Created by former sportswriter, TV producer and businessman Fred Raphael in 1978, the Legends tournament was an immediate hit with the older players, the galleries and TV audiences, and its success inspired the 1980 unveiling of the first Senior Tour season.

The event was played for 17 years in Austin, Texas, before the jump to the California desert in 1995. To enter the field, a player must have five or more victories on the PGA and/or Senior tours.

The event's new home, cut into the rugged desert terrain, sprang almost entirely from the devilish mind of Pete Dye.

"Alice [his wife] and I have built golf courses in cornfields, grazing meadows, swamps and coal country, but the worst piece of land we ever started with was the featureless, barren acreage that became the Stadium Course at PGA West," Dye said in his 1995 autobiography, *Bury Me in a Pot Bunker.*

In seeking to craft golf's ultimate challenge, Dye spared few tricks. "Length alone would not be the ultimate test," he said, "but I believed strategic hazards, deep bunkers, difficult angles across fairways, slightly offset greens, parallel lakes, and desert plants, when combined with cross-current winds, could provide the type of course [the owners] expected."

The par-5 16th, called "San Andreas Fault," begins the course's final theatrical flourish. Infamous bunkers, 20 feet deep, come into play on every shot leading to the green. "My purpose was to create a bunker shot that no one would forget," Dye has explained. Few who saw former Speaker of the House Tip O'Neill playing in the 1987 Bob Hope Desert Classic will forget how the Washington powerbroker finally escaped the sand pit: he threw his ball out.

A hole later there is "Alcatraz," the island-greened par-3 17th, before the players finish in a cheek-to-cheek tango with a fingered lake on the "Coliseum" hole.

According to the pros, Dye achieved what he set out to do. "I think it might be the most demanding course in the world," says Chi Chi Rodriguez.

TOURNAMENT-AT-A-GLANCE

Course: PGA West—TPC Stadium Course
Type: Resort
Location: 55920 PGA Blvd., La Quinta, CA 92253
Phone: (619) 564-7111
When: March 22–24, 1996
How To Get There: Take I-10 to Jefferson St. Go south for 9 miles. Jefferson dead-ends at PGA West.
Broadcast: ABC (1996)
Purse: $1.115 million (1995)
Tournament Record: 39-under-par 249 for 72 holes, Dale Douglass-Charles Coody, 1990 (Barton Creek, par 72)

"GO BUILD THE HARDEST DAMN GOLF COURSE IN THE WORLD."

—ERNIE VOSSLER & JOE WALSER,

LA QUINTA DEVELOPERS ISSUING INSTRUCTIONS TO ARCHITECT PETE DYE

WRONG CLUB CHOICE CAN MAKE "ALCATRAZ," THE PAR-3 17TH, HARD TO ESCAPE.

●TOUGHEST HOLE

The 18th is dubbed "Coliseum" to reflect the enhanced viewing that can accommodate thousands at this stern finishing hole. The tee shot on this long par-4 must cross a lake to reach a fairway guarded all along the left side by the water and on the right side by a series of fairway traps. The lake looms ominously close to the green too, which many pros will be approaching with long irons.

●BEST PLACE TO WATCH

Every hole is good for viewing at PGA West, but the sixth offers lots of excitement. This hole, called "Amen," is a long par-3. The tee shot requires a carry all the way over water with virtually no bail-out territory. There's water on three sides of the green. Lots of water balls here, particularly those tee shots that stray to the right.

●WHO THE COURSE FAVORS

Players who can grind, because there are no let-up holes.

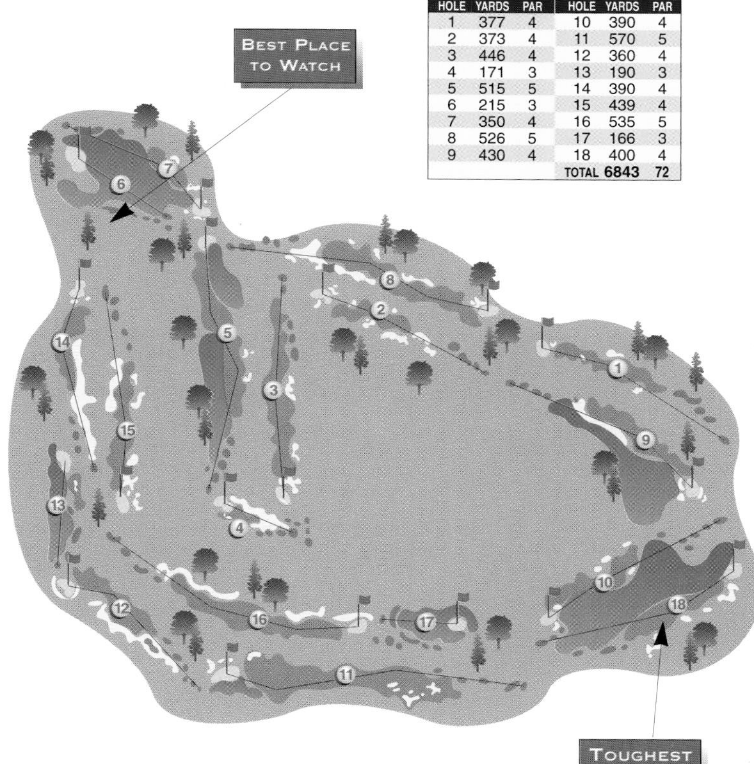

HOLE	YARDS	PAR	HOLE	YARDS	PAR
1	377	4	10	390	4
2	373	4	11	570	5
3	446	4	12	360	4
4	171	3	13	190	3
5	515	5	14	390	4
6	215	3	15	439	4
7	350	4	16	535	5
8	526	5	17	166	3
9	430	4	18	400	4
			TOTAL	6843	72

TPC STADIUM COURSE AT PGA WEST
ARCHITECT: PETE DYE (1986)

LODGING

$$$ La Quinta Hotel & Resort, 49499 Eisenhower Dr., La Quinta, Calif. (619) 564-4111. 5 minutes from PGA West.
$$$ Renaissance Esmeralda Resort, 44400 Indian Wells Ln., Indian Wells, Calif. (619) 773-4444. 15 minutes from PGA West.
$$ Holiday Inn, 74675 Hwy. 111, Palm Desert, Calif. (619) 340-4303. 20 minutes from PGA West.

DINING

La Quinta Cliffhouse, 78250 Hwy. 111, La Quinta, Calif. (619) 360-5991.
Devane's, 80755 Hwy. 111, Indio, Calif. (619) 342-5009.
Beachside Cafe, 78477 Hwy. 111, La Quinta, Calif. (619) 564-4577.

PUBLIC COURSES TO PLAY IN AREA

Indian Springs, 46080 Jefferson St., La Quinta, Calif. Public. (619) 775-3360. 18/6,409/71. 10 minutes from PGA West.
Rancho La Quinta, 79250 50th Ave., La Quinta, Calif. Semi-private. (619) 777-7799. 18/7,068/72. 10 minutes from PGA West.

TICKETS & ACCESSIBILITY

How to watch: Mon., Skins Match. Tue., golf clinic. Wed.-Thur., pro-am. Fri., tournament play, pro-am championship round. Sat.-Sun., tournament rounds. Daily tickets, $15. Liberty Mutual Legends of Golf, 55920 PGA Blvd., La Quinta, CA 92253. (619) 777-1150.
How to play: Four courses. Two resort courses open to public. Preferred times, tees for resort guests. TPC Stadium Course: 18/7,261/18. Jack Nicklaus Resort Course: 18/7,126/72. Must be a member or a guest to play the two private courses. (619) 564-7170.

Las Vegas Senior Classic

TPC AT SUMMERLIN

Summerlin, billed as "the best-selling master-planned community in America," is also the host of the most pro tournaments.

The luxury development, rising rapidly in the Nevada desert on property Howard Hughes purchased more than four decades ago, boasts five distinct villages, eight golf courses either in play or under construction, and both a PGA and Senior PGA Tour stop. A more appropriate two-tournament landlord than the Hughes Corp. would be hard to find: After all, Hughes himself was an amateur golf champion in the 1920s.

In 1997, the Las Vegas Classic will christen a new resort course at Summerlin designed by architect Bobby Weed and consultant Raymond Floyd. That track will capitalize on the dramatic desert terrain with an 18th green tucked between 30-foot rock walls. Until then, however, the Seniors could do worse than a time-share at Summerlin's Championship course with the PGA's Las Vegas Invitational.

In surging to victory here in 1994, Ray Floyd birdied five consecutive holes on the back nine. With Tom Wargo finishing second and Jim Dent third, Floyd posted a final-round 7-under-par 65 and tied the tournament record with a 13-under-par 203 total.

TOURNAMENT-AT-A-GLANCE

Course: TPC at Summerlin
Type: Private
Location: 1700 Village Center Cir., Las Vegas, NV 89134
Phone: (702) 382-6616
When: April 26–28, 1996
How To Get There: Take Rte. 95 North to Summerlin Pkwy. Exit. Follow Summerlin Pkwy. to end. Turn right to course.
Broadcast: ESPN (1995)
Purse: $1 million (1995)
Tournament Record: 13-under-par 203, Al Geiberger, 1987 (Desert Inn CC, Las Vegas) and Ray Floyd, 1994 (TPC at Summerlin)

Floyd missed just five greens all week to overcome some erratic putting. Both of his bogeys came on account of three-putt greens.

In 1995, victory went to the hometown hero. Though a New Jersey native, Jim Colbert now lives in Las Vegas—that is, when he's not traveling around the country playing golf. To secure his title, Colbert had to conquer wind gusts exceeding 45 miles per hour in the second round and a brief back-nine challenge from Floyd on the final day.

Colbert played steadily, while Floyd tried to be aggressive on the 16th hole, a 560-yard par-5. After a tee shot that plays a bit uphill, the hole tempts players to gun for the angled green, which is fronted by a lake. Floyd went for it from the rough.

"It came down to one shot," he said afterward. "It was 213 yards to the front. I almost laid up, but being behind and in the heat of the moment, I made a bad tactical decision. I maybe should have hit a 3-iron. I could have still made birdie laying up."

Instead, Floyd went for the green with a 2-iron and landed in the water, eventually settling into a three-way tie for second place, two shots behind Colbert.

"THESE GREENS ARE TOO DIFFICULT TO PUTT FROM WAY OFF. ANY LONG PUTT I HAD THIS WEEK, I NEVER GOT CLOSE."

—RAY FLOYD,

WHOSE PINPOINT APPROACHES PAVED HIS WAY TO VICTORY IN 1994

By J. Rick Martin

With desert waste bordering the hole's entire length, Summerlin's 15th has a tricky two-tiered green.

●TOUGHEST HOLE

Regularly one of the 15 toughest holes on the Senior Tour, the 18th at Summerlin presents myriad obstacles. First and foremost is length, at 433 yards. The tee shot on this dogleg left must carry to the right and nearly 200 yards across a wasteland to reach the fairway. However, a fairway trap on the right, at 242 yards out, forces the long hitter to keep his power in check. The comeback approach has to cross a pond situated to the left and left-front of the green, thus narrowing the target zone again. In the 1994 event, this rugged par-4 exacted its toll by playing to an average of 4.407 strokes.

●BEST PLACE TO WATCH

Mounds to the right of the par-4 12th offer great views of the players' encounters with a lake that runs from just beyond the tee-shot landing area all the way past the green. The lake gains an extra edge when the flagstick is moved the right side of the putting surface.

●WHO THE COURSE FAVORS

Length is certainly helpful at Summerlin, but precision from the tees may be more important. Advantages accrue to players whose fairway position allows accurate attacks on the tricky greens.

HOLE	YARDS	PAR	HOLE	YARDS	PAR
1	408	4	10	420	4
2	424	4	11	415	4
3	492	5	12	413	4
4	429	4	13	579	5
5	187	3	14	156	3
6	407	4	15	341	4
7	382	4	16	560	5
8	190	3	17	196	3
9	531	5	18	433	4
			TOTAL	6963	72

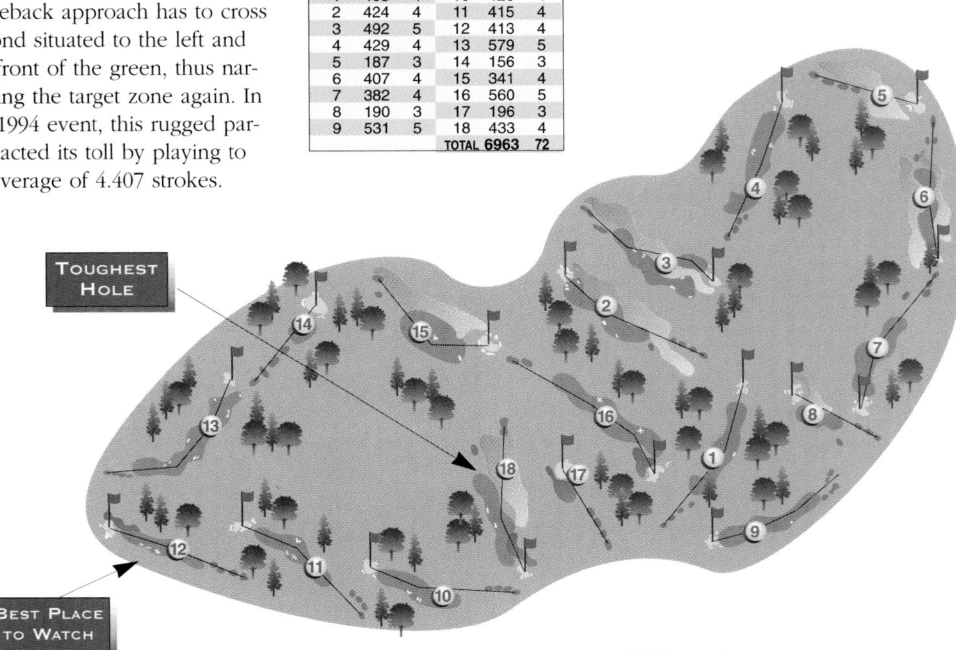

TPC at Summerlin
Architects: Bobby Weed and Fuzzy Zoeller (1992)

LODGING

$$$ Sheraton Desert Inn, 3145 Las Vegas Blvd. S, Las Vegas. (702) 733-4444. 25 minutes from TPC at Summerlin.
$$ Las Vegas Hilton, 3000 Paradise Rd., Las Vegas. (702) 732-5111. 25 minutes from TPC at Summerlin.
$$ MGM Grand, 3799 Las Vegas Blvd. S, Las Vegas. (702) 891-1111. 25 minutes from TPC at Summerlin.

DINING

Outback Steakhouse, 1950 N. Rainbow Blvd., Las Vegas. (702) 647-1035.
Chiasso Cafe, 4712 W. Sahara Ave., Las Vegas. (702) 877-2870.
Cadillac Grille, 2801 N. Tenaya Way, Las Vegas. (702) 255-5555.

PUBLIC COURSES TO PLAY IN AREA

Angel Park, 100 S. Rampart Blvd., Las Vegas. Public. (702) 254-4653. Mountain: 18/6,722/71. Palm: 18/6,530/70. 2 minutes from TPC at Summerlin.
Paiute Resort, 2 Nuvakai, Las Vegas. Public. (702) 658-1400. 18/7,158/72. 25 minutes from TPC at Summerlin.

TICKETS & ACCESSIBILITY

How to watch: Mon.-Tue., practice rounds. Wed., Super Senior Day. Thur., pro-am. Fri., pro-am, championship rounds. Sat., championship rounds, shoot-out. Sun., championship rounds. Daily grounds, $15. Season clubhouse, $50. Las Vegas Senior Classic, 801 S. Rancho Dr., Suite C3, Las Vegas, NV 89134. (702) 382-6616.
How to play: Private club. Must be a member, or member in TPC network of clubs, or guest.

PaineWebber Invitational

TOURNAMENT PLAYERS CLUB AT PIPER GLEN

Arnold Palmer, who has considerable business ties to the Charlotte area, was the designer chosen a decade ago to carve this TPC course out of hilly farmland and forest near the border between North and South Carolina.

Hurricane Hugo knocked out many of the strategically placed trees in 1989, and the rest of its forested areas have been thinned by the expansion of the exclusive Piper Glen residential community. As a result, large landing areas and zoysia-grass fairways can make the pro tournament look like a dart-throwing contest in which the object is to keep the greens' tiers and ridges from coming into play.

TOURNAMENT-AT-A-GLANCE

Course: Tournament Players Club at Piper Glen
Type: Private
Location: 4300 Piper Glen Dr., Charlotte, NC 28277
Phone: (704) 846-1212
When: May 3–5, 1996
How To Get There: Take I-77 to I-485 East to Rea Rd. Exit. Turn left, proceed on Rea to Piper Glen Dr. Turn right to course.
Broadcast: ESPN (1996)
Purse: $800,000 (1996)
Tournament Record: 13-under-par 203, Don Bies, 1992, Lee Trevino, 1994 and Bob Murphy, 1995

The course has what locals consider its own little "Amen Corner" in holes No. 13, 14 and 15. These three long par-4s are set off all by themselves on the far side of Rea Road.

Piper Glen's signature hole cost Ray Floyd dearly in 1995. Having just birdied No. 13 to take a one-shot lead, the former Masters, U.S. Open and PGA champ stumbled and crashed at the 14th.

At the 389-yard par-4, where a brook runs along the right side of the fairway and a pond protects the front of the green, Floyd drove into the creek. He then dropped out, but blocked his 7-iron approach into the pond. He needed a 10-footer to save double bogey, and made the putt.

Still en route to a 5-under 67, Floyd had two reachable par-5s ahead at forgiving Piper Glen. But Floyd drove into a tree on the 16th and topped his second shot while trying to slice a 3-wood out and onto the green. At No. 18, he drove into a spot that eliminated his angle to the green, and he was forced to settle for another par.

On the same stretch during the second round, eventual winner Bob Murphy made the most of his opportunities with a birdie at No. 14, an eagle at No. 15, and birdies at Nos. 17 and 18 en route to a 66.

Finishing holes also played a key part in the 1994 outcome. With two holes to go and victory in sight, Jimmy Powell—who had just birdied No. 16 to take the lead all by himself—suffered a watery ending in the lake behind the 17th green. That gave Lee Trevino the opening he needed for a one-shot victory over Powell and Jim Colbert.

Later, in describing his dismal fate on the 17th hole, Powell said his caddie and Trevino both thought his 9-iron from an elevated tee didn't have enough clout to reach the green. "Lee was hollering for the ball to get up, but I said, 'That's far enough.' And it was."

The ball landed in the rough behind the green and rolled into the lake.

●TOUGHEST HOLE
Any par-4 at 450 yards would be brutal enough just due to length. But No. 13 at Piper Glen also has a narrow fairway driving area, a mid- to long-iron approach over a lengthy series of traps and a teardrop-shaped, two-tiered green. Depending on pin placement, both the approach and the putting can be exceedingly difficult.

●BEST PLACE TO WATCH
Above and to the side of the 17th green. The view from here catches the action on a par-3 green guarded by water and the drives across the water to No. 18's distant fairway.

●WHO THE COURSE FAVORS
The experienced shotmaker has traditionally prevailed in the PaineWebber since it moved to Piper Glen. Length is a factor on a few occasions, but the bigger premium is on crisp approach shots and opportunistic putting.

HOLE	YARDS	PAR	HOLE	YARDS	PAR
1	378	4	10	384	4
2	511	5	11	435	4
3	430	4	12	183	3
4	210	3	13	450	4
5	419	4	14	389	4
6	529	5	15	410	4
7	374	4	16	501	5
8	189	3	17	142	3
9	435	4	18	514	5
			TOTAL	6883	72

TPC AT PIPER GLEN
ARCHITECT: ARNOLD PALMER DESIGN GROUP WITH ARNOLD PALMER (1985)

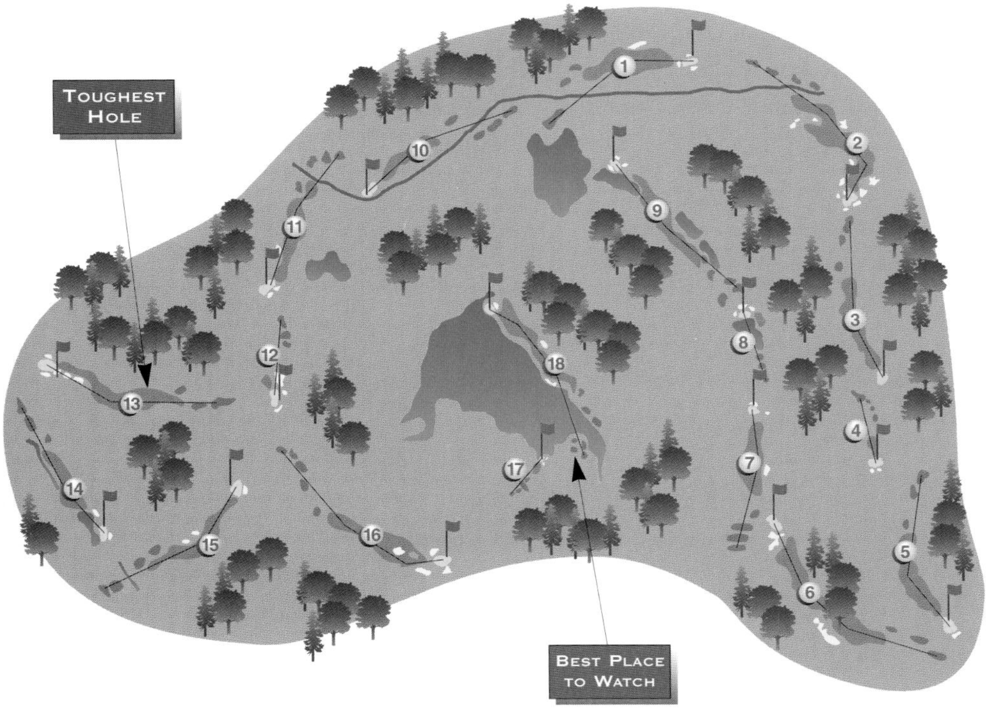

LODGING
$$ Hyatt Southpark, 6601 Carnegie Blvd., Charlotte. (704) 554-1234. 10 minutes from TPC at Piper Glen.
$$ Sheraton Airport, I-85 & Billy Graham Pkwy., Charlotte. (704) 392-1200. 15 minutes from TPC at Piper Glen.

DINING
La Biblioteque, 1901 Roxborough Rd., Charlotte. (704) 365-5000.
Manzetti's, 6401 Morrisson Blvd., Charlotte. (704) 364-9334.
Morton's, 227 W. Trade St., Charlotte. (704) 333-2602.

PUBLIC COURSES TO PLAY IN AREA
Charlotte Links, 11500 Providence Rd., Charlotte. Public. (704) 846-7990. 18/6,700/71. 15 minutes from TPC at Piper Glen.
Renaissance Park, 1525 W. Tyvola Rd., Charlotte. Public. (704) 357-3373. 18/7,500/72. 20 minutes from TPC at Piper Glen.

TICKETS & ACCESSIBILITY
How to watch: Mon.-Tue., practice rounds. Wed.-Thur., pro-am. Fri.-Sun., championship rounds. Season pass, grounds-only, $26. Season pass, clubhouse, $60. No one-day tickets. Ticket sales limited to 12,000 season-grounds and 3,000 season-clubhouse buyers. (704) 846-4699.
How to play: Private club. Charter and corporate members of any TPC club may bring or send guests to all courses in the network. Regular TPC members may bring guests to all clubs.

Nationwide Championship

GOLF CLUB OF GEORGIA

Golf Digest's choice as the best new private course in America in 1991, the Lakeside 18 at the Golf Club of Georgia welcomed the Nationwide Championship to its stunning stage in 1995.

On the front nine, designer Arthur Hills dispatched rolling, rippling fairways through pine and oak forest toward greens whose speed and severe contours recall a more famous Georgia course—Augusta National—an evident source of inspiration.

For much of the back nine, the layout winds along shimmering Lake Windward, and splashy penalties await most any shot that strays.

The course's par-3s are particularly unforgettable. The third hole drops dramatically to a shallow putting surface defended by a steep slope at its front edge. The picturesque sixth plays across the side of a placid pond to a distant green wrapped tightly by the coastline. And the downhill 17th, another par-3 that plays longer than 200 yards, is guarded by a stream that expands into a pond at the green's front left.

Tournament galleries find the Lakeside course perfect for watching the pros. Banks run along most of the fairways, affording sweeping views of each hole. And mounds surrounding the greens ensure that no spectator obstructed during a crucial putt.

In the Nationwide Championship's debut at the Golf Club of Georgia, Bruce Summerhays rocketed out to a first-round 63, but the course stood firm and proved that the event won't allow three sub-70 scores to its winner. In the end, Bob Murphy survived a final-round bogey on the 17th to take the title with a 13-under-par 203 total and a two-stroke margin over Summerhays and Hale Irwin.

A year earlier, Dave Stockton had brought the nearby Jack Nicklaus–designed Country Club of the South to its knees with a record-setting 18-under-par 198. (That year the players were aided by sloshy conditions that enabled them to clean and place the ball.) Making things interesting, the Tour writers' choice for Senior Tour Player of the Year topped his tee shot on the final hole and squirted it just 100 yards down the fairway. But Murphy, who had closed to within a stroke, missed a 35-foot attempt for birdie, and Stockton scrambled for a title-saving par.

TOURNAMENT-AT-A-GLANCE

Course: Golf Club of Georgia—Lakeside Course
Type: Private
Location: 1 Golf Club Dr., Alpharetta, GA 30202
Phone: (404) 393-4567
When: May 10–12, 1996
How To Get There: Take Ga. Rte. 400 to Exit 11. Go east on Windward Pkwy. 2.2 miles to Golf Club Dr. on right.
Broadcast: ESPN (1996)
Purse: $1.2 million (1996)
Tournament Record: 18-under-par 198, Dave Stockton, 1994 (CC of the South)

"I KIND OF PERK UP WHEN I'VE GOT ADVERSITY. I SCREWED UP, BUT I MADE 400 PEOPLE WALKING WITH ME SAY, 'HEY, THAT'S A SHOT LIKE I HIT'."

—DAVE STOCKTON,

WHO TOPPED HIS TEE SHOT ON THE FINAL HOLE IN 1994 BUT WON WITH A TOURNAMENT RECORD ANYWAY

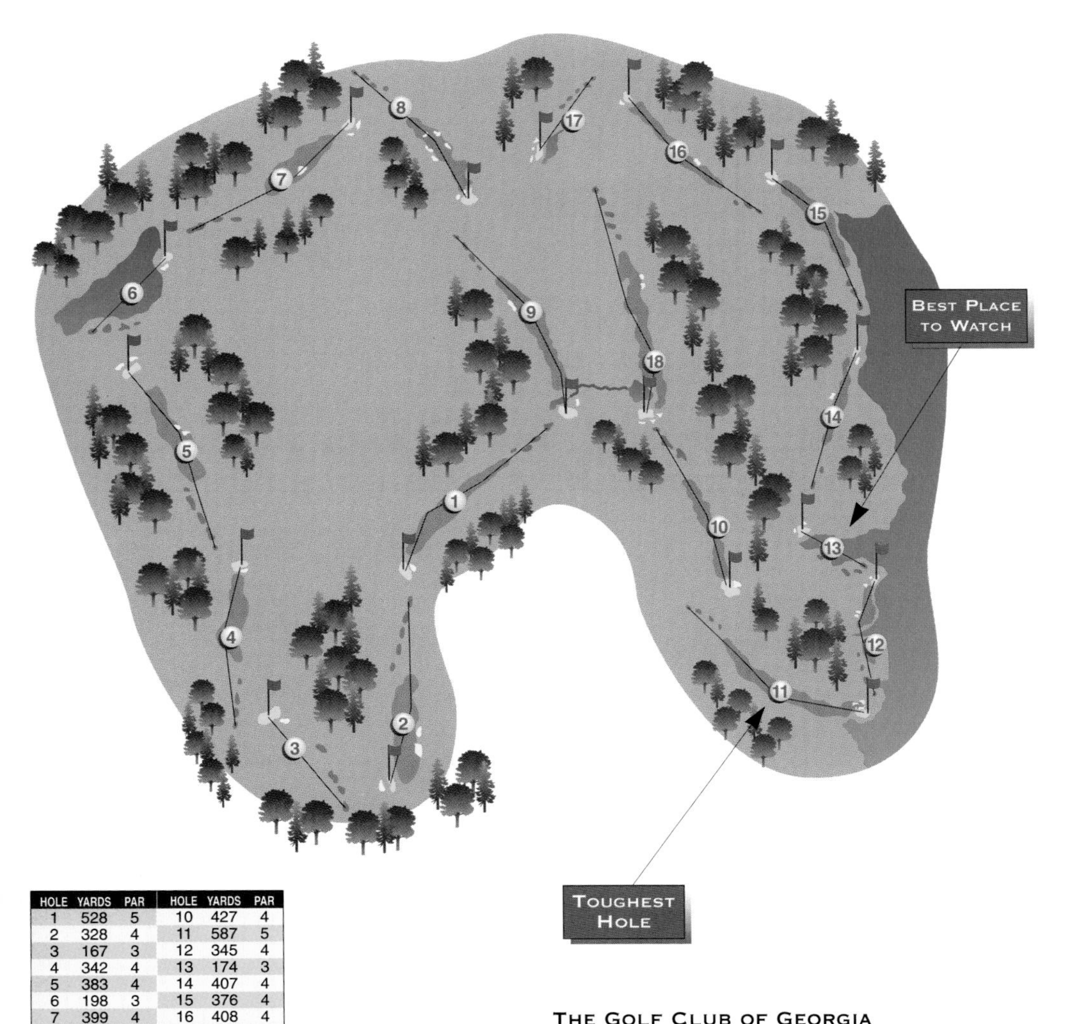

HOLE	YARDS	PAR	HOLE	YARDS	PAR
1	528	5	10	427	4
2	328	4	11	587	5
3	167	3	12	345	4
4	342	4	13	174	3
5	383	4	14	407	4
6	198	3	15	376	4
7	399	4	16	408	4
8	342	4	17	199	3
9	517	5	18	533	5
			TOTAL	6660	72

THE GOLF CLUB OF GEORGIA
ARCHITECT: ARTHUR HILLS (1991)

●TOUGHEST HOLE

The par-5 11th, one of the course's most scenic holes, is surely its most difficult. Players aim for a lone maple tree on the right to avoid treacherous, sloping rough on the left side of the tee-shot landing area. Gambling for the green in two is dangerous, since it juts into vast Lake Windward and is guarded to its front left by three bunkers.

●BEST PLACE TO WATCH

If you've never ventured to Augusta National, the scenic par-3 13th on this layout does a fair impression of the 12th at the venerable home of the Masters. Players confront a wide, calm inlet between the tee and a shallow green, which is overlooked by tall pines and adorned by azalea beds. A tricky mound in the back middle of the putting surface forces players to go right at the flagstick.

●WHO THE COURSE FAVORS

Maneuvering around the greens, first in terms of positioning approaches and then in the putting itself, will provide Senior pros the best opportunities for bettering par. Most greens contain mounds or tiers, which put the premium on positioning.

LODGING

$$ Courtyard By Marriott, 1500 Market Blvd., Roswell, Ga. (404) 992-7200. 10 minutes from GC of Georgia.
$$ Residence Inn, 5465 Windward Pkwy., Alpharetta, Ga. (404) 664-0664. 5 minutes from GC of Georgia.
$$ Holiday Inn, 1075 Holcomb Br., Roswell, Ga. (404) 992-9600. 15 minutes from GC of Georgia.

DINING

Grady's, 7900 North Point Parkway, Alpharetta, Ga. (404) 640-1620.
Macaroni Grill, 770 Holcomb Bridge Rd., Roswell, Ga. (404) 993-7115.

PUBLIC COURSES TO PLAY IN AREA

White Columns, 300 White Columns Dr., Alpharetta, Ga. Public. (404) 343-9025. 18/7,053/72. 22 minutes from GC of Georgia.
Champions, 15135 Hopewell Rd., Alpharetta, Ga. Semi-private. (404) 343-9700. 18/6,725/72. 18 minutes from GC of Georgia.

TICKETS & ACCESSIBILITY

How to watch: Mon., pro-am. Tue., junior clinic. Wed.-Thur., pro-am. Fri.-Sun., championship rounds. Season tickets, $35. (404) 933-8855.
How to play: Lakeside: 18/7,020/72. Creekside: 18/7,005/72. Private. Must be accompanied by a member of club.

Cadillac NFL Golf Classic

UPPER MONTCLAIR COUNTRY CLUB

There are many golf tournaments for Senior Tour professionals, and even a few for stars of other sports. But only one exists that combines both, and though it is still relatively young, the Cadillac NFL Golf Classic has become quite popular with the fans. The opportunity to see Arnold Palmer and Lee Trevino tee it up with football's Lawrence Taylor and Boomer Esiason is a magnetic attraction.

This is an event that began modestly as a long weekend of golf and fun for top Senior players and NFL players at the TPC Sawgrass course in Ponte Vedra, Fla. But a favorable response by all involved led organizers to create the Cadillac NFL Golf Classic and place it as a regular event on the Senior PGA Tour. The tournament became official in 1993 when it relocated to Upper Montclair Country Club in New Jersey. The first event attracted 77,000 fans for the week, and attendance continues to grow.

TOURNAMENT-AT-A-GLANCE

Course: Upper Montclair Country Club—West & South nines
Type: Private
Location: 177 Hepburn Rd., Clifton, NJ 07012
Phone: (201) 779-7505
When: May 17–19, 1996
How To Get There: From Newark Airport, take I-95 or Garden State Pkwy. north to N.J. Rte. 3. Go east from GSP at Exit 153; club entrance 100 yards on right. Go west from I-95 and loop around to reach club entrance on eastbound side of Rte. 3. From New York City, take Lincoln Tunnel. Follow Rte. 3 west; 12 miles to course.
Broadcast: ESPN (1996)
Purse: $950,000 (1995)
Tournament Record: 10-under-par 206, Raymond Floyd, 1994

In response to the public's love affair with the pro football players, the NFL portion of this event-within-an-event now stretches all the way through Saturday, albeit with several cuts along the way. Sunday is the sole day reserved for the Senior golfers. Tournament week is laced with special competitions, all geared toward the fans. Tuesday features the AT&T Long Drive for NFL players, won in 1995 by San Diego quarterback Stan Humphries with a blast of 293 yards; a special Merrill Lynch Shoot-Out, featuring two-man teams and won in '95 by senior golfer Jim Colbert and New York Giants quarterback Dave Brown; and a Cadillac Quarterback Scramble, won last year by Humphries and Green Bay signal caller Brett Favre. A two-day pro-am Wednesday and Thursday pairs two amateurs with a Senior Tour pro and an NFL player.

As for individual competition, 56 football players compete Wednesday and Thursday. There's a cut to 26 for Friday play, and then a final 12 on Saturday. Meanwhile, the Senior Tour championship rounds run Friday through Sunday.

On the NFL side of things, Houston placekicker Al Del Greco has clearly dominated, winning all three NFL player titles thus far. The Senior Tour champs have been Lee Trevino in '93, Ray Floyd in '94 and George Archer in '95.

The venue is a Robert Trent Jones design snugly nestled between two busy highways, N.J. Rte. 3 and the Garden State Parkway. On the outer holes, noise from whizzing automobiles can be annoying.

Upper Montclair previously hosted five Thunderbird events on the PGA Tour in the 1960s and four LPGA events under various sponsor banners in the late 1970s and early 1980s.

●TOUGHEST HOLE

The longest par-4 on the course, with a slight dogleg to the right, the ninth requires a long tee shot that must find short grass between or beyond a trio of fairway bunkers. From there, it's uphill to a small, elevated green cupped from behind by five more traps.

●BEST PLACE TO WATCH

Above and behind the 11th green. This par-5 hole requires a left-to-right tee shot to a landing area with a pond to its left and trees to its right. Then it's decision time. The players who go for the sloping green must clear an arm of a pond that also makes its pesence felt on the neighboring par-3 15th. There, the pros hit anything from a 7-iron to a 4-iron, depending on pin placement.

●WHO THE COURSE FAVORS

Players who can simply play the course as it lies. Most holes are framed by trees, but there's plenty of driving room. With most players reaching in regulation, putting should be a key. Also, a contender needs plenty of patience to put up with playing all those early rounds with football players.

HOLE	YARDS	PAR	HOLE	YARDS	PAR
1	323	4	10	410	4
2	319	4	11	478	5
3	182	3	12	408	4
4	386	4	13	340	4
5	507	5	14	357	4
6	398	4	15	168	3
7	525	5	16	360	4
8	164	3	17	195	3
9	420	4	18	550	5
			TOTAL	6490	72

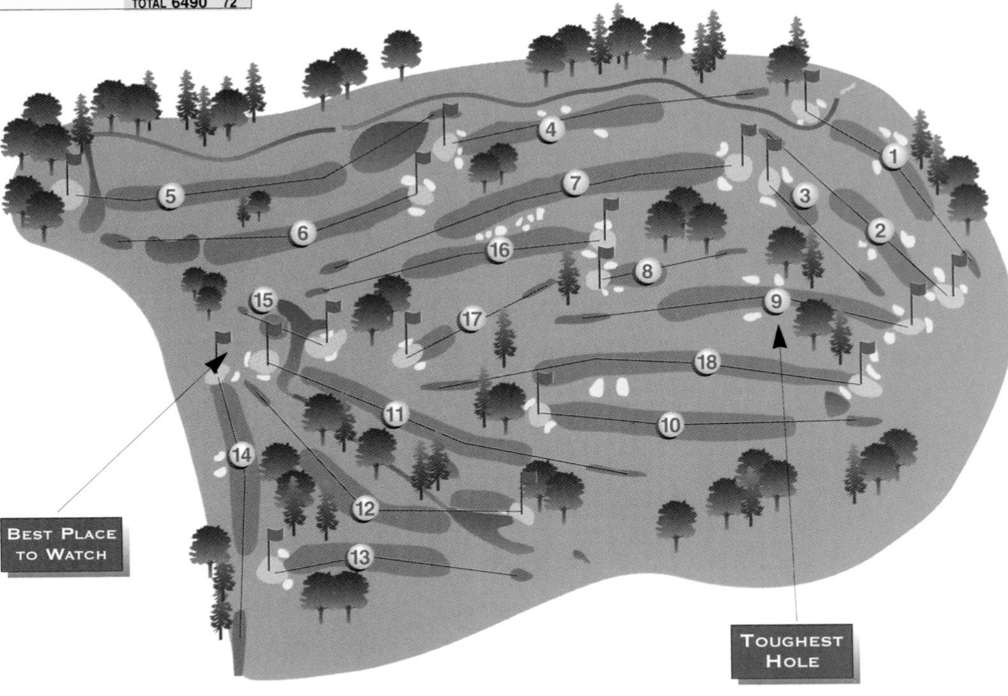

UPPER MONTCLAIR COUNTRY CLUB
ARCHITECT: A.W. TILLINGHAST (1901)
REMODELED BY ROBERT TRENT JONES (1958)

LODGING

$$$ Sheraton Tara, Kingsbridge Rd., Parsippany, N.J. (201) 515-2000. 25 minutes from course; official tournament hotel.
$$$ Meadowlands Hilton, 2 Harmon Plaza, Secaucus, N.J. (201) 348-6900. 10 minutes from Upper Montclair.
$$ Howard Johnson, 680 Rte. 3 West, Clifton, N.J. (201) 471-3800. 5 minutes from Upper Montclair.
$$ Ramada Inn, 265 Rte. 3 East, Clifton, N.J. (201) 778-6500. 7 minutes from Upper Montclair.

DINING

Bella Napoli, 1131 Bloomfield Ave., Clifton, N.J. (201) 365-8087.
Bel Vedere, 247 Piaget Ave., Clifton, N.J. (201) 772-5060.
Portuguese Tavern, 507 Crooks Ave., Clifton, N.J. (201) 772-9703.
Ashley's, 1065 Bloomfield Ave., Styertowne Shopping Center, Clifton, N.J. (201) 778-2253.

PUBLIC COURSES TO PLAY IN AREA

Galloping Hill Golf Course, Garden State Pkwy. at Exit 138, Union, N.J. Public. (908) 686-1556. 18/6,700/72. About 30 minutes from Upper Montclair.
Hendricks Field Golf Course, Franklin Ave., Belleville, N.J. Public. (201) 751-0178. 18/6,088/70. 10 minutes from Upper Montclair.

TICKETS & ACCESSIBILITY

How to watch: Mon.-Tue., practice rounds. Tue., AT&T NFL Long Drive, Merrill Lynch Shoot-Out & Cadillac Quarterback Scramble. Wed.-Thur., pro-am and 56 NFL players. Fri., senior pros and 26 NFL players. Sat., senior pros and 12 NFL players. Sun., senior pro final round. Season clubhouse is $150, season grounds $75. Mon.-Thur., daily ticket clubhouse $20, grounds $10. Fri.-Sun., daily ticket clubhouse $35, grounds $20. 30% discount by March 19, 20% discount by April 16. Advantage International, 1266 E. Main St., 7th fl., Stamford, CT 06902. (800) 964-4742.
How to play: You must be accompanied by a member. General manager or pro can extend invitation. (201) 777-5178.

BellSouth Senior Classic at Opryland

SPRINGHOUSE GOLF CLUB

Hard by the banks of Tennessee's broad Cumberland River and overlooked by towering limestone bluffs, this 1990 layout has the bubbly, open terrain of a classic links that's been tailored to fit the unique features of the land it occupies. In fact, it encompasses 20 acres of protected wetlands, providing habitat for bluebirds, purple martins and bats. Hummingbirds and butterflies feed at a planting bed next to the sixth tee.

Designed by Larry Nelson, a U.S. Open and two-time PGA champion, the course takes its name from the picturesque 1850s springhouse that still sits behind the green of the fourth hole.

In 1995, a 55-minute rain delay during the final round gave Jim Dent time to nap before winning. "It was perfect for me," said Dent. "I knew it wouldn't rain us out, so in that delay I took a nap and played the next 15 holes at 4-under-par."

Lee Trevino's record 17-under-par 199 in 1994 proved that this course will succumb to a scrambler who can answer its greenside mounds and grass bunkers with a bagful of creative shots.

TOURNAMENT-AT-A-GLANCE

Course: Springhouse Golf Club
Type: Public
Location: 18 Springhouse Ln., Nashville, TN 37214
Phone: (615) 871-7888
When: May 24–26, 1996
How To Get There: Take I-40 to Briley Pkwy. N/Opryland Exit or I-65 to Briley Pkwy. S/Opryland Exit. Take Briley Pkwy. to McGavock Pike (Exit 12A). Half-mile to course.
Broadcast: NBC (1996)
Purse: $1.1 million (1996)
Tournament Record: 17-under-par 199, Lee Trevino, 1994

●TOUGHEST HOLE

No. 11 has played marginally tougher than No. 4, but both rank among the 50 toughest on the Tour. On the long, par-4 11th, the Cumberland River runs the length of the hole along the right, but tee shots are aimed that way to avoid a fairway bunker. The narrow green is guarded by a long bunker to the right and three mounds to the right.

●BEST PLACE TO WATCH

The fourth is the layout's signature hole. Trees narrow the flight path of the tee shot; water stretches along the left side of the fairway and then crosses to the front and right of the green. The viewing fun comes in watching approach shots to a green that slopes downhill toward the creek and can severely penalize a fading approach.

●WHO THE COURSE FAVORS

A long hitter has a slight advantage, but a good putter and scrambler can make up for lack of length around the greens.

HOLE	YARDS	PAR	HOLE	YARDS	PAR
1	530	5	10	520	5
2	420	4	11	435	4
3	162	3	12	531	5
4	391	4	13	170	3
5	435	4	14	340	4
6	535	5	15	398	4
7	415	4	16	323	4
8	175	3	17	212	3
9	360	4	18	431	4
			TOTAL	6783	72

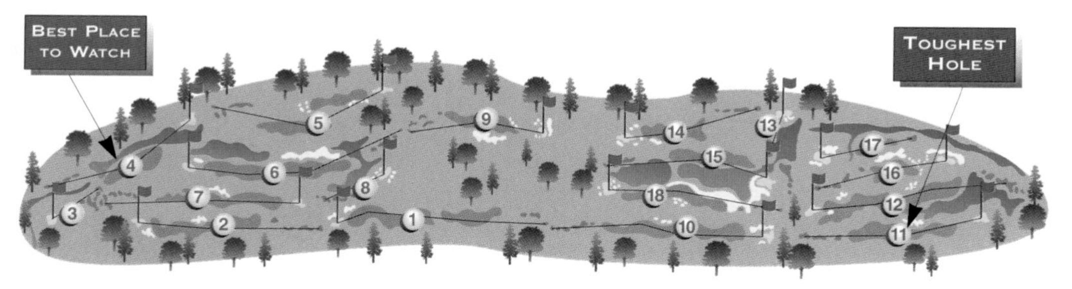

Springhouse Golf Club
Architect: Larry Nelson (1990)

LODGING

$$$ Opryland Hotel, 2800 Opryland Dr., Nashville. (615) 889-1000. 2 minutes from Springhouse GC.
$$ Sheraton Music City, 777 McGavock Pike, Nashville. (615) 885-2200. 10 minutes from Springhouse GC.
$$ Hermitage Hotel, 231 Sixth Ave., Nashville. (615) 244-3121. 20 minutes from Springhouse GC.

DINING

Old Hickory at Opryland, 2800 Opryland Dr., Nashville. (615) 871-6848.
Stockyard, 901 Second Ave., Nashville. (615) 255-6464.
Sunset Grill, 2001 Belcourt Ave., Nashville. (615) 386-3663.

PUBLIC COURSES TO PLAY IN AREA

Hermitage Golf Course, 3939 Old Hickory Blvd., Old Hickory, Tenn. (615) 847-4001. Public. 18/6,800/72. 20 minutes from Springhouse GC.
Legends Club of Tennessee, 1500 Legends Club Ln., Franklin, Tenn, (615) 790-1300. Public. North: 18/7,190/72. South: 18/7,113/71. 40 minutes from Springhouse GC.

TICKETS & ACCESSIBILITY

How to watch: Tue., Nisus Pro-Celebrity Shoot-Out, junior golf clinic. Wed.-Thur., pro-am. Fri.-Sun., championship rounds. Weekly pass, $30. BellSouth Senior Classic at Opryland, Springhouse Golf Club, 18 Springhouse Ln., Nashville, TN 37214. (615) 871-7888.
How to play: Public access course. (615) 871-7759.

Bruno's Memorial Classic

Greystone Golf Course

LODGING

$$$ Wynfrey Hotel, U.S. Hwy. 31 at The Galleria, Birmingham, Ala. (205) 987-1600. 25 minutes from Greystone GC.
$$ Sheraton Perimeter, 8 Perimeter Dr., I-459 at U.S. Hwy. 280, Birmingham, Ala. (205) 967-2700. 10 minutes from Greystone GC.
$$ Residence Inn, 3 Greenhill Pkwy. at U.S. Hwy. 280, Birmingham, Ala. (205) 991-8686. 5 minutes from Greystone GC.

DINING

Ruby Tuesday, 3407 Colonnade Pkwy., Birmingham, Ala. (205) 967-1384.
Chili's, 101 Inverness Corners, Birmingham, Ala. (205) 980-0290.
Longhorn Steakhouse, 10 Meadowview Dr., Birmingham, Ala. (205) 995-9044.

PUBLIC COURSES TO PLAY IN AREA

Bent Brook, 7900 Dickey Springs Rd., Bessemer, Ala. Public. (205) 424-2368. Brook: 9/3,570/35. Graveyard: 9/3,483/36. Windmill: 9/3,364/35. 30 minutes from Greystone GC.
Eagle Point Golf Club, 4500 Eagle Point Dr., Birmingham, Ala. Public. (205) 991-9070. 18/6,500/71. 5 minutes from Greystone GC.
Oxmoor Valley Golf Club, 100 Sun Belt Pkwy., Birmingham, Ala. Public. (205)290-0940. Ridge: 18/7,055/72. Valley: 18/7,292/72. 30 minutes from Greystone GC.

TICKETS & ACCESSIBILITY

How to watch: Tue., shoot-out. Wed.-Thur., pro-am. Fri.-Sun., championship rounds. Daily tickets: $12. Tickets discounted at area Bruno's retail locations. Bruno's Memorial Classic, 1200 Corporate Dr., Suite 410, Birmingham, AL 35242. (205) 939-4653.
How to play: Greystone Golf Club is a private course. You must be accompanied by a member.

TOURNAMENT-AT-A-GLANCE

Course: Greystone Golf Club
Type: Private
Location: 4100 Greystone Dr., Birmingham, AL 35242
Phone: (205) 980-5200
When: May 31–June 2, 1996
How To Get There: Take I-459, exit at U.S. Hwy. 280. Travel east, past Hwy. 119, to Hugh Daniel Dr. Turn left, go 1/2-mile to club entrance on left.
Broadcast: None (1995)
Purse: $1.05 million (1995)
Tournament Record: 15-under-par 201, Jim Dent, 1994 and Graham Marsh, 1995

The Bob Cupp and Hubert Green–designed Greystone course, located within a gated community in Birmingham, Ala., is long and fairly tight. It favors long or straight hitters off the tee and, indeed, three of the first four Bruno's titles went to acknowledged tee masters: George Archer in the 1992 inaugural, Jim Dent in '94 and Graham Marsh in '95. In '93, Bob Murphy rode a hot putter to victory.

Marsh's emphatic five-stroke victory in 1995 was the first Senior Tour triumph for the native Australian. He shot out of the gate with scores of 68 and 63 in the first two rounds, then coasted in with a 2-under 70 on his way to equaling the tournament's 54-hole record. Marsh isn't particularly long off the tee, but as he himself said, he's good at "getting the ball in position." That's key at Greystone.

•TOUGHEST HOLE

The No. 3 hole is a slight dogleg right, bordered by a ditch on the right of the fairway leading to a pond at the right of the angled green. A tight tee shot must be played left-center, toward the bordering hillside. Right-side shots will be fed sideways down toward the water. Pin placements on the right side of the green will force an approach to carry a considerable amount of water.

•BEST PLACE TO WATCH

The 14th is a medium-distance par-3 with a slight downhill shot from the tee to a green that has a creek crossing in front and meandering around a large greenside bunker on the right side. This is a fun hole to play and to watch.

•WHO THE COURSE FAVORS

Long, straight hitters should be able to set themselves up off the tee with a slight edge for approach.

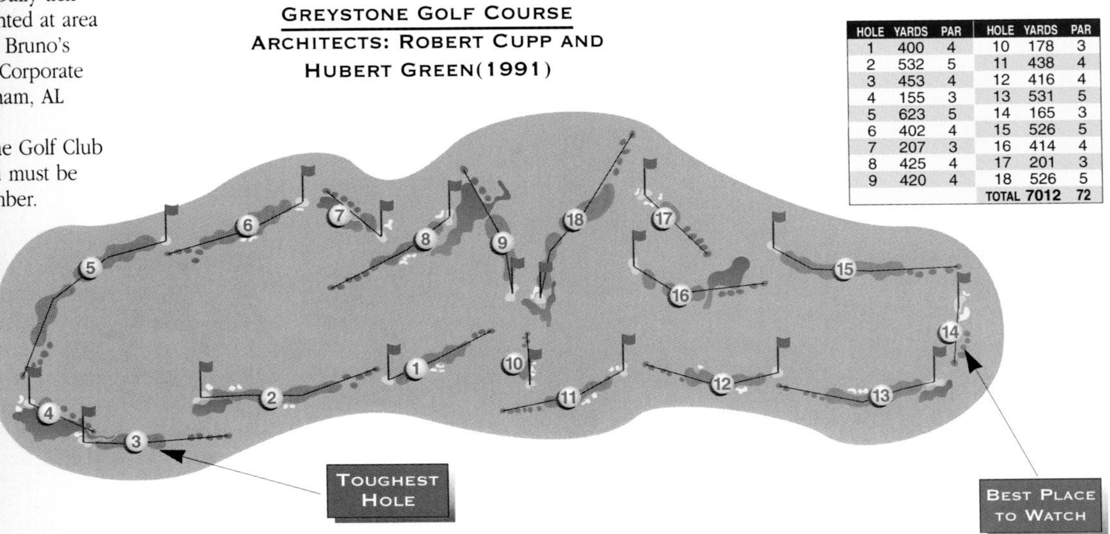

HOLE	YARDS	PAR	HOLE	YARDS	PAR
1	400	4	10	178	3
2	532	5	11	438	4
3	453	4	12	416	4
4	155	3	13	531	5
5	623	5	14	165	3
6	402	4	15	526	5
7	207	3	16	414	4
8	425	4	17	201	3
9	420	4	18	526	5
			TOTAL	7012	72

DALLAS REUNION

OAK CLIFF COUNTRY CLUB

A three-day pro-am is part of the unique format offered by the 54-hole Dallas Reunion. Inaugurated in 1985, the event moved to Oak Cliff in 1994.

The first winner at Oak Cliff, Larry Gilbert, propelled himself to a one-stroke victory with a dart of an 8-iron at the par-3 17th hole that stopped within a foot of the cup. It was the "shot of the tournament," said Gilbert.

Not a long course, Oak Cliff does ask for a degree of accuracy off the tee. Rocky Thompson failed on that count at the 16th hole, where he lost his lead in 1994 after finding a tree with his tee shot.

In 1995, Tom Wargo was a runaway, wire-to-wire seven-stroke victor. Wargo scrambled when he needed to, but attributed his rounds of 64, 64 and 69 to staying out of the trees. As startling as Wargo's numbers were, the 6,452, par-70 Oak Cliff course yielded only seven other sub-par totals.

TOURNAMENT-AT-A-GLANCE

Course: Oak Cliff Country Club
Type: Private
Location: 2200 W. Red Bird Lane, Dallas, TX 75232
Phone: (214) 331-4336
When: June 7–9, 1996
How To Get There: Take I-35 or I-20 to Hwy. 67. From I-35 go south to Red Bird Lane. Turn left. From I-20, go north to Red Bird Lane. Turn right.
Broadcast: None (1996)
Purse: $600,000 (1996)
Tournament Record: 15-under-par 201, Chi Chi Rodriguez, 1987 (at par-72 Bent Tree CC, Dallas)

●TOUGHEST HOLE

One of the most arduous par-4s on the Senior Tour, Oak Cliff's 15th hole is a dogleg left that presents two choices off the tee. Because of a 35-foot drop in the fairway, golfers may elect to use a driver and attempt to reach the lower, forward part of the fairway. A conservative tee shot would hold the plateau and leave a 170-yard approach that has to carry water. The danger in going all out from the tee is in having the ball kick left, where trees can block the approach. To cap it all off, there's a prominent swale on the right side of the green.

●BEST PLACE TO WATCH

Oak Cliff's seventh is a 172-yarder with an uphill tee shot to a green closely protected by five sand traps. Severely sloped, this green plays among the fastest on the course. This is a supurb spectating hole where fans get to see a challenging tee shot followed by a demanding putting test.

●WHO THE COURSE FAVORS

A player with a strong wedge game will do well here because of the need to get up and down at a number of small greens that are difficult to snag in regulation.

HOLE	YARDS	PAR	HOLE	YARDS	PAR
1	407	4	10	423	4
2	489	5	11	357	4
3	176	3	12	361	4
4	403	4	13	160	3
5	377	4	14	544	5
6	401	4	15	407	4
7	172	3	16	382	4
8	401	4	17	149	3
9	404	4	18	439	4
			TOTAL	6452	70

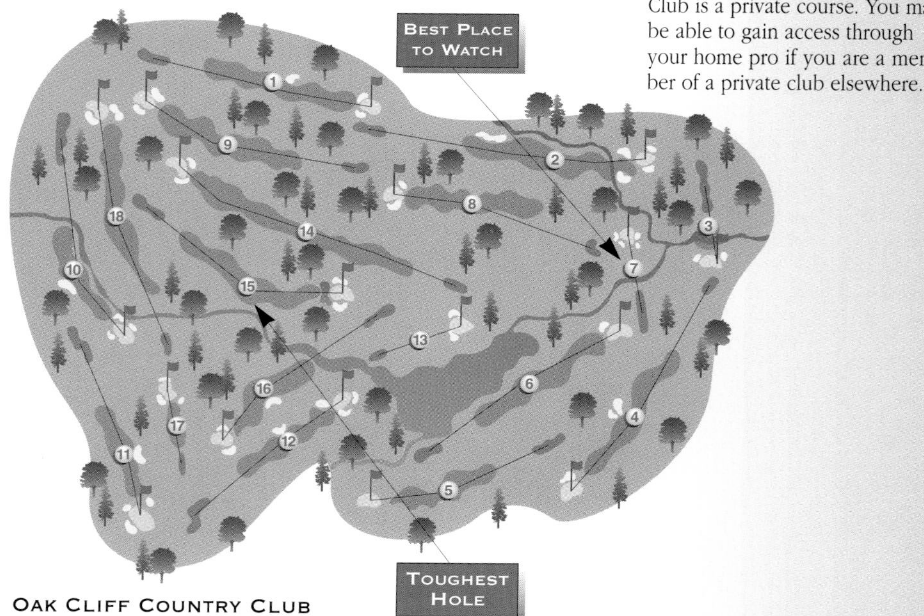

OAK CLIFF COUNTRY CLUB
ARCHITECT: PRESS MAXWELL (1953)

LODGING

$$ Hyatt Regency, 300 Reunion Blvd., Dallas. (214) 651-1234. 15 minutes from Oak Cliff CC.
$ Holiday Inn Southwest, 711 E. Camp Wisdom Rd., Duncanville, Texas. (214) 298-8911. 10 minutes from Oak Cliff CC.
$ Lexington Suites, 4150 Independence Blvd., Dallas. (214) 298-7014. 10 minutes from Oak Cliff CC.

DINING

Chili's, 7035 Marvin D. Love Fwy., Dallas. (214) 330-4829.
Black Eyed Pea, 3907 Camp Wisdom Rd., Dallas. (214) 780-9951.
Tia's Tex-Mex Grill, 7115 Marvin D. Love Fwy., Dallas. (214) 709-9927.

PUBLIC COURSES TO PLAY IN AREA

Steven's Park, 1005 N. Montclair, Dallas. Public. (214) 670-7506. 18/6,005/71. 10 minutes from Oak Cliff CC.
Country View, 240 W. Beltline Rd., Lancaster, Texas. Public. (214) 227-0995. 18/6,610/71. 30 minutes from Oak Cliff CC.

TICKETS & ACCESSIBILITY

How to watch: Tues., Skin's game. Wed.-Thur., pro-am. Fri., championship rounds. Sat., kid's clinic. Sat.-Sun., championship rounds. Daily ticket (Fri.-Sun.): $20. Weekly ticket: $40. Dallas Reunion Pro-Am, P.O. Box 140679, Dallas, TX 75214. (214) 827-4653.
How to play: Oak Cliff Country Club is a private course. You may be able to gain access through your home pro if you are a member of a private club elsewhere.

Pittsburgh Senior Classic

Quicksilver Golf Club

TOURNAMENT-AT-A-GLANCE

Course: Quicksilver Golf Club
Type: Public
Location: 2000 Quicksilver Rd., Midway, PA 15060
Phone: (412) 796-1811
When: June 14–16, 1996
How To Get There: Take Rte. 22 to Midway/McDonald Exit. Proceed south on Route 980, 2 1/2 miles to Quicksilver Rd. Turn right.
Broadcast: None (1995)
Purse: $1.1 million (1995)
Tournament Record: 9-under-par 207, Bob Charles, 1993

Less than three decades ago, when some of today's Senior Tour pros were just reaching their PGA Tour primes, the site of today's Quicksilver Golf Club was nothing but a strip mine. The property turned from coal production to pleasure in the early 1970s with the opening of the Fallen Timber Golf Club, but the course was best known for its length and the scars that mining had left behind.

That all changed in 1989, when renovations added dozens of bunkers, reshaped several greens and water hazards, and reseeded the whole layout. Arnold Palmer has since supervised additional changes to two holes.

The results: a layout now rated one of the best in the state. At 6,907 yards, Quicksilver is among the most challenging in the nation, giving up only a sprinkling of scores in the 60s.

●TOUGHEST HOLE

One of the 30 toughest holes on the Senior Tour, the 10th yielded just 10 birdies across three rounds of play in 1994. Out of bounds looms perilously close along the hole's right side, and the slope of the tee-shot landing area doesn't make things any easier. Players usually pull out a mid-iron to reach a green flanked in front by a pair of bunkers. Again, out of bounds awaits strayed shots—this time just 15 yards from the putting surface.

●BEST PLACE TO WATCH

Challenge and excitement blend at the superior finishing hole, where a hill behind the green provides plenty of room for crowds of seated spectators. The tee shot must thread several oddly shaped bunkers left and right of the fairway, including the dangerous "church pew" hazard.

●WHO THE COURSE FAVORS

With eight of its 10 par-4 holes exceeding 400 yards, the course favors a golfer either long off the tee or accurate with mid- to long-irons.

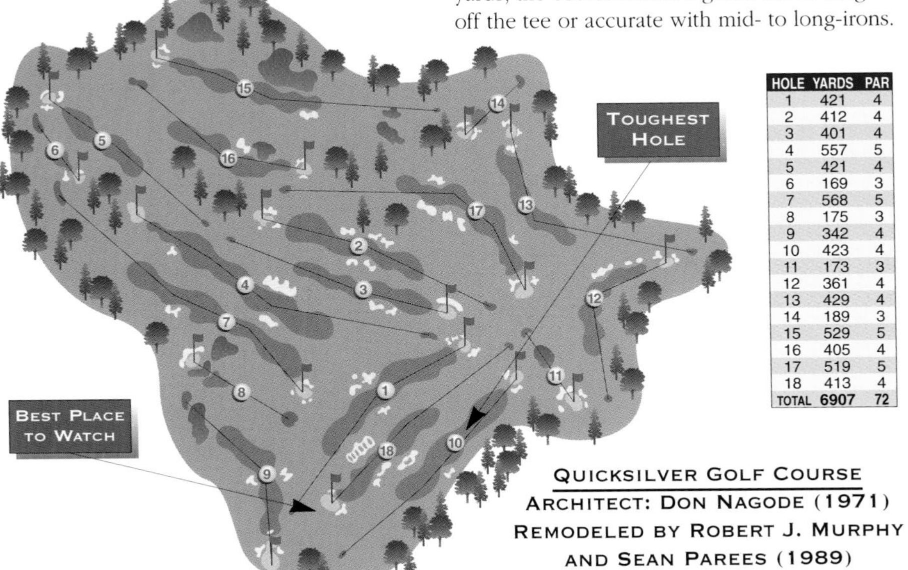

HOLE	YARDS	PAR
1	421	4
2	412	4
3	401	4
4	557	5
5	421	4
6	169	3
7	568	5
8	175	3
9	342	4
10	423	4
11	173	3
12	361	4
13	429	4
14	189	3
15	529	5
16	405	4
17	519	5
18	413	4
TOTAL	6907	72

Quicksilver Golf Course
Architect: Don Nagode (1971)
Remodeled by Robert J. Murphy and Sean Parees (1989)

LODGING

$$ Clubhouse Inn, 5311 Campbell's Run Rd., Robinson Township, Pa. (412) 788-8400. 30 minutes from Quicksilver GC.
$ Red Roof Inn, 6404 Steubenville Pike, Robinson Township, Pa. (412) 787-7870. 15 minutes from Quicksilver GC.
$ Comfort Inn, 7011 Old Steubenville Pike, Oakdale, Pa. (412) 787-2600. 15 minutes from Quicksilver GC.

DINING

Red Lobster, Robinson Town Center, Robinson Township, Pa. (412) 788-8700. 15 minutes from Quicksilver GC.
Dingbat's, Robinson Town Center,. Robinson Township, Pa. (412) 787-7010. 15 minutes from Quicksilver GC.
Red Bull Inn, 5205 Campbell's Run Rd., Robinson Township, Pa. (412) 787-2855. 15 minutes from Quicksilver GC.

PUBLIC COURSES TO PLAY IN AREA

Fort Cherry, 80 Fort Cherry Rd., McDonald, Pa. Public. (412) 926-4182. 18/6,205/70. 10 minutes from Quicksilver GC.
Hickory Heights, 116 Hickory Heights Dr., Bridgeville, Pa. Public. (412) 257-0300. 18/6,514/72. 25 minutes from Quicksilver GC.

TICKETS & ACCESSIBILITY

How to watch: Tue., Merrill Lynch Shoot-Out, junior clinic. Wed.-Thur., pro-am. Fri.-Sun., championship rounds. Daily, grounds-only: Mon., $5; Tue.-Thur., $15; Fri.-Sun., $20. Weekly, grounds-only, $85. Weekly clubhouse, $125. Pittsburgh Senior Classic, Quicksilver Golf Club, 2000 Quicksilver Rd., Midway, PA 15060. (412) 796-1825.
How to play: Public access facility. 18/7,085/72. (412) 796-1811.

Bell Atlantic Classic

CHESTER VALLEY GOLF CLUB

Not far from Philadelphia, Chester Valley quite definitely is in the Pennsylvania countryside—Northeastern trees, elevational changes from tee to fairway to green, subtle streams and ponds, sloping greens. And this course, designed by George Fazio, outranks all others on the Tour in degree of difficulty. It's the type many folks refer to when they talk about a "traditional" golf course in America.

And when they talk about tough, too. Four holes at Chester Valley registered among the 20 most difficult on the 1994 Tour; eight holes placed among the top 50. No other event that season came close. The U.S. Senior Open, which changes venues annually and was played on storied Pinehurst No. 2 that year, placed only six holes in the top 50. The PGA Seniors' Championship, anchored at PGA National's Champion course, had just five holes in the top 50. Overall, the field at the 1994 Bell Atlantic Classic averaged 4.183 strokes above the course par of 70.

"Long hitters have no advantage there," notes two-time winner Lee Trevino. "Chester Valley is a beautiful, challenging course. It is living proof that a golf course doesn't have to be 7,200 yards long to be difficult."

The Bell Atlantic, begun in 1985, is one of the older events on the Senior Tour, and Chester Valley consistently crowns a polished veteran. Besides Trevino, its roster of champions includes Don January, Gary Player, Chi Chi Rodriguez, Bruce Crampton and Bob Charles.

Though the Bell Atlantic can count on a quality field, the course usually wins. Don't expect to see many birdies here. Most pros are happy for long, unbroken strings of pars, which is just about what Jim Colbert settled for in '95 when he registered a 3-under-par 207 to win.

The year before, Trevino wasn't what anyone would call spectacular. Still, he was good enough to win his second Bell Atlantic in three years when he posted a 4-under-par 206 total to eclipse runner-up Mike Hill by two shots. In his final round, Trevino had three birdies and a bogey to go with 14 pars.

This is a place where the player who makes the least mistakes is likely to emerge the victor.

TOURNAMENT-AT-A-GLANCE

Course: Chester Valley Golf Club
Type: Private
Location: 430 Swedesford Rd., Malvern, PA 19355
Phone: (610) 647-4007
When: June 21–23, 1996
How To Get There: Take U.S. Rte. 30 to Church Rd. From east, turn right; from west, turn left. Follow Church to intersection with Swedesford Rd.
Broadcast: ESPN (1996)
Purse: $900,000 (1995)
Tournament Record: 8-under-par 202, Chi Chi Rodriguez, 1987

"CHESTER VALLEY IS NO COURSE TO MESS WITH. FIVE- OR 6-UNDER USUALLY WINS IT EVERY YEAR. YOU HAVE TO HAVE PATIENCE ON THIS GOLF COURSE."

—LEE TREVINO,
TWO-TIME BELL ATLANTIC CLASSIC CHAMPION

●TOUGHEST HOLE

On a course featuring more of the toughest holes on the Tour than any other Senior layout, No. 6 stands supreme in degree of difficulty. In 1994, this hole played closer to bogey than par, averaging a whopping 4.507 for the tournament and ranking third toughest among all the holes on the Tour that season. Yes, the hole allowed 119 pars in the '94 event. But it also held birdies to a mere seven, compared to 103 scores of bogey or more. This is a tough green to hit in regulation. Because of a creek that crosses the fairway, most players hit about a 3-wood to lay up short with the tee shot. But if the ball is left too short and doesn't reach the flat land just before the creek, the approach to the green will be a long iron off a downhill lie, one of the hardest shots in golf.

●BEST PLACE TO WATCH

A pinpoint tee shot is required to thread the tree-lined fairway of the 12th hole, where a rippled landing area usually presents players with an uphill lie that lengthens the approach shot to a steeply sloping green. Complicating the challenge from the tee is a creek that crosses the fairway and readily swallows balls that trail left. Were it not for No. 6, this would be the toughest hole on the course. In 1994, it averaged 4.463 for the tournament and was fifth toughest on Tour.

●WHO THE COURSE FAVORS

The player who can play every club in the bag. A guy like Lee Trevino. He's won the event twice (1992, 1994).

HOLE	YARDS	PAR	HOLE	YARDS	PAR
1	368	4	10	188	3
2	537	5	11	357	4
3	338	4	12	410	4
4	378	4	13	416	4
5	162	3	14	488	5
6	411	4	15	179	3
7	163	3	16	403	4
8	385	4	17	391	4
9	367	4	18	435	4
			TOTAL	6376	70

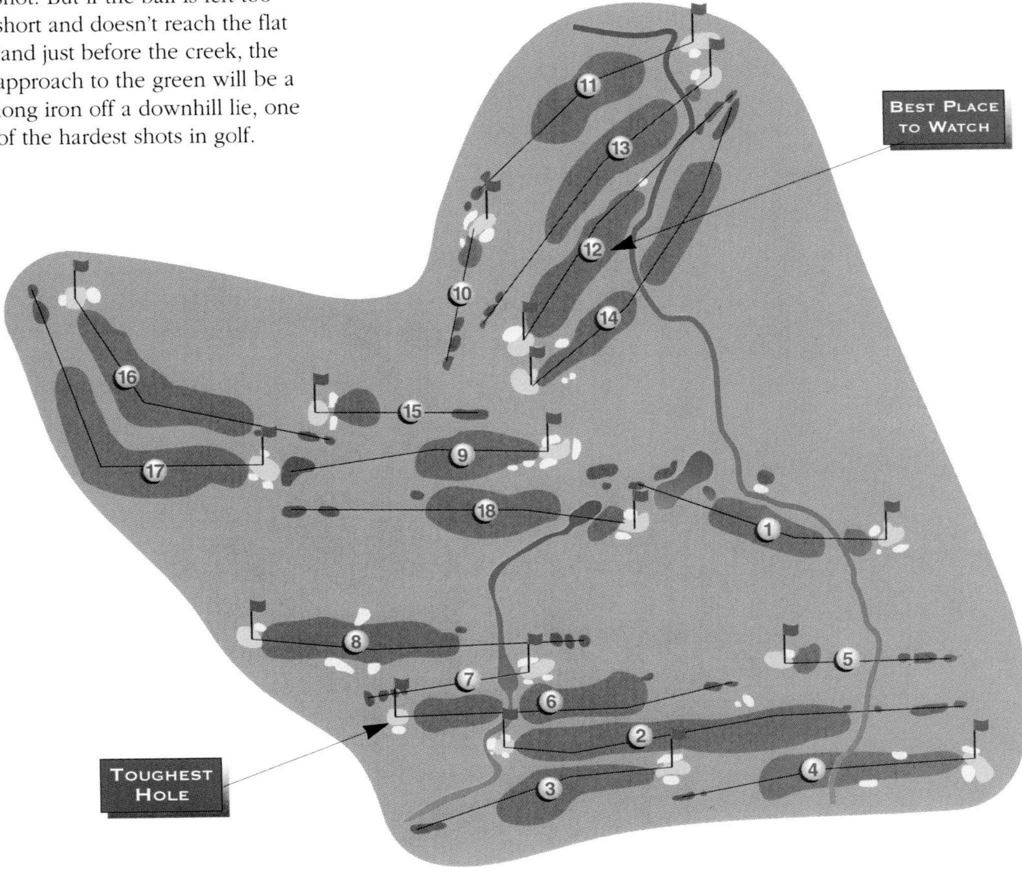

CHESTER VALLEY GOLF CLUB
ARCHITECT: DONALD ROSS (1928)
REMODELED BY GEORGE FAZIO (1969)

LODGING

$$$ Doubletree Guest Suites, 888 Chesterbrook Blvd., Wayne, Pa. (610) 647-6700. 10 minutes from Chester Valley GC.

$$$ Sheraton Great Valley, Rtes. 30 & 202, Frazer, Pa. (610) 524-5500. 4 minutes from Chester Valley GC.

$$ Hampton Inn Lionville, Rtes. 100 & 113, Lionville, Pa. (610) 363-5555. 14 minutes from Chester Valley GC.

DINING

Cafe Lagrande, 240 Lancaster Ave., Malvern, Pa. (610) 644-7334.

Casey's Dugout, 516 King Rd., Paoli, Pa. (610) 644-3084.

Il Primo, 237 W. Lancaster Ave., Paoli, Pa. (610) 296-7277.

PUBLIC COURSES TO PLAY IN AREA

Pickering Valley, S. Whitehorse Rd., Phoenixville, Pa. (610) 933-2223. 18/6,530/72. 15 minutes from Chester Valley GC.

Meadowbrook, 1415 State Rte. 29, Phoenixville, Pa. (610) 933-2929. 9/3,050/37. 15 minutes from Chester Valley GC.

TICKETS & ACCESSIBILITY

How to watch: Mon., PNC Bank pro-am. Tue., Merrill Lynch Shoot-Out, CertainTeed junior golf clinic. Wed.-Thur., pro-am. Fri.-Sun., championship rounds. Mon. admission free. Daily ticket, $20. Season ticket, $60. Bell Atlantic Classic, Tickets, P.O. Box 506, Malvern, PA 19355. (610) 644-2582.

How to play: Private club. Guests must be accompanied by member. Pro is authorized to extend reciprocal invitation.

Kroger Senior Classic

The Golf Center at Kings Island

An early entry in Jack Nicklaus' design portfolio, this collaboration with Desmond Muirhead has been called "an easier Muirfield" in reference to the signature course the team built elsewhere in Ohio.

The Grizzly, despite five lake holes, was meant to present a fair, playable challenge to the general public. The fairways are somewhat tight, often surrounded by moundings, but the relatively flat greens for the most part present open approaches in front.

For the Senior pros, there are always quite a few scores in the 60s here. In 1994, Jim Colbert registered rounds of 66, 64 and 69 en route to a two-shot victory over Ray Floyd. But it was Floyd's charge that testified as to how exciting the stretch run can be here. Despite turning a six-shot lead into 10 on the front side, Colbert was not home clear. Floyd eagled No. 9, then rang up four consecutive birdies to gain six strokes on the leader.

"I never felt seriously threatened, but I didn't feel completely comfortable either," Colbert said later. "I said, 'If Raymond is going to shoot 25 back here, God bless him.' "

TOURNAMENT-AT-A-GLANCE

Course: The Golf Center at Kings Island—Grizzly Course
Type: Public
Location: 6042 Fairway Dr., Mason, OH 45040
Phone: (513) 398-5742
When: June 28–30, 1996
How To Get There: Take I-71 to Exit 25 (northbound) or Exit 25B (southbound). Proceed west on Kings Mills Rd. to Fairway Dr.
Broadcast: ESPN (1996)
Purse: $900,000 (1996)
Tournament Record: 15-under-par 198, Gibby Gilbert, 1992

●TOUGHEST HOLE

They use the terms "beautiful" and "treacherous" together in describing the Grizzly's 18th hole. A lake comes into play from almost 200 yards out, but most players will opt not to cross it in two. Instead, they'll be flying wedges over the water to a green that slopes from back to front, leaving little room for error when the flagstick is placed up front.

●BEST PLACE TO WATCH

Also a par-5, the ninth is a scoring hole for the players, an entertaining hole for the fans. A large grandstand accommodates spectators. The lake here is 50 yards in front of the green; it's clearable, with fairway beyond. But this green is very reachable in two for the pros and will yield numerous putts for eagles.

●WHO THE COURSE FAVORS

The stronger player off the tee should have an advantage. With many greens providing accommodating openings in front, the approach is not so crucial. Shots that come up short of the green should still provide up-and-down opportunities.

HOLE	YARDS	PAR	HOLE	YARDS	PAR
1	437	4	10	366	4
2	437	4	11	398	4
3	374	4	12	198	3
4	518	5	13	412	4
5	163	3	14	441	4
6	402	4	15	369	4
7	377	4	16	186	3
8	215	3	17	403	4
9	489	5	18	546	5
			TOTAL	6731	71

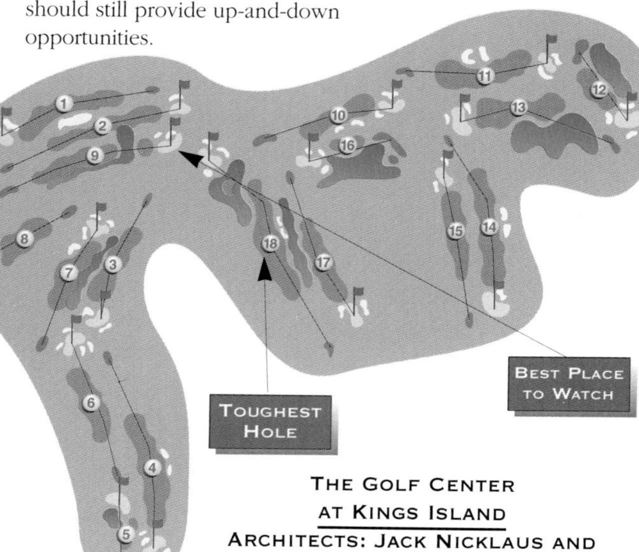

The Golf Center at Kings Island
Architects: Jack Nicklaus and Desmond Muirhead (1971)

LODGING

$$ Embassy Suites, 4554 Lake Forest Dr., Blue Ash, Ohio. (513) 733-8900. 15 minutes from Kings Island.
$$ Doubletree Guest Suites, I-275 and Reed Hartman Hwy., Sharonville, Ohio. (513) 489-3636. 15 minutes from Kings Island.
$$ Residence Inn, Reed Hartman Hwy., Cincinnati. (513) 530-5060. 15 minutes from Kings Island.

DINING

Houston, 4026 Route 42, Mason, Ohio. (513) 398-7377.
Golden Lamb Inn, 27 S. Broadway, Lebanon, Ohio. (513) 932-5065.
Black Forest, 8675 Cincinnati-Columbus Rd., Cincinnati. (513) 777-7600.

PUBLIC COURSES TO PLAY IN AREA

Blue Ash, 4040 Cooper Rd., Cincinnati. Public. (513) 745-8577. 18/6,600/72. 30 minutes from Kings Island.
Shaker Run, 4361 Greentree Rd., Lebanon, Ohio. Public. (513) 727-0007. 18/7,070/72. 30 minutes from Kings Island.

TICKETS & ACCESSIBILITY

How to watch: Wed.-Thur., pro-am. Fri.-Sun., championship rounds. Daily rounds, $25. Season clubhouse, $60. Kroger Senior Classic, P.O. Box 499, Mason, OH 45040. (513) 398-5742.
How to play: Public complex includes championship Grizzly Course, shorter Bruin Course (18/3,428/61), golf learning center, tennis courts, restaurant, banquet catering. (513) 398-7700.

VFW Senior Championship

Loch Lloyd Country Club

LODGING

$$$ Doubletree, 10100 College Blvd., Overland Park, Kan. (913) 451-6100. 20 minutes from Loch Lloyd CC.

$$ Marriott, 10800 Metcalf Ave., Overland Park, Kan. (913) 451-8000. 20 minutes from Loch Lloyd CC.

$$ Hyatt Regency Crown Center, 2345 McGee, Kansas City, Mo. (816) 421-1234. 40 minutes from Loch Lloyd CC.

DINING

Dick Clark's American Bandstand, 10975 Metcalf Ave., Overland Park, Kan. (913) 451-1600.

Smoke Stack Bar-B-Q, 13441 Holmes, Martin City, Mo. (816) 942-9141.

Stroud's, 1015 E. 85th St., Kansas City, Mo. (816) 333-2132.

PUBLIC COURSES TO PLAY IN AREA

Deer Creek, 7000 W. 133rd St., Overland Park, Kan. Semi-private (913) 681-3100. 18/6,890/72. 15 minutes from Loch Lloyd CC.

Longview Lake, 11100 View High Dr., Kansas City, Mo. Public. (816) 761-9445. 18/6,835/72. 20 minutes from Loch Lloyd CC.

TICKETS & ACCESSIBILITY

How to watch: Tue., Merrill Lynch Shoot-Out. Wed.-Thur., pro-am. Fri.-Sun., championship rounds. Daily tickets start at $10. Six-day passes are $40. Children under 12 free with paid adult. Loch Lloyd Country Club, Jim Kline, 10918 Elm Ave., Kansas City, MO 64134. (816) 765-6600.

How to play: Must be guest of member or pro may extend reciprocal invitation to private club members.

TOURNAMENT-AT-A-GLANCE

Course: Loch Lloyd Country Club
Type: Private
Location: 16750 Country Club Dr., Belton, MO 64012
Phone: (816) 322-1022
When: Aug. 2–4, 1996
How To Get There: Take I-435 to Holmes Rd. Exit and proceed south to 168th St.
Broadcast: ESPN (1996)
Purse: $900,000 (1996)
Tournament Record: 17-under-par 193, Gibby Gilbert, 1992

Designed by Donald Sechrest, this private course outside Kansas City is like two tracks in one. The first 10 holes are set on high, open ground, and they have a Scottish links-style flavor. At No. 11, however, the track tightens as it descends into a valley for a finish loaded with hazards. From there on, a creek meanders in and out of play, making its most dramatic appearance inside a 20-foot-wide moat at the par-4 15th.

Despite such treacherous hazards, Loch Lloyd has been proven vulnerable to low scores. Nine finishers in 1994 registered all three of their rounds in the 60s, led by Jim Colbert, who fashioned his second title in this event with a second-round 63.

● TOUGHEST HOLE

One of the 20 toughest holes on the Senior Tour, No. 17 runs uphill from the bottom of a valley. A creek meanders along the left side before crossing the fairway and joining a splash pool on the right side of the green. Further trouble is presented on the right by out of bounds. The three-tiered putting surface is deep, but not wide.

● BEST PLACE TO WATCH

Right behind the 11th hole, which shares its green with No. 17. From a hillside perch, spectators can see the action at 11, approaches to 17 and the tees at Nos. 12 and 18.

● WHO THE COURSE FAVORS

Accurate hitters off the tee will benefit from staying out of the long tournament rough, which can present problems to big hitters who miss the fairways and then have to attempt delicate approaches to well-protected greens.

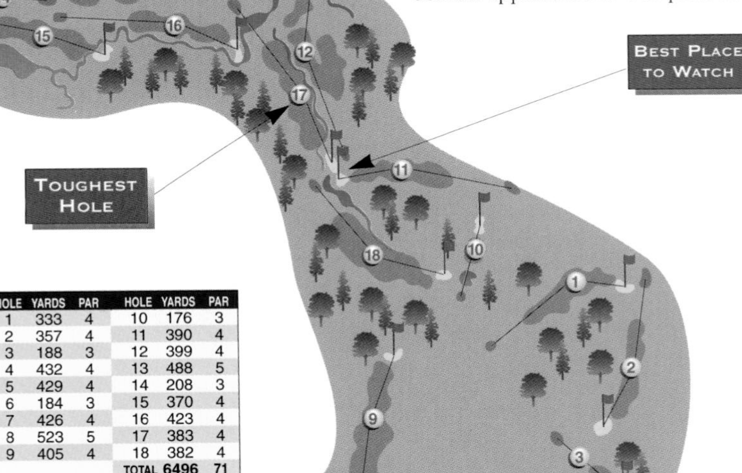

HOLE	YARDS	PAR	HOLE	YARDS	PAR
1	333	4	10	176	3
2	357	4	11	390	4
3	188	3	12	399	4
4	432	4	13	488	5
5	429	4	14	208	3
6	184	3	15	370	4
7	426	4	16	423	4
8	523	5	17	383	4
9	405	4	18	382	4
			TOTAL	6496	71

Loch Lloyd Country Club
Architect: Donald Sechrest (1990)

Burnet Senior Classic

BUNKER HILLS GOLF CLUB

There's a North woods feel to Bunker Hills, with its tall trees leafed at the top and thin-trunked below. The tournament layout is a combination of the three nines, with most of the holes coming from the original 18 and a handful from the newest nine. Some of the settings on this course are reminiscent of Pinehurst, the venerable North Carolina spread.

Weather is certainly a variable in the Minnesota summer. It can be warm and dry, as it was in 1994, when the Burnet was an August event, or drenchingly wet, as it was for much of the 1993 competition, when the tournament was held in June. During that inaugural, the Wednesday and Thursday pro-am tee times were delayed three hours due to heavy overnight rains. On both days, play began at 10 a.m. and was limited to nine holes per team. Heavy rains then forced suspension of play for two hours Saturday morning. Light rain continued through Sunday.

Somehow, the '93 Burnet pros got in 54 holes of golf. And, despite the weather, 151,000 fans crowded the fairways that week. Tournament officials attributed the good drainage to the course's being built on a glacial sand drift.

Chi Chi Rodriguez rode a 15-under 201 to win by two strokes over Bob Murphy and Jim Colbert. If there was a key to Rodriguez's victory, it was chipping in from 50 feet for a birdie on the fifth hole. In the final round, Rodriguez hit seven birdies in a nine-hole stretch. "I was in a zone out there," said Rodriguez. "When I get in a zone like this, nobody can touch me. I was in such a zone that I barely noticed the rain."

While the soggy conditions minimized the players' length off the tees, the rain did wonders for their iron play: every ball they hit seemed to hold the soft greens. Jack Kiefer faded on Saturday, but Friday's vulnerable targets helped him post a course-record-tying 64 in the first round.

In 1994, the weather was warm and dry and was just the ticket for Dave Stockton, who suffers from a bad back but plays better in warm weather. His 13-under sealed his second year in a row of $1 million in earnings.

TOURNAMENT-AT-A-GLANCE

Course: Bunker Hills Golf Club
Type: Public
Location: Foley Blvd. & Hwy. 242, Coon Rapids, MN 55433
Phone: (612) 783-8232
When: July 19–21, 1996
How To Get There: I-94 West to Rte. 252 North. Route 610 North to U.S. Hwy. 10. West to Foley Blvd.; proceed north to course.
Broadcast: ESPN (1996)
Purse: $1.1 million (1995)
Tournament Record: 15-under 201, Chi Chi Rodriguez, 1993

"I KNEW I WOULD WIN IT THEN, WHEN I CHIPPED IN; THAT WAS THE TURNING POINT. I WAS LOOKING AT BOGEY AND MADE BIRDIE. EVERY TOURNAMENT I'VE WON, I'VE ALWAYS MADE A SHOT LIKE THAT."

—CHI CHI RODRIGUEZ,

AFTER MAKING A 50-FOOT CHIP FOR BIRDIE ON NO. 5 TO HELP WIN THE '93 BURNET SENIOR CLASSIC

By Jeffrey G. Smith

THE RIGHT BUNKER ON NO. 8 HAS A DISTINCTIVE HIGH LIP.

●TOUGHEST HOLE

No. 14 is the course's toughest handicap hole. Though trees and out-of-bounds hem the fairway, the landing area is ample. An uphill lie greets the approach to a large green. Wind is often a factor.

●BEST PLACE TO WATCH

It may be only a par-3, but at 215 yards lots of things can happen at the eighth, especially when the wind kicks up. First, tee shots must carry both the water necking in from the right in front of the green and a deep trap on the shore side. Clear the water but come up short of the green, and the high lip of the bunker can cause fits. There's also a greenside trap to the left, but by comparison it is an easier extrication. The green tilts to the back and right, and front pin placement can make the approach difficult. Depending on the pin placement, the pros will hit anything from a 3-iron to a 3-wood.

●WHO THE COURSE FAVORS

Long-ball hitters, not only off the tee but on approach, have the advantage on this course, which generally affords plenty of driving room. There are six par-4 holes exceeding 400 yards, meaning the pressure will be on 3-iron and 4-iron approach shots. There are small trees lining most fairways, but there's little forest and very little water in play. All four par-3s are at least 180 yards, and the play on these can be a key to victory. The par-5s are reachable in two for the longer hitters. Greens are large, but not sloped.

HOLE	YARDS	PAR	HOLE	YARDS	PAR
1	425	4	10	410	4
2	530	5	11	370	4
3	180	3	12	515	5
4	365	4	13	200	3
5	535	5	14	430	4
6	420	4	15	390	4
7	400	4	16	410	4
8	215	3	17	180	3
9	384	4	18	535	5
			TOTAL	6894	72

BUNKER HILLS GOLF COURSE
ARCHITECT: DAVID GILL (1968)
REMODELED BY JOEL GOLDSTRAND (1987)

BEST PLACE TO WATCH

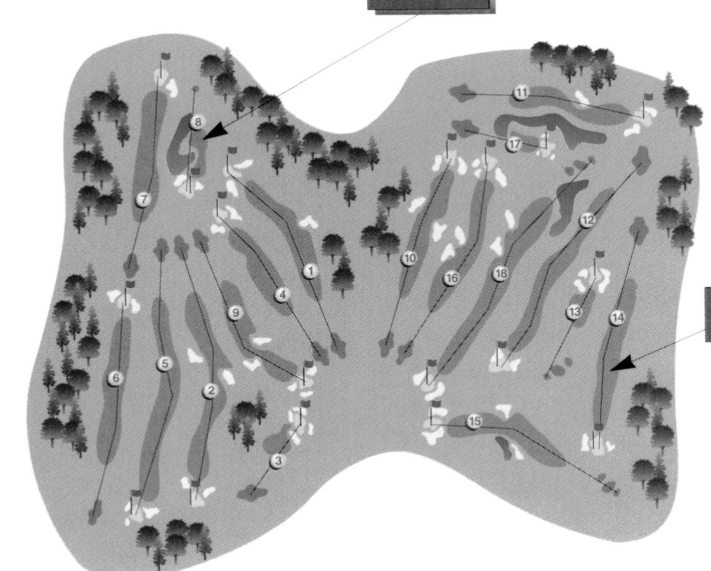

TOUGHEST HOLE

LODGING

$$$ Radisson Plaza, 35 S. Seventh St., Minneapolis. (612) 339-4900. 35 minutes from Bunker Hills.

$$ Country Suites, 155 N.W. Coon Rapids Blvd., Coon Rapids, Minn. (612) 780-3797. 10 minutes from Bunker Hills.

$ Super 8 Motel, 6445 James Circle, Brooklyn Center, Minn. (612) 566-9810. 10 minutes from Bunker Hills.

DINING

Shorewood, 6161 Hwy. 65 NE, Fridley, Minn. (612) 571-3444. 15 minutes from Bunker Hills.

Joe Senser's Sports Bar & Grill, 2350 N. Cleveland Ave., Roseville, Minn. (612) 631-1781. 25 minutes from Bunker Hills.

Dakota House, 1125 W. Main St., Anoka, Minn. (612) 388-7641. 15 minutes from Bunker Hills.

PUBLIC COURSES TO PLAY IN AREA

Links At Northfork, 153rd Ave., Ramsey, Minn. Public. (612) 241-0506. 18/6,988/72. 30 minutes from Bunker Hills.

Edinburgh USA, Edinburgh Crossing, Brooklyn Park, Minn. Public. (612) 424-7060. 18/6,701/72. 15 minutes from Bunker Hills.

TICKETS & ACCESSIBILITY

How to watch: Mon., Minnesota State Lottery celebrity Skins game. Tue., Norwest Shoot-Out. Wed., Norstan pro-am, 3M junior clinic. Thur., Norstan pro-am, Burnet Realty pro putting contest. Fri.-Sun., championship rounds. Season pass, $100; Daily Mon.-Thur., $15; Daily Fri.-Sun., $30. P.O. Box 33218, Coon Rapids, MN 55433-0218. (612) 783-9000 (within the Twin Cities) or (800) 546-8232.

How to play: Public access facility. North: 9/3,418/36. East: 9/3,381/36. West: 9/3,520/36. (612) 755-4141.

Ameritech Senior Open
KEMPER LAKES GOLF CLUB

Kemper Lakes, which straddles the Long Grove–Hawthorn Woods border 35 miles from downtown Chicago, deservedly enjoys a reputation as one of the top public-access courses in the United States, perhaps the best in the Midwest.

The challenges of the Ameritech Senior Open's new host site are plentiful: it's a long course, there are lots of fairway and greenside traps, and there's water in play on half the holes. Many greens have considerable undulation; many more, at least for championship events, can be exceedingly fast. Toss in a little wind, and the course can become downright brutal. Still, the public beats a path to the first tee, willingly paying $100 per round for greens fees with cart. Less skilled players, however, should not be playing here.

If there's a drawback to Kemper, it's aesthetics. Designed by Tom Killian and Dick Nugent, Kemper seems a bit contrived. It strikes the beholder as less natural in its setting than, say, Cog Hill No. 4 to the south, host site for a regular PGA Tour event. But, with a lot of elbow room for each hole, Kemper is certainly a better-than-average spectator's course.

Owned by a corporation bearing the same name, the Kemper Lakes course, annual home of the Illinois PGA sectional championship, has played host to a variety of major competitions: the 1989 PGA Championship, the 1992 U.S. Women's Amateur and the PGA Grand Slam of Golf (1986, 1988-'90).

TOURNAMENT-AT-A-GLANCE

Course: Kemper Lakes Golf Club
Type: Public
Location: Old McHenry Rd., Long Grove, IL 60049
Phone: (708) 820-8887
When: July 26–28, 1996
How To Get There: Take I-94/I-294 to Route 22 Exit. Go west, approximately 8 miles to Old McHenry Rd. Turn right. Club is 1 mile on left.
Broadcast: CBS (1996)
Purse: $850,000 (1996)
Tournament Record: 16-under-par 200, Mike Hill, 1991 (at Stonebridge CC, Aurora, Ill.)

The 16th, 17th and 18th holes at Kemper are conceded to be among the toughest final three holes in golf, and they have played a part in determining winners and losers many times before.

In the final round of the 1989 PGA, Mike Reid came to the 16th with a three-shot edge before the roof fell in. First, he barely saved bogey on 16. Then, on the 17th, a par-3 surrounded by water, his 4-iron rolled just off the collar, 25 feet above the hole. Instead of chipping and running the ball, Reid attempted a lob shot, which came up 15 feet short. His first putt grazed the cup and stopped 2 feet away. His second putt hit the right side of the hole and spun out. Reid made 5, a double bogey, and Payne Stewart became PGA champion.

In 1989, winds whipping at 25 to 35 mph dominated the one-day PGA Grand Slam, which brings together the winners of the four men's majors. Curtis Strange won at 1-over 73, while Greg Norman, who finished fourth, didn't even bother to turn in his card. In 1990, Andy North prevailed, but what is notable about that year is that when an ill Curtis Strange withdrew, former Chicago Bears football coach Mike Ditka, a 7-handicapper, filled in against North, Craig Stadler and Stewart. Ditka was popular with the 3,000 local fans, but returned a no-card.

"IT'S THE FIRST TIME MY DAD HAD EVER SEEN ME WIN IN PERSON. THIS IS SOMETHING THAT DOESN'T HAPPEN VERY OFTEN ON THE SENIOR TOUR."

—DALE DOUGLASS,
1992 AMERITECH SENIOR OPEN CHAMPION

Courtesy of Ameritech Senior Open

KEMPER LAKES' 18TH TOPS THREE FINISHING HOLES CONSIDERED AMONG THE FINEST IN GOLF.

●TOUGHEST HOLE

The par-4 ninth plays as long as, or longer than, its listing. The tee shot must be negotiated between two sets of bunkers guarding both sides of the fairway. The approach is a long, uphill shot to a deep but relatively narrow green. The hole requires length and accuracy off the tee, length and pinpoint precision on approach. Putting should be the least of the worries here.

●BEST PLACE TO WATCH

The 11th hole is a par-5 that doglegs to the right and makes for great spectator sport. The approach drops in elevation to a wide but narrow green. The putting surface is guarded by a pond in front and a bunker in the back, accentuating the peril of the green's lack of depth. With the downward angle, many of the pros can reach this hole in two shots, but the dangers on approach are considerable. It's exciting and intriguing for spectators to guess and see what the pros will attempt and, ultimately, achieve. The final three holes are among the game's toughest closing trio, and many titles have been decided on that critical home stretch. Mike Reid's double-bogey on the watery par-3 17th cost him the 1989 PGA Championship. Vicki Goetze won the 1992 U.S. Women's Amateur by hitting the 18th green while her match-play opponent, Annika Sorenstam, caught the water in front and could only salvage bogey.

●WHO THE COURSE FAVORS

The course is regarded as fair to all types of players, but when the tees are set back, the longer hitter has a slight advantage. Being off the fairway is treacherous, so accuracy off the tee may be as key as length.

HOLE	YARDS	PAR	HOLE	YARDS	PAR
1	378	4	10	416	4
2	357	4	11	502	5
3	141	3	12	369	4
4	496	5	13	183	3
5	423	4	14	377	4
6	166	3	15	557	5
7	513	5	16	426	4
8	392	4	17	172	3
9	428	4	18	384	4
			TOTAL	6680	72

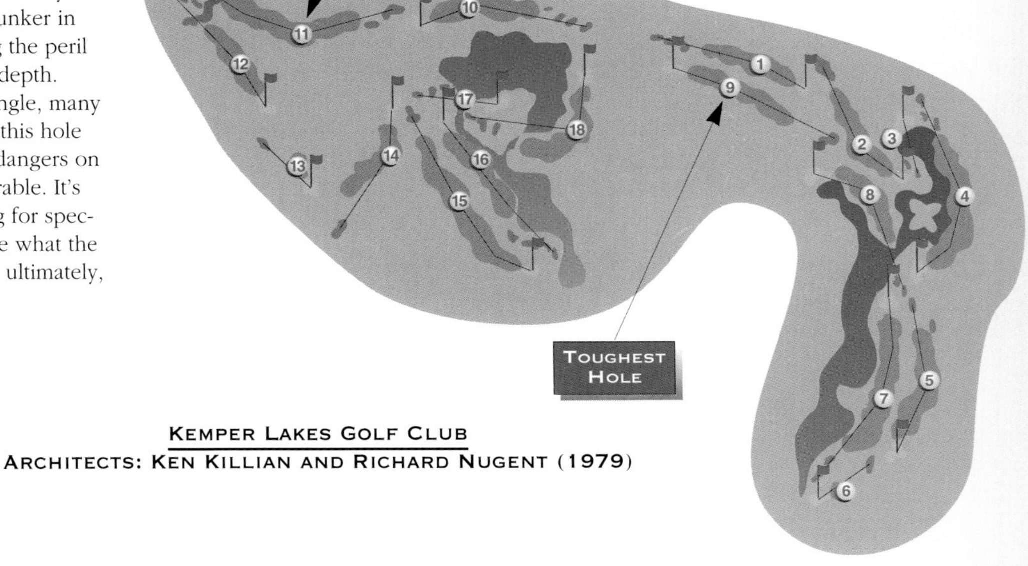

KEMPER LAKES GOLF CLUB
ARCHITECTS: KEN KILLIAN AND RICHARD NUGENT (1979)

LODGING

$$$ Marriott Lincolnshire, 10 Marriott Dr., Lincolnshire, Ill. (708) 634-0100. 15 minutes from Kemper Lakes GC.
$$$ Hyatt Deerfield, 1750 Lake Cook Rd., Deerfield, Ill. (708) 945-3400. 20 minutes from Kemper Lakes GC.
$$ Courtyard Marriott, 505 Milwaukee Ave., Lincolnshire, Ill. (708) 634-9555. 15 minutes from Kemper Lakes GC.

DINING

Bob Chinn's Crabhouse, 393 S. Milwaukee Ave., Wheeling, Ill. (708) 520-3633.
Julio's, 95 S. Rand Rd., Lake Zurich, Ill. (708) 438-3484.
Le Titi De Paris, 1015 W. Dundee Rd., Arlington Heights, Ill. (708) 506-0222.

PUBLIC COURSES TO PLAY IN AREA

Pine Meadow, 1 Pine Meadow Lane, Mundelein, Ill. Public. (708) 566-4653. 18/7,141/72. 20 minutes from Kemper Lakes GC.
Golf Club of Illinois, 1575 Edgewood Rd., Algonquin, Ill. Public. (708) 658-4400. 18/7,011/71. 30 minutes from Kemper Lakes GC.

TICKETS & ACCESSIBILITY

How to watch: Wed.-Thur., pro-am. Fri.-Sun., championship rounds. Daily tickets, $17 advance, $20 at gate; Season tickets, $50. Ameritech Senior Open, Brian Fitzgerald, 30 S. Wacker Dr., Chicago, IL 60606. (800) 736-4671.
How to play: Kemper Lakes Golf Club is a public course. (708) 320-3450.

First of America Classic

EGYPT VALLEY GOLF CLUB

This western Michigan event, born in 1986, now borrows holes from the back nines of two Arthur Hills–designed courses at Egypt Valley. The club itself is long on tradition, but the Hills layouts are new, set among woods, meadows and wetlands that give the track a mature look and feel.

The first Classic at Egypt Valley, in 1994, was shortened to 36 holes by rain and fog, but Tony Jacklin played brilliantly on Sunday to capture his first Senior Tour title just five weeks after turning 50. Jacklin eagled the par-5 13th and birdied the 14th hole en route to a second consecutive 68. Runner-up Dave Stockton had two birdies on the final four holes but failed to force a playoff at the 18th, missing a 25-foot putt for birdie. Jacklin recalled: "It was the first time I had a chance to win in a long time. I had to remember what to do."

TOURNAMENT-AT-A-GLANCE

Course: Egypt Valley Golf Club—Ridge/Valley courses
Type: Private
Location: 7333 Knapp St. NE, Ada, MI 49301
Phone: (616) 676-2626
When: Aug. 9–11, 1996
How To Get There: Take Hwy. 96 to East Beltline Exit. Go north to Knapp, then east about 5 miles to Egypt Valley.
Broadcast: regional syndication (1995)
Purse: $700,000 (1995)
Tournament Record: 14-under-par 199, George Archer, Jim Colbert and Chi Chi Rodriguez, 1993 (at The Highlands, Grand Rapids, Mich.)

●TOUGHEST HOLE

The ninth hole is a dogleg right presenting a sloping fairway and a small green. There is a fairway trap guarding the left side at 240 yards. Thus, golfers want to steer to the right, but not too far, as the fairway drops off on the right side, pushing wayward drives toward a stand of tall trees. The approach is downhill to a small, two-tiered green protected by sand traps on the left, a grass bunker in front and a drop-off on the right.

●BEST PLACE TO WATCH

A vantage at the fourth green affords a view of play here, and at No. 5, and parts of Nos. 3 and 6. A large pond sits on the left side of No. 4, so a lot of players will bail out right, but the rough on that side presents an awkward, blind shot to the green.

●WHO THE COURSE FAVORS

Players with proficient short games can come through in fine fashion. Because so many greens are missed in regulation, proficiency with flop shots and pitch-and-runs gains in importance.

HOLE	YARDS	PAR	HOLE	YARDS	PAR
1	411	4	10	423	4
2	394	4	11	423	4
3	515	5	12	184	3
4	389	4	13	526	5
5	408	4	14	369	4
6	189	3	15	423	4
7	534	5	16	162	3
8	153	3	17	518	5
9	426	4	18	417	4
			TOTAL	6864	72

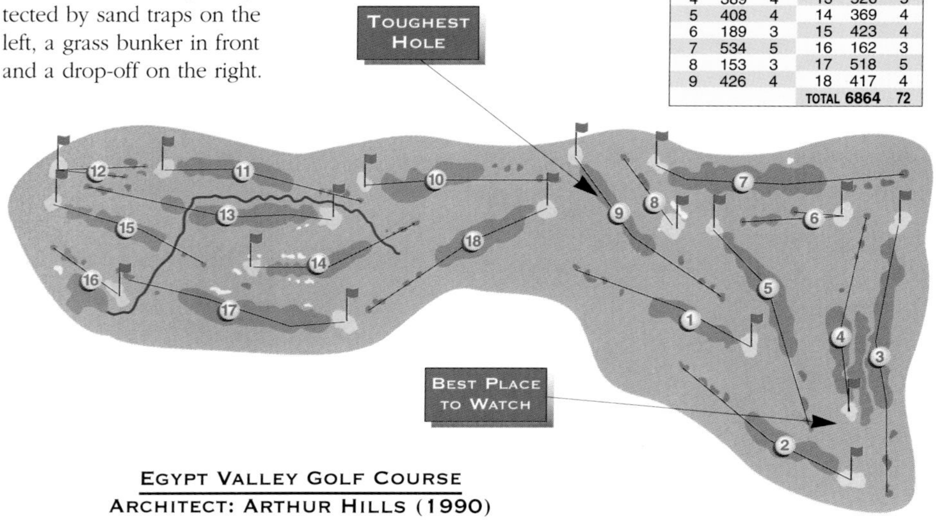

TOUGHEST HOLE

BEST PLACE TO WATCH

EGYPT VALLEY GOLF COURSE
ARCHITECT: ARTHUR HILLS (1990)

LODGING

$$ Holiday Inn Crowne Plaza, 5700 28th St. S.E., Grand Rapids, Mich. (616) 957-1770. 25 minutes from Egypt Valley GC.
$ Hampton Inn, 4981 28th St. S.E., Cascade Township, Mich. (616) 956-9304. 25 minutes from Egypt Valley GC.
$ Comfort Inn, 4155 28th St. S.E., Grand Rapids, Mich. (616) 957-2080. 30 minutes from Egypt Valley GC.

DINING

Olive Garden, 3883 28th St. S.E., Grand Rapids, Mich. (616) 940-1632.
Chili's, 4580 28th St. S.E., Grand Rapids, Mich. (616) 949-5892.
Cheddar's, 4284 28th St. S.E., Kentwood, Mich. (616) 940-1837.

PUBLIC COURSES TO PLAY IN AREA

Grand Rapids, 4300 Leonard St. N.E., Grand Rapids, Mich. Public. (616) 949-2820. Red: 9/3,050/36. White: 9/3,429/37. Blue: 9/3,066/35. 10 minutes from Egypt Valley GC.
Grand Haven, 17000 Lincoln Ave., Grand Haven, Mich. Public. (616) 842-4040. 18/6,789/72. 45 minutes from Egypt Valley GC.

TICKETS & ACCESSIBILITY

How to watch: Tue., clinic, Skins game, practice rounds, plus Holland pro-am at Holland CC. Wed., Vantage Classics pro-am at Wallinwood GC. Wed.-Thur., First of America Classic pro-am. Fri.-Sun., championship rounds. Tickets: Holland pro-am, free. Tue., $5. Wed.-Thur., $8. Fri.-Sun., $11 advance/$15 at gate. Weekly grounds-only, $25. Weekly with clubhouse, $100. Parking: Fri.-Sun., $5 per car, includes program and shuttle transportation. First of America Classic, 233 E. Fulton St., Suite 104, Grand Rapids, MI 49503. (616) 235-0943.
How to play: Egypt Valley is a private course. You must be accompanied by a member. Ridge: 18/6,663/72. Valley: 18/6,618/72.

Northville Long Island Classic

Meadow Brook Country Club

LODGING

$$$ Huntington Hilton, 598 Broad Hollow Rd. (Rte 110), Melville, N.Y. (516) 845-1000. 15 minutes from Meadow Brook.
$$$ Melville Marriott, 1350 Old Walt Whitman Rd. (just off Rte 110), Melville, N.Y. (516) 423-1600. 15 minutes from Meadow Brook.
$$ East Norwich Inn, Rte 25A (Northern Blvd.), E. Norwich, N.Y. (516) 922-1500. 5 minutes from Meadow Brook.

DINING

Maine Maid Inn, Rte. 106, Jericho, N.Y. (516) 935-6400.
Capriccio, 399 Jericho Tpk., Jericho, N.Y. (516) 931-2727.
Frank's Steaks, 4 Jericho Tpk, Jericho, N.Y. (516) 338-4595.

PUBLIC COURSES TO PLAY IN AREA

Bethpage State Park, Quaker Meetinghouse Rd., Farmingdale, N.Y. State Park. (516) 293-8899. Red: 18/6,756/70. Blue: 18/6,684/72. Green: 18/6,267/71. Yellow: 18/6,316/71. Black: 18/7,065/71. 25 minutes from Meadow Brook.
Marriott Wind Watch GC, 1717 Vanderbilt Motor Pkwy., Hauppauge, N.Y. Resort. (516) 232-9850. 18/6,425/71. 20 minutes from Meadow Brook.

TICKETS & ACCESSIBILITY

How to watch: Mon., one-day pro-am. Tue., Merrill Lynch Shoot-Out and junior golf clinic. Wed.-Thur., two-day pro-am. Sat., Dennis Walters golf show. Season pass $40 in advance, $45 at gate. Daily Mon.-Thur., $10 advance, $12 at gate; Fri.-Sun., $18 advance, $22 at gate. Free parking. Northville Long Island Classic Tournament Office, 25 Melville Park Rd., Melville, NY 11747. (516) 674-4653.
How to play: You must be the guest of a member. (516) 935-6500.

TOURNAMENT-AT-A-GLANCE

Course: Meadow Brook Country Club
Type: Private
Location: Cedar Swamp Rd., Jericho, NY 11753
Phone: (516) 935-6500
When: Aug. 16–18, 1996
How To Get There: Long Island Expwy. to Exit 41 north. Rte. 107 north to course.
Broadcast: ESPN (1995)
Purse: $800,000 (1995)
Tournament Record: 16-under-par 200, Lee Trevino, 1994

One of the top courses in the New York City area, Meadow Brook remains somewhat underpublicized. Designed by Dick Wilson in 1953, the course presents a contrast of nines. The front side traverses woods; the back nine provides a more wide-open feel, but all the holes are distinctive in their doglegs, fairway trapping, approaches and green settings.

For half a century, Meadow Brook was lodged at another location, but its membership was forced by highway construction to relocate in the mid 1950s, taking over an estate whose fields had previously hosted hunt club activities and polo. The current course draws rave reviews from the Senior pros, including Chi Chi Rodriguez who claimed, "This is about the toughest course I've ever seen for the Seniors."

After a streak in which George Archer won three straight Northville titles, Ray Floyd won in 1993 and Lee Trevino in '94. For five years, Trevino had been frustrated by Meadow Brook before his record 16-under-par 200. "This course has been beating me up," he admitted.

●TOUGHEST HOLE

The ninth, a 417-yard, par-4 dogleg right, annually ranks among the 10 toughest holes on the Senior Tour. The first challenge is to launch a strategic but lengthy drive past the dogleg. The approach will be a mid- to long iron uphill to a sharply sloping green protected by large bunkers.

●BEST PLACE TO WATCH

Long before stadium courses were built, this course's unique par-3 finishing hole had all the perfect traits: an ample amount of hillside to watch players hit from a recessed tee area to an elevated green. The spectator perch here also allows a sweeping panorama of the driving range and just about the entire front nine.

●WHO THE COURSE FAVORS

Because the greens may be the largest this side of the ridiculous Concord Monster, New York's Concord Resort Hotel course known for its sprawling greens, it's imperative to be accurate with approach shots. Otherwise, three-putting is a distinct possibility.

MEADOW BROOK COUNTRY CLUB
ARCHITECT: DICK WILSON (1953)

TOUGHEST HOLE

BEST PLACE TO WATCH

HOLE	YARDS	PAR	HOLE	YARDS	PAR
1	537	5	10	506	5
2	389	4	11	389	4
3	478	5	12	420	4
4	195	3	13	412	4
5	419	4	14	340	4
6	367	4	15	209	3
7	171	3	16	401	4
8	373	4	17	585	5
9	417	4	18	167	3
			TOTAL	6775	72

Bank of Boston Senior Classic

NASHAWTUC COUNTRY CLUB

After 12 years of hosting a stop on the Senior Tour, Nashawtuc Country Club had clearly become comfortable for the pros.

"I love this course, and I know most of the other players do too," said Lee Trevino, looking forward to the 1994 event. "It's not overly long, but that's good. We can come out here and play a number of different shots. I like that."

Nashawtuc's wide fairways flow almost without interruption into its large, true-rolling greens. Mature trees frame almost every hole; shallow bunkers keep a polite distance from the putting surfaces.

From 1986 to 1988, Chi Chi Rodriguez owned the course, beating par by at least two strokes in every round to claim three consecutive titles. In 1991, Rocky Thompson found a shortcut over the dogleg on the par-5 fifth on his way to victory with an 11-under-par 205.

So before the 1994 tournament got under way, golf course architect Brian Silva tried to toughen the challenge of the original Geoffrey Cornish design by moving tees back and pushing bunkers closer to the greens.

The results? Hardly a change. The course still belongs to the birdiemakers who can drop enough putts on the ridged and tiered greens.

In recent years, the "blue-collar" players have found a way to succeed at Nashawtuc. Former club pros Bob Betley and Jim Albus won the event in 1993 and 1994 respectively.

Albus, a model of concentration, rode back-to-back birdies on the 16th and 17th holes to a two-shot winning margin. Despite his relative anonymity, Albus overcame playing the final round with Lee Trevino and Raymond Floyd, where the crowds can be hectic and intimidating. "It actually helps to play with those two," said Albus. "They're always patting you on the back. They're just terrific to play with."

Cheered on by his wife and their son Mark, his caddie, Albus refused to wilt, even after his lead was cut to one stroke at No. 14, where he drove into trees and took just his second bogey of the tournament. He missed a 3-foot putt for birdie on the next hole, but instead of getting rattled he turned to his son and said, "Let's play golf from here on in."

And Nashawtuc was kind enough to yield him two more birdies in the last three holes.

TOURNAMENT-AT-A-GLANCE

Course: Nashawtuc Country Club
Type: Private
Location: 1861 Sudbury Rd., Concord, MA 01742
Phone: (508) 369-6420
When: Aug. 23–25, 1996
How To Get There: Take Rte. 128 to Exit 26 (Rte. 20E). Bear right off exit toward Waltham. Go through traffic light, stay in the left lane, and immediately after the gas station on the left you will see a small sign to Rte. 117, and a blinking yellow light. Turn left. Follow to the end. At intersection, turn left onto Rte. 117. Travel approx. 7 miles. Go straight through lights at Rte. 126, and the next set of lights is Sudbury Rd. Turn left.
Broadcast: ESPN (1996)
Purse: $800,000 (1995)
Tournament Record: 18-under-par 198, Chi Chi Rodriguez, 1987

●TOUGHEST HOLE

The seventh hole is a long, straight par-4 with plenty of wide-open fairway, but there's also a copious amount of rough both left and right. A fairway wood or long-iron is required to finish the journey to the large, sloped green, which has an open entrance but plenty of trouble in back if the approach won't stick.

●BEST PLACE TO WATCH

The approach on the par-4 16th must carry a pond to a two-tiered green. Unless the tee shot catches rough, the hazards here aren't much trouble, but if a player leaves a long putt, 216watch out.

●WHO THE COURSE FAVORS

Players who can post scores in the 60s. In other words, the birdiemakers.

By Bill Mavodones

THE GREEN ON NO. 8 IS NOT HARD TO HIT, BUT ITS SLOPING, TWO-TIERED CONTOUR MAKES PUTTING AN ADVENTURE.

LODGING

$$$ Westin, 70 Third Ave., Waltham, Mass. (617) 290-5600. 20 minutes from Nashawtuc CC.
$$$ Doubletree, 550 Winter St., Waltham, Mass. (617) 890-6767. 20 minutes from Nashawtuc CC.
$$ Best Western, 477 Totten Pond Rd., Waltham, Mass. (617) 890-7800. 20 minutes from Nashawtuc CC.

DINING

Michael's, 208 Fitchburg Turnpike, Concord, Mass. (508) 371-1114.
Rossini's, 9 Acre Corner, Concord, Mass. (508) 371-3280.
Sierra's, 470 North Rd., Sudbury, Mass. (508) 443-0820.

PUBLIC COURSES TO PLAY IN AREA

Stow Acres CC, 58 Randall Rd., Stow, Mass. Public. (508) 568-8690. North: 18/6,909/72. South: 18/6,520/72. 10 minutes from Nashawtuc CC.
Wayland CC, 121 Old Sudbury Rd., Sudbury, Mass. Public. (508) 358-4775. 18/5,974/72. 15 minutes from Nashawtuc CC.

TICKETS & ACCESSIBILITY

How to watch: Mon., practice. Tue., shoot-out. Wed.-Thur., pro-am. Fri.-Sun., championship rounds. Daily tickets, Wed.-Thur., $10; Fri.-Sun., $12. Season pass, $40. Bank of Boston Senior Classic, 1861 Sudbury Rd., Concord, MA 01742. (508) 371-0116.
How to play: Private club. Must be guest of member or club pro, who can extend reciprocal privileges.

BEST PLACE TO WATCH

TOUGHEST HOLE

HOLE	YARDS	PAR	HOLE	YARDS	PAR
1	387	4	10	510	5
2	189	3	11	423	4
3	372	4	12	413	4
4	294	4	13	199	3
5	518	5	14	367	4
6	365	4	15	342	4
7	454	4	16	408	4
8	192	3	17	176	3
9	540	5	18	521	5
			TOTAL	6670	72

NASHAWTUC COUNTRY CLUB
ARCHITECT: GEOFFREY CORNISH (1960)
REMODELED BY BRIAN SILVA (1994)

Franklin Quest Championship

PARK MEADOWS GOLF CLUB

TOURNAMENT-AT-A-GLANCE

Course: Park Meadows Golf Club
Type: Resort
Location: 2000 Meadows Dr., Park City, UT 84060
Phone: (801) 649-2460
When: Aug. 30–Sept. 1, 1996
How To Get There: Take I-80 to Park City Exit. Go north on State Hwy. 224 to Park Meadows.
Broadcast: The Golf Channel (1996)
Purse: $900,000 (1995)
Tournament Record: 19-under-par 197, Dave Stockton, 1993

Located in the historic mining town and popular ski resort of Park City, about 45 minutes from Salt Lake City, the Park Meadows Golf Club course was designed by Jack Nicklaus and opened for play in 1983. Set 7,000 feet high in the Wasatch Mountains, the open, treeless track bears a Scottish pattern, with bridges over meandering trout streams, 105 sand bunkers, and, of course, the obligatory double green, which is shared by the 11th and 17th holes. True to Nicklaus' ideas, it has generous driving areas but challenging greens, often guarded by ponds or those wandering "burns." The Wasatch Range looms large as a backdrop to the course, which is often ranked the very best in Utah.

The Franklin Quest Championship originated in 1982 as a 72-hole tournament played at another great Park City mountain course—the Arnold Palmer and Ed Seay–designed Jeremy Ranch. That inaugural was won by Billy Casper with an 8-under-par 279. For a few years thereafter, the tournament was contested as a team event, but it converted again to a 54-hole individual title event in 1987, when Miller Barber won the first of two consecutive "Showdown Classic" titles.

Dave Stockton blitzed the event's new venue in 1993 en route to a nine-stroke victory over runner-up Al Geiberger. Stockton opened with 68 and 66, then closed with a course-record, 9-under 63 for a tournament-record 197 total. Stockton's 54-hole total was the second lowest of the year and the winning margin tied the all-time Senior PGA Tour standard set in 1992 by Gibby Gilbert at the Southwestern Bell Classic.

Stockton obviously takes well to the Park Meadows course. He returned to the chase the following year, only to lose in a playoff to Tom Weiskopf after the pair had tied in regulation at 204. Stockton had seemed to have the tournament locked up for a second straight year when he birdied the par-5 17th hole, but Weiskopf—playing with uncommon purpose—birdied 16, 17 and 18 to force the playoff. Weiskopf then sank a 25-foot putt on the first playoff hole to win the title.

Weiskopf had nearly withdrawn from the tournament when his friend, fellow competitor Bert Yancey, died at the course on Friday from a massive heart attack. Instead, Weiskopf dedicated himself to winning his first Senior Tour event as a tribute to his longtime touring pal. After his finishing flourish of four consecutive birdies, Weiskopf said he would ask to have Yancey's name added to the trophy. "We traveled together for 15 years," Weiskopf said. "I loved him; I won this tournament because of him. Bert made me win this."

"I WON THIS TOURNAMENT BECAUSE OF BERT [YANCEY]. IF YOU WANT TO TALK ABOUT DESTINY, THE LAST THREE HOLES WOULD HAVE TO BE IT."

—TOM WEISKOPF,

DEDICATING HIS 1994 FRANKLIN QUEST TRIUMPH TO HIS FRIEND YANCEY, WHO DIED OF A HEART ATTACK AT THE GOLF COURSE ON FRIDAY OF THE EVENT

Courtesy of Franklin Quest Championship

Jack Nicklaus cut a Scottish-style course out of treeless mining country 7,000-feet high in the Wasatch range.

●TOUGHEST HOLE

The dogleg at No. 9 can stretch to 483 yards from the back tees, with a stingy par of 4, but for the Senior tournament it will play at "only" 451 yards. Sand traps left and right guard the fairway landing area. The green, just 28 yards deep, angles away from the golfers, from its front left to back right, favoring a faded approach. Many players have trouble holding approaches to this green, whose right-side approach line is protected by a series of greenside sand traps.

●BEST PLACE TO WATCH

The area around holes Nos. 14, 15 and 16. The three holes are clumped relatively close together, so spectators can take in a variety of action down the stretch on what are par-5, par-4 and par-3 holes, respectively. The 187-yard 16th hole requires a tee shot over water to an hourglass-shaped green guarded in front by a grass bunker and left and right by sand. On the front side, the par-5 sixth is intriguing because of a double fairway that provides a shortcut to the green if a player is willing to risk a tee-shot to the narrow island landing area on the right side. The terrain is relatively flat and open, making it easy to track your group of choice.

●WHO THE COURSE FAVORS

Maybe it's the air, but this is one of the longer courses the Senior Tour sets up, at 6,881 tournament yards. Thus, the edge goes to the long-hitter who is accurate not only with the driver, but with long irons too. Maybe that's why Tom Weiskopf, one of the Tour's longest drivers and a marksman with a 2-iron, won his first Senior event here.

Hole	Yards	Par	Hole	Yards	Par
1	403	4	10	436	4
2	401	4	11	420	4
3	201	3	12	404	4
4	412	4	13	167	3
5	160	3	14	508	5
6	502	5	15	363	4
7	379	4	16	187	3
8	502	5	17	553	5
9	451	4	18	432	4
			Total	6881	72

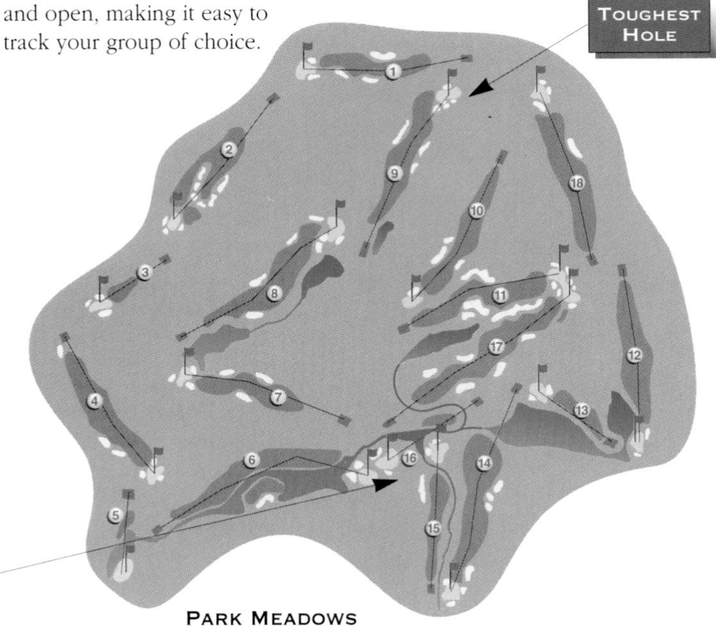

Park Meadows
Architect: Jack Nicklaus (1983)

LODGING

$$ Yarrow Hotel, 1800 Park Ave., Park City, Utah. (801) 649-7000. 5 minutes from Park Meadows GC.
$$ Olympia Park, 1895 Sidewinder Dr., Park City, Utah. (801) 649-2900. 5 minutes from Park Meadows GC.
$$ Radisson, 2346 N. Hwy. 224, Park City, Utah. (801) 649-5000. 5 minutes from Park Meadows GC.

DINING

Adolph's, Lower Park Ave., Park City, Utah. (801) 649-7177. 8 minutes from Park Meadows GC.
Barking Frog, 368 Main St., Park City, Utah. (801) 649-6222. 10 minutes from Park Meadows GC.
Grub Steak, Prospector Square, Park City, Utah. (801) 649-8060. 10 minutes from Park Meadows GC.

PUBLIC COURSES TO PLAY IN AREA

Park City Municipal, Lower Park Ave., Park City, Utah. Public. (801) 649-8701. 18/6,754/72. 8 minutes from Park Meadows GC.
Mountain Dell, Parleys Canyon, Salt Lake City. Public. (801) 582-3812. Lake: 18/6,709/71. Canyon: 18/6,787/72. 30 minutes from Park Meadows GC.

TICKETS & ACCESSIBILITY

How to watch: Mon., practice rounds, pro-am. Tue., senior clinic, Merrill Lynch shoot-out. Wed-Thur., pro-am. Fri.-Sun. championship rounds. Tickets available at area business establishments and through tournament office, $10 daily, $15 weeklong pass. Individual, group and sponsor ticket information available. Franklin Quest Championship, 2200 W. Parkway Blvd., Salt Lake City, UT 84119. (801) 977-1446 (year round). 2000 Meadow Dr., Park City, UT 84068. (801) 647-5896 (tournament).
How to play: Park Meadows is a public course. Area hotels offer special arrangements. (801) 649–2460.

Northwest Classic

INGLEWOOD COUNTRY CLUB

Trees. Big, tall, Northwest timber. What else would you expect? Inglewood looks the part, with tree-lined fairways and greens carved into wooded semi-circles. This venerable club has been part of the Seattle/Puget Sound neighborhood since 1927 and has hosted this Senior event since 1987, the tournament's second year of existence.

The 1994 edition wound up as another showdown between U.S. Senior Open champ Simon Hobday and runner-up Jim Albus, who both birdied the downhill finishing hole to force a playoff. On the third playoff hole, Hobday prevailed with a birdie.

In the 1993 event, Dave Stockton rolled to a four-stroke victory. But he arrived at the second hole in a three-way tie for the lead before landing his tee shot under a tree. No problem. Stockton extricated himself with a low 4-iron that bounced in front of the green and rolled within 20 feet, then dropped the putt for birdie.

TOURNAMENT-AT-A-GLANCE

Course: Inglewood Country Club
Type: Private
Location: 6505 Inglewood Rd. NE, Kenmore, WA 98028
Phone: (206) 488-7000
When: Sept. 6–8, 1996
How To Get There: Take I-5 to 145th St. Exit (from northbound, turn right; southbound, turn left). Follow 145th St. to Lake City Way (Bothell Way) and turn left. Follow Bothell Way through Lake Forest Park to 68th Ave. Turn right, proceed to Simonda Rd.; Country Club on the right.
Broadcast: Local (1995)
Purse: $600,000 (1995)
Tournament Record: 18-under-par 198, Mike Hill, 1991

●TOUGHEST HOLE

The par-4 ninth is annually one of the toughest holes on the Senior PGA Tour and is considered one of the most difficult holes in all of the Northwest golfing realm. The premium is on a tee shot that must find the fairway and avoid out-of-bounds both left and right. The long second shot targets a narrow green, heavily trapped.

●BEST PLACE TO WATCH

The 18th is a scoring hole. It's a short par-5 that plays downhill. Though the second shot may be from a downhill or sidehill lie and the green is well-bunkered, the hole is reachable by pros in two. It will provide eagle opportunities and certainly produce quite a few birdies.

●WHO THE COURSE FAVORS

Length is not a major obstacle, so the player who is pinpointing approaches and sinking putts can post low numbers.

Hole	Yards	Par	Hole	Yards	Par
1	452	5	10	384	4
2	370	4	11	375	4
3	285	4	12	148	3
4	365	4	13	351	4
5	398	4	14	404	4
6	175	3	15	425	5
7	557	5	16	200	3
8	200	3	17	397	4
9	390	4	18	500	5
			Total	6376	72

INGLEWOOD COUNTRY CLUB
ARCHITECTS: A. VERNON MCCANN AND ROBERT JOHNSTON (1921)
REMODELED BY JOHN HARBOTTLE (1994)

LODGING

$$ Wyndham Garden Hotel, 19333 N. Creek Pkwy., Bothell, Wash. (206) 485-5557. 15 minutes from Inglewood CC.
$$ Embassy Suites Hotel, 20610 44th Ave. W., Lynnwood, Wash. (206) 775-2500. 25 minutes from Inglewood CC.
$$ Residence Inn, 11920 N.E. 195th St., Bothell, Wash. (206) 485-3030. 15 minutes from Inglewood CC.

DINING

Lake Washington Grill House & Taproom, 6161 N.E. 175th St., Bothell, Wash. (206) 486-3313.
Teo's Mia Roma, 7614 N.E. Bothell Way, Bothell, Wash. (206) 486-6200.
Grazie Ristorante, 23207 Bothell-Everett Hwy., Bothell, Wash. (206) 402-9600.

PUBLIC COURSES TO PLAY IN AREA

Wayne, 16721 96th Ave. N.E., Bothell, Wash. Public. (206) 485-6237. 18/4,326/65. 10 minutes from Inglewood CC.
Bellevue, 5500 140th Ave. N.E., Bellevue, Wash. Public. (206) 451-7250. 18/5,800/71. 25 minutes from Inglewood CC.

TICKETS & ACCESSIBILITY

How to watch: Mon., practice rounds. Tue., practice rounds, junior clinic, Merrill Lynch shoot-out. Wed.-Thur., Weyerhaeuser pro-am. Fri.-Sun., championship rounds. Tickets: Daily grounds, $12 adult, $7 senior citizen, $2 junior; season pass with clubhouse, $60 (2-for-1 until Aug. 15). GTE Northwest Classic, P.O. Box 82797, Kenmore, WA 98028. (206) 488-7889.
How to play: Inglewood Country Club is a private course. You may be able to gain access through your home pro if you are a member of a private club elsewhere.

Brickyard Crossing Championship

Brickyard Crossing

LODGING

$$$ Holiday Inn Crowne Plaza, 123 W. Louisiana St., Indianapolis. (317) 631-2221. 5 minutes from Brickyard Crossing.
$$$ Hyatt Regency, 1 S. Capitol Ave., Indianapolis. (317) 632-1234. 12 minutes from Brickyard Crossing.
$$$ Adam's Mark, 2544 Executive Dr., Indianapolis. (800) 444-2326. 10 minutes from Brickyard Crossing.

DINING

St. Elmo Steak House, 127 S. Illinois St., Indianapolis. (317) 637-1811.
Keystone Grill, 8650 Keystone Crossing, Indianapolis. (317) 848-5202.
Union Jack's, 6225 W. 25th St., Indianapolis. (317) 243-3300.

PUBLIC COURSES TO PLAY IN AREA

Brownsburg, 8525 N. State Rd. 267, Brownsburg, Ind. Semi-private. (317) 852-5530. 9/3,228/36. 10 minutes from Brickyard Crossing.
Eagle Creek, 8802 W. 56th St., Indianapolis. Public. (317) 297-3366. Two courses: 18/7,189/72; 9/2,980/36. 15 minutes from Brickyard Crossing.

TICKETS & ACCESSIBILITY

How to watch: Mon., practice rounds. Tue., BankOne senior clinic, First of America Skins game, Merrill Lynch shoot-out. Wed.-Thur., Coca-Cola Carrier pro-am. Fri.-Sun., championship rounds. Tickets: Daily grounds, $20; season grounds, $50; season clubhouse, $100. Individual, group and sponsor tickets available. Brickyard Crossing Championship, P.O. Box 24486, Speedway, IN 46224. (317) 484-6709.
How to play: Brickyard is a public golf course. (317) 484-6572.

TOURNAMENT-AT-A-GLANCE

Course: Brickyard Crossing
Type: Public
Location: 4400 W. 16th St., Indianapolis, IN 46222
Phone: (317) 484-6572
When: Sept. 20–22, 1996
How To Get There: From I-65, exit at 16th St. Go west to Indianapolis Motor Speedway and course.
Broadcast: Local (1995)
Purse: $750,000 (1995)
Tournament Record: 17-under-par 199, George Archer, 1991 and Ray Floyd, 1992 (at Broadmoor CC, Indianapolis)

Yes, there really is a golf course at Indianapolis Motor Speedway. It's scenic, too, feeling more like the countryside than one of the world's most famous racetracks.

The origins of the course go back to the late 1920s, when racetrack owner and World War I flying hero Eddie Rickenbacker commissioned Bill Biddel to design the Speedway Golf Course—a public facility with greens fees of 75 cents weekdays and $1 weekends. It featured nine holes inside the racing oval and nine outside. In the 1960s, the Speedway hosted a PGA event and built an additional nine holes outside the racetrack.

In the early 1990s, architect Pete Dye revamped the whole layout, moving 1.5 million cubic yards of earth to create rolling, tree-lined fairways, deep bunkering and some severely swaled greens. Little Eagle Creek wends through the course, and, with the addition of three lakes, water comes into play on 11 holes. Four holes were constructed inside the racing oval, Nos. 7 through 10, with the other 14 outside the backstretch straightaway.

The tournament began in 1988 as the GTE North Classic at the Broadmoor course in Indianapolis. It moved to the Speedway in 1994, where Isao Aoki prevailed in a rain-curtailed affair. Aoki played 36 holes without a bogey and said the greens and ever-present hazards reminded him of courses in his native Japan.

•TOUGHEST HOLE

The fifth hole is a slight dogleg right. Pros aim to cut off as much as they can on the right side, but they must avoid a long, deep waste bunker that borders the fairway. Drives to the left, however, leave a longer approach to a large, undulating green. Depending on pin placement, some putts will break considerably.

•BEST PLACE TO WATCH

Around the eighth green. It's one of four holes inside the racetrack, and allows access to viewing No. 9 as well. "I find the eighth hole intimidating but beautiful," says auto racing driver Rick Mears, a four-time winner of the Indy 500.

•WHO THE COURSE FAVORS

Placement off the tee is important to set up opportunistic approaches.

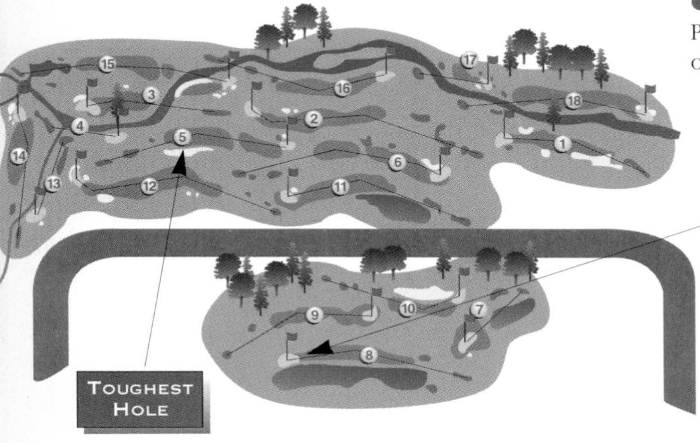

Hole	Yards	Par	Hole	Yards	Par
1	360	4	10	313	4
2	540	5	11	400	4
3	365	4	12	525	5
4	194	3	13	178	3
5	405	4	14	311	4
6	525	5	15	499	5
7	155	3	16	415	4
8	400	4	17	183	3
9	370	4	18	420	4
			Total	6558	72

BRICKYARD CROSSING
ARCHITECT: BILL BIDDELL (1929)
REMODELED BY BILL BIDDEL (1965), PETE DYE (1992)

Bank One Classic

KEARNEY HILL LINKS

Designed by Pete Dye and P.B. Dye and operated by the Lexington-Fayette county parks department, Kearney Hill Links has been called by amateur players the best public course in Kentucky. It's a Scottish-style links layout, meaning that it's fairly open and atypical of what the senior pros usually encounter. For the spectator, links-style means some unobstructed views across nearby holes and an opportunity to keep personal tabs on the action to a greater degree than at most other Tour stops. Only one tree comes into any significant play on the course, at No. 16, where a large, greenside hackberry guards the second-shot approach.

A historic graveyard lines the first fairway, but Kearney Hill is defined visually by two of Pete Dye's signature holes. The 175-yard, par-3 15th plays across a lake with a railroad-tie bulkhead to an undulating green encircled by large mounds. The green at the par-5 finishing hole is framed by a picturesque stone terrace, more large mounds and the white-columned clubhouse. Many of the pros can reach this hole in two, but any shot that strays to the left is penalized by a 150-yard-long ravine that is lined with sand.

The par-5s present eagle opportunities, especially when there's a tailwind off the tee. In 1994, Isao Aoki eagled the third hole, propelling him to a final-round 69 and a comfortable three-stroke victory that ended a two-year winless streak on the Senior Tour. Second-place finisher Chi Chi Rodriguez eagled the 531-yard 18th to keep Aoki honest.

In 1994, 58-year-old Gary Player broke a dry spell of his own by charging out to five consecutive birdies at the start of the final round.

The 1996 edition of the Bank One Classic will be the 14th for a multi-titled tournament that has had six title sponsors over that same span. The event for its first seven years was held at Marriott's Griffin Gate course, then moved to Kearney Hill Links in 1990.

With its series of tee options, the course presents a fair challenge for the average handicapper and the Senior pros alike.

TOURNAMENT-AT-A-GLANCE

Course: Kearney Hill Links
Type: Public
Location: 3403 Kearney Rd., Lexington, KY 40511
Phone: (606) 253-1981
When: Sept. 13–15, 1996
How To Get There: I-75 to Exit 120; proceed west on Ironworks Pike. Left on Georgetown Rd.; right on Kearney Rd.
Broadcast: None (1995)
Purse: $600,000 (1995)
Tournament Record: 15-under-par 201, Rives McBee, 1990

Courtesy of Bank One Classic

TRUE TO ITS NAME, KEARNEY HILL LINKS IS WIDE OPEN WITH ONLY ONE TREE ENTERING PLAY SIGNIFICANTLY.

●TOUGHEST HOLE

It's never easy to make the course's largest green in two on No. 13, a long dogleg par-4 that plays into the wind. Pot bunkers guard the right side of the fairway landing area, and the approach is either a fairway wood or a long-iron to a well-bunkered green.

HOLE	YARDS	PAR
1	431	4
2	154	3
3	497	5
4	423	4
5	366	4
6	340	4
7	551	5
8	189	3
9	436	4
10	356	4
11	375	4
12	190	3
13	435	4
14	524	5
15	175	3
16	365	4
17	422	4
18	531	5
TOTAL	6760	72

●BEST PLACE TO WATCH

The 18th hole provides amphitheater seating around the green and an opportunity to watch the big hitters go for this par-5 hole in two. There's plenty of green to aim for with a fairway wood. In 1994, Chi Chi Rodriguez locked up a $48,400 runner-up check by reaching the 18th in two and then sinking his eagle-putt en route to a final-round 66.

The 14th green provides an overview of Nos. 15, 16 and 17 as well.

●WHO THE COURSE FAVORS

The key element at Kearney Hill is putting—mastering the speed and the breaks on the greens. In 1993, Gary Player rode a hot putter in the final round to his three-stroke victory. The native South African dropped birdie putts on his first five holes en route to a 66 and a total of 202.

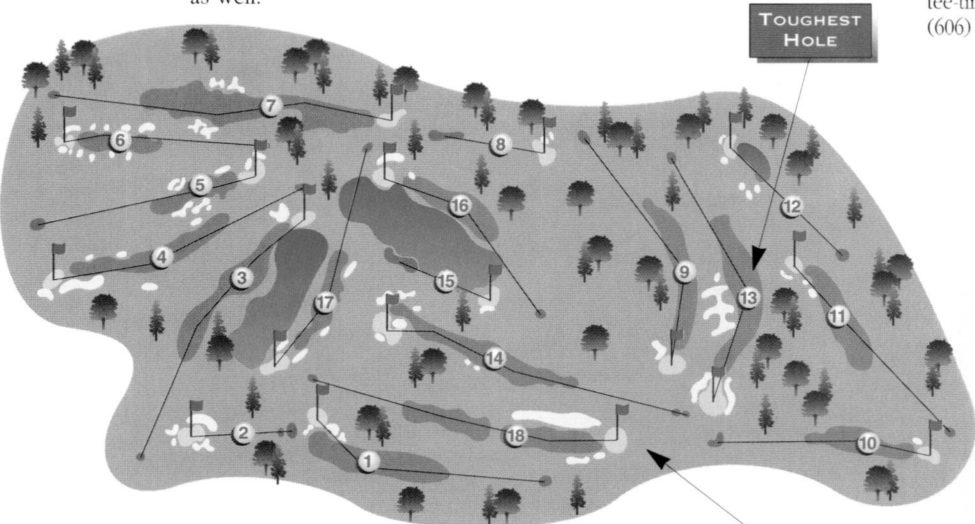

KEARNEY HILLS LINKS
ARCHITECTS: PETE DYE AND P.B. DYE (1989)

LODGING

$$$ Marriott's Griffin Gate, 1800 Newtown Pike, Lexington, Ky. (606) 231-5100. 10 minutes from Kearney Hill.
$$$ Radisson Plaza, 369 W. Vine St., Lexington, Ky. (606) 231-9000. 25 minutes from Kearney Hill.
$$ Residence Inn by Marriott, 1080 Newtown Pike, Lexington, Ky. (606) 231-6191. 17 minutes from Kearney Hill.

DINING

Coach House, 855 S. Broadway, Lexington, Ky. (606) 252-7777. 25 minutes from Kearney Hill.
New Orleans House, 1510 Newtown Pike, Lexington, Ky. (606) 254-3474. 7 minutes from Kearney Hill.
Bravo, 401 W. Main St., Lexington, Ky. (606) 255-2222. 25 minutes from Kearney Hill.

PUBLIC COURSES TO PLAY IN AREA

Lakeside Golf Course, 3725 Richmond Rd., Lexington, Ky. Public. (606) 263-5315. 18/6,890/72. 20 minutes from Kearney Hill.
Tates Creek Golf Course, 1400 Gainesway Dr., Lexington, Ky. Public. (606) 272-3428. 18/6,240/72. 20 minutes from Kearney Hill.

TICKETS & ACCESSIBILITY

How to watch: Wed.-Thur., pro-am. Fri.-Sun., championship rounds. Daily: $10. Ticket information available from Bank One Classic, P.O. Box 117, Lexington, KY 40501. (606) 259-1825.
How to play: Advance telephone tee-time reservations or walk-up. (606) 253-1981.

Vantage Championship

TANGLEWOOD PARK

Many of the Senior pros view this event as an unacknowledged fifth major, and there are ample reasons why. Played at a bucolic North Carolina retreat on a great Robert Trent Jones course that once hosted the PGA Championship, the Vantage is one of the richest events on the Senior circuit, and it caps a season-long money race among the Tour's over-50 crowd.

Tanglewood, formerly the country estate of tobacco scion William Reynolds, is now a meticulously landscaped, abundantly flowered public park that's congenial to nature lovers, horse breeders and small business conventions alike. Its two Robert Trent Jones courses fit the milieu to a tee.

Built in 1957, just six years after "Mr. Will" deeded Tanglewood to the public, the Championship course was thoroughly refashioned by its creator in the early 1970s. Preparing the stage for the 1974 PGA Championship, Jones lengthened the course to more than 7,000 yards, added 45 bunkers, enlarged 65 others, created a lake at the 12th hole and reduced the average size of the putting greens by one-fifth. R.J. Reynolds would fund a modernization program in 1989, but Jones had already established Tanglewood as one of the nation's top public courses and a personal favorite in his substantial portfolio.

TOURNAMENT-AT-A-GLANCE

Course: Tanglewood Park—Championship Course
Type: Public
Location: Highway 158 West, Clemmons, NC 27012
Phone: (910) 766-5082
When: Sept. 27–29, 1996
How To Get There: Take I-40 to the Tanglewood/ Bermuda Run Exit.
Broadcast: ESPN (1996)
Purse: \$1.5 million (1995)
Tournament Record: 18-under-par 198, Lee Trevino, 1993 and Larry Gilbert, 1994

Senior Tour hero Lee Trevino won his first PGA Championship here in 1974 by holding off Jack Nicklaus and conquering the difficult 425-yard, par-4 finishing hole (now the ninth hole). After a drive to the dogleg that's best hit with a fade, a Trevino trademark, the second-shot approach is long and uphill. A severe slope at the front of the elevated green means players need to keep the ball below the hole, but the 35-year-old Trevino found himself having to two-putt from 15 feet past the cup in order to edge Jack Nicklaus. Unfazed, Trevino did just that.

In 1993, Trevino relived that glorious weekend at Tanglewood with a record-setting 18-under-par 198. This time the victory came by a comfortable five strokes, and the title was the Vantage Championship, which had been the first event on the Senior Tour to award a purse of \$1 million.

The prize money clearly inspired Trevino. "This gives me a chance to win the money title," he said of the \$225,000 winner's check that put him in the hunt for the year's top-player honors. But a week later, Dave Stockton beat Trevino by a stroke at the Transamerica Senior Golf Championship and never looked back on his way to two straight earnings titles.

"IT'S LIKE WINNING THREE-AND-A-HALF TOURNAMENTS. IT'S LIKE THE SUPER BOWL; BY FAR THE MOST MEANINGFUL TOURNAMENT OF THE YEAR."

—JIM COLBERT,
1991 AND 1992 VANTAGE CHAMPIONSHIP WINNER

Courtesy of Vantage Championship

KATE B. REYNOLDS, WIFE OF TOBACCO BARON WILLIAM, NAMED TANGLEWOOD AFTER THEIR ESTATE'S WILD, DENSE FOREST.

●TOUGHEST HOLE

A pair of par-5s are listed as the No. 1 and 2 handicap holes on the Championship course scorecard. The fifth hole, which plays at 546 yards in the Senior Tour event, can stretch to 608 yards at full length. When the PGA Championship was contested on this course in 1974, no player managed to muscle the ball to the green in two. A cluster of three bunkers at the bend of the dogleg forces most seniors to take the long way around the turn, and their second shots are critical in setting up birdie chances. The other par-5 is the 17th. Again, it's shortened for the seniors. It's a fairly straightaway hole, but the green is protected by numerous bunkers from about 100 yards out and treacherous rough awaits balls that elude the sand. Going for it in two is fraught with peril, but a well-placed second shot can open up a chance for birdie.

●BEST PLACE TO WATCH

There are plenty of bleachers to accommodate spectators at the 10th hole, a short dogleg par-4. Players try to drop precision tee shots short of the pines and bunkers that guard the bend. The tee is elevated, and the drive is to a valley, leaving a tough club choice for an uphill approach to a green that slopes from back to front.

●WHO THE COURSE FAVORS

Players who are patient, thoughtful, methodical and able to maneuver the ball, going with the flow of the course. There's no need to try to overpower the layout. It's plenty playable.

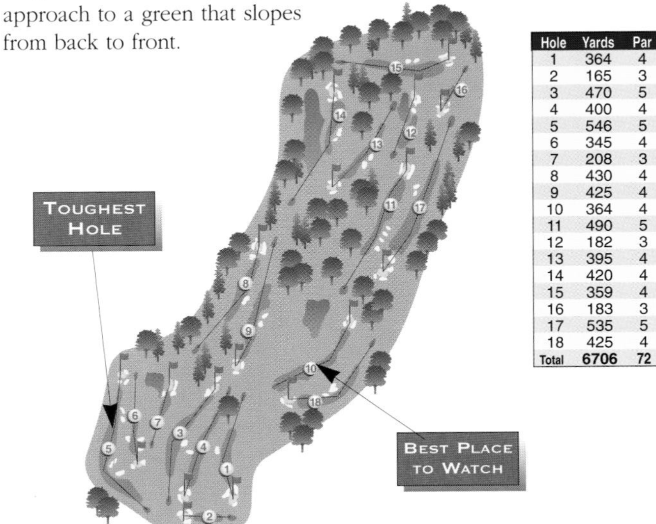

Hole	Yards	Par
1	364	4
2	165	3
3	470	5
4	400	4
5	546	5
6	345	4
7	208	3
8	430	4
9	425	4
10	364	4
11	490	5
12	182	3
13	395	4
14	420	4
15	359	4
16	183	3
17	535	5
18	425	4
Total	6706	72

TANGLEWOOD PARK
ARCHITECT: ROBERT TRENT JONES (1957)
REMODELED BY ROBERT TRENT JONES (1972)

LODGING

$$$ Adam's Mark, 460 No. Cherry St., Winston-Salem, N.C. (910) 725-1234. 15 minutes from Tanglewood Park.
$$ Holiday Inn, Lewisville–Clemmons Rd., I-40 Exit 184, Clemmons, N.C. (910) 766-9121. 5 minutes from Tanglewood Park.
$$ Hampton Inn, I-40 at Stratford Rd., Winston-Salem, N.C. (910) 767-9009. 15 minutes from Tanglewood Park.

DINING

Lone Star, 504 Hanes Mall Blvd., Winston-Salem, N.C. (910) 760-9720. 15 minutes from Tanglewood Park.
Olive Garden, 466 Hanes Mall Blvd., Winston-Salem, N.C. (910) 765-9008. 15 minutes from Tanglewood Park.
Cracker Barrel, 4402 Faison Pl., Greensboro, N.C. (910) 294-0911. 30 minutes from Tanglewood Park.

PUBLIC COURSES TO PLAY IN AREA

Reynolds Park, 2450 Reynolds Park Rd., Winston-Salem, N.C. Public. (910) 650-7660. 18/6,320/71. 20 minutes from Tanglewood Park.
Winston Lake, 3535 Winston Lake Rd., Winston-Salem, N.C. Public. (910) 727-2703. 18/6,213/71. 25 minutes from Tanglewood Park.

TICKETS & ACCESSIBILITY

How to watch: Wed.-Thur., pro-am. Fri.-Sun., championship rounds. Daily: $14 advance, $16 at gate, grounds-only. Season: $55 advance, $70 at gate, grounds-only; Daily, grounds and clubhouse: $25. Vantage Championship, P.O. Box 1720, Clemmons, NC 27012. (910) 766-2400, (800) 222-2204.
How to play: Public access facility. Championship course: 18/7,022/72. Reynolds course: 18/6,469/72. (910) 766-5082.

Ralphs Senior Classic

Wilshire Country Club

The Ralphs Senior Classic, which takes its name from the oldest supermarket chain in the western U.S.—Ralphs Grocery Co., founded 1873—moved to a course of appropriate age in 1995. The Wilshire County Club course, designed by Norman Macbeth, opened in 1919. It's located on a relatively small piece of property, just south of Hollywood, in an area known as Hancock Park. The course is split by Beverly Boulevard, with the front nine on the far side of the road and the back nine and clubhouse on the other.

Though not long, all three par-5 holes are considered three-shot affairs, primarily because their greens are so well-protected. A baranca (or creek) runs through the course, delving into 14 of the 18 holes. The course is tight off the tee and slick on the greens. The fairways and greens consist of Poa grass. For putting, that means there is essentially no grain to read and speeds are very fast. Putting is very important.

For five seasons, from 1990 to 1994, this event, briefly known as the Security Pacific Senior Classic, was contested at Rancho Park, a well-regarded public course. In moving to Wilshire, the tournament switched to a site that hosted the Los Angeles Open in 1928, 1931 and 1933.

TOURNAMENT-AT-A-GLANCE

Course: Wilshire Country Club
Type: Private
Location: 301 N. Rossmore Ave., Los Angeles, CA 90004
Phone: (213) 934-1121
When: Oct. 4–6, 1996
How To Get There: Take Hwy. 101 (Hollywood Fwy.) to Santa Monica Blvd. Exit. Travel west 1 mile to Vine St. Turn left, drive 1 mile (street becomes Rossmore Ave.) to club on the right.
Broadcast: Local (1995)
Purse: $800,000 (1995)
Tournament Record: 18-under-par 195, Ray Floyd, 1992

●TOUGHEST HOLE

Water plays a prominent part at the 18th hole. A creek crosses in front of the tee, runs down the right side of the fairway, cuts across to the left and then circles around the green. The long-iron approach from the fairway should aim for the right side of a narrow green.

●BEST PLACE TO WATCH

The clubhouse area affords views of the par-3 10th hole, whose tee is situated above the 18th green, plus the green at No. 16 and the tee at No. 17.

●WHO THE COURSE FAVORS

Shotmakers who can target approach shots, then make the putts. This is not a long course.

LODGING

$$$ Sheraton Universal, 333 Universal Terrace Pkwy., Universal City, Calif. (818) 980-1212. 20 minutes from Wilshire CC.
$$ Universal Hilton, 555 Universal Terrace Pkwy., Universal City, Calif. (213) 617-0666. 20 minutes from Wilshire CC.
$ Holiday Inn Hollywood, 1755 N. Highland, Hollywood, Calif. (213) 462-7181. 20 minutes from Wilshire CC.

DINING

Gladstone's Citywalk, 17300 Pacific Coast Hwy., Pacific Palisades, Calif. (310) 454-3474.
Hamburger Hamlet, 6914 Hollywood Blvd., Hollywood, Calif. (213) 467-6106.
Hard Rock Cafe Beverly Center, 8600 Beverly Blvd., Los Angeles. (310) 276-7605.

PUBLIC COURSES TO PLAY IN AREA

Rancho Park Golf Course, 10460 W. Pico Blvd., Los Angeles. Public. (310) 839-4374. 18/6,585/71. 20 minutes from Wilshire CC.
Griffith Park, 4730 Crystal Springs Dr., Los Angeles. Public. (213) 664-2255. Harding: 18/6,536/72. Wilson: 18/6,942/72. Roosevelt Executive: 9/2,478/30. 20 minutes from Wilshire CC.

TICKETS & ACCESSIBILITY

How to watch: Mon.-Tue., practice. Wed.-Thur., pro-am. Fri.-Sun., championship rounds. Tickets: Daily, $15 (discounts for juniors and seniors). Individual, group and sponsor tickets available. Ralphs Senior Classic, 555 E. Hardy, Inglewood, CA 90301. (310) 412-4653.
How to play: Wilshire Country Club is a private course. You must be a member or accompanied by one.

WILSHIRE COUNTRY CLUB
ARCHITECT: NORMAN MACBETH (1919)

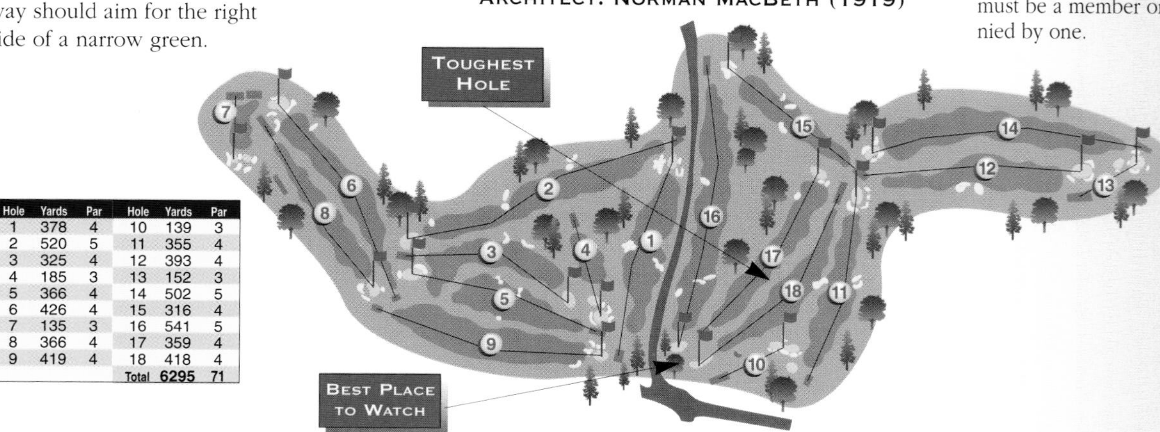

Hole	Yards	Par	Hole	Yards	Par
1	378	4	10	139	3
2	520	5	11	355	4
3	325	4	12	393	4
4	185	3	13	152	3
5	366	4	14	502	5
6	426	4	15	316	4
7	135	3	16	541	5
8	366	4	17	359	4
9	419	4	18	418	4
			Total	6295	71

THE TRANSAMERICA

SILVERADO COUNTRY CLUB

LODGING

$$$ Silverado Resort, 1600 Atlas Peak Rd., Napa, Calif. (707) 257-0200. On site.
$$$ Marriott, 3425 Solano Ave., Napa, Calif. (707) 253-7433. 5 minutes from Silverado CC.
$ Best Western, 100 Soscol Ave., Napa, Calif. (707) 257-1930. 7 minutes from Silverado CC.

DINING

Royal Oak Room, 1600 Atlas Peak Rd., Napa, Calif. (707) 257-0200.
Rutherford Grill, 1180 Rutherford Rd., Rutherford, Calif. (707) 963-1792.
Don Giovanni's, 1145 St. Helena Hwy., Napa, Calif. (707) 224-3300.

PUBLIC COURSES TO PLAY IN AREA

Chardonnay Club, 255 Jameson Canyon Rd., Napa, Calif. Semi-private. (707) 257-8950. Vineyards: 18/6,811/71. 10 minutes from Silverado CC.
Adobe Creek GC, 1901 Frates Rd., Petaluma, Calif. Semi-private. (707) 765-3000. 18/6,963/72. 25 minutes from Silverado CC.

TICKETS & ACCESSIBILITY

How to watch: Mon., practice round, free admission. Tue., practice round, $5. Wed.-Thur., pro-am. Fri., first round, $12. Sat.-Sun., $15. Season ticket, includes clubhouse access, $40 (25% less before Aug. 20). Daily parking, $3. (707) 252-8687.
How to play: Silverado's North and South courses are restricted to members, guests of members and resort hotel guests. Reciprocal play available if home pro calls to make arrangements.

TOURNAMENT-AT-A-GLANCE

Course: Silverado Country Club—South Course
Type: Resort
Location: 1600 Atlas Peak Rd., Napa, CA 94558
Phone: (707) 257-0200
When: Oct. 11–13, 1996
How To Get There: From San Francisco/Oakland Bay Bridge take I-80 East to Hwy. 37 Exit. Turn right onto Hwy. 29 North. Right onto Trancas St.; proceed to Atlas Peak Rd. Turn left for course. 62 miles.
Broadcast: ESPN (1996)
Purse: $650,000 (1995)
Tournament Record: 16-under 200, Bob Charles, 1992

Originally just one course, opened in 1955, Silverado was reconfigured as two 18-hole layouts by Robert Trent Jones Jr. in 1967. Visitors from the East and Midwest will feel right at home at this Napa Valley resort: the tournament South Course is often described as traditional or old-style, with a wide variety of mature trees, sculpted greenside bunkers and large, fast putting surfaces. Fairways provide a multitude of sidehill lies, and the course requires more than a dozen water crossings.

Low scores are a distinct and exciting possibility on this course. In 1994 Isao Aoki played the last 10 holes of regulation at 10-under for a final-round, record-equaling 63, thus gaining a playoff with Kermit Zarley. But Aoki pulled his tee shot on the first extra hole, the 18th, into trees while Zarley birdied the par-5 playoff hole to win the event.

●TOUGHEST HOLE

One of the 50 toughest holes on the Senior Tour, No. 8 presents more than length as a challenge, though length is a formidable component. The green, tucked behind a dogleg right, is not visible from the teeing ground. The fairway is bordered by deep rough to the left and out of bounds to the right. It's an uphill tee shot to a level landing area, followed by a second shot usually in the 200-yard range. Greatest peril on the approach is to the right, where the edge of the green is just five paces from out-of-bounds territory.

●BEST PLACE TO WATCH

Near the ninth green. It's a downhill dogleg left, with water guarding the front of the green. Guess whether a pro will try to reach in two, then watch what happens.

●WHO THE COURSE FAVORS

The player who hits it well left to right has an advantage. With few exceptions, length is not a necessity. Reading putts is important on greens that present double and triple breaks.

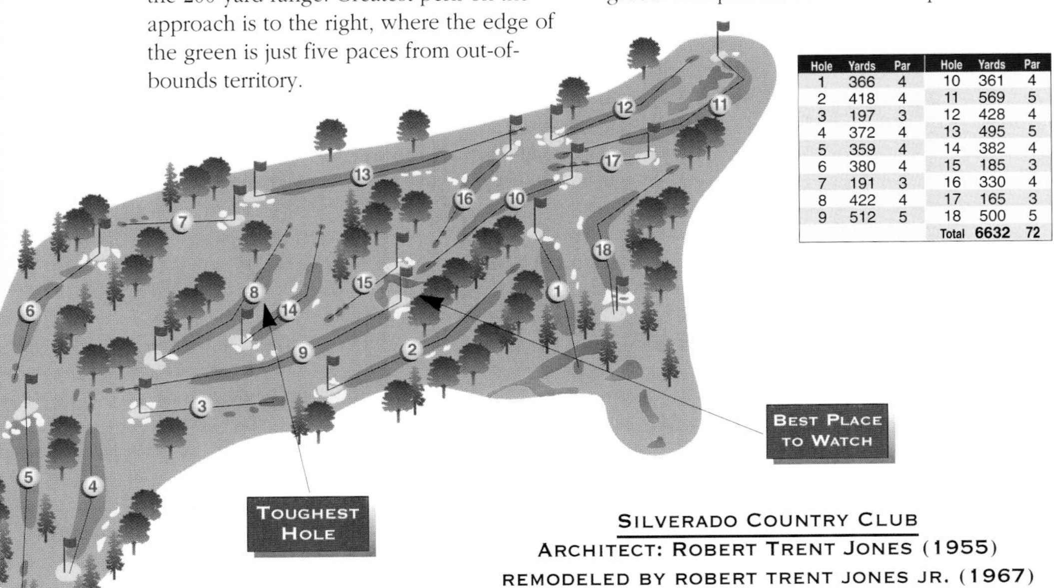

Hole	Yards	Par	Hole	Yards	Par
1	366	4	10	361	4
2	418	4	11	569	5
3	197	3	12	428	4
4	372	4	13	495	5
5	359	4	14	382	4
6	380	4	15	185	3
7	191	3	16	330	4
8	422	4	17	165	3
9	512	5	18	500	5
			Total	6632	72

SILVERADO COUNTRY CLUB
ARCHITECT: ROBERT TRENT JONES (1955)
REMODELED BY ROBERT TRENT JONES JR. (1967)

Raley's Senior Gold Rush

RANCHO MURIETA COUNTRY CLUB

Situated in a residential community not far from Sacramento, the Burt Stamps–designed North Course at Rancho Murieta opened in 1971. Its rolling fairways are pinched by strategically planted trees of all varieties and its greens are amply guarded by sand, but water comes into play on only two holes. Dramatic elevation changes test placement and club selection on several holes, and numerous rock gardens adorn both the fairways and greens. In 1995, Rancho Murieta ranked as the fifth-toughest course on the Senior Tour, as the pros averaged nearly two strokes over par on each round.

TOURNAMENT-AT-A-GLANCE

Course: Rancho Murieta North Course
Type: Resort
Location: 7000 Alameda Dr., Rancho Murieta, CA 95683
Phone: (916) 354-3400
When: Oct. 18–20, 1996
How To Get There: Take I-80, exit at Sunrise Blvd. Go south to Jackson Rd., turn left and proceed to Rancho Murieta.
Broadcast: None (1995)
Purse: $700,000 (1995)
Tournament Record: 15-under-par 201, Bob Charles, 1992

The Raley's Senior Gold Rush has been played on this track ever since its 1987 debut, when Orville Moody captured the title. George Archer, who lives nearby in the Lake Tahoe area, has won the event three times. Through 1994, no one else had won it twice.

More than 90,000 people attend the week's festivities, and the whole affair has a community feel to it. Many of the spectators know each other, or are renewing annual acquaintances.

In the 1994 Gold Rush, the 18th hole saw more decisive action than any other. Not only did it weather its share of play during three championship rounds, but when Bob Murphy and Dave Eichelberger tied after 54 holes, they returned five times to the 429-yard, par-4 final hole before deciding a winner. Four times in a row, the duo parred the hole, which normally requires a long-iron or fairway wood uphill to a well-bunkered green. Then came the fifth time, and it was the charm, sort of, for Murphy. Actually, Murphy three-putted for bogey but Eichelberger had already pushed his tee shot out of bounds and was destined for at least a double-bogey.

Earlier Murphy had birdied the 18th in regulation to pull even with the charging Eichelberger.

"I didn't think we'd finish," Murphy said after he sank the concluding 1-footer.

In 1993, Chi Chi Rodriguez tied the course record in the first round with a 7-under 65. But he wound up tied for second with defending champion Bob Charles, one stroke behind George Archer. Again, the 18th hole was the key. Tied for the lead as he came to the final hole, Archer pulled out one more birdie for a 68–202 and his third victory.

"IT WASN'T THE GREATEST WAY TO WIN A TOURNAMENT, BUT NO. 18 IS DIFFICULT."

—BOB MURPHY,

WINNER OF THE 1994 RALEY'S SENIOR GOLD RUSH WITH A BOGEY AT NO. 18, THE FIFTH PLAYOFF HOLE

●TOUGHEST HOLE

The fairway landing area is hidden from the tee on No. 4, a long par-4 requiring a left-to-right drive. The approach for the pros will be a mid- to long iron; for amateurs a long iron or wood. The approach will be difficult to hold on a green that slopes away from the player. Upfront pin placements are difficult because it's arduous trying to get the ball to stop at the front. A draw shot is practically required if the flagstick is placed in the back-left portion of the green. Another tough hole is the 435-yard, par-4 13th, where an uphill approach with a long iron or fairway wood must often carry a bunker to the front left of the green.

●BEST PLACE TO WATCH

The 10th hole provides an amphitheater-like setting. It's not a long par-4, but the tee shot is blind to a fairway sloping away from the players. The approach comes via a short-iron over water. There's danger for shots hitting up front on the green and spinning back, but the spectator excitement owes more to the myriad birdie opportunities presented. Bleachers surround the green on the difficult par-4 18th, which Bob Murphy and Dave Eichelberger played five consecutive times in 1994's sudden-death playoff before Eichelberger misstruck a tee shot.

●WHO THE COURSE FAVORS

A player who can work the ball left to right with deft placement off the tee should have the upper hand here because the doglegs primarily swing to the right. But this isn't a regular stop for Lee Trevino. Maybe three-time winner George Archer, a local hero, has a fourth title in him.

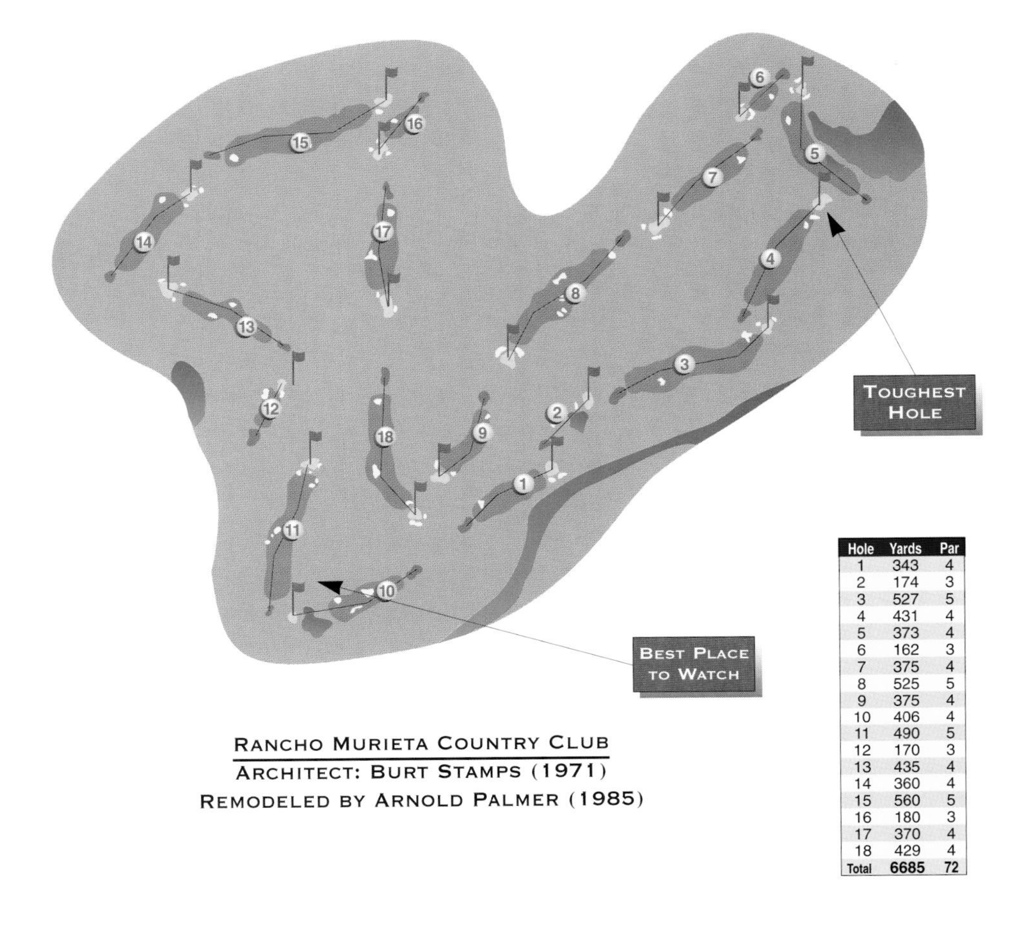

Rancho Murieta Country Club
Architect: Burt Stamps (1971)
Remodeled by Arnold Palmer (1985)

Hole	Yards	Par
1	343	4
2	174	3
3	527	5
4	431	4
5	373	4
6	162	3
7	375	4
8	525	5
9	375	4
10	406	4
11	490	5
12	170	3
13	435	4
14	360	4
15	560	5
16	180	3
17	370	4
18	429	4
Total	6685	72

LODGING

$$$ Sheraton, 11211 Point East Dr., Rancho Cordova, Calif. (916) 638-1100. 15 minutes from Rancho Murieta.
$$ Hallmark Suites, 11260 Point East Dr., Rancho Cordova, Calif. (916) 638-4141. 15 minutes from Rancho Murieta.
$$ Radisson Lake Natoma, 702 Gold Lake Dr., Folsom, Calif. (916) 351-1500. 20 minutes from Rancho Murieta.

DINING

Sheepherders, 11275 Folsom Blvd., Rancho Cordova, Calif. (916) 635-6886.
Cliff House, 9900 Greenback Ln., Folsom, Calif. (916) 989-9243.
Old Spaghetti Factory, 12401 Folsom Blvd., Rancho Cordova, Calif. (916) 985-0822.

PUBLIC COURSES TO PLAY IN AREA

Cordova, 9425 Jackson Rd., Sacramento. Public. (916) 362-1196. 18/5,287/63. 20 minutes from Rancho Murieta.
El Dorado Hills, 3775 El Dorado Hills Blvd., El Dorado Hills, Calif. Public. (916) 933-6552. 18/4,400/61. 40 minutes from Rancho Murieta.

TICKETS & ACCESSIBILITY

How to watch: Mon., U.S. Bank pro-am. Tue., Classics Skins Game, Reno Challenge of Champions, Merrill Lynch shoot-out. Wed., Cellular One pro-am first round. Thur., Cellular One pro-am second round, Raley's Classic pro-am. Fri.-Sun., championship rounds. Tickets: Mon., free admission; Tue.-Thur., $12 daily, Fri.-Sun., $17 daily; weekly grounds, $35 advance/$55 gate; weekly clubhouse, $55 advance/$75 gate. Rancho Murieta Country Club, P.O. Box 990, Rancho Murieta, CA 95683. (916) 354-2345.
How to play: Ranch Murieta is a resort course open to the public. Two courses: North and South (18/6,886/72). (916) 354-3440.

Hyatt Regency Maui Kaanapali Classic

KAANAPALI GOLF CLUB

THE KAANAPALI COURSES ARE BUILT OVER THE SAME LAND ON WHICH EARLY RULERS OF MAUI PLAYED THEIR GAME *ULU MAIKA*, A DISTANT RELATION OF LAWN BOWLING.

The Kaanapali golf courses sit just below the West Maui mountain range, in an area that formerly served as a sugar plantation. In fact, a steam-engine-powered Sugar Cane Train—a.k.a. the Lahaina, Kaanapali & Pacific Railroad—provides tourists with an entertaining ride through the South Course on its way to the nearby historic whaling town of Lahaina.

The tournament itself traverses the North Course, one of just two layouts in Hawaii that were fashioned by Robert Trent Jones. The North is the granddaddy of championship golf in the state, opened in 1962 with Bing Crosby on hand. Two years later, Arnold Palmer and Jack Nicklaus teamed here to win the Canada Cup (now the World Cup).

Kaanapali, which means "rolling hills" in Hawaiian, provides just that for the front nine of the tournament (the sequence of holes for the Senior Tour is changed from normal resort play). The front nine treks across gradual slopes that provide spectators on the uppermost portions with panoramic views of the Kaanapali resort village, the bustling town of Lahaina, the Pacific Ocean and the nearby islands of Lanai and Molokai. The generally flatter finishing nine requires slightly greater length.

The atmosphere for the Hyatt Regency Maui Kaanapali Classic is relaxed for both spectators and contestants. For fans, there's no admission charge all week long, a rarity on tour. For the players, the event comes as the season is nearing its end, and many pros make it a family trip. For everyone, there's plenty of elbow room, with spectators for the entire week estimated at 15,000 to 20,000.

The most dramatic Kaanapali Classic was undoubtedly the 1993 version in which Player of the Year Dave Stockton, all-time Senior Tour victories leader Lee Trevino and 1969 Masters champ George Archer deadlocked after 54 holes of regulation at 14-under 199. To reach the playoff, Archer had to pull off a minor miracle. Entering Sunday's play, he was four shots behind leader Stockton, with 10 other golfers either ahead or tied with him. But an 8-under-par 63 got Archer even with Stockton while Trevino gained a playoff berth by ramming in a 20-foot birdie putt from the collar of the 18th green. For the playoff, the trio returned to the 18th. After Stockton two-putted from 40 feet, Archer dropped his double-breaking birdie putt into the center of the cup and emerged the champion when Trevino fell 2 inches short with his 8-foot birdie attempt.

TOURNAMENT-AT-A-GLANCE
Course: Kaanapali Golf Club—North Course
Type: Resort
Location: Kaanapali Pkwy, Lahaina, HI 96761
Phone: (808) 661-3691
When: October 25–27, 1996
How To Get There: From Kahului Airport, take Hwy 30 west/north. 30 miles to course. From West Maui Airport, take Hwy 30 south. 2 miles to course.
Broadcast: ESPN (1996)
Purse: $600,000 (1995)
Tournament Record: 18-under 195, Bob Murphy, 1994

●TOUGHEST HOLE

In 1964, after competing in what is now known as the World Cup, an event that at the time drew two-man teams from 34 nations, Arnold Palmer labeled the 18th at Kaanapali North one of the most challenging holes he'd ever encountered. Many locals call it the best finishing hole in Hawaii. The rigors begin at the tee, where bunkers 220 yards out jut halfway across the fairway from the left, urging golfers to drive toward the right. However, the entire right side of the hole, from the tee well past the green, is bordered by a dangerous, blue lagoon. A drive center-right on the fairway means the approach will have to carry a neck of water guarding the right front of the green. Many a player has misjudged and misclubbed here, plunking an approach shot short and into the lagoon.

●BEST PLACE TO WATCH

The 18th is ringed with stands and, considering both its toughness and often-dramatic impact on the tournament's outcome, guarantees exciting viewing. But for a combination of golf spectating and breathtaking panorama, a perch on the high ground just above the seventh green/ eighth tee provides a majestic view of the entire course, the hotel district beyond the course and the Pacific Ocean.

●WHO THE COURSE FAVORS

Essentially long hitters, but if the trade winds are blowing above 20 mph, adept wind play and safe approach shots are essential. Because of the prevailing breezes, fairways are fairly open, tree factors are minimal and the large greens accommodate a fair margin of error.

Hole	Yards	Par
1	349	4
2	165	3
3	502	5
4	460	4
5	380	4
6	370	4
7	395	4
8	400	4
9	185	3
10	541	5
11	185	3
12	410	4
13	360	4
14	423	4
15	480	5
16	400	4
17	155	3
18	430	4
Total	6590	71

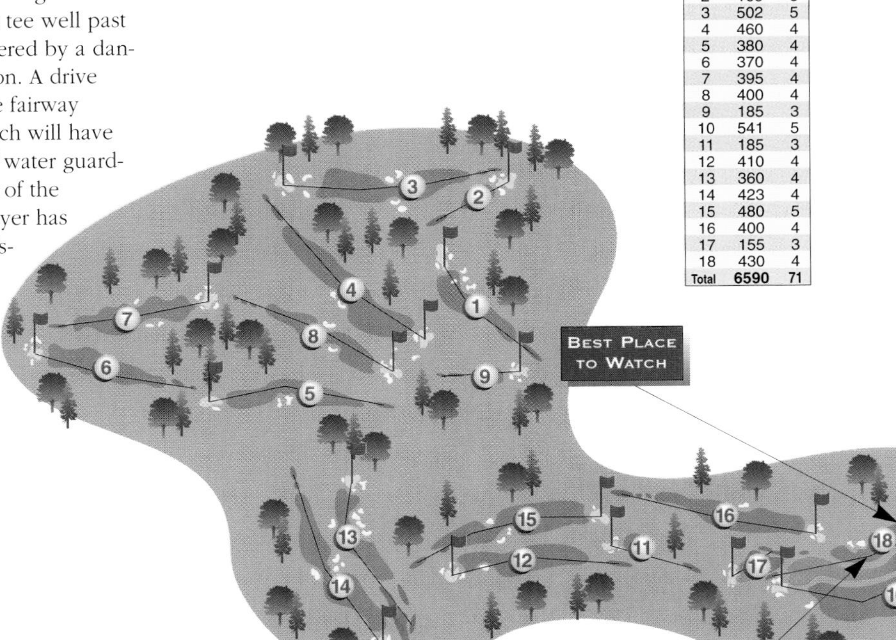

Royal Kaanapali North Course
North Course Architect: Robert Trent Jones (1968)

LODGING

$$$ Hyatt Regency, 200 Nohea Kai Dr., Lahaina, Hawaii. (808) 661-1234. Adjacent to Kaanapali.
$$$ Maui Marriott, 100 Nohea Kai Dr., Lahaina, Hawaii. (808) 667-1200. Adjacent to Kaanapali.
$$$ Westin Maui, 2365 Kaanapali Pkwy, Lahaina, Hawaii. (808) 667-2525. Adjacent to Kaanapali.

DINING

Swan Court, 200 Nohea Kai Dr., Lahaina, Hawaii. (808) 661-1234. In adjacent Hyatt Regency.
Kimo's, 845 Front St., Lahaina, Hawaii. (808) 661-4811. 15 minutes from Kaanapali.
Longhi's, 888 Front St., Lahaina, Hawaii. (808) 667-2288. 15 minutes from Kaanapali.

PUBLIC COURSES TO PLAY IN AREA

Kapalua Golf Course, 2000 Plantation Club Dr., Lahaina, Hawaii. Semi-private. (808) 669-8044. Bay: 18/6,600/72. Plantation: 18/7,263/73. Village: 18/6,632/71. 20 minutes from Kaanapali.
Wailea Golf Course, 120 Kaukahi St., Wailea, Hawaii. Semi-private. (808) 879-2966. Blue: 18/6,943/72. Orange: 18/6,810/72. Gold: 18/6,915/72. 40 minutes from Kaanapali.

TICKETS & ACCESSIBILITY

How to watch: Wed.-Thur., Super Senior pro-am on South Course, Classic pro-am on North Course. Fri.-Sun., championship rounds. Admission free to tournament, open to the public at all times. Hyatt Regency Maui Kaanapali Classic, P.O. Box 1521, Lahaina, HI 96767. (808) 661-1885.
How to play: Resort courses open to public; preferred tee times, fees for guests of adjacent hotels. In addition to North Course, Kaanapali GC includes South Course, 18/6,555/71. Limited play on South Course during tournament week. (808) 661-3691.

Emerald Coast Classic

THE MOORS GOLF CLUB

A new event came to a fairly new course in 1995 when the Emerald Coast Classic arrived at The Moors. The course, designed by John LaFoy, opened in June 1993 and hosted Nike Tour events in 1994 and early 1995.

With mostly broad fairways and flat bunkers, the Moors is a course that blends Scottish-flavor and Florida-style golf, with gently rolling terrain, few trees and luxury homes adjacent to the layout. A privately owned daily-fee course, The Moors is located just 5 miles east of Pensacola. Its 10,000-square-foot clubhouse resembles a more renowned edifice at Scotland's venerable Muirfield Golf Club.

The course record here is 62, set by Ron Philo in the first round of the '94 Nike Pensacola Classic. That round gave Philo a Nike Tour–record six-stroke lead after one round, but he finished second by a shot behind Bruce Vaughan's 13-under 271.

TOURNAMENT-AT-A-GLANCE

Course: The Moors Golf Club
Type: Public
Location: 3220 Avalon Blvd., Milton, FL 32583
Phone: (904) 995-4653
When: Nov. 1-3, 1996
How To Get There: Take I-10 to Exit 7. Go north on Avalon Blvd. 1 mile to club.
Broadcast: The Golf Channel (1996)
Purse: $1 million (1995)
Tournament Record: New event in 1995

●TOUGHEST HOLE

The long par-4 ninth, rated among the top 40 toughest on the Nike Tour in 1994, averaged 4.27 strokes and gave up just 27 birdies against 88 bogeys. The tee shot is presented with out-of-bounds to the right and a lateral hazard on the left. The approach must carry 85 yards of water fronting a large green.

●BEST PLACE TO WATCH

A perch behind the 16th green gives you a view of that par-3 hole, which features a wide but not-too-deep, elevated green protected by bunkers on the right and rear. Fans can also see the 12th tee and green, the 11th green, first green and 17th tee—all from this location.

●WHO THE COURSE FAVORS

The holes at The Moors vary, and they will play best for a golfer with a well-rounded game. At times, the demand is for a long and straight tee shot. Other times the premium is on a pinpoint approach to a large green, or skill in putting the more undulated surfaces.

Hole	Yards	Par
1	532	5
2	397	4
3	210	3
4	406	4
5	418	4
6	408	4
7	503	5
8	178	3
9	448	4
10	404	4
11	547	5
12	203	3
13	400	4
14	405	4
15	414	4
16	203	3
17	435	4
18	428	4
Total	6949	71

THE MOORS GOLF CLUB
ARCHITECT: JOHN LAFOY (1993)

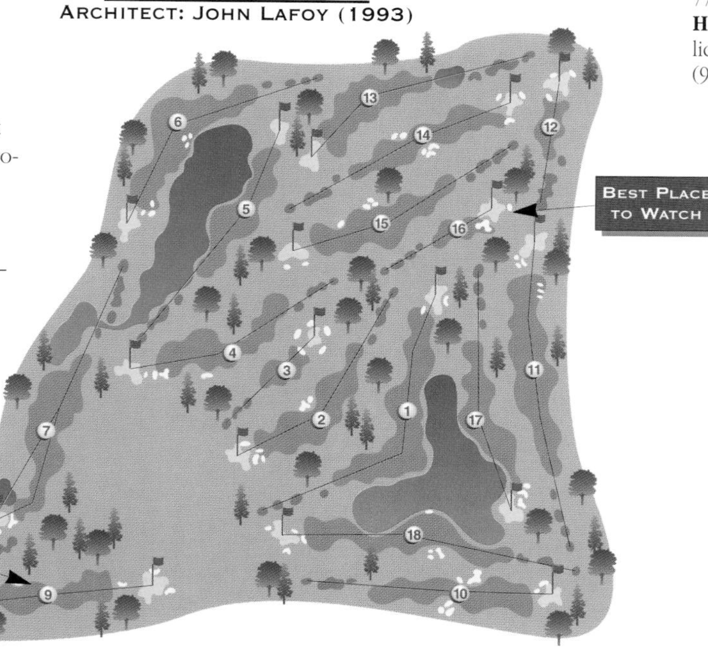

LODGING

$$ Holiday Inn University Mall, 7200 Plantation Rd., Pensacola, Fla. (904) 474-0100. 15 minutes from The Moors GC.
$$ Residence Inn, 7230 Plantation Rd., Pensacola, Fla. (904) 479-1000. 15 minutes from The Moors GC.
$ Best Western Village Inn, 8240 N. Davis Hwy., Pensacola, Fla. (904) 479-1099. 20 minutes from The Moors GC.

DINING

McGuire's, 600 E. Gregory St., Pensacola, Fla. (904) 433-6789.
Hall's, 920 E. Gregory St., Pensacola, Fla. (904) 438-9019.
Seville, 130 Government St., Pensacola, Fla. (904) 434-6211.

PUBLIC COURSES TO PLAY IN AREA

Marcus Pointe, 2500 Oak Pointe, Pensacola, Fla. Semi-private. (904) 484-9770. 15 minutes from The Moors GC. 18/6,732/72.
Hidden Creek, 3070 PGA Blvd., Navarre, Fla. Public. (904) 939-1939. 45 minutes from The Moors GC. 18/6,800/72.

TICKETS & ACCESSIBILITY

How to watch: Tue., practice round, Reunion Skins game, senior clinic. Wed., Food World pro-am, junior clinic. Thur., AmSouth pro-am. Fri.-Sun., championship rounds. Daily tickets: $12; Muirfield Club season pass, $100. Individual, group and sponsor tickets available. Emerald Coast Classic, 25 W. Cedar St., Suite 620, Pensacola, FL 32501. (904) 438-7700.
How to play: The Moors is a public, daily-fee course. 18/6,956/71. (904) 995-4653.

Energizer Senior Tour Championship

Dunes Golf and Beach Club

TOURNAMENT-AT-A-GLANCE

Course: Dunes Golf and Beach Club
Type: Resort
Location: 9000 N. Ocean Blvd., Myrtle Beach, SC 29572
Phone: (803) 449-5236
When: Nov. 7-10, 1996
How To Get There: Take U.S. Hwy 17 to N. Ocean Blvd.
Broadcast: ESPN (1995)
Purse: $1.5 million (1995)
Tournament Record: 15-under-par 273, Ray Floyd, 1994

Myrtle Beach bills itself as the Golf Capital of the World, with a concentration of more than 75 courses within a 35-mile radius. The Dunes, designed by Robert Trent Jones in 1949 and '50 on what was formerly prime turkey-hunting ground, was at the forefront of the region's rise as a golf mecca.

This season-ending championship, which brings together the year's top 31 Senior players, moved to the Dunes from Puerto Rico in 1994 and adopted a PGA-style 72-hole format after four years as a 54-hole event. In '95, a Super Seniors competition was added to the tournament, with the top 16 60-and-over pros vying for their own $400,000 purse.

The Dunes features lots of water, marsh hazards and several protected wetland tracts. In 1994, Jay Sigel set a course record when he shot a final-round 63 that included a double-eagle on the 15th. Ray Floyd's victory that year, his second in this event, was determined by a birdie on the fifth playoff hole after his final-round 66 brought him from six strokes back to tie Jim Albus in regulation.

Prior to the Senior PGA Tour's arrival, the Dunes had most notably been host to the 1962 U.S. Women's Open, when Murle Lindstrom recorded her first professional victory.

LODGING

$ Southern Sands Bar Harbor, 1st Ave. North, Myrtle Beach, S.C. (803) 449-7200. 20 minutes from Dunes Golf & Beach Club.
$ Coral Reef, 2706 S. Ocean Blvd., Myrtle Beach, S.C. (803) 448-8471. 30 minutes from Dunes Golf & Beach Club.
$ Dunes Village, 5200 N. Ocean Blvd., Myrtle Beach, S.C. (803) 449-5275. 10 minutes from Dunes Golf & Beach Club.

DINING

Cagney's, Hwy. 17, Myrtle Beach, S.C. (803) 449-3824.
Thoroughbreds, 9706 N. Kings Hwy., Myrtle Beach, S.C. (803) 497-2636.

PUBLIC COURSES TO PLAY IN AREA

Arcadian Shores, 701 Hilton Rd., Myrtle Beach, S.C. Public. (803) 449-5217. 18/6,938/72. 5 minutes from Dunes Golf & Beach Club.
Myrtlewood, 48th Ave. North, Myrtle Beach, S.C. Public. (803) 449-5134. Palmetto: 18/6,957/72. Pinehills: 18/6,640/72. 10 minutes from Dunes Golf & Beach Club.

TICKETS & ACCESSIBILITY

How to watch: Mon.-Tue., practice rounds. Wed., pro-am. Thur.-Sun., championship rounds. Daily grounds, Mon.-Tue., $10; Wed.-Fri., $20; Sat.-Sun., $25. Daily clubhouse, $40. Season grounds, $75; season clubhouse, $200. Many hotels offer lodging and tournament ticket packages. Individual, group and sponsor tickets available. Energizer Senior Tour Championship, 7700 N. King's Hwy., Suite 103, Myrtle Beach, S.C. 29572. (803) 444-4782.
How to play: You must be the guest of a member or be a hotel guest. 18/7,021/72. (803) 449-5236.

THE DUNES GOLF CLUB
ARCHITECT: ROBERT TRENT JONES (1949)

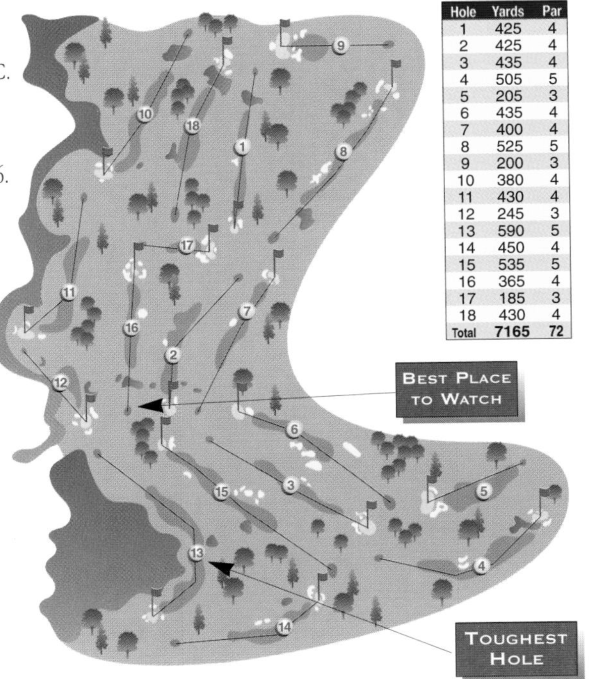

Hole	Yards	Par
1	425	4
2	425	4
3	435	4
4	505	5
5	205	3
6	435	4
7	400	4
8	525	5
9	200	3
10	380	4
11	430	4
12	245	3
13	590	5
14	450	4
15	535	5
16	365	4
17	185	3
18	430	4
Total	7165	72

●TOUGHEST HOLE

Par-5s don't often play toughest on a given course, but the 13th at the Dunes does. It's an uphill dogleg right around a lake. The tee shot must favor the right side of the fairway. The second shot must carry 200 to 215 yards over water. The third is an approach to a bunkered two-tiered green with a scant 20-foot opening front-center. Regarded as one of the world's great par-5s, it reportedly has been reached in two shots only once, when 1960s slugger Mike Souchak accomplished the feat.

●BEST PLACE TO WATCH

Teeside at No. 16 affords a view of the 15th green plus easy access to Nos. 2 and 3.

●WHO THE COURSE FAVORS

There's less emphasis off the tee and a greater demand for deft play around the greens here. With the Dunes' abundance of turtle-back putting surfaces, a solid short game is important.

Lexus Challenge

LA QUINTA HOTEL GOLF CLUB

Opened in 1926, the La Quinta Hotel is the area's oldest. With a classic Spanish-flavored architectural style and a soothing ambience, it has wooed Hollywood legends for decades, including Clark Gable, Bette Davis, Joan Crawford, Marlene Dietrich, Errol Flynn and director Frank Capra. The hotel was the creation of San Francisco oystering tycoon Walter Morgan.

Subsequent owners commissioned Pete Dye to design and construct what are now three courses. The newest of the links is Citrus (1987), which hosts the Lexus Challenge.

TOURNAMENT-AT-A-GLANCE

Course: La Quinta Hotel Golf Club—Citrus Course
Type: Resort
Location: 50-503 Jefferson St., La Quinta, CA 92253
Phone: (619) 564-7620
When: Dec. 21–22, 1996
How To Get There: Take I-10 to Jefferson St. Exit. Go south 3 miles to course.
Broadcast: NBC (1996)
Purse: $1 million (1995)
Tournament Record: New event in 1995

It's natural to compare La Quinta's two resort courses. Whereas Dunes places its highest premium on pinpoint approach shots, Citrus provides more room for bump-and-run into the greens. The Citrus layout is nestled in a grove at the base of the nearby mountains. You can literally pick and eat grapefruit between holes.

The greens on the Citrus course are generally kept fast, and the undulations of its putting surfaces are sometimes obvious, sometimes quite hidden. "The fun just begins on the greens. There's no guarantee putting anywhere," says one of the club pros. Wind can also be a factor. It tends to gust in the afternoons, so players with early starts usually get a break in that department.

The Lexus Challenge, hosted by Raymond Floyd, pairs some of golf's greatest names with a marquee lineup of celebrities. On the roster to join Floyd for the event's 1995 inaugural were fellow pros Arnold Palmer, Jack Nicklaus, Lee Trevino and Chi Chi Rodriguez along with celebs Sylvester Stallone, Clint Eastwood, Michael Douglas and Jack Nicholson. The format for Lexus lists a field of 12 Senior Tour pros and 12 celebrity golfers paired by random draw for a 36-hole betterball championship.

"I've always had the dream of one day hosting a very special event," said Floyd. "I had a vision of recreating the old Bing Crosby Clambake for the Senior PGA Tour. The event will be more than just a golf tournament. It's an opportunity for 24 friends to come together in the spirit of the season for a special holiday reunion."

> "THE TOURNAMENT WILL SHOWCASE THE BEST AGAINST THE BEST—THE WORLD'S MOST OUTSTANDING GOLFERS AGAINST ENTERTAINMENT'S MOST FAMOUS CELEBRITIES."
>
> —RAY FLOYD,
>
> ANNOUNCING THE CREATION OF THE LEXUS CHALLENGE

Courtesy of KSL Recreation Corporation

PETE DYE'S CITRUS COURSE PROVIDES AMPLE ROOM FOR BUMP-AND-RUN APPROACHES TO ITS QUICK GREENS.

●TOUGHEST HOLE

The finishing hole on the Citrus course requires a long but well-placed tee shot. The greatest peril on the drive is presented by a 100-yard-long bunker guarding the left side of the fairway, but a drive too far right will catch rough and severely hinder an attempt to reach the green in two shots. The amoeba-shaped green is protected by a large lake whose banks are lined with railroad ties.

●BEST PLACE TO WATCH

The ninth hole is a relatively short par-4, considered a fun hole for the pros, spectators and, when the tournament's not in town, for just-plain amateur enthusiasts. A drive with a slight draw to the middle of the fairway sets up an approach to an oblong green. There is definite birdie potential here.

●WHO THE COURSE FAVORS

Players who have a finely honed short game, followed by putting acumen. A lot of greens get missed, thus placing emphasis on being able to get up and down.

Hole	Yards	Par	Hole	Yards	Par
1	419	4	10	386	4
2	570	5	11	418	4
3	224	3	12	375	4
4	467	4	13	163	3
5	378	4	14	567	5
6	454	4	15	427	4
7	142	3	16	147	3
8	581	5	17	538	5
9	377	4	18	473	4
			Total	7106	72

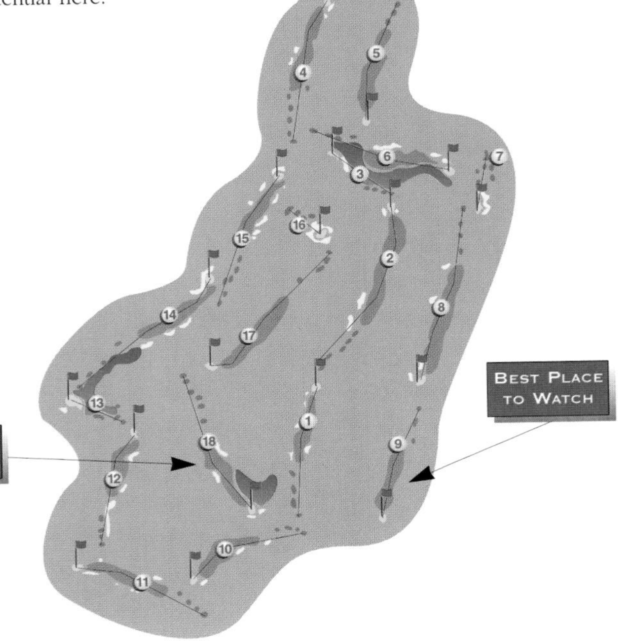

LA QUINTA CITRUS COURSE
ARCHITECT: PETE DYE (1987)

LODGING

$$$ Hyatt Grand Champions, 44-600 Indian Wells Ln., Indian Wells, Calif. (619) 341-1000. 20 minutes from La Quinta.
$$ La Quinta Hotel, 49-499 Eisenhower Dr., La Quinta, Calif. (619) 564-4111. At La Quinta.
$$ Stouffer Renaissance Esmeralda Resort, 44-400 Indian Wells Ln., Indian Wells, Calif. (619) 773-4444. 10 minutes from La Quinta.

DINING

Adobe Grill, at La Quinta Hotel, 49-499 Eisenhower Dr., La Quinta, Calif. (619) 564-4111.
Cliffhouse, 78250 Hwy. 111, La Quinta, Calif. (619) 360-5991.
Ruth's Chris Steak House, 74040 Hwy. 111, Palm Desert, Calif. (619) 779-1998.

PUBLIC COURSES TO PLAY IN AREA

Indian Palms, 48-630 Monroe St., Indio, Calif. Semi-private. (619) 347-2326. 18/6,700/72. 5 minutes from La Quinta.
Indian Springs, 46-080 Jefferson St., La Quinta, Calif. Public. (619) 775-3360. 18/6,601/71. 10 minutes from La Quinta.

TICKETS & ACCESSIBILITY

How to watch: Thur., pro/celebrity-am, scramble format. Fri., pro/celebrity-am, net best ball. Sat.-Sun., pro-celebrity better-ball championship. Tickets: Limited supply available to Lexus owners only, through lottery; register by calling (800) 255-3987.
How to play: The La Quinta Hotel courses are resort courses. Reduced fees for hotel guests. Two courses: Citrus and Dunes (50-200 Ave. Vista Bonita, La Quinta, Calif., 18/6,861/72). Third course, Mountain, is private and restricted to members. (619) 564-7620.

Courtesy of The Provincial Archive of Alberta, Canada and the du Maurier Ltd. Classic

TOURNAMENT HISTORIES

All results for tournaments played after mid-August 1995 are not included.
- Amateur
@ - Rain shortened
@@ - Rain delayed
* - Won sudden-death playoff
† - Won 18-hole playoff

THE MASTERS

AUGUSTA NATIONAL GOLF CLUB, AUGUSTA, GA.

YEAR	WINNER	SCORE	RUNNER-UP
1934	Horton Smith	284	Craig Wood
1935	*Gene Sarazen (144)	282	Craig Wood (149)
1936	Horton Smith	285	Harry Cooper
1937	Byron Nelson	283	Ralph Guldahl
1938	Henry Picard	285	Ralph Guldahl, Harry Cooper
1939	Ralph Guldahl	279	Sam Snead
1940	Jimmy Demaret	280	Lloyd Mangrum
1941	Craig Wood	280	Byron Nelson
1942	*Byron Nelson (69)	280	Ben Hogan (70)
1943	No tournament-World War II		
1944	No tournament-World War II		
1945	No tournament-World War II		
1946	Herman Keiser	282	Ben Hogan
1947	Jimmy Demaret	281	Byron Nelson, Frank Stranahan
1948	Claude Harmon	279	Cary Middlecoff
1949	Sam Snead	282	Johnny Bulla, Lloyd Mangrum
1950	Jimmy Demaret	283	Jim Ferrier
1951	Ben Hogan	280	Skee Riegel
1952	Sam Snead	286	Jack Burke Jr.
1953	Ben Hogan	274	Ed Oliver Jr.
1954	*Sam Snead (70)	289	Ben Hogan (71)
1955	Cary Middlecoff	279	Ben Hogan
1956	Jack Burke Jr.	289	Ken Venturi
1957	Doug Ford	282	Sam Snead
1958	Arnold Palmer	284	Doug Ford, Fred Hawkins
1959	Art Wall Jr.	284	Cary Middlecoff
1960	Arnold Palmer	282	Ken Venturi
1961	Gary Player	280	Charles R. Coe, Arnold Palmer
1962	*Arnold Palmer (68)	280	Gary Player (71), Dow Finsterwald (77)
1963	Jack Nicklaus	286	Tony Lema
1964	Arnold Palmer	276	Dave Marr, Jack Nicklaus
1965	Jack Nicklaus	271	Arnold Palmer, Gary Player
1966	*Jack Nicklaus (70)	288	Tommy Jacobs (72), Gay Brewer Jr. (78)
1967	Gay Brewer Jr.	280	Bobby Nichols
1968	Bob Goalby	277	Roberto DeVicenzo
1969	George Archer	281	Billy Casper, George Knudson, Tom Weiskopf
1970	*Billy Casper (69)	279	Gene Littler (74)
1971	Charles Coody	279	Johnny Miller, Jack Nicklaus
1972	Jack Nicklaus	286	Bruce Crampton, Bobby Mitchell, Tom Weiskopf
1973	Tommy Aaron	283	J.C. Snead
1974	Gary Player	278	Tom Weiskopf, Dave Stockton
1975	Jack Nicklaus	276	Johnny Miller, Tom Weiskopf
1976	Ray Floyd	271	Ben Crenshaw
1977	Tom Watson	276	Jack Nicklaus
1978	Gary Player	277	Hubert Green, Rod Funseth, Tom Watson
1979	*Fuzzy Zoeller	280	Ed Sneed, Tom Watson
1980	Seve Ballesteros	275	Gibby Gilbert, Jack Newton
1981	Tom Watson	280	Johnny Miller, Jack Nicklaus
1982	*Craig Stadler	284	Dan Pohl
1983	Seve Ballesteros	280	Ben Crenshaw, Tom Kite
1984	Ben Crenshaw	277	Tom Watson
1985	Bernhard Langer	282	Curtis Strange, Seve Ballesteros, Ray Floyd
1986	Jack Nicklaus	279	Greg Norman, Tom Kite
1987	*Larry Mize	285	Seve Ballesteros, Greg Norman
1988	Sandy Lyle	281	Mark Calcavecchia
1989	*Nick Faldo	283	Scott Hoch
1990	*Nick Faldo	278	Ray Floyd
1991	Ian Woosnam	277	Jose Maria Olazabal
1992	Fred Couples	275	Ray Floyd
1993	Bernhard Langer	277	Chip Beck
1994	Jose Maria Olazabal	279	Tom Lehman
1995	Ben Crenshaw	274	David Love III

UNITED STATES OPEN

YEAR	WINNER	SCORE	RUNNER-UP	COURSE
1895	Horace Rawlins	173-36 holes		Willie Dunn, Newport GC, Newport, R.I.
1896	James Foulis	152-36	Horace Rawlins	Shinnecock Hills GC, Southampton, N.Y.
1897	Joe Lloyd	162-36	Willie Anderson	Chicago GC, Wheaton, Ill.
1898	Fred Herd	328-72	Alex Smith	Myopia Hunt Club, Hamilton, Mass.
1899	Willie Smith	315	George Low Val Fitzjohn W.H. Way	Baltimore CC, Baltimore
1900	Harry Vardon	313	J.H. Taylor	Chicago GC, Wheaton, Ill.
1901	*Willie Anderson (85)	331	Alex Smith (86)	Myopia Hunt Club, Hamilton, Mass.
1902	Laurie Auchterlonie	307	Stewart Gardner	Garden City GC, Garden City, L.I., N.Y.
1903	*Willie Anderson (82)	307	David Brown (84)	Baltusrol GC, Short Hills, N.Y.
1904	Willie Anderson	303	Gil Nicholls	Glen View Club, Golf, Ill.
1905	Willie Anderson	314	Alex Smith	Myopia Hunt Club, Hamilton, Mass.
1906	Alex Smith	295	Willie Smith	Onwentsia Club Lake Forest, Ill.
1907	Alex Ross	302	Gil Nicholls	Philadelphia Cricket Club, Chestnut Hill, Pa.
1908	*Fred McLeod (77)	322	Willie Smith (83)	Myopia Hunt Club, Hamilton, Mass.
1909	George Sargent	290	Tom McNamara	Englewood GC, Englewood, N.J.
1910	*Alex Smith (71)	298	John McDermott (75) Macdonald Smith (77)	Philadelphia Cricket Club, Chestnut Hill, Pa.
1911	*John McDermott (80)	307	Mike Brady (82) George Simpson (85)	Chicago GC, Wheaton, Ill.
1912	John McDermott	294	Tom McNamara	CC of Buffalo, Buffalo
1913	*Francis Ouimet (72)	304	Harry Vardon (77) Edward Ray (78)	The Country Club, Brookline, Mass.
1914	Walter Hagen	290	Charles Evans Jr.	Midlothian CC, Blue Island, Ill.
1915	Jerome Travers	297	Tom McNamara	Baltusrol GC, Short Hills, N.J.
1916	Charles Evans Jr.	286	Jock Hutchison	Minikahda Club, Minneapolis
1917-18	No championships played-World War I			
1919	*Walter Hagen (77)	301	Mike Brady (78)	Brae Burn CC, West Newton, Mass.
1920	Edward Ray	295	Harry Vardon Jack Burke Leo Diegel Jock Hutchison	Inverness CC, Toledo, Ohio
1921	James M. Barnes	289	Walter Hagen Fred McLeod	Columbia CC, Chevy Chase, Md.
1922	Gene Sarazen	288	John L. Black Robert T. Jones Jr.	Skokie CC, Glencoe, Ill.
1923	*R.T. Jones Jr. (76)	296	Bobby Cruickshank (78)	Inwood CC, Inwood, L.I., N.Y.
1924	Cyril Walker	297	Robert T. Jones Jr.	Oakland Hills CC, Birmingham, Mich.
1925	*W. MacFarlane (147)	291	R.T. Jones Jr. (148)	Worcester CC, Worcester, Mass.
1926	Robert T. Jones Jr.	293	Joe Turnesa	Scioto CC, Columbus, Ohio
1927	*Tommy Armour (76)	301	Harry Cooper (79)	Oakmont CC, Oakmont, Pa.
1928	*Johnny Farrell (143)	294	R.T. Jones Jr. (144)	Olympia Fields CC, Matteson, Ill.
1929	*R.T. Jones Jr. (141)	294	Al Espinosa (164)	Winged Foot GC, Mamaroneck, N.Y.
1930	Robert T. Jones Jr.	287	Macdonald Smith	Interlachen CC, Hopkins, Minn.
1931	*Billy Burke (149-148)	292	George Von Elm	Inverness Club, Toledo, Ohio
1932	Gene Sarazen	286	Phil Perkins Bobby Cruickshank	Fresh Meadows CC, Flushing, N.Y.
1933	Johnny Goodman	287	Ralph Guldahl	North Shore CC, Glenview, Ill.
1934	Olin Dutra	293	Gene Sarazen	Merion Cricket Club, Ardmore, Pa.
1935	Sam Parks Jr.	299	Jimmy Thompson	Oakmont CC, Oakmont, Pa.
1936	Tony Manero	282	Harry Cooper	Baltusrol GC, Springfield, N.J.
1937	Ralph Guldahl	281	Sam Snead	Oakland Hills CC, Birmingham, Mich.
1938	Ralph Guldahl	284	Dick Metz	Cherry Hills CC, Denver
1939	*Byron Nelson (68-70)	284	Craig Wood (68-73) Denny Shute (76)	Philadelphia CC, Philadelphia
1940	*Lawson Little (70)	287	Gene Sarazen (73)	Canterbury GC, Cleveland
1941	Craig Wood	284	Denny Shute	Colonial Club, Fort Worth
1942-45	No championships played-World War II			
1946	*Lloyd Mangrum (72-72)	284	Vic Ghezzi (72-73) Byron Nelson (72-73)	Canterbury GC, Cleveland
1947	*Lew Worsham (69)	282	Sam Snead (70)	St. Louis CC, Clayton, Mo.
1948	Ben Hogan	276	Jimmy Demaret	Riviera CC, Los Angeles
1949	Cary Middlecoff	286	Sam Snead Clayton Heafner	Medinah CC, Medinah, Ill.
1950	*Ben Hogan (69)	287	Lloyd Mangrum (73) George Fazio (75)	Merion Golf Club, Ardmore, Pa.
1951	Ben Hogan	287	Clayton Heafner	Oakland Hills CC, Birmingham, Mich.
1952	Julius Boros	281	Ed Oliver	Northwood CC, Dallas
1953	Ben Hogan	283	Sam Snead	Oakmont CC, Oakmont, Pa.
1954	Ed Furgol	284	Gene Littler	Baltusrol GC, Springfield, N.J.
1955	*Jack Fleck (69)	287	Ben Hogan (72)	Olympic Club, San Francisco
1956	Cary Middlecoff	281	Ben Hogan Julius Boros	Oak Hill CC, Rochester, N.Y.
1957	*Dick Mayer (72)	282	Cary Middlecoff (79)	Inverness Club, Toledo, Ohio
1958	Tommy Bolt	283	Gary Player	Southern Hills CC, Tulsa
1959	Billy Casper	282	Bob Rosburg	Winged Foot GC, Mamaroneck, N.Y.
1960	Arnold Palmer	280	Jack Nicklaus	Cherry Hills CC, Denver
1961	Gene Littler	281	Bob Goalby Doug Sanders	Oakland Hills CC, Birmingham, Mich.
1962	*Jack Nicklaus (71)	283	Arnold Palmer (74)	Oakmont CC, Oakmont, Pa.
1963	*Julius Boros (70)	293	Jacky Cupit (73) Arnold Palmer (76)	The Country Club, Brookline, Mass.
1964	Ken Venturi	278	Tommy Jacobs	Congressional CC, Washington
1965	*Gary Player (71)	282	Kel Nagle (74)	Bellerive CC, St. Louis
1966	*Billy Casper (69)	278	Arnold Palmer (73)	Olympic Club, San Francisco

1967	Jack Nicklaus	275	Arnold Palmer	Baltusrol GC, Springfield, N.J.
1968	Lee Trevino	275	Jack Nicklaus	Oak Hill CC, Rochester, N.Y.
1969	Orville Moody	281	Deane Beman Al Geiberger Bob Rosburg	Champions GC, Houston, Texas
1970	Tony Jacklin	281	Dave Hill	Hazeltine GC, Chaska, Minn.
1971	*Lee Trevino (68)	280	Jack Nicklaus (71)	Merion Golf Club, Ardmore, Pa.
1972	Jack Nicklaus	290	Bruce Crampton	Pebble Beach GL, Pebble Beach, Calif.
1973	Johnny Miller	279	John Schlee	Oakmont CC, Oakmont, Pa.
1974	Hale Irwin	287	Forrest Fezler	Winged Foot GC, Mamaroneck, N.Y.
1975	*Lou Graham (71)	287	John Mahaffey (73)	Medinah CC, Medinah, Ill.
1976	Jerry Pate	277	Tom Weiskopf Al Geiberger	Atlanta Athletic Club, Duluth, Ga.
1977	Hubert Green	278	Lou Graham	Southern Hills CC, Tulsa
1978	Andy North	285	Dave Stockton J.C. Snead	Cherry Hills CC, Denver
1979	Hale Irwin	284	Gary Player Jerry Pate	Inverness Club, Toledo, Ohio
1980	Jack Nicklaus	272	Isao Aoki	Baltusrol GC, Springfield, N.J.
1981	David Graham	273	George Burns Bill Rogers	Merion GC, Ardmore, Pa.
1982	Tom Watson	282	Jack Nicklaus	Pebble Beach GL, Pebble Beach, Calif.
1983	Larry Nelson	280	Tom Watson	Oakmont CC, Oakmont, Pa.
1984	*Fuzzy Zoeller (67)	276	Greg Norman (75)	Winged Foot GC, Mamaroneck, N.Y.
1985	Andy North	279	Dave Barr T.C. Chen Denis Watson	Oakland Hills CC, Birmingham, Mich.
1986	Ray Floyd	279	Lanny Wadkins Chip Beck	Shinnecock Hills GC, Southampton, N.Y.
1987	Scott Simpson	277	Tom Watson	Olympic Club Lake Course, San Francisco
1988	*Curtis Strange (71)	278	Nick Faldo (75)	The Country Club, Brookline, Mass.
1989	Curtis Strange	278	Chip Beck Mark McCumber Ian Woosnam	Oak Hill CC, Rochester, N.Y.
1990	Hale Irwin (74)+3	280	Mike Donald (74)+4	Medinah CC, Medinah, Ill.
1991	Payne Stewart (75)	282	Scott Simpson (77)	Hazeltine National GC, Chaska, Minn.
1992	Tom Kite	285	Jeff Sluman	Pebble Beach GL, Pebble Beach, Calif.
1993	Lee Janzen	272	Payne Stewart	Baltusrol GC, Springfield, N.J.
1994	*Ernie Els (74)+4,4	279	Loren Roberts (74)+4,5 Colin Montgomerie (78)	Oakmont CC, Oakmont, Pa.
1995	Corey Pavin	280	Greg Norman	Shinnecock Hills GC, Southampton, N.Y.

BRITISH OPEN

YEAR	WINNER	SCORE	RUNNER-UP	COURSE
1860	Willie Park	174	Tom Morris Sr.	Prestwick, Scotland
	(the first event was open only to professional golfers)			
1861	Tom Morris Sr.	163	Willie Park	Prestwick, Scotland
	(the second annual open was open to amateurs also)			
1862	Tom Morris Sr.	163	Willie Park	Prestwick, Scotland
1863	Willie Park	168	Tom Morris Sr.	Prestwick, Scotland
1864	Tom Morris Sr.	160	Andrew Strath	Prestwick, Scotland
1865	Andrew Strath	162	Willie Park	Prestwick, Scotland
1866	Willie Park	169	David Park	Prestwick, Scotland
1867	Tom Morris Sr.	170	Willie Park	Prestwick, Scotland
1868	Tom Morris Jr.	154	Tom Morris Sr.	Prestwick, Scotland
1869	Tom Morris Jr.	157	Tom Morris Sr.	Prestwick, Scotland
1870	Tom Morris Jr.	149	David Strath Bob Kirk	Prestwick, Scotland
1871	No championship played			
1872	Tom Morris Jr.	166	David Strath	Prestwick, Scotland
1873	Tom Kidd	179	Jamie Anderson	St. Andrews, Scotland
1874	Mungo Park	159	No record	Musselburgh, Scotland
1875	Willie Park	166	Bob Martin	Prestwick, Scotland
1876	Bob Martin	176	David Strath	St. Andrews, Scotland
1877	Jamie Anderson	160	R. Pringle	Musselburgh, Scotland
1878	Jamie Anderson	157	Robert Kirk	Prestwick, Scotland
1879	Jamie Anderson	169	A. Kirkaldy J. Allan	St. Andrews, Scotland
1880	Robert Ferguson	162	No record	Musselburgh, Scotland
1881	Robert Ferguson	170	Jamie Anderson	Prestwick, Scotland
1882	Robert Ferguson	171	Willie Fernie	St. Andrews, Scotland
1883	*Willie Fernie	159	Robert Ferguson	Musselburgh, Scotland
1884	Jack Simpson	160	D. Rolland Willie Fernie	Prestwick, Scotland
1885	Bob Martin	171	Archie Simpson	St. Andrews, Scotland
1886	David Brown	157	Willie Campbell	Musselburgh, Scotland
1887	Willie Park Jr.	161	Bob Martin	Prestwick, Scotland
1888	Jack Burns	171	B. Sayers D. Anderson	St. Andrews, Scotland
1889	*Willie Park Jr.	155 (158)	Andrew Kirkaldy (163)	Musselburgh, Scotland
1890	John Ball	164	Willie Fernie	Prestwick, Scotland
1891	Hugh Kirkaldy	166	Andrew Kirkaldy Willie Fernie	St. Andrews, Scotland
	(championship extended from 36 to 72 holes)			
1892	Harold H. Hilton	305	John Ball Hugh Kirkaidy	Muirfield, Scotland
1893	William Auchterlonie	322	John E. Laidlay	Prestwick, Scotland
1894	John H. Taylor	326	Douglas Rolland	Royal St. George's, England
1895	John H. Taylor	322	Alexander Herd	St. Andrews, Scotland
1896	*Harry Vardon	316 (157)	John H. Taylor (161)	Muirfield, Scotland
1897	Harold H. Hilton	314	James Braid	Hoylake, England
1898	Harry Vardon	307	Willie Park Jr.	Prestwick, Scotland
1899	Harry Vardon	310	Jack White	Royal St. George's, England
1900	John H. Taylor	309	Harry Vardon	St. Andrews, Scotland
1901	James Braid	309	Harry Vardon	Muirfield, Scotland
1902	Alexander Herd	307	Harry Vardon	Hoylake, England
1903	Harry Vardon	300	Tom Vardon	Prestwick, Scotland
1904	Jack White	296	John H. Taylor	Royal St. George's, England
1905	James Braid	318	John H. Taylor Rolland Jones	St. Andrews, Scotland
1906	James Braid	300	John H. Taylor	Muirfield, Scotland
1907	Arnaud Massy	312	John H. Taylor	Hoylake, England
1908	James Braid	291	Tom Ball	Prestwick,Scotland
1909	John H. Taylor	295	James Braid Tom Ball	Deal, England
1910	James Braid	299	Alexander Herd	St. Andrews, Scotland
1911	Harry Vardon	303	Arnaud Massy	Royal St. George's, England
1912	Edward (Ted) Ray	295	Harry Vardon	Muirfield, Scotland
1913	John H. Taylor	304	Edward Ray	Hoylake, England
1914	Harry Vardon	306	John H. Taylor	Prestwick, Scotland
1915-1919	No championships played			
1920	George Duncan	303	Alexander Herd	Deal, England
1921	*Jock Hutchison	296 (150)	Roger Wethered (159)	St. Andrews, Scotland
1922	Walter Hagen	300	George Duncan James M. Barnes	Royal St. George's, England
1923	Arthur G. Havers	295	Walter Hagen	Troon, Scotland
1924	Walter Hagen	301	Ernest Whitcombe	Hoylake, England
1925	James M. Barnes	300	Archie Compston Edward Ray	Prestwick, Scotland
1926	Robert T. Jones Jr.	291	Al Watrous	Royal Lytham, England
1927	Robert T. Jones Jr.	285	Aubrey Boomer	St. Andrews, Scotland
1928	Walter Hagen	292	Gene Sarazen	Royal St. George's, England
1929	Walter Hagen	292	Johnny Farrell	Muirfield, Scotland
1930	Robert T. Jones Jr.	291	Macdonald Smith Leo Diegel	Hoylake, England
1931	Tommy D. Armour	296	J. Jurado	Carnoustie, Scotland
1932	Gene Sarazen	283	Macdonald Smith	Prince's, England
1933	*Denny Shute (149)	292	Craig Wood (154)	St. Andrews, Scotland
1934	Henry Cotton	283	S.F. Brews	Royal St. George's, England
1935	Alfred Perry	283	Alfred Padgham	Muirfield, Scotland
1936	Alfred Padgham	287	J. Adams	Hoylake, England
1937	Henry Cotton	290	R.A. Whitcombe	Carnoustie, Scotland
1938	R.A. Whitcombe	295	James Adams	Royal St. George's, England
1939	Richard Burton	290	Johnny Bulla	St. Andrews, Scotland
1940-1945	No championships played			
1946	Sam Snead	290	Bobby Locke Johnny Bulla	St. Andrews, Scotland
1947	Fred Daly	293	R.W. Horne Frank Stranahan	Hoylake, England
1948	Henry Cotton	294	Fred Daly	Muirfield, Scotland
1949	*Bobby Locke	283 (135)	Harry Bradshaw (147)	Royal St. George's, England
1950	Bobby Locke	279	Roberto DeVicenzo	Troon, Scotland
1951	Max Faulkner	285	A. Cerda	Portrush, Ireland
1952	Bobby Locke	287	Peter Thomson	Royal Lytham, England
1953	Ben Hogan	282	Frank Stranahan D.J. Rees Peter Thomson A. Cerda	Carnoustie, Scotland
1954	Peter Thomson	283	S.S. Scott Dai Rees Bobby Locke	Royal Birkdale, England
1955	Peter Thomson	281	John Fallon	St. Andrews, Scotland
1956	Peter Thomson	286	Flory Van Donck	Hoylake, England
1957	Bobby Locke	279	Peter Thomson	St Andrews, Scotland
1958	*Peter Thomson	278 (139)	Dave Thomas (143)	Royal Lytham, England
1959	Gary Player	284	Fred Bullock Flory Van Donck	Muirfield, Scotland
1960	Kel Nagle	278	Arnold Palmer	St. Andrews, Scotland
1961	Arnold Palmer	284	Dai Rees	Royal Birkdale, England
1962	Arnold Palmer	276	Kel Nagle	Troon, Scotland
1963	*Bob Charles	277 (140)	Phil Rodgers (148)	Royal Lytham, England
1964	Tony Lema	279	Jack Nicklaus	St. Andrews, Scotland

1965	Peter Thomson	285	Brian Huggett Christy O'Connor	Southport, England
1966	Jack Nicklaus	282	Doug Sanders Dave Thomas	Muirfield, Scotland
1967	Roberto DeVicenzo	278	Jack Nicklaus	Hoylake, England
1968	Gary Player	289	Jack Nicklaus Bob Charles	Carnoustie, Scotland
1969	Tony Jacklin	280	Bob Charles	Royal Lytham, England
1970	*Jack Nicklaus	283 (72)	Doug Sanders (73)	St. Andrews, Scotland
1971	Lee Trevino	278	Lu Liang Huan	Royal Birkdale, England
1972	Lee Trevino	278	Jack Nicklaus	Muirfield, Scotland
1973	Tom Weiskopf	276	Johnny Miller	Troon, Scotland
1974	Gary Player	282	Peter Oosterhuis	Royal Lytham, England
1975	*Tom Watson	279 (71)	Jack Newton (72)	Carnoustie, Scotland
1976	Johnny Miller	279	Jack Nicklaus S. Ballesteros	Royal Birkdale, England
1977	Tom Watson	268	Jack Nicklaus	Turnberry, Scotland
1978	Jack Nicklaus	281	Ben Crenshaw Tom Kite Ray Floyd Simon Owen	St. Andrews, Scotland
1979	Seve Ballesteros	283	Ben Crenshaw Jack Nicklaus	Royal Lytham, England
1980	Tom Watson	271	Lee Trevino	Muirfield, Scotland
1981	Bill Rogers	276	Bernhard Langer	Royal St. George's, England
1982	Tom Watson	284	Nick Price Peter Oosterhuis	Royal Troon, Scotland
1983	Tom Watson	275	Andy Bean	Royal Birkdale, England
1984	Seve Ballesteros	276	Tom Watson Bernhard Langer	St. Andrews, Scotland
1985	Sandy Lyle	282	Payne Stewart	Royal St. George's, England
1986	Greg Norman	280	Gordon Brand	Turnberry GL, Scotland
1987	Nick Faldo	279	Paul Azinger Rodger Davis	Muirfield, Gullane, Scotland
1988	Seve Ballesteros	273	Nick Price	Royal Lytham and St. Anne's, St. Anne's-on-the-Sea, England
1989	*Mark Calcavecchia	275	Wayne Grady Greg Norman	Royal Troon GC, Troon, Scotland
1990	Nick Faldo	270	Payne Stewart Mark McNulty	St. Andrews, Scotland
1991	Ian Baker-Finch	272	Mike Harwood	Royal Birkdale, England
1992	Nick Faldo	272	John Cook	Muirfield, Gullane, Scotland
1993	Greg Norman	267	Nick Faldo	Royal St. George's GC, Sandwich, England
1994	Nick Price	268	Jesper Parnevik	Turnberry GC, Scotland
1995	John Daly	282	Constantino Rocca	St. Andrews, Scotland

PGA CHAMPIONSHIP

YEAR	WINNER	SCORE	RUNNER-UP	COURSE
1916	James M. Barnes	1 up	Jock Hutchison	Siwanoy CC, Bronxville, N.Y.
1917-18	No championships played-World War I			
1919	James M. Barnes	6 & 5	Fred McLeod	Engineers CC, Roslyn, L.I., N.Y.
1920	Jock Hutchison	1 up	J. Douglas Edgar	Flossmoor CC, Flossmoor, Ill.
1921	Walter Hagen	3 & 2	James M. Barnes	Inwood CC, Far Rockaway, N.Y.
1922	Gene Sarazen	4 & 3	Emmet French	Oakmont CC, Oakmont, Pa.
1923	Gene Sarazen	1 up (38)	Walter Hagen	Pelham CC, Pelham, N.Y.
1924	Walter Hagen	2 up	James M. Barnes	French Lick CC, French Lick, Ind.
1925	Walter Hagen	6 & 5	William Mehlhorn	Olympia Fields, Olympia Fields, Ill.
1926	Walter Hagen	5 & 3	Leo Diegel	Salisbury GC, Westbury, L.I., N.Y.
1927	Walter Hagen	1 up	Joe Turnesa	Cedar Crest CC, Dallas
1928	Leo Diegel	6 & 5	Al Espinosa	Five Farms CC, Baltimore
1929	Leo Diegel	6 & 4	Johnny Farrell	Hillcrest CC, Los Angeles
1930	Tommy Armour	1 up	Gene Sarazen	Fresh Meadow CC, Flushing, N.Y.
1931	Tom Creavy	2 & 1	Denny Shute	Wannamoisett CC, Rumford, R.I.
1932	Olin Dutra	4 & 3	Frank Walsh	Keller GC, St. Paul, Minn.
1933	Gene Sarazen	5 & 4	Willie Goggin	Blue Mound CC, Milwaukee
1934	Paul Runyan	1 up (38)	Craig Wood	Park CC, Williamsville, N.Y.
1935	Johnny Revolta	5 & 4	Tommy Armour	Twin Hills CC, Oklahoma City
1936	Denny Shute	3 & 2	Jimmy Thomson	Pinehurst CC, Pinehurst, N.C.
1937	Denny Shute	1 up (37)	Harold McSpaden	Pittsburgh Field Club, Aspinwall, Pa.
1938	Paul Runyan	8 & 7	Sam Snead	Shawnee CC, Shawnee-on-Delaware
1939	Henry Picard	1 up (37)	Byron Nelson	Pomonok CC, Flushing, N.Y.
1940	Byron Nelson	1 up	Sam Snead	Hershey CC, Hershey, Pa.
1941	Vic Ghezzi	1 up (38)	Byron Nelson	Cherry Hills CC, Denver
1942	Sam Snead	2 & 1	Jim Turnesa	Seaview CC, Atlantic City
1943	No championship played-World War II			
1944	Bob Hamilton	1 up	Byron Nelson	Manito G & CC, Spokane, Wash.
1945	Byron Nelson	4 & 3	Sam Byrd	Morraine CC, Dayton, Ohio
1946	Ben Hogan	6 & 4	Ed Oliver	Portland GC, Portland, Ore.
1947	Jim Ferrier	2 & 1	Chick Harbert	Plum Hollow CC, Detroit
1948	Ben Hogan	7 & 6	Mike Turnesa	Norwood Hills CC, St. Louis
1949	Sam Snead	3 & 2	Johnny Palmer	Hermitage CC, Richmond, Va.
1950	Chandler Harper	4 & 3	Henry Williams Jr.	Scioto CC, Columbus, Ohio
1951	Sam Snead	7 & 6	Walter Burkemo	Oakmont CC, Oakmont, Pa.
1952	Jim Turnesa	1 up	Chick Harbert	Big Spring CC, Louisville
1953	Walter Burkemo	2 & 1	Felice Torza	Birmingham CC, Birmingham, Mich.
1954	Chick Harbert	4 & 3	Walter Burkemo	Keller GC, St. Paul, Minn.
1955	Doug Ford	4 & 3	Cary Middlecoff	Meadowbrook CC, Detroit
1956	Jack Burke	3 & 2	Ted Kroll	Blue Hill CC, Boston
1957	Lionel Hebert	2 & 1	Dow Finsterwald	Miami Valley CC, Dayton, Ohio
1958	Dow Finsterwald	276	Billy Casper	Llanerch CC, Havertown, Pa.
1959	Bob Rosburg	277	Jerry Barber Doug Sanders	Minneapolis GC, St. Louis Park, Minn.
1960	Jay Hebert	281	Jim Ferrier	Firestone CC, Akron, Ohio
1961	*Jerry Barber (67)	277	Don January (68)	Olympia Fields CC, Olympia Fields, Ill.
1962	Gary Player	278	Bob Goalby	Aronomink GC, Newtown Square, Pa.
1963	Jack Nicklaus	279	Dave Ragan Jr.	Dallas Athletic Club, Dallas
1964	Bobby Nichols	271	Jack Nicklaus Arnold Palmer	Columbus CC, Columbus, Ohio
1965	Dave Marr	280	Billy Casper Jack Nicklaus	Laurel Valley CC, Ligonier, Pa.
1966	Al Geiberger	280	Dudley Wysong	Firestone CC, Akron, Ohio
1967	*Don January (69)	281	Don Massengale (71)	Columbine CC, Littleton, Colo.
1968	Julius Boros	281	Bob Charles Arnold Palmer	Pecan Valley CC, San Antonio
1969	Ray Floyd	276	Gary Player	NCR CC, Dayton, Ohio
1970	Dave Stockton	279	Arnold Palmer Bob Murphy	Southern Hills CC, Tulsa
1971	Jack Nicklaus	281	Billy Casper	PGA National GC, Palm Beach Gardens, Fla.
1972	Gary Player	281	Tommy Aaron Jim Jamieson	Oakland Hills CC, Birmingham, Mich.
1973	Jack Nicklaus	277	Bruce Crampton	Canterbury GC, Cleveland
1974	Lee Trevino	276	Jack Nicklaus	Tanglewood GC, Winston-Salem, N.C.
1975	Jack Nicklaus	276	Bruce Crampton	Firestone CC, Akron, Ohio
1976	Dave Stockton	281	Ray Floyd Don January	Congressional CC, Bethesda, Md.
1977	*Lanny Wadkins	282	Gene Littler	Pebble Beach GL, Pebble Beach, Calif.
1978	*John Mahaffey	276	Jerry Pate Tom Watson	Oakmont CC, Oakmont, Pa.
1979	*David Graham	272	Ben Crenshaw	Oakland Hills CC, Birmingham, Mich.
1980	Jack Nicklaus	274	Andy Bean	Oak Hill CC, Rochester, N.Y.
1981	Larry Nelson	273	Fuzzy Zoeller	Atlanta Athletic Club, Duluth, Ga.
1982	Raymond Floyd	272	Lanny Wadkins	Southern Hills CC, Tulsa
1983	Hal Sutton	274	Jack Nicklaus	Riviera CC, Pacific Palisades, Calif.
1984	Lee Trevino	273	Gary Player Lanny Wadkins	Shoal Creek, Birmingham, Ala.
1985	Hubert Green	278	Lee Trevino	Cherry Hills CC, Denver
1986	Bob Tway	276	Greg Norman	Inverness CC, Toledo, Ohio
1987	*Larry Nelson	287	Lanny Wadkins	PGA National, Palm Beach Gardens, Fla.
1988	Jeff Sluman	272	Paul Azinger	Oak Tree GC, Edmond, Okla.
1989	Payne Stewart	276	Mike Reid	Kemper Lakes GC, Hawthorn Woods, Ill.
1990	Wayne Grady	282	Fred Couples	Shoal Creek, Birmingham, Ala.
1991	John Daly	276	Bruce Lietzke	Crooked Stick GC, Carmel, Ind.
1992	Nick Price	278	John Cook Jim Gallagher Gene Sauers Nick Faldo	Bellerive CC, St. Louis
1993	*Paul Azinger	272	Greg Norman	Inverness Club, Toledo, Ohio
1994	Nick Price	269	Corey Pavin	Southern Hills CC, Tulsa
1995	*Steve Elkington	267	Colin Montgomerie	Riviera CC, Pacific Palisades, Ca.

*Winners in playoffs. Figures in parentheses indicate scores.

MERCEDES CHAMPIONSHIPS

Desert Inn CC, Las Vegas (1953-66). Stardust CC, Las Vegas (1967-68). LaCosta CC, Carlsbad, Calif. (1969-95).

TOURNAMENT OF CHAMPIONS

1953 Al Besselink 280
1954 Art Wall 278
1955 Gene Littler 280
1956 Gene Littler 281
1957 Gene Littler 285
1958 Stan Leonard 275
1959 Mike Souchak 281
1960 Jerry Barber 268
1961 Sam Snead 273
1962 Arnold Palmer 276
1963 Jack Nicklaus 273
1964 Jack Nicklaus 279
1965 Arnold Palmer 277
1966 *Arnold Palmer 283
1967 Frank Beard 278
1968 Don January 276
1969 Gary Player 284
1970 Frank Beard 273
1971 Jack Nicklaus 279
1972 *Bobby Mitchell 280
1973 Jack Nicklaus 276
1974 Johnny Miller 280

MONY TOURNAMENT OF CHAMPIONS

1975 *Al Geiberger 277
1976 Don January 277
1977 *Jack Nicklaus 281
1978 Gary Player 281
1979 Tom Watson 275
1980 Tom Watson 276
1981 Lee Trevino 273
1982 Lanny Wadkins 280
1983 Lanny Wadkins 280
1984 Tom Watson 274
1985 Tom Kite 275
1986 Calvin Peete 267
1987 Mac O'Grady 278
1988 @Steve Pate 202
1989 Steve Jones 279

INFINITI TOURNAMENT OF CHAMPIONS

1990 Paul Azinger 272
1991 Tom Kite 272
1992 *Steve Elkington 279
1993 Davis Love III 272

MERCEDES CHAMPIONSHIPS

1994 *Phil Mickelson 276
1995 *Steve Elkington 278

UNITED AIRLINES HAWAIIAN OPEN

Waialae CC, Honolulu.

HAWAIIAN OPEN

1965 *Gay Brewer 281
1966 Ted Makalena 271
1967 *Dudley Wysong 284
1968 Lee Trevino 272
1969 Bruce Crampton 274
1970 No tournament
1971 Tom Shaw 273
1972 *Grier Jones 274
1973 John Schlee 273
1974 Jack Nicklaus 271
1975 Gary Groh 274
1976 Ben Crenshaw 270
1977 Bruce Lietzke 273
1978 *Hubert Green 274
1979 Hubert Green 267
1980 Andy Bean 266
1981 Hale Irwin 265
1982 Wayne Levi 277
1983 Isao Aoki 268
1984 *Jack Renner 271
1985 Mark O'Meara 267
1986 Corey Pavin 272
1987 *Corey Pavin 270
1988 Lanny Wadkins 271
1989 @Gene Sauers 197
1990 David Ishii 279

UNITED HAWAIIAN OPEN

1991 Lanny Wadkins 270

UNITED AIRLINES HAWAIIAN OPEN

1992 John Cook 265
1993 Howard Twitty 269
1994 Brett Ogle 269
1995 John Morse 269

NORTEL OPEN

El Rio G&CC, Tucson, Ariz. (1945-62). 49er CC, Tucson, Ariz. (1963-64). Tucson National GC, Tucson, Ariz. (1965-78, 1980, 1995). Randolph Park Municipal GC, Tucson, Ariz. (1979, 1981-86). TPC at StarPass, Tucson, Ariz. (1987-1993, 1995). Tucson (Ariz.) National Golf Resort (1994).

TUCSON OPEN

1945 Ray Mangrum 268
1946 Jimmy Demaret 268
1947 Jimmy Demaret 264
1948 Skip Alexander 264
1949 Lloyd Mangrum 263
1950 Chandler Harper 267
1951 Lloyd Mangrum 269
1952 Henry Williams 274
1953 Tommy Bolt 265
1954 No tournament
1955 Tommy Bolt 265
1956 Ted Kroll 264
1957 Dow Finsterwald 269
1958 Lionel Hebert 265
1959 Gene Littler 266
1960 Don January 271

HOME OF THE SUN INVITATIONAL

1961 *Dave Hill 269

TUCSON OPEN

1962 Phil Rodgers 263
1963 Don January 266
1964 Jack Cupit 274
1965 Bob Charles 271
1966 *Joe Campbell 278
1967 Arnold Palmer 273
1968 George Knudson 273
1969 Lee Trevino 271
1970 *Lee Trevino 275
1971 J.C. Snead 273
1972 Miller Barber 273

DEAN MARTIN TUCSON OPEN

1973 Bruce Crampton 277
1974 Johnny Miller 272
1975 Johnny Miller 263

NBC TUCSON OPEN

1976 Johnny Miller 274

JOE GARAGIOLA TUCSON OPEN

1977 *Bruce Lietzke 275
1978 Tom Watson 276
1979 Bruce Lietzke 265
1980 Jim Colbert 270
1981 Johnny Miller 265
1982 Craig Stadler 266
1983 *Gil Morgan 271

SEIKO-TUCSON MATCH PLAY CHAMPIONSHIPS

1984 Tom Watson 2 & 1
1985 Jim Thorpe 4 & 3
1986 Jim Thorpe 6 & 7

SEIKO-TUCSON OPEN

1987 Mike Reid 268

NORTHERN TELECOM TUCSON OPEN

1988 David Frost 266
1989 No tournament
1990 Robert Gamez 270

NORTHERN TELECOM OPEN

1991 #Phil Mickelson 272
1992 Lee Janzen 270
1993 Larry Mize 271
1994 Andrew Magee 270
1995 Phil Mickelson 269

PHOENIX OPEN

Phoenix CC, Phoenix (1935-86), alternating with Arizona CC, Phoenix (1955-73). TPC of Scottsdale, Scottsdale, Ariz. (1987-95).

1935 Ky Laffoon 281
1936-1938 No tournaments
1939 Byron Nelson 198
1940 Ed Oliver 205
1941-1943 No tournaments
1944 *Harold McSpaden 273
1945 Byron Nelson 274
1946 *Ben Hogan 273
1947 Ben Hogan 270
1948 Bobby Locke 268
1949 *Jimmy Demaret 278
1950 Jimmy Demaret 269
1951 Lew Worsham 272
1952 Lloyd Mangrum 274
1953 Lloyd Mangrum 272
1954 *Ed Furgol 272
1955 Gene Littler 275
1956 Cary Middlecoff 276
1957 Billy Casper 271
1958 Ken Venturi 274
1959 Gene Littler 268
1960 *Jack Fleck 273
1961 *Arnold Palmer 270
1962 Arnold Palmer 269
1963 Arnold Palmer 273
1964 Jack Nicklaus 271
1965 Rod Funseth 274
1966 Dudley Wysong 278
1967 Julius Boros 272
1968 George Knudson 272
1969 Gene Littler 263
1970 Dale Douglass 271
1971 Miller Barber 261
1972 Homero Blancas 273
1973 Bruce Crampton 268
1974 Johnny Miller 271
1975 Johnny Miller 260
1976 Bob Gilder 268
1977 *Jerry Pate 277
1978 Miller Barber 272
1979 @Ben Crenshaw 199
1980 Jeff Mitchell 272
1981 David Graham 268
1982 Lanny Wadkins 263
1983 *Bob Gilder 271
1984 Tom Purtzer 268
1985 Calvin Peete 270
1986 Hal Sutton 267
1987 Paul Azinger 268
1988 *Sandy Lyle 269
1989 Mark Calcavecchia 263
1990 Tommy Armour III 267
1991 Nolan Henke 268
1992 Mark Calcavecchia 264
1993 Lee Janzen 273
1994 Bill Glasson 268
1995 *Vijay Singh 269

AT&T PEBBLE BEACH NATIONAL PRO-AM

Held simultaneously at Rancho Santa Fe CC, San Diego (1937-42); Cypress Point CC, Monterey Peninsula, Calif. (1947-90); Monterey Peninsula CC, Monterey Peninsula, Calif. (1947-67); Pebble Beach GC, Monterey Peninsula, Calif. (1947-95); Spyglass Hill GC, Monterey Peninsula, Calif. (1968-95); Poppy Hills GC, Monterey Peninsula, Calif. (1991-95).

BING CROSBY PROFESSIONAL-AMATEUR

1937 Sam Snead 68
1938 Sam Snead 139
1939 Dutch Harrison 138
1940 Ed Oliver 135
1941 Sam Snead 136
1942 Tie-Lloyd Mangrum
Leland Gibson 133
1943-1946 No Tournaments
1947 Tie-Ed Furgol
George Fazio 213
1948 Lloyd Mangrum 205
1949 Ben Hogan 208
1950 Tie-Sam Snead
Jack Burke Jr.
Smiley Quick
Dave Douglas 214
1951 Byron Nelson 209
1952 Jimmy Demaret 145

THE BING CROSBY PROFESSIONAL-AMATEUR INVITATIONAL

1953 Lloyd Mangrum 204
1954 Dutch Harrison 210
1955 Cary Middlecoff 209

BING CROSBY NATIONAL PROFESSIONAL-AMATEUR GOLF CHAMPIONSHIP

1956 Cary Middlecoff 202
1957 Jay Heber 213
1958 Billy Casper 277

BING CROSBY NATIONAL

1959 Art Wall 279
1960 Ken Venturi 286
1961 Bob Rosburg 282
1962 *Doug Ford 286
1963 Billy Casper 285

BING CROSBY NATIONAL PROFESSIONAL-AMATEUR

1964 Tony Lema 284
1965 Bruce Crampton 284
1966 Don Massengale 283
1967 Jack Nicklaus 284
1968 *Johnny Pott 285
1969 George Archer 283
1970 Bert Yancey 278
1971 Tom Shaw 278
1972 *Jack Nicklaus 284
1973 *Jack Nicklaus 282
1974 @Johnny Miller 208
1975 Gene Littler 280
1976 Ben Crenshaw 281
1977 Tom Watson 273
1978 *Tom Watson 280
1979 Lon Hinkle 284
1980 George Burns 280
1981 @*John Cook 209
1982 Jim Simons 274
1983 Tom Kite 276
1984 *Hale Irwin 278
1985 Mark O'Meara 283

AT&T PEBBLE BEACH NATIONAL PRO-AM

1986 @Fuzzy Zoeller 205
1987 Johnny Miller 278
1988 *Steve Jones 280
1989 Mark O'Meara 277
1990 Mark O'Meara 281
1991 Paul Azinger 274
1992 *Mark O'Meara 275
1993 Brett Ogle 276
1994 Johnny Miller 281
1995 Peter Jacobsen 271

BOB HOPE CHRYSLER CLASSIC

Rotates among Bermuda Dunes CC, Palm Springs, Calif.; Tamarisk CC, Palm Springs, Calif.; Thunderbird CC, Palm Springs Calif.; La Quinta CC, La Quinta, Calif.; Indian Wells CC, Indian Wells, Calif.; Eldorado CC, Palm Springs, Calif.; and PGA West/Palmer Course, La Quinta, Calif. (1960-95).

PALM SPRINGS GOLF CLASSIC

1960 Arnold Palmer 338
1961 Billy Maxwell 345
1962 Arnold Palmer 342
1963 *Jack Nicklaus 345
1964 *Tommy Jacobs 348

BOB HOPE DESERT CLASSIC

1965 Billy Casper 348
1966 *Doug Sanders 349
1967 Tom Nieporte 349
1968 *Arnold Palmer 348
1969 Billy Casper 345
1970 Bruce Devlin 339
1971 *Arnold Palmer 342

1972	Bob Rosburg	344
1973	Arnold Palmer	343
1974	Hubert Green	341
1975	Johnny Miller	339
1976	Johnny Miller	344
1977	Rik Massengale	337
1978	Bill Rogers	339
1979	John Mahaffey	343
1980	Craig Stadler	343
1981	Bruce Lietzke	335
1982	*Ed Fiori	335
1983	*Keith Fergus	335

BOB HOPE CLASSIC

1984	*John Mahaffey	340
1985	*Lanny Wadkins	333

BOB HOPE CHRYSLER CLASSIC

1986	*Donnie Hammond	335
1987	Corey Pavin	341
1988	Jay Haas	338
1989	*Steve Jones	343
1990	Peter Jacobsen	339
1991	*Corey Pavin	331
1992	*John Cook	336
1993	Tom Kite	325
1994	Scott Hoch	334
1995	Kenny Perry	335

BUICK INVITATIONAL OF CALIFORNIA

MOVED ANNUALLY (1952-61). STARDUST CC, SAN DIEGO (1962-67). TORREY PINES GC, LA JOLLA, CALIF. (1968-95).

SAN DIEGO OPEN

1952	Ted Kroll	276
1953	Tommy Bolt	274
1954	#Gene Littler	274

CONVAIR-SAN DIEGO OPEN

1955	Tommy Bolt	274
1956	Bob Rosburg	270

SAN DIEGO OPEN INVITATIONAL

1957	Arnold Palmer	271
1958	No tournament	
1959	Marty Furgol	274
1960	Mike Souchak	269
1961	*Arnold Palmer	271
1962	*Tommy Jacobs	277
1963	Gary Player	270
1964	Art Wall	274
1965	*Wes Ellis	267
1966	Billy Casper	268
1967	Bob Goalby	269

ANDY WILLIAMS–SAN DIEGO OPEN INVITATIONAL

1968	Tom Weiskopf	273
1969	Jack Nicklaus	284
1970	*Pete Brown	275
1971	George Archer	272
1972	Paul Harney	275
1973	Bob Dickson	278
1974	Bobby Nichols	275
1975	*J.C. Snead	279
1976	J.C. Snead	272
1977	Tom Watson	269
1978	Jay Haas	278
1979	Fuzzy Zoeller	282
1980	*Tom Watson	275

WICKES/ANDY WILLIAMS SAN DIEGO OPEN

1981	*Bruce Lietzke	278
1982	Johnny Miller	270

ISUZU/ANDY WILLIAMS SAN DIEGO OPEN

1983	Gary Hallberg	271
1984	*Gary Koch	272
1985	*Woody Blackburn	269

SHEARSON LEHMAN BROTHERS ANDY WILLIAMS OPEN

1986	@*Bob Tway	204
1987	George Burns	266

SHEARSON LEHMAN HUTTON ANDY WILLIAMS OPEN

1988	Steve Pate	269

SHEARSON LEHMAN HUTTON OPEN

1989	Greg Twiggs	271
1990	Dan Forsman	275

SHEARSON LEHMAN BROTHERS OPEN

1991	Jay Don Blake	268

BUICK INVITATIONAL OF CALIFORNIA

1992	@Steve Pate	200
1993	Phil Mickelson	278
1994	Craig Stadler	268
1995	Peter Jacobsen	269

NISSAN OPEN

MOVED ANNUALLY (1926-44, 1954-55, 1968). RIVIERA CC, PACIFIC PALISADES, CALIF. (1945-53, 1973-95). RANCHO MUNICIPAL GC, LOS ANGELES (1956-67, 1969-72).

LOS ANGELES OPEN

1926	Harry Cooper	279
1927	Bobby Cruikshank	282
1928	Mac Smith	284
1929	Mac Smith	285
1930	Densmore Shute	296
1931	Ed Dudley	285
1932	Mac Smith	281
1933	Craig Wood	281
1934	Mac Smith	280
1935	*Vic Ghezzi	285
1936	Jimmy Hines	280
1937	Harry Cooper	274
1938	Jimmy Thomson	273
1939	Jimmy Demaret	274
1940	Lawson Little	282
1941	Johnny Bulla	281
1942	*Ben Hogan	282
1943	No tournament	
1944	Harold McSpaden	278
1945	Sam Snead	283
1946	Byron Nelson	284
1947	Ben Hogan	280
1948	Ben Hogan	275
1949	Lloyd Mangrum	284
1950	*Sam Snead	280
1951	Lloyd Mangrum	280
1952	Tommy Bolt	289
1953	Lloyd Mangrum	280
1954	Fred Wampler	281
1955	Gene Littler	276
1956	Lloyd Mangrum	272
1957	Doug Ford	280
1958	Frank Stranahan	275
1959	Ken Venturi	278
1960	Dow Finsterwald	280
1961	Bob Goalby	275
1962	Phil Rodgers	268
1963	Arnold Palmer	274
1964	Paul Harney	280
1965	Paul Harney	276
1966	Arnold Palmer	273
1967	Arnold Palmer	269
1968	Billy Casper	274
1969	*Charles Sifford	276
1970	*Billy Casper	276

GLEN CAMPBELL LOS ANGELES OPEN

1971	*Bob Lunn	274
1972	*George Archer	270
1973	Rod Funseth	276
1974	Dave Stockton	276
1975	Pat Fitzsimons	275
1976	Hale Irwin	272
1977	Tom Purtzer	273
1978	Gil Morgan	278
1979	Lanny Wadkins	276
1980	Tom Watson	276
1981	Johnny Miller	270
1982	*Tom Watson	271
1983	Gil Morgan	270

LOS ANGELES OPEN

1984	David Edwards	279
1985	Lanny Wadkins	264
1986	Doug Tewell	270

LOS ANGELES OPEN PRESENTED BY NISSAN

1987	*Tze-Chung Chen	275
1988	Chip Beck	267

NISSAN LOS ANGELES OPEN

1989	Mark Calcavecchia	272
1990	Fred Couples	266
1991	Ted Schulz	272
1992	*Fred Couples	269
1993	@Tom Kite	206
1994	Corey Pavin	271

NISSAN OPEN

1995	Corey Pavin	268

DORAL-RYDER OPEN

DORAL CC (BLUE), MIAMI.

DORAL CC OPEN INVITATIONAL

1962	Billy Casper	283
1963	Dan Sikes	283
1964	Billy Casper	277
1965	Doug Sanders	274
1966	Phil Rodgers	278
1967	Doug Sanders	275
1968	Gardner Dickinson	275
1969	Tom Shaw	276

DORAL-EASTERN OPEN INVITATIONAL

1970	Mike Hill	279
1971	J.C. Snead	275
1972	Jack Nicklaus	276
1973	Lee Trevino	276
1974	Brian Allin	272
1975	Jack Nicklaus	276
1976	Hubert Green	270
1977	Andy Bean	277
1978	Tom Weiskopf	272
1979	Mark McCumber	279
1980	*Ray Floyd	279
1981	Ray Floyd	273
1982	Andy Bean	278
1983	Gary Koch	271
1984	Tom Kite	272
1985	Mark McCumber	284
1986	*Andy Bean	276

DORAL-RYDER OPEN

1987	Lanny Wadkins	277
1988	Ben Crenshaw	274
1989	Bill Glasson	275
1990	*Greg Norman	273
1991	*Rocco Mediate	276
1992	Ray Floyd	271
1993	Greg Norman	265
1994	John Huston	274
1995	Nick Faldo	273

HONDA CLASSIC

INVERRARY G&CC (EAST), LAUDER-HILL, FLA. (1972-83). TPC AT EAGLE TRACE, CORAL SPRINGS, FLA. (1984-91). WESTON HILLS G&CC, FORT LAUDERDALE, FLA. (1992-95).

JACKIE GLEASON'S INVERRARY CLASSIC

1972	Tom Weiskopf	278

JACKIE GLEASON'S INVERRARY NATIONAL AIRLINES CLASSIC

1973	Lee Trevino	279

JACKIE GLEASON'S INVERRARY CLASSIC

1974	Leonard Thompson	278
1975	Bob Murphy	273
1976	Hosted Tournament Players Championship	
1977	Jack Nicklaus	275
1978	Jack Nicklaus	276
1979	Larry Nelson	274
1980	Johnny Miller	274

AMERICAN MOTORS INVERRARY CLASSIC

1981	Tom Kite	274

HONDA INVERRARY CLASSIC

1982	Hale Irwin	269
1983	Johnny Miller	278

HONDA CLASSIC

1984	*Bruce Lietzke	280
1985	*Curtis Strange	275
1986	Kenny Knox	287
1987	Mark Calcavecchia	279
1988	Joey Sindelar	276
1989	Blaine McCallister	266
1990	John Huston	282
1991	Steve Pate	279
1992	*Corey Pavin	273
1993	*@Fred Couples	207
1994	Nick Price	276
1995	Mark O'Meara	275

BAY HILL INVITATIONAL

RIO PINAR CC, ORLANDO, FLA. (1966-78). BAY HILL CLUB, ORLANDO, FLA. (1979-95).

FLORIDA CITRUS OPEN INVITATIONAL

1966	Lionel Hebert	279
1967	Julius Boros	274
1968	Dan Sikes	274
1969	Ken Still	278
1970	Bob Lunn	271
1971	Arnold Palmer	270
1972	Jerry Heard	276
1973	Brian Allin	265
1974	Jerry Heard	273
1975	Lee Trevino	276
1976	*Hale Irwin	270
1977	Gary Koch	274
1978	Mac McLendon	271

BAY HILL CITRUS CLASSIC

1979	*Bob Byman	278

BAY HILL CLASSIC

1980	Dave Eichelberger	279
1981	Andy Bean	266
1982	*Tom Kite	278
1983	*Mike Nicolette	283
1984	*Gary Koch	272

HERTZ BAY HILL CLASSIC

1985	Fuzzy Zoeller	275
1986	@Dan Forsman	202
1987	Payne Stewart	264
1988	Paul Azinger	271

THE NESTLÉ INVITATIONAL

1989	*Tom Kite	278
1990	Robert Gamez	274
1991	@Andrew Magee	203
1992	Fred Couples	269
1993	Ben Crenshaw	280
1994	Loren Roberts	275
1995	Loren Roberts	272

THE PLAYERS CHAMPIONSHIP

MOVED ANNUALLY (1974-76). SAWGRASS, PONTE VEDRA, FLA. (1977-81). TPC AT SAWGRASS, PONTE VEDRA, FLA. (1982-95).

TOURNAMENT PLAYERS CHAMPIONSHIP

1974	Jack Nicklaus	272
1975	Al Geiberger	270
1976	Jack Nicklaus	269
1977	Mark Hayes	289
1978	Jack Nicklaus	289
1979	Lanny Wadkins	283
1980	Lee Trevino	278
1981	*Ray Floyd	285
1982	Jerry Pate	280
1983	Hal Sutton	283
1984	Fred Couples	277
1985	Calvin Peete	274
1986	John Mahaffey	275
1987	*Sandy Lyle	274

THE PLAYERS CHAMPIONSHIP

1988	Mark McCumber	273
1989	Tom Kite	279
1990	Jodie Mudd	278
1991	Steve Elkington	276
1992	Davis Love III	273
1993	Nick Price	270
1994	Greg Norman	264
1995	Lee Janzen	283

FREEPORT-MCDERMOTT CLASSIC

City Park GC, New Orleans, (1938-62). Lakewood CC, New Orleans, (1963-88). English Turn G&CC, New Orleans, (1989-95).

GREATER NEW ORLEANS OPEN INVITATIONAL

1938	Harry Cooper	285
1939	Henry Picard	284
1940	Jimmy Demaret	286
1941	Henry Picard	276
1942	Lloyd Mangrum	281
1943	No tournament	
1944	Sammy Byrd	285
1945	*Byron Nelson	284
1946	Byron Nelson	277
1947	No tournament	
1948	Bob Hamilton	280
1949-1957 No tournaments		
1958	*Billy Casper	278
1959	Bill Collins	280
1960	Dow Finsterwald	270
1961	Doug Sanders	272
1962	Bo Wininger	281
1963	Bo Wininger	279
1964	Mason Rudolph	283
1965	Dick Mayer	273
1966	Frank Beard	276
1967	George Knudson	277
1968	George Archer	271
1969	*Larry Hinson	275
1970	*Miller Barber	278
1971	Frank Beard	276
1972	Gary Player	279
1973	*Jack Nicklaus	280
1974	Lee Trevino	267

FIRST NBC NEW ORLEANS OPEN

1975	Billy Casper	271
1976	Larry Ziegler	274
1977	Jim Simons	273
1978	Lon Hinkle	271
1979	Hubert Green	273

GREATER NEW ORLEANS OPEN

1980	Tom Watson	273

USF&G NEW ORLEANS OPEN

1981	Tom Watson	270

USF&G CLASSIC

1982	@Scott Hoch	206
1983	Bill Rogers	274
1984	Bob Eastwood	272
1985	@Seve Ballesteros	205
1986	Calvin Peete	269
1987	Ben Crenshaw	268
1988	Chip Beck	262
1989	Tim Simpson	274
1990	David Frost	276
1991	*Ian Woosnam	275

FREEPORT-McMORAN CLASSIC

1992	Chip Beck	276
1993	Mike Standly	281
1994	Ben Crenshaw	273
1995	Davis Love III	274

DEPOSIT GUARANTY GOLF CLASSIC

Hattiesburg CC, Hattiesburg, Miss. (1968-93). Annandale GC, Madison, Miss. (1994).

MAGNOLIA STATE CLASSIC

1968	*B.R. McLendon	269
1969	Larry Mowry	272
1970	Chris Blocker	271
1971	Roy Pace	270
1972	Mike Morey	269
1973	Dwight Nevil	268
1974	@Dwight Nevil	133
1975	Bob Wynn	270
1976	Dennis Meyer	271
1977	Mike McCullough	269
1978	Craig Stadler	268
1979	Bobby Walzel	272
1980	@*Roger Maltbie	65
1981	*Tom Jones	268
1982	Payne Stewart	270
1983	@Russ Cochran	203
1984	@*Lance Ten Broeck	201
1985	@*Jim Gallagher Jr.	131

DEPOSIT GUARANTY CLASSIC

1986	Dan Halldorson	263
1987	David Ogrin	267
1988	Frank Conner	267
1989	@*Jim Booros	199
1990	Gene Sauers	268
1991	*Larry Silveira	266
1992	Richard Zokol	267
1993	Greg Kraft	267
1994	@*Brian Henninger	135
1995	Ed Dougherty	272

Note: 1983-85 TPS Event

MCI CLASSIC

Harbour Town GL, Hilton Head, S.C.

HERITAGE CLASSIC

1969	Arnold Palmer	283
1970	Bob Goalby	280

SEA PINES HERITAGE CLASSIC

1971	Hale Irwin	279
1972	Johnny Miller	281
1973	Hale Irwin	272
1974	Johnny Miller	276
1975	Jack Nicklaus	271
1976	Hubert Green	274
1977	Graham Marsh	273
1978	Hubert Green	277
1979	Tom Watson	270
1980	*Doug Tewell	280
1981	Bill Rogers	278
1982	*Tom Watson	280
1983	Fuzzy Zoeller	275
1984	Nick Faldo	270
1985	*Bernhard Langer	273
1986	Fuzzy Zoeller	276

MCI HERITAGE CLASSIC

1987	Davis Love III	271
1988	Greg Norman	271
1989	Payne Stewart	268
1990	*Payne Stewart	276
1991	Davis Love III	271
1992	Davis Love III	269
1993	David Edwards	273
1994	Hale Irwin	266
1995	*Bob Tway	275

KMART GREATER GREENSBORO OPEN

Rotated between Sedgefield CC, Greensboro, N.C., and Starmount Forest CC, Greensboro, N.C. (1938-60). Sedgefield CC (1961-76). Forest Oaks CC, Greensboro, N.C. (1977-95).

GREATER GREENSBORO OPEN

1938	Sam Snead	272
1939	Ralph Guldahl	280
1940	Ben Hogan	270
1941	Byron Nelson	276
1942	Sam Byrd	279
1943-1944 No tournaments		
1945	Byron Nelson	271
1946	Sam Snead	270
1947	Vic Ghezzi	286
1948	Lloyd Mangrum	278
1949	*Sam Snead	276
1950	Sam Snead	269
1951	Art Doering	279
1952	Dave Douglas	277
1953	*Earl Stewart	275
1954	*Doug Ford	283
1955	Sam Snead	273
1956	*Sam Snead	279
1957	Stan Leonard	276
1958	Bob Goalby	275
1959	Dow Finsterwald	278
1960	Sam Snead	270
1961	Mike Souchak	276
1962	Billy Casper	275
1963	Doug Sanders	270
1964	*Julius Boros	277
1965	Sam Snead	273
1966	*Doug Sanders	276
1967	George Archer	267
1968	Billy Casper	267
1969	*Gene Littler	274
1970	Gary Player	271
1971	*Bud Allin	275
1972	*George Archer	272
1973	Chi Chi Rodriguez	267
1974	Bob Charles	270
1975	Tom Weiskopf	275
1976	Al Geiberger	268
1977	Danny Edwards	276
1978	Seve Ballesteros	282
1979	Raymond Floyd	282
1980	Craig Stadler	275
1981	*Larry Nelson	281
1982	Danny Edwards	285
1983	Lanny Wadkins	275
1984	Andy Bean	280
1985	Joey Sindelar	285
1986	Sandy Lyle	275
1987	Scott Simpson	282

KMART GREATER GREENSBORO OPEN

1988	*Sandy Lyle	271
1989	Ken Green	277
1990	Steve Elkington	282
1991	*Mark Brooks	275
1992	Davis Love III	272
1993	*Rocco Mediate	281
1994	Mike Springer	275
1995	Jim Gallagher Jr.	274

SHELL HOUSTON OPEN

Moved annually (1946-50, 1972-74). Memorial Park GC, Houston (1951-63). Sharpstown CC, Houston (1964-65). Champions GC, Houston (1966-71). Woodlands CC, The Woodlands, Texas (1975-84). TPC at The Woodlands, The Woodlands, Texas (1985-95).

TOURNAMENT OF CHAMPIONS

1946	Byron Nelson	274
1947	Bobby Locke	277
1948	No tournament	
1949	John Palmer	272

HOUSTON OPEN

1950	Cary Middlecoff	277
1951	Marty Furgol	277
1952	Jack Burke Jr.	277
1953	*Cary Middlecoff	283
1954	Dave Douglas	277
1955	Mike Souchak	273
1956	Ted Kroll	277
1957	Arnold Palmer	279
1958	Ed Oliver	281

HOUSTON CLASSIC

1959	*Jack Burke Jr.	277
1960	*Bill Collins	280
1961	*Jay Hebert	276
1962	*Bobby Nichols	278
1963	Bob Charles	268
1964	Mike Souchak	278
1965	Bobby Nichols	273

HOUSTON CHAMPION INTERNATIONAL

1966	Arnold Palmer	275
1967	Frank Beard	274
1968	Roberto DeVicenzo	274
1969	Hosted U.S. Open	
1970	*Gibby Gilbert	282
1971	*Hubert Green	280

HOUSTON OPEN

1972	Bruce Devlin	278
1973	Bruce Crampton	277
1974	Dave Hill	276
1975	Bruce Crampton	273
1976	Lee Elder	278
1977	Gene Littler	276
1978	Gary Player	270
1979	Wayne Levi	268

MICHELOB HOUSTON OPEN

1980	*Curtis Strange	266
1981	@Ron Streck	198
1982	*Ed Sneed	275

HOUSTON COCA-COLA OPEN

1983	David Graham	275
1984	Corey Pavin	274

HOUSTON OPEN

1985	Ray Floyd	277
1986	*Curtis Strange	274

BIG I HOUSTON OPEN

1987	*Jay Haas	276

INDEPENDENT INSURANCE AGENT OPEN

1988	*Curtis Strange	270
1989	Mike Sullivan	280
1990	@*Tony Sills	204
1991	Fulton Allem	273

SHELL HOUSTON OPEN

1992	Fred Funk	272
1993	@*Jim McGovern	199
1994	Mike Heinen	272
1995	*Payne Steuart	276

BELLSOUTH CLASSIC

Atlanta CC, Marietta, Ga.

ATLANTA CLASSIC

1967	Bob Charles	282
1968	Bob Lunn	280
1969	*Bert Yancey	277
1970	Tommy Aaron	275
1971	*Gardner Dickinson	275
1972	Bob Lunn	275
1973	Jack Nicklaus	272
1974	Hosted TPC	
1975	Hale Irwin	271
1976	Hosted U.S. Open	
1977	Hale Irwin	273
1978	Jerry Heard	269
1979	Andy Bean	265
1980	Larry Nelson	270
1981	*Tom Watson	277

GEORGIA-PACIFIC ATLANTA GOLF CLASSIC

1982	*Keith Fergus	273
1983	@*Calvin Peete	206
1984	Tom Kite	269
1985	*Wayne Levi	273
1986	Bob Tway	269
1987	Dave Barr	265
1988	Larry Nelson	268

BELLSOUTH ATLANTA GOLF CLASSIC

1989	*Scott Simpson	278
1990	Wayne Levi	275
1991	*Corey Pavin	272

BELLSOUTH CLASSIC

1992	Tom Kite	272
1993	Nolan Henke	271
1994	John Daly	274
1995	Mark Calcavecchia	271

GTE BYRON NELSON CLASSIC

Oak Cliffs CC, Dallas (1958-67). Preston Trail Golf Club, Dallas (1968-82). Las Colinas Sports Club, Irving, Texas (1983-85). TPC at Las Colinas, Irving, Texas (1986-95).

DALLAS OPEN

1944	Byron Nelson	276
1945	Sam Snead	276
1946	Ben Hogan	284
1947-1955 No tournaments		
1956	Don January	268
1956A	*Peter Thomson	267
1957	Sam Snead	264
1958	*Sam Snead	272
1959	Julius Boros	274
1960	*Johnny Pott	275
1961	Earl Stewart Jr.	278
1962	Billy Maxwell	277
1963	No tournament	
1964	Charles Coody	271
1965	No tournament	
1966	Roberto DeVicenzo	276
1967	Bert Yancey	274

BYRON NELSON GOLF CLASSIC

1968	Miller Barber	270
1969	Bruce Devlin	277
1970	*Jack Nicklaus	274
1971	Jack Nicklaus	274

1972	*Chi Chi Rodriguez	273
1973	*Lanny Wadkins	277
1974	Brian Allin	269
1975	Tom Watson	269
1976	Mark Hayes	273
1977	Ray Floyd	276
1978	Tom Watson	272
1979	*Tom Watson	275
1980	Tom Watson	274
1981	*Bruce Lietzke	281
1982	Bob Gilder	266
1983	Ben Crenshaw	273
1984	Craig Stadler	276
1985	*Bob Eastwood	272
1986	Andy Bean	269
1987	*Fred Couples	266

GTE BYRON NELSON GOLF CLASSIC

1988	*Bruce Lietzke	271
1989	*Jodie Mudd	265
1990	@Payne Stewart	202
1991	Nick Price	270
1992	@*Billy Ray Brown	199
1993	Scott Simpson	270
1994	@*Neal Lancaster	132
1995	Ernie Els	263

KEMPER OPEN

PLEASANT VALLEY CC, SUTTON, MASS. (1968). QUAIL HOLLOW CC, CHARLOTTE, N.C. (1969-79). CONGRESSIONAL CC, BETHESDA, MD. (1980-86). TPC AT AVENEL, POTOMAC, MD. (1987-95).

KEMPER OPEN

1968	Arnold Palmer	276
1969	Dale Douglass	274
1970	Dick Lotz	278
1971	*Tom Weiskopf	277
1972	Doug Sanders	275
1973	Tom Weiskopf	271
1974	*Bob Menne	270
1975	Ray Floyd	278
1976	Joe Inman	277
1977	Tom Weiskopf	277
1978	Andy Bean	273
1979	Jerry McGee	272
1980	John Mahaffey	275
1981	Craig Stadler	270
1982	Craig Stadler	275
1983	*Fred Couples	287
1984	Greg Norman	280
1985	Bill Glasson	278
1986	*Greg Norman	277
1987	Tom Kite	270
1988	*Morris Hatalsky	274
1989	Tom Byrum	268
1990	Gil Morgan	274
1991	*Billy Andrade	263
1992	Bill Glasson	276
1993	Grant Waite	275
1994	Mark Brooks	271
1995	*Lee Janzen	272

MASTERCARD COLONIAL

COLONIAL CC, FORT WORTH.

COLONIAL NATIONAL INVITATION TOURNAMENT

1946	Ben Hogan	279
1947	Ben Hogan	279
1948	Clayton Heafner	272
1949	No tournament	
1950	Sam Snead	277
1951	Cary Middlecoff	282
1952	Ben Hogan	279
1953	Ben Hogan	282
1954	Johnny Palmer	280
1955	Chandler Harper	276
1956	Mike Souchak	280
1957	Roberto DeVicenzo	284
1958	Tommy Bolt	282
1959	*Ben Hogan	285
1960	Julius Boros	280
1961	Doug Sanders	281
1962	*Arnold Palmer	281
1963	Julius Boros	279
1964	Billy Casper	279
1965	Bruce Crampton	276
1966	Bruce Devlin	280
1967	Dave Stockton	278
1968	Billy Casper	275
1969	Gardner Dickinson	278
1970	Homero Blancas	273
1971	Gene Littler	283
1972	Jerry Heard	275
1973	Tom Weiskopf	276
1974	Rod Curl	276
1975	Hosted TPC	
1976	Lee Trevino	273
1977	Ben Crenshaw	272
1978	Lee Trevino	268
1979	Al Geiberger	274
1980	Bruce Lietzke	271
1981	Fuzzy Zoeller	274
1982	Jack Nicklaus	273
1983	*Jim Colbert	278
1984	*Peter Jacobsen	270
1985	Corey Pavin	266
1986	@*Dan Pohl	205
1987	Keith Clearwater	266
1988	Lanny Wadkins	270

SOUTHWESTERN BELL COLONIAL

1989	Ian Baker-Finch	270
1990	Ben Crenshaw	272
1991	Tom Purtzer	267
1992	*Bruce Lietzke	267
1993	Fulton Allem	264
1994	*Nick Price	266
1995	Tom Lehman	271

MEMORIAL TOURNAMENT

MUIRFIELD VILLAGE GC, DUBLIN, OHIO.

MEMORIAL TOURNAMENT

1976	*Roger Maltbie	288
1977	Jack Nicklaus	281
1978	Jim Simons	284
1979	Tom Watson	285
1980	David Graham	280
1981	Keith Fergus	284
1982	Ray Floyd	281
1983	Hale Irwin	281
1984	*Jack Nicklaus	280
1985	Hale Irwin	281
1986	Hal Sutton	271
1987	Don Pooley	272
1988	Curtis Strange	274
1989	Bob Tway	277
1990	@Greg Norman	216
1991	*Kenny Perry	273
1992	*David Edwards	273
1993	Paul Azinger	274
1994	Tom Lehman	268
1995	Greg Norman	269

BUICK CLASSIC

WESTCHESTER CC, HARRISON, N.Y.

WESTCHESTER CLASSIC

1967	Jack Nicklaus	272
1968	Julius Boros	272
1969	Frank Beard	275
1970	Bruce Crampton	273
1971	Arnold Palmer	270
1972	Jack Nicklaus	270
1973	*Bobby Nichols	272
1974	Johnny Miller	269
1975	*Gene Littler	271

AMERICAN EXPRESS WESTCHESTER CLASSIC

1976	David Graham	272
1977	Andy North	272
1978	Lee Elder	274

MANUFACTURERS HANOVER WESTCHESTER CLASSIC

1979	Jack Renner	277
1980	Curtis Strange	273
1981	Ray Floyd	275
1982	Bob Gilder	261
1983	Seve Ballesteros	276
1984	Scott Simpson	269
1985	*Roger Maltbie	275
1986	Bob Tway	272
1987	*J.C. Snead	276
1988	*Seve Ballesteros	276
1989	*Wayne Grady	277

BUICK CLASSIC

1990	Hale Irwin	269
1991	Billy Andrade	273
1992	David Frost	268
1993	Vijay Singh	280
1994	Lee Janzen	268
1995	*Vijay Singh	278

CANON GREATER HARTFORD OPEN

WETHERSFIELD CC, HARTFORD, CONN. (1952-83). TPC OF CONNECTICUT, CROMWELL, CONN. (1984-90). TPC AT RIVER HIGHLANDS, CROMWELL, CONN. (1991-95).

INSURANCE CITY OPEN

1952	Ted Kroll	273
1953	Bob Toski	269
1954	*Tommy Bolt	271
1955	Sam Snead	269
1956	*Arnold Palmer	274
1957	Gardner Dickinson	272
1958	Jack Burke Jr.	268
1959	Gene Littler	272
1960	*Arnold Palmer	270
1961	*Billy Maxwell	271
1962	*Bob Goalby	271
1963	Billy Casper	271
1964	Ken Venturi	273
1965	*Billy Casper	274
1966	Art Wall	266

GREATER HARTFORD OPEN INVITATIONAL

1967	Charlie Sifford	272
1968	Billy Casper	266
1969	*Bob Lunn	268
1970	Bob Murphy	267
1971	*George Archer	268
1972	*Lee Trevino	269

SAMMY DAVIS JR. GREATER HARTFORD OPEN

1973	Billy Casper	264
1974	Dave Stockton	268
1975	*Don Bies	267
1976	Rik Massengale	266
1977	Bill Kratzert	265
1978	Rod Funseth	264
1979	Jerry McGee	267
1980	*Howard Twitty	266
1981	Hubert Green	264
1982	Tim Norris	259
1983	Curtis Strange	268
1984	Peter Jacobsen	269
1985	*Phil Blackmar	271

CANON SAMMY DAVIS JR. GREATER HARTFORD OPEN

1986	*Mac O'Grady	269
1987	Paul Azinger	269
1988	*Mark Brooks	269

CANON GREATER HARTFORD OPEN

1989	Paul Azinger	267
1990	Wayne Levi	267
1991	*Billy Ray Brown	271
1992	Lanny Wadkins	274
1993	Nick Price	271
1994	David Frost	268
1995	Greg Norman	267

MOTOROLA WESTERN OPEN

MOVED ANNUALLY (1899-1973). BUTLER NATIONAL GC, OAK BROOK, ILL. (1974-90). COG HILL CC (DUBSDREAD), LEMONT, ILL. (1991-95).

WESTERN OPEN

1899	*Willie Smith	156
1900	No tournament	
1901	Laurie Auchterlonie	160
1902	Willie Anderson	299
1903	Alex Smith	318
1904	Willie Anderson	304
1905	Arthur Smith	278
1906	Alex Smith	306
1907	Robert Simpson	307
1908	Willie Anderson	299
1909	Willie Anderson	288
1910	#Chick Evans Jr.	6 & 5
1911	Robert Simpson	2 & 1
1912	Mac Smith	299
1913	John McDermott	295
1914	Jim Barnes	293
1915	Tom McNamara	304
1916	Walter Hagen	286
1917	Jim Barnes	283
1918	No tournament	
1919	Jim Barnes	283
1920	Jock Hutchinson	296
1921	Walter Hagen	287
1922	Mike Brady	291
1923	Jock Hutchinson	281
1924	Bill Mehlhorn	293
1925	Mac Smith	281
1926	Walter Hagen	279
1927	Walter Hagen	281
1928	Abe Espinosa	291
1929	Tommy Armour	273
1930	Gene Sarazen	278
1931	Ed Dudley	280
1932	Walter Hagen	287
1933	Mac Smith	282
1934	*Harry Cooper	274
1935	John Revolta	290
1936	Ralph Guldahl	274
1937	*Ralph Guldahl	288
1938	Ralph Guldahl	279
1939	Byron Nelson	281
1940	*Jimmy Demaret	293
1941	Ed Oliver	275
1942	Herman Barron	276
1943-1945	No tournaments	
1946	Ben Hogan	271
1947	Johnny Palmer	270
1948	*Ben Hogan	281
1949	Sam Snead	268
1950	Sam Snead	282
1951	Marty Furgol	270
1952	Lloyd Mangrum	274
1953	Dutch Harrison	278
1954	*Lloyd Mangrum	277
1955	Cary Middlecoff	272
1956	*Mike Fetchick	284
1957	*Doug Ford	279
1958	Doug Sanders	275
1959	Mike Souchak	272
1960	*Stan Leonard	278
1961	Arnold Palmer	271
1962	Jacky Cupit	281
1963	*Arnold Palmer	280
1964	Chi Chi Rodriquez	268
1965	Billy Casper	270
1966	Billy Casper	283
1967	Jack Nicklaus	274
1968	Jack Nicklaus	273
1969	Billy Casper	276
1970	Hugh Royer	273
1971	Bruce Crampton	279
1972	Jim Jamieson	271
1973	Billy Casper	272
1974	Tom Watson	287
1975	Hale Irwin	283
1976	Al Geiberger	288
1977	Tom Watson	283
1978	*Andy Bean	282
1979	*Larry Nelson	286
1980	Scott Simpson	281
1981	Ed Fiori	277
1982	Tom Weiskopf	276
1983	Mark McCumber	284
1984	*Tom Watson	280
1985	#Scott Verplank	279
1986	*Tom Kite	286

BEATRICE WESTERN OPEN

1987	@D.A. Weibring	207
1989	*Mark McCumber	275

CENTEL WESTERN OPEN

1990	Wayne Levi	275
1991	Russ Cochran	275
1992	Ben Crenshaw	276

SPRINT WESTERN OPEN

1993	Nick Price	269

MOTOROLA WESTERN OPEN

1994	Nick Price	277
1995	Billy Mayfair	279

ANHEUSER-BUSCH GOLF CLASSIC

Silverado CC, Napa, Calif. (1968-80). Kingsmill GC, Kingsmill, Va. (1981-95).

KAISER INTERNATIONAL OPEN INVITATIONAL

1968	Kermit Zarley	273
1969	@Miller Barber	135
1969+	*Jack Nicklaus	273
1970	*Ken Still	278
1971	Billy Casper	269
1972	George Knudson	271
1973	*Ed Sneed	275
1974	Johnny Miller	271
1975	Johnny Miller	272
1976	J.C. Snead	274

ANHEUSER-BUSCH GOLF CLASSIC

1977	Miller Barber	272
1978	Tom Watson	270
1979	John Fought	277
1980	Ben Crenshaw	272
1981	John Mahaffey	276
1982	@Calvin Peete	203
1983	Calvin Peete	276
1984	Ronnie Black	267
1985	*Mark Wiebe	273
1986	Fuzzy Zoeller	274
1987	Mark McCumber	267
1988	*Tom Sieckmann	270
1989	*Mike Donald	268
1990	Lanny Wadkins	266
1991	*Mike Hulbert	266
1992	David Peoples	271
1993	Jim Gallagher	269
1994	Mark McCumber	267
1995	Ted Tryba	272

NEW ENGLAND CLASSIC

Pleasant Valley CC, Sutton, Mass.

CARLING WORLD OPEN

1965	Tony Lema	279

KEMPER OPEN

1968	Arnold Palmer	276

AVCO GOLF CLASSIC

1969	Tom Shaw	280
1970	Billy Casper	277

MASSACHUSETTS CLASSIC

1971	Dave Stockton	275

USI CLASSIC

1972	Bruce Devlin	275
1973	Lanny Wadkins	279

PLEASANT VALLEY CLASSIC

1974	Victor Regalado	278
1975	Roger Maltbie	276
1976	Bud Allin	277
1977	Ray Floyd	271

AMERICAN OPTICAL CLASSIC

1978	John Mahaffey	270
1979	Lou Graham	275

PLEASANT VALLEY JIMMY FUND CLASSIC

1980	*Wayne Levi	273
1981	Jack Renner	273

BANK OF BOSTON CLASSIC

1982	Bob Gilder	271
1983	Mark Lye	273
1984	George Archer	270
1985	George Burns	267
1986	*Gene Sauers	274
1987	@Sam Randolph	199
1988	Mark Calcavecchia	274
1989	Blaine McCallister	271
1990	Morris Hatalsky	275

NEW ENGLAND CLASSIC

1991	*Bruce Fleisher	268
1992	Brad Faxon	268
1993	Paul Azinger	268
1994	Kenny Perry	268
1995	Fred Funk	268

FEDEX ST. JUDE CLASSIC

Colonial CC, Memphis (1958-71). Colonial CC, Cordova, Tenn. (1972-88). TPC at Southwind, Germantown, Tenn. (1989-95).

MEMPHIS INVITATIONAL OPEN

1958	Billy Maxwell	267
1959	*Don Whitt	272
1960	*Tommy Bolt	273
1961	Cary Middlecoff	266
1962	*Lionel Hebert	267
1963	*Tony Lema	270
1964	Mike Souchak	270
1965	*Jack Nicklaus	271
1966	Bert Yancey	265
1967	Dave Hill	272
1968	Bob Lunn	268
1969	Dave Hill	265

DANNY THOMAS MEMPHIS CLASSIC

1970	Dave Hill	267
1971	Lee Trevino	268
1972	Lee Trevino	281
1973	Dave Hill	283
1974	Gary Player	273
1975	Gene Littler	270
1976	Gibby Gilbert	273
1977	Al Geiberger	273
1978	*Andy Bean	277
1979	*Gil Morgan	278
1980	Lee Trevino	272
1981	Jerry Pate	274
1982	Ray Floyd	271
1983	Larry Mize	274
1984	Bob Eastwood	280

ST. JUDE MEMPHIS CLASSIC

1985	*Hal Sutton	279

FEDERAL EXPRESS ST. JUDE CLASSIC

1986	Mike Hulbert	280
1987	Curtis Strange	275
1988	Jodie Mudd	273
1989	John Mahaffey	272
1990	*Tom Kite	269
1991	Fred Couples	269
1992	Jay Haas	263
1993	Nick Price	266
1994	*Dicky Pride	267
1995	Jim Gallagher Jr.	267

BUICK OPEN

Warwick Hills G & CC, Grand Blanc, Mich. (1958-69, 1978-95). Flint Elks CC, Flint, Mich. (1972, 1974-77). Benton Harbor Elks CC, Benton Harbor, Mich. (1973).

BUICK OPEN INVITATIONAL

1958	Billy Casper	285
1959	Art Wall	282
1960	Mike Souchak	282
1961	Jack Burke Jr.	284
1962	Bill Collins	284
1963	Julius Boros	274
1964	Tony Lema	277
1965	Tony Lema	280
1966	Phil Rodgers	284
1967	Julius Boros	283
1968	Tom Weiskopf	280
1969	Dave Hill	277

VERN PARSELL BUICK OPEN

1972	Gary Groh	273

LAKE MICHIGAN CLASSIC

1973	(2T) Wilf Homenuik	215

FLINT ELKS OPEN

1974	(2T) Bryan Abbott	135
1975	(2T) Spike Kelley	208
1976	(2T) Ed Sabo	279
1977	Bobby Cole	271

BUICK GOODWRENCH OPEN

1978	*Jack Newton	280
1979	*John Fought	280
1980	Peter Jacobsen	276

BUICK OPEN

1981	*Hale Irwin	277
1982	Lanny Wadkins	273
1983	Wayne Levi	272
1984	Denis Watson	271
1985	Ken Green	268
1986	Ben Crenshaw	270
1987	Robert Wrenn	262
1988	Scott Verplank	268
1989	Leonard Thompson	273
1990	Chip Beck	272
1991	*Brad Faxon	271
1992	*Dan Forsman	276
1993	Larry Mize	272
1994	Fred Couples	270
1995	Woody Austin	270

THE SPRINT INTERNATIONAL

Castle Pines GC, Castle Rock, Colo.

1986	Ken Green	Plus 12
1987	John Cook	Plus 11
1988	Joey Sindelar	Plus 17
1989	Greg Norman	Plus 13
1990	Davis Love III	Plus 14
1991	Jose M. Olazabal	Plus 10
1992	Brad Faxon	Plus 14
1993	Phil Mickelson	Plus 45
1994	Steve Lowery	Plus 35

NEC WORLD SERIES OF GOLF

Firestone Country Club, South Course, Akron, Ohio. (From 1962-1975, played as a four-man, 36-hole exhibition; 1994 event played on North Course.)

1962	Jack Nicklaus	(135)
1963	Jack Nicklaus	(140)
1964	Tony Lema	(138)
1965	Gary Player	(139)
1966	Gene Littler	(143)
1967	Jack Nicklaus	(144)
1968	Gary Player	(143)
1969	Orville Moody	(141)
1970	Jack Nicklaus	(136)
1971	Charles Coody	(141)
1972	Gary Player	(142)
1973	Tom Weiskopf	(137)
1974	Lee Trevino	(139)
1975	Tom Watson	(140)
1976	Jack Nicklaus	275
1977	Lanny Wadkins	267
1978	*Gil Morgan	278
1979	Lon Hinkle	272
1980	Tom Watson	270
1981	Bill Rogers	275
1982	*Craig Stadler	278
1983	Nick Price	270
1984	Denis Watson	271
1985	Roger Maltbie	268
1986	Dan Pohl	277
1987	Curtis Strange	275
1988	*Mike Reid	275
1989	*David Frost	276
1990	Jose Maria Olazaba	262
1991	*Tom Purtzer	279
1992	Craig Stadler	273
1993	Fulton Allem	270
1994	Jose Maria Olazabal	269

GREATER MILWAUKEE OPEN

Northshore CC, Mequon, Wis. (1968-70). Tripoli GC, Milwaukee (1971-72). Tuckaway CC, Franklin, Wis. (1973-93). Brown Deer GC, Milwaukee (1994-95).

GREATER MILWAUKEE OPEN

1968	Dave Stockton	275
1969	Ken Still	277
1970	Deane Beman	276
1971	Dave Eichelberger	270
1972	Jim Colbert	271
1973	Dave Stockton	276
1974	Ed Sneed	276
1975	Art Wall	271
1976	Dave Hill	270
1977	Dave Eichelberger	278
1978	*Lee Elder	275
1979	Calvin Peete	269
1980	Bill Kratzert	266
1981	Jay Haas	274
1982	Calvin Peete	274
1983	*Morris Hatalsky	275
1984	Mark O'Meara	272
1985	Jim Thorpe	274
1986	*Corey Pavin	272
1987	Gary Hallberg	269
1988	Ken Green	268
1989	Greg Norman	269
1990	*Jim Gallagher Jr.	271
1991	Mark Brooks	270
1992	Richard Zokol	269
1993	Billy Mayfair	270
1994	Mike Springer	268

BELL CANADIAN OPEN

Moved annually (1904-76). Glen Abbey GC, Oakville, Ontario (1977-79, 1981-95).

1904	J.H. Oke	156
1905	George Cumming	148
1906	Charles Murray	170
1907	Percy Barrett	306
1908	Albert Murray	300
1909	Karl Keller	309
1910	Daniel Kenny	303
1911	Charles Murray	314
1912	George Sargent	299
1913	Albert Murray	295
1914	Karl Keller	300
1915-1918 No tournaments		
1919	J. Douglas Edgar	278
1920	*J. Douglas Edgar	298
1921	W.H. Trovinger	293
1922	Al Watrous	303
1923	C.W. Hackney	295
1924	Leo Diegel	285
1925	Leo Diegel	295
1926	Mac Smith	283
1927	Tommy Armour	288
1928	Leo Diegel	282
1929	Leo Diegel	274
1930	*Tommy Armour	273
1931	*Walter Hagen	292
1932	Harry Cooper	290
1933	Joe Kirkwood	282
1934	Tommy Armour	287
1935	Gene Kunes	280
1936	Lawson Little	271
1937	Harry Cooper	285
1938	*Sam Snead	277
1939	Harold McSpaden	282
1940	*Sam Snead	281
1941	Sam Snead	274
1942	Craig Wood	275
1943-1944 No tournaments		
1945	Byron Nelson	280
1946	*George Fazio	278
1947	Bobby Locke	268
1948	C.W. Congdon	280
1949	Dutch Harrison	271
1950	Jim Ferrier	271
1951	Jim Ferrier	273
1952	John Palmer	263
1953	Dave Douglas	273
1954	Pat Fletcher	280
1955	Arnold Palmer	265
1956	#Doug Sanders	273
1957	George Bayer	271
1958	Wesley Ellis Jr.	267
1959	Doug Ford	276
1960	Art Wall Jr.	269
1961	Jacky Cupit	270
1962	Ted Kroll	278
1963	Doug Ford	280
1964	Kel Nagle	277

1965 Gene Littler 273
1966 Don Massengale 280
1967 *Billy Casper 279
1968 Bob Charles 274
1969 *Tommy Aaron 275
1970 Kermit Zarley 279
1971 *Lee Trevino 275
1972 Gay Brewer 275
1973 Tom Weiskopf 278
1974 Bobby Nichols 270
1975 *Tom Weiskopf 274
1976 Jerry Pate 267
1977 Lee Trevino 280
1978 Bruce Lietzke 283
1979 Lee Trevino 281
1980 Bob Gilder 274
1981 Peter Oosterhuis 280
1982 Bruce Lietzke 277
1983 *John Cook 277
1984 Greg Norman 278
1985 Curtis Strange 279
1986 Bob Murphy 280
1987 Curtis Strange 276
1988 Ken Green 275
1989 Steve Jones 271
1990 Wayne Levi 278
1991 Nick Price 273
1992 *Greg Norman 280
1993 David Frost 279
1994 Nick Price 275

QUAD CITY CLASSIC

Crow Valley CC, Bettendorf, Iowa (1972-74). Oakwood CC, Coal Valley, Ill. (1975-95).

QUAD CITIES OPEN
1972 Deane Beman 279
1973 Sam Adams 268
1974 Dave Stockton 271**ED**

McMAHON–JAYCEES QUAD CITY OPEN
1975 Roger Maltbie 275
1976 John Lister 268
1977 Mike Morley 267
1978 Victor Regalado 269
1979 D.A. Weibring 266

QUAD CITIES OPEN
1980 Scott Hoch 266
1981 *Dave Barr 270

MILLER HIGH-LIFE QUAD CITIES OPEN
1982 Payne Stewart 268
1983 *Danny Edwards 266
1984 Scott Hoch 266

LITE QUAD CITIES OPEN
1985 Dan Forsman 267

HARDEE'S GOLF CLASSIC
1986 Mark Wiebe 268
1987 Kenny Knox 265
1988 Blaine McCallister 261
1989 Curt Byrum 268
1990 *Joey Sindelar 268
1991 D.A. Weibring 267
1992 David Frost 266
1993 David Frost 259
1994 Mark McCumber 265

B.C. OPEN

En Joie CC, Endicott, N.Y.

BROOME COUNTY OPEN
1971 *Claude Harmon Jr. 69

B.C. OPEN
1972 Bob Payne 136
1973 Hubert Green 266
1974 *Richie Karl 273
1975 Don Iverson 274
1976 Bob Wynn 271
1977 Gil Morgan 270
1978 Tom Kite 267
1979 Howard Twitty 270
1980 Don Pooley 271
1981 Jay Haas 270
1982 Calvin Peete 265
1983 Pat Lindsey 268
1984 Wayne Levi 275
1985 Joey Sindelar 274
1986 Rick Fehr 267
1987 Joey Sindelar 266
1988 Bill Glasson 268
1989 *Mike Hulbert 268
1990 Nolan Henke 268
1991 Fred Couples 269
1992 John Daly 266
1993 Blaine McCallister 271
1994 Mike Sullivan 266

BUICK CHALLENGE

Green Island CC, Columbus, Ga. (1970-90). Callaway Gardens Resort, Pine Mountain, Ga. (1991-95).

GREEN ISLAND OPEN INVITATIONAL
1970 Mason Rudolph 274

SOUTHERN OPEN INVITATIONAL
1971 Johnny Miller 267
1972 *DeWitt Weaver 276
1973 Gary Player 270
1974 Forrest Fezler 271
1975 Hubert Green 264
1976 Mac McClendon 274
1977 Jerry Pate 266
1978 Jerry Pate 269
1979 *Ed Fiori 274
1980 Mike Sullivan 269
1981 *J.C. Snead 271
1982 Bobby Clampett 266
1983 *Ronnie Black 271
1984 Hubert Green 265
1985 Tim Simpson 264
1986 Fred Wadsworth 269
1987 Ken Brown 266
1988 *David Frost 270
1989 Ted Schulz 266

BUICK SOUTHERN OPEN
1990 *Kenny Knox 265
1991 David Peoples 276
1992 @Gary Hallberg 206
1993 *John Inman 278
1994 *Steve Elkington 200

LAS VEGAS INVITATIONAL

Held simultaneously at three courses, rotating among Las Vegas CC, Las Vegas; Desert Inn CC, Las Vegas; Dunes CC, Las Vegas; Showboat CC, Las Vegas; TPC at Summerlin, Las Vegas (1992-93, 1995); Las Vegas Hilton CC (1994).

PANASONIC LAS VEGAS PRO-CELEBRITY CLASSIC
1983 Fuzzy Zoeller 340

PANASONIC LAS VEGAS INVITATIONAL
1984 Denis Watson 341
1985 Curtis Strange 338
1986 Greg Norman 333
1987 @Paul Azinger 271
1988 @Gary Koch 274

LAS VEGAS INVITATIONAL
1989 *Scott Hoch 336
1990 *Bob Tway 334
1991 *Andrew Magee 329
1992 John Cook 334
1993 John Inman 331
1994 Bruce Lietzke 332

WALT DISNEY WORLD/ OLDSMOBILE CLASSIC

Rotates among Palm, Walt Disney World, Lake Buena Vista, Fla.; Magnolia, Walt Disney World, Lake Buena Vista, Fla.; and Lake Buena Vista CC, Lake Buena Vista, Fla.

WALT DISNEY WORLD OPEN INVITATIONAL
1971 Jack Nicklaus 273
1972 Jack Nicklaus 267
1973 Jack Nicklaus 275

WALT DISNEY WORLD NATIONAL TEAM CHAMPIONSHIP
1974 Hubert Green/ Mac McClendon 255
1975 Jim Colbert/ Dean Refram 252
1976 *Woody Blackburn/ Bill Kratzert 260
1977 Gibby Gilbert/ Grier Jones 253
1978 Wayne Levi/ Bob Mann 254
1979 George Burns/ Ben Crenshaw 255
1980 Danny Edwards/ Dave Edwards 253
1981 Vance Heafner/ Mike Holland 275

WALT DISNEY WORLD GOLF CLASSIC
1982 *Hal Sutton 269
1983 Payne Stewart 269
1984 Larry Nelson 266

WALT DISNEY WORLD OLDSMOBILE CLASSIC
1985 Lanny Wadkins 267
1986 *Ray Floyd 275
1987 Larry Nelson 268
1988 *Bob Lohr 263
1989 Tim Simpson 272
1990 Tim Simpson 264
1991 Mark O'Meara 267
1992 John Huston 262
1993 Jeff Maggert 265
1994 Rick Fehr 269

LACANTERA TEXAS OPEN

Rotated among several courses (1922-60, 1967-76). Oak Hills CC, San Antonio (1961-66, 1977-95).

TEXAS OPEN
1922 Bob MacDonald 281
1923 Walter Hagen 279
1924 Joe Kirkwood 279
1925 Joe Turnesa 284
1926 Mac Smith 288
1927 Bobby Cruikshank 272
1928 Bill Mehlhorn 297
1929 Bill Mehlhorn 277
1930 Denny Shute 277
1931 Abe Espinosa 281
1932 Clarence Clark 287
1933 No tournament
1934 Wiffy Cox 283
1935-1938 No tournaments
1939 Dutch Harrison 271
1940 Byron Nelson 271
1941 Lawson Little 273
1942 *Chick Harbert 272
1943 No tournament
1944 Johnny Revolta 273
1945 Sam Byrd 268
1946 Ben Hogan 264
1947 Ed Oliver 265
1948 Sam Snead 264
1949 Dave Douglas 268
1950 Sam Snead 265
1951 *Dutch Harrison 265
1952 Jack Burke Jr. 260
1953 Tony Holguin 264
1954 Chandler Harper 259
1955 Mike Souchak 257
1956 Gene Littler 276
1957 Jay Hebert 271
1958 Bill Johnston 274
1959 Wes Ellis 276
1960 Arnold Palmer 276
1961 Arnold Palmer 270
1962 Arnold Palmer 273
1963 Phil Rodgers 268
1964 Bruce Crampton 273
1965 Frank Beard 270
1966 Harold Henning 272
1967 Chi Chi Rodriguez 277
1968 No tournament
1969 *Deane Beman 274

SAN ANTONIO TEXAS OPEN
1970 Ron Cerrudo 273
1971 No tournament
1972 Mike Hill 273
1973 Ben Crenshaw 270
1974 Terry Diehl 269
1975 *Don January 275
1976 *Butch Baird 273
1977 Hale Irwin 266
1978 Ron Streck 265
1979 Lou Graham 268
1980 Lee Trevino 265

TEXAS OPEN
1981 *Bill Rogers 266
1982 Jay Haas 262
1983 Jim Colbert 261
1984 Calvin Peete 266
1985 *John Mahaffey 268

VANTAGE CHAMPIONSHIP
1986 @Ben Crenshaw 196

NABISCO CHAMPIONSHIPS OF GOLF
1987 Tom Watson 268

TEXAS OPEN PRESENTED BY NABISCO
1988 Corey Pavin 259
1989 Donnie Hammond 258

H-E-B TEXAS OPEN
1990 Mark O'Meara 261
1991 *Blaine McCallister 269
1992 *Nick Price 263
1993 Jay Haas 269
1994 Bob Estes 265

THE TOUR CHAMPIONSHIP

Oak Hill CC, San Antonio (1986-87). Pebble Beach (Calif.) GL (1988). Harbour Town GL, Hilton Head, S.C. (1989). Champions GC, Houston (1990). Pinehurst No. 2, Pinehurst, N.C. (1991-92). The Olympic Club, San Francisco (1993-94).

VANTAGE CHAMPIONSHIP
1986 @Ben Crenshaw 196

NABISCO CHAMPIONSHIPS OF GOLF
1987 Tom Watson 268

NABISCO GOLF CHAMPIONSHIPS
1988 *Curtis Strange 279

NABISCO CHAMPIONSHIPS
1989 *Tom Kite 276
1990 *Jodie Mudd 273

THE TOUR CHAMPIONSHIP
1991 *Craig Stadler 279
1992 Paul Azinger 276
1993 Jim Gallagher 277
1994 *Mark McCumber 274

LINCOLN-MERCURY KAPALUA INTERNATIONAL

Bay Course, Kapalua GC, Kapalua, Maui, Hawaii (1983-90). Plantation Course, Kapalua GC, Kapalua, Maui, Hawaii (1991-94).

KAPALUA INTERNATIONAL
1983 Greg Norman 268
1984 Sandy Lyle 266

ISUZU KAPALUA INTERNATIONAL
1985 Mark O'Meara 275
1986 Andy Bean 278
1987 Andy Bean 267
1988 Bob Gilder 266
1989 *Peter Jacobsen 270
1990 David Peoples 264

PING KAPALUA INTERNATIONAL
1991 *Mike Hulbert 276

LINCOLN-MERCURY KAPALUA INTERNATIONAL
1992 Davis Love III 275
1993 Fred Couples 274
1994 Fred Couples 279

FRANKLIN TEMPLETON SHARK SHOOTOUT

SHERWOOD CC, THOUSAND OAKS, CALIF.

RMCC INVITATIONAL

1989	Curtis Strange/ Mark O'Meara	190
1990	Ray Floyd/ Fred Couples	182

SHARK SHOOTOUT BENEFITING RMCC

1991	Tom Purtzer/ Lanny Wadkins	189

FRANKLIN FUNDS SHARK SHOOT OUT

1992	Davis Love III/ Tom Kite	191
1993	Steve Elkington/ Ray Floyd	188
1994	Fred Couples/ Brad Faxon	190

THE SKINS GAME

DESERT HIGHLANDS CC, SCOTTSDALE, ARIZ. (1983-84). BEAR CREEK CC, MURIETTA, CALIF. (1985). TPC AT PGA WEST, LA QUINTA, CALIF. (1986-91). BIGHORN GC, PALM DESERT, CALIF. (1992-95).

1983	Gary Player	$170,000
1984	Jack Nicklaus	$240,000
1985	Fuzzy Zoeller	$255,000
1986	Fuzzy Zoeller	$370,000
1987	Lee Trevino	$310,000
1988	Ray Floyd	$290,000
1989	Curtis Strange	$265,000
1990	Curtis Strange	$225,000
1991	Payne Stewart	$260,000
1992	Payne Stewart	$220,000
1993	Payne Stewart	$280,000
1994	Tom Watson	$210,000

JCPENNEY CLASSIC

ROTATED ANNUALLY (1960-76). BARDMOOR CC, LARGO, FLA. (1977-89). INNISBROOK RESORT, TARPON SPRINGS, FLA. (1990-95).

HAIG & HAIG SCOTCH FOURSOME

1960	*Jim Turnesa	
	Gloria Armstrong	+139
1961	Dave Ragan	
	Mickey Wright	272
1962	Mason Rudolph	
	Kathy Whitworth	272
1963	Dave Ragan	
	Mickey Wright	273
1964	Sam Snead	
	Shirley Englehorn	272
1965	Gardner Dickinson	
	Ruth Jessen	281
1966	Jack Rule	
	Sandra Spuzich	276

PEPSI-COLA MIXED TEAM

1976	Chi Chi Rodriguez	
	JoAnn Washam	275
1977	Jerry Pate	
	Hollis Stacy	270

JCPENNEY CLASSIC

1978	*Lon Hinkle	
	Pat Bradley	267
1979	Dave Eichelberger	
	Murle Breer	268
1980	Curtis Strange	
	Nancy Lopez	268
1981	Tom Kite	
	Beth Daniel	270
1982	John Mahaffey	
	JoAnne Carner	268
1983	Fred Couples	
	Jan Stephenson	264
1984	Mike Donald	
	Vicki Alvarez	270
1985	Larry Rinker	
	Laurie Rinker	267
1986	Tom Purtzer	
	Juli Inkster	267
1987	Steve Jones	
	Jane Crafter	268
1988	John Huston	
	Amy Benz	269
1989	*Bill Glasson	
	Pat Bradley	267
1990	Davis Love III	
	Beth Daniel	266
1991	*Billy Andrade	
	Kris Tschetter	266
1992	Dan Forsman	
	Dottie Mochrie	264
1993	Mike Spring	265
	Melissa McNamara	
1994	*Brad Bryant	262
	Marta Figueras-Dotti	

MERRILL LYNCH SHOOT-OUT CHAMPIONSHIP

ROTATED ANNUALLY (1987-94).

1987	Fuzzy Zoeller
1988	David Frost
1989	Chip Beck
1990	John Mahaffey
1991	Davis Love III
1992	Chip Beck
1993	Vijay Singh
1994	Corey Pavin

THE RYDER CUP

1927	Worcester Country Club, Worcester, Mass.	June 3-4	U.S.	9½	Britain	2½
1929	Moortown, England	May 26-27	Britain	7	U.S.	5
1931	Scioto Country Club, Columbus, Ohio	June 26-27	U.S.	9	Britain	3
1933	Southport & Ainsdale Courses, England	June 26-27	Britain	6½	U.S.	5½
1935	Ridgewood Country Club, Ridgewood, N.J.	Sept. 28-29	U.S.	9	Britain	3
1937	Southport & Ainsdale Courses, England	June 29-30	U.S.	8	Britain	4
1939-1945	Ryder Cup matches not held during World War II.					
1947	Portland Golf Club, Portland, Ore.	Nov. 1-2	U.S.	11	Britain	1
1949	Ganton Golf Course, Scarborough, England	Sept. 16-17	U.S.	7	Britain	5
1951	Pinehurst Country Club, Pinehurst, N.C.	Nov. 2-4	U.S.	9½	Britain	2½
1953	Wentworth, England	Oct. 2-3	U.S.	6½	Britain	5½
1955	Thunderbird Ranch and CC, Palm Springs, Calif.	Nov. 5-6	U.S.	8	Britain	4
1957	Lindrick Golf Club, Yorkshire, England	Oct. 4-5	Britain	7½	U.S.	4½
1959	Eldorado Country Club, Palm Desert, Calif.	Nov. 6-7	U.S.	8½	Britain	3½
1961	Royal Lytham and St. Anne's Golf Club, St. Anne's-on-the-Sea, England	Oct. 13-14	U.S.	14½	Britain	9½
1963	East Lake Country Club, Atlanta	Oct. 11-13	U.S.	23	Britain	9
1965	Royal Birkdale Golf Club, Southport, England	Oct. 7-9	U.S.	19½	Britain	12½
1967	Champions Golf Club, Houston	Oct. 20-22	U.S.	23½	Britain	8½
1969	Royal Birkdale Golf Club, Southport, England	Sept. 18-20	U.S.	16 Tie	Britain	16
1971	Old Warson Country Club, St. Louis	Sept. 16-18	U.S.	18½	Britain	13½
1973	Muirfield, Scotland	Sept. 20-22	U.S.	19	Britain	13
1975	Laurel Valley Golf Club, Ligonier, Pa.	Sept. 19-21	U.S.	21	Britain	11
1977	Royal Lytham and St. Anne's Golf Club, St. Anne's-on-the-Sea, England	Sept. 15-17	U.S.	12½	Britain	7½
1979	Greenbrier, White Sulphur Springs, W.Va.	Sept. 13-15	U.S.	17	Europe	11
1981	Walton Heath Golf Club, Surrey, England	Sept. 18-20	U.S.	18½	Europe	9½
1983	PGA National GC, Palm Beach Gardens, Fla.	Oct. 14-16	U.S.	14½	Europe	13½
1985	The Belfry GC Sutton, Coldfield, England	Sept. 13-15	Europe	16½	U.S.	11½
1987	Muirfield Village Golf Club, Dublin, Ohio	Sept. 24-27	Europe	15	U.S.	13
1989	The Belfry GC, Sutton Coldfield, England	Sept. 22-24	U.S.	14 Tie	Europe	14
1991	The Ocean Course, Kiawah Island, S.C.	Sept. 26-29	U.S.	14½	Europe	13½
1993	The Belfry GC, Sutton Coldfield, England	Sept. 24-26	U.S.	15	Europe	13

RECAPITULATION: 29 Events, U.S. 22 wins-Europe or Britain 5 wins-Ties 2.

U.S. WOMEN'S OPEN CHAMPIONSHIP

YEAR	WINNER	SCORE	RUNNER-UP	COURSE
1946	Patty Berg	5 & 4	Betty Jameson	Spokane CC, Spokane, Wash.
1947	Betty Jameson	295	(a) Sally Sessions	Starmount Forest CC,
			(a) Polly Riley	Greensboro, N.C.
1948	Babe Zaharias	300	Betty Hicks	Atlantic City CC, Northfield, N.J.
1949	Louise Suggs	291	Babe Zaharias	Prince Georges CC, Landover, Md.
1950	Babe Zaharias	291	(a) Betsy Rawls	Rolling Hills CC, Wichita, Kan.
1951	Betsy Rawls	293	Louise Suggs	Druid Hills GC, Atlanta
1952	Louise Suggs	284	Marlene Hagge	Bala GC, Philadelphia
			Betty Jameson	
1953	† Betsy Rawls (70)	302	Jackie Pung (77)	CC of Rochester, Rochester, N.Y.
1954	Babe Zaharias	291	Betty Hicks	Salem CC, Peabody, Mass.
1955	Fay Crocker	299	Mary Lena Faulk	Wichita CC, Wichita, Kan.
			Louise Suggs	
1956	† Kathy Cornelius (75)	302	B. Mcintire (82)	Northland CC, Duluth, Minn.
1957	Betsy Rawls	299	Patty Berg	Winged Foot GC, Mamaroneck, N.Y.
1958	Mickey Wright	290	Louise Suggs	Forest Lake CC, Detroit
1959	Mickey Wright	287	Louise Suggs	Churchill Valley CC, Pittsburgh
1960	Betsy Rawls	292	Joyce Ziske	Worcester CC, Worcester, Mass.
1961	Mickey Wright	293	Betsy Rawls	Baltusrol GC, Springfield, N.J.
1962	Murle Breer	301	Jo Anne Prentice	Dunes GC, Myrtle Beach, S.C.
			Ruth Jessen	
1963	Mary Mills	289 (-3)	Sandra Haynie	Kenwood CC, Cincinnati
			Louise Suggs	
1964	† Mickey Wright (70)	290 (-2)	Ruth Jessen (72)	San Diego CC, Chula Vista, Calif.
1965	Carol Mann	290 (+2)	Kathy Cornelius	Atlantic City CC, Northfield, N.J.
1966	Sandra Spuzich	297 (+9)	Carol Mann	Hazeltine Nat. GC, Minneapolis
1967	(a) Catherine LaCoste	294 (+10)	Susie Berning	Hot Springs GC, Hot Springs, Va.
			Beth Stone	
1968	Susie Berning	289 (+5)	Mickey Wright	Moselem Springs GC,
				Fleetwood, Pa.
1969	Donna Caponi	294 (-2)	Peggy Wilson	Scenic Hills CC, Pensacola, Fla.
1970	Donna Caponi	287 (-1)	Sandra Haynie	Muskogee CC, Muskogee, Okla.
			Sandra Spuzich	
1971	JoAnne Carner	288 (E)	Kathy Whitworth	Kahkwa CC, Erie, Pa.
1972	Susie Berning	299 (+11)	Kathy Ahern	Winged Foot GC, Mamaroneck, N.Y.
			Pam Barnett	
			Judy Rankin	
1973	Susie Berning	290 (+2)	Gloria Ehret	CC of Rochester, Rochester, N.Y.
1974	Sandra Haynie	295 (+7)	Carol Mann	La Grange CC, La Grange, Ill.
			Beth Stone	
1975	Sandra Palmer	295 (+7)	JoAnne Carner	Atlantic City CC, Northfield, N.J.
			Sandra Post	
			(a) Nancy Lopez	
1976	† JoAnne Carner (76)	292 (+8)	Sandra Palmer (78)	Rolling Green CC, Springfield, Pa.
1977	Hollis Stacy	292 (+4)	Nancy Lopez	Hazeltine Nat. GC, Chaska, Minn.
1978	Hollis Stacy	289 (+5)	JoAnne Carner	CC of Indianapolis, Indianapolis
			Sally Little	
1979	Jerilyn Britz	284 (E)	Debbie Massey	Brooklawn CC, Fairfield, Conn.
			Sandra Palmer	
1980	Amy Alcott	280 (-4)	Hollis Stacy	Richland CC, Nashville
1981	Pat Bradley	279 (-9)	Beth Daniel	La Grange CC, La Grange, Ill.
1982	Janet Anderson	283 (-5)	Beth Daniel	Del Paso CC, Sacramento
			Sandra Haynie	
			Donna White	
			JoAnne Carner	
1983	Jan Stephenson	290 (+6)	JoAnne Carner	Cedar Ridge CC, Tulsa
			Patty Sheehan	
1984	Hollis Stacy	290 (+2)	Rosie Jones	Salem CC, Peabody, Mass.
1985	Kathy Baker	280 (-8)	Judy Dickinson	Baltusrol GC, Springfield, N.J.
1986	† Jane Geddes (71)	287 (-1)	Sally Little (73)	NCR GC, Dayton, Ohio
1987	† Laura Davies (71)	285 (-3)	Ayako Okamoto (73)	Plainfield CC, Plainfield, N.J.
			JoAnne Carner (74)	
1988	Liselotte Neumann	277 (-7)	Patty Sheehan	Baltimore CC, Baltimore
1989	Betsy King	278 (-4)	Nancy Lopez	Indian Wood G&CC, Lake
				Orion, Mich.
1990	Betsy King	284 (-4)	Patty Sheehan	Atlanta Athletic Club, Duluth, Ga.
1991	Meg Mallon	283 (-1)	Pat Bradley	Colonial CC, Fort Worth
1992	† Patty Sheehan	280 (-4)	Juli Inkster	Oakmont CC, Oakmont, Pa.
1993	Lauri Merten	280 (-8)	Donna Andrews	Crooked Stick GC, Carmel, Ind.
			Helen Alfredsson	
1994	Patty Sheehan	277 (-7)	Tammie Green	Indianwood G&CC, Lake
				Orion, Mich.
1995	Annika Sorenstam	278 (-2)	Meg Mallon	Broadmoor GC, Colorado
				Springs, Co.

MCDONALD'S LPGA CHAMPIONSHIP

YEAR	WINNER	SCORE	RUNNER-UP	COURSE
1955	†† Beverly Hanson	220 (4 & 3)	Louise Suggs	Orchard Ridge CC, Ft. Wayne, Ind.
1956	*Marlene Hagge	291	Patty Berg	Forest Lake CC, Detroit
1957	Louise Suggs	285	Wiffi Smith	Churchill Valley CC, Pittsburgh
1958	Mickey Wright	288	Fay Crocker	Churchill CC, Pittsburgh
1959	Betsy Rawls	288	Patty Berg	Sheraton Hotel CC, French Lick, Ind.
1960	Mickey Wright	292	Louise Suggs	Sheraton Hotel CC, French Lick, Ind.
1961	Mickey Wright	287	Louise Suggs	Stardust CC, Las Vegas
1962	Judy Kimball	282	Shirley Spork	Stardust CC, Las Vegas
1963	Mickey Wright	294 (+10)	Mary Lena Faulk	Stardust CC, Las Vegas
			Mary Mills	
			Louise Suggs	
1964	Mary Mills	278 (-6)	Mickey Wright	Stardust CC, Las Vegas
1965	Sandra Haynie	279 (-5)	Clifford A. Creed	Stardust CC, Las Vegas
1966	Gloria Ehret	282 (-2)	Mickey Wright	Stardust CC, Las Vegas
1967	Kathy Whitworth	284 (-8)	Shirley Englehorn	Pleasant Valley CC, Sutton, Mass.
1968	Sandra Post (68)	294 (+2)	Kathy Whitworth (75)	Pleasant Valley CC, Sutton, Mass.
1969	Betsy Rawls	293 (+1)	Susie Berning	Concord GC, Kiameshia Lake, N.Y.
			Carol Mann	
1970	Shirley Englehorn	285 (-7)	Kathy Whitworth	Pleasant Valley CC, Sutton, Mass.
1971	Kathy Whitworth	288 (-4)	Kathy Ahern	Pleasant Valley CC, Sutton, Mass.
1972	Kathy Ahern	293(+1)	Jane Blalock	Pleasant Valley CC, Sutton, Mass.
1973	Mary Mills	288 (-4)	Betty Burfeindt	Pleasant Valley CC, Sutton, Mass.
1974	Sandra Haynie	288 (-4)	JoAnne Carner	Pleasant Valley CC, Sutton, Mass.
1975	Kathy Whitworth	288 (-4)	Sandra Haynie	Pine Ridge GC, Baltimore
1976	Betty Burfeindt	287 (-5)	Judy Rankin	Pine Ridge GC, Baltimore
1977	Chako Higuchi	279 (-9)	Pat Bradley	Bay Tree Golf Plantation
			Sandra Post	N. Myrtle Beach, S.C.
			Judy Rankin	
1978	Nancy Lopez	275 (-13)	Amy Alcott	Jack Nicklaus GC, Kings Island, Ohio
1979	Donna Caponi	279 (-9)	Jerilyn Britz	Jack Nicklaus GC, Kings Island, Ohio
1980	Sally Little	285 (-3)	Jane Blalock	Jack Nicklaus GC, Kings Island, Ohio
1981	Donna Caponi	280 (-8)	Jerilyn Britz	Jack Nicklaus GC, King's Island, Ohio
			Pat Meyers	
1982	Jan Stephenson	279 (-9)	JoAnne Carner	Jack Nicklaus GC, Kings Island, Ohio
1983	Patty Sheehan	279 (-9)	Sandra Haynie	Jack Nicklaus GC, Kings Island, Ohio
1984	Patty Sheehan	272 (-16)	Beth Daniel	Jack Nicklaus GC, Kings Island, Ohio
			Pat Bradley	
1985	Nancy Lopez	273 (-15)	Alice Miller	Jack Nicklaus GC, Kings Island, Ohio
1986	Pat Bradley	277 (-11)	Patty Sheehan	Jack Nicklaus GC, Kings Island, Ohio
1987	Jane Geddes	275 (-13)	Betsy King	Jack Nicklaus GC, Kings Island, Ohio
1988	Sherri Turner	281 (-7)	Amy Alcott	Jack Nicklaus GC, Kings Island, Ohio
1989	Nancy Lopez	274 (-14)	Ayako Okamoto	Jack Nicklaus GC, Kings Island, Ohio
1990	Beth Daniel	280 (-4)	Rosie Jones	Bethesda CC, Bethesda, Md.
1991	Meg Mallon	274 (-10)	Pat Bradley	Bethesda CC, Bethesda, Md.
			Ayako Okamoto	
1992	Betsy King	267 (-17)	JoAnne Carner	Bethesda CC, Bethesda, Md.
			Karen Noble	
			Liselotte Neumann	
1993	Patty Sheehan	275 (-9)	Lauri Merten	Bethesda CC, Bethesda, Md.
1994	Laura Davies	279 (-5)	Alice Ritzman	Du Pont CC, Wilmington, Del.
1995	Kelly Robbins	274 (-10)	Laura Davies	Du Pont CC, Wilmington, Del.

NABISCO DINAH SHORE

MISSION HILLS COUNTRY CLUB, RANCHO MIRAGE, CALIF. (DESIGNATED MAJOR COMMENCING 1983.)

YEAR	WINNER	SCORE	RUNNER-UP
COLGATE DINAH SHORE			
1972	Jane Blalock	213 (-3)	Carol Mann, Judy Rankin
1973	Mickey Wright	284 (-4)	Joyce Kazmierski
1974	*Jo Ann Prentice	289 (+1)	Jane Blalock, Sandra Haynie
1975	Sandra Palmer	283 (-5)	Kathy McMullen
1976	Judy Rankin	285 (-3)	Betty Burfeindt
1977	Kathy Whitworth	289 (+1)	JoAnne Carner, Sally Little
1978	*Sandra Post	283 (-5)	Penny Pulz
1979	Sandra Post	276 (-12)	Nancy Lopez
1980	Donna Caponi	275 (-13)	Amy Alcott
1981	Nancy Lopez	277 (-11)	Carolyn Hill
NABISCO DINAH SHORE			
1982	Sally Little	278 (-10)	Hollis Stacy, Sandra Haynie
1983	Amy Alcott	282 (-6)	Beth Daniel, Kathy Whitworth
1984	*Juli Inkster	280 (-8)	Pat Bradley
1985	Alice Miller	275 (-13)	Jan Stephenson
1986	Pat Bradley	280 (-8)	Val Skinner
1987	*Betsy King	283 (-5)	Patty Sheehan
1988	Amy Alcott	274 (-14)	Colleen Walker
1989	Juli Inkster	279 (-9)	Tammie Green
			JoAnne Carner
1990	Betsy King	283 (-5)	Kathy Postlewait, Shirley Furlong
1991	Amy Alcott	273 (-15)	Dottie Mochrie
1992	*Dottie Mochrie	279 (-9)	Juli Inkster
1993	Helen Alfredsson	284 (-4)	Amy Benz, Tina Barrett
1994	Donna Andrews	276 (-12)	Laura Davies
1995	Nanci Bowen	285 (-3)	Susie Redman

DU MAURIER LTD. CLASSIC (Designated major commencing 1979.)

YEAR	WINNER	SCORE	RUNNER-UP	COURSE
LA CANADIENNE				
1973	*Jocelyne Bourassa	214 (-5)	Sandra Haynie Judy Rankin	Montreal GC, Montreal
PETER JACKSON CLASSIC				
1974	Carole Jo Callison	208 (-11)	JoAnne Carner	Candiac GC, Montreal
1975	*JoAnne Carner	214 (-5)	Carol Mann	St. George's CC, Toronto
1976	*Donna Caponi	212 (-4)	Judy Rankin	Cedar Brae G & CC, Toronto
1977	Judy Rankin	214 (-4)	Pat Meyers Sandra Palmer	Lachute G & CC, Montreal
1978	JoAnne Carner	278 (-14)	Hollis Stacy	St. George's CC, Toronto
1979	Amy Alcott	285 (-7)	Nancy Lopez	Richelieu Valley CC, Montreal
1980	Pat Bradley	277 (-11)	JoAnne Carner	St. George's CC, Toronto
1981	Jan Stephenson	278 (-10)	Nancy Lopez Pat Bradley	Summerlea CC, Dorion, Quebec
1982	Sandra Haynie	280 (-8)	Beth Daniel	St. George's CC, Toronto
DU MAURIER LTD. CLASSIC				
1983	Hollis Stacy	277 (-11)	JoAnne Carner Alice Miller	Beaconsfield GC, Montreal
1984	Juli Inkster	279 (-9)	Ayako Okamoto	St. George's G & CC, Toronto
1985	Pat Bradley	278 (-10)	Jane Geddes	Beaconsfield CC, Montreal
1986	*Pat Bradley	276 (-12)	Ayako Okamoto	Board of Trade CC, Toronto
1987	Jody Rosenthal	272 (-16)	Ayako Okamoto	Islesmere GC, Laval, Quebec
1988	Sally Little	279 (-9)	Laura Davies	Vancouver GC, Coquitlam, B.C.
1989	Tammie Green	279 (-9)	Pat Bradley Betsy King	Beaconstield GC, Montreal
1990	Cathy Johnston	276 (-16)	Patty Sheehan	Westmount G & CC, Kitchener, Ontario
1991	Nancy Scranton	279 (-9)	Debbie Massey	Vancouver GC, Coquitiam, B.C.
1992	Sherri Steinhauer	277 (-11)	Judy Dickinson	St. Charles CC, Winnipeg, Manitoba
1993	*Brandie Burton	277 (-11)	Betsy King	London Hunt and CC, London, Ontario
1994	Martha Nause	279 (-9)	Michelle McGann	Ottawa Hunt Club, Ottawa

\# - Amateur
@ - Rain shortened
@@ - Rain delayed
* - Won sudden-death playoff
† - Won 18-hole playoff
†† - Won match-play final

CHICK-FIL-A CHARITY CHAMPIONSHIP

EAGLE'S LANDING CC, STOCKBRIDGE, GA.

SEGA WOMEN'S CHAMPIONSHIP
1992	Dottie Mochrie	277 (-11)

ATLANTA WOMEN'S CHAMPIONSHIP
1993	Trish Johnson	282 (-6)
1994	Val Skinner	206 (-10)

CHICK-FIL-A CHARITY CHAMPIONSHIP
1995	Laura Davies	201 (-15)

SPRINT CHAMPIONSHIP

KILLEARN CC & INN, TALLAHASSEE, FLA. (1990-95).

CENTEL CLASSIC
1990	Beth Daniel	271 (-17)
1991	Pat Bradley	278 (-10)
1992	Da. Ammaccapane	208 (-8)

SPRINT CHAMPIONSHIP
1993	Kristi Albers	279 (-9)
1994	Sherri Steinhauer	273 (-15)
1995	Van Skinner	273 (-15)

CENTEL SENIOR CHALLENGE

KILLEARN CC & INN, TALLAHASSEE, FLA.

1991	Sandra Palmer	143 (-3)
1992	Sandra Palmer	139 (-7)
1993	Sandra Palmer	138 (-8)
1994	Sandra Palmer	143 (-1)
1995	Sandra Palmer	138 (-8)

STAR BANK LPGA CLASSIC

CC OF THE NORTH, BEAVER CREEK, OHIO (1994-95).

1994	*Maggie Will	210 (-6)

STAR BANK LPGA CLASSIC
1995	Chris Johnson	210 (-6)

CHRYSLER-PLYMOUTH TOURNAMENT OF CHAMPIONS

GRAND CYPRESS RESORT, ORLANDO (1994-95).

1994	Dottie Mochrie	287 (-1)
1995	Dawn Coe Jones	281 (-7)

FRIENDLY'S CLASSIC

CRESTVIEW CC, AGAWAM, MASS (1995).

1995	Becky Iverson	276 (-12)

GHP HEARTLAND CLASSIC

FOREST HILLS CC, ST. LOUIS.

HEARTLAND CLASSIC
1994	Liselotte Neumann	278 (-10)

INAMORI CLASSIC

MOVED ANNUALLY (1980-87). STONE RIDGE CC, POWAY, CALIF. (1988-93).

INAMORI CLASSIC
1980	Amy Alcott	280 (-12)
1981	*Hollis Stacy	286 (-6)
1982	Patty Sheehan	277 (-15)
1983	@Patty Sheehan	209 (-10)
1984	No tournament	

KYOCERA INAMORI GOLF CLASSIC
1985	Beth Daniel	286 (-2)
1986	Patty Sheehan	278 (-10)
1987	Ayako Okamoto	275 (-13)

SAN DIEGO INAMORI GOLF CLASSIC
1988	Ayako Okamoto	272 (-12)

RED ROBIN KYOCERA INAMORI CLASSIC
1989	Patti Rizzo	277 (-7)
1990	Kris Monaghan	276 (-8)

INAMORI CLASSIC
1991	Laura Davies	277 (-11)
1992	Judy Dickinson	277 (-11)
1993	Kris Monaghan	275 (-13)

CUP NOODLES HAWAIIAN LADIES OPEN

TURTLE BAY RESORT (1987-89). KO OLINA GC, EWA BEACH, OAHU, HAWAII (1990-95).

TSUMURA LADIES OPEN
1987	Cindy Rarick	207 (-9)

ORIENT LEASING HAWAIIAN LADIES OPEN
1988	Ayako Okamoto	213 (-3)

ORIX HAWAIIAN LADIES OPEN
1989	Sherri Turner	205 (-11)
1990	Beth Daniel	210 (-6)
1991	Patty Sheehan	207 (-9)

CUP NOODLES HAWAIIAN LADIES OPEN
1992	Lisa Walters	208 (-8)
1993	Lisa Walters	210 (-6)
1994	Marta Figueras-Dotti	209 (-7)
1995	Barb Thomas	204 (-12)

JAL BIG APPLE CLASSIC

WYKAGYL CC, NEW ROCHELLE, N.Y.

1990	Betsy King	273 (-15)
1991	Betsy King	279 (-5)
1992	Juli Inkster	273 (-11)
1993	Hiromi Kobayashi	278 (-6)
1994	*Beth Daniel	276 (-8)
1995	Tracy Kerdyk	273 (-11)

JAMIE FARR TOLEDO CLASSIC

GLENGARRY CC, TOLEDO, OHIO (1984-84). HIGHLAND MEADOWS GC, SYLVANIA, OHIO (1989-95).

1984	Lauri Peterson	278 (-10)
1985	Penny Hammel	278 (-10)
1986	No tournament	
1987	Jane Geddes	280 (-8)
1988	Laura Davies	277 (-11)
1989	Penny Hammel	206 (-7)
1990	Tina Purizer	205 (-8)
1991	*Alice Miller	205 (-8)
1992	Patty Sheehan	209 (-4)
1993	Brandie Burton	201 (-12)
1994	*Kelly Robbins	204 (-9)
1995	Kathryn Marshall	205 (-8)

TORAY QUEENS CUP

MOVED ANNUALLY (1973-95). LPGA JAPAN CLASSIC (UNOFFICIAL EVENT.)

1973	Jan Ferraris	216 (even)
1974	Chako Higuchi	218 (-4)
1975	Shelley Hamlin	218 (-1)

MIZUNO JAPAN CLASSIC
1976	Donna Caponi	217 (-5)
1977	Debbie Massey	220 (-2)
1978	*Michiko Okada	216 (-6)
1979	Amy Alcott	211 (-11)

MAZDA JAPAN CLASSIC
1980	Tatsuko Ohsako	213 (-9)
1981	Patty Sheehan	213 (-9)
1982	Nancy Lopez	207 (-9)
1983	Pat Bradley	206 (-10)
1984	Nayoko Yoshikawa	210 (-6)
1985	Jane Blalock	206 (-10)
1986	*Ai-Yu Tu	213 (-3)
1987	Yuko Moriguchi	206 (-10)
1988	*Patty Sheehan	206 (-10)
1989	Elaine Crosby	205 (-11)
1990	@Debbie Massey	133 (-11)
1991	Liselotte Neumann	211 (-5)
1992	*Betsy King	205 (-11)

TORAY QUEENS CUP
1993	Betsy King	205 (-11)
1994	*Ko Woo-Soon	206 (-10)

JCPENNEY LPGA SKINS GAME

STONEBRIAR CC, FRISCO, TEXAS (UNOFFICIAL EVENT).

1990	Jan Stephenson	6 skins
1991	No tournament	
1992	Pat Bradley	8 skins
1993	Betsy King	7 skins
1994	Patty Sheehan	11 skins
1995	Dottie Mochrie	8 skins

JCPENNEYCLASSIC

DORAL CC, MIAMI (1976). BARDMOOR CC, LARGO, FLA. (1977-89). LNNISBROOK RESORT, TARPON SPRINGS, FLA. (1990-94). (UNOFFICIAL EVENT.)

PEPSI-COLA MIXED TEAM CHAMPIONSHIP
1976	JoAnn Washam/ Chi Chi Rodriguez	275 (-13)
1977	Hollis Stacy/ Jerry Pate	270 (-18)

JCPENNEY CLASSIC
1978	Pat Bradley/ Lon Hinkle	267 (-21)
1979	Murle Breer/ Dave Eichelberger	268 (-20)
1980	Nancy Lopez/ Curtis Strange	268 (-24)
1981	Beth Daniel/ Tom Kite	270 (-18)
1982	JoAnne Carner/ John Mahaffey	268 (-20)
1983	Jan Stephenson/ Fred Couples	264 (-24)
1984	Vicki Alvarez/ Mike Donald	270 (-18)
1985	Laurie Rinker/ Larry Rinker	267 (-21)
1986	Juli Inkster/ Tom Purtzer	265 (-23)
1987	Jane Crafter/ Steve Jones	268 (-20)
1988	Amy Benz/ John Huston	269 (-19)
1989	Pat Bradley/ Bill Glasson	267 (-21)
1990	Beth Daniel/ Davis Love III	266 (-18)
1991	*Kris Tschetter/ Billy Andrade	266 (-18)
1992	Dottie Mochrie/ Dan Forsman	264 (-20)
1993	Melissa McNamara/ Mike Spring	265 (-19)
1994	*Marta Figueras-Dotti/ Brad Bryant	262 (-22)

LADY KEYSTONE OPEN

SPORTMAN'S GC (1975-76). ARMITAGE GC (1977). HERSHEY (PA.) CC (1978-94).

1975	Susie Berning	142 (-2)
1976	Susie Berning	215 (-1)
1977	Sandra Spuzich	201 (-9)
1978	Pat Bradley	206 (-10)
1979	Nancy Lopez	212 (-4)
1980	JoAnne Carner	207 (-9)
1981	JoAnne Carner	203 (-13)
1982	Jan Stephenson	211 (-5)
1983	Jan Stephenson	205 (-11)

1984	Amy Alcott	208 (-8)
1985	Juli Inkster	209 (-7)
1986	*Juli Inkster	210 (-6)
1987	Ayako Okamoto	208 (-8)
1988	*Shirley Furlong	205 (-11)
1989	Laura Davies	207 (-9)
1990	Cathy Gerring	208 (-8)
1991	Colleen Walker	207 (-9)
1992	Da. Ammaccapane	208 (-8)
1993	Val Skinner	210 (-6)
1994	Elaine Crosby	211 (-5)

LAS VEGAS LPGA AT CANYON GATE

Desert Inn CC, Las Vegas.

DESERT INN LPGA INTERNATIONAL

1990	Maggie Will	214 (-2)
1991	Penny Hammel	211 (-5)

LAS VEGAS LPGA INTERNATIONAL

1992	Dana Lofland	212 (-4)

LAS VEGAS LPGA AT CANYON GATE

1993	Trish Johnson	209 (-7)

CORNING CLASSIC

Corning (N.Y.) CC.

1979	Penny Pulz	284 (+4)
1980	Donna Caponi	281 (-7)
1981	Kathy Hite	282 (-6)
1982	Sandra Spuzich	280 (-8)
1983	Patty Sheehan	272 (-16)
1984	JoAnne Carner	281 (-7)
1985	Patti Rizzo	272 (-16)
1986	Laurie Rinker	278 (-10)
1987	Cindy Rarick	275 (-13)
1988	Sherri Turner	273 (-15)
1989	Ayako Okamoto	272 (-12)
1990	Pat Bradley	274 (-10)
1991	Betsy King	273 (-15)
1992	Colleen Walker	276 (-12)
1993	*Kelly Robbins	277 (-11)
1994	Beth Daniel	278 (-10)
1995	Alison Nicholas	275 (-13)

McCALL'S LPGA CLASSIC AT STRATTON MOUNTAIN

Stratton Mountain (Vt.) CC.

STRATTON MOUNTAIN LPGA CLASSIC

1990	*Cathy Gerring	281 (-7)
1991	M. McNamara	278 (-10)

McCALL'S LPGA CLASSIC AT STRATTON MOUNTAIN

1992	F. Descampe	278 (-6)
1993	Dana Dormann	275 (-13)
1994	Carolyn Hill	275 (-13)
1995	Dottie Mochrie	204 (-12)

McDONALD'S CHAMPIONSHIP

White Manor CC (1981-86). Du Pont CC, Wilmington, Del. (1987-95).

McDONALD'S KIDS CLASSIC

1981	Sandra Post	282 (-6)
1982	JoAnne Carner	276 (-12)
1983	*Beth Daniel	286 (-2)
1984	Patty Sheehan	281 (-7)

McDONALD'S CHAMPIONSHIP

1985	Alice Miller	272 (-16)
1986	Juli Inkster	281 (-7)
1987	Betsy King	278 (-6)
1988	Kathy Postlewait	276 (-8)
1989	Betsy King	272 (-12)
1990	Patty Sheehan	275 (-9)
1991	Beth Daniel	273 (-11)
1992	Ayako Okamoto	205 (-8)
1993	Laura Davies	277 (-7)

EDINA REALTY LPGA CLASSIC

Edinburgh USA GC, Brooklyn Park, Minn.

NORTHGATE CLASSIC

1990	Beth Daniel	203 (-13)

NORTHGATE COMPUTER CLASSIC

1991	*Cindy Rarick	211 (-5)
1992	Kris Tschetter	211 (-5)
1993	Hiromi Kobayashi	205 (-11)

MINNESOTA LPGA CLASSIC

1994	Liselotte Neumann	205 (-11)

EDINA REALTY CLASSIC

1995	Julie Larsen	205 (-11)

NICHIREI INTERNATIONAL US-JAPAN TEAM CHAMPIONSHIP

Moved annually (1979-92). Ami GC Ibaragi-Ken, Japan (1993-95). (Unofficial event.)

	individual	team

PIONEER CUP

1979	Yuko Moriguchl	USA
1980	Amy Alcott	USA
1981	Chako Higuchi	Japan
1982	Nayako Yoshikawa	USA

SPORTS NIPPON TEAM MATCH

1983	Chako Higuchi	USA

NICHIREI INTERNATIONAL US-JAPAN TEAM CHAMPIONSHIP

1984	Hollis Stacy	Japan
1985	Jan Stephenson	USA
1986	Ayako Okamoto	USA
1987	Fukumi Tani	USA
1988	Beth Daniel	USA
1989	Colleen Walker	USA
1990	No ind. competition	USA
1991	No ind. competition	USA
1992	No ind. competition	USA
1993	Laura Davies	USA
1994	No ind. competition	USA

OLDSMOBILE CLASSIC

Walnut Hills CC, East Lansing, Mich.

OLDSMOBILE CLASSIC

1992	Barb Mucha	276 (-12)
1993	Jane Geddes	277 (-11)
1994	Beth Daniel	268 (-20)
1995	Dale Eggeling	274 (-14)

HEALTHSOUTH CLASSIC

Deer Creek CC (1980-85). Stonebridge G&CC (1986-89). Wycliffe G&CC, Lake Worth, Fla. (1990-94). Eagle Pines GC, Walt Disney World Resort, Lake Buena Vista, Fla. (1995)

WHIRLPOOL CHAMPIONSHIP OF DEER CREEK

1980	JoAnne Carner	282 (-10)
1981	Sandra Palmer	284 (-8)
1982	*Hollis Stacy	282 (-6)

MAZDA CLASSIC OF DEER CREEK

1983	Pat Bradley	272 (-16)
1984	Silvia Bertolaccini	280 (-8)
1985	Hollis Stacy	280 (-8)

MAZDA CLASSIC

1986	Val Skinner	280 (-8)
1987	*Kathy Postlewait	286 (-2)
1988	Nancy Lopez	283 (-5)

OLDSMOBILE LPGA CLASSIC

1989	*Dottie Mochrie	279 (-9)
1990	*Pat Bradley	281 (-7)
1991	Meg Mallon	276 (-12)
1992	*Colleen Walker	279 (-9)

HEALTHSOUTH PALM BEACH CLASSIC

1993	*Tammie Green	208 (-8)
1994	Dawn Coe-Jones	201 (-15)
1995	Pat Bradley	211 (-5)

PING AT&T WIRELESS SERVICES LPGA GOLF CHAMPIONSHIP

Rotated among Portland GC, Columbia Edgewater CC, and Riverside G & CC, Portland, Ore. (1972-94).

PORTLAND CLASSIC

1972	Kathy Whitworth	212 (-7)
1973	@Kathy Whitworth	144 (-2)
1974	JoAnne Carner	211 (-5)
1975	Jo Ann Washam	215 (-1)
1976	*Donna Caponi	217 (-2)

PORTLAND PING TEAM CHAMPIONSHIP (Unofficial event.)

1977	*JoAnne Carner/ Judy Rankin	202 (-17)
1978	*Donna Caponi/ Kathy Whitworth	203 (-16)
1979	Nancy Lopez/ Jo Ann Washam	198 (-21)
1980	Donna Caponi/ Kathy Whitworth	195 (-24)
1981	*Donna Caponi/ Kathy Whitworth	203 (-16)
1982	*Sandra Haynie/ Kathy McMullen	196 (-20)

PORTLAND PING CHAMPIONSHIP

1983	*JoAnne Carner	212 (-4)
1984	Amy Alcott	212 (-4)
1985	Nancy Lopez	215 (-1)

PING–CELLULAR ONE GOLF CHAMPIONSHIP

1986	Ayako Okamoto	207 (-9)
1987	Nancy Lopez	210 (-6)
1988	Betsy King	213 (-3)
1989	M. Spencer-Devlin	214 (-2)
1990	Patty Sheehan	208 (-8)
1991	Michelle Estill	208 (-8)
1992	*Nancy Lopez	209 (-9)
1993	Donna Andrews	208 (-8)
1994	Missie McGeorge	207 (-9)

PING/WELCH'S CHAMPIONSHIP (MASSACHUSETTS)

Radisson-Ferncroft CC (1980-84). Sheraton Tara Hotel/ Resort at Ferncroft (1985-90). Blue Hill CC, Canton, Mass. (1992-94).

BOSTON FIVE CLASSIC

1980	Dale Eggering	276 (-12)
1981	Donna Caponi	276 (-12)
1982	Sandra Palmer	281 (-7)
1983	Patti Rizzo	277 (-11)
1984	Laurie Rinker	286 (-2)
1985	Judy Dickinson	280 (-8)
1986	Jane Geddes	281 (-7)
1987	Jane Geddes	277 (-11)
1988	Colleen Walker	274 (-14)
1989	Amy Alcott	272 (-16)
1990	*Barb Mucha	277 (-11)

LPGA BAY STATE CLASSIC

1991	Juli Inkster	275 (-13)

WELCH'S CLASSIC

1992	Dottie Mochrie	278 (-10)

PING/WELCH'S CHAMPIONSHIP (Boston)

1993	*Missie Berteotti	276 (-12)
1994	Helen Alfredsson	274 (-14)
1995	Beth Daniel	271 (-17)

PING/WELCH'S CHAMPIONSHIP (ARIZONA)

Randolph Park North, Tucson, Ariz.

ARIZONA COPPER CLASSIC

1981	Nancy Lopez	278 (-14)
1982	*Ayako Okamoto	281 (-7)

TUCSON CONQUISTADORES OPEN

1983	Jan Stephenson	207 (-9)
1984	Chris Johnson	272 (-16)

CIRCLE K LPGA TUCSON OPEN

1985	Amy Alcott	279 (-9)
1986	Penny Pulz	276 (-12)
1987	Betsy King	281 (-7)
1988	Laura Davies	278 (-10)
1989	Lori Garbacz	274 (-14)
1990	Colleen Walker	276 (-12)

PING/WELCH'S CHAMPIONSHIP (Tucson)

1991	Chris Johnson	273 (-15)
1992	Brandie Burton	277 (-11)
1993	Meg Mallon	272 (-16)
1994	Donna Andrews	276 (-12)
1995	Dottie Mochrie	278 (-10)

ROCHESTER INTERNATIONAL

Locust Hill CC, Pittsford, N.Y.

BANKERS TRUST CLASSIC

1977	Pat Bradley	213 (-6)
1978	Nancy Lopez	214 (-5)

SARAH COVENTRY

1979	Jane Blalock	280 (-12)
1980	Nancy Lopez	283 (-9)
1981	Nancy Lopez	285 (-7)

ROCHESTER INTERNATIONAL

1982	*Sandra Haynie	276 (-12)
1983	Ayako Okamoto	282 (-6)
1984	*Kathy Whitworth	281 (-7)
1985	Pat Bradley	280 (-8)
1986	Judy Dickinson	281 (-7)
1987	Deb Richard	280 (-8)
1988	*Mei-chi Cheng	287 (-1)
1989	*Patty Sheehan	278 (-10)
1990	Patty Sheehan	271 (-17)
1991	Rosie Jones	276 (-12)
1992	Patty Sheehan	269 (-19)
1993	Tammie Green	276 (-12)
1994	Lisa Kiggens	273 (-15)
1995	*Patty Sheehan	278 (-10)

SAFECO CLASSIC

Meridian Valley CC, Kent, Wash.

1982	Patty Sheehan	276 (-12)
1983	Juli Inkster	283 (-5)
1984	Kathy Whitworth	279 (-9)
1985	JoAnne Carner	279 (-9)
1986	Judy Dickinson	274 (-14)
1987	Jan Stephenson	277 (-11)
1988	Juli Inkster	278 (-10)
1989	Beth Daniel	273 (-15)
1990	Patty Sheehan	270 (-18)
1991	*Pat Bradley	280 (-8)
1992	Colleen Walker	277 (-11)
1993	Brandie Burton	274 (-14)
1994	Deb Richard	276 (-12)

SARA LEE CLASSIC

Hermitage GC, Old Hickory, Tenn.

1988	*Patti Rizzo	207 (-9)
1989	Kathy Postlewait	203 (-13)
1990	Ayako Okamoto	210 (-6)
1991	Nancy Lopez	206 (-10)
1992	*Maggie Will	207 (-9)
1993	*Meg Mallon	205 (-11)
1994	Laura Davies	203 (-13)
1995	Michelle McGann	202 (-14)

SHOPRITE LPGA CLASSIC

Marriott Seaview CC & Resort (1986-87). Sands CC (1988-90). Greate Bay Resort & CC, Somers Point, N.J. (1991-95).

ATLANTIC CITY CLASSIC

1986	Juli Inkster	209 (-4)
1987	Betsy King	207 (-6)
1988	*Juli Inkster	206 (-7)
1989	Nancy Lopez	206 (-4)
1990	Chris Johnson	275 (-5)
1991	Jane Geddes	208 (-5)

SHOPRITE LPGA CLASSIC

1992	Anne-Marie Palli	207 (-6)
1993	Shelley Hamlin	204 (-9)
1994	Donna Andrews	207 (-6)
1995	Betsy King	204 (-9)

STANDARD REGISTER PING

HILLCREST GC (1980-82). ARIZONA BILTMORE CC (1983-86). MOON VALLEY CC, PHOENIX (1987-95).

SUN CITY CLASSIC

1980	Jan Stephenson	275 (-13)
1981	Patty Hayes	277 (-15)
1982	*Beth Daniel	278 (-10)

SAMARITAN TURQUOISE CLASSIC

1983	Anne-Marie Palli	205 (-14)
1984	Chris Johnson	276 (-12)
1985	*Betsy King	280 (-8)

STANDARD REGISTER TURQUOISE CLASSIC

1986	M.B. Zimmerman	278 (-10)
1987	Pat Bradley	286 (-6)
1988	Ok-Hee Ku	281 (-7)
1989	Allison Finney	282 (-6)
1990	Pat Bradley	280 (-12)

STANDARD REGISTER PING

1991	Da. Ammaccapane	283 (-9)
1992	Da. Ammaccapane	279 (-13)
1993	Patty Sheehan	275 (-17)
1994	Laura Davies	277 (-15)
1995	Laura Davies	280 (-12)

STATE FARM RAIL CLASSIC

RAIL GC, SPRINGFIELD, ILL.

JERRY LEWIS MUSCULAR DYSTROPHY CLASSIC

1976	*Sandra Palmer	213 (-3)

STATE FARM RAIL CHARITY GOLF CLASSIC

1977	Hollis Stacy	271 (-17)
1978	Pat Bradley	276 (-12)
1979	Jo Ann Washam	275 (-13)
1980	Nancy Lopez	275 (-13)
1981	JoAnne Carner	205 (-11)
1982	JoAnne Carner	202 (-14)
1983	*Lauri Peterson	210 (-6)
1984	Cindy Hill	207 (-9)
1985	Betsy King	205 (-11)
1986	*Betsy King	205 (-11)
1987	Rosie Jones	208 (-8)
1988	Betsy King	207 (-9)
1989	Beth Daniel	203 (-13)
1990	Beth Daniel	203 (-13)
1991	Pat Bradley	197 (-19)
1992	*Nancy Lopez	199 (-17)
1993	*Helen Dobson	203 (-13)
1994	Barb Mucha	203 (-13)

CHICAGO CHALLENGE

OAK BROOK GC (1991). WHITE EAGLE CC, NAPERVILLE, ILL. (1992-94).

CHICAGO SUN-TIMES SHOOT-OUT

1991	Martha Nause	275 (-13)

SUN-TIMES CHALLENGE

1992	*Dottie Mochrie	216 (E)
1993	Cindy Schreyer	272 (-16)

CHICAGO CHALLENGE

1994	Jane Geddes	272 (-16)

WORLD CHAMPIONSHIP OF WOMEN'S GOLF

MOVED ANNUALLY (1980-93). NAPLES NATIONAL GC, NAPLES, FLA. (1994).

CHEVROLET WORLD CHAMPIONSHIP OF WOMEN'S GOLF

1980	Beth Daniel	282 (-6)
1981	Beth Daniel	284 (-4)
1982	JoAnne Carner	284 (-4)
1983	JoAnne Carner	282 (-6)
1984	Nancy Lopez	281 (-7)

NESTLE WORLD CHAMPIONSHIP

1985	Amy Alcott	274 (-14)
1986	Pat Bradley	279 (-9)
1987	Ayako Okamoto	282 (-6)
1988	Rosie Jones	279 (-9)
1989	Betsy King	275 (-13)

TROPHEE URBAN–WORLD CHAMPIONSHIP OF WOMEN'S GOLF

1990	Cathy Gerring	278 (-10)

Daikyo World Championship of Women's Golf

1991	Meg Mallon	216 (-3)

WORLD CHAMPIONSHIP OF WOMEN'S GOLF

1992	No tournament	
1993	Dottie Mochrie	283 (-5)
1994	Beth Daniel	274 (-14)

YOUNGSTOWN-WARREN LPGA CLASSIC

AVALON LAKES GC, WARREN, OHIO (1994-95).

PHAR-MOR IN YOUNGSTOWN

1990	*Beth Daniel	207 (-9)
1991	*Deb Richard	207 (-9)
1992	*Betsy King	209 (-7)

YOUNGSTOWN-WARREN LPGA CLASSIC

1993	Nancy Lopez	203 (-13)
1994	Tammie Green	206 (-10)
1995	*Michelle McGann	205 (-11)

PGA SENIORS' CHAMPIONSHIP

PGA SENIORS' CHAMPIONSHIP

YEAR	WINNER	SCORE	COURSE
1937	Jock Hutchinson	223	Augusta National GC, Augusta, Ga.
1938	*Fred McLeod	154	Augusta National GC, Augusta, Ga.
1939	No tournament		
1940	*Otto Hackbarth	146	North Shore CC & Bobby Jones GC, Sarasota, Fla.
1941	Jack Burke Sr.	142	Sarasota Bay CC & Bobby Jones GC, Sarasota, Fla.
1942	Eddie Williams	1 3	Fort Myers G & CC, Fort Myers, Fla.
1943-1944	No tournament		
1945	Eddie Williams	148	PGA National GC, Dunedin, Fla.
1946	*Eddie Williams	146	PGA National GC, Dunedin, Fla.
1947	Jock Hutchinson	145	PGA National GC, Dunedin, Fla.
1948	Charles McKenna	141	PGA National GC, Dunedin, Fla.
1949	Marshall Crichton	145	PGA National GC, Dunedin, Fla.
1950	Al Watrous	142	PGA National GC, Dunedin, Fla.
1951	*Al Watrous	142	PGA National GC, Dunedin, Fla.
1952	Ernie Newnham	146	PGA National GC, Dunedin, Fla.
1953	Harry Schwab	142	PGA National GC, Dunedin, Fla.
1954	Gene Sarazen	214	PGA National GC, Dunedin, Fla.
1955	Mortie Dutra	213	PGA National GC, Dunedin, Fla.
1956	Pete Burke	215	PGA National GC, Dunedin, Fla.
1957	*Al Watrous	210	PGA National GC, Dunedin, Fla.
1958	Gene Sarazen	288	PGA National GC, Dunedin, Fla.
1959	Willie Goggin	284	PGA National GC, Dunedin, Fla.
1960	Dick Metz	284	PGA National GC, Dunedin, Fla.
1961	Paul Runyan	278	PGA National GC, Dunedin, Fla.
1962	Paul Runyan	278	PGA National GC, Dunedin, Fla.
1963	Herman Barron	272	Port St. Lucie CC, Port St. Lucie, Fla.
1964	Sam Snead	279	PGA National GC, Palm Beach Gardens, Fla.
1965	Sam Snead	278	Fort Lauderdale CC, Fort Lauderdale, Fla.
1966	Freddie Haas	286	PGA National GC, Palm Beach Gardens, Fla.
1967	Sam Snead	279	PGA National GC, Palm Beach Gardens, Fla.
1968	Chandler Harper	279	PGA National GC, Palm Beach Gardens, Fla.
1969	Tommy Bolt	278	PGA National GC, Palm Beach Gardens, Fla.
1970	Sam Snead	290	PGA National GC, Palm Beach Gardens, Fla.
1971	Julius Boros	285	PGA National GC, Palm Beach Gardens, Fla.
1972	Sam Snead	286	PGA National GC, Palm Beach Gardens, Fla.
1973	Sam Snead	268	PGA National GC, Palm Beach Gardens, Fla.
1974	Roberto DeVicenzo	273	Port St. Lucie CC, Port St. Lucie, Fla.
1975	*Charlie Sifford	280	Walt Disney World (Magnolia), Orlando
1976	Pete Cooper	283	Walt Disney World (Magnolia), Orlando
1977	Julius Boros	283	Walt Disney World (Magnolia), Orlando
1978	*Joe Jimenez	286	Walt Disney World (Magnolia), Orlando
1979	*Jack Fleck	289	Walt Disney World (Magnolia), Orlando
1979	+Don January	270	Turnberry Isle CC, North Miami, Fla.
1980	*Arnold Palmer	289	Turnberry Isle CC, North Miami, Fla.
1981	Miller Barber	281	Turnberry Isle CC, North Miami, Fla.
1982	Don January	288	PGA National GC (Champion), Palm Beach Gardens, Fla.
1983	No tournament		
1984	Arnold Palmer	282	PGA National GC (Champion), Palm Beach Gardens, Fla.

GENERAL FOODS PGA SENIORS' CHAMPIONSHIP

YEAR	WINNER	SCORE	COURSE
1984	+Peter Thomson	286	PGA National GC (Champion), Palm Beach Gardens, Fla.
1985	No tournament		
1986	Gary Player	281	PGA National GC (Champion), Palm Beach Gardens, Fla.
1987	Chi Chi Rodriguez	282	PGA National GC (Champion), Palm Beach Gardens, Fla.
1988	Gary Player	284	PGA National GC (Champion), Palm Beach Gardens, Fla.
1989	Larry Mowry	281	PGA National GC (Champion), Palm Beach Gardens, Fla.

PGA SENIORS' CHAMPIONSHIP

YEAR	WINNER	SCORE	COURSE
1990	Gary Player	281	PGA National GC (Champion), Palm Beach Gardens, Fla.
1991	Jack Nicklaus	271	PGA National GC (Champion), Palm Beach Gardens, Fla.
1992	Lee Trevino	278	PGA National GC (Champion), Palm Beach Gardens, Fla.
1993	*Tom Wargo	275	PGA National GC (Champion), Palm Beach Gardens, Fla.
1994	Lee Trevino	279	PGA National GC (Champion), Palm Beach Gardens, Fla.
1995	Ray Floyd	277	PGA National GC (Champion), Palm Beach Gardens, Fla.

THE TRADITION

THE TRADITION AT DESERT MOUNTAIN

YEAR	WINNER	SCORE	COURSE
1989	Don Bies	275	GC at Desert Mountain (Cochise), Scottsdale, Ariz.
1990	@Jack Nicklaus	206	GC at Desert Mountain (Cochise), Scottsdale, Ariz.
1991	Jack Nicklaus	277	GC at Desert Mountain (Cochise), Scottsdale, Ariz.

THE TRADITION

YEAR	WINNER	SCORE	COURSE
1992	Lee Trevino	274	GC at Desert Mountain (Cochise), Scottsdale, Ariz.
1993	Tom Shaw	269	GC at Desert Mountain (Cochise), Scottsdale, Ariz.
1994	Ray Floyd	271	GC at Desert Mountain (Cochise), Scottsdale, Ariz.
1995	Jack Nicklaus	276	GC at Desert Mountain (Cochise), Scottsdale, Ariz.

FORD SENIOR PLAYERS CHAMPIONSHIP

SENIOR TOURNAMENT PLAYERS CHAMPIONSHIP

YEAR	WINNER	SCORE	COURSE
1983	Miller Barber	278	Canterbury GC, Cleveland
1984	Arnold Palmer	276	Canterbury GC, Cleveland
1985	Arnold Palmer	274	Canterbury GC, Cleveland
1986	@Chi Chi Rodriguez	206	Canterbury GC, Cleveland

MAZDA SENIOR TOURNAMENT PLAYERS CHAMPIONSHIP

YEAR	WINNER	SCORE	COURSE
1987	Gary Player	280	Sawgrass CC, Ponte Vedra, Fla.
1988	Billy Casper	278	PC at Sawgrass (Valley), Ponte Vedra, Fla.
1989	Orville Moody	271	PC at Sawgrass (Valley), Ponte Vedra, Fla.
1990	Jack Nicklaus	261	Dearborn CC, Dearborn, Mich.

MAZDA PRESENTS THE SENIOR PLAYERS CHAMPIONSHIP

YEAR	WINNER	SCORE	COURSE
1991	Jim Albus	279	Dearborn CC, Dearborn, Mich.
1992	Dave Stockton	277	Dearborn CC, Dearborn, Mich.

FORD SENIOR PLAYERS CHAMPIONSHIP

YEAR	WINNER	SCORE	COURSE
1993	Jim Colbert	278	Dearborn CC, Dearborn, Mich.
1994	Dave Stockton	271	TPC of Michigan, Dearborn, Mich.
1995	*J.C. Snead	272	TPC of Michigan, Dearborn, Mich.

UNITED STATES SENIOR OPEN

YEAR	WINNER	SCORE	COURSE
1980	Roberto DeVicenzo	285	Winged Foot GC (East), Mamaroneck, N.Y.
1981	*Arnold Palmer	289	Oakland Hills CC (South), Birmingham, Mich.
1982	Miller Barber	282	Portland GC, Portland, Ore.
1983	*Billy Casper	288	Hazeltine National GC, Chaska, Minn.
1984	Miller Barber	286	Oak Hill CC, Rochester, N.Y.
1985	Miller Barber	285	Edgewood Tahoe GC, Stateline, Nev.
1986	Dale Douglass	279	Scioto CC, Columbus, Ohio
1987	Gary Player	270	Brooklawn CC, Fairfield, Conn.
1988	*Gary Player	288	Medinah CC, Medinah, Ill.
1989	Orville Moody	279	Laurel Valley CC, Ligonier, Pa.
1990	Lee Trevino	275	Ridgewood CC, Paramus, N.J.
1991	*Jack Nicklaus	282	Oakland Hills CC (South), Birmingham, Mich.
1992	Larry Laoretti	275	Saucon Valley CC, Bethlehem, Pa.
1993	Jack Nicklaus	278	Cherry Hills CC, Englewood, Colo.
1994	Simon Hobday	274	No. 2 Course, Pinehurst Resort & CC, Pinehurst, N.C.
1995	Tom Weiskopf	275	Congressional CC, Bethesda, Md.

HYATT SENIOR TOURNAMENT OF CHAMPIONS

LaCosta CC, Carlsbad, Calif. (1984-94). Hyatt Dorado Beach, Dorado Beach, Puerto Rico (1995)

MONY SENIOR TOURNAMENT OF CHAMPIONS

1984 Orville Moody 288
1985 Peter Thomson 284
1986 Miller Barber 282
1987 *Don January 287
1988 @Dave Hill 211
1989 Miller Barber 280
1990 George Archer 283

INFINITI SENIOR TOURNAMENT OF CHAMPIONS

1991 Bruce Crampton 279
1992 Al Geiberger 282
1993 Al Geiberger 280

MERCEDES SENIOR CHAMPIONSHIP

1994 Jack Nicklaus 279

SENIOR TOURNAMENT OF CHAMPIONS

1995 *Jim Colbert 209

SENIOR SKINS GAME

Turtle Bay GC, Oahu, Hawaii (1988). La Quinta GC, La Quinta, Calif. (1989). Mauna Lani Resort, Kohala Coast, Hawaii (1990-94). (Unofficial event.)

1988 Chi Chi Rodriguez $300,000
1989 Chi Chi Rodriguez $120,000
1990 Arnold Palmer $240,000
1991 Jack Nicklaus $310,000
1992 Arnold Palmer $205,000
1993 Arnold Palmer $190,000
1994 Ray Floyd $240,000
1995 Ray Floyd $420,000

ROYAL CARIBBEAN CLASSIC

Links at Key Biscayne, Key Biscayne, Fla.

GUS MACHADO SENIOR CLASSIC

1987 Gene Littler 207
1988 Lee Elder 202
1989 No tournament

ROYAL CARIBBEAN CLASSIC

1990 Lee Trevino 206
1991 Gary Player 200
1992 Don Massengale 205
1993 Jim Colbert 199
1994 *Lee Trevino 205
1995 *J. C. Snead 209

SENIOR SLAM OF GOLF

Club de Campestre Queretaro, Queretaro, Mexico (1994). Cabo del Sol GC, Cabo San Lucas, Mexico (1995).

SENIOR SLAM AT QUERETARO

1994 Tom Shaw 139

SENIOR SLAM OF GOLF

1995 Ray Floyd 139

GREATER NAPLES INTELLINET CHALLENGE

The Club at Pelican Bay, Naples, Fla. (1988-90). The Vineyards G & CC (South), Naples, Fla. (1991-94).

AETNA CHALLENGE

1988 Gary Player 207
1989 Gene Littler 209
1990 Lee Trevino 200
1991 Lee Trevino 205
1992 Jimmy Powell 197
1993 Mike Hill 202
1994 Mike Hill 201
1995 @Bob Murphy 137

GTE SUNCOAST CLASSIC

Tampa Palms CC, Tampa (1988-91). TPC of Tampa Bay at Cheval, Tampa (1992-93). TPC off Tampa Bay at Lutz, Fla. (1994).

GTE SUNCOAST SENIORS CLASSIC

1988 Dale Douglass 210
1989 *Bob Charles 207

GTE SUNCOAST CLASSIC

1990 Mike Hill 207
1991 Bob Charles 210
1992 *Jim Colbert 200
1993 Jim Albus 206
1994 Rocky Thompson 201
1995 Dave Stockton 204

FHP HEALTH CARE CLASSIC

Mountaingate CC, Los Angeles (1985-86). Wood Ranch GC, Simi Valley, Calif. (1987-88). Ojai Valley Inn & CC, Ojai, Calif. (1989-95).

AMERICAN GOLF CARTA BLANCA JOHNNY MATHIS CLASSIC

1985 Peter Thomson 205

JOHNNY MATHIS SENIOR CLASSIC

1986 Dale Douglass 202

GTE CLASSIC

1987 Bob Charles 208
1988 Harold Henning 214

GTE WEST CLASSIC

1989 Walter Zembriski 197
1990 No tournament
1991 @Chi Chi Rodriguez 132
1992 Bruce Crampton 195
1993 Al Geiberger 198
1994 *Jay Sigel 198

FHP HEALTH CARE CLASSIC

1995 *Bruce Devlin 130

SBC PRESENTS THE DOMINION SENIORS

Dominion CC, San Antonio.

THE DOMINION SENIORS

1985 Don January 206

BENSON & HEDGES INVITATIONAL AT THE DOMINION

1986 Bruce Crampton 202

VANTAGE AT THE DOMINION

1987 Chi Chi Rodriguez 203
1988 Billy Casper 205

RJR AT THE DOMINION

1989 Larry Mowry 201

VANTAGE AT THE DOMINION

1990 Jim Dent 205
1991 @Lee Trevino 137
1992 Lee Trevino 201
1993 J.C. Snead 214
1994 Jim Albus 208

SBC PRESENTS THE DOMINION SENIORS

1995 Jim Albus 205

DALLAS REUNION PRO-AM

Bent Tree CC, Dallas (1985-88). Stonebriar CC, Frisco, Texas (1989-93). Oak Cliff CC, Dallas (1994).

SENIOR PLAYERS REUNION PRO-AM

1985 Peter Thomson 202
1986 Don January 203
1987 Chi Chi Rodriguez 201
1988 *Orville Moody 206

MURATA SENIORS REUNION

1989 Don Bies 208

MURATA REUNION PRO-AM

1990 Frank Beard 207
1991 *Chi Chi Rodriguez 208
1992 *George Archer 211
1993 Dave Stockton 211

DALLAS REUNION PRO-AM

1994 Larry Gilbert 202
1995 Tom Wargo 197

LAS VEGAS SENIOR CLASSIC

Desert Inn CC, Las Vegas. (1986-93). TPC at Summerlin, Las Vegas (1994).

LAS VEGAS SENIOR CLASSIC

1986 Bruce Crampton 206
1987 Al Geiberger 203

GENERAL TIRE LAS VEGAS CLASSIC

1988 Larry Mowry 204
1989 *Charles Coody 205

LAS VEGAS SENIOR CLASSIC

1990 Chi Chi Rodriguez 204
1991 Chi Chi Rodriguez 204
1992 Lee Trevino 206
1993 Gibby Gilbert 204
1994 Ray Floyd 203
1995 Jim Colbert 205

LIBERTY MUTUAL LEGENDS OF GOLF

Onion Creek CC, Austin, Texas (1978-89). Barton Creek CC, Austin, Texas (1990-94). (Unofficial event.)

LEGENDS OF GOLF

1978 Sam Snead/Gardner Dickinson 193
1979 Julius Boros/Roberto DeVicenzo 195

LIBERTY MUTUAL LEGENDS OF GOLF

1980 Tommy Bolt/Art Wall 187
1981 Gene Littler/Bob Rosburg 257
1982 @SamSnead/Don January 183
1983 Rod Funseth/Roberto DeVicenzo 258
1984 Billy Casper/Gay Brewer 258
1985 Don January/Gene Littler 257
1986 Don January/Gene Littler 255
1987 Bruce Crampton/Orville Moody 251
1988 *Bruce Crampton/Orville Moody 254
1989 Harold Henning/Al Geiberger 251
1990 Dale Douglass/Charles Coody 249
1991 Lee Trevino/Mike Hill 252
1992 Lee Trevino/Mike Hill 251
1993 *Harold Henning 204
1994 Dale Douglas/Charles Coody 188
1995 Mike Hill/Lee Trevino 195

PAINEWEBBER INVITATIONAL

Quail Hollow CC, Charlotte, N.C. (1980-88). PC at Piper Glen, Charlotte, N.C. (1989-94). (Unofficial event 1980-82.)

WORLD SENIORS INVITATIONAL

1980 *Gene Littler 211
1981 Miller Barber 282
1982 Gene Littler 280
1983 Doug Sanders 283

WBTV WORLD SENIORS INVITATIONAL

1984 Peter Thomson 281

PAINEWEBBER WORLD SENIORS INVITATIONAL

1985 Miller Barber 277
1986 Bruce Crampton 279
1987 @*Gary Player 207

PAINEWEBBER INVITATIONAL

1988 Dave Hill 206
1989 No event (Hurricane Hugo)
1990 Bruce Crampton 205
1991 Orville Moody 207
1992 Don Bies 203
1993 Mike Hill 204
1994 Lee Trevino 203
1995 Bob Murphy 203

BELL ATLANTIC CLASSIC

Chester Valley GC, Malvern, Pa.

UNITED HOSPITALS SENIOR GOLF CHAMPIONSHIP

1985 @Don January 135
1986 Gary Player 206
1987 Chi Chi Rodriguez 202

UNITED HOSPITALS CLASSIC

1988 *Bruce Crampton 205

BELL ATLANTIC/ ST. CHRISTOPHER'S CLASSIC

1989 *Dave Hill 206

BELL ATLANTIC CLASSIC

1990 *Dale Douglass 204
1991 Jim Ferree 208
1992 Lee Trevino 205
1993 Bob Charles 204
1994 Lee Trevino 206
1995 Jim Colbert 207

CADILLAC/NFL GOLF CLASSIC

Upper Montclair CC, Clifton, N.J.

1993 Lee Trevino 209
1994 Ray Floyd 206
1995 George Archer 205

VFW SENIOR CHAMPIONSHIP

Quail Creek G & CC, Oklahoma City (1987-90). Loch Lloyd CC, Belton, Mo. (1991-95).

SILVER PAGES CLASSIC

1987 Chi Chi Rodriguez 200

SOUTHWESTERN BELL CLASSIC

1988 *Gary Player 203
1989 *Bobby Nichols 209
1990 Jimmy Powell 208
1991 Jim Colbert 201
1992 Gibby Gilbert 193
1993 Dave Stockton 204
1994 Jim Colbert 196

VFW SENIOR CHAMPIONSHIP

1995 Bob Murphy 195

BURNET SENIOR CLASSIC

Bunker Hills GC, Coon Rapids, Minn.

1993 ChiChi Rodriguez 201

1994 Dave Stockton 203
1995 Ray Floyd 201

KROGER SENIOR CLASSIC

Jack Nicklaus Sports Center (Grizzly), Kings Island, Ohio.

1990 @Jim Dent 133
1991 Al Geiberger 203
1992 *Gibby Gilbert 203
1993 Simon Hobday 202
1994 Jim Colbert 199
1995 Mike Hill 196

AMERITECH SENIOR OPEN

Canterbury, GC, Cleveland (1989). Grand Traverse Village, Mich. (1990). Stonebridge CC, Aurora, Ill. (1991-94).

1989 Bruce Crampton 205
1990 Chi Chi Rodriguez 203
1991 Mike Hill 200
1992 Dale Douglass 201
1993 George Archer 133
1994 John Paul Cain 202
1995 Hale Irwin 267

FIRST OF AMERICA CLASSIC

Elks CC, Grand Rapids, Mich. (1986-89). The Highlands, Grand Rapids, Mich. (1990-93). Egypt Valley GC, Ada, Mich. (1994).

GREATER GRAND RAPIDS OPEN

1986 *Jim Ferree 204
1987 Billy Casper 200
1988 Orville Moody 203
1989 John Paul Cain 203
1990 @Don Massengale 134

FIRST OF AMERICA CLASSIC

1991 *Harold Henning 202
1992 Gibby Gilbert 202
1993 *George Archer 199
1994 @Tony Jacklin 136
1995 Jimmy Powell 201

NORTHVILLE LONG ISLAND CLASSIC

Meadow Brook Club, Jericho, N.Y.

THE NORTHVILLE INVITATIONAL

1988 Don Bies 202

NORTHVILLE LONG ISLAND CLASSIC

1989 @*Butch Baird 183
1990 George Archer 208
1991 George Archer 204
1992 George Archer 205
1993 Ray Floyd 208
1994 Lee Trevino 200

BANK OF BOSTON CLASSIC

Marlboro CC, Marlborough, Mass. (1981-83). Nashawtuc CC, Concord, Mass. (1984-94).

MARLBORO CLASSIC

1981 Bob Goalby 208
1982 Arnold Palmer 276
1983 Don January 273

DIGITAL MIDDLESEX CLASSIC

1984 Don January 209

DIGITAL SENIORS CLASSIC

1985 *Lee Elder 208
1986 Chi Chi Rodriguez 203
1987 Chi Chi Rodriguez 198
1988 Chi Chi Rodriguez 202
1989 Bob Charles 200
1990 Bob Charles 203
1991 Rocky Thompson 205
1992 @*Mike Hill 136

BANK OF BOSTON CLASSIC

1993 Bob Betley 204
1994 Jim Albus 203

FRANKLIN QUEST CHAMPIONSHIP

Jeremy Ranch GC, Park City, Utah. (Unofficial event 1983-86). Park Meadows GC, Park City, Utah (1994).

THE SHOOTOUT AT JEREMY RANCH

1982 Billy Casper 279
1983 Bob Goalby/
Mike Reid 256
1984 Don January/
Mike Sullivan 250
1985 Miller Barber/
Ben Crenshaw 257

SHOWDOWN CLASSIC

1986 Bobby Nichols/
Curt Byrum 249
1987 Miller Barber 210
1988 Miller Barber 207
1989 Tom Shaw 207
1990 Rives McBee 202
1991 Dale Douglass 209

FRANKLIN SHOWDOWN CLASSIC

1992 @*Orville Moody 137
1993 Dave Stockton 197

FRANKLIN QUEST CHAMPIONSHIP

1994 Tom Weiskopf 204

BRUNO'S MEMORIAL CLASSIC

Greystone GC, Birmingham, Ala.

1992 George Archer 208
1993 Bob Murphy 203
1994 Jim Dent 201
1995 Graham Marsh 201

PITTSBURGH SENIOR CLASSIC

Quicksilver CC, Midway, Pa.

1993 Bob Charles 207
1994 Dave Eichelberger 209
1995 Dave Stockton 208

NORTHWEST CLASSIC

Sahalle CC, Redmond, Wash. (1986). Inglewood CC, Kenmore, Wash. (1987-94).

1986 Bruce Crampton 210
1987 Chi Chi Rodriguez 206
1988 Bruce Crampton 207
1989 Al Geiberger 204
1990 George Archer 205
1991 Mike Hill 198
1992 Mike Joyce 204
1993 Dave Stockton 200
1994 *Simon Hobday 209

BRICKYARD CROSSING CHAMPIONSHIP

Broadmoor CC, Indianapolis. (1988-1993). Brickyard Crossing GC (1994).

GTE NORTH CLASSIC

1988 Gary Player 201
1989 @Gary Player 135
1990 *Mike Hill 201
1991 George Archer 199
1992 Ray Floyd 199
1993 Bob Murphy 134

BRICKYARD CROSSING CHAMPIONSHIP

1994 @Isao Aoki 133

BANK ONE CLASSIC

Griffin Gate GC, Lexington, Ky. (1983-1989). Kearney Hill Links, Lexington, Ky. (1990-94).

CITIZENS UNION SENIOR GOLF CLASSIC

1983 Don January 269
1984 Gay Brewer 204
1985 @Lee Elder 135

BANK ONE SENIOR GOLF CLASSIC

1986 *Gene Littler 201

VANTAGE PRESENTS BANK ONE SENIOR GOLF CLASSIC

1987 Bruce Crampton 197
1988 Bob Charles 200

RJR BANK ONE CLASSIC

1989 Rives McBee 202

VANTAGE BANK ONE CLASSIC

1990 Rives McBee 201

BANK ONE CLASSIC

1991 *DeWitt Weaver 207
1992 Terry Dill 203
1993 Gary Player 202
1994 Isao Aoki 202

NATIONWIDE CHAMPIONSHIP

CC of the South, Alpharetta, Ga.

1991 Mike Hill 212
1992 @Isao Aoki 208
1993 Lee Trevino 205
1994 Dave Stockton 198
1995 Bob Murphy 203

BELLSOUTH CLASSIC AT OPRYLAND

Springhouse GC, Nashville, Tenn. (1994-95).

1994 Lee Trevino 199
1995 Jim Dent 203

VANTAGE CHAMPIONSHIP

Tanglewood Park, Clemmons, N.C.

VANTAGE CHAMPIONSHIP

1987 Al Geiberger 206
1988 Walt Zembriski 278

RJR CHAMPIONSHIP

1989 Gary Player 207

VANTAGE CHAMPIONSHIP

1990 Charles Coody 202
1991 Jim Colbert 205
1992 @Jim Colbert 132
1993 Lee Trevino 198
1994 Larry Gilbert 198

THE TRANSAMERICA

Silverado CC (South), Napa, Calif.

TRANSAMERICA SENIOR GOLF CHAMPIONSHIP

1989 Billy Casper 207
1990 Lee Trevino 205
1991 Charles Coody 204
1992 Bob Charles 200
1993 Dave Stockton 203
1994 *Kermit Zarley 204

RALEY'S SENIOR GOLD RUSH

Rancho Murieta CC (North), Rancho Murieta, Calif.

RANCHO MURIETA SENIOR GOLD RUSH

1987 Orville Moody 205
1988 Bob Charles 207
1989 Dave Hill 207

GOLD RUSH AT RANCHO MURIETA

1990 George Archer 204

RALEY'S SENIOR GOLD RUSH

1991 George Archer 206
1992 Bob Charles 201
1993 George Archer 202
1994 *Bob Murphy 208

RALPHS SENIOR CLASSIC

Rancho Park GC, Los Angeles.

SECURITY PACIFIC SENIOR CLASSIC

1990 Mike Hill 201
1991 *John Brodie 200

RALPH'S SENIOR CLASSIC

1992 Ray Floyd 195
1993 *Dale Douglass 196
1994 Jack Kiefer 197

HYATT REGENCY MAUI KAANAPALI CLASSIC

Royal Kaanapali GC (North), Maui, Hawaii.

GTE KAANAPALI CLASSIC

1987 @Orville Moody 132
1988 Don Bies 204
1989 @Don Bies 132
1990 Bob Charles 206

FIRST DEVELOPMENT KAANAPALI CLASSIC

1991 Jim Colbert 195

KAANAPALI CLASSIC

1992 Tommy Aaron 198
1993 George Archer 199
1994 Bob Murphy 195

ENERGIZER SENIOR TOUR CHAMPIONSHIP

Tryall Golf & Beach Club, Sandy Bay, Jamaica (1985-87). Hyatt Dorado Beach (East) Dorado, Puerto Rico (1988-93). Dunes Golf and Beach Club, Myrtle Beach, S.C. (1994).

MAZDA CHAMPIONS (Unofficial event 1985-89.)

1985 Don January/
Alice Miller 127
1986 Bob Charles/
Amy Alcott 193
1987 Miller Barber/
Nancy Lopez 191
1988 Dave Hill/
Colleen Walker 186
1989 Mike Hill/
Patti Rizzo 191

NEW YORK LIFE CHAMPIONS

1990 *Mike Hill 201

SENIOR TOUR CHAMPIONSHIP

1991 Mike Hill 202
1992 Ray Floyd 197
1993 Simon Hobday 199

GOLF MAGAZINE SENIOR TOUR CHAMPIONSHIP

1994 *Ray Floyd 273